C000271885

The
Norwich Knowledge

An A-Z of Norwich – The Superlative City

By Michael Loveday

Contents

Thanks

Although creating this tome has been a long term, personal ambition and indeed obsession, I must thank some people in particular who have assisted, guided and prodded me to actually do the deed and transform aspiration into reality. I tend not to be extravagant with praise so this won't be an Oscar-like accolade to everyone who has ever known me.

Thanks to the Heritage Economic & Regeneration Trust, and my colleagues working for it, for providing advice, access to information and materials and for agreeing to assist with the publication – I hope that we make a modest return and if we do, some of that will go into HEART's coffers.

Thanks to my long time friend and colleague Brian Ayers for proofing the manuscript and preventing me (hopefully) from making any horrendous historical errors, apart from the ones we disagreed over, obviously.

Thanks to my daughter Vik who provided a vast amount of research on the 'Norwich Fringe' and a whole new insight into the 'mills legacy' of the area.

Thanks to my two step daughters, Laura and Katy, for research on what the City offers to young adults as well as reality checks on content and bibliographies.

Thanks to Jonathan Plunkett for free access to the outstanding Plunkett Photographic Archive, to the Norfolk Museums Service and Picture Norfolk for access to images, and to Norfolk Historic Environment Service.

Thanks to the UEA's School of Computing, and David Drinkwater in particular, for the stunning virtual reality images of the City's lost heritage.

Thanks to Anne Reekie for taking on the huge job of knocking 200,000 words and 1500 images into something visually stunning.

And finally, thanks to my wife Gwyn, for continually jibing me that I'd 'never actually finish it' and provoking me into, for the first time ever probably, being a completer finisher.

Sorry if I missed someone, no slight intended.

Michael Loveday

Written and published by Michael Loveday
© Michael Loveday 2011
ISBN 978-0-9570883-0-6

An introduction to Norwich Knowledge

'The Knowledge' is a rigorous initiation that London taxi drivers are put through before they are granted an operating license. It is the most exacting test for cabbies in the World and equips them to be the 'font of all knowledge' not just for where everything is in London, geographically, but also what the history of places and people is, how to discover unusual shops, bars, restaurants, museums, galleries, clubs and other venues and how to impart information on just about anything relevant to the Capital. So whether the passengers are a City gent or a Japanese tourist, a newly arrived student or a family from the Home Counties out on a day trip, a visiting academic or a resident of Southwark visiting Stoke Newington, they can deploy exactly the right quota of useful information required to inform and indeed inspire the passenger.

Norwich Knowledge takes this principle, applies it to Greater Norwich and puts it in a book. Like 'The Knowledge' it's designed to appeal to everyone and is presented in a handy guide book size and alphabetical format to make that easy. A very obvious target for the book

constituency. Newly arrived students at the UEA, NUCA, City College, Easton or the language schools can have an instant guide to where everything is from the best clubs, pubs and gigs to a vast range of opportunities to engage their interests through local venues, organisations, clubs and societies. At a broader level, it'll give them a feel of what their adopted city is like now and has been like in the past and, if their course is related to anything like tourism, history or culture then the guide provides an unparalleled reference to unlock those areas locally. The Norwich Knowledge will also be a handy tool for local people seeking more information about their city since 'locals' are notoriously poorly supported in knowing what's here for them. From the business perspective it can assist companies to be more informed about the local context in meeting the needs of their clients and, of course, it can even do the job for taxi drivers!

The obvious question is 'do I really need this?' If I want to find somewhere I'd look in an A to Z, if I needed to check out some history I'd buy a history book or if I needed a guide book I'd get one. Well you could do that but this puts all of the answers in one place and, to date, no other information resource has provided the depth of knowledge that the Norwich Knowledge does. A much

simpler question is 'couldn't I just Google it?' Again, that's possible in some instances but if the information is there, and that's not always the case, it would require multiple searches to find the right site and of course you need to ask the right question. Additionally, many of the

"To spend time in this thriving, pluralistic, proud, vital place, that lives simultaneously in its many-layered past and its present – is a tonic experience, its values at the core of our identity, it seems to me: vigorously productive, sceptical of external authority, assertive of its achievements, democratic in its structures, rooted in its origins, its eye on the ball of the immediate future, but its heavenly vision one of the freedom of the greater citizenship. I was moved; I still am."
Simon Callow

sites are sponsored so if you Google 'best pub' you're very unlikely to get the best pub but rather one that's paid to get its name on the site – Norwich Knowledge isn't sponsored and provides clear, objective information.

So if you need to find the only UK pub to win CAMRA's National Pub of the year twice running, if you want to find out about the first woman to write a book in English or where Jimi Hendrix and Ginger Baker performed and current bands now perform, where the best civic portrait collection in the UK can be viewed or one of the best private art collections or where the World's biggest collection of bladder stones is kept (!) or even where to get the best cup of coffee – then it's all here.

"The present is shaped by the past and history provides us with an essential sense of perspective."
Rt Reverend Peter Nott, former Bishop of Norwich

is visitors aiming to get a quick view of the best and most appealing bits. The guide, however, aims to do much more than that in terms of meeting the needs of the largest possible

Foreword

There is a romantic view of 'dear old Norwich' – a place which has not changed from its halcyon, medieval past. In this idealised vision, change is a modern phenomenon and therefore a threat to be resisted. Experience, however, shows us that the opposite is true. Through its rich, varied and turbulent history, leading by example or adapting to outside pressures, Norwich has only evolved to become such a diverse and attractive City by making change work for it rather than doggedly resisting it.

Over 12 centuries of change, invasions, wars, rebellions, fires, plagues, depressions and economic booms have all shaped the City into the complex and diverse place that it is today. The really striking point is that for more than a millennium, the City has not been one place but many.

Throughout its history, Norwich has absorbed diverse cultures, from Viking Age Danes to invading Normans, Bretons and Jews, to persecuted Dutch, Flemish, Walloon and French weavers in their thousands, from the rural poor of the 18/19th centuries to American and other Allied Service personnel in the last War and in more recent times, Chileans fleeing the military junta, 'new Europeans' taking advantage of the expanding EU and now over 100 nationalities at the UEA, Research Park and University Hospital. All have made a contribution to enriching the life and character of the City and have added to its interest.

Norwich has grown to be one of the most attractive cities in Europe by taking a radical and positive approach to harnessing change – not by seeing it as a threat. Of course, change has resulted in some tragic losses – how wonderful if we could have retained the 12 City Gates, the Market Cross, the Duke of Norfolk's Palace or some of the monastic complexes swept away by the Reformation. However, as Sir Roy Strong rightly observes, without the loss of such treasures there would be no impetus for renewal and creativity. Without the City's willingness to experiment and adapt and with a more cautionary view of change

we may have missed many such opportunities – the Sainsbury extension at the UEA, London Street – Britain's first pedestrianised traditional shopping street, City Hall – Britain's finest example of interwar municipal architecture, and Edwardian splendours such as the Royal Arcade or the Marble Hall, which themselves replaced gems of the medieval period, Michael Innes' remarkable Castle Mall complex, Hopkins Architects' new Cathedral Hostry and their Forum building replacing David Percival's award winning 1960s Central Library – and so on all the way back through the City's history.

Below: The Romanesque Cathedral and C21st Hostry.
Opposite: The C15th splendour of St Peter Mancroft reflected in the imposing, C21st Forum building.

The Sainsbury Centre for Visual Arts at the University of East Anglia.

The essence of the City's success is that, for the most part, it has managed to retain the inherited features of its rich history while accommodating pressures for change in ways which have enhanced its character. The purpose of this book is to present an accessible gazetteer of the multitude of components, past and present, which together make up the 'Fine City' – people, streets, buildings, events are all here and presented in a handy reference form. There can be few historic cities that demonstrate the process of adaptation and renewal over 1200 years so effectively. Equally, there can be few examples in Britain or indeed Europe where continuing pressures for change in an historic city have been harnessed so effectively and continuously to bring about the regeneration of an area's character and environment. This point, however, is true of Norwich in the 'big picture' sense and will be more so in the future as Growth Point status expands the built up area population to something akin to Nottingham. Previous works on Norwich have, understandably, concentrated on the Walled City, since this was 'Norwich' up until the C19th, and have largely ignored the remainder of the built up area and in particular the suburban parishes. Whatever the vagaries of municipal boundaries and jurisdictions in the past, present and future, it is clear that Norwich always has had a complex relationship functionally with these areas over the centuries and will continue to do so – the great merchant families that ruled the City during and beyond the medieval period had their country houses in the outlying villages, the ecclesiastical foundations

Norwich has been many things...

- Seat of the Saxon Earls of East Anglia
- Capital of the most populous region in Norman England
- Walled City covering an area bigger than London by the C14th
- One of Medieval Europe's great seedbeds of religious art and architecture
- A major trading centre in the orbit of the Hanseatic cities
- A truly European City with significant Dutch, French, Flemish and Walloon communities in the C16th
- England's second city and chief seat of textile manufacture in the C18th
- A great Victorian industrial centre with the largest shoe factory in England and a prodigious brewery with a greater output than any in London
- An early C20th focus of innovation producing the first all metal aircraft and largest airship frame
- The epicentre for 'aircraft carrier East Anglia' which delivered the US 8th Army Air Force's assault on Nazi Germany
- A modern European regional capital combining the best of heritage and culture with the cutting edge of innovative research and lifestyle opportunities.

held lands in these areas and the people that lived there came into the City to buy and sell things and for entertainment. The same applies today. Norwich provides half of the jobs in the County, it is one of the foremost retail centres in the UK because it is supported by a large rural hinterland and its great institutions, ranging from the Theatre Royal to Norwich City Football Club, attract regular patronage from a very wide area. In that context, the emotional tie is by far the most significant thing. Like Sir John Pettus, individuals who live in places like Rackheath, well beyond the medieval City Walls, will regard themselves as 'Norwich People' just as much as those within the sound of St Peter Mancroft's bells. As if to reinforce the point, a very large proportion of that church's regular congregation live outside the boundaries of 'municipal Norwich'. Reflecting these points, this book takes a generous interpretation of the geographical scope of Norwich and strays well into the hinterland of influence. This book will guide you on

Work of the Medieval Norwich School of Glass painters.

a journey of discovery through 1200 years of history in 'the City' in the widest sense and give you a taste of the present and a glimpse of possible futures. Whether you are a visitor needing inspiration, a newcomer wishing to uncover the secrets of your new home, a resident wanting to drill more deeply into your City's past, a consultant trying to impress a client with that little knowledge edge, a taxi driver needing

to know a bit more about the patch or even someone who likes to set Norwich trivia pub quizzes.

"Norwich may be minute compared with London, Paris or Rome, but nevertheless it lives its life as a city on the same level of dignity."
J. B. Priestley

Rather unusually, perhaps, Norwich Knowledge isn't set out as an historical or thematic narrative but rather as an alphabetical gazetteer.

From left: historic Princes Street and sun setting over the River Wensum.

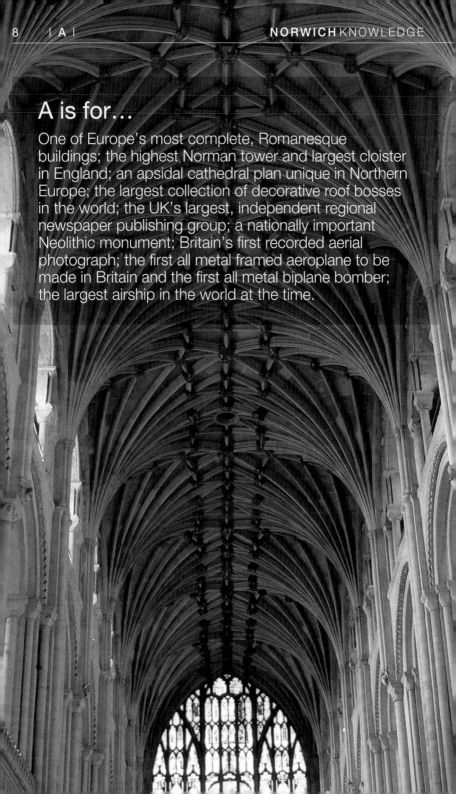

A is for...

One of Europe's most complete, Romanesque buildings; the highest Norman tower and largest cloister in England; an apsidal cathedral plan unique in Northern Europe; the largest collection of decorative roof bosses in the world; the UK's largest, independent regional newspaper publishing group; a nationally important Neolithic monument; Britain's first recorded aerial photograph; the first all metal framed aeroplane to be made in Britain and the first all metal biplane bomber; the largest airship in the world at the time.

ABC Cinema

See Regent Theatre.

ABC Wharf

Historic Wharf. Located on the east side of King Street just north of Wensum Lodge, the wharf represents one of the few remaining examples of riverside industrial structures in the City Centre. This cobbled yard with a cluster of sheds and warehouses includes a remarkable corrugated iron structure on the water front.

Abolition Movement

Fight against slavery. Although William Wilberforce is the figure celebrated in English history for the 'abolition of slavery' the realities are much more complicated. One of the centres spearheading the cause for abolition was Norwich and Norfolk with the Quakers at the forefront. Wilberforce was a regular visitor to the Gurneys at Earlham and his success in getting the trade in slaves abolished in 1807 received massive support from petitions signed by thousands of Norfolk people in the decades before. In 1794 the freed slave and principal black campaigner in the abolition movement, Olaudah Equiano, spoke publicly in Norwich generating a hugely positive public reaction. The local media were also very active in promoting the abolition movement. Equiano was able to support lectures, tours and publications by getting people to subscribe to his book charting the horrors of slavery from the victim's perspective. In Norfolk there were 250 subscribers to the 8th edition ranging from the gentry (the Ives who had provided generations of Mayors), through the middle classes (the lawyers De Hagues and merchants Barnards) to working class dyers and leather cutters. Supporters also included a large number of women such as Amelia Alderson (later Opie) and Miss Jarrold. When Wilberforce stepped down, Elizabeth Fry's brother in law, Thomas Fowell Buxton, took up the lead and finally secured the abolition of slavery in 1833.

About Anglia

Iconic regional news programme. Established in the 1960s by Anglia TV anchor man Dick Joyce, About Anglia became a firm favourite with local audiences until its demise 30 years later in July 1999. Some of the stalwarts continue to be local media personalities.

Adam & Eve

City's oldest pub. The Adam and Eve pub, on the corner of Bishopgate, is said to be the oldest public house in Norwich. Cathedral documents refer to the building as early as 1249 and it may have been developed originally as a brewhouse for the builders of the Cathedral. It is said that the dying Lord Sheffield was brought to the pub after a battle in August 1549 when his men were defeated at Palace Plain during Kett's Rebellion. Lord Sheffield is said to still haunt the pub today. During the C19th it was frequented by the crews of wherries bringing sea sand from Yarmouth for use in pub spittoons and on floors. The landlady in the mid C19th owned her own wherry called Adam & Eve. Among the pub's more notorious clientele was the Victorian murderer James Bloomfield Rush. The pub retains a Norwich Brewery Company sign – a device invented by Grand Metropolitan to generate some faux local provenance after it had taken over and then closed all of the independent Norwich breweries in the 1960s.

Opposite: Nave of the Anglican Cathedral.
Above: Adam & Eve – possibly the City's oldest pub.
Right: ABC Wharf just off King Street.

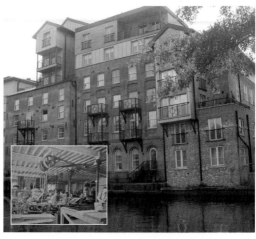

Above: detail from the Agricultural Hall. Right: Albion Mills after restoration (inset, Albion Mills interior in 1905).

Agricultural Hall

Former Agricultural Hall. Built in 1882 and designed by J.B. Pearce the hall was intended as a venue for agricultural shows and exhibitions and this is reflected in the exterior architectural motifs. The Agricultural Hall was opened by the Prince of Wales (later Edward VII) in November 1882. Additional to its agricultural role, the Hall played host to public meetings, including a speech by Prime Minister Gladstone, aged 80, in 1890 and a lecture by Jerome K Jerome in 1894. The Great Blondin, famed for his tightrope walk over Niagara Falls in 1859, returned to Norwich (he had performed at the Theatre in 1869) two weeks before his 70th birthday, to wheel a Norwich citizen in a wheel barrow along a tightrope strung across the Agricultural Hall, over the heads of a captivated audience.

The Hall was also a venue for other entertainments, including circuses and some of the first silent film shows in the City (and indeed the country). After a brief spell with the Army during the Second World War and use as an extension to the next door main post office sorting office, it was bought by the Council in 1957 and ultimately united with the next door Hardwick House, via a bridging link by David Luckhurst of Feilden and Mawson, to provide the new headquarters of Anglia TV. The interior has been largely butchered by the inclusion of sound studios but some modest remnants of the original cast iron splendour remain.

Agricultural Hall Plain

Post Medieval Street. One of the very few streets to be added to the City's street pattern after the medieval period, the Plain connects the also newly developed Prince of Wales Road (opened 1862) to Castle Meadow. Its three principal buildings are the Agricultural Hall, from which it takes its name, Hardwick House (the former Crown Bank and later central post office) and the Royal Hotel.

Airport

See Norwich International Airport.

Alan Partridge

TV character. Alan Partridge was a comedy character portrayed by actor Steve Coogan as a DJ on the fictional local BBC station Norwich Radio. His presentation of the area tended to reinforce stereotypes of Norfolk being a haven for yokels and in-breeding and prompted an adverse reaction from some local City and County councillors to the extent that one blamed this unfortunate association with the failure of Norwich to progress in its bid as European Capital of Culture in 2002.

Albion Mills

Former early C19th textile mill. Built in 1836 in an attempt to revive the City's flagging textile industry, the mills were used towards the late C19th as Coopers Biscuit Factory but had become derelict by the 1930s when they were taken over by R.J. Read Ltd and converted to flour mills in 1932. The business expanded over the majority of the C20th but closed in the 1990s. P.J. Livsey converted the mills to an imaginative housing scheme in the early C21st. The original works had included a very early steam engine, produced by the Norwich company of Riches & Watts in 1858 and reconditioned by the same company in 1896. It was eventually replaced in 1934 by an L,S&E electric motor.

Alderson Place

1960s housing scheme. Located behind St John de Sepulchre and in a triangle formed by Queens Road, Finklegate and Ber Street, Alderson Place is a two and three storey local authority housing scheme designed by City Architect David Percival and built between 1959 and 1960. It thoughtfully replicates the line of the, now lost, historic City Wall with a modern flint wall and was awarded a bronze medal and diploma by the then Minister of Housing & Local Government for good design. It takes its name from Alderson's Street, a row of small Victorian cottages connecting Finklegate to Queens Road, formerly on the same site and demolished as part of the Council's slum clearance scheme. The Alderson in question was Dr James Alderson, a noted local surgeon, of St Clement's parish, whose daughter Amelia Alderson was to become the author, poet and social campaigner Amelia Opie.

Aldrich, John

Former Mayor. John Aldrich, or Aldrych, a grocer, was sheriff in 1551 and mayor in 1558 and 1570, as his father Thomas had been, and burgess to Parliament in 1555, 1558 and 1572. The remnant of his house, formerly the house of the Priors of Ixworth and more recently the old Labour Exchange, where he lived with his wife Elizabeth Sotherton (daughter of Alderman Nicolas Sotherton) survives as a single storey flint structure on the south side of Colegate, adjacent to St Clement's church. Aldrich was buried there following his death in 1582, and is commemorated by an impressive memorial. His son married a daughter of Augustine Steward. Aldrich, with Mayor Thomas Codd, had engaged with the rebels during Kett's Rebellion in an effort to moderate their actions but had clearly managed to persuade the authorities that his actions had been motivated in the cause of the Government rather than the rebels as evidenced by his later survival and successes. He is commemorated by the residential Aldryche Road, just north of Plumstead Road.

Alexandra

Queen of England. In 1918, Queen Alexandra unveiled a memorial to the Norfolk nurse Edith Cavell who was shot by the Germans three years earlier, to the day, for aiding the escape of allied soldiers from behind German lines during the First World War. The memorial was originally located in front of the Maids Head on a traffic island in Tombland but was moved to a small garden beside the Erpingham Gate in the 1980s.

Allcock, Terry

Former Norwich City footballer. The Canaries all time second highest scorer, Terry Allcock, nicknamed 'the count', netted 127 goals in 389 games. He came to Norwich from Bolton Wanderers in 1958 and played for the club for 11 years with one of his most famous performances being during the 1959 FA Cup run, where he scored against Tottenham at White Hart Lane. In addition to his overall tally, his records include the highest number of goals scored in one season (37), the most FA Cup goals scored (12), the second most League Cup goals scored (9) and the remarkable record of scoring in six successive games.

Right: Footballer Terry Allcock.
Below: Door of the house of John Aldrich.

Clockwise from top: All Saints Great Melton, Branthwaite tomb All Saints Hethel, All Saints Hethel.

From top: All Saints Horsford, All Saints Intwood.

All Saints Church, Fyebridge

Lost Walled City church. Probably founded in the C11th, All Saints' church was positioned so close to the gate in the C11th defences that it is thought to be originally part of the gate structure. The church appears to have been taken down in the mid C16th after what turned out to be groundless promises from the Cathedral about its retention. In March 1551 the canons of Norwich Cathedral leased All Saints' to the mayor and people of Norwich for five hundred years, but by the end of June, after the Dean had assured parishioners that the church had not been given away or sold, it was pulled down and its parish amalgamated with that of St Paul. Evidence suggests that it is likely that the church was split up and sold, the nave to one buyer and the chancel to another. There is a possibility that substantial amounts of flint in the walls to the rear of the Cat & Fiddle pub were recycled from the church and burials were excavated to the east in 2005.

All Saints Church, Great Melton

Medieval parish church. All Saints church contains elements from the C11th but is principally C14th and C15th when the tower was rebuilt. J.B. Pearce undertook a major refurbishment in 1883. Inside there are late C15th benches, some good Victorian stained glass and a C14th coffin lid.

All Saints Church, Hethel

Medieval parish church. The Saxon origin church of All Saints has a strange collection of styles ranging from the square Saxon tower, with later additions, to the C14th/C15th body of the church then the rather incongruous brick mausoleum dating from 1730, to the Branthwaite family. Inside there is a range of interesting monuments to the Branthwaite family and particularly the grand alabaster tomb to Miles Branthwaite of c.1612. The churchyard also has the distinction of supporting the oldest living hawthorn tree in East Anglia and probably in the UK at 700 years old.

All Saints Church, Horsford

Suburban medieval parish church. Originally C13th with the 'new' tower developed in the mid C15th, and an interesting thatched chancel restored in 1703. The whole building was heavily restored and Victorianised in 1869. Inside there is a Norman Purbeck marble font, suggesting a post Conquest foundation, and an early C16th screen as well as a few medieval stained glass fragments and some late Victorian glass from the Royal Bavarian Institute for Stained Glass.

All Saints Church, Intwood

Medieval parish church. All Saints, has a round, probably Norman, tower and a Norman origin nave. There was a major restoration by Henry Hobart in 1590 and a further Victorian renovation by John Brown in 1852. Most of the inside content is Victorian including a font and pews of 1852, some stained glass of 1888 and a brass to Clement Unthank of 1900.

From top: All Saints Keswick, All Saints Postwick.

All Saints Church, Keswick

Medieval parish church.
All Saints is a round-towered church. A previous church existed on this site until it was demolished in 1597, and a new church was constructed at Intwood instead using materials from the demolished church when the parishes of Keswick and Intwood were consolidated. It was the Gurneys who restored All Saints in the 1890s. The original east wall of the chancel still remains to the east of the current church structure and part of the tower may be of Saxon

*Right: All Saints Westlegate.
Below: All Saints Rackheath.*

origin although it was heavily restored in 1893. Inside there is some stained glass signed William Morris.

All Saints Church, Postwick

Suburban medieval parish church. This was a pre Conquest dedication but the present church was begun at least in the C13th, with the chancel dating from that period, while the tower dates from a century later. One of the bells was relocated from the demolished St Paul's in Norwich.

All Saints Church, Rackheath

Redundant, suburban medieval parish church.
Declared redundant in 1971 this predominantly early C14th church, restored in the 1840s, now stands alone in fields in the lost village of Rackheath Magna, isolated from the modern New Rackheath. The Interior provides clues to the former glories of the area with impressive monuments to the once influential mayors of Norwich, the Pettus family, and to the Straceys, the subsequent owners of Rackheath Hall. There is also a font dating from 1639 and some mid C19th stained glass.

All Saints Church, Westlegate

Redundant medieval Walled City church.
The existing church is a C15th rebuild of a much earlier structure. All that remains of the original church is a stump of thicker wall by the tower end of the arcade. The chancel dates from the first half of the C14th and is in the Decorated style. The tower is C15th and plain, without buttresses. Its corners were rebuilt in brick in the C19th, and the top stage was constructed in 1913. It has no staircase and ascent of the tower is by ladders. The three-light west window is C15th and lined with Tudor brick. The nave windows are in the late C15th Perpendicular style and provide an interesting comparison to the pointed chancel windows, which are earlier in date. The large east window in the C14th Decorated style, is actually a Victorian replica. The porch is a later addition evidenced by it 'lapping over' the nave plinth. Rough masonry where the west side meets the nave shows where a stair turret went to the upper room, or 'parvise'. The parvise was a bedsitting room for the priest and

Left: All Saints Westlegate interior.
Above: All Saints Westlegate stained glass.

provided a view into the church. If the priest had accommodation elsewhere, the parvise was used as a treasury or watching-chamber. A drawing of the church dated 1828 shows that the chancel roof was thatched, originally. The walls of the church are faced with whole and split flints and C19th brickwork replaces decayed stone. In the south-east corner of the east wall is an ancient stone with indents for a chalice brass and inscription. This was moved from the floor inside the church, where it marked the burial place of a priest. The Reformation in the 1530s brought major changes to the fabric of the building. The rood screen was dismantled creating a more open space, windows were filled with clear glass, images of saints were removed and the wall paintings were covered in a layer of paint. Emphasis on the visual was replaced with the written word: boards inscribed with the Ten Commandments were swiftly erected to fill the empty spaces. The antiquarian, Francis Blomefield, noted that the "fine old font" was

decorated with carvings of the twelve apostles, Saint Michael and many of the confessor saints, as well as a splendid dragon. This now resides in St Julian's.

The north aisle windows are glazed with fragments of original C15th glass. In the 1860s, the church was refurnished in the High Anglican tradition with an elaborate reredos, a new rood beam, and a stained glass window depicting the Virgin and Child. The window is now at St John Timberhill.

The church contains a C17th wall monument to William Clabburn, who was a leading manufacturer of the fashionable Norwich shawl. The Clabburns' commitment to All Saints is reflected in Thomas Clabburn's 1816 bequest for bread and coal to be distributed each February to the poor of the parish. In the C19th the Clabburn textile manufacturers made the highest quality silk shawls and their customers included members of the Royal family.

All Saints is known as the bell founders' church, as bells were cast nearby. Many of the bells in Norfolk

and Suffolk churches were cast here between c1580 and 1680. The oldest bell in the tower was cast by William Dawe of London (1385-1418).

The church was declared redundant in 1973 yet £8,000 had to be spent on making it watertight to prevent further deterioration. In 1979 it was leased to the All Saints Centre to be used as a place of Christian hospitality and in 1996 it was visited by the then Archbishop of Canterbury, George Carey.

All Saints Green

Historic public space.
Originally known as the Swinemarket or the Old Swinemarket, from the activity that went on in front of All Saints Church, the name changed to Timbermarket when the swinemarket moved to Orford Hill in 1270. It had become Alhalowe Green or Alderhllen Green from the Old English ealra halena meaning All Hallows or All Saints, after the church, by the C16th. The street extends from the church to the former Brazen Door within the City Walls. It was a densely populated part of

the City until 1930s slum clearance moved people out to New Lakenham. Although wartime bombing and post war redevelopment have changed much of the street in a dramatic way, the south side particularly retains much of its Georgian character, with a fine run of C18th buildings and evidence of earlier structures. Further towards the south west, St Catherine's Close and Ivory House represent excellent survivors of the street's former character.

Almary Green

Part of Cathedral Close. Almary Green lies just inside and to the south of the Ethelbert Gate. It takes its name from the monastic Almonry, now lost. Important buildings include the substantial range to the west, built in 1702 with a slightly later façade (1758)

and earlier buildings, although dated 1701, to the south, built for Jeremy Vynn who was Sheriff in 1677, Mayor in 1690, and died on December 1, 1705, aged 73. He is buried in a vault at the entrance to St Luke's Chapel in the cathedral. Beneath the grassed area of the Green lies the lost medieval church of St Ethelbert, destroyed in the Riot of 1272.

Almonry

See *Anglican Cathedral Almonry*.

Alms Lane

Historic lane within the Walled City. Located between Muspole Street and St Georges Street the lane takes its name from seven alms houses endowed on the site by widow Alice Crome in 1516. The current buildings on the north side date from the C19th but

incorporate wall fragments from the C16th and C17th. A dig on the south side, preceding development of the current houses, revealed development from the C12th onwards.

Alnwick Gate

C15th gateway. Started by Bishop Alnwick, probably in 1435 and finished by Bishop Lyhard, this represented the main entry to the Bishop's palace and now to the Bishop's House. It has a carriage and pedestrian entrance and both doors are medieval. There is a brick vault beneath which was used as the Bishop's Prison. The Gate is a Scheduled Ancient Monument.

Alnwick, William

C15th Bishop. William Alnwick was Bishop of Norwich between 1426 and 1436 and during part of this time he was Keeper of the

Left: Plaque in Alms Lane.

Below (clockwise from left):
Decorative boss of Bishop beneath Alnwick Gate,
Alnwick Gate south side, Alnwick Gate north side.

Privy Seal. His principal architectural contributions to the City were the remodelling of the west front of the Cathedral, the completion of the cloister reconstruction and commencing the Alnwick Gate.

Anchor Brewery
See *Bullard's*.

Anchorites/ Anchoresses
Religious recluses. Anchorites were people who withdrew from secular life to devote themselves to prayer and contemplation. They normally lived alone, often walled up in a cell with the necessities of daily life (very basic food, water and a chamber pot) being delivered through a hole in the wall. Norwich had more hermits and anchorites between 1370 and 1549 than any other English city including London and its suburbs. The most famous anchoress was Mother Julian of Norwich but other examples include Katherine Mann, who was installed in a cell attached to the north side of Blackfriars.

Anderson's Meadow
Public park. Located in the west of the built up area in the historic hamlet of Heigham, between the River Wensum and the Marriott's Way long distance footpath, Anderson's Meadow provides an extensive area of flat grass, surrounded by trees, for passive, outdoor recreation.

Angel Inn
Lost medieval inn. Originally on the site of the Royal Arcade, the Angel had its origins in the C15th at a time when the Market Place was surrounded by four dozen inns. The Inn was at its most popular in the C17th, C18th and early C19th when it was the venue for all manner of bizarre and enticing public performance. Mrs Pease, for instance, exhibited 'twoe meeremayds and a devouring great Quaker' in 1675 and this was followed by a pair of elephants ten years later. At the other extreme, the Inn entertained illustrious visitors including the Dukes of York and Wellington in 1820. The other main role of the Angel was a coaching inn. From 1814, a new fast, light weight coach called the Telegraph made the Norwich to Whitechapel run in 13 hours for 25 shillings. By 1830, The Times was making the morning run, leaving at 5.45am and The Royal Mail left at 5pm. In 1840 the Inn was the subject of a substantial refurbishment and reopened as the Royal Hotel but this, in turn, was largely redeveloped in 1899 for the Royal Arcade.

Angel Road
Residential road just beyond the City Walls. This principally residential road to the north of the City Centre takes its name from the Angel Pleasure Gardens which existed there in the C19th. The Victorian Angel Gardens pub still survives from that period half way along on the south side. The houses are an eclectic mixture of mid Victorian, terraced cottages, bay fronted Edwardian terraces, inter war local authority housing, post war Council flats and more recent private houses. There are substantial school buildings on both sides including Angel Road Infant School (formerly First School) and Angel Road Junior School with 325 pupils (formerly Middle School), which is the largest junior school building in Norfolk. Angel Road provides one of the principal entrances to Waterloo Park.

Anglia Square
1960s redevelopment scheme. Anglia Square was typical of many post war redevelopment schemes inflicted upon historic cities by modernist architects in the name of progress and, in this case, jobs. The scheme was driven by the dual aims of providing a solution to the need to accommodate traffic and also to facilitate the relocation of Her Majesty's Stationery Office (HMSO) to Norwich. The scheme obliterated the historic street network, which had been there in broadly the same form since pre Conquest times, as well as a fairly large number of locally and nationally important historic buildings. This part of historic Norwich, which had won a Civic Trust Award less than ten years earlier for its sensitive conservation and rehabilitation, was replaced by the Inner Ring Road, including the Magdalen Street Flyover, offices for HMSO and the Computer Services Division, a new Odeon cinema, a 750 space multi storey car park, some night clubs and a range of small and medium sized shops including a Sainsbury supermarket, all designed by Alan Cooke & Partners. Perhaps the most ironic part of the scheme was a first floor level, access road to the car park from the Ring Road, called Green Lane – either the most optimistic piece of road naming in Norwich or unprecedented tongue in cheek humour

From top: Anglia Square from St Augustines, Anglia Square Panorama.

from the Council's road naming section. Large derelict sites were also created for subsequent phases which never materialised. To begin with, the scheme was relatively successful, providing significant jobs, modern leisure facilities and reasonable shops although the aspiration that these would help to regenerate the flagging Magdalen Street never materialised. Following the development of large new superstores on the periphery of the City, Sainsbury's closed their store and, despite a range of regeneration proposals for the vacant sites and the Square as a whole, other 'nails' in the coffin followed

with Odeon pulling out and HMSO vacating Sovereign House while retail vacancy was a perpetual issue. In the 1990s the Square established itself as a focus of 'value retailing' and did reasonably well, in relative terms. The development passed to a succession of owners who variously floated regeneration proposals or gave up and sold it on again. In 2007 a major redevelopment was proposed to provide improved retail and a large number of apartments but, following the recession, the scheme was cut back to provide little more than a large superstore box sitting on ground level parking decks. It remains to be seen

whether this scheme will be any more viable than the many unrealised proposals that have preceded it and in the vein of achieving something which delivers real and distinctive regeneration rather than a rerun of the 1960s scheme in barely disguised modern garb, it might be better if the current proposal went the way of its predecessors. Currently (2011), the Square provides a fair degree of value retailing, an independent cinema and quite a lot of derelict land and buildings.

Anglia Television

Local Independent TV station. Established in 1959, in the former Agricultural Hall, as an independent company, Anglia TV served a large region reaching through Lincolnshire to South Yorkshire and southwards to the Essex suburbs of Greater London. Its iconic symbol was a large, silver, mounted knight. Apart from the successful news programme About Anglia, the company developed a niche for wildlife productions (Survival), quiz shows (Sale of the Century), 'Lifestyle TV' (Vanessa and Trisha) and drama (Roald Dahl's Tales of the Unexpected). In 2002 the station lost its separate identity and is now known as ITV Anglia. The company is part of ITV plc and currently broadcasts to Norfolk, Suffolk, Cambridgeshire, Essex (excluding the parts closest to the Greater London boundary), southern Lincolnshire, Northampton-shire, a small part of southern Leicestershire, northern Buckinghamshire, and northern Hertfordshire.

Anglican Cathedral

The Cathedral of the Holy and Undivided Trinity

The principal structure

The founder Herbert de Losinga had the cathedral church and cloisters designed as a whole. The first phase of building was begun in 1096 at the eastern end of the church so that the essential ecclesiastical elements were in place and it could be consecrated as soon as possible. This phase, up to the 5th bay of the nave and the tower to the top of the church roof, was completed, in Caen stone brought from France, by 1119 when Losinga died, but he never saw his design fully realised. The western portion of the nave, the remaining nine bays and upper storeys of the tower, were completed by Bishop Eborard also in Caen stone and Barnack stone from Northampton-shire. The whole church was built in just 50 years. At its completion the cathedral was the largest building in East Anglia and measuring 141m (461ft) long and, with the transepts, 54m (177ft) wide. The church has the 2nd longest nave and the largest decorated Norman tower in England.

Damage & Reconstruction

Today the building still retains its almost entirely unaltered original Norman ground plan, despite the havoc wreaked on the building over the years by devastating gales, fires, riots and wars. Just 23 years after the completion of the building, in 1169, lightning struck the tower and set fire to the building. The chapel of St Saviour at the eastern end was particularly badly damaged but repairs were soon made by Bishop de Turbe. Lightning struck again in 1271 but damage was minimal as a rain storm doused the fire but one year later, the Norwich Riot of 1272 resulted in extensive damage to the cathedral precinct. The timber roofs and timber furnishings caught fire and the extensive repair work took six years to complete. The cathedral was reconsecrated in 1278 and remains of a consecration cross survive on the north wall of the nave in the fifth bay from the west.

Norman north doorway of the Cathedral.

Repair work continued well into the C14th and several additions were also made to the cathedral and the buildings within The Close including a wooden spire, erected in 1297 on top of the Norman tower. Unfortunately the spire was to be the cause of yet another disaster when it was blown down by severe gales in January 1361 or 1362. The fallen spire badly damaged the presbytery and this allowed Bishop Percy to bring more light into the presbytery by rebuilding the upper half with the soaring windows

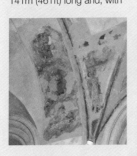

Opposite: Anglican Cathedral.
Above: Wall painting, possibly Bishop Herbert.
Right: Cathedral arcading.

that survive today. Percy ensured that the design of the new windows matched the earlier Norman architecture below. The spire was also rebuilt, this time in stone, but in 1463 it was damaged by fire. Bishop Goldwell rebuilt it again, this time in brick with a stone facing, and it survives today as the second highest spire in England (after Salisbury).

When lightning struck the spire in 1463, the nave was severely damaged when fire spread throughout the wooden roofs.

Evidence of this and later fires that ravaged the cathedral can still be seen on some of the stonework in the walls, the stone having turned pink through the heat of the fires. In the 1460s Bishop Lyhart took substantial measures to stop such fires ever taking hold again and completely replaced the nave roof with a stunning stone vault which was completed in the year of Lyhart's death, 1472. He also added the spectacular west window to light the beauty of his roof and its colourful bosses. The cathedral bosses total some

1106, including those of Lyhart's nave roof; the presbytery vault, added in 1480 by Bishop Goldwell, the transept vaults, added in 1509 by Bishop Nykke after a further fire and the cloister. The bosses represent an incomparable collection of medieval roof bosses and carvings and depict scenes from both the old and new testaments.

Henry VIII's Dissolution of the Monasteries brought an end to Bishop Losinga's Benedictine priory. In 1538 the Dean and Chapter was established but this did not herald less turbulent times for the cathedral. During Edward VI reign (1547-1553) the building was pillaged and many wall paintings whitewashed over. Equally disastrous were the years of the English Civil War (1642-1651). In May 1643 the cathedral was ransacked by Puritans who demanded further reform of the English Church. The inside of the cathedral was destroyed, the window glass was smashed, the wall paintings defaced, the vestments and books stolen, the tombs and monuments defaced or demolished and gunmen filled the cathedral drinking,

smoking and shooting. However, when Cromwell was asked by the Puritans of Great Yarmouth whether they could pull the cathedral down so that they could use the stone to strengthen their harbour and build new workhouses he refused. Unlike many of the churches in Norwich, the cathedral managed to escape the devastation caused by the 1942 Baedeker raids of the Second World War despite a large number of incendiaries falling on or close to it.

Interior elements

The Nave

The nave is striking because of its great height and length. The 14 arcaded, Romanesque bays exhibit a remarkable harmony with Bishop Lyhart's late C15th vaulted, Gothic roof. The roof bosses function as key stones to hold the roof together and here, in the nave, they tell a series of stories. Of the 250 in the nave, the set in the first seven bays, from the east end, tell the story of the Old Testament from Creation to the coming of Christ while the second set of seven bays cover the New Testament. Remarkably, most of the

Reconstruction of Cathedral south elevation in 1250.

Cathedral roof bosses.

bosses were carved and painted in situ. There are also two curious barley-sugar twist piers in the nave. These represent the original western extent of the first nave sanctuary and the location of the nave altar. The piers' two bays east are also barley twist but they are now concealed by a later covering. At the end of the nave, the great west window was also built by Walter Lyhart although the glass dates from 1854 by George Hedgeland. Towards the east end of the nave is the nave altar, Lyhart's pulpitum screen and the nave sanctuary. On the north side of the sanctuary a small chapel to Norwich's own saint, St William, would have stood. There is now a Chapel for Holy Innocents in the sanctuary.

Elsewhere in the nave there is a large brass font which was once a boiling pan used at the Nestlé chocolate factory that stood on the site of what is now Chapelfield shopping mall. The font was given to the cathedral when Nestlé closed their factory and moved from Norwich in 1996, the 900th anniversary of the foundation of the cathedral.

North Nave Aisle

Within the North Nave Aisle there are a number of interesting features including the table tomb of Sir James Hobart, Attorney General to Henry VII. There is also a monument to the remarkable Osbert Parsley who sang at daily services from 1535, when the Benedictine monks still inhabited the Cathedral, through 1549 when Latin services were translated into English and 1553 when services were back in Latin again, up until 1585 when they were again delivered in English. He also composed church music including a Magnificat performed during the visit of Elizabeth I in 1578.

South Nave Aisle

At the extreme east of the South Nave Aisle, close to the pulpitum screen and in the upper Norman vaulting, is the earliest surviving wall painting. Dating from about 1175, this shows Herbert de Losinga paying the King for his bishopric. Close to this is the skeletal, Elizabethan monument to Thomas Gooding who was reputedly buried standing up. Also in this section of the nave is the elaborate tomb of Bishop Nykke dating from 1536. Next door is a memorial to Dean Fairfax, relative of the commander of the New Model Army and victor at Naseby. References to him on the tablet were subsequently scratched out

Clockwise from top: Choir stalls, ambulatory, Anglo Saxon style detailing.

by Royalist sympathiser Bishop Moore.

Choir

The choir holds an interesting collection of stalls which occupy the same position as those in the original priory. Most date to the time of Bishop Lyhart and Bishop Goldwell who restored the cathedral after the fire of 1463, but some were provided by Bishop Wakering and date from 1420. The stalls have misericords: folding seats that have built in 'pity shelves' on which clerics could lean during long services. Misericords are often highly decorated and those in the cathedral are carved with a range of designs including the seven

deadly sins, St George and the Dragon, a crowned head and a huntsman with stag and hounds. Three misericords were missing so it was decided that they would be replaced by local carpenter Joe Dawes in celebration of the Millennium. The carvings depict The University of East Anglia, Norwich City Football Club, and Queen Elizabeth II's visit to Norwich to distribute the Maundy money in 1996. Above the choir stalls is the organ, built in 1942 with 6655 pipes but some were part of previous reconstructions dating back as far as 1660. The earliest recorded reference to an organ is 1333. Finally, beneath the tower space, is the C14th Pelican lecturn.

North Transept

On the north wall is the Norman Bishop's door, originally providing a direct link from the Bishop's Palace, and above this are triangular decorative features and carved heads. These are thought to be Anglo Saxon in style and may have been recycled from an earlier, demolished church, possibly Christ Church. The stained glass above these features is modern and includes works by John Hayward, produced for the Millennium, and Keith New, produced from pieces originally in St Stephen's Walbrook (London). The altar is from St Saviour's Chapel and the reredos behind it was painted by Norwich artists between

1385 and 1430 and was moved here from St Michael at Plea. East of the transept is St Andrew's Chapel.

South Transept

On the east side is St Catherine's Chapel and beside it is the blocked door to what was St Peter and St Paul's Chapel. The 75 roof bosses were the last to be produced and were just completed at the time of the Reformation.

Presbytery

The presbytery, at the east end of the nave, is thought to be based on the basilica of the Imperial Palace in Trier, built in 300 A.D. This element of the Cathedral is composed of ground and first floor Norman arcading begun in 1096, with a delicate clerestory level built by Bishop Percy from 1362 all crowned by Bishop Goldwell's vaulted roof knitted together by 128 bosses. His elaborate tomb is on the south side. At the far eastern end of the presbytery there is a wooden throne or cathedra constructed in 1960 but with a more recently added back. More impressive, however, are the pieces of weatherworn stone at the base of the chair. These probably date to the C8th and are the oldest element of the cathedral church. They are thought to be the remains of a much earlier throne brought from North Elmham, the original centre of the Bishops of East Anglia. Norwich cathedral is also the only cathedral in Northern Europe to have always kept its throne facing the congregation and behind the high altar. Usually the throne is sited to one side of the altar. In the middle of the presbytery, a black slab marks the tomb of Cathedral founder Herbert de Losinga. Just beyond Goldwell's tomb is the shield of the Boleyn family. William, grandfather of Anne Boleyn is buried south of the high altar sanctuary.

Ambulatory

The ambulatory is a horseshoe shaped walkway, wrapping around the presbytery and providing access to a range of small chapels. Jesus Chapel on the north east side of the Ambulatory, dates from the very beginning of the

---

Above: Bishop's Throne. Below (clockwise): St Saviour's Chapel, effigy of St Felix, St Luke's Chapel.

Cathedral's construction. The stained glass, although mainly Victorian, includes a small Flemish C16th roundel, originally in Surrey House and C14th fragments relocated from Norfolk and Suffolk churches. There are surviving fragments of C13th wall paintings and the displayed panel painting, 'Adoration of the Magi', is thought to be by Martin Schwarz of Rothenburg, with a date of 1480. The chapel also contains a rare example of a sealed medieval mensa – an altar top designed to contain religious relics. The wall paintings are copies of C12th originals.

Next, in clockwise order, is St Saviour's Chapel, separated from the ambulatory by an elaborate iron screen designed by Stephen Dykes Bower and made by Eric Stevenson. The Chapel is the Regimental Chapel of the Royal Norfolk Regiment and commemorates its fallen from the Regiment's formation to more recent wars. It contains an outstanding triptych painted between 1385 and 1430 by Norwich screen painters.

Before reaching St Luke's Chapel there is a very early statue in a niche, thought to be St Felix, first Bishop of East Anglia. It was originally located above and outside the Bishop's Door, where a replica is now positioned. St Luke's chapel on the south east side of the Ambulatory was also part of the first phase of the building and acts now as the parish church for The Close,

replacing the lost parish church of St Mary in the Marsh. Stained glass includes the Virgin and Child dating from the 1460s and relocated from Ringland church. There is also an impressive surviving element of a C13th wall painting scheme which originally extended throughout the building. The C15th Seven Sacraments font was relocated from the now lost St Mary in the Marsh. The Despenser Reredos or Retable, the painted screen behind the altar, was only saved from destruction by clever-thinking clergy who disguised it as a table top. The stunning retable, one of the finest C14th painted panels in Europe was possibly painted by Thomas Okell and was only rediscovered in 1847 and restored in 1958.

The Bauchon Chapel is located on the south side of the Ambulatory and was added in 1325-35, with the vaulted roof being completed just after 1460. The stained glass depicts the Benedictine order and is modern, designed by Moira Forsyth and made by G. King & Sons in 1964. There

is a strong possibility that C14th wall paintings survive beneath the whitewash. The painting, 'Presentation in the Temple' is by John Opie and dated 1791.

Reliquary Arch

Directly north of the high altar and spanning the ambulatory or walkway around the presbytery is the reliquary arch. This was added in the late C13th to house the cathedral's holy relics. These relics could include the bones of a saint or holy person, fragments of their clothing or some of their possessions. The room above the arch would have kept the relics safely away from pilgrims or any disturbances – it is likely that the arch was built after the riots of 1272. Since 1972, the room has stored the cathedral's treasury. The treasury holds plate from churches throughout Norfolk as well as some 27 pieces of silver from churches within Norwich. This includes spoons, cups, flagons and dishes. The reliquary room also contains the most extensive collection of surviving wall paintings within the

Cathedral Treasury.

Reconstruction of the pre Reformation Cathedral and Priory.

cathedral. They date from the C14th but much earlier wall paintings, possibly c 1175, can be found in the south aisle of the nave. They are in an area that once housed the Lady Chapel and the fragments show the Nativity scene.

Anglican Cathedral Almonry

Lost monastic buildings providing hospitality to the poor and pilgrims. The Almonry of the Benedictine friary at the Cathedral was located just inside the precinct wall and to the south of the Ethelbert Gate in what is now the south west corner of Almary Green. The Almonry would have dispensed food and other provisions to the poor (including lepers) and provided lodging and hospitality to pilgrims although more well to do guests would have been accommodated at the Hostry. The Almonry also contained a school for poor scholars by the C13th, making it the earliest school of its kind. By the C14th fee paying borders from the

wealthy classes were also accepted into the school. Nothing remains of the complex apart from a few imprints on the precinct walls against which the Almonry buildings were constructed.

Anglican Cathedral Belfry

Lost bell tower. Just inside The Close and south of the Erpingham Gate is the site of the Cathedral Bell Tower or Clocher. This was a substantial masonry structure 14m (45 ft) square. Bartholemew Cotton says that it was in existence before the 1272 Riot and the Cathedral's Customary of 1260 refers to the 'greater bells' as distinct from those within the Cathedral tower. This pre Riot date is supported by the probability that the monks used the Belfry as an archery platform to snipe at the citizens in Tombland during the Riot. It also perhaps explains why the citizens regarded it as a legitimate target and burned it down when they broke into the precinct. The Sacrist Roll indicates that rebuilding

work started in 1291 but probably wasn't completed until some time between 1298 and 1307. The rebuilt Belfry was made of Caen and Barnack limestone and crowned by a lead spire. While the bells above the Choir, in the Cathedral tower were used for daily services, the five 'greater bells' in the Belfry were reserved for major feasts and festivals and were in a special structure partly at least because it was better able to cope with their weight and vibration than the main tower structure of the Cathedral. It is also suggested that the Belfry had a functional relationship with the lay cemetery in the north west of the precinct and the charnel house (Carnary College). The Belfry was still surviving in Cunningham's perspective of 1558 but was partly demolished in 1569. The foundations were unearthed by Cathedral Surveyor J.H. Brown in 1881 confirming its location and scale, while a fragment survives in the cellar of No. 71.

Anglican Cathedral Chapter House

Lost element of the former priory. The Chapter House played an important role in the ecclesiastical ritual of the monastery but also acted as a pivotal administrative space while providing a burial place for people deemed to be sufficiently important by the prior – it was the first designated resting place of St William. Located immediately to the east of the cloisters and forming part of their outer wall, the only surviving element of the Chapter House is the screen originally linking the two buildings and constructed in the 1320s. The building itself would have been built in the early C12th and its dimensions were 25.9m (85 ft) by 13.7m (45 ft). It is probable that it was a two storey construction with a polygonal apse and two windows in each of seven bays and that it was rebuilt in this form after the 1272 Riot. The building was demolished in the 1560s and some of the masonry was used to block up the openings in the entrance. These were subsequently unblocked in 1850.

North Cloister range.

Anglican Cathedral Cloisters

Largest cathedral cloisters in England. The cloisters are reputedly the largest surviving monastic cloisters in England. Unfortunately the original single storey Norman cloisters were damaged by fire during the 1272 riots prompting an extensive remodelling. The buildings around the south, west and east sides of the cloister contain remnants of C12th masonry, including arcading, and the western buildings retain five circular windows with splayed openings. The majority of the cloister, however, dates from the late C13th to mid C14th. The new two-storey cloisters were paid for from the monks' own funds and took 133 years to complete because of lack of money and the outbreak of the Black Death (1347-1350). Bishop Walpole began work on the east walk in 1297 as reflected in the Geometric architectural style of the windows. Walpole's successor, Bishop Salmon, continued building with the south walk and the west and north walks then followed. The cloisters are considered to have been completed by about 1350 in the Decorated architectural style of the late C13th to mid C14th. The window tracery of the north walk, however, seems not to have been finished until the late C14th or was modified during this time as it contains window designs in the Perpendicular style.

The north walk contains beautiful Elizabethan wall paintings of the Coats of Arms of dignitaries who were associated with the 1578 visit of Elizabeth I. On the green at the centre of the cloister is a labyrinth built in 2002 to commemorate the Golden Jubilee of the current queen, Elizabeth II.

At the south east corner of the nave, next to the south transept, is the more spectacular of two doors leading from the priory cloisters into the cathedral church – the Prior's Door. The door dates to about 1300 and has a finely carved arch decorated with thin piers at its sides and decorated recesses in the arch. These recesses contain statues of Christ at the top, John the Baptist and possibly Aaron to the left, and David and Moses bearing a scroll detailing the Ten Commandments to the right. To the right of the doorway are three sedilia, or seats, recessed into the wall of the cloister.

Anglican Cathedral Hostry

New Cathedral education/visitor centre.
Located directly adjacent to the west wall of the cloisters, the Hostry was intended to be accommodation for favoured guests at the monastery. The original surviving elements include the back (east) wall and the porch. It is probable that the main internal structure, like the refectory, had the equivalent of a two storey floor to ceiling height. The building was substantially demolished after the Reformation. Designed by Hopkins Architects, the new, £12.5m Hostry provides education, exhibition and choir school facilities for the Anglican Cathedral. It utilises surviving elements of the medieval Hostry to recreate the historic space using glass, oak and limestone. The building was part funded by the Heritage Lottery Fund and opened in late 2009.The official opening, by the Queen in May 2010 was followed by an RIBA award in the same month.

Anglican Cathedral Infirmary

Lost priory hospital.
Located, unusually for monastic infirmaries, just south of the monastic Refectory, the Infirmary was constructed by John of Oxford in 1183 and may have replaced an earlier structure destroyed in a fire of 1171. The principal structure was an aisled hall but there were extensive additional elements including an infirmary cloister, the infirmarer's chamber, the latrine and an infirmary garden. Even after the Reformation, the Hall survived relatively intact until 1804 when it was substantially demolished to improve the view of the Deanery. A number of local artists recorded the Hall prior to or during demolition. The surviving remnants were decimated further by bombing in 1942. All that survives now is a section of south wall, incorporated into No. 64 The Close, and four column remnants sitting in the car park.

Anglican Cathedral Precinct

See *Cathedral Close*.

Anglican Cathedral Refectory

Rebuilt Monastic Refectory.
The original monastic refectory was built between 1125 and 1145. It was located directly adjacent to the south side of the cloisters and significant proportions of the north, south and east walls survive. Overall, the refectory was very large, measuring 51.8 m (170 ft) by 13.7 m (45 ft) making it one of the biggest in the whole country. It was also relatively unusual, having the dining area at ground level rather than on the 1st floor, but with a very substantial, at least two floor equivalent floor to ceiling height. The original arcading of 24 Romanesque window openings had been reduced to just four by 1873 but replicas were subsequently reinstated. Following the Reformation the original use ceased and in 1620 a prebendary house was constructed over the eastern end, retaining and incorporating much of the building's walls, but this was in turn demolished in 1873. The western section became a walled orchard and garden. Sitting on the footprint of the medieval refectory and utilising the surviving historic walls, the new refectory building, by Hopkins Architects, provides restaurant facilities and improved access to the Cathedral's Library. The principally timber and glass structure opened in 2005.

The Prior's Door.

Anglo-Scandinavian Norwich

Pre Conquest Borough

It is probable that Norwich began not as a single urban centre but as a series of urban nodes. Northwic, probably the largest, was a relatively densely developed settlement north of the river built around Fybrigate.
It was contained within a defensive, D-shaped enclosure following approximately the lines of modern Blackfriars Street, Cowgate, Botolph Street and Calvert Street, defended to the south by the river and additionally to the east by the Dalymond and to the west by the Muspole stream. Extramural development west of Northwic was based on modest clustering around

the churches of St Mary and St Michael. Mirroring this across the Coslany river crossing, more modest clustering occurred around St Gregory and the crossroads of two probable Roman roads (modern St Benedicts and a north to south road running from Oak Street to Ber Street).

Further nodal development occurred along the river margins, clustered around churches and key road/river intersections. Additional nodal development took place along the Roman roads.

Some concentrations of essentially industrial activity, developed most notably at Pottergate (pottery), the modern Forum site (gold working), modern Rose

Lane (iron and silver working), Berstrete Ridge (excavation of building materials), Parmentergate (leather working).

Following the attack of 1004 when Sweyn Forkbeard 'completely ravaged and burned the borough' (it is reasonable to assume that 'the borough' referred to Northwic and not to the whole urban area) the centre of urban activity shifted from north of the river to the south focussed around Tombland.

Between the attack and the Conquest it is probable that the redeveloped borough emerged as a grid iron settlement, with a new civic infrastructure around the previous 'empty space' – Tombland. It is probable that

Reconstruction of Anglo-Scandinavian Tombland.

the space then took on the role of 'town square' and the function of a very significant market, linked to the area around St Martins Church. Archaeological finds provide some flavour for the goods that may have been traded here. These would have included locally produced and imported pottery, soapstone bowls, antler work (fastening pins, tools, knife handles, combs, gaming pieces) flat Saxon type disc brooches with Scandinavian Borre (interlaced) or Jellinge (stylised animal) style ornamentation, silver and gold armlets and rings, decorative horse furniture in the Ringerike style in iron and bronze, Norwegian hone stones, glass linen smoothers, iron tools, swords, axes and spears, leather goods, raw materials such as gold and silver from

Anglo-Scandinavian period brooch excavated locally.

mainland Europe, tin from Cornwall, copper and lead from the Pennines, crucibles from Lincolnshire, whale bone and walrus ivory from Scandinavia and the North Atlantic, and a variety of food stuffs including imported Rhineland wine. Although small, live animals would probably have been traded here too (poultry), it is probable that, as in the later medieval period, special purpose livestock markets (cattle, swine, horses, sheep) would have been located elsewhere in the borough.

On Tombland was the Palace of the Earls of East Anglia, occupied in the immediate pre Conquest period by Gyrth Godwinson, the King's brother. Mottram intriguingly refers to the stone undercroft of the Earl's Palace just outside the Priory gate (Ethelbert Gate) and a record from the Cathedral refers to rent of 6s paid by Simon de Stonhus for the Stonehouse which belonged to the Priory. If this stonehouse stood on the site of the Earl's Palace which de Losinga may have caused to be demolished in the last decade of the C11th, it is plausible that a Saxon undercroft may have survived forming the

structural platform for a later Norman stone house. However, the fabric evidence for a Saxon undercroft is not compelling and while other writers have speculated about the Earl's Palace being just outside the later Ethelbert Gate, there is no evidence to support this hypothesis. An alternative but radical proposition is that the Palace was located elsewhere in Tombland and survives in part. The outside wall of the western Cathedral cloister contains small, round, splayed Saxon style windows. The wall in which they sit could conceivably have formed part of a Saxon Hall. The location of such a building on the south east junction of Holmestrete and the north/south route defining the eastern edge of the great Saxon market square would have most certainly been a prestige location in keeping with a building of this stature. If the Palace was built of stone and did sit in this location, it is probable that the Cathedral builders may have recycled it prudently into the later cathedral structure. Another speculative possibility is that Bishop Herbert recycled the Palace into his own Palace, just as he possibly reused elements of the Saxon Christchurch in his chapel. If either of these speculations is true, then the palace remnant is the only surviving example of a secular Saxon building in the England.

St Michael's Church was developed at the southern end of Tombland, possibly sitting within the space, rather than on the perimeter. This was the principal church of the borough and a hint of its stature is provided

by a walrus ivory cross excavated from its site in the C19th, during the construction of the underground toilets, and now displayed in the Castle Museum, on loan from the V&A. On the north side of Tombland, it is reputed that the Bishop had a house (site of the later Maids Head Hotel).

East of Tombland and probably located strategically on the north east corner of Holmestrete and the north/south St Martins to St Vedast route (i.e. beneath the later Cathedral), the church of the Holy Trinity or Christchurch was located. The dedication suggests a church of some importance and there is evidence that it also had a monastic function – in 1076 Abbot Ingulphus of Croyland refers to 14 monks from Christchurch Norwich. Since the decree to include a Benedictine Priory within the Norman Cathedral was not issued until Christmas Day 1100, this early post Conquest reference suggests an existing priory at the Saxon Christchurch.

Beyond this civic centre it is probable that the new borough stretched from the river in the north to a defensive bank and ditch in the south, running roughly along the line of the current Mountergate and Stepping Lane, and from the Great Cockey in the west to the river marshlands in the east, and was laid out on a relatively regular grid pattern with churches on many of the intersections. Archaeological investigation, evidence of 'lost lanes' from historic maps and references in the surviving street topography largely support this proposition. The principal west/east grid structure is likely to have been:

- Elm Hill, passing St Simon & St Jude, extended through the Wensum Street frontage and street block eastward to emerge in Palace Plain (this extended route has been identified from archaeological excavation), passing north of St Martins and to continue along the now disappeared Worlds End Lane.
- Waggon and Horses Lane leading to Palace Street and thus, south of St Martins, to the first section of Bishopgate.

- Holmestrete (St Benedicts/Bishopgate Roman Road) itself, passing St Christophers, St Peter Hungate, Christ Church and St Helens.
- Bedford Street (then Pottergate) leading, via St Michael Motstowe, to Queen Street, via St Mary the Less through

Above: Remnant of a walrus ivory cross excavated in Tombland. Right: Anglo-Scandinavian style townscape.

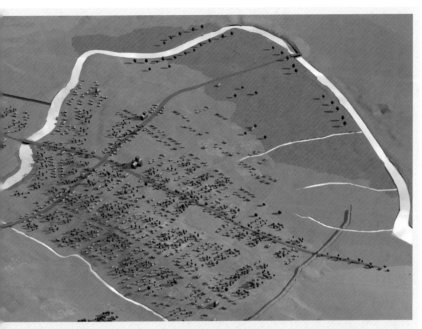

Reconstruction of the Anglo-Scandinavian Borough looking to the north east.

Tombland via St Michaels, and then to what is currently the main route through the Cathedral Close, passing St Ethelbert and St Mary in the Marsh.

• The western end of London Street (Hosyergate), passing modern Jarrold, cutting through modern Castle Meadow obliquely (a much later insertion), to link, south of St Cuthberts along the now lost Beugate or Neugate, with St Faith's Lane.

• Beginning approximately at the eastern end of Davey Place (previously Kings Head Yard), cutting through the Castle then through King St, across the later Franciscan Friary site to join an extant lane north of St Vedast.

• An east-west route, beginning at what was later to be White Lion Street (Saddlegate), cutting across the later Castle Bailey (now Castle Mall) past the Anglia TV Stave church and St John the Evangelist to link with Rose Lane and then St Vedast.

• Little Orford Street (approx the rear of Debenhams), running along the south side of Orford Hill, cutting through the corner of Orford Street to link with Farmers Avenue and another church discovered during the Castle Mall excavation, linking to a now lost lane cutting east from Cattlemarket Street to connect with a lane running to the north of St Peter Parmentergate and eastward across King Street following a further extant lane.

The final east-west grid route is also suggested as the intramural route defining a southern defensive bank and ditch. While the existence of such a defensive structure is speculative, there is some archaeological evidence to support at least parts of it – notably excavations at Stepping Lane in 2000 revealing a 4m wide, 2m deep ditch and also some indications from excavations on the Castle Mall site. The road within the ditch would most probably have taken the following route:

From the Great Cockey in the west (which would have formed the western defensive perimeter of the planned borough) at a point roughly equivalent to St Stephens Plain, running up Westlegate (formerly Wasetlgate – street of pastry

View looking north from the Gate on Ber Street.

or white bread makers) past All Saints, picking up a series of extant lanes running east from Ber Street, through the now lost Scoles Green to Stepping Lane and Mountergate. Recent excavations here have uncovered the original road line, relocated to the north when the Austin friary enclosed the site later. The defences would have stopped at the mashy river margins in the area now east of Mountergate but the intramural road would have turned north to form the eastern boundary of the settlement. Interestingly, Mountergate and the westerly section of Recorder Road were originally known as St Faith's Lane and it is not surprising therefore that the continued route runs along Recorder Road, through some surviving lanes in The Close to pick up the north-south line of Bishopgate and connect with the end of the now extant Worlds End Lane

The north-south alignments are more speculative since the development of the later Cathedral obliterated much of the evidence but excavations on the Franciscan Friary site in 1993 and subsequently at Palace Street, reveal the ends of routes which, in all likelihood, originally spanned the Cathedral site. The suggested routes running parallel to the St Faith's route described above were likely to have been:

• From Palace Plain west of St Martins, and possibly an early river crossing on the site of modern Whitefriars Bridge, through The Close and through the nave of the later Cathedral, the probable site of the pre conquest Christchurch (works to the Norman Bishop's Palace in 1960 uncovered skeletons to the north of the Cathedral, probably forming part of Christchurch graveyard) and St Mary in the Marsh, to emerge from The Close along the north-south dog leg of St Faith's Lane and thence to Rose Lane and St Vedast.

Reconstruction of the view across Fyebridge to Northwic.

Evangelist and St Peter Parmentergate.

- From modern Monastery Court, just south of the river, past St Peter Hungate and St Michael Motstowe, along modern Redwell Street (known earlier as Hundegate) and Bank Plain, through the modern Castle Mall site and past the Anglia TV Stave church, crossing Cattlemarket Street and entering the now extant Globe Lane and thus to the southern defences.

- From the current St Georges Bridge, which may have been the site of another early river crossing, along St Georges Street (Neubriggate) and up St Andrews Hill, cutting across the site of Castle Mall and possibly passing through the site of the later Castle Keep – while excavating a well beneath the keep in 1784, workmen found a 'beaten foot-path used before the hill (Castle Mound) was thrown up' at the same level as the ground outside the ditches – passing the Farmers Avenue excavated church and St John de Berstrete (now St John Timberhill) before joining Berstrete.

- From a street block on Palace Street into The Close and across the west front of the later Cathedral, running along the eastern edge of the Upper Close and passing St Ethelberts, leaving The Close and entering the former Franciscan Friary precinct the route picks up two excavated sections of early roadway and terminates at Rose Lane.

- Fybrigatte to Conesfordgate passing St Simon & St Jude, St Michaels, St Cuthberts, St John the

It is interesting that at this point, Berstrete splays suggesting it formed a junction receiving the two converging routes from the north.

There is additionally the possibility of a route running along the inside of the Great Cockey with modern Red Lion Street known originally as Baxtergate or Bakers street. This would have crossed modern White Lion Street (Saddlegate) and continued along Back of the Inns/Castle Street (Cockey Lane), crossing Hosyergate (London Street) and eventually emptying into the Wensum.

This 'other Norwich' is all the more fascinating because, while the Cathedral and Castle precinct developments of the post Conquest period obliterated large proportions of the Anglo Scandinavian Borough, what survived, formed the basis of the latter medieval and therefore the modern City. A great deal of the City's modern urban structure and what we move around on today was therefore laid out originally by our Anglo Scandinavian forebears almost exactly a thousand years ago.

Anglo-Scandinavian buildings.

Clockwise from top: Civic portrait of Mayor Thomas Anguish, Anguish memorial in St George's Tombland, door lintel at Anguish's House.

Anguish, Thomas

Philanthropist.
Former Sheriff and Mayor of the City, Anguish, was a wealthy grocer who lived on the site of the current Maid's Head. He was appalled by child poverty and when he died in 1617 he made provision in his will for a site in Fishergate to be used as a hospital "for the keeping and bringing up and teaching of very poor children". Accommodation was originally for boys but his legacy enabled the provision of a Girls Hospital in Lakenham by the C19th. Today the Anguish Education Foundation run by the Norwich Consolidated Charities is worth about £8.5m. Grants are made currently to applicants aged under 24. A monument to Anguish was erected in St Georges Tombland, at his death, and shows him kneeling with his seven sons, wife, two babies and three daughters. The skulls held by the children denote that they died prior to their father.

Anne of Bohemia

Queen of England. The wife of Richard II, Anne of Bohemia became Queen at the age of 16 in 1382, the year before the couple visited Norwich on a national progress of thanks to areas that had been particularly diligent in suppressing the Peasants' Revolt of 1381.

As well as coming with the prestige position of the 'new Queen of England' she was also a high profile figure in European terms, being the daughter of the Holy Roman Emperor Charles IV and the sister of Wenceslas IV of Bohemia. To commemorate the visit, Bishop Despenser, who had personally led the suppression off the Peasants' Revolt in Norfolk, had the ceiling of the church of St Helen painted with 252 eagles – a symbolic gesture of tribute to the Holy Roman Empire. The Eagle Roof survives today as one of the City's outstanding examples of medieval art. Good Queen Anne, as she was known, was well regarded by the 'common folk' and created a stir by riding side saddle in her procession through the City.

Appleyard, William

First mayor. William Appleyard, son of Norwich MP Sir Bartholemew Appleyard, became the City's first Mayor in 1403/4. William was also a burgess to Parliament for Norwich

Eagle Roof of the Great Hospital commemorating the visit of Anne of Bohemia.

nine times and a knight. He was re-elected Mayor for the two succeeding sessions after his first term and again in 1411, 1412 and 1418. He lived in what is now the Bridewell Museum with his wife Margaret, who was one of the notable Clere family of Ormsby. He died in 1419 leaving money to the Carmelite friary. He is commemorated by a stone plaque at the Bridewell and in the name of Appleyard Crescent at Mile Cross.

Arcade
See *Royal Arcade*.

Archant
Newspaper & publishing business. Archant is the largest, independent regional newspaper publishing group in the UK. In 1845 Jacob Henry Tillett, Jeremiah Colman, John Copeman and Thomas Jarrold started the Norwich-based Norfolk News. The Eastern Weekly Press was launched in 1867 and in 1870 was renamed the Eastern Daily Press. The Eastern Evening News was launched in 1882 and both papers continue in production (end 2011). As the business grew it moved premises in 1902 to London Street, 1959 to Redwell Street and again in the late 1960s to its present headquarters location the purpose-designed Prospect House at the top of Rouen Road.

At the end of the sixties, Eastern Counties Newspapers began its corporate expansion with the coming together of ECN with the East Anglian Daily Times Company to form Eastern Counties Newspapers Group (ECNG). ECNG developed further with the launch of

Early production of the EDP and EEN.

Community Media Limited (CML) in 1981, a weeklies publishing operation based in Bath which launched and acquired titles in Scotland and the West Country. In 1985 ECNG purchased the East Anglia-based Advertiser group of weekly free newspapers. These businesses operated as separate entities until the mid 1990s when they were brought together under the ECNG banner. ECNG itself grew in 1993 when it bought four weekly newspapers in Huntingdon, Ely, Wisbech and March from Thomson. The acquisition of

Peterhead-based P Scrogie followed shortly afterwards. In September 1996 ECNG entered the rapidly developing world of electronic publishing with the launch of its own internet publications and website design services. In April 1998 ECNG bought Home Counties Newspapers Holdings plc with an agreed bid of approximately £58m. HCNH published a range of 26 weekly paid and free titles across Greater London and the Home Counties. The title portfolio included the Hampstead & Highgate Express, the South Essex Recorder series, the Herts Advertiser series, the Comet series, the Herald group and the Welwyn & Hatfield Times.

Consumer magazine publisher Market Link Publishing, now Archant Specialist, based in Essex was acquired by ECNG for £5m in autumn 1999. Its titles now include Photography Monthly, Professional Photographer, Pilot and Sport Diver. The launch of a county magazine in Norfolk in 2000 saw the beginning of what is now Archant Life, the country's biggest publisher of county magazines. The division was subsequently given scale through acquisitions in the North West, the Cotswolds and the South and South East of England. In March 2002, ECNG changed its name to Archant, a move prompted by the broadening geographic scope and growing range of its activities. In December 2003, Archant purchased 27 weekly newspapers from Independent News and Media in two separate deals worth up to £62m. The titles included the Islington Gazette, the East London Advertiser, the Barking & Dagenham Post and the Kentish Times series. In early 2005, Archant acquired two magazine publishers Romsey Publishing Group, which became part of Archant Specialist, and Highbury Local Publications, which became part of Archant Life and Archant London. In summer 2005, Archant Anglia was merged with Archant Norfolk and the newly created Archant Herts & Cambs, a division of Archant Regional. In early 2006, Metropolis Publishing's six London lifestyle magazine titles were added to the Archant Life stable. They were quickly joined by six county magazine titles in the Midlands from Advent Media. In April 2007, Archant Scotland's eight newspaper titles were sold to Johnston Press for around £11m. The company retains its headquarter location in Norwich with functions split between Prospect House and £40m Print Centre at Broadland Business Park. The company turns over £175m annually and employs 1,000 people.

Argyle Street

Famous City squat. Argyle Street formed part of the wave of terraced housing development which took place within the Walled City following the approval of Artisan's Dwelling Act of 1875. In this case, most of the escarpment between King Street and Ber Street was developed by tightly packed, 2 up/2 down terraced houses. These survived for less than 100 years and the majority of them were redeveloped by

the radical City Council clearance scheme of the late 1950s/early 1960s when the character of the area was changed totally with the development of Normandie Tower, Rouen Road, cluster block housing and industrial sheds. Argyle Street, however, avoided this redevelopment and by the late 1970s there was a move for the University to purchase the surviving terraced houses from the City Council for student accommodation. The plans faltered when the Government refused financial assistance and as the houses sat empty waiting for alternative proposals, 120 squatters moved in over night to begin Britain's longest running squat. The following year, the squatters formed a co-operative and, supported by the Council, sought financial aid from the Government funded Housing Corporation. In 1981 the principle of a £1m renovation grant was agreed but the following year the Department of the Environment blocked proposals for the Council to sell or lease the properties to the co-operative. By 1984

there seemed little prospect of concluding the issue positively and the Council resolved to demolish Argyle Street and redevelop it for new Council properties. In 1985 the bailiffs moved in, the 'Republic of Argyle Street' was evicted and the bulldozers quickly demolished the properties. New properties were built shortly after.

Armada House
See *Garsett House*.

Arminghall

Suburban village. Located in the parish of Bixley, Arminghall is around three miles south east of Norwich City Centre. The church here is St Mary's and although it has its origins in the medieval period, it was heavily restored in the C19th. Arminghall Old Hall, on Arminghall Lane, was built around 1600, and was notable for an elaborately carved C14th arch, which had been relocated there, after the dissolution of the Carmelite or White Friars friary in Norwich but the hall was demolished in 1906. Arminghall is perhaps best known for the Arminghall Henge, a prehistoric timber

Below: Argyle Street in the late 1950s.
Right: The Arminghall Arch located now within the Courts building.

circle and henge monument discovered 1.5 miles north of the village in 1929 from aerial photography and first excavated in 1935. It consists of two concentric ring ditches with a horseshoe shaped arrangement of post hole pits within. Through radiocarbon dating, it is thought to date back to the Neolithic period between 3650 and 2650 BC.

Arminghall Arch

Surviving relic of the lost Carmelite friary. Built between 1343 and 1382 and thought to be part of the overall rebuild of the Carmelite friary in Whitefriars, the elaborate arch survived in situ until the Reformation when it was relocated and incorporated in the new manor at Arminghall, built by the Mingay family. It remained there until the early C20th but by that time the manor had become dilapidated and in 1906 the Colman family demolished the surviving buildings, recycling the important archaeological remnants to Crown Point, including the arch. In 1985, the development of the new Magistrates Courts complex just south of the river from

Sainsbury Centre for Visual Arts.

the original friary site, provided the opportunity to bring the arch back home (almost) and it now forms an internal feature within the courts foyer.

Art Galleries

Venues for viewing or buying art. Galleries for viewing art include principally those listed on the highlighted panel. Additionally, changing public exhibitions can be viewed periodically at the Assembly House, the Castle Museum supported by the East Anglia Art Foundation, The Forum, Norwich Arts Centre, Norwich University College

of the Arts, Sainsbury Centre for the Visual Arts, Wensum Lodge, the Playhouse and occasionally at open air venues such as St Peter Mancroft's railings. Galleries for viewing and buying art include:

- Fairhurst Gallery, Bedford Street
- Grapevine, Unthank Road
- King of Hearts, Fye Bridge Street
- Mandell's Gallery, Elm Hill
- Norwich Studio Art gallery, Upper St Giles
- Outpost, Wensum Street
- St Giles Gallery, St Giles Street
- Tudor Galleries, Noverre House, Theatre Street.

Art Galleries

Abstract & Constructivist – 400 works by artists who share a fascination with basic geometric shapes and bold primary colours *(Sainsbury Centre)*

Art Nouveau: Anderson Collection – extensive collection ranging from Tiffany and Lalique to unknown designers *(Sainsbury Centre – 3 yearly cycle, next exhibition Spring 2010)*

Civic Portrait Collection – selection of portraits of former Mayors of Norwich *(St Andrew's & Blackfriars Halls & City Hall)*

Norwich School of Artists – the most comprehensive collection of the work of the Norwich School of Artists in existence. The collection covers three generations of some fifty artists who form the nucleus of the School *(Castle Museum)*

Rembrandt Etchings – almost 100 etchings by Rembrandt, considered the fourth most important collection in the country after the British Museum, the Ashmolean Museum and the Fitzwilliam Museum *(Castle Museum)*

Robert & Lisa Sainsbury Collection – ancient and modern art spanning 5,000 years from across the globe *(Sainsbury Centre)*

Clockwise from right: Assembly House – dining room, south range, foyer, detail from former College of St Mary, and exterior.

Below: Footballer Ron Ashman.

Ron Ashman
played 1944 to 1963
appearances 662

Art School
See *Norwich University College of the Arts*.

Asger, John
Former mayor. Mayor of Norwich in 1426, John Asger provides an example of the strong linkages between Norwich and the Low Countries during the medieval period. Asger was also a Merchant of Bruges and, in 1431, petitioned Parliament for his Flanders born wife, his Zeeland born son and all his heirs to be treated 'in all things as true and loyal leiges'. He lived on the site of what was later to be Strangers Hall and one of his other houses, next to St Lawrence's, was given to a group of women for use as a beguinage.

Ashman, Ron
Norwich City footballer. Ron Ashman is regarded as one of the Norwich City Football Club greats, having spent all of his playing career with the Canaries. He put in 662 appearances (the second highest ever) between 1947 and 1963 and captained the famous 1959 Cup squad. When he finished playing, he spent four years as manager, finally leaving in 1966, moving on to manage Scunthorpe, where he enabled Kevin Keegan to gain his first break in professional football.

Assembly House
The quintessential Regency Assembly Rooms. 'No other town of its size in England has anything like it' said architectural historian Nikolaus Pevsner and this observation relates not only to the splendour of the Regency assembly rooms but also to the fact that, in

part, they represent a clever re-use of a medieval college. John le Brun founded a hospital north west of St Stephen's church, on the site of the current Assembly House, in 1248 dedicated to the Virgin Mary. In a short time, the foundation was changed to a College for Secular Canons. The first building also served as a Great Hall within which much of the City's civic business was conducted prior to the building of the Guildhall. This included a famous breakfast when the Earl of Surrey presented venison to the City and he, and the Bishop and Abbot of St Benet at Holm, had breakfast at the Chapel-in-the-Fields and 'there was great cheer made between them'. At the Reformation, the collegiate church and cloister were demolished but other buildings were first incorporated into domestic use and then into the Assembly House built by Thomas Ivory in 1755. During alterations to the Assembly House in 1901, it became clear that what is now the Music Room contains the core of the medieval Great Hall. Additionally, the medieval undercroft survives beneath the current Assembly House kitchens. The Assembly House hosted civic 'assemblies' on Guild Day where, as in 1802, 'the dresses of the ladies were elegant and highly becoming', sumptuous dinners such as that celebrating Nelson's victory at Trafalgar and performances and exhibitions including notably appearances by Liszt and Madame Tussaud before she established herself in London. The building was later used by Norwich High

School for Girls, and, during the Second World War, Oliver Messel, appointed by the War Office used the building as a camouflage school. He went on to become a famous costume and theatrical set designer.

After the war the house underwent considerable restoration programme, encouraged by Messel and funded by leading Norwich shoe manufacturer, H. J. Sexton. The house was reopened once again as a centre for entertainment and the arts.

Following a severe fire in 1995, the complex was subject to another major restoration which restored it to its former glory. The rooms of the Assembly House appear now almost exactly as they did at the height of the Regency period. The complex is now used for exhibitions, concerts and a variety of events and contains a restaurant, cafe and cake shop managed by local chef Richard Hughes. The surviving elements of the former College of St Mary are a Scheduled Ancient Monument.

ATM terminals

Location of automated cash machines. There is a reasonable coverage of accessible cash machines within the City generally and at least a dozen within the centre. Key locations include the Railway Station, Guildhall Hill (Tesco), Gentleman's Walk (Lloyds, Halifax), London Street (HSBC, NatWest, Nationwide), St Stephens Street (Halifax), Surrey Street (NatWest), Red Lion Street (Nationwide) and the two shopping malls (Chapelfield and The Mall).

Atthill, Capt. A.W.M.

Founder of the Royal Norfolk Veterans Association. In 1893 Captain Atthill appealed for funds to entertain old soldiers from the City who had seen active service. This proved to be very successful and led ultimately to the founding of the Royal Norfolk Veterans Association in 1898. Edward VII became patron in 1902 and Capt. Atthill remained chairman of the association for 28 years. He is commemorated by Atthill Road, just south of Waterworks Road.

Augustine Steward's House

Tudor merchant house. Augustine Steward's House lies on the opposite side of Tombland to the Cathedral. It is a crooked-looking C16th timber framed building that is now used as offices and as an antiques and collectables centre. Originally it was the home, shop and warehouse of three times Mayor Augustine Steward, one of Norwich's most important cloth merchants and politicians.

Augustine Steward's House in the 1930s.

Reconstruction of the pre Reformation Austin Friary looking north west.

WWII fighter pilot Douglas Badar.

Austin (Augustinian) Friary

Lost medieval friary.
The Austin Friars came to Norwich at the beginning of the reign of Edward I, settling on a site to the east of King Street and just south of modern Mountergate on land owned by Roger Miniot. In 1293, 1325 and 1335 they obtained licenses from Edward I, II and III respectively to extend their site and in 1348 they were allowed to absorb the church of St Michael at Conesford and nearly all of the land between Mountergate and the river. Between 1360 and 1368, they demolished St Michael's and constructed a substantial priory church dedicated to Our Lady & St Augustine. William of Worcester gives dimensions of the church as 60 paces long by 36 wide but this is likely to refer to just the length of the nave, excluding the choir and belfry passage, since Kirkpatrick gives the whole length as 140 paces. William also gives dimensions of a south cloister but excavations in the 1960s also reveal, unusually, a north cloister. The church was a centre of pilgrimage since it contained one of only three Scala Sancti in Britain (the others

being at Westminster Abbey and St Botolph's in Boston). The original Scala Sancta or Ladder of Heaven was in Jerusalem and comprised the 28 steps which led to the Praetorium of Pontius Pilate. These were moved to Rome by the mother of Constantine the Great and pilgrims were granted an indulgence if they ascended the 28 steps on their knees. The same indulgence applied to the chapel in Norwich. In 1419, Sir Thomas Erpingham paid for the glazing of the great east window of the priory church which commemorated 107 noblemen who had died childless since the coronation of Edward III. In 1457, Margaret, widow of Alderman Wetherby, gave 100 marks for a new library. The site also played an important education role with the order having the status as a School of Philosophy attracting students from all over Europe. The site was dissolved on 29th August 1538 and although redevelopment in the 1960s for a major brewery depot was thought to have destroyed the archaeology, recent excavations have revealed elements of the original friary.

Avenues, The

Out of Centre residential area. Located in the 'Golden Triangle' area west of the centre and leading from just beyond the City Centre towards the UEA from Park Lane, the Avenues housing largely dates from the 1920s. The Avenues means 'a way of approach', or a road bordered by trees. Heigham Park is located off The Avenues, and was opened in 1924 as Norwich's first, inter war, purpose-built park.

Aviation Museum

See *City of Norwich Aviation Museum*.

Aviation Pioneers

Innovators in aviation.
Just two years after the first manned balloon flight in the world had taken place in Paris in 1793, James Decker rose 'in the most beautiful manner, with considerable rapidity' from Quantrell's Pleasure Gardens in Norwich, to the delight of the watching crowd, and flew all the way to Loddon. This had been the first manned balloon flight from Norwich and was followed by many others including a display by the eminent balloonist Windham Sadler in 1815. In 1895,

Albert Coe took the first recorded aerial photograph in Britain from a hot air balloon flying over Thorpe Station. In 1912 Benfield Hucks, the first British aviator to 'loop the loop' made the first recorded aeroplane flight into Norwich in a Bleriot XI monoplane. In 1917 the Royal Flying Corps produced the earliest known aerial photo mosaic picture which depicted the Walled City of Norwich. The first all metal framed aeroplane to be made in Britain was produced by Boulton & Paul and exhibited at the Paris Exhibition of 1919. This was followed by the first all metal biplane bomber, the Sidestrand, which was taken into service by No. 101 Squadron RAF in 1926. In 1929 the airframe for the largest airship in the world at the time, the R101, was built by Boulton & Paul at the Riverside Works. In 1931 Aviation pioneer Amy Johnson piloted her Gypsy Moth into Norwich aerodrome at Mousehold and the same year the first air mail letter arrived in the City on 15th May. On 9th July 1940, Norwich had the dubious privilege of being the first place of any size to be bombed in the UK. It was also the first British City to be mentioned by name in official records relating to the Luftwaffe's bombing campaign. In 1941 British WWII fighter air aces Douglas Bader and Stanford Tuck took advantage of the City's leisure attractions when stationed at Coltishall airfield as did the volunteer American Eagle Squadron, before the official entry of the US into the War, and Free Polish squadrons from 1944. Most recently the City of Norwich Aviation Museum was the first aviation museum in the country to register with the Museums and Galleries Commission.

Aviva
See *Norwich Union*.

Aylsham Road
Radial Road. The road takes its name from its purpose being the main route from Norwich to the market town of Aylsham, a principal coaching stop on the Norwich-Cromer road. There is evidence of early occupation, with an early Saxon (C5th/C6th) cremation cemetery having been discovered in 1898 near Eade Road. A cremation urn and fragments of others as well as a square headed brooch were found. Despite this, subsequent development activity was minimal and, as late as the 1838 Ordnance Survey, there was very little development along the road. The map shows mainly open land, with the area east of Aylsham Road and south of modern Philadelphia Lane identified as Chalk Farm. North of the later Philadelphia Lane and east of Aylsham Road there are some very limited frontage building plots while the west side of the road is entirely undeveloped, apart from three mills. These included the St Clement's Mill, which was roughly opposite Philadelphia Lane in Press Lane. The Philadelphia Tower Mill, as it was also known, was built in 1875 but preceded by two post mills, the first dating from at least 1741. The last one was still there at the time of the 1898 Ordnance survey and although a photograph survives of it under repair in 1906, it was severely damaged by fire in 1913 and eventually demolished in 1920. Further north, and on the east side of the road

C19th housing for the middle classes.

there was a tower mill down a lane behind the surviving Windmill pub and opposite the pub on the site of the later Half Mile Road, a further tower mill. By the end of the C19th, Victorian terraced housing had been developed at the southern end, with a substantial school on its eastern side where it met the walled City (later to be bombed and redeveloped for the St Augustines Pool, now itself redeveloped). Further terraced housing followed in the Edwardian period although Chalk Farm still appears on the 1907 Ordnance Survey. Substantial Council housing was developed immediately after the First World War to the west at Mile Cross and Waterloo Park followed, on the east side. Notable buildings include the Norwood Rooms (see Capitol), St Catherine's Church, Mile Cross Methodist Church and the mock Georgian Territorial Army centre, built in 1939 as the headquarters for the newly formed 78th Heavy Anti Aircraft Regiment of the TA. Today the road provides the principal entry route from the north and acts as a local centre for the large area of housing on its east and west sides.

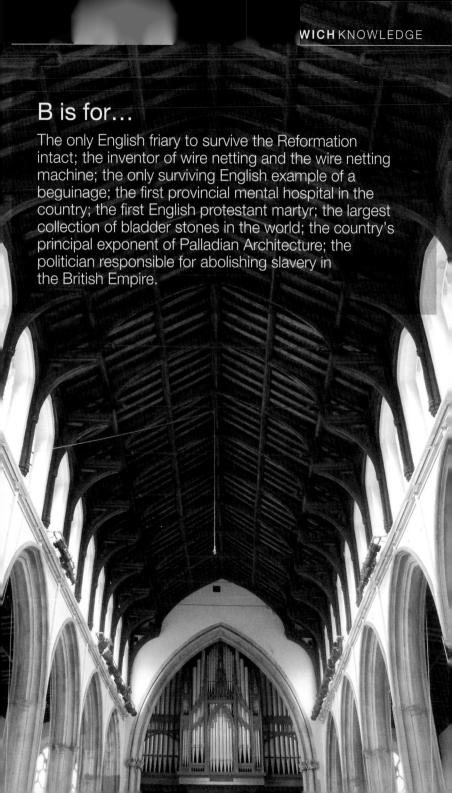

B is for...

The only English friary to survive the Reformation intact; the inventor of wire netting and the wire netting machine; the only surviving English example of a beguinage; the first provincial mental hospital in the country; the first English protestant martyr; the largest collection of bladder stones in the world; the country's principal exponent of Palladian Architecture; the politician responsible for abolishing slavery in the British Empire.

*Opposite: Blackfriars Friary.
Left: Henry Bacon's
House, Colegate.
Above: Interior of
Bacon's House.*

Back of the Inns

Ancient thoroughfare.
Now running from White
Lion Street to Castle Street
but originally including
Castle Street, until the
C19th when the two
became separate, Back of
the Inns was originally called
Cockey Lane. This reflected
its very early role as a path
running beside the Great
Cockey which defined the
western edge of the pre
Conquest borough. 'Cockey
Lane' was used from the
earliest records to the C17th
when the appearance of
major inns, and later
coaching inns, along the
Walk rebranded the street
as Back Lane then Backside
of the Inns, later shortened
to Back of the Inns. The Inns
in question included the
C15th Angel (later the
Royal), the Bear, the King's
Head, the Star and the Half
Moon. On the eastern side
the Castle Hotel also
backed onto the
thoroughfare. This is one of
the few streets in the City
that has always been a
pedestrian only route
despite the plea from the
Norwich Directory of 1783
that 'if the Back of the Inns
would admit carriages from
Hogg Hill to London Lane it

would be a safer
thoroughfare'. The street
suffered severe bomb
damage during the Second
World War but the post War
rebuilding, although not architecturally distinguished,
has maintained the medieval
feel of the street. Michael
Innes's Castle Mall entrance
of the early 1990s also sits
comfortably within its
historic setting, providing a
more distinguished
replacement for the rather
dull, post War rebuild of the
Castle Hotel.

Back's

See the *Curat House.*

Bacon's House

Medieval merchant house.
Bacon's House on the North
side of Colegate, is one of
the finest houses in the
street and has its origins in
the western range, running
up St Georges Street and
probably dating from the
mid C15th. Henry Bacon,
Sheriff in 1548 and mayor in
1557 and 1566, developed
this early range into a
substantial courtyard
mansion in the mid C17th.
The building became
subdivided subsequently
and was eventually used as
a shoe factory. By the 1970s

it was in an appalling state
of disrepair but was rescued
by the City Council and
refurbished/converted by
the City Architects
department (John Pogson)
into flats, a studio, a private
members club and a store
for the Civic Portrait
Collection.

Bacon, Richard Mackenzie

**Musical innovator and
journalist.** Born in
Costessey in 1776, Bacon
was notable as a writer on
music and proprietor then
later editor of the Norwich
Mercury. As a respected
printer, he formed a
partnership with Francis
Noverre and John Gilbert in
1807 to develop one of the
first Fourdrinier paper
making machines in the
country at Taverham Paper
Mill. He founded and edited
the Quarterly Musical
Magazine and Review
(London, 1818-30), the first
English journal devoted
exclusively to writing on
music. A strong proponent
of serious, all-sung English
opera, he also produced
two treatises on singing.
He is credited with founding
the Triennial Music Festival
which was to develop into

Baedeker Raids, clockwise from top: Heinkel III, St Bartholomew Heigham, St Stephen's Plain looking towards Buntings, St Benedict's Gate.

the Norfolk & Norwich Festival. His son Richard succeeded him as editor of the Mercury and went on to promote public works in the City including the Jenny Lind Children's Hospital and the Waterworks.

Baedeker Raids

Devastating wartime air raids. In 1942 the RAF 'area bombed' the historic, Hanseatic city of Lubeck. Outraged by this 'Terrorangriff' (terror attack), Hitler ordered reprisal raids on historic British cities. Reich Aussenministerium spokesman Baron Gustav von Stumm declared that historic buildings identified in Karl Baedeker's tourist guide would be obliterated. A Luftwaffe bomber force was assembled to deliver the attacks and was reinforced by units from as far afield as Russia and Sicily. On the moonlit night of

Monday 27th April 1942, and subsequently Wednesday 29th, parachute flares ignited over the NW of the City illuminating the way for 30 Dornier Do 217s and Heinkel He 111s of Kampfgeschwader 2 and Erprobungs Kommando 17, flying from North Holland and Lille, to deliver the largest fire bomb raid on any East Anglian target in the whole of the War – the 'Firebomb Blitz'. Within two hours, on the first night, 50 tons of high explosives were dropped on the City and on the Wednesday a further 45 tons of high explosive and 20,000 incendiaries rained down around the Castle and Cathedral. Many buildings which had survived from the C16th, including several medieval inns, were engulfed. Farmers Avenue and the north side of Timberhill were virtually obliterated. Opposite

St John's churchyard, an early Tudor group of buildings in Ber Street which survived a road widening proposal in 1936, ironically, was burnt out. Close by, Bonds store, the Norman church of St Michael at Thorn, the Saxon church of St Julian and the Jewish Synagogue were all gutted. The area around Orford Place, Rampant Horse Street and the eastern end of St Stephens was one of the worst devastated as was St Benedict's Gate. Some incendiaries hit the Cathedral but while 663 fires raged in the heart of the City, the Cathedral, Castle and the City's other medieval churches were spared. Beyond the centre, severe damage was also inflicted around Heigham, Earlham Road, Aylsham Road/Mile Cross, Drayton Road and Rupert Street. The fire service was so overwhelmed that many buildings were left to burn themselves out. On the first night 162 people were killed and 84 were dug out of the rubble. 69 died during the second night. One Heinkel was brought down by a Spitfire of 610 Sqd. over the Norfolk coast while a Dornier was destroyed by a 151 Sqd. Mosquito over the North Sea. The boasts from Dr. Goebbels' propaganda ministry the following day of 'the havoc wrought by last night's attack' and that 'extensive fires have ravaged the target area' were, for once, an accurate reflection of the situation.

Bagleys Court

Historic courtyard. Bagleys Court, located on the south side of Pottergate, probably takes its name from builder, Charles Bagley who was listed in the 1912 Kelly's Directory as being located there. However the buildings are much earlier than this, being of predominantly C18th construction with some earlier, possibly C16th walls. Originally the court would probably have been the courtyard of a merchant house and later the yard of the Farriers Arms pub which operated between 1839 and 1895 and is commemorated by one of the Norwich Lanes/HEART pavement sculptural plaques. The court had fallen into decline by the 1970s but an imaginative restoration scheme in 1982 produced an attractive range of speciality shops which continue to trade successfully.

Balderston Court

Georgian cottages. Balderstone Court is a group of restored Georgian cottages on Calvert Street.

Having fallen into a delapidated state, they formed part of the European Architectural Heritage Year, Heritage Over the Wensum scheme in 1975, and were converted to flats. Their name commemorates parish residents the Balderstone family. Sheriff and twice mayor Timothy Balderstone lived there in the early C18th and has an impressive memorial by Thomas Rawlins in St Georges Colegate. Later, Matthew Balderstone was a benefactor for poor children and the Bethel Hospital.

Bally

See *Haldestein's & Sons*.

Baltic Wharf

Modern housing development. Taking its name from an historic trading wharf which recalls the maritime connections between Norwich and the Baltic States, this 2006 housing development by Hopkins Homes is located to the east of Mountergate on the west bank of the Wensum.

Bank Plain

Historic thoroughfare. Originally a very ancient thoroughfare running past what is now St Michael at Plea, but was originally St Michael Motstowe in the pre

Conquest period, the street was also known as Motstowe. Later it became Redwell Plain, commemorating the red well at its northern end then Bank Plain when the Gurneys founded their bank there in 1775. This became Barclays and the original bank was redeveloped with the current building (now Open) appearing in 1929. Writer Ralph Motram was born at Gurney's Bank House in 1883.

Banks

Bank locations. All of the main clearing banks are represented within the City Centre with some presence at the larger suburban shopping areas. The key central locations include Gentleman's Walk (Lloyds TSB, Halifax), London Street (HSBC, NatWest, Nationwide), St Stephens Street (Halifax), Surrey Street (NatWest & Lloyds TSB) and Red Lion Street (Nationwide, Barclays).

Barclays

See *Gurneys*.

Bar Gate/Barregate

Lost City gate. This was the gate in the City Walls at Pockthorpe, also known as Pockthorpe Gate, and was built in 1338. The Gate was rebuilt after extensive

Reconstruction of Bar Gate or Barregate, also known as Pockthorpe Gate.

The former Barking Dickey Public House 1938.

damage caused during Kett's Rebellion in 1549 and was eventually demolished in 1792.

Barking Dickey

Former historic pub. Number 20 Westlegate is one of only five original thatched houses left in the City, after the 1507 fires that devastated many parts of Norwich. The C16th building has had a very varied past. During the C19th the property was a public house, known as the Light Dragoon. It later became known as the Barking Dickey because of the badly painted sign that depicted a mounted Light Dragoon – the sign looked more like a donkey braying (or indeed 'barking'), rather than a dragoon's horse – 'dickey' being the Norfolk dialect term for donkey. The first recorded licensee was James Moneyment, in 1830; the last was Edward Ringer in 1856. Subsequently, the building was used as a greengrocer's shop and then a bank. The building underwent significant repairs in the 1950s and the thatching was restored in the 1960s. Most recently it changed use to a café and hairdressers.

Barnard, Bishop & Barnard

Industrial innovator & inventor of the wire netting loom. In 1826 Charles Barnard started an iron mongery business in the Market Place. By 1844 he had responded to the need of farmers to protect their crops and had developed a rudimentary loom for weaving wire fencing. This rather basic invention made him the creator of the first wire netting machine in the world and, effectively the inventor of wire netting. The original machine survives in the Bridewell Museum. In 1846, John Bishop joined the partnership and its expansion necessitated a move to St Georges. His sons also became partners and Barnards became Barnard, Bishop & Barnard employing 105 people.

Further expansion required another move to Coslany Street and the establishment of the Norfolk Iron Works, where the company remained until the 1970s.

The respected designer Thomas Jeykll became associated with the company and produced imaginative, oriental fire place designs which the company produced. Jeykll went on to design gates which won medals in London and were eventually given to the Prince of Wales in 1864 and now form the entrance to the Royal Park at Sandringham.

By the 1870s Barnards had become even more ambitious and exhibited an iron pagoda at the 1976 Philadelphia Exhibition at which it was awarded a medal. Two years later the Pagoda was exhibited at the Paris Exhibition and subsequently purchased by the Norwich Corporation for £500. It was erected in Chapelfield Gardens and became a City landmark until it deteriorated and was demolished in the 1950s. Some of the sunflower motifs were incorporated in

Below: Barnards City Station Bridge.
Opposite (clockwise from top): Barnards Pagoda in Chapelfield, Barnard & Bishop Works, Coslany St 1938, Barnards replica gates in Chapelfield to a Thomas Jeykel design, and Barnards wire netting weaving machine.

the entrance to Heigham Park and reproductions have been introduced recently as gates to Chapelfield Gardens on Chapelfield East. During their 'pagoda' period, Barnards expanded into bridges and structural architecture including the surviving bridge on St Crispins Road, intended originally to access City Station, and the railway bridge at Lenwade. Architectural developments included the roof of the Agricultural Hall in 1881 and the roof of City Station in 1886.

By the late C19th the company had developed a more sophisticated wire netting machine and was supplying miles of wire fencing to Australia to combat the problem of rabbit infestation.

During the First World War, Barnards supplied the Government with 7,000 miles of wire fencing for use in the Egyptian desert, hand woven wire lattice for the Balkan theatre, stoves for the US Army Expeditionary Corps in France, castings for the Admiralty and a variety of other contributions to the War effort. After the War a site at the Mousehold Aerodrome was purchased and pressed into use for the new, and stronger, chain link fencing.

During the Second World War, the Mousehold factory majored in the production of artillery shells and parts for Hawker Hurricane fighters. Telegraph poles were constructed for the North African campaign and the ever present wire netting was pressed into service in creating temporary airfield runways. This contribution to the War effort did not go un-noticed by the Germans who bombed the factory in July 1940 and February 1941, although production was not seriously affected.

After the War, Barnards was taken over by the Sheffield based Tilney company who continued to make fencing. The company continued to innovate and by the 1970s had invented a wire to reinforce under sea oil pipes for the off shore oil industry. However, industrial amalgamations and the growth of property values meant that the Coslany Street site was sold to the Council for the Barnards Yard/Mary Chapman Court housing development in the 1970s and the Mousehold Aerodrome site at Salhouse Road was sold as a retail park in the 1980s. The only trace of Barnards now is the name of the housing scheme and the original wire netting machine in the Bridewell.

Barn Road

Orbital road. Originally the extramural route around the western section of the City Walls, Barn Road developed in the C19th as the City began to spill outside the Walls and Victorian yards and terraces were built between Dereham Road and Heigham Street. The road took its name from the Barn Tavern, developed in 1859 but destroyed during the devastating air raids of April 1942. The pub was quickly re-established as a temporary wooden hut until being replaced by the present building in 1956. It ceased to be a pub in 1991. The street itself housed a gas works by the 1870s but this became a timberyard, which still survives. In the 1960s the development of the Inner Ring Road swept away the eastern section of terraces exposing substantial sections of the City Wall. In the 1970s the Colman's Wincarnis (tonic wine) works just inside the City Wall was sold and redeveloped for Toys R Us and the 'Cathedral Retail Park'.

Barracks

See *Britannia Barracks* and *Nelson Barracks*.

Barrack Street

Orbital road. Known originally as Pockthorpe Street, after the hamlet of Pockthorpe, then Bargate after the City gate originally at what is now the Silver Road junction, then St James Street, after the church at its western extremity, the street eventually became Barrack Street to commemorate the Nelson Barracks which sat on its north side from 1791 until the early 1970s. Like Barn Road, the street accommodated spillage from the Walled City and as well as the substantial Barracks, it was home to Steward & Patteson's Pockthorpe Brewery. Also like Barn Road, its domestic scale transformed in the 1960s as the Inner Ring Road created the Cowgate roundabout and widened sections of the street. It stands ready for further transformation as the redevelopment of the Jarrold Printing Works and inter War Council flats will provide a new mixed use quarter for the City in the form of St James' Place.

Barwell's Court

Former historic court. Now a hideous, windowless alley running between the former Woolworth building (now M&S) and shops in St Stephens, Barwell's Court had been the site of an Elizabethan mansion up until 1915 and other ancient houses survived there until the Baedeker Raids obliterated most of it in 1942. Barwell's were a local wine merchant family who had premises there and John Barwell was dealing in foreign wines from St Stephens as early as 1802 although later company advertising literature claimed that they had been established prior to 1755. The dynasty survived here until after the War then moved to the Pigeons in Charing Cross, later the Hog In Armour.

Bassingham Gateway

Historic gateway. John Bassingham was a prominent goldsmith in the City in the reign of Henry VIII. His wealth was reflected in the elaborateness of his premises at 57 London Street and, in particular, the lavishly ornamented gateway. In 1857, when London Street was widened and his former premises were demolished, the gateway was bought by William Wilde and re-erected at the entrance to the Magistrates Court at the Guildhall.

Bates, Sidney 'Basher'

War hero. Originally from Camberwell London, Sidney Bates joined the Royal Norfolks in 1940 and secured the nickname 'Basher' from his exploits in the boxing ring. Two months after D Day in 1944 Sidney's company of the Norfolk's was attacked by the crack 10th Waffen SS Panzer Division 'Frundsberg' near Sourdevalle, in France, and were in danger of being overwhelmed. Sidney picked up a bren gun from one of his dead comrades and attacked the enemy single handed, killing at least 50 and causing the attacking force to retreat before he was mortally wounded. He received the Victoria Cross posthumously for his exploits. A memorial

Bassingham Gateway in the Guildhall.

commemorates his exploits in France and a road, Bates Green, bears his name in Norwich.

Bawburgh

Suburban village.
Situated 8km (5 miles) west of Norwich and with a population of 466, Bawburgh provides several points of historical interest. Its name is of Old English derivation and means 'Gadfly Fort'. The Flemish gabled Bawburgh Hall was completed around 1634 and its first owner was Sir Henry Jernegan, by grant of Queen Mary. By the first half of the C19th the Hall was however being used as a farmhouse. In 1856 the hall went up for auction and was purchased by Lord Strafford and incorporated into the Costessey Estate. It was sold on again after the First World War and had deteriorated by the Second World War. It was last sold on to Philip Vincent of Wramplingham Hall before its eventual demolition in 1963. However, the Slipper Chapel and Folly (The Hermit's House) still survive in the gardens of the Hall Farm Place residential

complex and date from the same period as the Hall although they contain earlier, recycled materials, probably from a demolished ecclesiastical structure. The early C14th St Mary and St Walston's church is Grade I listed with a round, probably pre Conquest, tower. The church is interesting for its dedication to St Walston, the patron saint of farmers, who may have been born in Bawburgh. The foundation of the church pre-dates the St Walston legend, but around 1015 St Walston's body was placed at the site of the current church and where his body lay Bawburgh Well is said to have sprung up. This well has been a site of pilgrimage ever since. Bawburgh Watermill was rebuilt in 1876, but a mill was first mentioned in the Domesday Book. The C19th mill still exists today but has been converted into residential property. Other historic properties include the Grade II* Listed Church Farmhouse, with remnants dating from 1278; the Kings Head pub, dating from 1602; the Grade II* Listed Lodge Farm, dating from

about 1630; Child's Terrace, which is mainly C17th but with some C15th material and the 400 year old Post Office Cottage.

BBC East

Regional HQ of the BBC.
This is the eastern region of the BBC serving Norfolk, Suffolk, north Essex, Cambridgeshire, Hertfordshire, south Northamptonshire, Bedfordshire, Bucking-hamshire and south Lincolnshire. Its flagship news programme is Look East which began in 1959, making it the longest running regional news programme on the BBC. The region is also the controlling centre for BBC Radio Cambridgeshire, BBC Essex, BBC Radio Northampton, BBC Radio Norfolk, BBC Radio Suffolk and BBC Three Counties Radio. Established originally at Thomas Ivory's 1780 mansion St Catherines Close in All Saints Green, which the BBC expanded in 1975 and 1988, BBC East moved to Sir Michael Hopkins Forum building in 2001.

Clockwise: Bawburgh Slipper Chapel, Bawburgh Folly, Bawburgh Mill, Bawburgh Church Farm, Bawburgh cottages.

Beatles

British Pop Group. In 1963 on May 17th, the Beatles made their one and only appearance in Norwich and performed to a crowd of 1700 at the Grosvenor Rooms on Prince of Wales Road (now redeveloped as the Grosvenor House office block) for a fee of £250. Their appearance came immediately after their first No. 1 single and their first album topped the charts. Following the 'gig' they enjoyed fish and chips with fans at Valori's in Rose Lane. In 2002 Paul Macartney, former Beatle and popular music legend, returned and visited the University of East Anglia to make a public poetry reading.

From top: Queen Post roof in Bedford's, Bedford Street. Inset: Moulded head on Bedford Street building.

Bedford's

Medieval merchant house. Located in Old Post Office Yard, off Bedford Street, Bedford's is a Grade II* listed building. It houses one of the 26 scheduled ancient monuments in Norwich, a substantial medieval undercroft, and includes a first floor range with the finest Queen Post roof in the City. Surviving the Great Fire of Norwich in 1507 the building was taken over by John Clifford, a book-binder, whose business flourished in the early C17th. The building was transformed subsequently into a public house, the Nelson Tavern, although this was briefly renamed the Pink Dominoes between August 1880 and September 1881. This pub was just one of several in an area that became well-known as the venue for bare-knuckle boxing contests. After the First World War the building reverted to more domestic trades – a stationer, a confectioner and tobacconist, and a tea-merchant all occupied the building in their turn. During the 1970s the building was restored and re-designed by the City Council Architects Department (architect Jim Chapman) and converted into a restaurant, bar, shops and offices.

Bedford Street

Anglo Scandinavian period street. This street gets its name from the Bedford Alms public house (at 13 Bedford Street; known as the Duke of Wellington between 1822 and 1865) – this was closed in 1975. Bedford Street was originally part of Pottergate, and was formally known as Lobster Lane. However, the street's origins go back to a much earlier period. The most

Above: Beeston Hall and Beeston Red Hall.
Right: Britons Arms, former beguinage.

significant development cluster outside pre Conquest Northwic (the Anglo Scandinavian development north of the Wensum) was probably the area around modern Bedford Street/Lobster Lane, known during this period and later as Pottergate – street of the potters. It is possible that the Danes introduced industrial scale pottery making into both Thetford and Norwich on the same basis as the Baltic settlement of Hedeby where they developed a specialised manufacturing quarter producing pottery on a very large scale. It is also possible that, under Danish sponsorship, Rhineland potters were imported to start the industry here. The presence of an early pottery industry is supported by archaeological finds of kilns on both sides of Bedford Street and Lobster Lane as well as large quantities of Thetford type ware water vessel fragments

Beeston St Andrew

Deserted Village. The parish of Beeston St Andrew is located 4.8km (3 miles) north of Norwich and was named in the Domesday Book as 'Bestina' which meant 'sedge or bent grass enclosure'. The parish now has a tiny population of only

39 people (2001 Census) and encompasses a few farms and plantations as well as Beeston Hall and Beeston Park. Samuel Lewis writing in 1848 referred to the 'Old Hall' as having been built in 1610 and being 'a fine specimen of domestic architecture' but was redeveloped for the 'New Hall' which appears on Faden's map of 1797. This in turn was demolished in 1846 and the surviving Hall is a replica built in 1897 between two surviving C17th walls – the latter are listed but the former isn't. The parish church, which originally dated from around the time of the Conquest, was in ruins by the C16th and its conjectural location is based on crop marks and ploughed up tiles. The only surviving structures are the C18th Oak Lodge Farm and Red Hall which has Victorian additions.

Beguinages

Institutions for 'Lay Sisters'. Norwich is the only English city to have supported beguinages – religious sisterhoods living as nuns but without formal vows and retaining the power to return 'to the world' if they wished. Three communities are recorded. One lived in what was later to become the Britons Arms in Elm Hill, another lived in

the tenement of John Pellet in St Swithins parish from 1427 to 1444 and a third group, of three sisters, lived in the tenement of John Asger, a merchant of Bruges, in the parish of St Laurence.

Bell Avenue

Lost street. Bell Avenue developed after the Cattlemarket was established on the former Castle ditches. It provided a route from the Bell Hotel to the junction of Rose Avenue and Market Avenue (rear of Anglia TV). Additional to being one of the main routes across the Old Cattlemarket it achieved fame in the C20th as a departure point for coach tours notably by companies like Red Car and Votiers/Mascot. It also hosted a local pet shop institution, which claimed establishment in the reign of George IV, and had been relocated there after the redevelopment of Cattlemarket Street. Bell Avenue was redeveloped as part of the Castle Mall scheme and disappeared beneath the new Castle Green.

Bell Founders

Local bell makers. Norwich had a long tradition of bell founding which served a wide area of Norfolk and beyond with the concentration of foundries

The Bell Hotel. Inset: Advert for the old Bell Hotel.

David Bullock, Town Crier.

being in the Timberhill area in the C15th. Excavations in 1989 located a bell founding pit and bell fragments north of St John's Timberhill. In the C15th the Brayser family were the preeminent founders and their work survives in the Anglican Cathedral, St George's Colegate, St Julian's and St Michael at Coslany. All Saints Church had become the bell founders' church by the mid C16th and many generations of the Brends are buried there. In the first half of the C17th the Brend family were the main founders, with their foundry at the southern end of the All Saints Green triangular space (roughly beneath what was the Carlton/ Gaumont cinema) and their survivals are even more prolific including again the Cathedral, St Andrew's, St Clement, St George's Colegate and Tombland, St Giles, St Helen, St James, St Lawrence, St Michael Coslany, St Peter Hungate and a number of out of centre churches. Thomas Newman seems to have

taken up the mantle in the C18th but after that most of the Norwich bells were sourced from further afield.

Bell Hotel

Historic Coaching Inn.

The Bell is one of only two historic coaching inns to survive within the Walled City (the other being the Maids Head). Originally the Bluebell, it has its origins in the late C15th/early C16th, and it is probably a reasonable proposition that it took its name from the close proximity of bell foundries. The Bell is most well known for its associations with various clubs and societies. In 1793 the Revolution Club was formed there by supporters of the French Revolution. Another notorious organisation was the Hell Fire Club which sought, among other things, to 'crush the Methodists'. The Wesleys preached nearby and were victims of aggressive receptions from the Club. By the C20th the Bell had become a genteel hotel and drinking

establishment and after a period of misuse and vacancy in the 1970s/80s it was partly converted to a bank and partly restored as a pub by the Wetherspoon chain, who included a commendable amount of historic interpretation within the scheme.

Bellman

Town Crier. Bellmen date back to the Roman period when news was despatched by a bellmen, standing at strategic points, reading out proclamations or relaying momentous events like victories in wars. Bellman was the term used in Norwich for what is often referred to as Town Crier and the post here goes back to the early medieval period when few people could read so got their news by word of mouth. The first recorded reference to a Bellman in Norwich was 1272, in a Bull of Pope Gregory. The Norwich Bellman survived until the early First World War when the post was abolished, the last encumbent being Harry Moulton (usually

Historic buildings in Ber Street.

accompanied by his dog Prince). Immediately prior to this, William Childerhouse had held the post between 1877 and 1905, allegedly 'cri-ing' 600,000 times and walking 70,000 miles during his tenancy. The post was reinstated as Town Crier in 1986 with David Bullock being the first new encumbent and still holding it at the time of publication (2011).

Benedictine Priory
See *Anglican Cathedral*.

Ber Street
Ancient thoroughfare.
Part of one of the probable north/south Roman Roads transecting the site of the later City, the street was known as Berstrete in the C12th and Bergstrete in the C13th. 'Berg' is taken to mean hill or mound, as the hill runs along a ridge. Different variations followed – such as Bear Street in the 17th and 18th centuries. From an early period this was the centre of the butchery trade and the Mayor's Court Rolls in the Elizabethan period state that this was the only place within the Walls that cattle could be killed. Not surprisingly therefore it became known as 'blood and guts' street by the C18th due to the profusion of butchers and this was even reflected in the pub names, including the notable C18th Jolly Butchers (no longer a pub). In the C19th the street became a centre for the new immigrant Italian community with densely packed residential yards and courts. Slum clearance and Wartime bombing took their toll of the area and while characters like Black Anna helped to lend a Bohemian appeal to Ber Street it increasingly developed a forlorn and seedy air and became known as a centre for street prostitution. Although originally rich with medieval and Tudor buildings, the only survivors are St John de Sepulchre church and the early C17th, jettied Black's Hall – a significant proportion of the non survivors falling victim to pre War slum clearance and War time bombing. It is now a rather marginal part of the centre looking for a new role.

Ber Strete Gate
Lost City Gate. The Ber Strete Gate or Porte de Berstrete was the key entrance from the south along the line of the old Roman road. Built in the early C14th it was rebuilt in 1340 and rebuilt again in 1727 but finally demolished in 1807. A Moray Smith mural on the southern end of the Berstrete Gates pub gives an impression of how it once appeared.

Bethel Hospital
First psychiatric hospital.
Built on the site of the Committee House, destroyed in the Great Blowe of 1648 on a 'wast peece of ground' leased on a peppercorn rent to Mary Chapman in 1712, the

Reconstruction of Ber Strete Gate.

Bethel Hospital.

Bethel opened in 1713 as the first provincial mental hospital in the country. Its founder lived on the site until her death in 1724. Until the County Asylum opened in 1814 the Bethel was the only facility available in Norwich for people with psychiatric disorders. The site was extended and remodelled by local architect Edward Boardman in 1899 and continued to deliver psychiatric services until the 1980s. It has now been converted into residential use.

Bethel Street

Street of Norman origin. Developed as part of the Norman Borough for the 'Franci de Norwic', the street was originally called Neuport or Neweport reflecting this as a principal street in the Norman 'new town' ('port' meaning town with market rights). In the C17th the street became briefly Committee Street after the Committee House but following the demolition of this structure by the Great Blowe of 1648, it was renamed Bethel Street after the Bethel Hospital of 1713.

Although the western end, with buildings like the Coach and Horses, retains much of its original character, the eastern half has been dramatically transformed by clearances, first for the City Hall and Fire Station (1936) then for the new central library in the early 1960s, later replaced by The Forum.

Sir Samuel Bignold.

Bichil

Ancient site. Located on the northern edge of what was later to be Palace Plain, the Bichil, meaning Bitch's Hill or Beak-like Hill, was a consolidated surface used for beaching river craft and for loading and unloading goods – some of these would have been sold in the adjacent open space.

Bignold Family

Insurance Barons. Merchant Thomas Bignold founded the Norwich Union Society for the Insurance of Houses, Stock and Merchandise from Fire in 1797. In 1808 he followed this with the establishment of the Norwich Union Life Insurance Society. His son Samuel took over both insurance companies from his father in 1818 and was company secretary for 60 years. In parallel though he was also active in local commerce and industry, establishing the Norwich Joint Stock Banking Company in 1827 and Norwich Yarn Company in 1834 – both enterprises failed however. He set up a committee for the construction of the Norwich to London railway in 1834 and opened the Eastern Union Railway in 1849. In 1854 he was knighted following the resolution of the Council to pledge loyal support to the Queen's declaration of war on Russia. In 1864 he took over the Amerciable Society, which had been the first insurance company in the world (founded by Samual Talbot in 1706). Additional to his business role, Bignold was Sheriff in 1830 and Mayor in 1833, 1848, 1853 and 1872 – the last person to hold the position three times had been Thomas

Hyrne in 1604, 1609 and 1616. He was a great philanthropist supporting a range of public works and helping the poor. He died in 1875 and is commemorated by a statue outside Surrey House and by the naming of Bignold School and Bignold Road at Mile Cross.

Bigod Family

Influential Norman dynasty. Roger Bigod (or Bigot) came over with the Conqueror and founded the Bigod dynasty in England. His second son, Hugh became the 1st Earl of Norfolk, Constable of Norwich Castle and Governor of the City of Norwich in 1122. Originally a favourite of Henry I, initially he supported Stephen over Matilda, following Henry's death, but subsequently rebelled with a group of dissenting barons and supported Matilda's son, the eventual Henry II. Rewarded by Henry on his accession, Bigod became disenchanted again and in 1173 when, with an army of Flemings, he took and held Norwich against the King in favour of the king's son 'Young Henry'. The King prevailed and Hugh eventually came to an accommodation with the King, dying in Palestine in 1177. Hugh's son Roger became 2nd Earl of Norfolk in 1189 following a lengthy dispute about the succession and Constable of Norwich. He was a close ally of King John but perversely negotiated the release of Richard the Lionheart from prison and was one of the signatories to the Magna Carta. After the French Dauphin had occupied Norwich in 1216, Henry III returned control of the City to Bigod.

Thomas Bilney, from Foxe's Book of Martyrs.

Billy Bluelight

Local character. Born William Cullum in 1859, Billy Bluelight's principal claim to fame was that he would attempt to race the SS Jenny Lind (by running along the river bank) from Foundry Bridge to Thorpe Reach, although sometimes he would run all the way to Yarmouth, and often in the reverse direction. He would call out to the passengers 'my name is Billy Bluelight, my age is 45, I hope to get to Carrow Bridge before the boat arrive'. He would then collect tips from the enthusiastic passengers on disembarkation. During the winter months, when racing ships was more arduous, he dressed up in a military style uniform and sold cough sweets outside the Royal Arcade. He died at the age of 90 in 1949 and a pub on Hall Road commemorated his memory for a decade from 1994 until reverting to its original name of the Freemason's Arms.

Bilney, Thomas

First Protestant Martyr. Recorded in Foxe's Book of Martyrs, Thomas Bilney is generally regarded as the first protestant martyr on the road to the Reformation of the Church in England.

He had read law at Trinity Hall Cambridge and was ordained as a priest at Ely in 1524. From 1516 he had developed a reformist view of the church at the time having read the Erasmus' translation of the New Testament. He preached against the abuses of the monasteries and was twice brought before Cardinal Wolsley who let him off with a warning not to preach 'Lutheran heresay'. In 1531 he came to Norwich, preaching outside and distributing copies of Tyndale's translation of the New Testament, which had been banned. He returned to London but was arrested and sent back to Norwich where Bishop Nix convicted him as a relapsed heratic. The chancellor of the Norwich diocese blocked an appeal direct to the King and he was condemned to be burned as a heretic. Held in the Guildhall the night before, he prepared himself for the ordeal by holding his finger in a candle flame. The next day he was taken to Lollards Pit where he suffered an agonising death as the wind blew the flames away from him so he was roasted before the fire consumed him. Following his death there was uproar.

Bishop Bridge, and moulded head beneath Bishop Bridge.

Bishop's Garden.

Sir Thomas Moore interrogated the City MP Edward Reed and Alderman John Curat while Bishop Nix was accused of excecuting Bilney without State approval and had his property confiscated. Bilney is commemorated by plaques at Riverside Road and the Guildhall.

Bishop Bridge

City's oldest bridge. There has been a river crossing on this site for a very long time, originally linking the Roman Road, Holmestrete, to the port of Brundall. The first mention of a bridge is a reference to repairs carried out by the Bishop in 1249. The current bridge was part of the defensive works undertaken by Richard Spynk and was built around 1340, originally with a fortified gatehouse at the west end, which was demolished in 1791 due to its structural impact on the bridge. This is the oldest surviving river bridge in the City and one of the oldest in England. The bridge is a Scheduled Ancient Monument.

Bishop's Garden

Secret garden. There has been a garden on the site north of the Cathedral since the first Bishop built his Palace just before1100 although in the C14th Bishop Salmon extended it further to the north, creating the current 'kink' in Bishopgate. The garden covers four acres and is surrounded by a substantial flint perimeter wall. The general form of the present garden was laid down 300 years ago. The garden has an interesting range of elements and features including the large traditional herbaceous borders, a small woodland walk, boxed rose beds and a long shade border with hostas, meconopsis and tree ferns. There is also a large wild grass labyrinth, extensive shrubberies containing many rare and unusual plants, among these being a Hebe planted from a sprig taken from Queen Victoria's wedding bouquet in 1840, an organic kitchen garden and bamboo walk. The Bishop and his wife open the Garden several times a

year with the proceeds going to local charities.

Bishopgate

Ancient Roman route. Holmestrete or the Holmestrete Way ran from the probable Roman port at Brundall in the east to the settlement of Ashill (south east of Swaffham) forming a junction with the north-south Roman Peddars Way in the west. It entered the City at modern Pilling Park and crossed the river at the site of Bishop Bridge. A causeway along modern Bishopgate lifted the road above the level of the marsh and the road then passed through the site of the later Cathedral, along the alignment of the nave, to emerge in Tombland. There was some development along Saxon Holmestrete towards the west end between Tombland and the Bichil (later St Martin at Palace Plain) but much of the remainder was marsh. The development of the cathedral radically changed the street both in character and alignment as the cathedral precinct and

Bishops Palace required it to divert to the north and, indeed, renamed it. The other major intervention in the street was the Great Hospital of 1249 which then expanded over the next 750 years. The construction of Bishop Bridge also made the street a more strategic entry to the City from the east, which it remained until Foundry Bridge took its place in the C19th. Apart from the Great Hospital, other ancient points of interest include the Adam & Eve, allegedly the oldest pub in the City although the oldest fabric is C17th, and the C17th Hermitage, built into the Precinct Wall and one of only five thatched buildings surviving within the Walled City. The rest of the street remainder largely undeveloped until the C19th when a major gas works appeared on the north side and some limited terrace housing developed at the east end. Further development arrived in the C20th with a major courts complex, a WRVS housing scheme by Feilden & Mawson at Queen Elizabeth Close and substantial housing association residential development at

Cotman Fields. Even now though, the street maintains a fairly open aspect with the Norwich School playing fields and Close on the south side and the grounds of the Great Hospital on the north.

Bishop Hall's Palace
See *Dolphin*.

Bishop Reynolds' Chapel
C17th Bishop's Chapel. In 1672 Bishop Edward Reynolds built a new chapel on the site of the end of Bishop Salmon's C14th Great Hall, reusing the original foundations as well as the tracery and masonry from Salmon's destroyed chapel. Bishop Reynolds was buried in the chapel in 1676 and his marble monument survives there. The chapel was converted to the Norwich School Library in 1970.

Bishop Salmon's Hall
Surviving ruin. In association with a remodelling of the Bishop's Palace in the first half of the C14th, Bishop John Salmon constructed a huge Hall on the site of an early chapel.

Bishop Salmon's Porch.

The Hall measured 60 ft (18.3 m) by 120 ft (36.6 m) and was only exceeded in scale by the Archbishop's Hall at Canterbury. The Hall was completed in 1325, but pulled down in 1662. The only surviving element is the two storey porch which led to the Hall. This remains as a ruin in the Bishop's Garden.

Bishop's Palace and Chapel
Surviving Norman palace. Although looking outwardly like an unexceptional, large, Victorian mansion, what is

Right: Bishop Reynolds' Chapel.
Below: Norman arch dogtooth detailing on Bishop Reynolds' Chapel.

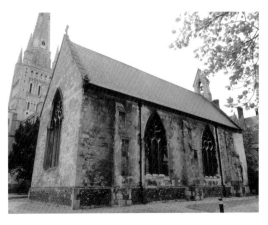

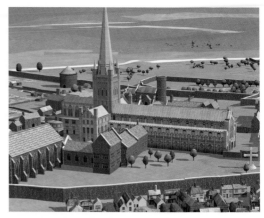

Top left: East elevation of surviving Bishop's Palace in the Norwich School.
Bottom left: West elevation. Right: Reconstruction of the pre Reformation Bishop's Palace.

now the principal building of the Norwich School hides a remarkable complex of historic buildings dating back to the C11th. Begun by Herbert de Losinga at or just before the construction of the Cathedral, the Palace was like a miniature, fortified, Norman keep connected to the north side of the Cathedral nave by a covered, barrel vaulted passage. Just to the east of the Palace was the Bishop's Chapel (now lost). The interesting point here is that the Palace and Chapel were on the same alignment but this was a different alignment to the Cathedral. This suggests that either they were started before the alignment of the Cathedral was finalised or that they used pre existing Saxon elements which were aligned in a different way. Gilchrist suggests that the chapel may indeed have been the Saxon church of the Holy Trinity.

The keep of probably 1096 and the slightly later, two storey connecting passage were developed further by Bishop Salmon in the C14th by the insertion of a four bay, rib vaulted undercroft, probably used as a kitchen. A Queen Post roof was added to the keep in the C15th. The provenance of the ensemble was lost in 1859 when the buildings were drastically remodelled and the link to the Cathedral removed.

Bixley

Deserted Village. Located around 4.8km (3 miles) south of Norwich, Bixley has a population of only 144, but is notable for several historic buildings. The name derives from the Old English meaning 'box wood grove'. The church of St Wandregesilius dates back to 1272 and is the only church in the country dedicated to the C7th Frankish abbot St Wandregisel or Wandrille, the patron saint of weavers. Although the church was refurbished in 1868, the structure was severely damaged during an arson attack in 2004 and now stands derelict, in isolation from any other buildings. Bixley Tower Mill can be

found today in the grounds of Bixley Manor, now the home of Sir Timothy Colman. The mill was originally 11 stories in height, probably making it the highest in the country. It was built in 1838 to replace Bixley Smockmill, which dated from at least 1797. The tower mill was reduced in size to only seven stories around 1872 when it was purchased by the Colman family. Bixley Hall was located just over a mile to the south of the Manor. Only the overgrown remains of the Hall's cellars are visible today, but the Hall was designed in the early C18th by John Buxton and built for Sir Edward Ward to replace his earlier, C16th house. The estate was sold to the Colman family around 1884, but the empty hall fell into disrepair and was finally demolished around 1904. Arminghall Henge is also located within the parish.

Blackfriars Bridge

See *St George's Bridge*.

Black Friars

(Dominican) Friary
Surviving medieval friary.

The Dominican or Blackfriars, also known as the Friars Preachers, were originally established in 1226 in a small house on the north side of Colegate in the parish of St John the Baptist on land granted by Sir Thomas Gelham. The Black Friars were unique in Norwich in that they were given money for their cause by royal order, unlike the other religious orders of friars at this time. In 1272, Henry III ordered the Sheriff to give the Black Friars ten marks, and in 1289 Edward I also donated money, highlighting the growing importance of the order in the City. In 1307 they took over the site of the Sack Friars (just north of later Blackfriars Hall) and by 1310 had acquired additional land which was ultimately to include the original line of Elm Hill running through to St Andrew's Plain. After initially adapting Becket's Chapel for their use, they built a Chapter House shortly after 1310 (now lost) and the Choir (Blackfriars Hall) between 1310 and 1320, measuring 60 paces (102 ft) long including the passage between it and the nave. By the middle of the century the Friars completed the preaching nave (St Andrew's Hall), measuring 75 paces (127 ft) long and 41 paces (70 ft) wide, and the cloisters with their refectory over the west wing and the dormitory over the east. Tragically, in 1413, only just over 50 years after works had been completed, a fire almost entirely destroyed the building and the friars moved back to their original site in Colegate while rebuilding took place.

Clockwise from top: early vaulted undercroft at Blackfriars, Blackfriars preaching nave (St Andrew's Hall), and reconstruction of the pre Reformation Blackfriars Friary.

The seven-light east window of the choir survived, as did substantial sections of the choir walls, along with five windows and the south wall of the nave. The cost of rebuilding the nave was borne by Sir Thomas Erpingham and, later, his son and this is commemorated by the Erpingham arms between the clerestory windows. The beams of both the hammerbeam roof of the nave and the roof of the choir were gifted by the Paston family and their generosity is commemorated by their arms engraved in an oak door in the south porch. The Friars moved back in 1449 although building works were not completed until 1465. A central walkway separated the nave from the choir and this was crowned by a tower donated by Simon de Felbrigg, standard bearer to Richard II, in 1462. At the time of the Reformation, when most of the other monastic sites were sold by the King and subsequently demolished, Blackfriars was bought by the Norwich Corporation for use as a Common Hall. Over the intervening period the complex has served a very wide range of uses including a mint, a library and a Dutch church. Today it is used for concerts, banquets, lectures and the largest provincial beer festival in the UK. The Heritage Economic & Regeneration Trust (HEART) recently undertook an extensive range of preparatory work to facilitate an ambitious multi million pound project to regenerate the complex into a regional stature concert, conference and community events centre which could have

Exterior view of City Wall at Black Tower.

unified the cultural venues in the immediate area into a significant 'cultural quarter'. However, the economic downturn resulted in the City Council putting the project on ice. The site remains the only surviving, intact Dominican Friary complex in the UK.

Black Prince

Prince. Edward, the Black Prince, visited the City with many noblemen in 1350 to attend a great tournament at the Gildencroft and was entertained at the expense of £37 4s 6d.

Black Tower

City defences.
Also known as the Commander's, Governor's or Boteler's Tower, this is the largest and most architecturally complex of the surviving towers on the City Walls. Located on the southern end of the Ber Street Ridge, this defensive work has a diameter of 10m and a height of over 11m. As well as its original purpose, the tower has been used as pest house for plague victims in 1665/6, a prison, a snuff mill and a cotton spinning mill. The site is accessible from the City Walls Walk.

Bladder stones

Medical curiosity. The Norfolk & Norwich University Hospital holds the largest collection of bladder stones in the world which represents a legacy reflecting both the outstanding medical skills present in the area and a remarkably quirky local medical affliction. Between 1727 and 1737 the work undertaken by the Norwich School of Lithotomy, and by William Cheselden and Benjamin Gooch specifically, represented the cutting edge of bladder stone treatment in England at the time. A principal reason for such innovative work taking place in the City was that the incidence of bladder stone admissions to the relatively new Norfolk & Norwich Hospital (N&N) was significantly greater than to any other provincial hospital in England. In 1779, for instance, one in 55 admissions into the N&N was for 'the stone' while at Addenbrooke's (Cambridge) it was one in 1650. In 1817 the Norwich rate had actually risen to one in 38 exceeding to 'an astonishing degree' the rate for any other hospital for which records were available. The reason was a quite unprecedented occurrence of the bladder stone in Norfolk during the C18th/C19th particularly compared with any other part of England. Between 1772 and 1909, 1498 bladder stone operations were undertaken and the stones along with their operation registers survive today. After the pioneering surgical work in the early C18th other innovative surgeons followed including William Donne, Sir Astley Cooper and Philip Meadows

Boar's Head prior to wartime bombing.

Martineau referred to in Paris as 'le lithotomiste le plus eminent et le plus heureux de son epoque'. The collection of the stones stopped in 1909 by which time the endemic bladder stone had ceased to be a major medical affliction.

Blomefield, Francis

Eminent local historian. Born in 1705 and educated at Gonville & Caius College Cambridge, Blomefield became rector of Fersfield, near Diss in 1729, though his passion was local history. He devoted himself to writing the history of Norfolk beginning in 1733 and during his researches, discovered the Paston Letters at Oxnead in 1735. He decided to publish his Norfolk history himself and bought a printing press for the purpose. His first volume sold out and had to be reprinted twice. He moved to Norwich to write the second volume, living in Willow Lane, and became rector of St Georges Tombland. He completed volume II but before he was able to complete the third volume he contracted smallpox and died at the age of 46.

Bly, Terry

NCFC striker. Prolific striker and top scorer in the 1958/9 'cup run' season (29 goals) destined to become one of the top ten highest goal scorers in a season in the English League ever after moving to Peterborough.

Blyth, Dr Ernest

First Lord Mayor. Ernest Egbert Blyth was the last Mayor and first Lord Mayor of Norwich. A solicitor by profession. Dr Blyth entered public life to improve educational provision and to address the challenges of slum housing. He is commemorated by Blyth Road, just off Elm Grove Lane although his more appropriate memorial, the former Blyth School, has been recently renamed Sewell Park College.

Boar's Head

Lost medieval inn. Built in 1456 at the junction of Surrey Street and St Stephens, the inn was first known as the Greyhound. In 1790, the Norgate family occupied the building and erected their arms, including a boar's head, over the main entrance. From then onwards the inn became known as the Boar's Head. By 1854 the concert room of the inn had become the venue for the first Norwich music hall, 'The Shades' and in the same year the Norwich Licensed Victuallers Association was created at the Boar's Head. The inn survived remarkably intact in its medieval form, with a thatched range running along Surrey Street and four thatched gables fronting St Stephens until April 1942 when the infamous Baedeker Raids resulted in it being gutted. It remained derelict until 1952 when it was demolished and a faux Georgian style pub was built on its site as part of the redevelopment of St Stephens. In 1966, following a short closure, the new Boar's Head reopened entirely renovated internally in the Flemish/Dutch style, complete with tapestries and a model windmill. In 1972 all of the internal decorations were stripped out to create a stark dancing space with a stage for musicians. The pub closed finally in 1974 to go through a range of catering incarnations – it remains a sandwich takeaway shop with nothing surviving to indicate its former historic pedigree.

Boardman, Edward

Noted local architect. Boardman was a local architect of great distinction. Boardman and Son's architectural business began in 1860 as the first proper architectural business in Norwich and it continued until 1966. Boardman was responsible not only for the conversion of Norwich Castle from a prison into a museum and for the late C19th redevelopment of the Norfolk and Norwich Hospital but also for the

Above: William Boleyn's house in King Street as it appeared in 1946.

Above right (clockwise): Architect Edward Boardman, Boardman House, Princes Street, Cosseyware lettering on Boardman's office, Old Bank of England Court.

design of many of Norwich and Norfolk's Nonconformist churches. Over the years, the firm Boardman and Son was responsible for the design of Princes Street United Reformed church, Trinity United Reformed church, St Peter's Methodist church, Chapel Field Road United Methodists Chapel and Queens Road Primitive Methodists Chapel. Outside the City Boardman designs include St Andrew's church in Trowse and the church of St Mary the Virgin in Marlingford. Boardman's son (also Edward) was Mayor in 1905, served on the Council for 20 years and was founder president of the Norfolk Association of Architects.

Boleyn House

Ancient remnant. Just south of Dragon Hall, nos. 125-9 King Street formed the city house of Sir William Boleyn, grandfather of Anne Boleyn and great grandfather of Elizabeth I. Remarkably it survived until

the 1940s when a local furniture retailer obliterated the ground floor for a showroom leaving only the first floor which survives today – just about. Immediately south of this was the house of Sir Miles Stapleton, one of the original Knights of the Garter.

Boileau Memorial

Statuary. Originally forming part of a fountain at the junction of Newmarket Road and Ipswich Road, the statue was designed by Sir John Boehm in 1876 and erected by Sir John Boileau to commemorate his wife Catherine. Sir John was a benefactor to the former Norfolk & Norwich Hospital. The statue was moved to the grounds of the hospital in 1965 when the fountain was demolished to accommodate traffic engineering works.

Bombazines

Textiles. Introduced by Flemish weavers in 1575, Bombazines were first made

in Norwich as a combination of silk and worsted with the warp being the former and the weft the latter. Although other colours were produced, the principal colour was black and the main use was for the production of mourning garments. The material was popular until well into the C19th peaking with the death of Prince Albert.

Bonds

Local department store, now John Lewis Partnership. Robert Herne Bond moved to Norwich in 1879 and took over 'Mr Woodland's' existing drapery shop at 19 Ber Street to instigate a retail phenomenon in Norwich which was to endure for over 100 years. Robert's wife, Mary Anne, specialised in millinery and developed a roaring trade in hats for the modest business. Within seven years they had prospered and expanded by acquiring three adjacent premises including the Jubilee pub, as well as a satellite business in St George's. Robert's second son, John became an architect and, as well as designing extensions to the family business he went on the head up one of the most successful practices in Norwich – J. Owen Bond. The successful business in Ber Street led to significant expansion in 1914 when the Bonds opened its Arcade in All Saints Green. Millinery soon became a staple of the new store and by the 1930s Bonds had 20 milliners making hats and 30 shop assistants selling them – the store sold 1,000 hats on a typically busy Saturday. The founder died in 1924 and his sons William and Ernest took over. They targeted the county set, to become known as 'the carriage trade' until well into the modern period. In 1930 they took over the Thatched Cinema and used it as a restaurant, conference hall and ballroom which had one of the first sprung floors in the UK. It was used for display and storage of furniture during the day but had to be cleared for

Saturday evening dances and evening functions. The company had a commendable training policy 'bringing up' staff from apprenticeships to showroom staff. By the outbreak of WWII Bonds had become a major institution providing for all family needs 'from cradle to grave' and it employed over 200 staff. During the infamous Baedeker raids of late April 1942 the whole premises were gutted including the former Thatched Cinema. Undaunted, Bonds had commissioned a fleet of old buses from which to retail within days of the raid and was operating its restaurant out of an old corrugated iron shed on the car park. The restaurant later moved into St Catherine's House in All Saints Green while some of the store's departments occupied other buildings such as the current Barclays in Orford Place and premises on Thorpe Road. Within nine years of the raids a brand new store, by the architect son J. Owen Bond, had risen from the ashes. It prospered and in 1979

celebrated its centenary having undertaken significant modernisation works. In 1982 the family succumbed to the pressures of being a large independent in an increasingly globalised sector and sold out to the John Lewis Partnership (JLP) – the employees became 'partners'. In 1988 JLP commenced a large scale regeneration programme which absorbed and converted a row of Georgian cottages on All Saints Green but renovation revealed much earlier, possibly C16th roof timbers, indicating that the Georgian front disguised much earlier buildings. The renovated cottages became offices and a Boardroom but retained many of the original features including cast iron fire places, a bread oven and a lead sink. In 1990 the company demolished the Surrey Chapel and built a major new multi storey car park. In 2001 JLP decided to lose its quirky local store names and what had been Bonds for 112 years became rebranded as the John Lewis Partnership.

Bonds in 1935 operating from the former Thatched Cinema.

The Boom Towers.

Boom Towers

River defences. Built in 1344 the twin towers provided the river defence element of the City Walls just north of the King Street or Connesford Gate. A double chain of Spanish iron was pulled up between the towers by windlass to stop approaching ships. In the event they were never used to prevent a river borne assault but proved much more effective as a means of extracting taxes from merchant vessels. After out living their original use, the tower on the southern bank was employed as a coke oven in the C18th and the coke was used by nearby maltings to malt barley for beer. Remarkably the towers survived to a significant height until before the Second World War.

Borrow, George

C19th author. Born in Dereham, Borrow lived intermittently in Norwich, latterly in Willow Lane at Borrow House which now has a memorial plaque to him on the outside. He specialised in travelogues and semi auto biographical works involving Romani peoples. One of his first jobs was to work as a writer and translator for the British & Foreign Bible Society which sent him to St Petersburg then to Spain and Portugal. This expedition resulted in his first significant publication The Bible in Spain which was a great success, selling almost 20,000 copies in its first year – three times more than the first edition of the Pickwick Papers. Following this, Borrow travelled across

Europe to Constantinople which resulted in the publication of Lavengro in 1851. In 1857 he wrote Romany Rye. After more domestic, walking tours in Norfolk, Cornwall, Wales, Scotland and Ireland, he produced Wild Wales (1862) and Celtic Bards, Chiefs and Kings but this wasn't published until much later. He didn't create anything of critical acclaim after this and died in 1881. It is ironic that, as with many artists and writers, he was celebrated more after his death than during his life. Apart from some roads (and a pub) named either after him or his works, his greatest memorial is the City's motto 'A Fine City' which derives from a line in Lavengro – 'A fine old city, truly, is that, view it from whatever side you will.'

Botolph Street

Ancient thoroughfare. Originally a street linking St Augustines to Magdalen Street, Botolph Street takes its name from the East Anglian saint Botolph who founded a monastery at 'Icanhoe' (probably Iken in Suffolk) in 654. St Botolph's church stood roughly on the site of modern Anglia

George Borrow plaque, Willow Lane.

Kings Arms, Botolph Street, 1936.

Square and was a pre conquest foundation. It was dissolved at the Reformation and demolished in 1546. The association of the street with the church suggests it also had a pre Conquest provenance although most anciently the street was known as Merholt, after the adjacent boundary wood. With the development of the Inner Ring Road and Anglia Square in the 1960s, some important buildings were lost from the street. These included the former Chamberlin's clothing factory, designed by A.F. Scott in 1903 and described by Pevsner as 'the most interesting factory building in Norwich.' He added 'There was little in England and indeed Europe quite so functional and unfussy then. Yet it is by no means purely utilitarian.' Additionally the Kings Arms, which had survived from1646, and the remarkable Art Deco Odeon, also disappeared. Only a small remnant of the original street survived, linking St Augustines to Anglia Square, while the dislocated northern rump of St Georges Street was renamed Botolph Street too.

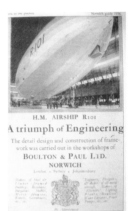

Clockwise from top: Surviving remnant of the Boulton & Paul Works in Rose Lane, R101 Airship, and Boulton & Paul Sidestrand bomber.

Boudica

Iceni queen. Boudica was queen of the Iceni, who inhabited East Anglia at the time of the Roman occupation. The tribe's religious centre and possibly her palace were at Thetford although it is likely that she would have also been closely associated with Venta Icenorum – Market of the Iceni, just outside Norwich. Her famous revolt of 61 A.D. and remarkable successes at Colchester, London and St Albans' before being finally routed by the Romans at Watling Street, still stands as one of the great patriotic gestures of English history.

Boudica's Way

Long distance footpath. This is a 60km (38 miles) walk running from Norwich to Diss via the Roman settlement of Venta Icenorum (Caistor St Edmund) and passing the Tasburgh hill fort and the Scole Roman settlement along the line of the Roman Pye Strete.

Boulton & Paul

Industrial innovator. In 1797, William Moore founded a company in London Street (then Cockey Lane) which was to become, eventually, Boulton and Paul Ltd. The ironmongery company relocated to Rose Lane in 1865. Over the next 50 years they diversified enormously producing everything from sausage machines to pre fabricated field hospitals and portable churches and by the C20th they were innovating further with products ranging from motorboats to the sledges for Robert Falson Scott's ill-fated Antarctic expedition. The First World War produced orders for naval hospitals, aircraft hangers and aircraft – an enormous breakthrough. In 1919, Boulton and Paul exhibited the first all metal framed aeroplane with the first ever major use of plastic at the Salon d'Aeronautique in Paris in 1919. They went on to build bombers for the newly established RAF and flyingboat hulls for the Royal Navy but in 1926 they produced the first ever example of an all metal biplane bomber, the Sidestrand, for 101 Squadron RAF. This was followed, shortly, by the company's production of the airframe for the largest airship in the world at the time, the R101. Shortly after, the aircraft division moved to Wolverhampton where the famous Boulton Paul Defiant was produced. The Norwich site survived into the 1990s, principally making joinery products but then closed down to be redeveloped for the Riverside leisure, retail and residential development. The only surviving physical remnant of the company within the City Centre is its former headquarter office building on Rose Lane, the Arts & Crafts Movement Tudor Hall, and the façade wall of the Rose Lane factory, retained in Mountergate.

Boundary Crosses

Demarcation of the City's jurisdiction. Flowing from charters in the C15th and C16th, the City erected 12 crosses to denote its boundary as a City & County, distinct from the County of Norfolk. Due to the changes in boundary over the centuries, the crosses have been re-sited, substituted or have just disappeared. Known sites are as follows:

- Boundary Road Cross at the junction of Boundary & Drayton Roads: heavily restored in 1902 with 5 ft of the original cross shaft and surviving today
- Carrow Cross at the junction of Bracondale & King Street: lost
- Catton Cross on the west of St Clement's Hill: lost
- Hardley Cross at the junction of the Rivers Yare and Chet was restored in 1676 and survives today
- Hellesdon Cross is in Hellesdon churchyard E of the church: restored in 1902 with 6 ft of the original cross shaft and surviving today
- Magdalen Cross north of the Lazar House: lost
- Needham Cross outside St Stephen's Gate: lost
- Nether Earlham Cross by the river on Earlham Road: lost

Clockwise from top: Surviving boundary cross in Hellesdon churchyard, boundary cross at Hardley Cross, remnant of boundary cross at the Boundary Public House.

- Our Lady's Cross between Hall Road and Grove Road: lost
- St Faiths Cross (or Le Whytecrosse) on Aylsham Road outside the Boundary pub: restored in 1902 with 5 ft of the original shaft but the base only survives today
- Thorpe Wood Cross east of St Leonards Hill: lost
- Trowse in the middle of Trowse Bridge: lost when the bridge was redeveloped.

Bowthorpe

Suburban settlement. Originally an ancient hamlet whose name, in Old Norse, means 'Bo's settlement'. It was depopulated by the C15th leaving the remains of the church, currently a Scheduled Ancient Monument, and Bowthorpe Hall, the C16th Manor House of the Yaxleys but remodelled from 1700. In 1973 the Council bought the site and extended the City boundary to the west. It produced a masterplan for the site which involved the development of a balanced community based around three 'villages' provided with a broad range of social facilities and an extensive employment area. The villages of Clover Hill, Chapel Break and Three Score were intended to each accommodate 4500 people. The Bowthorpe Main Centre hosted the first superstore to arrive in the City (Sainsbury's) although the company subsequently moved out to a larger retail park site (Longwater) leaving local entrepreneur Roys to take over the site. The development was characterised by a relatively high quality standard of design and a layout dominated by pedestrians and cyclists from which cars were largely excluded.

Bowthorpe Marsh

Public open space.
Bowthorpe Marsh borders the River Yare to the west of Norwich and is a local nature reserve. It can be reached from Earlham Road, turning into Wilberforce Road and then Bland Road. The site is essentially a 5.7 hectare (ha) area of low lying, undulating tall-herb fen and unimproved grassland on the river margin with public access and users should be aware that horses are routinely grazed in the area.

Boxing

Boxing provenance. Apart from having a strong tradition from the very early days of prize fighting, with 'greats' such as Jem Mace, the 'father of modern boxing', the City has had recent success with former British and European Lightweight Champion Jon Thaxton (recently retired) and reigning (Mar 2011) English Light Heavyweight Champion Danny McIntosh. Herbie Hide (born Herbert Okechukwu Maduagwu in Nigeria) is also locally based and is former twice WBO World Heavyweight Champion and current WBC International Cruiserweight Champion.

Bracondale

Located just west of Carrow and to the south east of the City Centre and meaning bracon valley from the Old English, Bracondale is a conservation area centred around the road which links Queen's Road to Martineau Lane. The earliest surviving building is the Manor House (No. 54) probably built in 1620 for Anne Kempe, the widow of a local grocer (despite what the 1578 date on the outside suggests). It was extended and improved in 1656 as a town house for Augustine Reve of Wacton Hall. Although divided into flats in 1951 it was restored in the 1980s. Close by on the south side of the road, a fine C18th three storied house obscures the early C17th Tower House. Nos. 62-62 are clearly C17th also with some later work. Additionally there are fine examples of C18th extramural housing development for the affluent classes including notably No. 66 dating from the 1760s. On the north side there are good examples of late Georgian/early Victorian housing of the same character. Bracondale Tower Mill was built in 1829, but although it appeared on the 1884 Ordnance Survey it had been demolished by the 1890s. More recently, Bracondale Court provided an interesting art deco style development of 28 flats (numbered 1-29 but excluding a No. 13) to the south of the road in 1937. To the south of Bracondale at the opposite end to the Walled City, William Wilkins developed a substantial house, for the Martineau Family, called Bracondale Lodge in 1792 which had a significant landscaped garden by Repton. The house was demolished in 1966 to make way for County Hall, designed by Slater & Uren while much of the landscaped garden was tarmaced for a huge surface car park. The only remnant of the original site is a small amount of woodland and a remnant of a garden folly constructed by Dr Phillip Martineau in 1813 from the remnants of the Anglican cathedral Infirmary, demolished in 1804.

Bradbury, Sir Malcolm

Author. Co-founder, with Angus Wilson, of the University of East Anglia's Creative Writing Course, which is widely regarded as the most prestigious and successful of its kind in the country, Bradbury was a professor at the UEA from 1970 to 1995. He was knighted in 2000. His most well known book is The History Man.

Left to right: Bracondale Manor House, Bracondale Georgian houses, Art Deco Bracondale Court.

Reconstruction of Brazen Gate.

Brazen Doors

Lost City Gate. Located at the All Saints Green entry point to the Walled City this postern gate is of uncertain date but likely to have been built in the first quarter of the C14th. It was made wide enough for coaches in 1726 but this didn't save it from demolition in 1792.

Brettingham, Matthew

Eminent C18th architect. Born the son of a brick layer in Norwich, Matthew went on to become one of the great architects of his day and a principal exponent of the Palladian style although much of his innovative work in London has been demolished subsequently and other schemes have been remodelled. Holkham Hall perhaps remains his most notable achievement. Other schemes included Heydon, Honningham, Langley and Gunton Hall, all in Norfolk and Euston in Suffolk. In London he designed Norfolk House for the 9th Duke of Norfolk in St James' Square. Although the exterior was criticised at the time, the interior was to set the standard for the English town house over the next century. Two more houses for the nobility followed in St James' Square and then Egremont House in Piccadilly, for Lord Egremont, which was later the home of Palmerston. Brettingham was then commissioned by Nathaniel Curzon, Lord Scarsdale to design Kedleston Hall. Although he completed the design and began the work, Curzon took the project away from him and commissioned Robert Adam to finish it to Brettingham's design. Undaunted, Brettingham went on to design York House in Pall Mall for the King's brother, the Duke of York.

His work in Norwich included modifications to the Castle and Cathedral, the Shirehouse (where his brother Robert undertook the flintwork), 15 Surrey Street and Holkham House in Cow Hill (although this may have been his brother Robert's work).

Brewing

Beer production in Norwich. Norwich had a long history of beer production. The brewhouse at the Benedictine Priory (Cathedral) is referred to in records of 1285 and the earliest known hop in England was discovered south of the river in Whitefriars in 1979 suggesting the production of hopped beer some considerable time before the practice was traditionally thought to have been introduced to England by the Flemings in the 1400s. There are later references to the hop fields of the Franciscans friars on what is now Prince of Wales Rd. By 1836 there were no fewer than 27 breweries operating in the City but with amalgamations and takeovers, this figure fell to 12 by 1858 and seven by 1875. By the 1920s the 'big four' had absorbed all of the others and Bullard's (Anchor Brewery, Coslany St), Morgans (King Street), Steward and Pattesons

Left to right: Brettingham Memorial, St Augustine's Church, Brettingham's Egremont House in Piccadilly, later the home of Lord Palmerston.

Steward & Patteson Ltd.
brewers of
FINE NORFOLK ALES
Established 1793
POCKTHORPE BREWERY, NORWICH

Left to right: Beer revival, The Star Brewery, product of the Norwich Brewery Company, and 1950s Steward & Patteson advertising.

(Pockthorpe Brewery) and Youngs, Crawshay and Youngs (Crown Brewery, King Street) managed to prosper until the 1950s. Further takeovers then saw Bullard's and S&P absorb the other two breweries and what was intended originally as a trading agreement with Watneys saw the national giant take over the two remaining breweries and close them both by 1968. Although Watneys continued to brew in King Street and even attempted a sop to local distinctiveness by rebranding the operation

The Norwich Brewery Company, it stopped brewing in the 1980s and eventually closed the whole operation. Micro breweries rose to the challenge subsequently with the Golden Star and Reindeer breweries coming then going. At the time of publication, operating breweries include the Chalk Hill Brewery (Coach & Horses, Thorpe Rd), Winters Brewery (Keelan Close), the Bear Brewery, the Northcote (Sweetbriar Industrial Estate) and the Fat Cat Brewery (The Shed, Lawson Road).

At a wider level, Norfolk now claims to have the second largest number of breweries of any English county.

Bridewell

Former medieval merchant house and prison, now a museum. In the early C14th Geoffrey de Salle built a house on the site of the current Bridewell Museum. The museum, however, is housed within a later building commissioned by Bartholomew Appleyard c1370. Bartholomew was a rich merchant who needed a grand house befitting his

Left to right: The refurbished Bridewell, Bridewell undercroft – the largest in Norwich, original entrance to the Bridewell.

The Britons Arms, transformed for the feature film Stardust.

Religious radical. Expelled from the Church of England in 1636 for preaching 'Puritanism' at St Georges Tombland, Bridge became a minister of the English Church in the Netherlands and founded the Independents who ultimately became the Congregationalists. 23 years after his death, they established the first Congregationalist church in Norwich – the Old Meeting House – which was to be the first of the City's non conformist chapels.

Britons Arms

Unique Medieval beguinage. The Briton's Arms is a building of medieval date but it was not built as a tavern nor as a house. The building was probably purpose built as a beguinage: a home for a small community of lay, pious women who chose to dedicate their lives to prayer and to helping the parish poor and sick. Beguinages were popular in Northern France, Germany, the Netherlands, Belgium and Luxembourg and are still found there today. In England, however, beguinages were much less common but towns and cities with strong Continental connections, such as Ipswich, York and Norwich housed such communities. There is written evidence to suggest three such medieval institutions in Norwich and the Briton's Arms is thought to be one of them. It is now the only surviving medieval beguinage in England.

Architecturally the building is also remarkable. The timber framing on the top floor at the west end has an arched top arcade. Also, a three storey building is unusual as most medieval Norwich

status; his son William, who became the first mayor of Norwich in 1403, further enlarged the house. William's coat of arms can be seen in Bridewell Alley on a plaque on the western wall of the house.

The building has four ranges set around a central courtyard. The northern and eastern ranges contain the largest undercrofts in Norwich and these would have been used by the merchant owners to store their goods. The northern wall of the house, which faces onto the back of St Andrew's church, is impressive since it is constructed in close regular courses of squared black flint and is said by some to be the finest piece of flintwork in England. The late C15th entrance to the building on St Andrew's Hill has an excellent carved wooden doorframe and is a Scheduled Ancient Monument.

The merchant's house was bought by the City in 1583 and part of it was converted into a Bridewell, or prison, for women and beggars. These prisoners were occupied with manual work and some were taught a trade. In 1751 much of the building was destroyed by fire but was rebuilt and continued in use as a prison for a further seventy-seven years until the new City Gaol was built on Earlham Road where the Roman Catholic Cathedral now stands. From 1828 the Bridewell building was put to use as a tobacco factory, leather warehouse and boot and shoe factory. It was bought in the 1920s and turned into a museum of local industry. Following a grant from the Heritage Lottery Fund, the Museums Service closed the museum for a substantial refurbishment in 2009 and it is planned to reopen in 2012.

houses are thought to have been only two storeys high. Furthermore, the attic of the Briton's Arms is one of the earliest examples of an attic being purpose built as a living space. Attics were not commonly used as living or storage space until the C16/17th. Similarly, the whole plan of the building is also more reminiscent of C16/17th buildings. Medieval buildings normally consisted of a large communal room plus a few private rooms. Fireplaces were restricted to the private rooms and to the homes of the rich. However, C16/17th buildings had smaller, heated rooms that were used for particular purposes much like the rooms in our own homes today. The Briton's Arms was designed along these lines making it the earliest surviving example of its type in the country. Each floor is divided into two rooms heated by a fireplace and each floor is reached by a small staircase that runs up the eastern side of the building. Such a layout suggests that the building was built to house a number of people living as individuals – a community like the beguines. Furthermore, at second floor level a

Britannia Barracks.

door leads out into the churchyard of St Peter Hungate, giving the beguines easy access to the church for regular worship.

By 1760 the building had been turned into a pub called the Kings Arms but by 1800 a wave of republican fervour had gripped the City and the pub became the Briton's Arms. The pub has gone but the name survives as the ancient structure is now a popular coffee house and restaurant.

Britannia Barracks

Victorian former infantry barracks. Built in 1887 and extended in 1897, Britannia Barracks were built in a prominent position overlooking the City as the home of the Norfolk Regiment. The name

derives from the regimental insignia (Britannia) which, formerly as the 9th Regiment of Foot, was awarded to the regiment either by Queen Anne after the Battle of Almanza in 1707 or by George III in 1799. In 1959 when the Norfolks amalgamated with the Suffolks and moved to Bury St Edmunds the decline of the institution began. In 1967 the 4th Territorial Battalion was disbanded and by 1987 the barracks had closed as a military installation. The buildings subsequently became part of Norwich Prison.

Broads

Protected wetlands. A 'broad' is a shallow lake formed when peat excavations became flooded. Historically peat was excavated as early as Roman times and during the medieval period peat provided an important fuel for the growing City of Norwich while reeds harvested from the Broads provided a convenient source of thatching materials. The term Broads is used to describe an area of over 300 sq km predominantly in Norfolk (hence the generic term The Norfolk Broads) but also

Left to right: The Broads – Ranworth Conservation Centre, The Broads in winter.

Bronze Age ceremonial dagger.

in Suffolk, which includes 200km of navigable waterways, marshes, fens and 63 broads. This extensive area of wetlands is not only an important landscape and wildlife habitat, with a protection status equivalent to a national park, but it is also a major tourism resource attracting over two million visitors annually. Visitor activity is centred around boating activities including holidays on Broads cruisers or yachting. Other activities such as bird watching provide an important element of the tourism offer. The area is administered by the Broads Authority who have jurisdiction not only over the Broads area but also over the River Wensum within the heart of Norwich.

Bronze Age

Activity between 2000 and 800 BC. Excavations in 2000 on the former Busseys garage site, between Palace Street and Quayside, revealed post holes of a very early Bronze Age building (2000 BC), flints and a Biconical Urn from the same period. In the same year, a small post-hole structure and quantities of Beaker pottery, were discovered in the River Valley at Bowthorpe. Evidence of another structure was recorded during excavations at Harvey Lane in 1999. Bronze Age barrows have been found in Ber Street and, beyond the City, at Harford Farm, Bixley and Ketteringham. A late Bronze Age 'hoard' (950-700 BC) and including socketed axes, spearheads, gouges, rapier fragments and a possible sword scabbard guard, was discovered in 2007 at Eaton and represents the largest late Bronze Age assemblage of metalwork found in Norfolk.

At a wider level, the Oxborough Dirk, a 27.9 inch long ritual dagger, and the remnants of the ritual site 'Seahenge' discovered at Holme, are both of international importance and illustrate the significance of Bronze Age activity in early Norfolk.

Browne's Meadow

Lost open space. Taking its name from the eminent physician and philosopher, the Meadow was leased to Sir Thomas Browne from 1669, by the Dean and Chapter, 'during his naturell life.' Located south of what used to be the canal running from Pulls Ferry west to the Cathedral, the Meadow was probably an extension of Browne's exotic garden at his house in the Haymarket – what diarist John Evelyn called 'a cabinet of rarities.' After Browne had died it became a vegetable garden for the Dean then allotments for the residents of The Close before eventually being used as a car park from the 1970s.

Browne, Sir Thomas

Physician, philosopher & writer. Browne was the greatest scholar and most original thinker to have lived in Norwich. He was a physician, philosopher and one of the great writers of English prose in the C17th. He could speak six languages and was also a naturalist and antiquarian of some distinction. His most celebrated work – Religio Medici – concerned his own religious faith in relation to his profession as a physician. It was published in eight languages. In 1671,

From left: Religio Medici by Sir Thomas Browne, Sir Thomas Browne's house before demolition.

Charles II 'knighted the so famous Browne, Whose worth and learning to the world are Known', noted poet Matthew Stephenson at the time. The ceremony took place in St Andrew's Hall. His mansion survived in the Haymarket until 1842 and his ancient garden house to the rear, until 1961. Today he is commemorated by a statue by Henry Pegran (1905) in Hay Hill and by more recent sculptures by Anne & Patrick Poirier (2007).

Clockwise from top left: Bullard's Fermentation Building while still in operation, Bullard's Chimney the night before demolition, Bullard's Fermentation Block derelict, 1970s.

Bullard's

Lost brewer. The Bullard dynasty started in a partnership between James Watts and Richard Bullard, when the two brewers founded the Anchor Brewery at St Miles Bridge in 1837 although the surviving buildings carry a boundary marker dated 1773 so it is probable that they occupied existing premises. The premises were extended in 1857 and the massive, four storey Fermentation Block on the corner of Coslany Street and Westwick Street appeared in 1868. The importance of the company within the City is reflected in the fact that the founder's son, Harry Bullard, became Sheriff in 1877 and Mayor in 1878, 1879 and 1886 and was elected City MP in 1890 and 1895. By the time that Bullard's became a limited company in 1895, its number of owned pubs had risen from an 1837 level of 33 to 280. The company proved to be a remarkable success and expanded to cover seven acres on both side of Coslany Street by 1900 and even had its own light railway. Bullard's commissioned artist Sir Alfred Munnings to develop promotional materials. The

company expanded further in the late C19th/early C20th, absorbing breweries as far afield as Thetford, Eye and Setchy, near Kings Lynn. In 1958 they took over Youngs, Crawsay & Youngs, one of the only four surviving Norwich breweries and four years later, jointly with Steward & Pattesons, they gobbled up Morgans – it was said that the two Norwich giants decided on how they would divide Morgans pubs by cutting a pack of cards. This success attracted the attention of Watney Mann who took Bullard's over in 1963 and closed them in 1968. Proposals emerged for the wholesale demolition of the Anchor Brewery site for offices in 1974 but these were resisted and the whole complex was converted to residential use by Scolapoint in the early 1980s. Sadly, the famous landmark chimney was demolished in July 1982 but the base remains.

Bull Close Road

Extra mural road. This road running outside the north east section of the City Wall and taking its name from the space where cattle from within the walled City were taken to graze during the day, links Magdalen Street to Silver Road. Significant elements of the old C13th wall survive along Bull Close Road.

Buntings

Lost iconic retailer. In 1866 Arthur Bunting opened a large drapery store on the junction of St Stephen's and Rampant Horse Street utilising existing medieval and later buildings. In 1912, Augustus Scott designed and built an iconic new store utilising innovative reinforced concrete. The building prospered until 1942 when it was gutted during the Baedeker Raids although the current ornate façade survived and it was partly rebuilt to form the NAAFI Club, a

Buskers performing on the streets of Norwich.

recreational venue for service personnel. Buntings moved to London Street and after the War the site was fully reconstructed and reopened by Marks & Spencer in 1950. In the 1990s M&S expanded into the nextdoor Woolworth store and in 2011 incorporated and redeveloped the remaining street block elements to make it one of the UK's largest M&S stores.

Bureaux de Change

Locations for foreign currency exchange. Most banks provide foreign currency exchange services and in addition the main post office in Castle Mall provides the service as does Marks & Spencers store in Rampant Horse Street.

Business Hours

See *Opening Hours*.

Buskers

Street Entertainers. Norwich has a long tradition of street entertainers ranging from the usual musicians to more unusual 'acts'. The tradition continues today with a varied range of street entertainment located principally along the Walk or in London Street but sometimes in other locations such as outside The Forum.

Bus Station

Main bus station. The bus station was developed on orchards to the south of St Stephen's Street in the early 1930s following the acquisition of the tram company by the Eastern Counties Omnibus Company. The bus station was an extensive Art Deco structure with a substantial bus garage occupying half of the site area, a control building and information and ticket office to the north end of the site either side of the Surrey Street entrance and a run of bus bays along the southern perimeter. By the 1990s the site was felt to be inefficient and inappropriate for modern customer needs so was entirely redeveloped. The present bus station is reckoned to be the most advanced in the UK and was developed in 2004/5 with the aid of Government funding and designed by Norfolk Property Services (architect Michael Spicer). It provides real time information, ticket machines, an information centre, waiting facilities, toilets and a café. Services using the bus station are principally for County destinations or further afield. Some Park & Ride services also terminate here.

Bus Stops

Principal bus and coach stop locations. Although the new bus station provides a terminus for principally County services, the majority of City Services stop along a 'bus spine' running from the south end of St Stephens Street to the north end of Castle Meadow. The 'spine' is equipped with modern shelters, real time departure information displays and 'pre purchase' ticket machines.

Butler, Barry

Former Norwich City footballer. Barry Butler came from Sheffield Wednesday to Norwich in 1957. He was a key member of the 1959 Cup Run side and played every game in the promotion winning run of the following season. Two years latter he was a member of the side that won the Football League Cup. He was considered the best un-capped centre half in the country. He became club captain in 1963 and amassed an impressive 349 appearances while at the club, 208 in a consecutive, un-broken run. Tragically, his career was cut short at the age of 31 in 1966 when he was killed in a car accident. He is commemorated by the clubs Player of the Year award which was named the Barry Butler Memorial Trophy in his honour.

REMEMBER
THOMAS FOWELL BUXTON Bt
MEMBER OF PARLIAMENT
WHOSE EFFORTS LED TO THE
EMANCIPATION OF 700,000
SLAVES ON 1ST AUGUST 1834

Memorial to Sir Thomas Fowell Buxton in the Cathedral.

Butter Hills

Extra Mural site. Originally known as Gosehill and located just south of the most southerly section of City Wall, this area was recorded as being in the ownership of John le Boteler in 1175-86. Botelleres hil or Botylereshil remains in common usage until the C16th when it begins to be corrupted to Butterhills. Today it is a largely overgrown area with no public access.

Buxton, Thomas Fowell

Anti slavery campaigner. While Wilberforce is traditionally regarded as being responsible for the abolition of the slave trade, it was Thomas Fowell Buxton who set about outlawing slavery. He took over from Wilberforce in the House of Commons as leader of the abolition movement when Wilberforce retired and, in 1833, his efforts resulted in slavery being abolished in the British Empire and the freeing of 700,000 slaves then held in the West Indies and elsewhere. Buxton became a close friend of Joseph Gurney and Elizabeth Fry. He worked with Elizabeth Fry to improve conditions in prisons and reduce the number of crimes deemed worthy of the death penalty. He spoke at the Friends Meeting House and used St Andrews Hall to organise meetings in favour of his various causes. He married Joseph Gurney's sister Hannah in 1807 and spent much time in Norwich. He is commemorated by a plaque erected by the Heritage Economic & Regeneration Trust (HEART) at the Friends Meeting House.

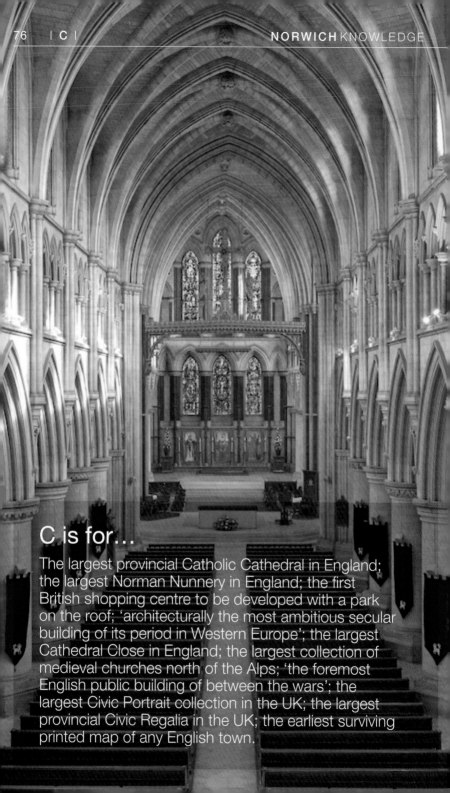

C is for...

The largest provincial Catholic Cathedral in England; the largest Norman Nunnery in England; the first British shopping centre to be developed with a park on the roof; 'architecturally the most ambitious secular building of its period in Western Europe'; the largest Cathedral Close in England; the largest collection of medieval churches north of the Alps; 'the foremost English public building of between the wars'; the largest Civic Portrait collection in the UK; the largest provincial Civic Regalia in the UK; the earliest surviving printed map of any English town.

Cadge, Dr William

Medical innovator. A distinguished graduate of University College Hospital, Cadge worked as a surgeon at the Norfolk and Norwich Hospital from 1854 until 1890. He spearheaded much of the work which led to the hospital's modernisation, sinking £20,000 of his own money into improvements and leaving a further £5,000 in his will. When he died, his work was commemorated in a stained glass window in the Cathedral and doctors from 22 different countries attended its unveiling in 1904. He is remembered in the name of Cadge Road in Earlham.

Caistor St Edmund

Suburban parish and abandoned Roman town. Located to the south of Norwich on the River Tas, the current village of Caistor St Edmund has a population of only 270 people, but is probably best known as the site of the remains of a Roman market town and the cantonal capital, Venta Icenorum, or 'market place of the Iceni'. The remains of the town are currently in the care of the Norfolk Archaeological Trust and South Norfolk Council, and have been open to the public since 1995. A number of features of the town continue to be visible today. Although the walls are largely covered by an earth bank, on the north side the town wall still stands to its full height of around 6m with one wall bastion remaining and overlooking the River Tas. The outline of the streets can be seen in dry weather as brown marks in the grass and the former amphitheatre can be seen only as a crop mark. The church here is St Edmunds, located to the southeast of the Roman town. A church has stood in this location at least since the time of Edward the Confessor, and is thought to have been in use for more than 950 years. The nave is the oldest part of the building and there have been several alterations to the church over the centuries, including the addition of red tiles recovered from the Roman town. Away from the site of the Roman town, Caistor Old Hall was built for Thomas Pettus in 1612 and the 'new' Hall almost opposite was built for the Dashwood family in 1805 and now functions as a hotel. There was once a mill in the village on the River Tas, on a site upstream from the Roman town. It is likely that the Romans had a mill too, and certainly a mill was still present in the area in 1838 where one is marked on the ordnance survey map, although this no longer exists today.

Caius, John

Physician and scholar. Born in King Street in 1510, Caius went on to be physician to Edward VI, Mary Tudor and Elizabeth I. He produced innovative scientific texts and following generous endowments to Gonville College Cambridge, he became its Master.

Caley's

Noted confectionery company. J. Caley came to Norwich in 1857 and established a chemist's business in London Street and, in 1863, he started making mineral waters in a small cellar at the back of his shop. The business expanded rapidly and after his son, Edward J. Caley, joined the business in 1878 they took over a building in Chapelfield. Although successful in the new premises, the manufacture of mineral water was seasonal so Caley looked for something else to fill the seasonal gap and to avoid having to lay off staff. In 1883, he started manufacturing cocoa and that led to the making of chocolate in 1886. In 1890 the large new Fleur de Lys works was erected on a site at Chapelfield utilising two Artesian wells. In 1897 to give additional work to the girls employed on preparing the frills for the chocolate boxes, Caley's started

Opposite: Cathedral of St John the Baptist, interior.
Below, from left: Walls of former Roman Venta Icenorum, Caistor Old Hall, Caistor New Hall.

Caley's packing department early C20th.
Inset: Early Caley's advertising.

making Christmas crackers. By 1904 they were employing 700 people and their chocolates and crackers were being shipped to the most remote quarters of the world. They had agencies in Canada, South Africa, Australia and India, and there was a large demand for Caleys' crackers in Paris. At the beginning of the C20th Caley's had noted that 'quality' chocolate was being imported from Switzerland so they set out to substitute a domestic product for this import by sourcing the highest quality ingredients including milk from a Whitlingham herd of red poll cattle. During the First World War, Caley's produced their famous Marching Chocolate for troops at the front and this was to become one of the signature products of the company.

In 1918, the company was purchased by The African and Eastern Trade Corporation, who, in 1932, sold it to John Mackintosh & Sons Limited of Halifax for £138,000. The first pack of 'Rolo' was manufactured in Norwich in 1937, and its popularity spread around the world being exported to over 100 countries. The main 'Rolo' plant at Norwich produced two tons an hour. In April 1942 the 'fire bomb blitz' on Norwich totally

destroyed the works and rebuilding the began in 1946 allowing limited production facilities to operate, with the first phase of the reconstruction being completed in 1949. The whole rebuilding scheme was not completed until 1952. The confectionary product line continued to prosper with the addition of Week-End, Munchies, Caramac and Good News. The mineral water business was sold to a local brewery after the war and 1953 the Christmas cracker manufacturing side of the business merged with Tom Smiths who maintained production at their Salhouse Road factory.

In 1969 Mackintosh merged with Rowntree of York. The Norwich factory continued successfully over the next 25 years, employing over 1,000 people and producing over 40 million chocolate eggs for Easter alone. In 1988 the Swiss company Nestles took over the factory and by 1995 had rationalised operations and closed it with the loss of 900 jobs. After some years of negotiation a scheme for redevelopment, by Bovis Lendlease, eventually emerged providing a mix of new retail and 150 homes as well as 2,000 new jobs. The former factory managers also produced a

phoenix from the ashes by purchasing the rights to make Caley's chocolate from Nestles and opening the Caley's Cocoa Café which still prospers in the Guildhall.

Calvert Street Methodist Chapel

Lost Walled City chapel. In 1810, the 'Free Methodists' built a chapel at what is now the end of Calvert Street, on the site of modern St Crispin's Road. Calvert Street Methodists Chapel was a red brick building with round arched windows and internally, a panelled gallery and a high spacious pulpit with seating for at least ten speakers. It was designed to hold 1050 people but over the years underwent several refurbishments. In 1858 the Wesleyan reformers took over the chapel, making some improvements, but in 1894 a major refurbishment was carried out by the architect A F Scott. This work included the installation of a new organ which may have still been in use in the 1960s. L.C. Martin wrote that the organ had a forty foot long pipe laid under the floor of the gallery and that when the organ was played it "made a rumble like thunder and set all the sash windows of the chapel rattling. The high-pitched treble notes with which the slow march began sounded like the wail of a deserted and dying child, threatened now and again by the roar of some formidable monster."

Unfortunately, despite being a listed building, the chapel was demolished to make way for the inner ring road and the congregation held their last service in the building on 26th June 1966. It was a huge loss, not only to the congregation but also architecturally. Some people considered it a building comparable in architectural importance to the Old Meeting House and the Octagon Chapel on Colegate.

Canary, Norwich

Emblematic local bird.
Sailors from the Spanish Netherlands captured finches from the Canary Isles on their travels and kept them as caged pets. When, in the mid C16th, Flemish and Dutch refugees fled from the Duke of Alva's persecution of 'religeous heretics' and came to Norwich to reinvigorate the textile industry, they brought their finches with them and developed canary breeding as a staple activity in the City. The Norwich Canary became a specialised breed to the extent that when the City established its own association football team in the early 1900s, Norwich City became the Canaries and the name has remained with them ever since. Canary breeding also remains a popular local pastime with the Norwich Plainhead and Norwich Crested being the principal types.

Capitol

Former cinema. Built in 1932, the 800 seat Capitol Cinema and ballroom, on Aylsham Road, was intended to serve the growing Mile Cross Estate. It survived the War and into the 1950s but closed in 1960 to be merged with the adjacent ballroom to become the Norwood Rooms. This continued as a popular dancing and function venue until it was converted to a bingo hall.

Huge inflatable canary celebrates NCFC promotion in 2004.

Car parking

Types and locations.
Norwich has a wide choice of parking options ranging from award-winning park and ride sites to central long and short stay car parks and on-street provision.

The key options include:
On-Street free parking
This is available on some streets outside the City Centre or within the centre after 6.30pm and before 7.30am. Users should take care to note if they are in a Controlled Parking Zone (CPZ), where controls are in place to protect residents, either visitor or residential permits are required to be displayed in all but specially designated areas.
On-Street Pay & Display Parking
This operates on most streets within the City Centre, except where yellow lines prevent parking, between 7.30am and 6.30pm. Payment is made in a machine and a ticket then affixed to the interior windscreen. The system is enforced by a vigilant band of parking attendants.
City Council-run Off Street
The City Council runs 1500 spaces in 15 sites which are open 24 hours a day/7 days a week. The principal sites include: 1084 spaces at St Andrews (Duke St entrance) located just north of the Lanes shopping area.

210 at Rose Lane (Mountergate entrance) located just south of the Castle. 206 spaces at St Saviours (St saviours entrance) located east of the Magdalen Street shopping area. 145 spaces at Barn Road (St Swithins Rd entrance) located west of St Benedicts shopping area. 145 spaces at Rouen Rd (Rouen Rd entrance) located south of Castle Mall. 134 spaces at St Helens Wharf (Bishopgate entrance) located just north of the Cathedral. 104 spaces at Westwick St (Westwick St entrance) located just west of St Benedicts shopping area. 86 spaces at Clegate (Golden Dog Lane entrance) located just west of Magdalen St shopping area. Additionally the Council operates the St Giles car park (330 spaces) from 7am to 1am Mon to Sun and this is located just north of City Hall.

Non Council-Run, off street car parks
959 spaces beneath the Chapelfield Shopping Centre accessed from Chapelfield Rd. 734 spaces at Riverside accessed from Koblenz Av. 700 spaces at the Mall Shopping Centre accessed from Rose Lane. 650 spaces at John Lewis accessed from Ber Street 260 spaces at NCP St Stephens accessed from Queens Rd. 209 beneath

The Forum accessed from Bethel St. Parking is also possible on some retail sites but these are generally time limited and proof of purchase is usually required (Sainsbury's Queens Rd, Morrisons Riverside).

County Council-run Park & Ride sites: Norwich has the largest Park & Ride facility of any city in the UK with five sites providing nearly 5,000 spaces, serving the key approach radials and the buses are painted in liveries unique to each site to make site recognition and return easier. Weekday operation is between 6.40am and 7.30pm (later Thursdays). Sat operation is 7am-7.30pm while on Sundays Airport, Postwick, Harford & Thickthorn operate between 9.30am and 5.30pm (others closed). Airport – access off A140 Cromer Rd for traffic from north – 620 spaces – journey time 20-25 mins. Sprowston – access of A1151 Wroxham Rd for traffic from north east – 792 spaces – journey time 20-25 mins. Postwick – access off A1242 Yarmouth Rd for traffic from east – 550 spaces – journey time 20-25 mins. Harford – access off A140 Ipswich Rd for traffic from south (Ipswich direction) – 1088 spaces – journey time 15-20 mins. Thickthorn – access off A11/A47 for traffic from south west (Cambridge direction) – 726 spaces – journey time 12-15 mins. Costessey – access off A47 roundabout Showground for traffic from west – 1100 spaces – journey time 20 mins.

Carlton Cinema
Former cinema, now bingo hall. This 900 seat venue in All Saints Green, by J. Owen Bond, was the first City cinema to be designed specifically for 'talkies' and it opened in 1932. A year later it was extended significantly and its organ was also enlarged. In 1939 it was taken over by the Odeon chain and 20 years later, when the old Gaumont closed in the Haymarket, it became the Gaumont. It finally ceased as a cinema in 1973 when it became a bingo hall.

Carmelite Friars
See *Whitefriars*.

Carnary College
Former medieval chapel. The Chapel of St John the Evangelist is said to stand on the site of an early charnel house. The charnel house was probably a two-storey building with a chapel above and an undercroft that housed exhumed bones from the City's overcrowded graveyards. This was replaced by Bishop Salmon in 1316 with the College and Chapel of St John the Evangelist. The chapel was built within the lay cemetery and the new undercroft of the chapel continued to be used as a charnel store. The building was designed with low round windows that allowed people to look into the undercroft and view the collection of bones. The chapel also still contains an early C14th porch door that may be original as well as its original roof constructed in 1316. This roof is therefore the oldest roof in the whole cathedral precinct. On the western side of the lay cemetery and built against the precinct wall was the main hall of the college. Eventually this hall was altered and extended eastwards so that it joined onto the chapel. By the mid C16th the chapel became part of the college, which with reference to its former

Clockwise from top left: Carnary College interior detail, Carnary College vaulted undercroft, Carnary College from Upper Close.

Old Carrow Bridge, built 1810.

use as a charnel house became known as Carnary College. In the late C18th Horatio Nelson was one of its pupils. Restored in 1941, the chapel is now part of Norwich School and is used by staff and pupils who welcome anyone who wishes to worship there. The College is a Scheduled Ancient Monument.

Carrow

Former hamlet. Located at the southern end of the probable Conesford Roman road, close to the confluence of the Yare and Wensum, the settlement was named from Old English meaning projecting spur in the bend of a river. There is very early evidence of occupation on and around the site with hand axes and flint flakes denoting Mesolithic activity having been found in 1927, 1947, 1963 and most recently in 2002 during excavations on the Football Club car park. Despite this there is little remaining to denote remnants of any settlement surviving for a lengthy period and instead what survives are remnants of large scale developments undertaken over relatively brief periods.

These include principally, the site of Carrow Works, the adjacent workers housing provided by the Colman Family and the grounds of the former Norman Carrow Priory which were incorporated into the estate of the Colman Family when they moved their factory to Norwich and had Carrow House built by James Minns in 1861. The large and recently restored Boulton & Paul conservatory was added in 1895. The house was, until recently, the home of the Norfolk Museum Service's Costume & Textile Study Centre – now moved to the Shirehall.

Carrow Bridge

The first Carrow Bridge, by Arthur Browne, was built as a fixed bridge in 1810 but 175 yards downstream from its current position on an alignment with the factory entrance of Colmans in King Street. This was replaced by a double bascule lifting bridge in 1833 to enable larger ships to gain access to the Port of Norwich. The bridge on the current site was designed by A.E. Collins (City Engineer) as a single leaf bascule. It was started in 1920 as part of an employment creation scheme and officially opened in June 1923 by the future King Edward VIII.

Carrow Priory

Lost medieval nunnery. Carrow Priory was a Benedictine priory of nuns, founded in Norwich in 1146. King Stephen gave the nuns all the uncultivated land between Ber Street, Southgate and Trowse Bridge and directed the nuns to build a priory there. The priory was dedicated to St Mary and St John and had a chapel to St John the Baptist on the south side and a chapel to St Catherine

Clockwise from top left: Carrow Priory – Norman Nunnery ruins, Prioress' Lodging, Gothic Revival restoration, and Medieval fireplace and panelling.

on the north side. Initially the priory had a prioress and nine nuns, though this later increased to twelve nuns. In 1199, the nuns were granted an important source of income in the shape of a three-day fair and Henry III later confirmed the charter.

A significant number of the nuns came from wealthy families in the City and this might account for its relative lack of popularity (compared to the friaries and parish churches) among the lay people of Norwich when the time came for them to consider their beneficiaries. Nevertheless, in a sample of 615 wills drawn up by Norwich citizens between 1370 and 1532 they received support from 16 per cent of the testators. Detailed accounts of the priory exist and reveal a process of economic diversification throughout the C15th/16th. The nuns were forced, through a combination of factors which included low rents and high prices, to adopt innovative money-making schemes such as sheep farming.

Community relations, as with many of the monastic houses in Norwich (and indeed between them: Carrow Priory engaged in long-running legal battles with the monks at the cathedral-priory), could be problematic. During an attack on Carrow Priory during the 1381 uprising, the prioress was forced to surrender documentation proving particular (contested) rights so that they might be burnt. This act not only destroyed the physical evidence supporting the priory's claim, but symbolised the rebels' dismissal of the claim. Subsequent prioresses did not

From top: Carrow Road Football Ground 1935, River End, and at the close of the 2010/11 season.

necessarily have more peaceful reigns. In 1416 the widow of a murdered man accused the prioress of harbouring her husband's killers and she was subsequently arrested and imprisoned before finally being acquitted of the crime.

The 1526 visitation revealed that with the exception of the beer (which was watery and thus too weak) the house was well run and not, as critics suggested, in debt. This provided a stark contrast to the 1492 visitation during which no accounts could be produced and the general picture was one of a house in disarray run by dishonest servants.

The priory was surrendered to the Crown in 1538 and the property was later owned by Sir John Shelton. Ruins of the cloister, dormitory undercroft, chapter house and church remain and the prioress' lodging remains intact although restored in the Gothic revival style.

Archaeological excavations in 1981 revealed C12th/13th tiled floors and nine graves of adult women. The Priory remains are a Scheduled Ancient Monument.

Carrow Road

Home of Norwich City Football Club. Located north of the Wensum from the hamlet of Carrow and the Carrow Works, the site was acquired from Colmans and first developed in 1935 to accommodate the club following their move from 'The Nest' on Rosary Road. Work was completed in a remarkable 82 days and the ground opened on 31st August 1935 to a crowd of 29,779 people who watched Norwich beat West Ham 4-3. Floodlights appeared in 1956 and new stands followed later with the Norwich & Peterborough being developed over the old River End in 1979, the Geoffrey Watling Stand replacing the old Main Stand destroyed by fire in 1984, the new Barclay arriving in 1993 and the 8,000 seater Jarrold Stand replacing the old south stand in 2004. In the same year major improvements were made to the pitch in terms of drainage and under soil heating. Subsequently, Holiday Inn developed a hotel in the north east corner of the ground. Over the last decade the Club has developed its conference, corporate hospitality and catering offer around the pitch to a significant degree.

Carrow Works
See *Colmans*.

Carter, R.G.
Construction company. As an apprenticed carpenter, George Carter got his first local job with the well established builders John Youngs. After the First World War, he worked for the London construction company Scott & Middleton but in 1922 he left and started his own business. His first Norwich job was for Bullard's Anchor Brewery and this secured him continued work with the company, and indeed with other brewers, until they were all taken over by Watneys in the 1960s. The company also moved into village halls and church buildings as well as public buildings. In 1925 R.G. Carter secured a large housing contract with the City Council at Drayton Road. The company weathered the recession and by the mid 1930s had absorbed other companies and employed 250 people. During WWII the company secured a number of service contracts and by 1946 George's son Bob had joined the team and by 1950 he was running the

business. A key element of Carter's work after the War was house building and between 1946 and 1960 they built 4,000 houses. One of the biggest schemes was the development of Norwich Union's Island Site as well as a wide range of other projects regionally. Between 1966 and 1971 turnover doubled to £15.3m and the workforce rose to 3,000. In 1967 the wheel moved full circle as the company took over John Youngs, who had first employed George Carter. The company continued to deliver major projects locally and despite the untimely death of the company's principal, Bob Carter, in 1974, the company continued to prosper under his eldest son, Robert. In the 1980s it augmented its commercial schemes with prison contracts, substantial work at the Football Ground, the Airport, the Norwich Sport Village and the Theatre Royal. Other major schemes followed including the prestigious Millennium Project, The Forum. Today Carters runs 14 companies throughout the East of England Region and employs 1500 people.

Cash Machines
See *ATM terminals*.

Castle, Castle Bridge, Castle Fee, Castle Gardens and Castle Green
See page 84-86.

Castle Mall
Innovative shopping centre. Following its takeover by the Mall Company, what started life over 25 years ago as Castle Mall is now know simply as 'The Mall'. In response to a perceived need for more retail space in the 1980s, at a time when the trend was to build large, out of town sheds, the development company Estates & General and their architect Michael Innes came forward in 1983 with an innovative proposal for a major 'in-town' scheme in the shadow of the Castle. Although the proposal started positively, the developer ran into financial difficulties and the Prudential produced a rival scheme in 1986. E & G eventually partnered with insurance giant Friends Provident and the City Council agreed to contribute their land holding so the scheme began, with one of the biggest archaeological digs in Europe, in 1989. The novel proposal involved the removal of 800,000 tons of earth and rubble to create

Castle Mall under development early 1990s.

Castle

'It was architecturally the most ambitious secular building (of its period) in Western Europe' T.A. Heslop

This was the most elaborate Norman Keep to be constructed in England and the first English castle to be built on a mound. Inside the keep, the largest provincial Civic Regalia collection in England resides. Inside the former prison buildings, the works of the unique Norwich School of Painters and the largest teapot collection in the World are both exhibited.

Royal Castle

The mound is artificial and was constructed by forced labour soon after the Conquest. A wooden keep followed shortly after and this structure was so substantial that it withstood a siege of three months duration in 1075 when Emma de Gauder, wife of a rebel baron, held out against the King's army and then only sued for peace when food ran out. The keep, built of stone from Caen in Normandy and Barnack in Northamptonshire, was begun in the 1090s and completed for Henry I to celebrate Christmas there in 1121. The building was notable for its elaborate, blind arcading on the exterior and fine detailing internally.

The original defensive ring earthworks encompassed an area of over nine acres in the later City and were topped with a series of defensive walls and gates. These defences have since been eroded by modern development. The Castle was first tested as a defensive structure in 1174 when Hugh Bigod sacked the City and occupied the Castle with a contingent of Flemings. In 1216 the Castle was again found wanting when the French Dauphin Louis occupied it for a year, installing William de Bello Monte as his garrison commander. In 1262 Hubert de Morley was paid £57 16/- to strengthen the structure and six years later a stone (or possibly flint) curtain wall and towers were erected around the top of the mound.

Prison

From the C13th onwards the Castle ceased to be a Royal Castle and was used predominantly as a prison. A Shirehouse was constructed in 1271 to augment this new function and reconstructed in 1326. The prison function became the exclusive use for the next 500 years. In 1746 a major fire destroyed the Shirehouse and Matthew Brettingham, the country's principal exponent of Palladian architecture and designer of Holkham Hall, built a handsome, new Shirehouse adjacent to and north of the keep. The earliest reliable survey of the keep, the Dove Survey, was completed in 1788 and preceded the development

of a new prison building, 'of Scotch granite', by the eminent architect Sir John Soane, adjacent to the east side of the keep between 1789 and 1794. This provided convenient accommodation for prisoners of the Napoleonic Wars who were 'marched out of the City singing the Marseillois' and 'met with the most humane treatment from Mr Armand, the keeper of the Castle.' In 1806 the Castle passed from the Crown to the County. Soane's prison had a very short life and following its demolition in 1824, William Wilkins built a new radial design, covering virtually the whole of the top of the mound, to house 224 inmates. 15 years later Anthony Salvin controversially refaced the keep in Bath stone. While producing a faithful reproduction of the blind arcading, based on detailed drawings by Wilkins, he reduced the number of battlements, used larger blocks of stone than the original keep facing, etched to look like small blocks and replaced the ground floor flint infilling with stone. Further modifications were made to the Wilkins prison in 1875 and communal areas were developed to accommodate more inmates.

Museum

The City Corporation bought the Castle in 1887 and in 1890, local architect Edward Boardman converted the keep and prison buildings into a museum at a cost of almost £4,000. The gaoler's house was demolished and replaced by sunken gardens, a fountain and a pool – all traces of the former prison use were erased or concealed. Inside the keep, the intention had

been to restore the original first floor level but budget constraints meant that only a balcony was constructed around the edge at this level. The new museum was opened formally in October 1894. Modifications continued throughout the next century with a new picture gallery at the end of the north wing in 1910, the Norfolk Room, for natural history collections, in 1930, the Colman Galleries for the Norwich School of Artists on former exercise yards in 1951 and a major refurbishment in 1963-9 when all of the former external spaces were built over to provide a new internal circulation space and café. A major Heritage Lottery funded scheme in the late 1990s saw the removal of back of house functions to the converted Shirehall to free up more space within the Castle. The original Norman features were much more effectively displayed, a new gallery depicting the history of Iceni Queen Boadica, and including the remarkable Snettisham Treasure, was developed and new art galleries, often hosting exhibitions from the Tate and other notable galleries, were completed. In 2004 a new Anglo Saxon and Viking Gallery was added exhibiting some of the most important finds in the UK. The ground floor area, previously used for storage, was opened to display original Norman vaulting and provide displays on how the Castle was built. More recently, the Arts of Living Gallery has been added, with substantial funding from the Heritage Economic & Regeneration Trust (HEART), exhibiting examples of

From top: Castle Keep and remnant of gate tower, Castle Keep interior, Arts of Living Gallery opened by Zandra Rhodes & Prof John Last 2009.

Opposite: Castle Fee as it would have appeared in the C13th/C14th.

costume and other decorative arts. Also, a new ground floor gallery has provided an impressive interpretation of the Castle's prison history, including the use of state-of-the-art virtual reality models to reveal lost elements of the former prison structure such as the treadmill. This has freed up space in the keep to provide capacity for loan exhibits from the British Museum's reserve collections following a recent partnership between the BM and the

Norfolk Museums Service. In the longer term there are plans to make more of the keep as a medieval resource.

Castle Bridge
Ancient Castle access.
The present bridge up to the Castle, although restored in 1830 and subsequently, is Norman in origin and probably built at the same time as the keep, also of Caen stone. The bridge originally spanned a gap twice as deep as the current drop to the gardens and excavations in 1990/92 revealed that below ground, nine courses of chamfered Caen stone sit beneath a faced wall also of Caen stone. This is the oldest bridge in Norwich and one of the oldest in England.

Castle Fee
Historic boundary of the Castle. From the Norman Conquest until 1345 the Castle Fee was the area of land around the Castle which was directly ruled by the Crown and not by the City authorities. Although it took up a large part of the City Centre, it was not part of Norwich in legal terms and the City laws, taxes and regulations did not apply within it. The Fee was controlled by the Sheriff, then as now a representative of the monarch, and it had its own courts, its own church and its own prison. Residents were known as 'The Men of the Fee'. The citizens of Norwich often resented this situation, because the Fee dwellers could make money by trading in the City but did not pay tax back to it. It was also because it was possible for inhabitants of the Fee to commit crimes in the City and then seek sanctuary

within the Fee. If they were tried at all, it was by a friendly jury. This eventually led to the Fee, apart from the Castle buildings themselves, being returned to the City's jurisdiction in 1345. In 2009 the Heritage Economic & regeneration trust (HEART) installed a series of pavement markers defining the extent of the

From top: Norman Castle Bridge, pavement marker denoting original extent of the Castle Fee, Castle Green Sculpture – Mask of Daedalus.

original Fee using replicas of the original Royal fee marker, discovered during archaeological excavations

Castle Gardens
Public Park. Originally the inner ditch of the Castle motte, the ditch outer mound had been substantially eroded on most sides by the C19th and in 1849, the surviving remnant, to the south east of the Castle, was transformed into a landscaped garden. This was extended to a series of masonry edged pathways running up the mound. In the C20th, the Whiffler Theatre was added to the northern end of the gardens. As part of an £11m regeneration scheme for the Castle in the 1990s the mound was cleared of trees and the paths were also removed. The gardens were remodelled to provide a clearer and more direct access to the Castle and this was augmented with a new glass lift and steps leading to the main bridge to the Castle and a ramp leading to Castle Green.

Castle Green
Public park. Located adjacent to the Castle and Castle Gardens, Castle Green is effectively a 4.5 acre (2 ha) roof garden on top of the Mall shopping centre. It provides terraced lawns, water features, a children's playground, sculpture and extensive viewpoints over the east of the City. It has 138 trees which have survived and flourished since the scheme opened in 1993 by being located in cylindrical concrete tubes which run through the geometry of the development.

one of the biggest holes in Europe at the time. This was then secured with a perimeter made up of 800 concrete piles. A development covering 1 million square feet and including nearly 400,000 square feet of retail space was inserted in 'the hole' to provide five large anchor stores and over 70 smaller units. The scheme also provided 1050 car parking spaces as well as a four acre roof top park. During construction 63,000 visitors came to look at the dig and the gradually filling hole from as far away as Thailand and Leningrad. The Russians were so impressed that they commissioned the architect to design a 'Castle Mallski' beside Red Square in Moscow. Although Castle Mall opened in the pit of the recession in September 1993 and only a handful of units were let, business picked up and after a relatively short period, the developers were able to announce that Disney considered their Castle Mall store to be their strongest opening in Europe, Boots Mall store was 'national store of the month' and Virgin exceeded their anticipated performance. In the late 1990s the centre increased its appeal by developing a Ster Century (now Vue) eight screen cinema at the Farmers Avenue level. The centre was taken over by the Mall Company in the new Millennium and this resulted in a revamping of the food court – a modification which was not to the taste of the original architect – and the insertion of a T.K. Maxx in the basement. Today, the scheme continues to offer a range of variety stores (Boots, Argos), a selection of high street standards

(Mothercare, Early Learning), fashion stores (New Look, Madhouse, La Senza), catering (principally from the food court) and speciality including the Norwich City Football Club shop. The Mall also houses the principal post office and most recently benefitted from the addition of an NHS 'drop-in centre'. It hosts a range of events including fashion and talent shows.

Castle Meadow
Historic space. Originally a meadow within the fortified Castle Bailey to the immediate east of the Castle Motte and, as the name suggests, the meadow on which the Castle's livestock were grazed, the name migrated to the road running to the north and west of the Castle once the former Bailey had passed into the control of the Corporation. The original meadow became part of the Cattlemarket and the 'new' Castle meadow was little more than an orbital track until the trams broke a route through to the west of the Bell Hotel, linking Prince of Wales Road/Agricultural Hall Plain to St Stephens and Red Lion Street thus transforming Castle Meadow into a significant through route. This role was further emphasised in 1927 when widening, at the expense of the Castle Mound, created a wide thoroughfare. Increasing volumes of traffic using this as a through route persuaded the Council, in the 1990s, to restrict access to buses and service traffic only. Further work more recently has increased pavement widths, provided pedestrian cross overs and improved bus facilities such as shelters, ticketing and real time information.

Castle Street
Ancient thoroughfare. Linking Back of the Inns to London Street and following the course of the Great Cockey (now culverted beneath the street), this street follows the outer line of the western Castle defences. Few significant buildings survive but one of the notable lost structures includes what was known as 'Tyces' at the junction of the street with Davey Place. Inspired by the Crystal Palace, this exceptional cast iron and glass structure was similar to the surviving Panks/Crystal House in Cattlemarket Street of the same date. When Tyce's closed in 1959 the building was sold and redeveloped despite protests from conservation bodies like the Norwich Society.

Cathedral, Anglican
See *Anglican Cathedral*.

Cathedral, Roman Catholic
See *Cathedral of St John the Baptist*.

The surviving historic sign in Castle Street, and the now lost Tyce's store (below).

Cathedral Close

Precinct of the former Benedictine Priory. The monastic precinct was established with the building of the Cathedral in the late C11th to provide sufficient space to support the emerging Benedictine monastery. It was defined by a substantial flint rubble wall with four fortified entry points – St Ethelbert's Gate, Erpingham Gate, Bishop's Gate and the Water Gate (Pull's Ferry) – and at least two other minor entries.

Unlike the City defences, all of the Gates survive in excellent condition as does a majority of the Wall, albeit, incorporated into later structures to some degree. The defensive nature of the structure was important since it not only needed to define the secular City from the ecclesiastical precinct but also, at times, it was required to perform a military function, as in the 1272 Riot. The Wall encloses an area of 18 Ha (44 acres), making the precinct the largest cathedral close in the country. The Close contains the densest concentration of significant historic and architectural structures in the City and one of the most important collections in the country. There are six scheduled Ancient Monuments and 65 Listed Buildings or groups of which five are Grade I and 43 are Grade II*.

Entering from the St Ethelbert Gate, which dates from 1316-20 and replaces an earlier structure seriously damaged in the 1272 Riot, the houses to the north, and backing onto the surviving precinct wall (Nos. 75, 74,73), are all Georgian dating from the very early 1800s. The first one (No. 75)

Reconstruction of the C14th Close looking east.

was the home of Thomas Tawell who founded the hospital and school for blind people. Further north No. 71a is one of the very few modern interventions into The Close and is a 1956 house (originally an office) designed by Fielden & Mawson. Next door, and adjacent to the 1416-25 Erpingham Gate, is the gabled No. 71 which was built as a prebendary house in 1628 on the site of the Cathedral Belfry or Clocher, destroyed during the 1272 Riot, rebuilt between 1298 and 1307 and demolished in 1569. Immediately north of the Erpingham Gate is the

Vergers Tenement, a small two bay structure with elements dating from the late C15th/early C16th. North of this and running along the north side of the Upper Close, No. 70 (School House) is a pleasant, apparently mid C19th house, with a façade designed by Wordingham in 1852. This however, hides the surviving hall house of Bishop Salmon, probably built in 1316 and extended in 1480 as the Carnary College to link with the chapel. At the same time, a new porch was added providing both access to the College, via a surviving early

C14th door, and the Chapel. This is decorated with the rebus of Bishop Lyhart. The Carnary Chapel itself dates from 1316 and was built by the famous masons William or John Ramsey. Next door, and butting onto the east end of the Carnary Chapel is School End (No. 69), started in 1543 by Dr. John Baret. It later became a canonry and the Dutch south gable was added in the C18th. Obliquely north east, and behind the Cathedral, the Norwich School incorporates the C11th Bishop's Palace. Along the east side of the Upper Close, the Cathedral itself

dominates the space with the 2009 Hostry building by Hopkins Architects providing the new entrance to the Cathedral and sitting against the west wall of the cloisters. South of the Hostry (Nos. 68, 67, 67a) the long range of flint buildings is the reused late C14th/early C15th Cellarer's warehouse and offices. The buildings retain a medieval, brick vaulted cellar, a C15th arch braced roof and a medieval door on the east side. Opposite to and south of the upper Close is Almary Green, the site of the monastic Almonry and containing an interesting collection of C17th and C18th buildings.

Turning east, and adjacent to Almonry Green, a substantial flint wall partially hides a Dutch gabled house (No. 6) dating from the C16th, with a attractive doorway. Next door, Holland Court, built in 1961 and 1964 by Feilden & Mawson, provides a rather unexciting range of offices. Opposite, again apparently later buildings (Nos. 65 and 64) disguise what was originally the medieval Infirmary Chambers which, following the Reformation, were converted to a prebendary house with a new C16th roof. Recent works to the building revealed wall paintings dating from 1550. The former Cathedral Herb Garden has been reestablished in front of these buildings.

Left to right, from top: Cathedral Close – former monastic Sextry (now houses), Prior's Hall (now the Deanery), former monastic granary (now house), former monastic brew house (now houses), Carnary College (now chapel of the Norwich School), Bishop Salmon's former house (now offices), former monastic infirmary (now car park and offices), Georgian houses incorporating former church of St Mary in the Marsh.

Moving to the Lower Close, the most striking building is the Prior's Hall or Deanery dating from the C13th and located on the north side of the space at the west end. Next door (nos. 56-51) are buildings which were originally the mid C13th monastic malt and wheat granary and they retain some of the original fabric, including arcading at the rear of 54/5. Within No. 56 there is a surviving medieval wall painting. On the east side of the Lower Close again ancient fabric survives in apparently later buildings. This range was the monastic bakehouse and brewhouse, clearly well located in relation to the storage of raw materials adjacent (granary). The C13th brewhouse (Nos. 32-3) still contains traces of the original fabric and an early cellar but was substantially remodelled as a town house in 1682. The bakehouse next door (No. 34) also retains evidence of its early origins including a medieval buttress. This became the Three Cranes pub at least by the 1570s and although the pub sign, allegedly painted by John Crome, showed three feathered cranes, it is probable that the pub name related to cranes used for unloading barges which brought goods up the now lost canal. The pub use continued until 1827 when the building became a residence. South of the green space, the buildings (Nos. 7-12) appear uniformly Georgian, dating from around 1775 by Stephen Moore, although the spine wall of 10-12 is the north wall of the pre Conquest church of St Mary in the Marsh while No. 12 incorporates a blocked C16th window and another, large C16th window on the 1st floor. East from this Georgian range are three Victorian villas (Nos. 13-15) dating from 1883 by George and Peto.

From the Lower Close, routes diverge north towards Life's Green, north east to Hook's Walk and east along the line of the former canal towards Pull's Ferry. Towards Life's Green, No. 57 is a Victorian Gothic villa by John Brown, built between 1862 and 1864. It occupies the site of the monastic Plumbery or Leadhouse, demolished in 1640, where lead for the

roofs and for stained glass windows was fashioned. Next door to the north, Nos. 58-60 occupy the site of the monastic Sextry, the office of the Sacrist who was responsible for the maintenance of the monastic estate. Remnants of the medieval Sextry fabric survive in the two northerly most buildings as does part of a minor gatehouse leading from The Close to Bishopgate. These buildings are principally C16th rebuilds while No. 58 dates from the C18th. Turning the corner eastwards, No. 60a is a 1964 house by S. Crosse sitting on the foundations of the pre Conquest church of St Helen while No. 61 is a flint faced, early C19th house. To the east of these, Nos. 44 and 43 sit in relative isolation, backing onto properties in Bishopgate. Their most interesting feature is the substantial re-used wall of the pre Conquest church of St Helen which forms the north wall of No. 44. The Dutch gabled buildings themselves date from 1670 and were built by James and Katherine Hobart of Beeston.

Returning to the Lower Close and progressing east along Hook's Walk, No. 50 was built in 1661 and later occupied by Dr Frank Sayer, a local antiquary and school contemporary of Nelson. No. 49 was originally the office of the monastic gardener and incorporates two C13th windows from the original building. It was extended in the early C15th and rebuilt in the early C17th. Nos. 47-8 are late C18th while across the lane to Bishopgate, Nos. 40 and

41 are C17th and C18th. Nos. 37-9 were built in 1633 by 'John Howell and Helen his wife' an inscription over the door tells us.

Returning to the Lower Close and following the line of the extant canal along Ferry Lane, No. 29 was the monastic boathouse adjacent to the former canal, although it has an early C19th façade, the core of the building is C16th and earlier. Next door, No. 27 has similarly early, C15th origins, evidenced by Bishop Lyhart's rebus in the east gable, but was subject to major reconstruction in 1646 and a Georgian façade in the C18th. It was occupied by the Bailiff of the Liberties of the Precinct.

Opposite, Nos. 16-18 are C18th/19th but No. 17 does incorporate a C17th wing. On the same side further east there is a range of C19th cottages opposite to an attractive run of C19th mews style stables. At the end of the lane, Pull's Ferry, the water gate, dates from the C15th with the 1647 Ferry House adjacent. It was previously called Sandling's Ferry, after one of the Cathedral Choir in the reign of Elizabeth I and the first man to hold the ferry license. It was Pull's Ferry Inn from 1796 to 1868 and operated by John Pull (or Poole) as both landlord and ferryman until his death in 1841.

The canal from the ferry was filled in around 1780 and the ferry itself ceased in 1943 when the last ferryman, Cecil Mollet, finished. The buildings were substantially restored by Cecil Upcher in 1947.

Cathedral of St John the Baptist

Catholic Cathedral

"Perhaps the finest example of Victorian Gothic revival in this country." Built on the site of the former City Gaol and endowed by the 15th Duke of Norfolk, construction began in 1882 to the plans of George Gilbert Scott Jr. The scheme was completed by his brother, John Oldrid Scott, after Gilbert Scott's death. The Duke's grand scheme celebrated an association with both the Howard family and the Catholic community in the City stretching back centuries. Gilbert Scott's intention was to build a seminal example of pure English Gothic and the result is regarded as, arguably, the finest example of Gothic revival ecclesiastical architecture in England.

The structure was built of stone from Devon and Derbyshire with marble brought from Durham but when the Devon stone was found to weather poorly, the building was completed in Ancaster and Clipsham stone. One of the most distinctive aspects of the stone employed is the thousands of fossils contained within it and the stone steps leading into the main entrance exhibit the point well. Once inside, this element is continued with more fossils speckling the black Frosterley marble pillars surrounding the nave.

The nave consists of ten bays, supported by massive cylindrical columns. It is over 49 m (160 ft) long and 18 m (60 ft) high. Inside, the work of Hardman & Powell represents some of the finest C19th stained glass in Europe. The pulpit and altar are by Anthony Rossi (1961). The building was completed in 1910 but at that time it was merely a very grand church. It wasn't until 1976 that Pope Paul VI recreated the Catholic Diocese of East Anglia and designated St John's as a cathedral. It is now the second largest Catholic cathedral in the country. A new educational and community centre, called the Narthex and designed by Cathedral Architect Russell Taylor, opened in early 2010.

Clockwise: Cathedral of St John at night, Cathedral of St John, view down nave, Cathedral of St John exterior view, Cathedral of St John view down into the nave from the tower.

Cathedral Cloisters

See *Anglican Cathedral Cloisters*.

Catherine of Aragon

Henry VIII's first queen. Queen Catherine of Aragon visited Norwich in 1520, with Cardinal Wolsley, and was presented with 100 marks by the City Corporation.

Catholic Cathedral

See *Cathedral of St John the Baptist*.

Catholic Chapel and Priest's House

Lost Chapel. The Roman Catholic Chapel and priest's house, built by the 10th Duke of Norfolk in 1764, had a turbulent history. Built within the grounds of the abandoned Duke's Palace in St Andrew's and currently occupied by St Andrew's car park, the priest's house and the adjoining chapel were of little note architecturally but the chapel was enhanced by a magnificent plaster ceiling. The ceiling was vaulted into four bays each with an ornate central plaster boss and two triangular panels. The arches of the ceiling sprung from the walls between each window and beneath this was plaster decoration in the form of winged cherubim. The ceiling is said to have been one of the best in Europe.

In 1786, when the 10th Duke died, the Roman Catholic priest and congregation were asked to leave the chapel and house because the 11th Duke of Norfolk was of Protestant faith. He rented the chapel to the Norwich Subscription Library but when they left in 1839 the Duke sold the chapel and house to the Norfolk and Norwich

Museum. After 55 years on the site the museum moved to Norwich Castle and the buildings were used for a further 44 years by the City as offices for various public services including the Guardians of the Poor and the Public Assistance Committee. In 1966, however, the buildings had gone out of use and, despite its glorious ceiling, the chapel and house were demolished to be replaced by a multi-storey car park, predecessor to the current one.

Cattle Market

See *Old Cattlemarket*.

Catton, New

Suburb. New Catton has its roots as a disputed 'no mans land' between the Walled City and the northern parishes of Catton, Sprowston, Hellesdon and the obscure, ancient manor of Tolthorpe. As such it tended to function as a venue for things that didn't fit particularly well within the City or the parishes – lepers particularly were stuck there (three Leper Houses originally), criminals or traitors were hanged and sometimes buried here and fairs happened here too. Although the main period of development, and indeed the name of the area, can be attributed to the C19th, New Catton's origins are much older. In the C5th, Pagan Saxons were burying their cremated dead here and the area was part of the very early parish of St Clement at Fybriggate, probably a C9th foundation, with New Catton then known as 'St Clement Without' – the naming of a principal north/south route through the area as St Clement's Hill underlines the point.

An early construction was the Leper Hospital or Lazar House on modern Sprowston Road in about 1100. Two other leper houses followed in the second half of the C13th outside the Magdalen and St Augustines Gates. The area remained largely agricultural until the C18th when enclosure and development by wealthy merchants for new country houses began to change the character of the area. In the decade following 1811 the City's population rose by a third, fuelled by a textile boom after the Napoleonic Wars, and most of this was accommodated north of the Walled City. St Clement Without increased by over 150 per cent, accommodating an extra 1100 people. Most of the new houses were small and poorly constructed but well built houses for the middle classes appeared in locations such as St Clements Hill. Other buildings included mills (three towermills near Philadelphia Lane and one on St Clements Hill), a new church (Christchurch), a Wesleyan Methodist Sunday School in Sun Lane and Chapel in Philadelphia Lane, a mixed school and a boys school. Up until the last quarter of the C19th however, the area was still sparsely developed and most of the explosion in suburban development occurred between 1875 and the early C20th. This is characterised by the swathe of surviving terrace housing and schools (Angel Road 1895).

Waterloo Park and Sewell Park were early examples of public open spaces although the former was developed in its present form in the 1920s. After WWI Council housing was developed around Duff

Road/Chamberlain Road, Wensum Park was developed (1925) and the Blyth School was built (1929). During the 1930s further, lower density development occurred in the north of the area with infill development and redevelopment of much of the early Victorian housing taking place after the War.

Catton, Old

Suburban village. Located around 4.8km (3 miles) to the north east of Norwich City Centre, Old Catton has a population of almost 6,000. Old Catton is perhaps best known as the location in which Anna Sewell wrote Black Beauty between 1871 and 1877 before her death five months after the publication of the book in 1878. Old Catton was documented in the Domesday Book and a number of buildings and locations of historic interest survive. St Margaret's Church is a flint construction with a round tower and has probably been present in the village since the late C11th. The tower is likely to be Norman although alterations to the church occurred in the C16th and C19th. Catton Park was laid out in 1788 by Humphrey Repton in the vicinity of Catton New Hall and is on the English Heritage Register of Parks and Gardens of Special Historic Interest. A vestige of the original garden can be seen today in a garden on Parkside Drive, including a clamshell fountain and oval pond. Catton New Hall was built in 1780 and was commandeered by the army during World War II. The Hall continues to be a residential property today. Catton Old Hall on Lodge Lane was built in 1632 as a

Clockwise from top left: Old Catton – C16th Manor door with Catton (cat – tun) rebus, Catton Old Hall, C19th cottages, Georgian Houses on Spixworth Rd.

Gentleman's House. Originally named Moregate, the house became Catton Old Hall after 1845 and is currently used as a guest house. The Manor House, in Church Street is originally C16th with later additions.

Catton Park

Suburban landscaped park. Originally owned by the Cathedral priory, then the Dean & Chapter and located to the south of Old Catton, the site of Catton Park had been acquired by a Mr Lincoln by the mid C18th and subsequently sold to Charles Buckle, Steward of the Manor of Catton. In

Catton Park by Repton.

1778 he applied to the magistrates to realign the Norwich to Catton road so that he might be able to unify his land holding. Ten years later prominent Worsted merchant Jeremiah Ives, Norwich Sheriff in 1782 and Mayor in 1786 and 1801, took over the Catton estate. He commissioned Humphry Repton in 1788 and again in 1790 to prepare a landscape scheme for the park. This involved a series of plantings as well as the removal of some trees to improve views to the Cathedral. At this time the estate amounted to 461 acres. Over the next half century, the estate reduced in extent by about two thirds but very little else occurred in the way of landscape works. In 1856 J.H. Gurney took over the estate and undertook major additional landscape works which saw the joining up of earlier plantations and the development of a significant tree belt around most of the site. The successor owner Samuel Gurney Buxton introduced deer to what is now known as the Deer

Park. The park is now run as a public resource by a trust.

Cavalry Barracks
See *Nelson Barracks*.

Cavell, Edith
Local heroine. Edith Cavell was born in Swardeston, south of Norwich, in 1865. She trained as a nurse and later became matron of a hospital in Brussels, Belgium. During the First World War German occupation of Belgium she was arrested and accused of helping hundreds of allied soldiers to escape. Edith did not deny these claims and was executed by firing squad in the early hours of the 12th October 1915. Her body was buried in Belgium but later exhumed and reburied at Norwich Cathedral. Edith Cavell is remembered not only for her heroism but also for her advances in nursing practice. Statues to her memory can be found at Tombland in Norwich and at St Martin's Place, outside the National Portrait Gallery, in London. Numerous hospitals and less obvious things are named after her throughout the world: in New Zealand there is Edith Cavell Bridge and Mount Edith Cavell can be found in the Canadian Rockies.

Central Library
Lost principal library. Plans for a new library for Norwich were gestated after WWII and the first scheme emerged in 1956 for a site between Theatre Street and Bethel Street, originally earmarked in the 1945 Plan as part of the proposed Civic Centre development. This was to be the first new post war civic building in Norwich and the first new library in the UK after the War. Work started in 1960 with the clearance of a dense network of buildings, some of considerable historic significance including the medieval White Swan. The new library was opened by the Queen Mother in January 1963. Hailed as a stunning example of modernist architecture the flint faced quadrangle by City Architect David Percival received a Civic Trust Award. The new complex provided for an archive centre in the basement, extensive lending and reference libraries on

Clockwise from below: Edith Cavell's memorial in Tombland, Edith Cavell's memorial in St Martin's Place, London, and Edith Cavell's grave in Cathedral Close.

Clockwise from top: New Millennium Library in The Forum, Central Library shortly after opening in 1963, Central Library being demolished after the 1994 fire.

the ground floor, as well as the USAAF Memorial Library, and a local studies library and lecture room on the first floor. There was a substantial 'book stack' feature in the west corner of the building.

The County Council took over library responsibility in 1974 and ultimately remodeled the complex, roofing in the formerly open, central courtyard. In August 1994, a plug shorted out while cleaners were cleaning the library prior to opening. The resultant fire swept through the site devastating the whole building and the book stock. The rich archives in the basement strongroom survived as did some material from the upper 'stacks'. The resulting redevelopment saw the provision of a new 'state of the art' library, as part of the Millennium Commission funded, Forum building, by Sir Michael Hopkins, which is now the most successful library in the UK.

Chalk Workings
See *Underground Norwich*.

Chamberlins
Local Department Store, now lost. In 1814 Henry Chamberlin moved from Scotland to found one of the City's first department stores, at the junction of Guildhall Hill and Dove Street (now Tesco). His son Robert joined the business shortly and spearheaded its development. The company expanded and Robert's success in the local community is reflected in him becoming Mayor in 1854, 1856 and 1871. By the turn of the century the business was being promoted as a high class department store with goods ranging from English and Continental draperies to furniture. Its buffet 'furnished in the most luxurious manner and the best possible taste' was provided for 'the convenience of country customers' and not with any intention of making a profit. The company also had its own clothing

Chamberlins Grand Salon.

production facility in Botolph Street and when WWI broke out production switched to meet the demands of the Admiralty and war office, particularly for the production of oil skins. After the War their store and factory re-equipped to meet changing needs and the business prospered up to and beyond WWII. In the 1950s it was taken over by Marshall & Snelgroves and the business eventually closed.

Chapelfield

Shopping centre. Following the closure of the former Rowntree Mackintosh chocolate factory in 1996, after its takeover by Nestles, the City Council worked with prospective owners to deliver a solution which both enhanced environment and facilities for local people and redressed the loss of 900 jobs. Initially, the Council resisted a number of inappropriate proposals but eventually entered into discussions with the international developer Lendlease (now Bovis Lendlease) and architects BDP to regenerate the site. The key components of the scheme were:

- A major new retail presence to satisfy unmet need
- Additional residential provision including affordable housing
- The careful integration of these facilities into the grain and fabric of the City
- The removal of intrusive 1960s offices and multi storey parking and the post-war factory
- The regeneration of St Stephens churchyard
- The creation of a landscaped City walls walk
- The provision of modern, underground parking
- A contribution to public realm improvements and park & ride.

The scheme opened in 2005 and was transferred to Capital Shopping Centres as new owners and managers. It adds a new department store to the City (House of Fraser), as well as previously unrepresented, large fashion and other retail units such as Clas Ohlssen, and additional catering offers such as Carluccio's. It also provides 1,000 parking spaces, new public spaces, 150 new homes and 2,000 new jobs.

Chapelfield Gardens

Public park. Originally cultivated fields associated with the medieval College of St Mary in the Fields (located on the current Assembly House site), Chapelfield has supported a range of activities and functions including a windmill recorded in 1343, in the C15th, training butts for archers, a location for tournaments, a training ground for the Yeomanry at the time of the Spanish Armada, a mass burial site at the time of the plague, a reservoir in 1792 (although this was subsequently abandoned when cholera swept the City) and ultimately an ornamental park, opened in 1880. The most significant structure in the Gardens was Barnard and Bishops remarkable iron pagoda, exhibited in 1876 in Paris and Philadelphia then re-erected in the Gardens in 1880. Sadly its condition deteriorated and it had to be demolished in 1949. Other features of note include a large equipped children's play area, extensive planted areas, over 190 trees representing 45 domestic and foreign species including impressive avenues of trees planted in

Right: Clearance of the old chocolate factory in preparation for the Chapelfield shopping centre.
Below: Chapelfield shopping centre view to House of Fraser.

Clockwise from top: Chapelfield Gardens winter panorama, Chapelfield Gardens Spring flower explosion, Chapelfield Gardens 1930s, Chapelfield Gardens aerial view.

the C18th, the 1880 bandstand, Mark Goldsworthy's 1999 sculpture of Will Kemp and the regular, but all too brief, spring show of crocuses and daffodils. The Gardens are within the ownership of the City Council but the Chapelfield Society exists to protect and promote this important historic and natural asset.

Chapelfield North

Historic terrace. Although only modest in length, this northern perimeter for Chapelfield Gardens provides an interesting run of buildings spanning a range of periods. At the eastern end, the imposing former Howes Garage is now 'The Garage', a performing arts academy. Adjacent St Mary's Croft, dating from 1881, is very unusual and contains Zulu pavilions on the top floor. Next door, built ten years later, is an imposing, red brick Jacobean revival style villa with mock Tudor chimneys. Further west there is a very attractive range of Regency buildings

(all listed) including the imposing, balconied Chapelfield House. In the centre of the frontages is the plain, Norwich Spiritualist Church dating from the late 1930s.

Chapelfield Road Methodist Chapel

In July 1881 the United Free Methodist Church was opened just beyond the medieval City walls, on Chapel Field Road. It was designed by the architect Edward Boardman and was established to provide a place of worship for a congregation of up to 1,000 people from the expanding southern and western suburbs of Norwich. Now known as Chapelfield Road Methodist Church, the outside is little changed from that of the late C19th. The inside has, however, undergone a certain amount of change in response to the modern needs of the congregation. Most recently, the upper rooms of the building, including the kitchen, have been refurbished and a lift has been installed.

Chapel in The Field

Lost City Centre chapel. Opened in 1858 at the junction of Chapelfield East and Chantry Road and designed by John James, this Independent Congregational non conformist chapel was a substantial building with a capacity of 900 and was built in a neo Romanesque style and flanked by two imposing spiral turrets. Damaged by wartime bombing it was eventually demolished in 1972 and the site has been a surface car park ever since. During the demolition of the main church a fascinating discovery was made. In the foundation stone of the church, the demolition team found a sealed jar containing number of documents written by Rev. J Alexander, the first minister of the church. These documents detailed meetings discussing the foundation of the church, the purchase of the land and fundraising for the building of the church; fascinating details that would otherwise have been lost.

Chaplin, Charlie

Silent Film Actor. In 1904 a young, would be actor, Charlie Chaplin appeared at the Theatre Royal in 'A Lancashire Lad'.

Chapman, Mary

Mental health pioneer. Born in 1647, Mary Chapman's later destiny was shaped when she married the Rev Samuel Chapman in 1682. Both of them had experienced mental illness in their respective families and had been appalled that society of the time regarded people with psychiatric disorders as either subjects of ridicule (the village idiot) or criminals that should be incarcerated indefinitely. The idea of curing mental illness was not contemplated in the England of the late C17th. Consequently, when he died, Samuel Chapmen left money for a hospital for 'poor lunatics' and it fell to Mary to deliver his last wish. She built a hospital on the site of the Committee House, destroyed in the Great Blowe the year after her birth. The Bethel opened in 1713 as the first provincial mental hospital in the country. The hospital provided medical supervision for patients and the emphasis of the institution was on cure rather than containment. The institution continued for a long time and by the late C19th was achieving a 60 per cent recovery rate. Mary lived at the hospital until her death in 1724. She is commemorated by Mary Chapman Court, a student housing development in Duke Street.

Charing Cross

Historic thoroughfare. This was originally known as Tonsoria, Medieval Latin, translated to mean "workshop where woollen cloth is shorn", and thus by the 1300s as Sherhill Cross / Shereshill / Sherergate / Shereman Rowe / Shearing Cross. Many of the City's shearers lived in and around this street, hence its name. There was also a stone cross situated here, although this was removed around 1730. However, it became known as Charing Cross in the C18th – the fashion was to copy the names of London streets and areas and perversely the London derivation probably had nothing to do with shearing – it is thought that Charing Cross derives from the French Chere Reine and refers to a devotional, processional route around crosses commemorating Queen Eleanor of Castile. The principal building on the street is the medieval Strangers Hall.

Charles II

King. In 1671 Charles II, with his queen, Catherine of Braganza, and the Dukes of York, Monmouth and Buckingham, visited the City and stayed at the recently completed Duke of Norfolk's Palace in St Andrew's Street. While here, he attended a service in the cathedral, visited Bishop Reynolds in his Palace, 'shewed himself to his citizens' from the balcony of the Guildhall and dined with the Corporation at the expense of £900. After dinner he knighted Sir Thomas Browne in St Andrew's Hall.

Cherry Lane Methodist Chapel

Lost Walled City chapel. The Cherry Lane Chapel was purpose built by the Methodist Society after their building on Timberhill, known as 'The Foundry', had become too small for their congregation. Work began on the chapel in early 1769 and it was completed by the October. A typically Georgian brick house was built in front of the chapel. At its centre was an arched passageway leading through to the chapel set at the back of the plot of land. The passageway had large heavy doors designed to shield the congregation from rioters who might try to disrupt the Methodist services. John Wesley himself gave the opening service at the chapel but within just two years he complained that the building was again too small for its congregation. Although a further small chapel was set up in Pottergate in 1806, it was not until 1810 that the Methodists began developing a new site on Calvert Street. At this time a small group of Congregationalists from the Old Meeting House on Colegate took over the Cherry Lane Chapel but by 1818 the Strict and Particular Baptists had bought the whole complex and renamed it 'Providence Chapel'. The buildings were all demolished in 1936.

Christchurch, Christchurch Road

Suburban, Victorian church. Designed by J.H. Brown and J.B. Pearce, this substantial church, sporting

Christchurch, just off Christchurch Road.

a distinctive octagonal pinnacle was built between 1873 and 1879. The west porch and south aisle were added by in 1912. The original bell was donated by the Cathedral but a new bell was cast in 1936.

Christchurch, Magdalen Road

Suburban, Victorian church. Designed by John Brown and built in the Gothic revival style in 1840-42, this is his first Norwich church. It contains a sumptuous Arts & Crafts style war memorial window.

Christchurch, Saxon Borough

Lost Walled City church. Christ Church or the Holy Trinity church was founded during the Saxon period and is mentioned in the Domesday Book of 1086. It was demolished c 1096 to make way for Norwich cathedral, at which point the cathedral took over the dedication of the Holy Trinity. The location of Christ Church was indicated in 1987 when several Christian burials were uncovered to the west of the north transept of the cathedral. The bodies are thought to

have originally been buried in the graveyard of Christ Church and therefore the church may have stood near the site of the north transept of the cathedral church. It has also been suggested that the north transept may incorporate some stone work from the Saxon building of Christ Church. The dedication suggests a church of some importance and there is evidence that it also had a monastic function – in 1076 Abbot Ingulphus of Croyland refers to 14 monks from Christchurch Norwich. Since the decree to include a Benedictine Priory within the Norman Cathedral was not issued until Christmas Day 1100, this early post Conquest reference suggests an existing priory at the Saxon Christchurch.

Christ Scientist Church

Former Christian Science church. In 1879 The Church of Christ, Scientist was founded in America by Mary Baker Eddy who believed in the healing powers of the Christian faith. Despite the great history of religious diversity in Norwich it was not until 1911 that a

Christian Scientist group was founded in the City. By 1921 the group had twenty-nine members and in 1934 the First Church of Christ Scientist was built at No. 3 Recorder Road. Mrs Herbert Jewson led the plan to build the church and she commissioned her brother-in-law Herbert G. Ibberson of Hunstanton to design it. Ibberson designed a brick church which shows the influence of the Arts and Crafts movement of the late C19th/early C20th as well as medieval Gothic architecture. The building has tall thin lancet windows and the interior has a barrel vaulted chancel and arched arcades to the aisles. In 1991 the building became a Grade II listed building along with its boundary walls, gates and gate piers. A reduction in the Christian Scientist congregation meant that in 1997 the church became the Greek Orthodox Church of The Mother of God, The Megalohari of Tinos. The Christian Science congregation now meets in the Christian Science Reading Room, a brick building next door to the church.

Reconstruction of the lost Christchurch from the south, Mousehold in the background.

Church of Christ Scientist, Recorder Road.

Churches, Medieval

The largest urban collection of medieval churches in Northern Europe. The old adage says that Norwich had a church for every week of the year and a pub for every day. By 1450, the City already had almost 60 churches within the City Walls, some surviving from the pre conquest period or just after. From the mid 1400s for almost a century, there was an explosion in rebuilding this significant resource. Much of the impetus came from the wealthy merchant class who had benefited from the City's emerging role as a European centre for the textile industry. Whether from a motivation to 'stake their claim' in the afterlife or merely to provide physical expressions of their wealth and power, the great families invested a fortune in sustaining a large proportion of the City's churches. The legacy that survives today is a testament to that investment. This activity supported a major class of artisans and artists including masons, plasterers, carpenters, plumbers and glaziers but less obviously perhaps, painters (muralists), leadbeaters (roofers), sculptors, brass workers (monumental brasses), and gold or silver smiths.

Although the Reformation, dereliction and the 2nd World War all took their toll on the Medieval churches, 32 still survive within the walls and more than a dozen more within the built up area giving Norwich the largest number of surviving pre Reformation churches of any city in Northern Europe. Each surviving church within the built up area and indeed the rural hinterland has a separate entry within the guide. There are also references for each of the 'lost' churches.

Churchman House

C18th merchant house. Begun in the early 1700s by Worstead weaver Thomas Churchman, at a time when Norwich was 'the chief seat of the chief manufacture in the realm' Churchman House set out to be a bold expression of commercial success in England's most successful industry of the period. Chuchman's son (also Thomas) took over his father's project and

Churchman House in the snow.

developed what had started as a modest town house, into the sumptuous mansion which survives today. The front rooms are in the fashionable mid C18th Rococo style and include astonishingly rich plaster decorations and paintings in the reception room, a fine paneled living room, a bedroom with a bed alcove and a sumptuous entrance hall. Churchman junior went on to become an alderman and mayor in 1761. When he took the congratulations of Norwich's citizens to George III on the occasion of his marriage he was knighted.

After Churchman's death, the house passed to the Reverend William Clayton

Reconstruction of the pre Reformation Norwich skyline dotted with church towers.

Churches

Surviving Structures

Church	Location	Status
All Saints, Great Melton	Rural Fringe	Church
All Saints, Hethel	Rural Fringe	Church
All Saints, Horsford	Rural fringe	Church
All Saints, Intwood	Rural Fringe	Church
All Saints, Keswick	Rural Fringe	Church
All Saints, Postwick	Rural Fringe	Church
All Saints, Rackheath	Rural fringe	Redundant
All Saints, Westlegate	Walled City	Day Centre
Holy Cross, Stoke Holy Cross	Rural Fringe	Church
St Andrew, Colney	Urban Fringe	Church
St Andrew, Eaton	Urban Fringe	Church
St Andrew, Kirby Bedon	Rural Fringe	Church
St Andrew, St Andrew's Street	Walled City	Church
St Andrew, Trowse	Rural Fringe	Church
St Augustine, St Augustines Street	Walled City	Redundant
St Clement Colegate	Walled City	Counselling Centre
St Edmund, Caistor	Rural Fringe	Church
St Edmund, Fishergate	Walled City	Advice Centre
St Edmund, Old Costessey	Rural Fringe	Church
St Edmund, Taverham	Rural Fringe	Church
St Etheldreda, Conesford	Walled City	Sculptor's Studio
St George's Colegate	Walled City	Church
St George's Tombland	Walled City	Church
St Gervase & St Protase, Little Plunstead	Rural Fringe	Church
St Giles, St Giles Street	Walled City	Church
St Gregory, St Gregory's Alley	Walled City	Arts Venue
St Helen, Bishopgate	Walled City	Church
St James Cowgate	Walled City	Puppet Theatre
St John de Sepulchre	Walled City	Vacant
St John Maddermarket	Walled City	Museum Church
St John the Baptist & All Saints, Old Lakenham	Built Up Area	Church
St John Timberhill	Walled City	Church
St Julian, St Julian's Alley	Walled City	Church & Shrine
St Laurence, St Benedict's Street	Walled City	Redundant
St Margaret, Drayton	Rural Fringe	Church
St Margaret, Old Catton	Urban Fringe	Church
St Margaret de Westwick	Walled City	Gallery
St Martin at Oak	Walled City	Vacant
St Martin at Palace	Walled City	Probation Centre
St Mary, Arminghall	Rural Fringe	Church
St Mary & All Saints, Little Melton	Rural Fringe	Church
St Mary & St Margaret, Sprowston	Urban Fringe	Church
St Mary & St Walstan, Bawburgh	Rural Fringe	Church
St Mary, Coslany	Walled City	Publisher's Office
St Mary, Earlham	Urban Fringe	Church
St Mary, East Carleton	Rural Fringe	Church
St Mary, Great Plumstead	Rural Fringe	Church
St Mary, Hellesdon	Urban Fringe	Church
St Mary Magdalen, Mulbarton	Rural Fringe	Church
St Mary, Swardeston	Rural Fringe	Church
St Mary the Less	Walled City	Dutch Study Centre
St Michael Coslany	Walled City	Vacant
St Michael at Plea	Walled City	Book Shop/café
St Peter, Cringleford	Rural Fringe	Church
St Peter, Crostwick	Rural Fringe	Church
St Peter Hungate	Walled City	Medieval Art Centre
St Peter, Ketteringham	Rural Fringe	Church
St Peter Mancroft	Walled City	Church

St Peter Parmentergate	Walled City	Martial Arts Centre
St Peter, Spixworth	Rural Fringe	Church
St Peter, Swainsthorpe	Rural Fringe	Church
St Remigius, Dunston	Rural Fringe	Church
St Remigius, Hethersett	Rural Fringe	Church
St Saviour, Magdalen Street	Walled City	Social Centre
St Simon & St Jude	Walled City	Dance School
St Stephen, Theatre Street	Walled City	Church
St Swithin, St Benedict's Street	Walled City	Arts Centre

Ruins

Church	Location	Status
St Andrew, Thorpe St Andrew	Urban Fringe	Ruin adj. to existing church
St Andrew, Whitlingham	Rural Fringe	Ruin isolated
St Bartholomew, Ber Street	Walled City	Ruin in street
St Bartholomew, Heigham	Built Up Area	Ruin in park
St Benedict, St Benedict's Street	Walled City	Tower only, housing site
St Mary, Great Melton	Rural Fringe	Ruin adj. to existing church
St Mary, Kirby Bedon	Rural Fringe	Ruin adj. to existing church
St Michael, Bowthorpe	Urban Fringe	Ruin isolated
St Peter, East Carleton	Rural Fringe	Ruin adj. to existing church
St Peter Southgate	Walled City	Ruin in park
St Wandregesilius, Bixley	Rural Fringe	Ruin burnt out isolated

Entirely lost churches

Church	Location	Status
All Saints, Fyebriggate	Walled City	Lost, poss remnants on site
Christchurch, Saxon Borough	Walled City	Lost, poss remnants Bisp Chap
St Andrew, Beeston	Rural Fringe	Lost, no remnants
St Botolph, Anglia Square	Walled City	Lost, no remnants
St Catherine, Surrey Street	Walled City	Lost, poss remnants in wall
St Christopher, Princes Street	Walled City	Lost, no remnants
St Clement Conesford	Walled City	Lost, no remnants
St Crowche, St Andrew's Street	Walled City	Lost, remnants on site
St Cuthbert, Upper King Street	Walled City	Lost, site excavated
St Edmund, Markshall	Rural Fringe	Lost, no remnants
St Edward, Conesford	Walled City	Lost, no remnants
St Ethelbert, Cathedral Close	Walled City	Lost, no remnants
St Helen, Bishopgate	Walled City	Lost but wall survives
St James, Carrow	Built Up Area	Lost, no remnants
St John the Baptist, Colegate	Walled City	Lost, no remnants
St John the Evangelist, Rose Lane	Walled City	Lost, no remnants
St Margaret in Combusto	Walled City	Lost, site excavated
St Margaret Newbridge	Walled City	Lost, no remnants
St Martin in the Bailey	Walled City	Lost, no remnants
St Mary in the Marsh	Walled City	Lost, remnants on site
St Mary, Swainsthorpe	Rural Fringe	Lost, no remnants
St Mary Unbrent	Walled City	Lost, poss residual material
St Matthew, Bishopgate	Walled City	Lost, no remnants
St Michael Conesford	Walled City	Lost, no remnants
St Michael at Thorn	Walled City	Lost, no remnants
St Michael Tombland	Walled City	Lost, no remnants
St Nicholas, Bracondale	Built Up Area	Lost, no remnants
St Olave King Street	Walled City	Lost, no remnants
St Olave Pitt Street	Walled City	Lost, no remnants
St Paul	Walled City	Lost, no remnants
St Vedast, Rose Lane	Walled City	Lost, no remnants
Unknown, Anglia TV	Walled City	Lost, site excavated
Unknown, Farmers Avenue	Walled City	Lost, site excavated

who built a grand ballroom (now the Walpole Room) and staircase in 1830. In 1875 the Norwich High School for Girls was founded in the house, where it remained until 1877 when the house reverted to private, domestic use. The Council bought it in 1919 and used it as offices for their public health functions until it was converted to the Norwich Register Office by the City Architect's Department (Vic Nierop Reading) in 1988. The building now offers two marriage rooms for the residents of Norwich, Broadland and parts of South Norfolk as well as registration services for births, deaths and marriages.

Cinema City

The City's Arts Cinema.
Cinema City was established as a local branch of the National Film Theatre in 1978 and opened by Joseph Losey. The 230 seat cinema and connected facilities were created within the former Stuart and Suckling Halls. Although hugely popular among niche cinema goers it struggled to be successful financially and

after much local heart searching it was eventually converted, with Heritage Lottery Fund support, into a three screen multiplex to be run by the international 'Picturehouse' chain – ironic since the City's most famous cinema of the past had borne the same name. Reopening in 2008 the new Cinema City has been a tour de force, even more successful than its predecessor and looking destined to carry Norwich's legacy of innovative cinema into the new millennium. It incorporates an attractive bar and restaurant. www.picturehouses.co.uk/cinema/cinema_city

Cinema Palace

Former cinema. Design by Morgan and Buckingham and built on the western side of Magdalen Street, just north of its Edward Street junction, this was the first purpose built cinema in Norwich (as opposed to a conversion). This ornate building seated 850 and was equipped with the only example of a 'silver screen' in Norwich. It adapted to the 'talkies' in 1930 and, avoiding destruction in the War, relaunched itself as the

A 1912 advertisement for Norwich Cinemas.

Mayfair, with a new tiled frontage in 1946. Ironically it was the first of the Norwich cinemas to close as part of the overall decline and shut its doors in 1956. It was redeveloped for the Norwich Bowl bowling alley which, after a relatively short life, eventually was converted to TV studios by Anglia TV and then became the home of EPIC, the training facility for media students.

From left: Cinema City's exterior courtyard, and Cinema City's bar – the former Suckling House.

Cinemas

Former and current cinema provision. In its heyday, Norwich boasted nearly two dozen cinemas but following a rash of closures in the 1950s/60s this had reduced to just three venues by the 1990s with seven screens between them. Separate entries in the guide provide information about the 'lost' cinemas. A major 'cinema need appraisal' undertaken during the 1990s, and praised by the then Planning Minister for its innovation, indicated enormous unmet potential for development in Norwich, due to the City's large catchment and high level of students. As a result, new cinemas were approved and the City now supports the eight screen Vue within the Castle Mall shopping centre (www.myvue.com), the three screen Cinema City in St Andrews (www.picturehouses. co.uk/cinema/cinema_city), the 14 screen Odeon at the Riverside complex, which has recently added a 3D IMAX facility, (www.odeon.co.uk) and the three screen Hollywood at Anglia Square (www.hollywoodcinemas.net).

Circus

'Big Top' tradition. Norwich has had a long standing record of associations with the circus over the centuries. From an early period, circus acts appeared at inns on the Market Place and ranged from a pair of elephants in 1685 at the Angel, through the first rhinoceros to be exhibited in mainland Europe to the largest Rattlesnake in England. Beyond exotic livestock, 'freak show' exhibits included the 8 foot 4 inch Irish Giant O'Brien in 1797, Daniel Lambert in 1808, at almost 53 stone, the heaviest man to have lived in England and Monsieur du Pain who visited the Angel Inn on the Walk and amazed audiences by dipping his feet in boiling lead. The Tombland Fair had also been a popular venue for circus type acts and when it moved to the Old Cattle Market, this provided a long running venue. P.T. Barham's Great American Show visited the City in 1844 and the famous dwarf, General Tom Thumb, appeared at the Theatre Royal. Seven years later, Robert Hales, the Norfolk Giant, returned to Norwich from an extended tour with Barnham & Bailey's Circus where he was billed as 'The Tallest Man in the World'. He told his life story for a penny a time to people on Gentlemans Walk. Another home grown talent was William Darby, who astutely adopted the sobriquet Pablo Fanque to become the country's first black circus proprietor. In 1899 Barnum and Bailey's Famous Show was back again in four trains which generated a procession three quarters of a mile in length. In two days, the shows attracted 42,000 people. Four years later Buffalo Bill's famous Wild West Show performed in the City. In the mid C20th, other circuses visited Norwich, including the famous Billy Smart and were accommodated at Eaton Park. More recently, the Chinese State Circus and the Moscow State Circus have appeared at Earlham Park and the Royal Norfolk Showground. The tradition has also been embraced by the Norfolk and Norwich Festival hosting the NoFit State Circus in the recent past.

City College

College of Further & Higher Education. With 16,000 enrolments annually and over 1,000 staff, City College is one of the largest further & higher educational establishments in the UK. While it had its roots in the late C19th, the present campus on Ipswich Road has been operating since 1953, although the designs were prepared in 1938 by City Architect L.G. Hannaford and work was halted during the War. Today the College has earned National Skills Academy status in the areas of Financial Service, Manufacturing, Hospitality, Retail and Creative & Cultural Industries. Other Schools include Health, Social Care & Early Education, Creative Arts, Hotel School, School of Technology and the School of Lifelong Learning. Recently proposals have been unveiled for a major redevelopment of the entire campus.

City and County Gaols

Lost prisons. Over the centuries there have been various places of incarceration within the City prior to the development of the current Norwich Prison. The Castle was used increasingly as a prison from the C13th onwards with the addition of shire houses and gaolers accommodation adjacent to the keep. Sir John Soane had produced a prison building within the keep by 1794 and a new prison building outside. This was short lived and by 1826 Wilkins had demolished Soane's buildings and developed a wholly new prison covering all of the top of the mound. This was modified subsequently until Boardman converted the whole ensemble into a museum which opened in 1894. Over the Castle's history, prisoners ranged from the mundane, through the infamous (James Blomefield Rush) to the veritably exotic such as Welsh rebels and French prisoners of war in 1797 From the development of the Guildhall in the early C15th, the earlier undercroft was pressed into service as a 'free prison' and cells were provided under the rest of the building which were still used up until the 1980s when the courts finally moved to St Martins.

The Norwich Gaol was established on the site of the later Norfolk & Norwich Subscription Library as a spillover facility from the Guildhall and although elaborate plans were prepared for a new gaol there by architect William Cubitt in 1822, these never materialised. The Bridewell was also established as a prison for beggars and vagrants from the C16th. In 1827 a purpose built goal to hold 120 prisoners was developed on the site of the current Catholic Cathedral at a cost of £30,000 to a design by Philip Barnes. This survived until 1878 when the current Norwich prison was developed.

From top: Wilkins' extensive prison built around the Norman Keep, Cubitt's proposals for a new gaol.

City Gates and Walls

Lost defended entries.
From the pre Conquest, Anglo Scandinavian period, Norwich had defences of sorts, beginning with a ditch and bank and developing to more substantial structures. The City Walls, as a piece, were instigated by a Murage Tax, granted by Edward I and they were developed between 1297 and 1334 although Gates in one form or another preceded this grand defensive work by some time. There is, for instance, a reasonable chance that a defensive gate existed half way up Fybriggate (Magdalen Street) prior to the Conquest and that this probably incorporated the now lost All Saints Church. There also would have been a gate on Botolph Street. To the south there is also evidence of a defended enclosure during this period and probable Gates on Ber Street and King Street.

Before the formation of the substantial, late C13th/early

Reconstruction of the Walled City from the south in the early C14th.

C14th defences there is some evidence of defences, and some gates at least, on the same alignment. In all, when the major circuit of defences were instigated in 1297, there were 12 Gates and 2.5 miles of walls. A wealthy merchant, Richard Spynke, supplemented the income from the Murage Tax to augment the grand construction. They were substantially completed by 1334. The Gates included, from the south and in clockwise direction, Conesford, Berstrete, Brazen Doors, St Stephens/Needham, St Giles, St Benedicts, Heigham, St Martins, St Augustines, Magdalen, Pockthorpe/Barre and Bishop Gate. Boom Towers were constructed to defend the River. In all there were 12 Gates and it is interesting to ponder why this might be. After all, there are streets which had been historically significant for some time (Pottergate) which stopped dead at the Wall so it wasn't a lack of orbital routes that restricted the number of Gates. Also it may be more than just a coincidence that a City with a church for every week of the year, a substantial Cathedral, a growing clutch of priories and other monastic foundations might be very comfortable with having a gate for each of the 12 apostles or, indeed, the same number of gates as the Holy City of Jerusalem. The Walls themselves were nearly 7m (20 ft high) and 1m (3 ft) thick. They absorbed 37,000 tonnes of masonry, enough to build 80 parish churches. This elaborate construction made Norwich the largest walled city in country and one of the largest in Europe. Today all the Gates have gone, demolished in the C18th to improve traffic circulation, but substantial sections of Wall remain.

City Hall

"The foremost English public building of between the wars."
Nikolaus Pevsner

This represents the definitive English inter war city hall. It boasts the longest balcony in England and the clock bell (Great George) is the largest, with the deepest tone in East Anglia. In response to prolonged pleas that former municipal premises were cramped and 'rat infested' the Ministry of Health finally agreed to loan sanction for the construction of a new city hall, that would be a 'national monument', in the early 1930s. The decision turned out to be inspired at the time of the Great Depression, when the project created hundreds of jobs for local people. The building was opened by the King in 1938 to the acclaim of the largest gathering of citizens in the City's history. The masterplan of C. H. James and S.Rowland-Pierce for the new civic centre, including the Market, and a detailed design for City Hall were the successful winners of a competition attracting 143 entries. As well as its imposing exterior architectural form, the building included striking art deco interiors, typified by the Council Chamber, as well as stunning artistic detailing such as the heraldic lions and rear

Clockwise from below: City Hall exterior, City Hall Council Chamber, official programme for City Hall opening, 1938.

City Hall's bronze doors celebrating local heroes and trades.

sculptures by Alfred Hardiman and the bronze front doors illustrating the City's history, by James Woodward. The 'ensemble' was also augmented by specially designed furniture and furnishings. Despite taunts by Lord Haw Haw that the new City Hall would be short lived, it was rumored that Hitler admired its architectural style as a potential seat of regional government. The building is Listed and forms one of the Norwich 12 group of iconic historic structures. Public areas are accessible during normal working hours and tours of less accessible parts are organised on special occasions such as Heritage Open Days.

City of Norwich Aviation Museum

Local aviation museum. Founded in 1977, initially on the supplementary runway at Norwich Airport, the museum started life with an Avro Anson, a Westland Whirland helicopter, a Sea Vixen and a French Dassault Mystere IV. In 1983 the collection acquired the iconic Avro Vulcan V-Bomber and two years later the Museum moved to its present site on the northern fringe of the Airport with access from Horsham St Faiths. The collection now has over a dozen aircraft including a Meteor, a Lockheed Shooting Star, an English Electric Lightning, two Hawker Hunters and a Jaguar as well as some civil

aircraft. In 2010 it acquired a Nimrod. The aircraft collection is supplemented by several buildings full of models, photographs and aviation memorabilia. The Museum is closed Mondays in summer and Mondays and Tuesdays in winter. www.cnam.co.uk

City of Norwich Plan 1945

First comprehensive regeneration plan for Norwich. The 1945 City of Norwich Plan was prepared by the two architects who had designed, then overseen construction of, City Hall in the late 1930s – C.H. James and S. Rowland Pierce. The very comprehensive proposals included new housing and employment development, roads, education and utility services and formed the cornerstone for post War reconstruction. Most prominent and dramatic were the redevelopment proposals for the City Centre where the architects proposed sweeping away historic structures to provide modern boulevards. Much of this impulsion for change was driven by a perceived need to accommodate traffic and if the plans had

Unrealised proposal for an elevated viaduct in the City of Norwich Plan 1945.

City of Norwich Aviation Museum – left to right from top: Avro Vulcan bomber, English Electric Lightning in Saudi livery, Dassault Mystere IVA, BAe Nimrod, Westland Whirlwind HAR 10, SEPECAT Jaguar GR 1, Gloster Meteor F8, Lockheed T-33A Shooting Star, Hawker Hunter.

City of Norwich School

Local secondary school. Founded in 1910 by a merger of the King Edward VI Middle School, the Duke Street Higher Grade School for Boys and the Presbyterian School, the 'CNS' was designed by C.J. Brown for the Norwich Education Committee as the principal secondary school in the City. It became the City's grammar school subsequently and then a comprehensive, changing its name to the Eaton CNS. Over the last two decades there have been significant infill developments all around the original school core. The School supports around 1,000 pupils.

City Road

Ancient route. Probably part of the Roman Pye Street running north from Colchester to Venta Icenorum, and continuing, via the site of later Norwich, to the Roman camp at West Runton. There is no surviving evidence of very early occupation of this road but, at the northern end, three of the earliest, but much modified, examples of C19th workers back-to-back housing survive at Nos. 27-33. Further south, and just east of City Road, Jubilee Terrace provides an excellent example of early C19th terraces. Close by, on

Very early terrace houses at Jubilee Terrace, off City Road.

reached fruition, much of Norwich today would look like St Stephens. To be fair though, proposals to take the Inner Ring Road around the outside of the City Walls would have been less damaging than the ill conceived elevated road

cutting across the historic street – the Magdalen Street Flyover. The dramatic nature of the City Centre proposals aside though, the Plan did provide a most effective tool, overall, for post War reconstruction.

City Station.

Civic Regalia on display in the Castle.

the west side of City Road, is St Marks church, built by John Brown in 1843-4 in the Perpendicular revival style.

City Station
Lost railway station.
Opened in 1882 on roughly the site of what is currently the Barn Road roundabout, City Station was originally designed to serve the Lynn & Fakenham Railway and was subsequently the terminus for the Midland and Great Northern Railway in Norwich. It was severely damaged by the 1942 air raids and never really recovered, closing to passengers in 1959 and for goods until 1969.

Civic Portraits
Largest civic portrait collection. This represents largest collection of civic portraits in the country, totalling 127 late 16th to 19th century paintings of Norwich Mayors, Sheriffs and other dignitaries. Artists include Gainsborough, Hoppner, Lawrence, Heins and Bardwell and Beechey (portrait of Nelson). The main collection is held in St Andrew's and Blackfriars Halls with other elements of the collection in City Hall,

the Castle and Strangers Hall. The Heritage Economic & Regeneration Trust (HEART) is currently working with the School of Computer Modelling at the UEA to provide virtual reality 'talking heads' of some of the collection.

Civic Regalia and Plate
Finest provincial regalia collection. The collection is centred around the civic sword, presented by the St Georges Company in 1705, and a Crystal Mace, presented by Augustine Steward in 1549. Other regalia pieces include maces, staves,

Magdalen Street in the 1950s after the Civic Trust Facelift.

medallions and chains. The Plate includes the Reade Salte, presented by Sir Peter Reade at his death in 1568 and made by Norwich silversmith William Cobbold. Other Cobbold pieces include silver gilt cups of 1561 and 1580 and an Elizabethan silver beaker. The overall collection includes an array of interesting novelties such as a silver model of a Boulton & Paul Overstrand bomber and a contemporary mustard pot by David Thomas (1962).

Civic Trust Scheme 1959
Civic regeneration initiative. In 1957 it was agreed that the Civic Trust and the City Council would collaborate to create a 'model' regeneration scheme for the area between Fye Bridge and Stump Cross – this would be the first scheme of its kind in the country leading to replication of similar 'Facelift' schemes across the UK. As the name suggests, the scheme concentrated on improving the look of properties and removing clutter but did not 'drill down' into more fundamental issues such as traffic or the regeneration of

urban functions. Opened by Duncan Sandys and hailed as successful, the scheme was more of a stay of execution as, less than ten years later, the bulldozers moved in to demolish a large part of the street as part of the Anglia Square and Magdalen Street Flyover developments. 50 years on, the street still remains one of the Council's priorities for regeneration.

Clarence Harbour

Unrealised scheme. This was a C19th proposal to build a new harbour, north of the present football ground, to re-invigorate sea borne trade. However, the arrival of the railways killed the scheme and the only tangible progress towards it was the building of the Clarence Harbour pub in 1837 on Carrow Road to serve the employees of the intended harbour. Despite the failure of the harbour to materialise, the pub survived for 165 years, in 1949 adding the attraction of a boxing gymnasium to its offers, but finally succumbed in 2002 to a redevelopment for housing.

Clarkson, Mabel

Female Lord Mayor. Mabel Clarkson was the first woman to be elected to the City Council (1913) and she became the City's first woman Sheriff in 1928 and second female Lord Mayor in 1931. She was a tireless campaigner for women's rights and a champion for the poor.

Clocks

Clockmaking and timepieces
The first European mechanical clocks appeared in the C13th and the earliest documentary evidence of

Norwich clocks, left to right from top: Royal Arcade, Norwich Union, H Samuel, St George Tombland, St Lawrence, St Michael at Plea.

the work of a clock maker in Norwich is the commission for Roger de Stoke to install an astronomical clock in the Cathedral between 1321 and 1325. This however, replaced an earlier clock dating from 1273, making it one of the earliest in Europe, although neither of these now survive. The oldest surviving clock in the City is thought to be that in St Laurence church. Made by Northumbrian monks (possibly at Hexham) in the C15th, it came to Binham Priory first and was then

acquired by the Rev Augustus Sutton for St Mary at Sporle in 1873, before moving to St Laurence 20 years later.

The Norwich clock making industry was begun by Low Countries and French immigrants in the first half of the C17th. The first recorded Norwich watch maker is John Gascoyne (1634) but Ahasuerus Fromanteel (b. Norwich 1607) is regarded as 'the godfather' of the English clock development, making a major contribution to the development of the pendulum clock, although most of this activity followed his move to London, as a fully qualified clock maker, in 1629. The earliest surviving Norwich clock is a lantern clock, signed by Elias Browne, a goldsmith working from 1633 to 1660. Another early Norwich clock maker was Cornelius Manley who worked in St Peter's Street between the last quarter of the C17th and the first of the C18th. One of his clocks survives in the Bridewell. Between 1680 and 1765 the area just north of the Guildhall was a particularly rich source of clock makers including Jeremiah Hardy, Edward Browne, Robert Gymer and John Harrison. Further noted clock makers continued the tradition into the C19th when the 'Norwich Clock' was developed in the first quarter. The industry was boosted by additional continental immigration in the C19th including the Zipfel dynasty. In 1930 John H. Willis developed the 'Willis World Clock' and more recently Martin Burgess produce the Gurney Clock, now located in Castle Mall, to celebrate the 200th anniversary of the founding of Barclays Bank by the Gurneys in 1775. This is reputedly the most accurate mechanical clock in the Britain. Today many fine examples of public clocks survive in the City.

Clubbing

Evening entertainment. Contrary to the prejudicial view that Norwich is a sleepy backwater, the City has a vibrant club scene, evidenced by the fact that around 30,000 young people

descend on the City Centre, on a Friday or Saturday night, from a very wide area to enjoy the entertainment on offer. The epicentre stretches from the Riverside leisure complex (bars, clubs, multiplex) beside the railway station, up Prince of Wales Road. It used to continue into Tombland but this has become more of an eating rather than clubbing location now. There are other clubs scattered around the City but the list below concentrates on those in this core area. The principal venues include:

- **Riverside** – Project/Project Live: converted from Lava & Ignite and reopened Feb 2011 after £2m refurb. Themed nights including nationwide indie and dance cub night. There is also a regular Comedy Club. Open Mon/Thurs/Fri/Sat.

- **King Street** – Waterfront: converted from a C19th brewery warehouse this venue has a capacity of 900. With three rooms featuring the best in live music, hard house and trance all the way through to heavy metal the Waterfront provides a unique venue. www.water-frontnorwich.com

- **Prince of Wales Road** – Chicago Rock Café: converted Victorian furniture shop. Café by

Prince of Wales Road clubbing area.

day, club by night.
Essence: Open from lunch till the early morning from Mon to Sat. Free entry on Thursday. Music includes RnB, Pop and House. Capacity 540.
Fluke: Opened in 2011. Can enjoy a different dj playing each night. Open Mon/Wed/Thurs/Fri/Sat.
Lola Lo's, formerly Po Na Na's: Converted ground floor of the former Edwardian Royal Hotel with a capacity of 400. Principally club classics and contemporary beats. Open Mon/Wed/Thurs/Fri/Sat. Mercy: a £4m refurbishment of the former ABC Cinema produced the largest venue in the City with a capacity of 2300. Offering impressive visual and sound effects Mercy had three different rooms, six bars, celebrity guests and a wide range of music. It was closed at time of publication for another large refurb to open again in later 2011. Mojos: two floors; street level and club basement. Music includes RnB/Hip Hop. Capacity 460. Open Mon/Wed/Thurs (student nights) Fri/Sat.
Pure: Variety of music which include urban, RnB and dj's special stuff before 12. Capacity 800. Open Thurs/Fri & Sat is dedicated to the ladies!
Qube: 250 people on the ground floor, 2nd/3rd floor for VIP and members only. Weds laid back grooves, Thurs/Fri/Sat/Sun dj's provide a mix of beats and club classics.
Sonic: With a capacity of 300 the venue is in a converted ground floor of a hotel and specialises in House music.
Tao, formerly Optic: Following a £2m refit of a

former club in 2003, Optic offered a stylish venue and diverse range of music from urban to commercial. Refurbished again it reopened in May 2011 offering nightclub, bar and secret garden with an oriental chic design. Dj's in the main nightclub which provides a mix of dancefloor classics and anthems. Live performances in the lounge/bar. Capacity 500. Open Mon/Wed/Thurs/Fri/ Sat.

- **Rose Lane** – MEDiA: includes what claims to be the best VIP lounge in the City, an outdoor terrace and a 300 capacity club this venue offers principally Funky House. The Loft: reopened 2011 after refurb. Principally gay club playing pop, RnB and classics. Kamp tastic is held on the 2nd and last Friday of the month.

- **Queen Street** – Knowhere: four bars spread over three floors. Weekly events and club nights using local dj's and live bands. Capacity: 300.

The other venue worthy of note, but well away from the 'evening economy' zone, is the University of East Anglia's LCR (Lower Common Room). Offering a huge capacity of 1450, the LCR provides an enormously wide choice from live bands to hard trance. Has themed 'student nights'.

Cnut

Scandinavian and English king. Cnut, or Canute as he is more commonly known in England, was the son of Sweyn Forkbeard, who had 'completely ravaged and burned the borough' (Norwich) in 1004. The poem Cnutsdrapa, celebrating the deeds of

Norwich Coat of Arms in various guises.

Cnut, tells us that he very much followed in his father's footsteps and that in 1016 'Gracious giver of mighty gifts you made corslets red in Norwich will you lose your life before your courage fails.' Cnut was king of England between 1016 and 1035, king of Denmark from 1018 and king of Norway and part of Sweden from 1028. The fact that such a powerful figure, and indeed his powerful father 12 years previously, had bothered to come to Norwich in person to ravage it, suggests that the borough was a place of some importance. During the archaeological excavations preceding the recent development of the Anglican Cathedral Hostry, a Cnut Silver Penny was discovered on the site of what would have been the civic heart of the Anglo Scandinavian borough prior to the Norman Conquest and the construction of the Cathedral. The penny was minted in Norwich by a moneyer called Ringulf between 1016 and 1023. It would have paid the wages of a peasant for about one

day. The coin is rare because it shows what is probably a comet behind the king's head, possibly commemorating a comet appearance in 1018.

Coat of Arms

City's official Arms. The coat of arms of the City of Norwich is composed of a three towered, silver castle above a golden lion passant, supported by two sword bearing angels, wings outstretched, all on a field of red. Various ancient and more recent sculptural examples adorn the exteriors and interiors of City buildings.

Cockeys

Former streams, now disappeared. Additional to the main river Wensum, the site of the historic City also supported more minor water courses which have either been culverted or have disappeared. The only evidence for their existence, apart from the survival of their valleys in the urban topography, are a few culvert outlets into the Wensum. Cockeys included

Lord Chief Justice Coke.

Aerial view of Colegate from the 1970s.

the Great Cockey, the Dalymond, the Muspole, the Dalingflete, the Fresflete and a further stream in the vicinity of Willow Lane.

Coke, Sir Edward

Lord Chief Justice. Coke was a Recorder of the City but, more significantly, Lord Chief Justice to James I. He was responsible for prosecuting both Sir Walter Raleigh and Guy Fawkes. He bought what is now Wensum Lodge in 1612 for £850. Coke's family retained it for over a century.

Colegate

Ancient thoroughfare. With a pre Conquest Anglo Scandinavian origin, the street takes its name from the old Danish 'gata' meaning street or way and the personal name 'Coli'. The street, in many respects a microcosm of the history of the City, provides probably the richest heritage thoroughfare, both in architectural and social terms, in the whole of Norwich – three surviving medieval, parish churches, two probably of pre conquest origin; the site of the original Dominican friars' foundation; medieval merchant houses; stunning non conformist chapels – one the most elegant in Europe according

to John Wesley; imposing Georgian houses of mayors and sheriffs; the largest shoe factory in Victorian England and, being Norwich, there were at least half a dozen pubs in the C19th. Add to that associations with three of the City's most notable daughters (Glover, Martineau and Opie) and a dozen or more of its most influential families and the place of this quiet street in the City's history becomes pivotal.

Collections

Art & object collections. Norwich boasts a varied range of spectacular, unusual, unique and just bizarre collections either on public display in museums and galleries or owned by institutions and private individuals. Some of the key examples are included in the adjacent table.

Below: Silver collection in the Anglican Cathedral Treasury, The Castle's teapot collection.

Collections

Archaeology – 2.75 million items spanning 250,000 years predominantly Norfolk based (Castle Museum).

Archives – one of the largest and most complete archive collections in the UK held in the most modern facility in Europe (Norfolk Archive Centre).

Art: Abstract & Constructivist – 400 works by artists who share a fascination with basic geometric shapes and bold primary colours (Sainsbury Centre).

Art: Norwich School of Artists – the most comprehensive collection of the work of the Norwich School of Artists in existence. The collection covers three generations of 50 artists who form the nucleus of the School (Castle Museum).

Art: Rembrandt Etchings – almost 100 etchings by Rembrandt, considered the fourth most important collection in the country after the British Museum, the Ashmolean Museum and the Fitzwilliam Museum (Castle Museum)

Art: Robert & Lisa Sainsbury Collection – ancient and modern art spanning 5000 years from across the globe (Sainsbury Centre for Visual Arts).

Art Nouveau: Anderson Collection – extensive collection ranging from Tiffany and Lalique to unknown designers (Sainsbury Centre for Visual Arts – three yearly cycle).

Anglo Saxon & Viking objects – one of the best collections in the UK including Spong Hill Man, the earliest English three dimensional representation of a human figure (Norwich Castle).

Aviation – City of Norwich Aviation Museum – a range of historic aircraft (Horsham St Faiths).

Bladder Stones – the largest collection in the world (Norfolk & Norwich University Hospital).

Butterflies – a collection of 22,000 butterflies made by Victorian lepidopterist Margaret Fountaine (Castle Museum)

Cats – the Langton Cat Collection, a group of ninety-four miniature cats made from a variety of materials and ranging in date from the C2nd to the C19th.

Civic Portraits – the largest provincial civic portrait collection in the UK (St Andrew's Hall and other locations)

Civic Regalia – the largest civic regalia collection in the UK (Castle Museum).

Costume & Textiles – one of the most significant collections in the UK (Shirehall and in private collections).

Military Subjects – artefacts and documents associated with the Royal Norfolk Regiment, its predecessors and successors (Castle Museum).

Silver – church and cathedral silver including pre Reformation patens and silver hallmarked in Norwich between 1565 and 1702 (Cathedral treasury).

Stained Glass – medieval art and stained glass specifically (Hungate Medieval Art Centre).

Teapots – the largest collection of teapots in the world (Castle Museum).

College of St Mary in the Fields

Lost ecclesiastical college. John le Brun founded a hospital north west of St Stephen's church, on the site of the current Assembly House, in 1248 dedicated to the Virgin Mary. In a short time, the foundation was changed to a College for Secular Canons. The first building also served as a Great Hall within which much of the City's civic business was conducted prior to the building of the Guildhall. This included assemblies relating to issues such as the regulation of the textile industry, negotiations over civic liberties, such as the Charter of 1404, and civic hospitality. The latter included a famous breakfast when the Earl of Surrey presented venison to the City and he, and the Bishop and Abbot of St Benet at Holm, had breakfast at the Chapel-in-the-Fields and 'there was great cheer made between them.' During alterations to the Assembly House in 1901, it became clear that what is now the Music Room contains the core of the medieval Great Hall. Additionally, the Hospital undercroft survives beneath the current Assembly House former kitchens and restaurant.

These renovations also revealed the extent of the other buildings. The collegiate church was longer than St Peter Mancroft, with a 90 ft, five bay nave incorporating a north aisle and a 60 ft, three bay chancel with north and south aisles. Within the church there were six altars, a rood loft and 46 marble grave stones – the floor was paved partly with marble and partly with yellow and green glazed tiles. There was a substantial

Reconstruction of the pre Reformation College of St Mary in the Fields.

tower to the west end of the church. To the south of the church, a leaded and glazed cloister, with a total length of 296 ft, functioned as a promenade and a library and a choir school. At the Dissolution the complex passed into secular use and eventually became absorbed into the Assembly House.

College Road

Suburban road. A late Victorian development linking Unthank and Earlham Roads, College Road takes its name from the Norwich and Ely Diocesan Training College, designed in 1892

by Oliver and Leeson in the Gothic revival style. The college fell victim to the April 1942 Baedeker Raids and was completely burnt out. The road now provides the spine of the 'Golden Triangle', the 'desirable' housing area of the City, occupied by professionals and university staff.

Colman Family

Influential dynasty. Jeremiah Colman was the founder of the mustard empire which was to provide the basis of one of Norwich's most influential families over nearly two centuries.

Left to right from top: Jeremiah James, Carrow Works in its heyday, the oldest surviving building on the Carrow site, interior of the Mustard Mill.

Beginning his business at Bawburgh then producing flour from a mill at Magdalen Gates he began the manufacture of mustard at Stoke Mill in 1814. His success and influence is reflected in the fact that he became Mayor in 1846. Jeremiah passed the business on to his nephew, Jeremiah James, who moved it to Carrow in 1854. He expanded the production facility and was making mustard, starch and laundry blue and milling paper. By 1866 he was making mustard for Queen Victoria and subsequently Napoleon III and Victor Emmanuel II. His products also won awards and medals at exhibitions in England, France and Russia. As significantly though, Colmans were industrial philanthropists in the vein of Robert Owen and Titus Salt. They built good quality workers' housing and provided schools, a library, dispensary, a savings bank, athletics ground, allotments, a works kitchen and the first industrial nurse in the UK. J.J. Colman became Sheriff in 1862 and Mayor in 1867. He went on to be Liberal MP for the City from 1871 to 1895 and was a personal friend of prime minister Gladstone. Locally he supported good causes and was a champion of heritage buildings and structures. His legacy was a great international company which managed to retain its identity until being taken over by Unilever in 1995 although the mustard brand remains a very distinctive international brand in that company's portfolio. Beyond the company the Colmans went on to play an important part in City life providing Norwich with its first female Lord Mayor and endowing galleries and libraries.

Colman's Mustard Shop

Iconic local shop.
Established in 1973 to celebrate the 150th anniversary of Colmans, the Mustard Shop and Museum was originally located in Bridewell Alley to retail a range of speciality mustards and ephemera and to display a range of historic, mustard related items. Its success and popularity led to the shop relocating to the Art Nouveau Royal Arcade in 1999 where it remains. In 2008, following the takeover of the Colman Company by the Anglo Dutch multi national Unilever some years earlier, they decided that running a mustard shop no longer fitted their corporate mission and contemplated closure. The Heritage Economic & Regeneration Trust (HEART) came to the rescue and, with an initial grant from Unilever, took over the management of the Mustard Shop in 2009.

Colney

Suburban village. Situated some 4.8km (3 miles) west of the centre of Norwich, just beyond the City boundary, the name may mean 'hill island', or the gravel river bed of the Yare by which it is located may have given it the Anglo-Saxon name from 'coln' (pebbles) 'ey' (water).

St Andrew's is the round-towered, pre Conquest parish church, restored in the C19th. The attractive rectory dates from 1715 and sports a prefabricated rear extension by Boulton & Paul from 1891. Colney Old Hall is a C17th Flemish gabled building with significant remodelling in the C19th/C20th. The much newer Colney Hall was built in 1834 for Joseph Hall, added to in the C19th then refurbished in the 1960s. There was probably a watermill at Colney in the past as there is a weir here on the River Yare, although there remains no evidence of the mill itself. Although Colney is only a small settlement with a population of 124, due to its location to the west of the U.E.A., it is the home to the Norwich Research Park, incorporating the John Innes Centre and the Institute of Food Research. It is also the location of the Norfolk and Norwich University Hospital, opened in 2004 by the Queen and the BUPA Hospital designed by Lambert, Scott & Innes in 1983. Other points of interest include the Norwich City F.C. training ground and the Woodland Burial Park located in Colney Wood, which opened in 2000.

Coltishall Aerodrome

C20th fighter base.
Coltishall was conceived in 1939 and designed as a bomber base. When it opened in 1940 the role was changed to fighters and it first hosted Spitfires of 66 Squadron followed shortly by the Canadian flown Hurricanes of 242 Squadron. Douglas Bader took command in July and in September was joined by the South African ace Sailor Malan and 66 Squadron. Badar left in October and Stanford-Tuck arrived with 257 Squadron's Hurricanes. At around the same time, the 133 Eagle Squadron also arrived briefly before moving to Duxford. In 1941 Beaufighter night fighters of 255 Squadron arrived to defend Norwich. The following year 255 was replaced by 68 Squadron commanded by Max Aitken and staffed by Czechs. In 1942 George VI visited and made history by being the first reigning monarch to present a squadron badge. Towards the end of the War, four Polish squadrons arrived. After the War the base became a permanent RAF base, flying Mosquitoes, Javelins and Lightnings. In 1963 the Anglo French SEPECAT Jaguar took over and remained until the base was disbanded in 2006.

Part of the Mustard Museum & Shop collection.

Colney Hall.

Polish Spitfires operated from Coltishall in the last year of the War.

Coltishall Memorial Aircraft
See *Spirit of Coltishall*.

Colton, John
Medieval benefactor.
Late one night in the C15th, John Colton was on his way home when he got lost, stumbled into marshy ground and was in danger of drowning. He was saved by the sound of St Giles bells which guided him to St Giles Gate and probably saved his life. When he died he left an acre of land in Earlham Road to the church on condition that a 'curfew bell' continue to be rung every night. The Angelus bell at the church has maintained this tradition since 1497.

Compass Tower
First high-rise flats.
Norwich's first excursion into high rise residential development, this 11 storey tower block was built on the Heartsease Estate by City Architect David Percival in 1963.

Condon, Dick
Theatre manager. Dick Condon is a legend not only in Norwich but in the theatre profession nationally. He took a failed local theatre (Theatre Royal) and made it the most successful provincial theatre in the UK. This legacy has provided a strong platform for subsequent charismatic Theatre Royal managers to create a sustainable model of outstanding cultural entrepreneurship, not just in terms of the breadth and depth of the cultural programme but also in terms of the robustness of the business model.

Concert venues

Norwich Theatre Royal – 1300 seats. No. 1 Touring Theatre – Major presenting house for musicals, drama, opera and ballet, concerts.

UEA Student Union – 1550 standing. Rock and Pop.

St Andrews Hall – circa 900 seats. Hall for hire/occasional concerts.

The Waterfront – 700 standing (200 seats). Rock/pop/club.

Maddermarket Theatre – 310 seats. Amateur theatre/occasional one night concerts.

Norwich Playhouse – 300 seats. Small-scale professional performing arts.

John Innes Centre at Norwich Research Park – 300 seats. Occasional Chamber Music.

Norwich Arts Centre – 250 standing/120 seats. Rock and pop/folk/comedy/theatre.

UEA Drama Studio – 200 seats. Student and professional, theatre and dance.

UEA Music School – 150 seats. Student and professional music.

Assembly House – rooms seat 50-300.

King of Hearts – 80 seats. Small recitals.

Concert Venues
Locations for music performances. Norwich offers venues for everything from full orchestral performances and pop concerts to small scale concerts. The venues range, at one extreme, from Norwich City Football Club, where the likes of George Michael and Elton John have performed recently, to more intimate pubs and clubs. Key locations are described in the adjacent table.

Conesford
Historic Ward. On of the original four wards of the City, Conesford took its name from the Danish meaning 'King's Ford'. The ward stretched from the southern boundary of Wymer Ward to the southern extend of the City Walls and the Wensum and included the parishes of St Peter Parmentergate, St Julian, St Etheldreda, St Peter Southgate, St John de Sepulchre, St Michael at Thorn, St John Timberhill and All Saints.

Conesford Gate
Lost City Gate. The Connesford or King Street Gates are referred to between 1175 and 1186, well before construction of the overall defensive scheme for the City began in 1297. They were regarded as important in providing defence from potential attack from the south although there is no record of them ever being assaulted. They had become dilapidated by the C17th and an advertisement in the Norfolk Chronicle dated March 1794 invites tenders for their demolition, which followed shortly after.

Cooke's Hospital
Lost caring institution. Founded in 1692 by Thomas and Robert Cooke on the north side of Rose

Cooke's Hospital.

Conesford Gate reconstruction looking north.

Lane, Cooke's Hospital was a group of alms houses for the poor. These were demolished in 1890 when the site was redeveloped but a new complex was built at the end of Chatham Street and opened in 1892. They survive today as a private housing development and have been renamed Mazly Court after a village in Northern France from whence the ancestor of local estate agent Frank Potter originated.

Copemans

Former grocery business.
In 1789, John Cozens, supported by his brother in law Jonathan Davey (builder of Davey Place) bought the old established Newman's retail and wholesale grocers on the Walk. The provisions stocked at the time included such exotic offerings as casks of sperm oil and whale oil, snuff in bladders and puncheons of molasses. John Copeman joined the business in 1801 and was a full partner in Cozens & Copeman by 1809. When Cozens retired in 1837 Copeman's son became the partner in Copeman & Son. The business prospered but wholesaling became the dominant element to the extent that Copemans sold the retail grocery business at 21 The Walk to Charles Underhill in 1873 while retaining the wholesale premises. By the turn of the century business was doing so well that the company bought adjoining premises in Castle Street and Davey Place which provided more space and improved facilities such as a cold store. Company head, Henry Copeman's role in the City was underlined by the fact that he became Mayor in 1911. At the outbreak of WWI the company was contracted to provide rations for troops and, at one period, were supplying rations and running canteens for 30,000 soldiers. Further success and expansion between the Wars resulted in a further move to substantial new premises providing in excess of 30,000 sq ft in Duke Street in 1939. In WWII the company again provided an important role in rationing and W.O. Copeman was appointed Chairman of the eastern Area Provisions and Groceries Advisory Committee to the Ministry of Food and received the O.B.E. for his work in this area. After the War Copemans looked to best practice in the US and Canada and introduced the collaborative grocers' system used there. They also continued to make an impact at home and in 1948 company chairman William Copeman was Lord Mayor and also chairman of Eastern Counties Newspapers Ltd. In 1960 Copemans established MACE, first locally then nationally, as the first and largest collaborative grocery grouping of its kind in the UK. In 1964 expansion again pressed them to move, this time to Drayton Road. The old premises were demolished and although ambitious plans emerged for them to be redeveloped as a five star hotel, the Dukes Palace, the plans never materialised and the site remained vacant until partly developed for a Premier Travel Inn in the early C21st. After a fire in 1970 the Drayton Road premises were redeveloped and expanded. In 1987 the company was taken over by Booker.

Co-op Bakery

Former Edwardian bakery.
Designed by Edward Boardman & Sons, the Queens Road Bakery was constructed in 1914.

Clockwise from above: Old Corn Exchange, New Corn Exchange in the 1930s,
New Corn Exchange pediment above the main door, salvaged as a Hethersett garden feature.

Corn Exchange

Lost corn exchange. The first Corn Exchange was built on the site of the medieval mansion Benjamin Wrench's Court in 1828 and said by White's Directory to have 'one of the largest rooms in the kingdom' at the time. This was clearly not large enough since it was demolished in 1860 and replaced the following year by a new Corn Exchange, which at 126 ft was 30 ft longer. As well as providing the venue to buy and sell agricultural commodities, the Corn Exchange was pressed into a range of other, perhaps surprising uses. Italian violinist, Niccolò Paganini performed two concerts in the Corn Exchange and composer Franz Liszt also performed there in the C19th. Boxing also proved to be a popular spectator sport there, although illegal in the early days. The Corn Exchange had lost its original use by the early 1960s and was redeveloped

in 1964 for Jarrold's department store extension. Part of the original decorative pediment above the main entrance survives in a garden in Hethersett.

Coslany

Ancient district. Located north of the Wensum and west of the defended Anglo Danish settlement of Northwic, Coslany's name is Danish in origin and may mean 'island with reeds' refecting the fact that originally the river was braided at this point with an island or islands sitting within the river and two bridges crossing along the line of what had been a Roman road.

Costessey, New

Suburban development. Situated approximately 6.4km (4 miles) to the west of Norwich and with a population of 5211 people, New Costessey was developed during the first half of the C20th. After World War I, Costessey Park

was divided up and sold off to families seeking to move from the crowded and insanitary conditions in the Walled City. Temporary wooden houses and railway carriages were used as housing by these families. Gradually between the 1930s and 1950s paths became more formalised streets and the temporary dwellings were converted into permanent brick housing. The majority of the initial permanent development was in the form of bungalows. St Helen's on Gurney Road is New Costessey's modern church.

Costessey, Old

Suburban village. Located 6.4km (4 miles) west of Norwich City Centre and bounded to the north by the River Wensum, Old Costessey has a population of 4611 people. The village dates from a Bronze Age farming community, although the Anglo-Saxons established a settlement here after 600 AD and the name 'Costessey' originates from this time, meaning 'Kost's Island'. In the Domesday Book, Costessey is recorded as having had a mill and a manor with eighty square miles of estate. St Edmund's church located on The Street is the oldest surviving building in Costessey dating from the rebuild of 1390. Within The Street there is a range of attractive C17th and later buildings and the barn at Church Farm dates from 1688. There was a postmill in Costessey known as Costessey Eastwood Mill or Stone Hills postmill, built in 1810, although demolished one hundred years later. The structure had a sixteen-sided wooden roundhouse. Costessey watermill was recorded in the Domesday Book, but there have most likely been a number of different structures over the centuries on this one particular site. The final structure was built in 1858 and was powered by water

and steam. In addition to Hellesdon Mill, it was one of the biggest mills in the county. The mill was finally destroyed by fire in 1924, but evidence of it can still be seen such as the old millrace and marks left from the water wheels. In 1989 the water authorities diverted the river around the old mill site via a new weir.

Perhaps the most interesting aspect of Costessey's long history, is that of the lost Costessey Hall, depicted on the village sign. In 1546, Henry VIII granted Costessey manor to Anne of Cleaves, and this was the predecessor to what was later known as Costessey Hall. Remains of this are still thought to exist in Costessey Park to the north of the River Tud. In 1555, Queen Mary granted Sir Henry Jerningham the manor of Costessey and he began to build his hall on an area of land to the south of the River Tud. This Tudor hall was later to be incorporated into a much

larger structure when in 1827 Sir George William Jerningham the 8th Lord Stafford commissioned the expansion of the original manor into a Gothic-style house with ornate chimneys, turrets and gables. The stables were allegedly designed by Sir John Soane. In 1884, the 10th Lord Stafford was certified a lunatic, so Costessey Hall estate was held by the Lunatic Commission. The 11th Lord Stafford died in 1911 and the contents of Costessey Hall went to auction. The last owner of the manor was the War Office between 1914 and 1918 when it was used for training troops. After World War I the Hall had unfortunately fallen into disrepair and the majority of the building was demolished with the 400 year old stone fire place and oak, linen-fold panelling being recycled in Hethersett Hall and the outstanding stained glass being sold for £17,000 (current value more than £500,000). During World War II, one of the remaining towers was struck by a Blenheim bomber. Today only the belfry tower remains of the Hall on what is Costessey Park Golf Course's 18th fairway and the stable block, by Sir John Soane, also survives.

Cotman House

Artist's home. Built by Samuel Pye on the site of the old White Swan around 1767, this handsome Georgian building may have been designed by Robert Brettingham who had owned the site, brother of the architect of Holkham Hall. In 1823 John Sell Cotman moved here and used it as a 'School for Drawing and Painting

---

Left to right from top: Old Costessey house exhibiting 'Cosseyware' detailing, Old Costessey C17th pub with C19th additions, Costessey Hall in 1933 before demolition, Costessey Lodge by Soane, 1784.

Cotman House, Palace Plain.

Above: Cotman commemorative plaque, John Sell Cotman.

Water-Colours' as well as for his home. He remained there only for 11 years when he moved to London to be drawing master at King's College School. The house was threatened by slum clearance in 1937 but was saved and eventually restored by the Norwich Amenities Preservation Society. It is currently a dental surgery.

Cotman, John Sell

Iconic artist. Born in 1782 in the parish of St Mary Coslany, Cotman started work with a London firm of engravers at the age of 16. He joined Dr. Thomas Monro's circle a year later where he studied by copying drawings in his host's collection. When only 18, he had his first exhibition at the Royal Academy and he was awarded the large silver palette by the Society of Arts. He was elected as an honorary member of the Society of United Friars of Norwich in 1801. After two tours of Wales and three of Yorkshire, he exhibited again at the Royal Academy in 1806 then returned to Norwich, setting up a drawing school in St Andrews Street. The following year he exhibited

for the first time with the Norwich Society of Artists. By 1811 he had become president of the Norwich Society of Artists and had exhibited twice with the Associated Painters in Water Colours in London. In 1817 and 1818 he made two tours of Normandy and published some volumes of architectural etchings as well as Architectural Antiquities of Norfolk and he contributed to two volumes of Excursions in the County of Norfolk. After a further Normandy tour he returned to Norwich and opened a drawing school at his home in St Martin at Palace Plain. He again became president of the Norwich Society of

Artists before moving back to London in 1834 and lived in Bloomsbury where he remained until his death in 1842. Some of Cotman's best Norwich paintings include Norwich Market Place 1809 (Tate Britain), St Luke's Chapel 1808 and the Castle 1808 and his best etchings include the Erpingham Gate 1817, the Bishop's Palace gate 1814 and St Ethelbert's Gate 1817. The Norwich Castle Museum holds examples of the artist's work as do the British Museum, V&A and Tate Britain. Cotman's sons, John Joseph and Miles Edmund also went on to become successful artists.

County Hall.

County Hall

County Council headquarters. Norfolk County Council had functioned previously from offices in Thorpe Road but by the 1960s they were operating far beyond capacity and a decision was made to build a new County Hall and Police Headquarters. The C18th Bracondale Lodge, designed by William Wilkins Snr, and its 31 acre Sir Humphrey Repton designed estate were purchased and leveled to provide the new offices and substantial surface car parking. A remnant of the original estate survives in a garden building erected in 1813 from the remains of the Cathedral Infirmary which had been demolished in 1804. The new County Hall was designed in 1966 by Slater & Uren and was the last major work by Reginald Uren who had been responsible for 1933 Hornsey Town Hall, the first major building in the UK to be constructed in the Modernist style. The building was opened by the Queen in May 1968.

Courts

Historic & current seats of justice. In 1985 Magistrates Court functions moved from the Guildhall to the newly completed, warehouse inspired courts in Bishopgate by the City Architect's Department (architect Robert Goodyear). A year later the new Crown and County Courts, by the Government's Property Services Agency, opened next door. A particularly interesting feature is a Norman stone house, discovered during pre development excavations and preserved in a sub basement below the scheme.

Courts and Yards

Residential groupings. Although many cities exhibited narrowly packed concentrations of high density housing tenements around pedestrian alleys, the Norwich Courts and Yards were unique because of their number, density and the enormous scale of appalling living conditions which they epitomised. Beginning life as substantial merchant houses with large gardens in the late medieval period, the yards and courts first developed as the merchant classes fled the Walled City for country estates and demand increased for inner city housing from the labouring classes. This began with the arrival of large numbers of Dutch, Flemish and Walloon refugees in the C16th and was inflated by an influx of the rural poor and later, tides of immigrants from France, Eastern Europe and Italy. The great houses were subdivided into tenements, with often whole families occupying just one room while the gardens were developed into shoddy, sub standard residential courts often accommodating up to 40 families. The names of these yards were often exotic, usually deriving from the pubs which occupied them – Arabian Horse, Bear & Staff, Boatswain's Call, Cardinals Cap, Cock & Pie, Eight Ringers, Elephant & Castle, Greenland Fishery,

Clockwise: Old Post Office Court, Wrights Court, lost yard off King Street.

Hampshire Hog, Labour in Vain, Queen of Hungary, World's End and Zipfels to name just a few. Inhabitants usually had to share a single privy and pump for drinking and washing. By the turn of the century, the walled City was home to over 80,000 people (the 2009 population is 8,000) predominantly living in 750 courts and yards. The Public Health Commissioners described these as 'the vilest slums in England' and the Council reacted in 1898 by passing the 'Courts & Yards' by-law which resulted in repaving, clean water supplies, new sanitary facilities and in severe cases, clearance. Within 13 years a third of the yards had been dealt with. Following the First World War there was a greater impetus to address the problem and the Council defaulted to wholesale clearance. While effective in sanitary terms, the implication was that dozens of stunning although dilapidated medieval gems were swept away. In 1927 the Council proposed to demolish Elm Hill as one of the worst remaining slums areas and it was only saved

by a concerted campaign by the Norwich Society and the casting vote of the Lord Mayor. The Norwich Heritage Projects Group has recently concluded a research and oral history project on the courts and yards and more information can be found on www.norwich-yards.co.uk

Cowgate

Ancient thoroughfare. A street of Anglo-Scandinavian origin originally indicating a track leading to the meadows where cows were grazed at Cowholme. The section running from Fybriggate (Magdalen Street) eastwards is most probably an intra mural route running south of the bank and ditch defences of Northwic. The north/south section was a post Conquest creation, as evidenced by excavations in 1992, possibly linking to a very early river crossing on the site of the later Whitefriars Bridge. In the pre Conquest period, Cowgate, within the defensive enclosure, probably stopped at a point roughly equivalent to the modern St Paul's tavern, where Peacock Street formed a north/south,

intra mural route running down to the river. Although once rich in impressive architectural structures, including the Carmelite Friary, Norman's Hospital, St Paul's Church, All Saints Church and the medieval City House of Sir John Fastolf (later the Ship at 104 Cowgate) as well as attractive domestic buildings (see Ninham's C19th view south), the street now has very little to commend it apart from the beleaguered church of St James.

Cow Hill

Historic thoroughfare. Known previously as St Giles Hill and taking its current name from the Red Cow pub, which stood just south of Holkham House until being demolished as being 'inconvenient in structure' and very old in 1908 and replaced by the parish hall. Holkham House itself was built by Matthew Brettingham for his brother Robert as a scaled down version of Holkham Hall which the former was responsible for designing. Aside from the attractive palladian exterior, Holkham House has a fine moulded

Cowgate, a C19th view by David Hodgson.

Gabled houses on Cow Hill.

Cow Tower.

plaster ceiling. At the top of the Hill, opposite the church of St Giles, is a range of gabled C17th houses with an earlier undercroft. One is used by the Christadelphins, and incorporates a baptismal device. It is possibly the oldest building used by this religious group in the world. Finally, it is worthy of note that the Hill was cobbled until 1925 when it was asphalted over.

Cow Tower

Ancient tower. Known originally as the Dungeon or Hospital Tower, the Cow Tower is one of the earliest artillery block houses in England, one of the earliest brick structures of this type and also one of the earliest example of gun loops in the country. Built originally as a toll house and prison on the river by the Prior of the Cathedral then passed to the Great Hospital, some time after 1249, it was given to the City authorities 'for ever' in 1378. The Chamberlain's Rolls of 1398/9 provide an astonishingly detailed account of how the building was reconstructed and refaced in brick as a free

standing artillery tower. Standing in the north east 'elbow' of the Wensum it provided, with the fortified Bishop Bridge, the only defensive construction on the east of the City. It incorporated artillery emplacements on the roof and two floors of loops for hand guns. The Tower saw action during Kett's Rebellion of 1549 and bombardment from the rebels at Mousehold caused damaged to the battlements and traces of burning remain today. It is alleged that the structure was used to imprison witches in the C16th before they were led away to be burned at Lollards Pit. There is very little evidence of any subsequent use. The Tower is a Scheduled Ancient Monument and maintained in good condition.

Cozens Road

See *Railway Cottages*.

Creative Writing Course

Seedbed for writers. The University of East Anglia's Creative Writing course was established by Angus Wilson and Malcolm Bradbury in

The Crescent in winter.

1970. Its MA is regarded as the most prestigious in the country. Alumni include Sir Ian McEwan, Kazuo Ishiguro, Anne Enright, Andrew Cowan, Deirdre Madden, Glenn Patterson, Kathryn Hughes, Suzannah Dunn, Erica Wagner, Phil Whitaker, Tracy Chevalier, Susan Elderkin, Jane Harris, Martyn Bedford, Trezza Azzopardi, Stephen Foster, Mick Jackson, John Boyne, Richard Beard, Toby Litt, Louise Doughty, Andrew Miller, Susan Fletcher, Owen Sheers, Panos Karnesis, Esther Morgan, Kathryn Simmonds, Adam Foulds, Diana Evans, Matt Fullerty, Tash Aw, Naomi Alderman, Clare Allen, Donna Daley-Clarke, Clare Wigfall, Mark McNay, James Scudamore, Joe Dunthorne, James Sorel-Cameron and Mohammed Hanif. Lecturers on the course have included Angela Carter, Rose Tremain, Andrew Motion, W.G. Sebald, Michèle Roberts and Patricia Duncker.

Crescent, The

Early town houses. These are some of the earliest examples of development outside the City Walls. Built between 1821 and 1827 by John Bunn and located to the west of Chapelfield Road, these 18, two storey houses grouped around a tri angular green have survived intact.

Cringleford

Suburban parish. Located approximately 4.8km (3 miles) south-west of the centre of Norwich on the main London road, Cringleford had a population of 2076 in the 2001 census, although this figure is predicted to have risen due to the development of the

Left to right: Cringleford Bridge, Cringleford Hall, Cringleford Mill.

area in the intervening period. Originally named 'Kringelforda' meaning 'circle ford' or 'the ford by the round hill' Cringleford has a long history indicated by the discovery of Neolithic flints in the area and Bronze Age burial mounts in Cantley Wood. Keswick Road is probably of Roman origin, and led from Caistor St Edmund; Roman pottery and coins have also been found in Cringleford. During the Tudor period, a stone bridge was constructed after 1519 when the original wooden structure was swept away during flooding. This bridge still exists today and is protected as a Scheduled Ancient Monument. Its image forms part of the village sign. Just after this time Cringleford was nearly completely destroyed by fire, but was subsequently rebuilt. Other notable buildings in the village include the 'Ford End' house, originally 'The George' pub, which had stood in Cringleford since the reign of Charles II and had a Dutch gable added to its structure in 1700. St Peter's church is probably of late Saxon or early Norman origin, although the tower dates from the C14th. An interesting stained glass collection exists from the 1898 restoration of the church. Cringleford Hall has

a C16th core but this is outwardly invisible due to late Georgian and Victorian rendering and extensions. There is a record of a watermill standing in Cringleford as early as the time of Edward the Confessor in 1042, although the final structure was destroyed by fire in 1916. However, the mill house of 1795 and sluice gates remain. There was also a postmill in the village, which was marked on a 1797 map, although this had been demolished by 1795 due to storm damage. The character of Cringleford has changed considerably throughout the C20th, with post- World War I housing along Intwood Road, Oakfields Road, Keswick Road and Colney Lane, and the 1930s saw the development of the Tudor Mill estate. The village continued to expand in the 1950s and 1960s. Today, the village is seeing yet further development in the form of the Round House Park, named after the surviving 1805 structure, which in 2007 was projected to double the population of the village.

Crome, John

Founder of the Norwich School of Artists. Known generally as 'Old Crome' to distinguish him from his

painter son John Bernay Crome, he was born in 1768 the son of a publican. Poorly educated he became an errand boy for Dr Edward Rigby at the age of 12 and went on to become apprentice to a sign painter. This nurtured his talent and eventually Thomas Harvey became his patron, allowing him to copy some of his collection including the works of Dutch artists like Hobbema and van Ruisdael. He became a drawing master to the Gurneys at Earlham Hall and also began to sell his own work. With Robert Ladbrookehe founded the Norwich Society of Artists in 1803 and became its president – this became the Norwich school of Artists. He made excursions to the Lake District, Wales and Hampshire and one trip to the continent but most of his subjects were local. He died in 1821 and is buried in St Georges Colegate. His best Norwich pictures include several river scenes, including New Mills, and Mousehold. The majority of his works are held at the Castle Museum or Tate Britain. After his death it was said that, with Turner and Constable, he was one of the three major English landscape painters of the C19th.

Cromwell, Oliver

Lord Protector. In 1643 Oliver Cromwell was in the City when news arrived of a possible Royalist insurrection at Lowestoft. With his five troopers and 800 Norwich volunteers, he left 'between 5 and 6 O'clock in the morning' to engage the insurrectionists but they surrendered without a blow'. He returned in 1653 to visit the Guildhall and inspect the reinforcement of the Castle's defences.

Crooks Place

Victorian development just outside the City Walls. Located south of Chapelfield Road, off St Stephen's Road, Crook's Place was primarily composed of C19th terraced housing and was one of the first areas to be developed beyond the City Walls. A tiny remnant of what the area would have looked like survives in St Stephens Square where a handful of very early C19th terraced houses remain. Crook's Place Towermill, otherwise known as the New City Mill, was built in 1826 but was demolished in 1890.

Civil War re-enactment.

Crook's Place School is now known as Bignold School. The area suffered extensive damage during bombing in World War II and after some decades as a derelict bomb site, was redeveloped for twin block extensions to the Norfolk and Norwich Hospital in the 1960s. These in turn were demolished when the hospital moved out of the City in 2002 to the new University Hospital site and have now been redeveloped as Fellowes Plain, a major residential scheme which recalls a number of the more notable former hospital staff in its street names.

Cross-Grove, Henry

Media innovator. Henry Cross-Grove became editor of the Norwich Gazette in 1707, which was set up in opposition to the Norwich Post, and he held that position for 36 years. He is credited with inventing the 'Letters to the Editor' feature.

Crotch, William

Musical Prodigy. William Crotch was born in Green's Lane (north of modern St Crispin's Road) in 1775. His musical prowess attracted public attention at a very early age and he performed for George III at the age of three and a half (Mozart was seven when he performed for the same monarch). By the age of 11 he was studying at Cambridge and had written his first composition by the age of 13. He graduated in music from St John's College Oxford and had been accepted as a professor there by the time he was 22. By 1822 he had become the first principal of the Royal College of Music. He composed many pieces but his best known is the Westminster Chimes which precede the striking of Big Ben.

Left to right: Memorial plaque to John Crome, St Georges Colegate. Back of New Mills, perhaps Crome's most famous picture.

Reconstruction of Cuningham's Prospect of the City.

Crown Bank

See *Hardwick House*.

Crown Brewery

See *Youngs, Crawshay & Youngs*.

Crystal House

Victorian industrial building. Inspired by the Great Exhibition of 1851, Holmes & Sons engineers developed this stunning cast iron and glass building in 1863 literally as a show case for their steam engines. Panks took the business over in 1902 and Kellers succeeded in 1983 and remained passionate about maintaining and exhibiting this excellent legacy to Victorian engineering enterprise. The building is now a designer furniture shop.

Cucking Stool

Medieval torture device. Located on Fye Bridge, the Cucking or Ducking Stool, was a device for punishing women who were accused of being a 'scold, harlot or strumpet'. Victims were paraded through the streets in a tumbrel, past jeering crowds, and at 1pm, were dumped three times in the cold and polluted waters of the Wensum. The last woman to suffer this fate was Margaret Grove in 1587.

Cuningham, William

Innovative cartographer. In 1559, Cuningham produced The Cosmographical Glasse which contained a panoramic prospect of the City of Norwich from the west as it was 'this present 1558'. This is believed to be the earliest surviving printed map of any English town. The Cosmographical Glasse also introduced triangulation into England for the first time, adapted from a work (Libellus de Locorum describendorum ratione by Gemma Frisius) published in Leuven/Louvain in 1533. The 1559 plan was reproduced again, by his original printer John Day, as part of 'Queen Elizabeth's Progress to Norwich' to commemorate the Queen's visit of 1578.

Curat House

Ancient merchant house. The Curat House has its origins in its early medieval cellars dating possibly from as early as the C13th and rumoured to be part of the Norwich Jewry. The cellars survive and cover an extensive area. The house was built by lawyer John Curat on the site of a much earlier property and an arch in the cellars bears Curat's rebus and the date of 1501. Curat became a successful

merchant reflected in his election as Sheriff in 1529. Significant parts of the medieval fabric survive, in the upper rooms particularly. The property continued as a residential building for much of its history but in the very early C19th the Back Family took it over beginning an association which was to last for over a century. During this period it included elegant dining rooms and a Wine Room, where clientele could enjoy a glass of Norwich Silk, a sherry unique to the Back company. It also boasted the longest bar in Norwich and, in its medieval cellars, the company bottled Guinness and French wines. A major fire in 1962 did severe damage to the property but the restoration was sensitive and included a replacement window provided 'through the generosity of Norwich Museum – from the house of William Coo in St Martins Oak Parish' and dated 1600. Backs revived but finally closed in 1976. The clothing chain Next refurbished the property in the 1980s, using the upstairs rooms as showrooms but when they moved out, access to the oldest parts of the building became restricted to the occasional Heritage Open

Clockwise from top left: Curat House – elaborate fire place, view to courtyard, courtyard entrance, and interior.

Days tour. The Curat House is a Scheduled Ancient Monument.

Curls
Retail Dynasty
In 1860, three Curl brothers moved from west Norfolk into Norwich and acquired the ancient Rampant Horse Inn, opposite modern Marks & Spencers, to establish a retail and warehousing business. By the turn of the century, Henley Curl, Chairman of the company, had become a key figure in the local community and an alderman. The store expanded to become one of the City's principal department stores by the 1930s. The Baedeker Raids of 1942 obliterated the store completely and left a large hole which was pressed into service as a surface car park after the War. In the early 1950s, reconstruction began and a new store with a floor area totalling almost 100,000 sq ft opened in 1956. As with other family department stores in Norwich, Curls was acquired by a national chain, in this case Debenhams, and all that remains to celebrate the provenance of the site is a mosaic of the Rampant Horse in the entrance way.

Cycle Routes
The National Cycle Route No. 1 passes through Norwich, arriving in the south east via the Wherryman's Way at Whitlingham Country Park and leaving in the north west along the Railway Path to Marriotts Way. A range of other orbital and radial cycle routes exist and can be downloaded from the City Council's web site. A diverse range of routes is available on quiet rural roads around the City.

Cycle Speedway
Dirt track cycle racing.
The principal team, the Norwich Stars, are based at Eaton Park which is the location of the main track.

Curl Bros 1905.

D is for...

A merchant trading hall unique in Europe; alchemist and physician to Tsar Michael I; the 'fighting bishop'; the first Delftware pottery to be established in England; one of the most important C14th art works in the country; founder of the country's first non denominational cemetery; one of the largest C16th Dutch communities in England.

Above: Davey Place – C19th view of Dakins, tea merchants and grocers. Right: elevated view looking west.

Dallingflete

Former watercourse. The Dallingflete stream rose just south of modern St Faiths Lane, within the precincts of the now lost Franciscan Friary, crossed St Faiths Lane under a stone bridge and entered the Wensum at Lovell's Staithe, just south of Pulls Ferry. It was filled in in the early C19th but the bridge survived until 1890.

Dalymond

Former watercourse. The next most significant minor water course after the Great Cockey was the Dalymond which entered the City north east of the junction of modern Edward Street and Magpie Road and, flowing broadly southwards, entered the Wensum just west of St Edmund's church, south of Fishergate. The stream was discovered to still be flowing underground through gravel beds during excavations in 1985.

Opposite: Dragon Hall – Crown Post Roof and Dragon Spandrel detail.

Danyel's Alms Houses, Surrey Street

Lost alms house. Danyel's almshouses in Surrey Street in St Stephen's parish, were founded in 1418 by John Danyel, merchant, and by Walter his brother. Nothing survives today.

Darby, William

See *Pablo Fanque.*

Danby Woods

Local nature reserve. Danby Woods is a local nature reserve located on the southern fringe of the built up area just west of Ipswich Road and north of Marston Lane. It is 3.4 ha. Broadleaved, semi-natural woodland developed over an old chalk quarry and although subterranean workings remain they are no longer accessible. The site offers good views over the Yare Valley and the location is noted for bat colonies.

Davey Place

'New street'. Virtually all of the City streets and lanes have origins in the medieval period or earlier but this is one of the few exceptions. In 1813, Alderman Jonathan

Davey announced in Council 'Gentlemen I mean to put a hole in the King's Head' but refused to explain further what he meant. This apparent threat to the life of George III by a known radical and French Revolutionary sympathiser resulted in a guard being placed at Davey's house and a watch being kept on the main London turnpike. A week later, Davey bought the King's Head in the Market Place and proceeded to 'put a hole in the King's head' linking the walk to Castle meadow and creating the first purpose made pedestrian street in the City. The new street became an important centre for grocery related trades including Copeman's, in which Davey was a partner, Dakins, a tea merchants and grocers established in the mid C19th and tea merchants Bonsers who adorned their premises with an enormous golden eagle.

Dean of Norwich

Senior Church Figure. The Dean is the head of the Chapter of Norwich Cathedral. The first Dean was William Castleton, who was appointed in 1538 and was the last Prior of the Benedictine Priory. The current Dean (Graham Smith at the time of publication) is the 38th to hold the position.

Defoe, Daniel

Writer. In 1724 Daniel Defoe visited Norwich and noted that it was 'an ancient, large, rich and populous city... the walls... taking in more ground than the City of London.' And that 'if (a stranger) was to view the City on the Sabbath Day, or any other public occasion, he would wonder where all the people could dwell, the multitude so great.'

Deal Ground

Former industrial site. This is an extensive 20 acre site south of the built up area, between the railway and the River Yare. It takes its name from the soft wood 'deals' which were seasoned on the site after being imported from the Baltic then used by Colmans to make packaging and barrels. The site also contained a label printing works and a kiln and was linked to the main works by a tunnel under the railway. Part of the site is of wildlife and landscape importance and contains Black Poplars and Willows, Pipistrelle bats and owls, kingfishers and Cetti's Warblers. The site is now substantially derelict but work is in progress to regenerate it.

Deanery

See *Prior's Lodging*.

Dee, Arthur

Alchemist. Eldest son of the noted mathematician, astronomer, astrologer, occultist, navigator and consultant to Queen Elizabeth I, Dr John Dee, Arthur became a physician

Dereham Road –
Early C19th town house.

to Michael I of Russia, the founder of the Romanov Dynasty, and resided in Moscow for fourteen years in the early C17th where he wrote his Fasciculus Chemicus, a collection of writings upon alchemy. Returning to England upon the death of his wife in 1637, Dee became physician to King Charles I. Upon his retirement Arthur Dee resided in Norwich where he became a friend of Sir Thomas Browne who commented 'I was very well acquainted with Dr. Arthur Dee, and at one time or another he has given me some account of the whole course of his life'. Arthur Dee died in October of 1651 and is buried in St Georges Tombland. Upon his death Browne was bequeathed the bulk of Arthur Dee's alchemical manuscripts and books.

Dereham Road

Radial Road. Originally Dereham Road was a continuation west of the Roman Holmestrete/Westwick Way. This was where Queen Elizabeth I left the City after her visit in 1578 and to commemorate the event the route was "Hanged with cords made of herbs and flowers, with garlands, coronets, pictures with cloths and a thousand

devices." She was so impressed that she said "I have laid up in my breast such good will as I shall never forget Norwich." Dereham Road remained substantially undeveloped until the C19th with just a few scattered farms along its length. The development of the new municipal cemetery in 1855 and the new Workhouse on Bowthorpe Road in 1859 provided impetus for further urbanisation along this important arterial road. Moving west from the Walled City, on the left, Valentine Street is an example of the early housing to be developed outside the Walled City for the more affluent classes. Further out on the right, the current Potters Church was designed for the Baptists as a Gothic revival expression in 1901 by A.F. Scott and formally opened by M.P. George White in 1904. Most of the development moving west is late Victorian/Edwardian or later but at the junction with Northumberland Street, an impressive early Victorian villa survives. Crossing the Outer Ring Road, the Gate House pub is recorded as having been there in 1868 but was damaged during the Baedeker Blitz of April 1942 and rebuilt after the War. Beyond this, development is exclusively inter War and post War Council housing development at north Earlham and the Larkman.

Despenser, Bishop Henry

The Warrior Bishop. The 'warrior' Bishop of Norwich spent proportionately more of his time fighting enemies of the state and church than tending to the pastoral needs of the community.

His most notable achievement was putting down the Lidster (or Lister/Litester) Rebellion – the Norfolk faction of Watt Tyler's Peasants revolt – in 1381 after the rebels had occupied Norwich, pillaged houses and killed civic officials. The Bishop captured Lidster, sentenced him to being hung, drawn and quartered, heard his last confession, granted him absolution, then walked him to the gallows. Despenser subsequently led a crusade in the Low Countries in favour of Pope Urban VI and against the 'anti Pope' Clement VII. In Norwich, the Bishop built a choir for the church of the Great Hospital and endowed the Despenser Reredos in St Luke's Chapel of the Cathedral.

Despenser Reredos or Retable

Medieval art work. Endowed by the warrior bishop Henry Despenser following his suppression of the Peasants' Revolt in Norfolk, the Reredos represents one of the most important pieces of C14th art in the country. It depicts scenes from the crucification and resurrection. There is a probability that it was painted by Thomas Okel, creator of the Wilton Diptych, now in the National Gallery. This is evidenced by the presence of oak leaves in the background of the Resurrection scene – a possible rebus of his name. The reredos was hidden probably at the time of the Reformation, to avoid destruction. It was rediscovered in 1847 having been used face down as a table top. It was restored and is now located in the Anglican Cathedral's St Luke's Chapel.

Dickens, Charles

Author. Early in January 1849 Dickens, who had been researching his novel David Copperfield in Yarmouth, visited the City. He was interested in the exploits of James Blomefield Rush who had murdered the Recorder of Norwich and Dickens visited Rush's execution site at the Castle, 'which we found fit for a gigantic scoundrel's exit' he noted. On 11th October a decade later Dickens returned to do a public reading at the Theatre Royal. He observed that the Norwich audience was the least responsive he had ever met. He stayed at the Maids Head. In October 1861 he was back again, this time staying at the Royal Hotel in the Market Place to do a further public reading, this time of David Copperfield, which was the first of an extensive provincial tour taking in 18 English cities and not concluding until January the following year.

Diocese of Norwich

Administrative area of the Anglican Church. Tracing its roots back to the Diocese of Dunwich in 630 AD, the Diocese moved to North Elmham then Thetford before finally moving to Norwich in 1094. It forms part of the Province of Canterbury with 577 parishes and 646 churches. Covering an area of 1800 square miles, the modern diocese extends over most of Norfolk and a tiny proportion of Suffolk while its medieval equivalent covered both counties.

Diocesan Training College

See *College Road*.

Dirty Shirt Club

Lost institution. The Rifleman pub in Cross Lane (latterly the Lille Portion Mission and now a residence) was where weavers paid their out workers on Saturday afternoons. The workers would arrive straight from their labours and often, therefore in 'dirty shirts'. Having collected their earnings they would stay, socialise and take some ale. A ceremonial silver pipe was used to initiate new members into the club and it cost them 7 shillings and 6 pence to smoke it. The Rifleman was artist John Crome's local and he too became a member of the Dirty Shirt Club. The club was re-established recently by the church of St George, Colegate.

Despenser Reredos, Norwich Cathedral.

Disability Parking

Parking for people with disabilities. Norwich operates a Blue Badge system to assist people with disabilities to obtain priority parking close to facilities. There are over 50 designated on-street spaces in the centre with additional free parking provision in designated off-street sites.

Dolphin

Historic inn in Heigham. Built in 1541 by former Sheriff Richard Browne the building is most famously known as the retreat of former Bishop Hall. Joseph Hall was appointed 45th Bishop of Norwich by Charles I in 1627 but he subsequently fell out with the Arch Bishop of Canterbury and the Parliamentary Government and was effectively exiled to what became known as Bishop Hall's Palace in Heigham. The Bishop died in 1656 and was buried in the local parish church. By the mid C18th it was owned by Thomas Burton who brewed and sold ale. In the early C19th another brewer, John Morse was in charge and it was known as the Dolphin by this period. The building continued as a pub until the Baedecker Raids of April 1942 when it was gutted. It remained derelict until the late 1960s when the local brewers Steward & Patteson undertook a respectable restoration and it was reopened, perhaps appropriately, by the 69th Bishop of Norwich Lancelot Fleming. The pub did not survive much beyond the Watney/Grand Metropolitan takeover of Norwich breweries and is now used for a house, offices and consulting rooms by a hypnotherapy practice.

Dolphin Bridge

Opened in 1909 by Mayor Ernest Blyth and designed by City Engineer Arthur Collins, the bridge was intended to link the developing residential areas around Heigham and Aylsham Road.

Dominican Friars Friary

See *Blackfriars Friary*.

Doughty's Hospital

Historic caring institution. In 1677, mariner William Doughty petitioned the Court of Mayorality to absolve him of all taxes if he endowed alms houses in the City. The proposal was accepted and in 1667 he produced a will which donated the considerable sum of £6,000 for the purchase of a site for the development of a 'hospital' to accommodate '14 poor aged men and eight poor aged women' as well as other properties which would produce a regular income for their care. When Doughty died in 1688, the trustees of his will purchased the site for the hospital, which survives today in Golden Dog Lane, for the construction of 32 alms houses around a symmetrical quadrangle. By 1728 the institution was prospering and a nurse had been appointed to care for the residents. Subsequent bequests helped to sustain the institution and by the C19th, physical improvements were made including the remodelling of three wings and the development of an upper storey. Further improvements continued in the early C20th with modern extensions and conversions in the latter half of the C20th raising the total number of units to 42. The institution survives today as a successful testament to the aspirations of its founder.

Dowson, John

Philanthropist. Born in 1800, John Withers Dowson went to the Norwich Grammar School then trained for his articles with London solicitors. He returned to Norwich to practice his profession. He tutored poor children whose parents couldn't afford to send them to school and, with James Martineau, started a free school at the Octagon Chapel in Colegate. He was founder and secretary of the Mechanics Institute, a member of the Board of Guardians and a trustee of the Coal & Soup Society. He died in 1879 and is buried in

The former Dolphin public house, formerly Bishop Hall's Palace.

From top: Doughty's Hospital – elevated view looking south east, Doughty's Hospital foundation plaque.

the Rosary Cemetery. He is remembered by Dowson First School and Dowson Road is named after him.

D'Oyley, Rev William

Road safety campaigner. A poor rural clergyman, William D'Oyley made it his life's work to raise money for road safety improvements, initially in the parishes to the south of Norwich. However, in his late 60s he decided to turn his attention to Briggs Lane (Brigg Street) in Norwich, whose narrowness was causing safety problems. He rode a total of 12,000 miles around the parishes to the east, west and south of Norwich raising a total of £400 for the Briggs Lane project. The works were not completed until 35 years after his death however.

Dragon Hall

See page 136.

Drayton

Suburban parish. Located north of the River Wensum around 8km (5 miles) to the north west of Norwich City Centre between Taverham and Hellesdon, Drayton has a population of 5150 people. Drayton appeared in the Domesday Book as 'Draituna', meaning 'place where logs are dragged', as indicated by the village sign which features a dray carrying a ton of logs. Drayton was probably

settled much earlier however, as Roman pottery has been unearthed in the area. Drayton was in the possession of Sir John Fastolf (the probable inspiration for Shakespeare's Falstaff from Henry IV) between 1432 and 1459, and Fastolf built Drayton Lodge in 1432. After his death in 1459, Drayton Lodge was passed on to John Paston although violent disputes with the Duke of Suffolk, who owned Costessey, followed in 1465 resulting in the destruction of Drayton Lodge by the Duke's forces in 1465. The ruins of the Lodge are still visible today off the Drayton High Road in the grounds of the present Drayton Old Lodge, which is around only a century old. St Margaret's on School Road is the parish church dating from the C13th, although the tower collapsed in 1850 resulting in extensive restoration. A stone entrance to an old stairway that had existed prior to the restoration was rescued after the addition of an aisle and the moving of the chancel and this entranceway now stands alone in the north arcade. The C14th but much restored village cross

Drayton Lodge surviving remnants.

Dragon Hall

'A survival unique in Europe of an early C15th Merchant Trading Hall built by an individual merchant for his own enterprise.' Norfolk & Norwich Heritage Trust

Principal features include an 88 foot long timber framed hall capped with a crown post roof structure dating from 1427; surviving undercroft dating from 1330 and incorporated into the later Hall; imposing, elaborately decorated C14th doorway possibly 'recycled' from the once adjacent Austin Friary following the Reformation

The site of Dragon Hall was originally settled in the Saxon period and in the C12th by two substantial houses at right angles to the river and separated by a road. These were the houses of the Abbot of Woburn and Bartholomew de Acre.

A third building was developed in 1330, for the Medday family, which was incorporated into the ground floor of the huge merchant trading hall, probably built by Robert Toppes in 1427. Following Toppes' death the Hall was converted for domestic use and occupied by some of the most notable local families. In the C19th it was converted to shops, a pub and tenements and the subdivisions resulted in the great crown post roof disappearing for many years. The building was 'rediscovered' in the 1980s and, after 20 years of effort from the Norfolk & Norwich Heritage Trust and committed volunteers, Heritage Lottery Funding was finally secured to

Clockwise from top: Dragon Hall – Crown Post Roof, exterior from east, C14th undercroft, and the main door (possibly recycled from the Austin Friary).

convert it into a heritage centre interpreting the Hall and the City's merchant

trading heritage. It is also available to book for private and corporate functions.

survives in the heart of the village and other structures of note include the former C17th Rectory, the Red Lion, dating from 1678, and several C17th former farm houses. Drayton is also home to the major local building company Carters.

Drayton Road

Arterial road. This ancient route leading to the village of Drayton from Magdalen Gate and St Augustine's Gate was virtually undeveloped until well into the C19th. The 1838 Ordnance Survey shows just farmland all the way to Drayton with the only building being the now lost Hellesdon Old Hall on what is now the southern section of Mile Cross Lane. By the 1850s the Ropemakers pub (later James I) had been developed just beyond the City Gates as had some cottages and a substantial area of chalk extraction and lime production. The first major development was Edwards & Holmes shoe factory which opened in 1912. The area was substantially developed between the Wars for Council housing (Mile Cross) and Wensum Park was developed on marginal land south of Drayton Road in 1925.

Drill Hall

Lost military complex. Located at the junction of Queens Road and Chapelfield North, the Drill Hall was developed in the Gothic castle revival style and opened by the Prince of Wales in 1866. Serving originally as the headquarters of various volunteer regiments, it was taken over by the 4th Battalion of the Norfolk Regiment in 1908. By the

Former Drill Hall, Chapelfield Road.

1960s it had become obsolete and was demolished to accommodate the Inner Ring Road and the Chapelfield Roundabout. Its only memorial is a line of flints mapping out the line of the former City Wall and tower, which had been incorporated into the Drill Hall development originally.

Drummond, Thomas

Founder of England's first non denominational cemetery. Born in 1764 and a Unitarian minister for most of his life, Drummond retired to Norwich (where he was

born and had preached earlier) in 1815. Being aware of the difficulties that non denominational burials faced, he put his energies into establishing the country's first non denominational cemetery on a former market garden site just north of Thorpe Road. Following approval of the Bishop and using a family bequest of £3,200, he bought and laid out the site of the Rosary which opened in 1821 – the first burial was his wife who had died two years earlier in childbirth. Drummond died in 1852 and was buried beside his wife.

Duke's Palace

See page 138.

Duke's Palace Bridge

The first bridge, designed by Henry Lock, dated from 1822 and was demolished in 1972 to make way for road widening. It was however saved by the Norwich Society and preserved until it was reused to face the main car park entrance for the Castle Mall shopping scheme in 1992.

Old Duke Street Bridge, later reused as the entrance to Castle Mall's main car park.

Reconstruction of Duke of Norfolk's Palace, view looking north.

Duke's Palace

Now demolished Palace of the Dukes of Norfolk. By the end of the medieval period, Norwich had more houses with in excess of ten hearths than any other provincial city in the kingdom. The greatest of these Great Houses was the Palace of the Dukes of Norfolk (now demolished), in the parish of St John Maddermarket, on the north side of Wymer St. (now St Andrew's Street). The original town house was established in 1547 but redeveloped into a Palace by the 4th Duke in 1602 using stone from the former St Benet's Abbey at Holm. He is said to have claimed that his 'estate was worth little less than the whole realm of Scotland' and that 'when I am in my own tennis court at Norwich, I think myself as great as a king.' Consequently, the Palace was regarded as one of the

greatest in England and according to Thomas Baskerville, cost the Duke '30 thousand pounds to build'. This is reflected in the fact that it had 60 hearths and was large enough to accommodate Charles II on his visit in 1671 along with the Dukes of Monmouth, York and Buckingham and the Queen – her retinue alone consisted of 55 people. Thomas Cory in October of that year noted

'All the house throughout was nobile and richlie furnished'. Macaulay, in a manuscript from 1664 waxes lyrical about the contents referring to 'prints and draughts done by most of the great masters' own hands. Stones and jewels, as onyxes, sardonyxes, jacinths, jaspers, amethysts &c, more and better than any prince in Europe.' The main Palace fronted Wymer St. (St Andrews) and

consisted of an east-west two storey principal Palace with a dormer storey and two north-south wings around a courtyard. A significant four storey development, referred to as the Duke's Palace Offices, was located north of the main Palace running north-south. After an acrimonious dispute with Mayor Thomas Havers the Duke demolished most of the Palace in 1711 although the 'Offices' survived to become a Workhouse. The historian Kirkpatrick made drawings in the previous year which give some clue to its scale and extent. The ornate doorway of 18 Colegate is said to have been recycled from the Palace.

Above: Duke of Norfolk's Palace, former door recycled into a house in Colegate. Left: Reconstruction of Duke of Norfolk's Palace, view of rear from north bank of Wensum.

Dunston

Suburban hamlet. Part of the parish of Stoke Holy Cross, the hamlet is short on population but includes some interesting buildings. St Remigius church is C13th in origin with C15th alterations and a major Victorian refurbishment in 1898 but contains some remarkable internal features. Dunston Manor dates from 1710 while its larger neighbour, Dunston Hall, is a Tudor revival mansion started by J.C. Buckler in 1859 but finished by Edward Boardman in 1878. After a long time in the wilderness as a furniture warehouse and then empty it was refurbished as a luxury hotel and is now run by the DeVere group as one of the two Five Star hotels in the City. At the other end of the scale, End House is a relatively rare, small, early C16th Hall House.

Dutch, Flemish and Walloons

Immigrants from the Low Countries. In 1565 the City authorities invited religious refugees from the Spanish Netherlands to settle in Norwich. Six households were French speaking Walloons, from modern day southern Belgium, and the other twenty four were Dutch or Flemish. Within fourteen years the 'Strangers' accounted for nearly 40 per cent of the City's population. They formed their own communities within the City with the Dutch speakers establishing a church in what is now Blackfriars Hall (where services continued in Dutch until 1921) and the Walloons in St Mary the Less. As well as skills which helped to reinvigorate the Norwich textile industry, the

Dunston Hall.

new citizens brought the City's first printer, the country's first Delftware pottery, gold and silver smithing, flower growing, landscape gardening and canary breeding. The Dutch and Flemish left their mark on the local dialect with words such as dwile, (floorcloth), fye out (clear out), push (a spot or boil) and foisty (mouldy) and also on the form of grammar. The unique Norfolk third person singular of the verb – he go (rather than he goes), she come from Norwich (rather than she comes) – is thought to have been established from Dutch speaking influence during this period. They also left their mark on the Norwich landscape with the naming of the uniquely Norwich named 'plains' deriving from the Dutch plein – St Martin at Palace Plain, St Mary's Plain, St Catherine's Plain.

The earlier Dutch influence prompted a great popularity for the Dutch style of landscape painting (Hobbema, Cuyp, de Koninck and the Ruysdaels) which carried an immense weight in the creation of the Norwich School of Painting.

E is for...

A street with more Tudor buildings than the whole of the City of London; the only English residents to have their portraits painted by Rembrandt; one of the most advanced broadcast production facilities in Europe; the Captain of the English Archers at Agincourt; one of England's foremost diarists who designed a Norwich garden for the Duke of Norfolk.

Eade, Sir Peter

Physician. A pupil of eminent surgeon John Greene Crosse, Eade was a physician at the Norfolk and Norwich Hospital from 1858, for a period of 57 years, a record at the time, and he was also a consultant at the Jenny Lind Hospital. He was made Sheriff in 1880 and Mayor in 1883, again in 1893 and May to November 1895, replacing Lt Col Bignold who died half way through his term. He was knighted in 1885. Beyond medicine, his passion was public open spaces and, with F.W. Harmer. He was principally responsible for the layout of Chapelfield Gardens and the Castle Gardens and for the acquisition of Mousehold Heath. He was also involved in the business life of the City being Vice President of the Norwich Union Life Assurance Society, a director of the London Accident Insurance Association and a trustee of the Norwich Savings Bank. Apart from a large number of medical publications he wrote a history of the Norfolk & Norwich Hospital and the Parish of St Giles. Eade died in 1915 aged 90. He is commemorated in the name of Eade Road.

Earlham

Ancient hamlet. Located remotely to the west of Norwich at a bridging point on the Yare from very early times and deriving its name from the Old English meaning the earl's homestead, the hamlet originates from the pre Conquest period. In the C12th the de Hauville family owned the manor and took the name de Earlham as their family name. St Mary Earlham dates from the C13th but with C15th additions although by this time the Black Death had left the village largely depopulated and by the C16th, the manor and the church were the only elements of the ancient hamlet to have survived.

The manor had passed to the Aleyns in 1401, then the Downes in 1571, followed by Sir Charles Cornwallis in 1594 and then to Sir Henry Hobart in 1608. The Houghtons held the manor by 1642 then it passed to Thomas Waller, onto the Bacons and finally the Franks. The bridge was rebuilt by a new stone structure in 1774 which survived until 1971. The Gurneys were tenants at the Hall between 1786 and 1912 and in 1925 the Norwich Corporation purchased the Hall and the grounds became a public park, before the University of East Anglia (UEA) leased the building from the Council in the 1960s. Earlham is a designated conservation area incorporating the University of East Anglia. Established in 1963, the UEA was designed by Sir Denys Lasdun and for the time, featured a number of innovative characteristics such as the Teaching Wall, raised walkways, a central square around which the main buildings were arranged and the well-known 'Ziggurats' of Norfolk and Suffolk Terrace, all of which still exist today – the structure is listed as an example of modernist architecture. In the grounds of the UEA beside the River Yare, the Sainsbury Centre for Visual Arts was opened in 1978 and designed by Sir Norman Foster. The Sports Park opened in 2001 after a grant from the Sport England Lottery Fund.

Earlham Cemetery

Principal cemetery. In April 1854 the Mayor received an Order from the Home Secretary that all burials in Norwich churches should cease immediately and that churchyard burials must be discontinued from 1st February 1855. This gave

---

Opposite:
View of Elm Hill looking east.
Below: Hamlet of Earlham –
C16th house to rear of church.

Below: Earlham Cemetery Lodge and general view.

Earlham Hall

Earlham Hall

Historic manor house.
In 1580, the first house, forming the core of the present Hall, was constructed on the southern edge of the 'lost' medieval hamlet of Earlham. In the C17th the manor passed from the Hobarts to the Houghton family and Thomas Houghton carried out extensive alterations by widening the C16th building and adding east and west wings. He sold the manor to Thomas Waller whose daughter married Francis Bacon. His son, Waller Bacon, extended the west wing and modernised the fireplaces in 1730. Waller Bacon's son, Edward, undertook further alterations in 1761 including the addition of a kitchen wing, out houses to the east and south and a dining room. He also converted the C16th chapel range into drawing room bedrooms. Between 1786 and 1912 the Hall was occupied by the Gurneys (and their relatives by marriage, the Ripleys) during which time the Hall was the family home of Elizabeth Fry, the noted prison reformer. In 1887 Joseph John Gurney and his wife 'puritanised' the house, ripping out paneling and removing decorations. They also plastered over the brickwork and painted it buff white to keep it as 'plain and drab as possible'. In 1905, Reginald Gurney added a billiard room and dining room in the north west and north east. He also added new windows in the heavily restored north facade and Dutch gables to the south and front of the house. The

Clockwise from top: Earlham Hall – exterior, panelled room, ceiling plasterwork, donkey engine, and fireplace.

Gurneys left in 1912 and the City Council bought the property and estate in 1924 for £20,000. The Parks & Gardens Dept pressed the grounds into service and the wider estate became a municipal golf course in the 1930s. While there was, initially a proposal for the Castle Museum to use the house as a study centre, this idea was opposed by a majority of councilors and, eventually, it was used for a range of alternative activity including, a nursing home, maternity home and school. In 1961 the Council agreed to allow the development of the University of East Anglia on the golf course and the Hall was leased to the University for administrative purposes. The remaining open space, not absorbed by the UEA development, was retained by the Council as Earlham Park. Subsequently the UEA Law School took over the Hall and, at the time of publication (2011), discussions are under way for the University to acquire the site to support the knowledge based industries sector.

Earlham Park viewed from across the Yare.

From left: Earlham Road – Curfew Lodge and Chester Place.

the Council less than a year to provide a cemetery for the 1250 people buried annually. The Council set up a Burials Board but acquisition of land proved difficult and the government granted an extension for the opening of the cemetery to August 1855. The land was finally acquired and purchased with a loan of £5,000 from Gurney's Bank. A request for a further extension of the opening date was granted to 1st January 1856. Estimates for developing the cemetery included a six foot perimeter wall, two mortuary chapels (one for the established church and one for non conformists), a cottage for the residence of a sexton, drainage, walks, gates and levelling the ground, together with the planting of trees and shrubs. A figure of £4,150 was produced for a plot of 60 acres and £6,400 for two square plots of 30 acres each. The original cemetery covered an area of 34 acres, 23 of which were put to immediate use and the remainder given over to agricultural purposes until required. The planting of trees and shrubs, which included spruce and Scotch firs was essential as in the C19th very few people could afford a headstone and the cemetery would have looked very bare without some additional landscape

features. In the first ten months of its opening, 745 burials took place but only four headstones were erected. By 1890 burials had increased to 1640 but only 214 (13 per cent) had headstones. Many of those buried in unmarked graves were soldiers from the Britannia Barracks. At that time mortality rates in the army was considerably higher than those of civilians of similar age, and in 1875 the Burials Board adopted a suggestion from a Mr. J.J. Winter that a piece of ground should be kept expressly for the burial of soldiers. Mr. Winter then proposed that a monument should be raised to the memory of soldiers who died while stationed in Norwich which would record their names. Money was raised by public subscription and a statue, The Spirit of the Army, was unveiled by Lord Waveney in 1878.

In the month the cemetery opened the Watch Committee was asked to provide policemen to be on duty on Sundays and eventually the Board employed a police pensioner at a wage of 2s.0d. a week 'to prevent the grounds being surrounded with children during the performance of funeral services' but this was eventually discontinued.

Earlham Hall
See opposite.

Earlham Park
Public Park. Originally the private parkland of Earlham Hall, Earlham Park is now a public park and is situated to the west of the City adjacent to the University of East Anglia. It is the least formal of Norwich parks, with 88 acres of open maintained grassland sloping down to the River Yare. It is the largest event park in the City and hosts events including a firework spectacular (20,000 people), the Race for Life, orchestral and pop concerts, circuses and funfairs. It is located three miles from the City Centre off the Earlham Road with easy access to the outer ring road.

Earlham Road
Arterial Road. Originally providing the route from St Giles Gate west to the hamlet of Earlham, this route now connects the City Centre to the University of East Anglia, the Norwich Research Park and the Norfolk & Norwich University Hospital. The earliest activity associated with Earlham Road was flint mining. This probably dates from the C16th when extensive tunnels were excavated beneath the road. These features were highlighted in 1988 when the famous No. 28 bus fell through into

a previously unknown gallery. Urban development along the road was earlier than most of the other radials with The Black Horse pub appearing in 1714 and The Grapes (now replaced by retirement housing) slightly later. Some early, extra mural housing was also developed in the first quarter of the C19th at Curfew Lodge, Heigham Grove and Grove Place. Heigham Grove House was also built at this time in the Elizabethan revival style along with various follies in the gardens but an air raid of 1942 obliterated the site. In 1856, the same year that Earlham Cemetery opened, Henry Trevor's house (now the Beeches Hotel) at No. 4 appeared followed by the remarkable Plantation Garden at the rear, while Edward Boardman completed Chester Place ten years later. In the last quarter of the C19th, St Thomas's church, by Ewan Christian, was built to serve the large area of terraced housing being developed either side of Earlham Road as was the Mitre pub, which was rebuilt in the Tudor revival style in 1932. The Cathedral of St John, which was built originally as a church, took shape at the City end of the road at the turn of the century when most of the remaining housing fronting the road began to develop. Following bombing of the Synagogue Street premises in 1942 a new synagogue was opened on Earlham Road after the War, incorporating some salvaged elements of the former building. In 1961 the modernist style Earlham House shopping centre and flats was designed by Chaplin and Burgoine, opposite the cemetery.

East Carleton – Curzon Hall Farm.

Earlham Woods

Nature reserve. Also known as Violet Grove and The Heronry, Earlham Woods are located on the western edge of Earlham Park. This extensive 7.8 ha. site includes a diverse range of habitat types including dense tall marsh, unimproved neutral grassland and a pond. There are also various woodland types mainly neutral and dominated by oak and ash, which have dense shrub layers. Access is from Earlham Park.

Earl Of Surrey's Palace

Now demolished Palace. Surrey House, the Palace of the Earl of Surrey, was in the parish of St Stephen on Newgate (now Surrey St.). This survived until the last century when it was demolished to provide Marble Hall/Surrey House as a corporate headquarters for Norwich Union. The house was built in the early 1540s and Kirkpatrick tells us that the first building on the Duke's Palace site, in St Andrew's, was exactly in the form of Surrey House in Newgate 'and the walls plastered with rough mortar in the same manner.'

The front, or west, range of Surrey House was located directly on the street frontage and included what appears to be a large gable fronted hall range running back through the site to form the south wing of a courtyard. Surviving photographs show mullioned windows in that range. It appears that the east and north ranges were redeveloped in the C18th. References to the Palace in the 1829 General History of Norfolk refer to Tudor frontages and ceiling. Some of the original stained glass survives in Skipper's Surrey House and parts of the Palace were recycled in Norwich Union's Pinebanks Social Club and in a director's house in Lime Tree Road.

East Carleton

Suburban parish. Located 9.7km (6 miles) to the south of Norwich and deriving its name from the Old English or Old Norse meaning 'eastern enclosure of the free peasants', the village is ancient and is mentioned in the Domesday Book. St Mary's East Carleton is a pre Conquest foundation but dates principally from the C13th although it was

From left: Easton – milestone and Easton College.

Eaton Tumuli

Burial mounds. Dating from the Bronze Age (c. 2000 BC), these burial mounds are located to the rear of the 10th green on Eaton Golf Course. The Tumuli are a Scheduled Ancient Monument.

Eaton

Suburban village. Located relatively remotely 3.2km (2 miles) to the south-west of the original Walled City, on the banks of the Yare at its crossing with the London road, its name is Old English and means 'enclosure by the river'. The parish is recorded in the Domesday Book where it is referred to as the King's land held by Edric of Laxfield. It passed to the church then to the Dean & Chapter by 1538. Historic maps show the parish extending north to Earlham and east to the site of the former Norfolk & Norwich Hospital, thus encompassing a large proportion of the later Unthank Road and Newmarket Road developments.

There is documentary reference to a 'mill pool' in 1290 and specific evidence of a mill in the village in 1473, having been rebuilt in 1379. The 'Great Wood' at Eaton is referred to in the C16th. The original village has a dozen listed buildings including the oldest, St Andrew's Eaton church, which dates from the C13th with a C15th tower, and is the only thatched church within the City boundary. Its most notable features are a set of C14th wall paintings discovered during restorations in 1860 by Thomas Jekyll. The church also has an unusual extension on the south side built in 1992-3. Also

largely rebuilt from 1881. In the same churchyard, a flint wall is the only surviving remnant of St Peter's East Carleton which was of a similar age to St Mary but united with St Mary's parish in 1441 and abandoned by 1550. East Carleton Manor was a late Georgian house built for John Steward, Norwich Mayor in 1810, and remained in the family until being sold at auction in 1921 to a Major Best. The architect George Skipper apparently prepared a scheme for its renovation but this was never implemented and the manor was auctioned again in 1923. The new owner remained there until the Second World War and after a short time as a furniture warehouse, it was demolished. In the 1960s the estate was bought by the then Lotus boss Colin Chapman and James Fletcher-Watson designed him a neo Georgian, New England colonial style mansion that was built in 1964. The Shooting Lodge for the Manor is a converted C17th farmhouse. Curzon Hall was the site of the C14th manor of the Curzon family although the surviving timber framed house with crow stepped end gables is C16th. Other buildings of note include the C17th Whitehouse farm on the Wymondham Road, the C16th and C17th North Farmhouse on the Intwood

Road, the early C16th open hall at Walnut Tree Cottage on Rectory Road and the C16th Majority Cottage, remodelled in 1848 as part of the Boileau Estate at Ketteringham Hall.

Easton

Suburban parish. Located 6.4km (4 miles) west of Norwich and just outside the built up area, Easton derives its name from the Old English meaning eastern enclosure and was recorded in the Domesday Book. Its oldest building is St Peter's church which is probably of Anglo Saxon origin but has surviving Norman features including an impressive doorway. Belle Vue is a C16th hall house, re worked in 1728 while West Lodge is very early C17th with a major renovation in 1743. Easton Hall, is now the headquarters for Easton College (School of Agriculture), and was built in the C18th. It has a C18th facade and brick vaulted cellar. The staircase of the same period is identical to that in Mayor Thomas Harvey's House in Colegate, Norwich. Other buildings of note include the C18th post office, the C18th Dog pub, with C17th elements and the C17th Mill farmhouse.

Eastern Counties Newspapers –

See *Archant*.

thatched are the C18th former Lamb pub, now the HSBC Bank, and just opposite in Eaton Street, and flint rubble cottages on the opposite side of the road to the C19th Cellar House pub. Other surviving historic buildings include the Dutch gabled Red Lion, dating from 1643, where Norwich Sheriff Robert Holmes operated a brewery during the mid C17th. 31-33 Church Lane and 30-32 Eaton Street are also both C17th in origin with later additions. Eaton's principal activity, historically, was plant nurseries, located mainly off Bluebell Lane (now Road). Major development activity took place from the late 1950s and infilled the area to the north east of the original village with largely uninspiring suburban residential development accessed off Church Lane and the new cul de sac Greenways. Eaton Street remained the main route to London until the unsightly bypass was built in the 1970s. The character of the village centre remained largely unchanged until a local retail entrepreneur built one of the first major Norwich supermarkets to the rear of the Red Lion in the 1970s. This was taken over subsequently by Waitrose. To the south of the village are large areas of marshland and Eaton Golf Course, established in 1910.

Eaton Common

Nature reserve. This is 6.2 ha local nature reserve located adjacent to the River Yare largely comprising neutral grassland which is marshy in places. In addition there are smaller areas of tall herb and some broad-leaved woodland. A circular walk can be completed in about an hour and the site has a good selection of more common dragonflies. The site can be accessed by walking down Mill Lane, from Church Lane Eaton.

Eaton Old Hall

Historic House. Located well outside the village of Eaton, just north of Unthank Road, the 'Hall' appears on Faden's 1797 map and Walter Rye speculates that it was originally a C18th farm, advertised to be let in 1782, but that the original Manor of Eaton was elsewhere. The 'Hall' was converted to flats in 1971 by City Architect David Percival and the grounds were developed for houses in 1976 by Edward Skipper. The Hall is Grade II Listed.

Eaton Park

Public park. Opened in 1928 by the Prince of Wales, the park had been a major job creation scheme during the inter war period of depression and high unemployment employing over 100 men for three and a half years in creating a bandstand, pavilions, and model boat and lily ponds, 40 tennis courts, cricket squares, bowling greens, other sports' and leisure areas and gardens. The scheme was designed by the Council's Parks Superintendent, Capt A. Sandys-Winsch, who was also responsible for developing the City's other inter war parks (Waterloo Park, Heigham Park, Wensum Park). In the

Clockwise from below: Eaton Old Hall, Eaton Park – view of yacht pond and rotunda, Eaton – Red Lion Public House.

Edmund Wood's House (King of Hearts) – spandrel and interior.

Edwards & Holmes shoe factory interior, 1905.

1960s a pitch and put course was added at the western end and the model railway was opened by the Norwich & District Society of Model Engineers, and extended in 1974. In 1998 a major grant from the Heritage Lottery Fund allowed the park to be substantially regenerated. Today the park provides a major area of formal and informal recreation for the City's western suburbs.

Ebenezer Chapel

See *Surrey Chapel*.

Edmund Wood's House

Medieval merchant House. Numbers 11-15 Fye Bridge St, formed the northern element of a substantial Tudor mansion built by grocer and Mayor Edmund Wood early in the C16th as an extension to the original late C15th street range. Originally the complex extended down to the junction with Fishergate. Edmund's son Robert, also a Mayor, was knighted by Queen Elizabeth I on her visit in 1578. The ground floor window in the rear range is the largest of its type to survive in the City while the ground and first floor Tudor ceilings remained hidden until renovation in the 1980s which converted the semi derelict structures into the King of Heart's arts

centre. Opposite, the Mischief Tavern was originally the house of Mayor and MP Alexander Thurston. A stone chimney piece in the front range bears his merchant mark and the date 1599.

Edward I

King. In 1278 Edward I and queen Eleanor were present for the service of re-consecration conducted by Bishop William de Middleton on advent Sunday following works to repair the Cathedral after 'the Riot' of 1272. They then spent several days in the City. He returned in 1285 to grant a new charter and was present in the City to confer it.

Edward II

King. In 1326 Edward II visited the City, confirmed the City's charters and issued musters to be made all over England and beacons to be lit in preparation for a possible French invasion. He also gave alms to the Blackfriars who gave him 53 apples – one from each friar.

Edward III

King. In 1340 Edward III and Queen Philippa attended 'a great tournament' in the City and they kept court at Bishop Bek's Palace. They visited again in 1342 and 1344.

Edward IV

King. The Paston letters suggest that the King was in the City in the Spring of 1469.

Edward VI Grammar School

See *Norwich School*.

Edward VII

King. In 1909 Edward VII visited the City to confer the title of Lord Mayor for the first time on the City's First Citizen, in St Andrew's Hall. He presented colours to local territorial Battalions in the Drill Hall and was entertained by 11,000 singing school children who covered an entire side of Mousehold. This was the first visit to the City by a reigning English monarch since Charles II visited in 1671.

Edwards & Holmes

Shoe making dynasty. Born in Norwich in 1868, Henry Holmes began modestly as an apprentice shoe maker. In 1891 he went into partnership with W.E. Edwards to initially form a two-man production operation in a four roomed cottage in Pottergate. The business grew and they took on staff, moving to premises in St Georges, Botolph Street and eventually, in 1896, they built a new factory in Esdelle Street. Although Edwards retired in 1899, the company retained the name and by 1912 it employed over 1,000 people in its new factory in Drayton Road and claimed to be the largest exporter of boots and shoes in the City. During the First World War their contributions included providing several thousand pairs of uppers for Cossack boots for the Imperial Russian Army. The company continued to grow after the War and the contribution to City life of its founder was recognised by him being elected Lord Mayor in 1921 and 1932. During this period he bought the Bridewell and gave it to the City as a museum of trades and industries. He was also president of the Norfolk and Norwich Aero Club, an enthusiastic flyer and also Chairman of the Philharmonic Society. Henry's son, Geoffrey took over the company subsequently but they received a severe blow when the Baedeker Blitz of April 1942 resulted in the factory being burnt out. It was rebuilt after the War and Geoffrey's son Peter later took charge. The factory was one of the last to survive the demise of the Norwich shoe industry but closed eventually in the 1990s to be redeveloped for housing.

Pastor Johannes Elison, portrait by Rembrandt.

Elgar, Sir Edward

Composer. In 1908 Sir Edward Elgar conducted the Dream of Gerontius at a Triennial Festival performance in St Andrews Hall.

Elison, Johannes

Dutch community pastor. Johannes (or John) Elison was senior minister of the Dutch congregation in Norwich, which held its services in Dutch in Blackfriars Hall. For more than 300 years the hall was known as the Dutch Church. Elison and his wife Mary had their portraits painted by Rembrandt in 1634 – they are the only English residents to have been portrayed by Rembrandt. Elison is buried beneath Blackfriars Hall as is commemorated by a major memorial tablet.

Elizabeth I

Queen. In 1578 Queen Elizabeth I, with the French Ambassador and the 'whole court' spent a week in the City, staying in the Bishop's Palace. She hunted in Costessey Park, visited the Earl of Surrey at his Palace just east of the Wensum and knighted the mayor, Robert Wood. It is rumoured that, following her visit, 4817 citizens died of the plague and that this was introduced by the Queen's entourage but this is now generally discounted.

Elizabeth II

Queen. One of the first significant visits of Queen Elizabeth II to Norwich was when she opened the newly completed County Hall at Martineau Lane on 24th May 1968. In 1975 the Queen opened the Cathedral Visitor Centre and celebrated the restoration of the roof, in the presence of the Lord Mayor, W.A. Spear and Bishop Wood. She returned two years later, in her Silver Jubilee year to open the new WRVS Housing Scheme. In 1996,

From left: Queen Elizabeth II visiting City Hall in 1996, and opening The Forum in 2002 flanked by The Forum Trust Chair, David McCall and Lord Mayor Derek Wood.

From top: Elm Hill looking west, Elm Hill in the 1930s looking east.

the Queen contributed to the Cathedral's 900th celebrations by attending the Royal Maundy Service there on 4th April. In 2002 she returned and opened the newly refurbished Castle Museum/Shirehall and the recently completed Forum.

Elm Hill

Tudor showpiece street. Probably the best collection of preserved Tudor buildings in Norwich, and also a street which lays claim to containing more Tudor buildings than the City of London, Elm Hill represents a remarkable survivor from the City's past. During the medieval period Elm Hill was the epicentre of society at the time with 16 mayors and sheriffs living there. Mayor Augustine Steward rebuilt the Pastons Place at 22-6 Elm Hill after the Great Fire. Steward's House incorporated the original courtyard entrance to the Pastons Place (Crown Court Yard) which bears his merchant mark. A little further down the street on the opposite side (41-3 Elm Hill) is the remnant of Pettus House where that family lived from 1550 until 1683.

Originally it extended all the way down to the church and Wrights Court would have formed its carriageway entrance. The family, mercers (cloth merchants) like Steward, served the City well and their monuments survive in the nearby church of St Simon and St Jude. Further down and opposite the church, nos. 34-6 were once a single large residence started in 1540. At the opposite end a further significant Tudor mansion can be found at nos. 12-16 but in most cases the best view, reflecting more of the original fabric of all of the even numbered properties can be gained at the rear from Elm Hill Gardens. Finally, just turning the corner at the top of the street, nos. 4-6 Princes St are the surviving mansion of Richard Mann, built around 1600. This is the only merchant house to survive of the 18 noble houses from this period illustrated on James Corbridge's map of 1727.

In the 1920s the Council decided to demolish Elm Hill as part of its slum clearance scheme but a spirited defence by the newly formed Norwich Society resulted in the street being saved by the casting vote of the Lord Mayor.

Ely, Reginald

Master Mason. Born possibly in Coltishall, Ely was a Master Mason and one of the greatest English architects of the C15th. He worked on the rebuilding of the Blackfriars friary from 1440 but his most notable work was King's College Chapel in Cambridge. He is also thought to have worked on Peterhouse and Queens College Old Hall.

From left: Sir Thomas Erpingham – effigy above the Erpingham Gate, Erpingham Gate west façade.

Empire Picture Palace

Former cinema. Located at 79, Oak Street, on the western side and just south of what is now St Crispins Road, the 1,000 seat Empire opened in 1913 and was famed as one of the venues where poor children could gain admission by presenting a jam jar rather than hard cash. It moved to 'talkies' in 1931 but was damaged badly in the infamous Baedeker Blitz of late April 1942 and it was never re-opened.

EPIC

Digital media hub. The East of England Production Innovation Centre (EPIC) was established in Magdalen Street, with support from the East of England Development Agency and Norfolk County Council, as a hub to support Norfolk's creative industries and to act as an educational and training facility in 2006, in a former Bowling alley subsequently converted in 1978 by Feilden and Mawson to Anglia TV Studios. EPIC is one of the most advanced broadcast production facilities in Europe, hiring HD studios and post production facilities to broadcasters and production companies. It has three studios, suitable for drama, light entertainment, sitcom, chat show, discussion and small channel hosting. There is also a real-time Virtual Studio. EPIC is a 'Living Lab' of the European E-Clic programme, internationally recognised as a centre for the development of new formats, services and digital communications technologies.

Erpingham Gate

Historic portal. The Erpingham Gate was built after Agincourt, between 1420 and 1435 and is generally thought to have been donated to the cathedral by Sir Thomas. However, the name 'Erpingham Gate' was not used for the gate until after the mid C18th and the statue of Erpingham kneeling that sits above the entrance arch was not placed there until the late 1600s at the earliest. Nevertheless, the gatehouse is decorated with the coat of arms of Sir Thomas plus those of his first and second wives so it is probable that he did pay for it. Erpingham may have donated the gateway to the cathedral as thanksgiving for his success and survival at Agincourt. Alternatively it may have been given as a way of currying favour with the cathedral where he hoped to be buried or perhaps it was built as his memorial when he died in 1428. The inscription 'Yenk' is carved onto the gate and has been given opposing interpretations by scholars as meaning 'thank', for Erpingham's success at Agincourt, or 'think', asking visitors to The Close to remember Erpingham. Whatever Erpingham's reason for building the gate, it is a splendid structure. There is fine carving of foliage and birds as well as twenty-four niches containing statues of the twelve apostles and twelve female saints, and the kneeling statue of Erpingham looks down on those entering the cathedral precinct. The Gate is a Scheduled Ancient Monument.

Erpingham, Sir Thomas

Soldier, Adventurer, Diplomat, Philanthropist. Born in north Norfolk, Thomas had served John of Gaunt in campaigns spanning Scotland, Spain France and Italy. He was a companion of Henry Bollingbroke (later Henry IV) and fought with the Teutonic Knights at the siege of Vilna in Lithuania, visiting Danzig and Konigsberg as well. He also traveled with Bollingbroke to Jerusalem visiting Prague and the court of King Wenceslas, Vienna, Rhodes, Cyprus, Venice, Padua, Milan, Chambery and Paris in the course of the journey. Erpingham's support for the House of Lancaster saw him rewarded as Chamberlain to Henry IV, Constable of Dover Castle, Warden of the Cinque Ports and Knight of the Garter in 1400. He went on to be Steward of the Royal Household and acting Marshall of England. With the accession of Henry V to the throne, Erpingham became Captain of English archers at Agincourt – 'stout Sir Thomas' as Shakespeare remembered him. The victory took place on St Crispin's Day, coincidentally the patron of shoemakers – a principal trade in the City then and destined to be the largest employer later in its history. The Cathedral's Erpingham Gate commemorates the role of Sir Thomas and his archers in this decisive victory (French casualties being almost 100 times those of the English) and the remarkably well preserved effigy over the gate gives us an idea of both the man and the costume of the time. Sir Thomas lived in St Martin's Plain and played an important part in City life. As well as performing a critical arbitration over the way the City was governed in the 'Composition of 1415', he paid for the great east window of the Austin friary in King Street and for much of the cost of rebuilding the nave of the Blackfriars (St Andrew's Hall). His son subsequently paid for the building of the clerestory in freestone.

Ethelbert Gate

See *St Ethelbert's Gate*.

Evelyn, John

Writer. The famous diarist visited Norwich with 'My Lord Henry Howard' on 17th October 1671 and on the following day visited the celebrated Sir Thomas Browne, noting that his whole house and garden were a paradise and 'cabinet of rarities'. Sir Thomas led him 'to see all the remarkable places of this ancient city, being one of the largest and noblest in England.' Evelyn's visit may have been associated with his earlier work for Lord Howard, to lay out 'My Lord's Garden' for him at Howard's City House in King Street.

Events

Festival activity. There is a significant range of events throughout the year in and around the City, varying from major 'one offs' like the Tour of Britain cycle race to the regular French Markets or Christmas festivities. The 'Festivals' entry provides information about the major regular activities while the Visit Norwich, Visit Norfolk and EDP24 web sites all provide up to date information.

Exchange Street

C19th new street. One of only a tiny handful of new streets built within the City Walls since the medieval

Events, from top: Lord Mayor's Procession, Norwich Half Marathon and Tour of Britain.

period, Exchange Street was cut northwards from the Market place through to St Andrew's Street in the first half of the C19th to accommodate the new Corn Exchange, built in 1828 at its top end. The first Corn Exchange was demolished in 1860 and replaced by a larger and grander version later in the same year. This survived until 1964 when it was replaced by Jarrold's store extension. The street also hosted the City's first post office in 1845 and new Museum further down beyond the Bedford Street junction, on the east side.

Excursions, left to right from top: Binham Priory, Blickling Hall, Ancient House Thetford, Castle Acre Priory, Coast at Happisburgh, Felbrigg Hall, Horsey Mill, Neatishead Radar Museum, Coast at Blakeney, Oxburgh Hall, Coast seal trips.

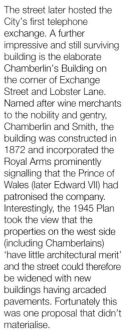

The street later hosted the City's first telephone exchange. A further impressive and still surviving building is the elaborate Chamberlin's Building on the corner of Exchange Street and Lobster Lane. Named after wine merchants to the nobility and gentry, Chamberlin and Smith, the building was constructed in 1872 and incorporated the Royal Arms prominently signalling that the Prince of Wales (later Edward VII) had patronised the company. Interestingly, the 1945 Plan took the view that the properties on the west side (including Chamberlains) 'have little architectural merit' and the street could therefore be widened with new buildings having arcaded pavements. Fortunately this was one proposal that didn't materialise.

Excursions

Visiting further afield beyond the immediate City area and its adjacent villages, there is a vast range of day and half day trips available. Some of the principal attractions include:

From left: Art Show, 2011,
at The Assembly House,
King James Bible Exhibition
at The Hostry.

- **Historic Houses** – Blickling, Felbrigg, Holkham, Oxburgh and Sandringham
- **Gardens** – Bressingham, Fairhaven, Fritton Lake, Mannington, Raveningham and Norfolk Lavender at Heacham
- **Mills** – literally dozens but the principal examples include Berney Arms, Billingford, Bircham, Cley, Dereham, Horsey, Letheringset watermill, Little Cressingham wind and watermill, Stracey Arms and Sutton
- **Transport** – Bressingham Steam Museum, Bure Valley Railway, Charles Burrell steam traction engine museum at Thetford, Muckleborough Collection of military vehicles at Weybourne, North Norfolk Railway at Sheringham and the Wells Walsingham Railway. Further afield still, the East Anglian Transport Museum at Carlton Colville and the Imperial War Museum at Duxford are worth a visit
- **Museums** – A number of rather quirky local museums include the Burston Strike School, Cockley Cley Iceni Village, Cromer Lifeboat Museum, Dickleborough 100th Bomb Group Museum, Fakenham Gas Museum, the Great Yarmouth Time

and Tide and Nelson Museums, Gressenhall Museum of Rural Life, Kings Lynn Museum and Old Gaol House, Neatishead Radar Museum, and the Thetford Ancient House Museum
- **Wildlife experiences** – Banham Zoo, Blakeney Seal Trips, Pensthorpe Wildfowl Reserve, the Sea Life Centres at Gt Yarmouth and Hunstanton and Thrigby Hall
- **Ancient Monuments** – Binham Priory, Burgh Castle, Castle Acre Castle and Priory, Castle Rising Castle, Grimes Graves, North Elmham Chapel, St Benets Abbey, Walsingham and Thetford Priory
- **Heritage Towns** – Diss, Fakenham, Holt, King's Lynn, North Walsham, Swaffham, Thetford, Walsingham and Wymondham
- **Attractions** – Gt Yarmouth Pleasure Beach, Pleasurewood Hills
- **Coast** – there are 93 miles of coast in Norfolk including everything from sandy beaches to wild dunes and bird reserves, with more just over the border in Suffolk. The coast is sprinkled with an eclectic range of towns and villages to suit all tastes.

Exhibitions
Changing displays.
The City hosts a large and diverse feast of exhibitions throughout the year ranging from spectacular art and photography to object and collection based subjects. The principal art venues are the Sainsbury Centre for Visual Arts at UEA, and the Castle, while the Assembly House and The Forum also host very frequent art and other exhibitions. The recently completed Hostry at the Anglican Cathedral and the Narthex at St John's Catholic Cathedral also offer an interesting and changing programme. NUCA offers frequent art exhibitions as do the Norwich Arts Centre, St Gregorys, SADAC and the numerous galleries in the centre. Some recent examples have included:

- King James Bible at The Hostry
- Art Show 2011 at the Assembly House
- H Factor (heritage) at The Forum
- Degree Show and 5 African Women Photographers at NUCA
- John Hedgecoe and Dorothy Bohm at the Sainsbury Centre
- Hubert Duprat at the Castle.

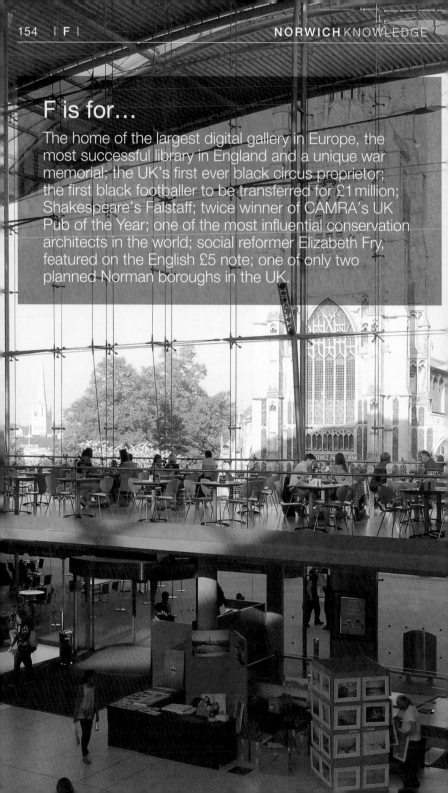

F is for...

The home of the largest digital gallery in Europe, the most successful library in England and a unique war memorial; the UK's first ever black circus proprietor; the first black footballer to be transferred for £1 million; Shakespeare's Falstaff; twice winner of CAMRA's UK Pub of the Year; one of the most influential conservation architects in the world; social reformer Elizabeth Fry, featured on the English £5 note; one of only two planned Norman boroughs in the UK.

Above: Pablo Fanque poster.
Opposite: The Forum.

Justin Fashanu, the UK's
first £1m black footballer.

Sir John Fastolf's house
in Cowgate.

Fanque, Pablo

First black circus proprietor. Pablo Fanque, real name William Darby, was born to a black father and white mother in Ber Street. He went on to shape his career in the circus, first performing equestrian feats in the Norwich Pleasure gardens, then in the north of England. He was to become the UK's first ever black circus proprietor. He is immortalised in the Beatles song Being for the Benefit of Mr Kite.

Farmers Avenue

Formerly historic street. Previously the southern boundary of the Old Cattle Market, Farmers Avenue retains only two vestiges of its formerly long history. The historic former Plough and Horses at the eastern end became La Rouen and in 2008, No. 12. At the other end, what appears to be an integral part of the Bell, is in fact the remnant of the first Norwich Excise Office, opened in 1643 at 1 Farmers Avenue by Adrian Parmenter. This can be seen as a single storey building in John Joseph Cotman's painting of the Castle. It was later

incorporated into the Bell subsequently. The street takes its name from the Jolly Farmers, which sat in the middle of the street façade originally surrounded, remarkably, by five other pubs. That all came to an abrupt halt when the Baedeker Blitz destroyed virtually all of the frontage in 1942. The site remained vacant for a long time and after a brief occupation by Zaks red and white striped hamburger caravan – a local institution in the 1970s/80s – it was redeveloped for Castle Mall.

Fashanu, Justin

Norwich City footballer. The son of a Nigerian barrister, Justin Fashanu went into a Dr Barnardo's home when his parents split up and he was subsequently brought up by foster parents in Norfolk. Joining Norwich City as an apprentice and turning professional in 1978, he quickly moved to the first team, scoring a spectacular 'BBC Goal of the Season' against Liverpool in 1980. Scoring a total of 40 goals between 1979 and 1981 in the first team he made headlines in 1981 as the

first black footballer to be transferred for £1m when he moved to Nottingham Forest.

Fastolf, Sir John

Shakespeare's Clown. It is probable that Sir John Fastolf was the inspiration for Shakespeare's Falstaff, and while most writers recognise this, a significant number assert that Falstaff is a cruel and inaccurate caricature of the factual figure who served his country loyally and with honour. Fastolf had significant land holdings in Norfolk and Suffolk but his principal estate was at Caister on Sea, where he was born in 1378 at the manor. He also had an estate in Southwark which included a town house and the Boar's Head Inn.

He made his living as a soldier in the Hundred Years War where he served with distinction. He was knighted for his service at Agincourt, where he would have served with local hero Sir Thomas Erpingham, as well as in other engagements. He acted as governor of Anjou and Maine from 1423 to

1426 and was made a Knight of the Garter in 1426. While commanding a supply convoy in 1429 he successfully repelled an attack by superior French and Scottish forces using herring barrels and thereby coining the title Battle of the Herrings. While his conduct was questioned following the defeat of the English by Joan of Arc at Patay in the same year, he seems to have ultimately persuaded his superiors that his withdrawal was governed by sound tactical considerations rather than cowardice.

Returning to England in 1432 he obtained a license to demolish the manor house at Caister and build a fortified house, or castle. This remains one of the best preserved brick built mid C15th houses in England. A year later, he took over the manors of Hellesdon and Drayton and built Drayton Lodge (the shell survives) to strategically command the Norwich Road and his manors generally. He returned permanently to England in 1440 and, while based mainly in Caister, he made use of his properties in Norwich which included a mansion on the site of the Samson and Hercules and Fastolf's Place, his City House in Pockthorpe. The latter stood on the west side of Cowgate facing St James' churchyard. Blomefield described a great hall within the building and elaborate stained glass. The house became the Ship Inn in the C19th but fell victim to the Council's slum clearance programme in the 1930s. While staying in Norwich we can speculate that Fastolf enjoyed the company of his great friend John Paston and Fastolf features prominently in the Paston

Fat Cat Brewery.

Letters. When he died in 1459 he left the majority of his properties to the Pastons, triggering two decades of acrimonious litigation and armed conflict to resolve ultimate ownership.

Fat Cat

Unique award winning pub. One of only two pubs in the UK to achieve the accolade of CAMRA National Pub of the Year twice (1998 and 2004) and The Good Pub Guide's Beer Pub of the Year 2008, this corner pub in Adelaide Street retains much of the character of a Victorian local while offering a remarkable range of real ales and other notable beers – 25 real ales dispensed by hand pump or gravity, a dozen draft continental beers and 30 bottled beers. Landlord Colin Keatley has been something of a monument in the movement to restore quality pubs in the City. The Fat Cat also has its own brewery located at its sister pub, The Shed.

Feilden, Sir Bernard

Internationally respected conservation architect. Regarded as one of the most influential conservation architects in the world, Bernard Feilden started his career after qualifying in 1949 with Edward Boardman's old practice where he designed the, now listed, Trinity United Reform Church on Unthank Road. He establish his own practice with David Mawson in 1954 and his earliest major scheme was to take over the delivery of the University of East Anglia campus from Denys Lasdun, who was proving too expensive. Following this, the Bishop of Norwich, Launcelot Fleming, asked him to advise on the Cathedral following the death of the Cathedral Architect. The major challenge was the structural stability of the spire which he managed to resolve with an innovative solution. He went on to tackle a range of other ecclesiastical structures, including York Minster, and he was also appointed surveyor to the fabric of St Paul's Cathedral. In 1975 he devised a plan to safeguard the centre of Chesterfield which won him a Europa Nostra medal. He lectured regularly at a range of conservation institutions including the Intergovern-mental International Centre for the Study of Preservation and Restoration of Cultural Property in Rome (ICCROM) from 1972 to 1994 and this led to him giving advice to architects and restorers in Iraq, Iran, India, Pakistan, Sri Lanka, China, New Zealand and Canada. In 1986, he received the Aga Khan award for architecture for his contribution to the conservation of the dome of Al Aqsa mosque in Jerusalem. Feilden received an OBE in 1969, CBE in 1976, and was knighted in 1985. He died in 2008 at the age of 89.

Festivals

Regular events. Norwich boasts a diversity of festival activity throughout the year.

Principal events include:

- **Dragon Festival** (Feb) – bi-annual event celebrating dragons in heritage, art, literature and performance

- **Spring Literary festival** – international writers at the UEA

- **Norfolk & Norwich Festival** (May) – the oldest City based music festival in the country

- **Norwich Fringe Festival** (May) – alternative arts festival

- **City of Ale Festival** (late May/early June) – newly inaugurated in 2011 to celebrate independent breweries within a 30 mile radius of Norwich

- **Norwich Comedy Festival** (June)

- **Lord Mayor's Celebrations** (July) – weekend of events culminating in major procession

- **Cathedral's Shakespeare Festival** (July) – celebration of Shakespeare at the Anglican Cathedral

- **Heritage Open Days** (early Sept) – the largest free heritage event in the UK or Ireland outside London

- **Norfolk Food Festival** (Sept) – celebrating local producers

- **Norwich Beer Festival** (Last week in Oct) – the largest provincial beer festival in the UK

- **Norwich Fashion Week** (Sept) – celebrating local fashion designers and retailers.

From top: St Benedicts redevelopment proposals from west, St Benedicts redevelopment proposals from east and the proposed extension to the Maids Head.

Fifties and Sixties

Decades of destruction. Despite the experience of the 1920s and 30s, when the City lost some stunning historic assets and very nearly lost some others, such as Elm Hill and the Guildhall, it seemed that Norwich in general and the local authorities in particular had learned nothing by the 1950s and 60s. Firstly, there was generally (although not exclusively) a 'sweep it away' attitude to what had been damaged during the War. While churches like St Julian's were reconstructed, others like St Paul and St Michael at Thorn were erased – the latter, which appeared to be salvageable, has been replaced by a surface car park. Equally ancient buildings like the Boar's Head, again apparently capable of restoration, were demolished. The same was true in the rural hinterland where impressive halls and country houses which had survived for centuries, were allowed to be flattened. The instigators of post War change ploughed on a course which was seen as 'progress' but was actually a blinkered drive principally to accommodate the motor car or to celebrate modernist architecture at any cost and sometimes both. Some of the greatest excesses against the City's heritage included the demolition of the centuries old White Swan to provide a surface car park, the levelling of large sections of the City Wall, the imposition of the destructive Inner Ring Road through the northern, medieval street pattern and the infliction of hideous abominations on the grain of the historic City such as Anglia Square, St Stephen's and the much reviled Westlegate Tower. Other less ancient structures such as the Cavalry Barracks, the Corn Exchange and the Steward & Patteson's Brewery all fell to the demolition ball to be replaced by nothing very remarkable. Towards the end of the period, the arrival of the City's first Planning Officer, Alfie Wood, and his team of passionate professionals, saw a major, positive change in the way that the City valued its heritage which has endured to the present day and has earned Norwich a number of national and international accolades in recent years.

Fifty Nine Cup Run

Norwich City's legendary FA Cup successes. As a lowly Third division side at the time, Norwich made a remarkable progression through the early rounds of the F.A. Cup dispatching Manchester United, in front of a home crowd of 38,000, Spurs and Sheffield United before losing 1-0 in a replay to Luton in the semi final. Although the club reached the semi finals again in 1989 (losing 1-0 to Everton) and again in 1992 (losing 1-0 to Sunderland) their giant killing 1959 performance represents one of their greatest achievements.

Finkelgate

Ancient thoroughfare. This was a common name in Scandinavian England and the suffix 'gata' also suggests a pre Conquest, Anglo Scandinavian origin which would be reinforced by the presence nearby of other 'gates' including Sandgate (Thorn Lane), Skythegate (Horns Lane) and Holgate (Mariners Lane). The meaning is less certain. Elsewhere, such as Finkel Street in York, it derives from an old Scandinavian personal name (Finnkell). It has also been suggested that it could mean fennel, denoting the location of a herb market but this seems a very odd location, well to the south of the original, defended pre Conquest borough and even far removed from other, later markets. Another suggestion is that finkle means to cuddle or pet and that this street was a location for sexual activity. Given the long history of Ber Street with street prostitution this may well denote one of the oldest locations of the oldest profession in the City.

Clockwise from below: Fires – C19th Dove St fire, Central Fire Station weather vane, Colmans Works Fire Engine.

Fires

Historic conflagrations.
As with most historic cities, fires have played a significant role in the development and renewal of Norwich over 1500 years. As early as 1004, the Anglo Saxon Chronicle tells us that Sweyn Forkbeard came with his fleet and completely burned and wasted the borough. This event is commemorated in the names of lost churches such as St Margaret in Combusto (the burnt area). After the Conquest, the 1293 Riot resulted in major fires which devastated the Benedictine Friary and the surrounding area while lightning caused a further major Cathedral fire in 1463. Further into the medieval period there were catastrophic fires in 1504 and 1507 which destroyed over a third of the City including all of Elm Hill apart from the Britons Arms while Kett's Rebellion of 1549 razed more of the City. Other significant fires included:

- 16th January 1913 – complete destruction of Sexton's Shoe Factory, Fishergate, causing over £100,000 of damage
- 22nd June 1934 – total devastation of the Theatre Royal
- 24th October 1934 – complete destruction of Hinde & Harveys silk factory, Botolph Street
- 27/29th April 1942 – Baedeker fire bomb raids which devastated huge areas of the City
- March 1962 – major damage to the Curat House
- 1st August 1970 – destruction of Garlands department store which had been established since 1862

Mountergate fish market plaque.

- 25th October 1984 – destruction of Norwich City's Main Stand and a proportion of its trophies
- 1st August 1994 – destruction of the Norwich Central Library
- 12th August 1995 – severe damage to the historic Assembly House.

Firs Stadium

Former home of Norwich Speedway. Opened in 1931 as a grass and dirt track stadium off the Cromer Road and opposite the surviving Firs pub (now a Tesco), the Firs Stadium developed to be one of the finest motorcycle speedway tracks in the whole country. It hosted some of the sport's greatest stars including the greatest of them all, the multiple World Championship winning Swede Ove Funden. Ironically, between 1955 and 1964, when the Norwich Stars were performing at their best, the venue went into decline and was sold for £75,000 and closed finally in October 1964. The final event was a stock car race. The site was subsequently redeveloped for housing.

Fishergate

Ancient thoroughfare.
Located on the north bank of the Wensum, within the

D shaped enclosure that was pre Conquest Northwic, this is a route of Anglo Scandinavian origin, meaning street of the fishermen. Archaeological excavations have uncovered C11th fish hooks and net weights and the presence of fishermen within the parish of St Edmund is recorded well into the medieval period. The church itself is likely to have been a pre Conquest foundation although the present structure is of later date. The only other building of note is the C17th former merchant house and latterly the Duke of Marlborough pub which functioned from 1760 until 1969 and is now in residential use. At the western end, the 1864 former Anguish Boys School, subsequently a Roman Catholic Chapel, in a Tudor/Gothic style, had survived into the 1980s but was redeveloped for the massive Norwich Corrugated Board factory.

Fishmarket

Location of fish markets.
Originally located close to the river, probably near the Bichel, the fish market moved to the centre of the City following the establishment of the Norman Great Market, and

Clockwise from top: 1912 floods in Westwick Street, Great Hospital meadow, flood marker at New Mills and 1912 floods news item.

was located close to the Tollhouse/Guildhall. By the C19th, seven centuries of piecemeal development had created a 'malodorous and dilapidated' collection of structures which, although historic and picturesque, were regarded as insanitary by the Corporation and swept away. In their place the Corporation's surveyor Mr Benest created a grand, neo classical style edifice in 1860. However, the new building had a short life, first being reused as offices in 1914 then demolished when the City Hall, Memorial Gardens and new Market layout were developed in the 1930s. A new wholesale Fishmarket was constructed in Mountergate and opened

on Christmas Eve 1913 by City Engineer Arthur Collins. Today, fish stalls survive at the front of the provision market and the old wholesale market is let for storage and light industrial purposes.

Flemish

See *Dutch and Flemish*.

Floods

Historic inundations. Following severe and persistent rain towards the end of August 1912 there was a record rainfall of over 7 inches (200mm) in one day which resulted in heavy flooding particularly around Heigham and Coslany. The flood level was 15 inches (400+ mm) higher than the

previously recorded highest flood mark of 1614. 3650 houses were devastated by the flood water and this led to some of the first slum clearance and social housing development in the City. The floods were so severe that they demolished or partly demolished bridges at Trowse and Lakenham. Miraculously only three people died.

Flowerday, Philippa

Britain's first industrial nurse. In 1872, Colmans employed Philippa Flowerday as the country's first industrial nurse. She trained at the Norfolk and Norwich Hospital and her duties at Colman's included

The Forum

'A unique collection of communicative media in an award winning C21st complex'.

Built in the old Norman borough, The Forum represents an example of turning adversity into remarkable good fortune. In 1994, an electrical fault caused a fire which gutted the former, award-winning library in just 20 minutes and left it irreparable. The resulting building by Sir Michael Hopkins was developed by a cocktail of Millennium Commission, City Council and County Council funding and represents probably the most striking piece of post war architecture in the City Centre. Not a mere building but a series of juxtaposed spaces and buildings within buildings, The Forum was designed to include a cutting edge, multi level Millennium Library incorporating the 8th USAAF Memorial Library and the Norfolk Heritage Library, a three level multimedia visitor attraction exploring the history of the City and its region, a new Tourist Information Centre and shop, the regional head-quarters for BBC Radio and TV, a business and learning centre, the European

Information Library, café and restaurants and major indoor and outdoor public spaces. In 2009 a major refurbishment saw the introduction of a Digital Gallery, an Open Studio and a conference suite. The structure boasts a number of spectacular claims including the largest digital gallery in Europe, the most successful library in England and a war memorial unique in the world.

Clockwise from top: The Forum at night, The Forum's Fusion Gallery, performance venue, and view out.

Philippa Flowerday – Britain's first industrial nurse.

helping the doctor and taking supplies to the sick at home, she would carry out approximately 45 visits a week.

Forbes, Duncan

Inspirational footballer. Forbes spent 33 years in total with Norwich City as a player, commercial staff member and chief scout. In 357 appearances he scored 12 times and was never sent off – a remarkable achievement for an assertive central defender. Duncan was captain in Norwich's first ever game in Division 1, he was the first City captain to receive the Division 2 trophy and the first to captain the club at Wembley, in the 1973 League Cup Final. He retired in May 2001.

Forum, The
See page 161.

Foundry Bridge
The foundation stone of the first Foundry Bridge, taking its name from the iron foundry located just down stream from it, was laid in August 1810. The second bridge replaced the first one in 1844 to accommodate additional traffic from the new Thorpe Station opened

in the same year. The development of Prince of Wales Road allied to further riverside industrial development and the impending completion of the new, much expanded Thorpe Station in 1886 led to the current iron bridge, designed by P.P. Marshal, being developed in 1884.

Franciscan Friars Friary
See *Greyfriars Friary*.

French Borough

Post Norman Conquest French 'new town'. The Borough is said to be one of only two planned French boroughs in the UK (with Nottingham's) and was established in a largely undeveloped area of common land to the west of the castle immediately following the Conquest. It boasted a new market place, on the spot where the current market still stands, to replace the Saxon Tombland market, two new principal streets running west from it – Upper Newport (St Giles) and Lower Newport (Bethel

Duncan Forbes – inspirational Norwich City captain.

Street) and by 1086 the new Borough housed 125 French inhabitants, the 'Franci de Norwic' (Domesday Book). The Normans further stamped their mark on the area with the construction of three new churches – St Peter Mancroft, St Giles' and St Stephen's. Later, in C13th, the ecclesiastical College of St Mary in the Fields was founded in the southern part of the French Borough but did not survive the Reformation of the 1530s. To the east of the Borough, and within the protective view of the Castle, lay the medieval Jewish Quarter, now the site of shops south and east of the Haymarket.

French Church –
See *St Mary the Less*.

French Refugees

French Immigrants. After the revocation of the Edict of Nantes (1685) enormous numbers of French Huguenots fled to England and many settled in Norwich helping to establish the crape and silk industries. The Crown encouraged further French refugees who introduced the art of calico printing to the City. In the 18th and early 19th centuries French ideas boosted the radical tradition in the area and, fuelled by thinkers of the period such as Thetford's Thomas Paine, one of the main contributors to the radical ideals which sparked the American Revolution, gave Norwich the label 'Jacobin City'. The City also attracted large numbers of expatriate French fleeing the Revolution. One such immigrant seeking a new life was David Soman who founded a shoe making company in Norwich in 1799 which became Haldestein's,

*David Soman,
French refugee.*

*Friends Meeting House,
Upper Goat Lane.*

one of the most significant manufacturers of quality shoes in the UK by the late C19th. In turn, this company merged with the Swiss giant Bally in 1933 to become a significant shoe maker on the international stage.

Fresflete

Lost stream. This was a small stream which flowed from roughly modern Mountergate into the Wensum south of the iron foundry that gave its name to Foundry Bridge. The stream ran along the eastern boundary of the New Spring Gardens.

Friars de Sacco

Sack Friars. The Friars Penitential, or Sack Friars – so called because they dressed in garments made of sacking, came from Marseilles and settled on a site north of the present Blackfriars Hall shortly after 1250. Their buildings were modest and their first was the surviving crypt, then unvaulted and roofed in timber. Subsequently, they added the surviving Becket's Chapel. In 1307 the Pope dissolved the order and Edward II gave the Blackfriars approval to take over the site provided that they took care of the Sack Friars prior, William de

Hoo, who was 'broken with age and nearly blind.'

Friars of Our Lady

Religious community. The friars of St Mary or De Domina arrived in Norwich in 1290 and settled in a house on the south side of St Julian's churchyard. After less than 60 years, the order in Norwich was extinguished by the Black Death.

Friars Quay

Iconic housing scheme. Designed by Feilden & Mawson in 1975, this 40 residential unit redevelopment of a former timberyard provided the centre piece of the Architectural Heritage Year scheme, Heritage over the Wensum and demonstrated one of the earliest city centre housing regeneration schemes in the UK. Adjacent to the houses, the former Wilson's Glassworks incorporates elements of the 1814 St Clement's Baptist Chapel where the radical non conformist Mark Wilkes preached.

Friends Meeting House

Quaker Chapel. In 1654 Thomas Symonds became the first person in Norwich to convert to the Religious Society of Friends or Quakers but it wasn't until 1679 that

the Friend's had a Meeting House of their own, built on Upper Goat Lane. By 1700 there were about 500 Quakers in Norwich and the Goat Lane buildings were soon expanded with almshouses for the poor and a school. Further improvements in 1826 saw John Thomas Patience design a new Meeting House replacing the old one with the current Classical style building. The financial burden of this new building and a decline in numbers did, however, nearly cause the end of Quaker worship in Goat Lane. The Friends nearly sold the Meeting House to the Wesleyan Methodists but when the deal fell through they held onto the site and still worship there today.

The Meeting House is also known particularly for its famous congregation. The prominent Norfolk banking family, the Gurney's worshiped here, as did Elizabeth Fry (1780-1845), prison reformer and campaigner for the sick and homeless. Fry worshiped in both the old and new Meeting Houses but her journals reveal that she often feigned sickness to skip the insufferably long services and the 'disagreeable' older Quakers.

Fry, Elizabeth

Social Reformer. Born in 1780 into the Quaker banker family of the Gurneys, Elizabeth spent her early years in the (surviving) family house in Magdalen Street (now Gurney Court) before moving to Earlham Hall at the age of six. After a relatively privileged upbringing, she was influenced by the preachings of Quaker William Savery and began to turn her attentions to assisting the

The Elizabeth Fry Building
was officially opened by
The Rt Hon Gillian Shephard MP
Secretary of State for Education
on Friday 30 June 1995

Elizabeth Fry Building,
University of East Anglia.

less fortunate members of late C18th/early C19th society. This included setting up a Sunday School to help poor children to read. In 1800, at the age of 20, she met and married Joseph Fry, another Quaker banker. The couple moved to London where they had 11 children. She became a Quaker Minister in 1811. In London she turned her attention to the condition of prisoners and after some initial charitable works, she began to introduce reforms at Newgate Prison in ernest in 1816 including the establishment of a school. She was instrumental in the founding of the Association for the Reformation of the Female Prisoners in Newgate, in 1817, and subsequently the creation of the British Ladies' Society for Promoting the Reformation of Female Prisoners, generally acknowledged as the first established women's organisation nationwide in the UK. Her brother in law, Thomas Fowell Buxton, was elected to Parliament and

began to lobby on her behalf. She became the first woman to present evidence to Parliament when, in 1818, she gave evidence to a House of Commons Committee on prisoners' conditions. Fry, and her brother John Joseph Gurney, lobbied the Government on capital punishment and prison reform and in 1823 persuaded Prime Minister Peel to introduce the Gaols Act, which introduced prison chaplains, women warders for women prisoners and payment of gaolers rather than making them dependent for their incomes by taking fees from prisoners.

Fry established a night shelter in London in 1820 and a 'Visiting Society' in Brighton in 1824, aimed at providing support to poor people in their homes. This model was replicated across the country. In 1840, she opened a training school for nurses at Guys Hospital and this inspired Florence Nightingale to take a team of Fry's nurses to the Crimea.

Although criticised by the Victorian establishment for promoting the role of women, she was well regarded by Queen Victoria who donated to her causes and granted her several audiences.

She is commemorated on the reverse of the five pound note as well as in a road name in Norwich, a faculty building (School of Social Work and Psychology) at the University of East Anglia and by plaques in both Norwich and London. There are also 21 Elizabeth Fry Societies across Canada which promote volunteering and social welfare programmes.

Future Radio

Community Radio Station.
Future Radio is a community radio station based in West Norwich, in the Larkman Estate, and funded by the East of England Development Agency (EEDA) and the North Earlham, Larkman and Marlpit Development Trust (NELM). It is part of Future Projects, an NR5 based arts, media and education charity. Future provides school inclusion projects for young people aged 13 to 16 years, post 16 support, music, media and radio training, education films/DVDs and much more. The station's mission statement is to 'promote social inclusion in its broadest sense, freedom of expression and the dissemination of information for the benefit of our local and wider communities'. Future Radio uses music of all genres to promote racial and social harmony, embrace social, cultural and economic diversity and promote tolerance, understanding and democracy. It seeks to use radio as an engagement tool for the local and wider communities, an education and training resource, an information and advice service and a platform for local talent. It can be accessed on 96.9 FM in the Norwich Area.
www.futureradio.co.uk

Fye Bridge

Historic bridge site.
The main north-south thoroughfare of the borough would have been Fybriggate (now Fye Bridge Street/ Magdalen Street), taking its name from the first wooden causeway crossing of the river. Excavations for a sewer trench in April 1896 revealed piles driven into the

river bed, suggesting a support structure for a causeway and earlier building works 'for foundations at Messrs Geldart's in Wensum St' revealed a roadway paved with round cobble stones sloping down towards the river and likely to have been the approach to the causeway. In 1999 archaeological excavations produced a further pile with bark but it was not possible to date it. The suggested early date of the crossing is perhaps supported by the discovery of C10th Thetford type ware close to the site in 1974. There are references to a bridge here in 1132 and 1283 and by the time of Henry IV the wooden bridge had been replaced by a stone bridge which, following the flood of 1570, was itself replaced by a new stone bridge in 1573. This survived until 1829 when Francis Stone replaced it.

The present bridge, completed in 1934, is supposed to be inspired by the medieval Bishop Bridge.

Fybriggate
Ancient thoroughfare.
Northward extension of the ancient King Street, Fybriggate, from the Old Danish meaning street to Fye Bridge, this route forms part of a probable Roman Road from Pye Strete/Venta Icenorum to Roman settlements in north Norfolk. The name Fybriggate was in use well into the C18th when the term Magdalen Street gradually began to replace it, at least as far south as the surviving 'rump' Fye Bridge Street, which now covers only the section from Colegate south. Magdalen Street takes its name from the chapel of St Mary Magdalen, the former leper house which survives on Sprowston Road. At its peak, Fybriggate had half a

dozen churches on it. Like its southern extension, King Street, the street also hosted major merchant mansions including the 1599 house of mayor and MP Alexander Thurston (now the Mischief Tavern), the 1540 mansion of Edmund and Robert Woode, knighted by Elizabeth I in Norwich in 1578, No. 29, which is part of the 1612 house of Thomas Shipdown, mayor in 1631 and Gurney Court which is C16th with a later, Georgian covering, while later Georgian houses testify to the one time prominence of the street. The southern section remains largely intact but the institutional vandalism of the Inner Ring Road and Anglia Square in the 1960s have ripped the heart out of the street, leaving the northern stump somewhat isolated and abandoned. The area is proposed by the Council as a focus for future regeneration activity.

Clockwise from below: Fybriggate – merchant houses, view south, Thurston's House, view to west, and Thomas Shipdown's House.

G is for...

The largest and most elaborate medieval 'city hall' in England; 'the most effective Parliamentary reformer of his generation'; Norwich City's top scorer of all time; the longest row of buildings surviving from the Tudor period in England; the inventor of the Tonic Sol-fa; subjects of a rare Hans Holbein double image portrait; the seat of King Harold's brother; a caring institution providing continuous service since 1249; a friary attended by a later Pope; the first recorded battle despatch in English history; the most accurate mechanical clock in Great Britain.

Galsworthy, John

Writer. In 1904 John Galsworthy stayed in the City at the Royal Hotel. He visited local bankers to sort out the estate of his cousin Ada, who was the inspiration for the character Irene in his classic novel The Forsyte Saga.

Galleries

See *Art Galleries*.

Garage

Cultural venue. The Garage is a creative industries training and performance venue located adjacent to Chapelfield Gardens. Although offering its services to all age ranges and backgrounds, the Garage targets particularly the 8-25 year old age group. The venue is the former Howes Garage (hence the name) transformed with the aid of New Deal for Communities funding into a range of facilities including a number of professional sprung floor dance and drama studios, meeting rooms and a high spec studio theatre which seats 110 people. www.thegarage.org.uk

Garrett, John

Parliamentarian.
Referred to by the Independent newspaper as 'the most effective Parliamentary reformer of his generation' John Garret served Norwich South as its MP from 1974-83 and from 1987-97. He played a major role in the reform of the Civil Service and was opposition spokesman for the Treasury on industry and energy and on the Civil Service. After retiring from Parliament in 1997 he became a local councillor on both the County and City Councils serving the

Garsett House, St Andrews, with detail from timbers.

Bowthorpe ward. He died in 2007 and is remembered by the annual John Garratt Memorial Lecture at the University of East Anglia.

Garsett House

Surviving merchant house.
Located opposite St Andrew's Hall, on Princes Street, Garsett House takes its name from former resident and Sheriff (1599) Robert Garsett who is commemorated in the Suckling Chapel of St Andrew's Church. The timber framed building probably dates from 1589 and is also known as Armada House because it has been suggested that the timbers may have come from one of the Spanish Armada galleons wrecked off the east coast during the previous year. The original house was truncated by the development of a new tram route in 1900 connecting Redwell Street to St Andrew's Plain and also lopping off part of the front of Suckling House. The house has previously been home to the Norfolk Archaeology Service and the Norfolk & Norwich Archaeological Society.

Gas Works

Gas manufacturing sites.
The Norwich Gas Light Company was formed in 1820 and developed a plant in St Stephen's parish. The British Gas Light Company, established in 1824, bought the Norwich company in 1825 and concentrated activity on the new site at Bishop Bridge (Gas Hill). By 1850 it had acquired a large site in St Martins and set about developing a new plant there, demolishing many historic buildings in the process. A further expansion in 1888 obliterated the ancient Worlds End Lane. The 1945 City of Norwich Plan slated the Gas Works – 'it is questionable whether a more unfortunate site could have been found' – and expressed concern that Thomas Ivory's Methodist Meeting House and Parsonage, which had been absorbed by the development, might be difficult to rescue – the Plan was right. It was suggested that the works be relocated to a site adjacent to the Power Station near Trowse Eye and eventually it was, only to become redundant itself in due course. The gas holders at Gas Hill remain as a testament to the City's industrial past.

Johnny Gavin – Norwich City football hero.

Gaumont
See *Carlton Cinema*.

Gay and Lesbian Norwich
See *Norwich Pride*.

Gavin, Johnny
Norwich City striker. Irish international Johnny Gavin was the Canaries top scorer of all time hitting the net 132 times in 338 games over two spells at the club between 1948 and 1958. He worked as a painter on Irish railways until City signed him for £1,500 in 1948. He had a brief excursion to Tottenham Hotspur in 1954/5 when he scored an impressive 15 goals in 32 games but then moved back to Norwich. After leaving Norwich in 1958 he played for Watford, Crystal Palace and Cambridge before settling down as a publican in that city.

From top: Gentleman's Walk in the C19th, prior to pedestrianisation looking south, and the north view today.

Gentlemans Walk
Principal street. Formed following the Conquest when the Norman Market was laid out, 'The Walk' was known as Le Nether Rowe from the early medieval period and sometimes Souter Rowe (Shoe Makers Row). The present name originates from the C17th when the gentry flocked to the City to shop, be entertained and to 'display'. Thomas Baskerville in 1681 talks about 'a fair Walk before the prime inns and houses of the market-place... called gentlemen's walk or walking place... kept clear for the purpose from the encumbrances of stalls, tradesmen and their goods.' Kirkpatrick tells us 'on Saturdays, at Sessions time and other occasions, when the Gentlemen of the County resort to ye City, this is the usual place of their walking for their diversion and having discourse together, as it is also for the Principal Citizens.' This civilised pursuit of strolling was brought to an abrupt halt with the arrival of

King George VI inspecting civil defence volunteers, 1940.

motorised traffic at the turn of the C20th. By the 1980s the street had become unpleasant and dangerous for pedestrians and the Councils showed courage and imagination in closing it to traffic. As well as making The Walk a more attractive place, the closure resulted in a 300 per cent increase in pedestrian flows at peaks, a reduction in accidents, an increase in property values and an improvement in air quality. Architecturally, The Walk, and its extension into the Haymarket, is a picture of the City's styles and periods in microcosm. From the London Street corner moving southwards, key examples include a Venetian revival style building (formerly Burtons) by Boardman from 1876; then another Boardman building (formerly Hope Brothers), of 1872 with minor ironwork by Thomas Jekyll; on the north corner of Davey Place the exuberant stone-faced Lloyds bank designed by H. Munro Cautley in 1928, and extended from four to six

bays in 1930; the assertively modernist stone, glass and ceramic structure from 1959 by E. Somake; Edward Skipper's spectacular Art Nouveau Royal Arcade (1899) is faced up by the surviving frontage of Joseph Stannard's Royal Hotel (1846); just south of the Arcade is an early C19th house which contains a surviving C17th stair turret at the rear; next to that is an impressive C17th building (currently W.H.Smith/Lush) with a C15th undercroft; opposite is a C19th shop (Booksale) with a C14th undercroft beneath.

George V

King. In 1911 George V visited Norwich and after a civic reception in St Andrew's Hall, where he knighted the Lord Mayor, he attended the Royal Norfolk Show, held at Crown Point Trowse, where he inspected 200 'old soldiers and sailors' of the Norfolk Veterans Association.

George VI

King. In 1938, George VI and the Queen Elizabeth opened City Hall and then attended a football match at Carrow Road between Norwich and Millwall. This was the first Second Division English Football League match to be attended by a reigning monarch. In 1940 he returned to boost morale.

Gibraltar Gardens

Historic pub. With the southern section dating from 1470 and the north and central sections from 1550 and 1600 respectively, this is one of the oldest pubs in the City. While originally built as a substantial dwelling, it is likely that the building was an inn before the end of the C17th and by 1753 Land

and Window Tax records indicate that it was a public house. Although one school of thought suggests the name is a corruption of 'Gibbet and Altar' it is more likely that it celebrates the capture of Gibraltar in 1704 by local admiral from North Norfolk Sir Cloudesley Shovell. The 'Gardens' element derives from the presence of gardens on site and as early as 1750, landlord John Cotton was advertising displays of 'beautiful carnations'.

Gildencroft

Ancient space. Once a large and ancient open space between Jenkins Lane and the northern run of City Wall, the name now refers to a thoroughfare (partly traffic free) between the junction of St Augustines/Botolph Street and Chatham Street, running south of St Augustine's churchyard. The name derives from the Old English gildenacroft or field of the guild brethren. Part of the original Gildencroft was called Justingacre and it is probable that jousting tournaments took place here. Edward the Black Prince reputedly attended a great tournament here in 1350. Standing along the south side of St Augustine's church, at Nos. 2 to 12 Gildencroft, is a row of Tudor cottages. They are the longest row of buildings surviving from the Tudor period in England. They do not survive in the original form as they have been altered in the C17th- C20th and have had later style windows inserted. They would have originally stood as a row of 12 homes but were restored by Norwich Corporation in 1956-57 and converted into six cottages.

From left: The Gildencroft, the Meeting House in the Gildencroft before WWII bombing, Gildencroft Burial Ground.

Gildencroft Meeting House

Replica Quaker meeting house. The Religious Society of Friends held its first meeting in Norwich in 1654 and then grew from strength to strength. The land on Gildencroft was bought as a burial ground in 1670 for £72 but by 1699 the Society had outgrown its original meeting house on Upper Goat Lane. A larger meeting house was therefore built on land next to the Gildencroft burial ground and was used as the main meeting house until a new building was built at Upper Goat Lane in 1826. The Gildencroft Meeting House was later leased to the Particular Baptists but was destroyed by bombing in April 1942. In 1958 a smaller building incorporating parts of the original structure was built on the site and is now used as a children's play centre. The Society of Friends still use the building when members are laid to rest in the adjoining burial ground.

Glover, Sarah Ann

Originator of the Tonic Sol-fa technique. Born in The Close in 1786, Sarah Ann Glover honed her talent for music in the congregation of her father, the curate of St Lawrence. She developed what was to be called the Norwich Tonic Sol-fa system, later popularised in the film The Sound of Music. In the 1820s she opened a school, with her sisters Christina and Margaret, in Black Boys Yard in Colegate and she also taught at the Norwich Workhouse and at the Central School (the teacher training establishment at the time). She taught music to the blind and worked as a Governess to the family of Sir Thomas Fowell Buxton. In Black Boys Yard they taught poor children scripture, writing, arithmetic, drawing and sewing but most notably, music by a revolutionary technique of sight reading using doh, ray, me, fah, soh, lah, tee and doh. It was a system of music notation designed to improve the standard of singing and to simplify the reading of music. Sarah used her Norwich Sol-fa system in her own teaching, but she also published a number of books and charts explaining and facilitating her methods. Her Manual of the Norwich Sol-fa System 'The Tetrachordal System designed to facilitate the acquisition of music by a return to First Principles', was published by Jarrold & Sons in Norwich and Novello in London. It was re-issued, with Sarah's up-dates, in many editions. The system became popular, and was used in a number of publications. Sarah also invented the Glass Harmonicon, an instrument designed to facilitate her Sol-fa system, to establish pitch and to train the ear. Sarah's instrument resembled a xylophone, with glass plates as keys, which were struck by hammers. A later instrument, probably made for the Great Exhibition of 1851 and now in the

The Glover Memorial in St Lawrence.

Bridewell Museum, Norwich, had a keyboard similar to that of a piano. It produced a very clear sound, ideal for the purpose of establishing pitch.

The technique was taken up by Revd John Spencer Curwen who was responsible for publishing on the approach and getting it adopted throughout the country. By 1870 there were over 5,000 retained teachers of the Sol-fa system and 1.5 million pupils. During her teaching period, Sarah lived in Pottergate then moved to Cromer, Reading and Hereford, eventually dying of a stroke in Great Malvern in October 1867. In 1891 a brass plaque was erected in St Lawrence to commemorate the jubilee of the Sol-fa system.

God's House in St Giles

Almshouse. During the reign of Edward I (1272-1307) John le Grant gave an almshouse in Lower Newport on the north side of St Giles Street between Willow Lane and Fishers Lane to the parish before 1306 and this was confirmed by his son in 1310. It was rebuilt 1472 by Bishop Walter Lyhart and nomination rights for inmates passed to the bishop. In 1534, as part of the Dissolution of the Monasteries, the land and buildings were confiscated and nothing of them remains today.

God's House in Westwick Street

Lost alms house. Robert de Aswardby founded God's House in St Margarets, for the benefit of the poor, in 1292 on a site on the west side of the churchyard of St Margaret Westwick. The alms houses have long since disappeared.

Thomas and John Godsalve portrait by Holbein.

Godsalve, Sir John

Prominent local figure.
Born in 1505 John Godsalve came to prominence partly as a result of his father's influence (Sir Thomas) and partly due to his finding favour with Thomas Cromwell. He held office in London and in 1539, Cromwell secured his nomination as MP for Norwich and he was elected with Augustine Steward. This was the start of various associations with the Commons and Lords lasting into the 1550s. In the same year, he was appointed Constable of Norwich Castle and Keeper of Norwich Gaol. In 1544 he accompanied the King on his French campaigns and was knighted at the coronation of Edward VI and was granted Comptrollership of the Tower Mint. It seems that he was back in Norwich by the end of the decade since accounts of Kett's Rebellion of 1549 tell us that Godsalve 'and a great company of others kept Sir William Paston's great pieces (artillery) that night in the Castle yard.' His son Thomas was held by the rebels and used by them to compose their demands.

He had inherited significant wealth on his father's death in 1542, including 49 houses in Norwich alone, and commanded an annual property income of £195 (roughly £750,000 in modern values). He retained his interests in the Mint into the reign of Queen Mary and, with Thomas Egerton, is credited with devising the coins showing the double face of Philip and Mary in 1554. Sir John had his portrait painted, in an unusual 'double portrait' with his father Sir Thomas by the Royal portrait painter Hans Holbein in 1528. This was followed by an individual portrait by the same artist in 1532.

Godwinson, Gyrth

Saxon Earl of East Anglia.
Gyrth Godwinson was Earl of East Anglia and brother to King Harold II. For the period, he was well travelled and cultured. He had lived in Bruges during the turbulent period that preceded Edward the Confessor's reign and, when Earl in 1061, he accompanied his brother Tostig on a diplomatic legation to visit the Pope in Rome. En route, the party had passed through Germany, probably visiting the German court, and via Burgundy, crossed the Alps. Gyrth's Palace was at the centre of the Saxon borough, in Tombland, close to St Michael's – the principal church in the City at that time. He fought beside the King at Stamford Bridge and was killed at Hastings.

Golden Triangle

Desirable residential district. Originally a term coined for the highly prosperous area of housing

Possible headquarters of the Goldsmiths' Guild.

bounded by Ipswich Road, Newmarket Road and Lime Tree Road from the mid C19th, the perception and geography changed in the later C20th to encompass a much larger area bounded broadly by Earlham Road, Newmarket Road, Mile End Road and Colman Road. Composed almost entirely of terrace houses built between the Artisan's Dwelling Act of 1875 and the early Edwardian period, the Golden Triangle now provides home to a large proportion of the City's professional classes (architects, doctors, senior public servants) as well as lecturers from the universities and staff from the Norwich Research Park. The area's hub is probably Unthank which provides a diverse mix of shops, pubs and other facilities and, to a lesser degree, Earlham Road.

Goldsmiths and silversmiths

Craft working heritage. The fact that the area generally had a rich and early heritage in working with precious metals (e.g. Snettisham Treasure), the presence of a mint in Norwich from at least the 930s and the very dense representation of ecclesiastical institutions which fueled a demand for plate all attest to goldsmiths

working in gold and silver from an early period in Norwich. The first documentary evidence is in 1141 and refers to a lease being granted to Salomon 'The Goldsmith' in the parish of St Peter Mancroft. The goldsmiths workshops were located between Dove Street and Swan Lane, from the late C13th, in 'Vicus de Aurifabria', later known as 'Le Goldsmythe Rowe'. It is locationally significant that the Guild was probably based on a site in the epicentre of this area, just north of the Guildhall, between Dove Street and Exchange Street, and was probably there from about the late C13th as a substantial stone house. The present building, 6-9 Guildhall Hill, probably built as a courtyard mansion at the time of Queen Anne, is likely to have incorporated some of the original stone building and served as the location of the Goldsmiths Guild until the Guild ceased. There is also a strong probability that the Norwich Assay was located here from its opening in 1565.

The gold and silversmiths were key players in the life of the City from the earliest times. The first goldsmith to become mayor was Richard Brasyer in 1456 and he was mayor again in 1463. The elaborate surviving entranceway to the mansion of John Bassingham testifies to the wealth of these artisans by the reign of Henry VIII. The volume of production was also significant. Before the Reformation, demand was fuelled by the vast number of churches and monastic institutions. It is no mere coincidence that more examples of pre Reformation Norfolk Paten

silver survive here than in any other county. After the Reformation the local smiths continued to be prolific, their work being fueled by recycling a vast number of pre Reformation items. Over 400 pieces of church plate survive from this period. The leaders of the Guild during this period included William Cobbold, William Rogers, Peter Peterson, George Fenne and John Bassingham.

The surviving Norwich Silver can be found principally in the Civic Regalia (Norwich Castle), the Anglican Cathedral treasury and the Ticktum Trust Collection.

Goldwell, Bishop James

Bishop. James Goldwell held the position of Bishop of Norwich from 1472 until 1499. Prior to that he had been Dean of Salisbury and a commissioner for Edward IV, sent to make peace with Denmark in 1465, to represent the King in Rome in 1468 and to make a peace treaty with the French in 1471. He was sent as King's Proctor to Pope Sixtus IV in 1472 and the Pope appointed him to the vacant see in Norwich. During his bishopric he is noted for having built the current spire, although shorter than his previous cathedral at Salisbury, and for extending the lierne rib vaulting to cover the presbytery. His tomb monument provides a remarkable and elaborate survival within the Cathedral.

Gothic Works

Victorian factory of Lawrence, Scott & Electromotors. The Gothic Works was built between 1896 and 1898 by Lawrence, Scott & Company

Bishop Goldwell's tomb, Norwich Cathedral.

Gothic works – headquarters of Lawrence Scott.

to make electric motors and generators. Located just south of the walled City, on the Wensum and close to the railway station, the site covered 7,500 sq ft and employed 150 people. In 1908 a Test Shop was added to the plant and during the First World War further extensions were developed to make shells. In 1937 a further extension doubled the area of the works and by that time it employed 3,000 people. New buildings were added in 1953 and 1957. A decline started in the 1980s and by 2008, substantial areas of the original site had been cleared and the workforce had fallen to 250. Various rescue packages had secured the future of the surviving company and enhanced its performance. While major redevelopment proposals for a mix of residential and commercial uses were aired in 2008, the then parent company had secured a lease to continue production on the remaining parts of the plant for a further three years.

Grant, Cary

Actor. In 1912 screen icon Cary Grant made his first performance at the Norwich Hippodrome under his real name – Archie Leach – as part of a Norwich acrobatic troupe called the 'Nippy

Nines'. The troupe were subsequently invited to perform in New York where Archie stayed, changed his name and made his fortune.

Great Blowe

Major C17th catastrophe. In 1648, at the close of the Civil War, Royalist sympathisers broke into the County Committee Rooms in Bethel Street with the intention of seizing arms and ammunition. During the bungled attempt, they managed to ignite the powder store and 96 barrels erupted, leveling the Committee Rooms, killing 100 people, blowing all of the stained glass out of St Peter Mancroft and damaging many surrounding buildings.

Great Cockey

Former watercourse. The largest watercourse after the Wensum was the Great Cockey which rose at Jack's Pit, near modern All Saints Green, within the Norwich Union/Aviva Island Site, and flowed north roughly along Back of the Inns/Castle St/Little London St to enter the Wensum to the east of the modern Duke St river crossing. The extent of the Great Cockey valley is most obvious when viewed from the eastern valley side at St Michael at Plea as it falls

westwards to roughly the Exchange Street Junction with St Andrews Street then rises again to St Benedicts. The Cockey was culverted in the C18th but was seen to still be flowing below ground in the 1980s.

Great Hall

C15th merchant house. A rather beleaguered survivor on the west side of Oak Street, very close to the northern limit of the City Walls. Following the threat of dramatic 1930s slum clearance, the Great Hall was saved by Col. Glendenning only to be almost obliterated by 1940s bombing and restored again in the 1950s. The Great Hall was originally an early C15th hall house, extended and remodelled, with the insertion of a floor, in the C16th. While its builder is unknown, research by the Centre for East Anglian Studies indicates a fairly intensive period of occupation by weavers in its early life and up until the late C18th. As is the case with many surviving medieval structures, the Hall became a pub in 1830 and remained in that use until 1907, taking the name of the Flower Pot, and giving that name to the yard in which it sat. Following the War it had a range of uses and is now the home of the Norwich Unemployed Workers Centre.

The Great Hall, Oak Street.

The Great Hospital

Medieval caring institution.
Founded in 1249 by Bishop Walter de Suffield, the hospital was originally known as the Hospital of St Giles and it provided care for poor, elderly clergy. In addition to this, a number of the poor of Norwich were given food and access to a fire during the winter months and on feast days and special anniversaries. The hospital was staffed by four chaplains, four lay brothers and four sisters who, in the interests of propriety, Suffield insisted were over 50 years old.

Only a small portion of Suffield's original building, the simple southern porch

to the church, survives. The remaining parts of the church and hospital date to a redevelopment during the late C14th/early C15th. The hospital buildings and layout resemble those of a monastery or priory and are set around a small cloister, reputedly the smallest in England. On the south side of the cloister is St Helen's church, with an unusually large chancel which was built in the 1380s by Bishop Despenser. It was completed by 1385 in time for the visit of King Richard II and his queen, Anne of Bohemia. The 252 panels of the roof are decorated with eagles and these are said to be Anne's emblem. In 2003 roof timbers from the nave and south aisle were dated through tree ring dating

techniques (dendrochronology) to between 1378 and 1403. Previously the nave was thought to have been built along with the south transept by Bishop Goldwell in about 1480. On the opposite side of the nave to the chancel is an equally large aisled infirmary hall and on its south west corner, a tower. Attached to the west side of the cloister is medieval refectory, with its crown post roof and dragon spandrels, and the Master's Lodge to the north. The Chaplain's Dormitory is on the north side of the cloister. The eastern side of the cloister would probably have led into the chapter house and other small rooms, as indicated by doorways remaining within the cloister walk. However, this eastern range of the hospital buildings, along with the south aisle of the Infirmary Hall and a kitchen that would have stood north of the cloister have since been destroyed. Nevertheless, much of the medieval hospital remains intact and represents an important survival of medieval buildings of this type. Unlike most other surviving medieval hospitals in England, a vast archive of hospital documents survive and are housed in the County archive.

At the dissolution of the Monasteries, the hospital of St Giles and the church of St Helen were taken from the cathedral priory by Henry VIII. For several years the future of the hospital was uncertain and it was not until the reign of Edward VI that the citizens of Norwich managed to successfully petition the King for its return to local control. Edward VI re-founded the

Great and Little Melton

Suburban parish. Located 11km (7 miles) south west of Norwich and deriving their name from the Old English for middle enclosure, both settlements are ancient in origin. Great Melton's oldest building is All Saints church which contains elements from the C11th but is principally C14th and C15th when the tower was rebuilt. J.B. Pearce undertook a major refurbishment in 1883. Inside there are late C15th benches, some good Victorian stained glass and a C14th coffin lid. Within the same churchyard, the dilapidated tower of St Mary, dates from 1440. Great Melton Hall was built in 1611 for Mayor Thomas Anguish and passed from a range of hands up until the C20th when it became dilapidated. Now only a ruin survives. Other significant buildings include Whiterails Farmhouse which is an early C16th hall house with C17th additions, the C17th Wong Farmhouse, the C17th Whipple Green house, and Circle Cottages, originally a C17th house. In Little Melton the church of St Mary and All Saints represents the oldest building, dating from 1300 and containing interesting elements such as a C13th font, C14th wall paintings and a C15th screen. Little Melton Manor dates from the early C17th with C19th additions. Other notable structures include the C16th timber framed hall house, Grey Cottage and the 1749 Steward's House. There is also a remnant of the 1830 tower mill which was operating fully in 1904 but had lost its sails by 1937.

hospital to care for the poor of Norwich and it continues its good work today, providing sheltered housing and a nursing home for the elderly of Norwich. When the hospital was re-founded the medieval buildings were modified. The church was reduced in size by separating off the chancel with a wall and turning it into a dormitory for the female patients. Access from the church into the Infirmary Hall was also blocked and the infirmary was turned into lodgings for the male residents. To increase capacity, both the chancel and infirmary were divided into two floors and a fireplace was inserted at either end. By 1839 both floors of these halls had been divided into individual cubicles with a small living room next to the fires. By

the late twentieth century the ground floor of the chancel was named the Pump Ward and the first floor the Eagle Ward, the ground floor of the infirmary was called Parker Ward, and the first floor Fawcett Ward. In the 1970s the residents were re-housed in modern flats nearby but most were sad to leave their comfortable little bed-sits in the medieval hospital. The Eagle Ward remains today as a museum of how the former accommodation was deployed.

The remainder of the site accommodates almshouses from the 1820s, the late Victorian/Edwardian Gothic Revival Birkbeck Hall and, to the north, St Helen's House, built by Thomas Ivory in the C18th and extended subsequently.

Opposite: Great Hospital – former ward converted from nave.
Above: Great Hospital – cloister view.
Below from left: Eagle Ward cubicle and refectory.

Reconstruction of the Monastery of the Greyfriars, looking north west.

Great and Little Plumstead

Suburban parish. Known as Plumstede in the Domesday book, meaning 'dwelling site near plums', the modern-day parish of Plumstead is situated approximately 9.7km (6 miles) east of Norwich City Centre, and is composed of three villages: Great Plumstead, Little Plumstead, and the garden village of Thorpe End. The parish church St Mary the Virgin is in Great Plumstead and dates originally from the C13th. The tower was rebuilt in 1711, and the church itself underwent a major redevelopment in 1875 after a fire destroyed the majority of the building. There are two medieval brasses in the nave. Little Plumstead's church St Gervase and St Protase is the parish's oldest building, and interestingly the only church in the country to be dedicated to these saints. The church has a Norman round-tower and adjoins an C18th estate including an Elizabethan revival hall built in 1889, lake and woodland, and until recently the hall was used as a hospital known from 1930 as the Little Plumstead Mental Deficiency Institution. The hospital is currently being renovated into a housing development. Although the parish is now mainly composed of C20th housing, in addition to the churches and hall, there is also the grade II listed Octagon Barn in Little Plumstead, one of only four such surviving structures in the country, which is currently being developed for commercial use.

Great Market

See *Market*.

Greyfriars (Franciscan) Friary

Lost Friary. Bartholomew de Cotton's Chronicle tells us that in 'A.D. 1226 The Minors (the Franciscan friars) settled in a house given to them by John de Hastingford, south of Tombland, and east of the Castle, between the churches of St Vedast and St Cuthbert'. The rule of the Grey Friars prevented them from accepting grants of land, other than that of property which adjoined their houses already in existence. This often forced the friars (not just the Grey Friars, but the Black, White and Austin Friars too) to close up roads and thoroughfares that ran through their 'precinct'. They expanded the area they

Little Plumstead Hall.

occupied, so that by the end of the C13th the Grey Friars owned 21 plots of land. Extensions were made to their houses between 1226 and 1284, where the order gained from a number of large benefactions. This was developed further when, in 1284, Edward I granted a royal licence that allowed the friars to enclose and take on some common land. By 1288 they were given permission to make purchases to enlarge their site – it seemed inevitable that, as numbers of Grey Friars in Norwich increased, there was a need for bigger and more permanent buildings to be constructed.

Additional grants of land were made between 1292-99, and a lane closed off to the north of the site, for further enlargement in 1297. Development of the site entailed the demolition of St John's church on King St.

Between 1283 and 1299 the site was extended to cover an area bounded to north by the cathedral precinct, to the west by King St and to the south by modern Rose Lane. Unlike the other orders, the Franciscans had no direct river access but in 1340 they obtained approval to use a stream which ran through the site and was bridged by the eastern boundary wall, close to the Horsefair.

There is archaeological evidence to suggest that the Grey Friars were not the first settlers to the site they occupied. Work has indicated that there may have been activity on the site as far back as the mid-Saxon period. This seems to have been mostly to the east of the area that the Grey Friars were later to settle on, on the margins of the River Wensum.

Buildings were growing and becoming more elaborate, and, from around 1290, the Grey Friars began constructing a large church, monastery (with cloisters that would have included a school-room and a library) and chapter house, on a site close to King Street. The buildings were of an impressive size. Measurements given by William of Worcester suggest that the church nave was 32 paces (105 feet) long, the choir 60 paces (102 feet) and the tower space 28 paces (48 feet). This compares approximately in scale to the Dominican friary (St Andrews Hall) which has a nave of 127 feet and a choir of 102. Additionally, there was a 61 pace (104 foot) long cloister beside chapter house which was used for civic meetings as well as friary business. Like the Austin friary, this site also, unusually had two cloisters – one to the south of the friary church, serving as a focus for domestic buildings and a second burial cloister on the east of the precinct. This cloister had a special indulgence attached to it and was known as the Pardon Cloister. The main gate was on the west side of the precinct on King St, close to modern Prince of Wales Rd.

There were chapels dedicated to the Blessed Virgin Mary (in the choir), St Saviour (on the south side of the church) and St Anne (in the church).

Indeed, these buildings seem far from the life of poverty the Franciscans had claimed to emulate. By 1324 the entire precinct had been walled in with a number of gates.

In 1336 Pope Benedict XII constituted 21 friaries as colleges of advanced study and Norwich was one. Like its Austin neighbour, the Franciscan college attracted students from all over Europe including Pietro Philarzi – the future Pope Alexander V.

The friary ceased during the Dissolution. After this, the site, church, and all its possessions were granted to Thomas, Duke of Norfolk who, in 1559 sold it to the City of Norwich. It was later broken up and sold as a number of small holdings. Today, nothing remains of the church or monastic buildings of the Grey Friars of Norwich, although parts of the cloisters were revealed in archaeological excavations.

Grosvenor Rooms

See *Prince of Wales Cinema*.

Guader, Emma de

Conspirator's wife. In 1075, King William gave his authority for the marriage of the daughter of his close lieutenant, William FitzOsbern, and Ralph de Gauder, Earl of Norfolk and Suffolk. At the bridal feast, de Gauder conspired with Roger, Earl of Hereford, and Waltheof, Earl of Northumbria, to stage a coup during the King's absence in Normandy and to solicit the assistance of the Danes and Bretons to bring about the King's defeat. The plot was uncovered however, and while de Gauder escaped to Brittany, his new wife was left to defend the Castle at Norwich. With a garrison of 50 soldiers plus some local retainers, Emma de Gauder had to face a besieging army, led by Bishop

Lanfranc and William de Warrene, of 300 armoured troops and crossbowmen. The garrison held out for three months before famine forced a surrender. The first recorded battle despatch in English history was sent to William I from Archbishop Lanfranc following the surrender of the rebellious garrison commanded by Emma de Guader at Norwich Castle in 1075 Either because the King was impressed by the courage of the defenders or, more probably, because Emma was a blood relative, he gave the defenders 40 days to leave the country. While the garrison escaped unscathed the City didn't. Arbitrary Norman justice was meted out in the form of property confiscation, blindings and death to locals who were deemed to be guilty by association.

Guader, Ralph de

Failed conspirator. Ralph de Guader was the son of a Breton mother and Norfolk born father. He had fought with William I at Hastings and had been rewarded with the Earldom of Norfolk and Suffolk and the stewardship of the Royal Castle at Norwich. The 'Conqueror' had also given leave for him to marry Emma FitzOsbern, daughter of William FitzOsbern, the King's close friend and cousin and the man who had been given joint regency, with the King's half brother – the soldier bishop Odo of Bayeux, of the subjugated England while William returned to Normandy.

De Guader played a key role in shaping the future City by laying out the Market and new French Borough. His promising career concluded abruptly with an

unsuccessful coup against his former sponsor. De Gauder survived the failed coup, being out of the country when it was discovered. His wife Emma had a rather more difficult time.

Guildhall
See opposite.

Guild of St George

Medieval guild. Established in Norwich in 1385, less than 40 years after St George became England's patron saint, the Guild of St George was to become one of the most important guilds in the City, numbering the rich and powerful among its membership. The pinnacle of the guild's activity was the St George's Day procession, on 23rd April, which included a re-enactment of the battle between St George and the dragon and included 'Snap', a dragon shaped hobby horse which was to feature in local pageantry for centuries. The Guild of St George was driven officially by religious, charitable and social objectives, specifically providing help for the poor. However, this 'exclusive club' will have proved important to its members in facilitating their economic and political ambitions. In its early years the guild had less prominence than other guilds but in 1417 Henry V granted the guild a Royal Charter elevating it to a position of more prominence. In 1452, following some dispute over the influence of the guild, Yelverton's Mediation resulted in the guild being very closely aligned to the City Corporation. In 1486 the Corporation allowed the guild to use the upper chamber in the Guildhall for

its meetings. In 1547 Edward VI sought to abolish all guilds but the St George's Charter and its ties with the Corporation gave it immunity from these moves. The following year, reflecting this hovering threat, the Guild changed its name to the Company and Citizens of St George, at the same time removing any religious connections. In 1584 the Corporation/Guild links were cemented by combining the St George's Feast Day and the Mayor Making Day on the same day (23rd June). The very close Corporation/ Company relationship continued and indeed strengthened until 1729 when Alderman William Clark mounted a sustained attack on the Company resulting in its eventual collapse and the surrender of all of its assets to the Corporation in 1731.

Gunn, Brian

Norwich City goalkeeper and manager. Not only one of NCFC's legendary goal keepers and holder of the 4th place in the club's history for most appearances (477), Gunn briefly took on the mantle of club manager in 2009. Previously he had been a Sherriff of Norwich and raised an enormous amount of money for leukaemia sufferers following his young daughter's death from the disease.

Gurney Clock

Public art and time piece. The Gurney clock was commissioned by Barclays Bank in 1974 to mark the bicentenary of the founding of the Gurney Bank in Norwich, the fore runner of Barclays. Martin Burgess was tasked with recreating a chronometer mechanism

The Guildhall

'Norwich Guildhall has no real parallel in England and it may be that its builders were inspired by… the great city halls which graced the wealthy cloth towns of the Low Countries'. Helen Sutermeister

- The largest medieval 'city hall' in England – C13th brick vaulted undercroft, beneath the east end, pre dating the present building.
- One of the finest Council Chambers in England containing C15th stained glass from the Norwich School of Glass Painters.

The Guildhall was constructed between 1407 and 1424, on the site of the Norman tollhouse, and extended up until the C16th. Despite its name, it had relatively little to do with guilds – it began its life as the City Hall and continued this role until 1938 when the new City Hall opened. It also functioned as a court and prison with notable prisoners including Thomas Bilney, Protestant martyr, burned for heresy in 1531, and Robert Kett. From these uses the building maintains the fine C18th Court of Record (now a café) and the slightly later Sword Room or Grand Jury Room.

From top: The Guildhall exterior east façade, Grand Jury or Sword Room, Court of Record.

Page 166: The Guildhall Council Chamber.

Clockwise from above: The original Gurney Bank, Bank Plain, the largest banking hall in England, Gurneys/Barclays boardroom.

first produced by John Harrison (1693-1776) linked to a sculpture by Michael Barber within a glass housing produced by Roy Foster. The installation was intended to represent the interaction of Barclays, depicted as scales, with the City, a Lion and Castle, through the circulation of money. The installation was beset by problems from the outset. Martin Burgess was unable to complete the chronometer replica until ten years after the original commission and once installed in Chapelfield Gardens, the Clock was subjected to periodic vandalism and functional failure. The Norwich Society headed up a campaign to relocate the Clock to a more supervised location and in 1999 it was relocated to the upper level of Castle Mall, just off Timberhill, where it remains. The move was sponsored principally by the company Auto Wrappers. It is said to be the most accurate mechanical clock in Great Britain.

Gurney Court

Historic courtyard. A third of the way up Magdalen Street on the east side, this very attractive courtyard is composed of a C16th north and east range, a C17th street range and a south range built in 1730. There is a fair degree of Georgian refacing to the earlier structures. Apart from the architectural quality, the court is remarkable because it was the home of the notable Quaker bankers the Gurneys before their move to Earlham Hall and the birthplace of two of England's most remarkable women, Elizabeth Fry and Harriet Martineau. It has been renovated relatively recently into residential accommodation.

Gurney, Henry

The Quaker Banker. A member of a family with roots in Norfolk reaching back to the conquest, and a staunch Quaker, Henry founded the Gurney Bank with his brother John in 1775 in Pitt Street. Henry's son Bartlett moved the bank to larger premises in

Redwell Plain two years later, on part of the site currently occupied by Edward Boardman's neo Georgian banking hall dating from 1929. As a result of the founding of the bank here, the street changed its name to Bank Plain. Richard Gurney joined the business in 1779 and subsequently married the only daughter of London banker David Barclay. By 1896 the firm was known as Gurney, Birkbeck, Barclay, Buxton and Company – this ultimately became the Barclays Bank empire.

Guttsman, Valerie

First foreign born, female Lord Mayor. Born in the former Czechoslovakia, Valerie Guttsman fled the Nazis in 1939 and made Britain her home. She arrived in Norwich in 1963 where her husband Willi became the founding librarian of the newly established University of East Anglia. The following year she was elected councillor for Crome Ward. She became the sixth female Lord mayor in 1979 and the

*Above: Gurney Court front
courtyard elevation.
Right: rear elevation.*

first foreign born holder of the post. Her key interests included championing improved conditions for children and the family. She was a governor of both the Heartsease and Hewitt Schools. She received an OBE in 1991 and died in 2009 at the age of 91.

Gybson, Robert

C16th philanthropist.
Alderman Robert Gybson was a brewer in the parish of St Lawrence in the C16th. He sought approval from the Corporation to be granted the rights to a well used in the parish since the C13th and this was approved subject to the condition that 'at his own charge in a conduit or a cock of lead he shall bring water from the well into the public street for the ease of the common people and should maintain the same.' Not only did he produce this 'conduit' in 1578 but he set it in an elaborate arched structure celebrating his achievement and displaying the Royal coat of arms and the inscription 'Vivat Regina' in honour of Elizabeth I's visit

in the same year. The conduit or well remained on the outside of the perimeter wall of the Anchor Brewery in Westwick Street until 1982 when it was moved inside the wall to protect it. The Well head had fallen into disrepair by the first decade of the C21st so in 2010/11 the Norwich Preservation Trust undertook a major renovation scheme to restore the structure to its former glory and protect it from damage. The Well is a Scheduled Ancient Monument. Gybson went on to become Sheriff in 1596 but fell out of favour seven years later. In 1603 a plague swept the City and the Mayor, deciding that drapes hanging from houses might harbour infection, asked residents to remove them. His gentle entreaties to Gybson in Westwick Street resulted in a tirade of abuse which Gybson repeated to a gathering of local people. The Corporation reacted harshly accusing him of 'reproachful, scornful, contemptuous and foul speeches and unfitting behaviour,' depriving him of

his Aldermanship and disenfranchising him from the freedom and liberties of the City. He died in 1606 and is buried within St Lawrence church.

Gybson's Well
See *Robert Gybson*, left.

*Robert Gybson's Well,
originally in Westwick Street.*

H is for…

The first church museum in the country; the 'first English satirist'; the oldest surviving hawthorn tree in England; founder of the House of Commons Record, Hansard; Mr Pastry the iconic 1950s entertainer; Norwich's first socialist councillor; the first English writer to use blank verse; the first English, graphic representation of a wheel barrow; one of the earliest and most ambitious works seeking to catalogue and describe the wild bird species of Britain.

*Left: Bally's 1946,
Princes Street.
Above: Haldestein's factory
complex in the C19th.*

Haldestein's & Sons

Shoe making dynasty.
In 1799 French emigre David Soman arrived in the City and set up a cap making business but soon switched to shoes. His daughter married Philip Haldestein who became a partner in the business in 1846 and developed the company in Queen Street. Four successive generations of Haldestein's went on to run the business with the last, George, retiring in 1946. The company prospered and by the turn of the century Haldestein's had factories not only in Norwich but in London, Kettering, Leicester and Wymondham employing 2,000 people and exporting all over the world. The product line was huge, ranging from the normal Norwich speciality line, women's fashion shoes, through men's and children's shoes, work boots and leisure footwear. The company established itself domestically with the major department stores and fashion shoe retailers before the War and, unlike many other manufacturers, came through the War relatively unscathed. After

the War the Swiss shoe giant Bally acquired the entire share capital of the company and supported the business locally including a branch in Lowestoft in 1955. The company found its central site, close to the Cathedral and Elm Hill, was a constraint on development and in 1969 a major new plant was developed on Hall Road. The old site was redeveloped for housing and offices. Success continued – a further factory was opened at Dereham in 1973 and further development was undertaken at Hall Road. The company continued to do well, specialising in the high end of women's fashion shoes, but as production costs came under pressure from cheaper imports and Bally became part of a Swiss conglomerate, the position of the UK operation came under review and the factory was closed in the 1990s. The site is now earmarked for a mixed use development of homes, shops and commercial uses.

Hall, Bishop Joseph

The first English satirist.
Hall moved from Exeter to Norwich in 1641 and already had a reputation of stature in both the church and literary world. His six 'Byting Satyres' supported his claim

to be the 'first English satirist' but he was also prolific in religious writings including sermons delivered at Court. At the time of the English Revolution he was in a precarious position as a Puritan but defender of the office of bishop. Although impeached and charged with treason he was released and, having been expelled from the bishopric, retired to his palace at Heigham where he continued to produce challenging literary works, uncensored. He died there in 1656 at the age of 82 and was buried in St Bartholomew's Heigham.

Hampshire Hog Yard

Historic yard. Just north of St Swithin's church, off St Benedict's Street, this surviving remnant of an historic yard contains one of the only five remaining thatched buildings within the Walled City. In 1822 it is recorded as the Hamshire Hog pub although there is a reference to Sir Peter Seaman, Mayor in 1707, leaving a Public House in St Swithin's Alley in his will. It remained as a pub until 1912 when the license ceased. From November 1880, the licensee was John 'Licker' Pratt who had beaten the famous Jem Mace in a two hour bare

Opposite: Hungate Medieval Art when it was the first church museum in the country.

The former Hampshire Hog Public House.

knuckle boxing match at Drayton in his early career. The Hampshire Hog's other claim to fame was that it was the last pub in Norwich, and even possibly England, where Logats was played. This was a hybrid of skittles and bowls employing 22 inch long clubs (the Logat) being thrown at a wheel shaped jack. The building had declined by the 1930s but was restored by the Norwich Amenities Preservation Society. Opposite the Hog and behind the church was a medieval, gabled rectory which was less fortunate and fell victim to the slum clearance scheme of 1938.

Hannent, Antoinette

Local character. Antoinette Hannent, know universally as Black Anna (from her mode of dress), was a cultural icon in the Ber Street community in the mid C20th. With origins in Ber Street's Italian community, she became landlady of the Jolly Butchers and a regular performer in a venue regarded as one of the key music establishments in the City of that period.

Hansard, Luke

First Diarist of the House of Commons. Born in St Mary's parish and baptised in the church, Luke trained as a printer in Norwich but moved to London at the age of 17 to work for the printers to the House of Commons, John Hughs. In 30 years, he rose through the firm and, by the time the proprietor retired, Hansard took over the company and gave it his name. Hansard is now the term in common usage for the daily diary of Parliament although few realise that it comes from a poor Norwich lad who arrived in London with just a guinea and died worth £80,000.

Hardwick House

Former Bank and Head Post Office. Hardwick House was built in 1866 as the headquarters of the Harvey and Hudson Bank. It was generally known as the Crown Bank on account of the Harvey family crest which adorns the building. This elaborate stonework was carved by local mason Barnabas Barrett of Redwell Street, who also carved the 12 apostles on the flying buttresses of Norwich Cathedral. Hardwick House was designed by Philip Charles Hardwick (1822-1892) who was responsible for the rebuilding of Charterhouse in 1872, as well as several other schools, but he developed a special reputation for grand Victorian bank offices. In the City of London he designed offices for Roberts, Curtis, and Lubbock, Barclay and Bevan, the Union Bank of London and Drummond's. Hardwick House is his only building in Norwich.

Constructed in expensive Bath stone, when buildings entirely faced in stone were still a rarity in Norwich, the building cost £13,000. The classical design, with its grand portico, represented the solid reliability considered essential for a bank. It formed part of a new 'commercial hub' created between the 1860s and the 1880s, joining the City Centre to Thorpe Station via the commercial properties of Prince of Wales Road. The Harvey and Hudson Bank was a solid and growing business in 1866, when it moved to its new headquarters from an 18th Century building on King Street, now occupied by the Norfolk Club. It was one of a large number of interconnected banks and insurance houses in the City, in which the same family names; Harvey, Gurney, Barclay, Bignold and so on, occur again and again. Unfortunately, the solid respectability of the Crown Bank was not to last long. In 1870, financial instability caused by the outbreak of the Franco-Prussian War uncovered something that put the Crown Bank in a hopeless position. Co-Owner Sir Robert Harvey had opened false accounts to finance unsuccessful share speculations, and the banks debts were greater than its assets. When the

Hardwick House as the main Post Office in 1938.

bankruptcy was uncovered Sir Robert committed suicide by shooting himself. The collapse of the Crown Bank could have been a major disaster for its savers and investors, but another large Norwich Bank, Gurney and Co. (later Barclays) stepped in to meet the weekly wages of farmers and manufacturers. They acquired the bank, but their own brand new headquarters was just across the road at Bank Plain, so they had no further use for the building.

After standing empty from 1871-75, Hardwick House was found a suitable use when it was bought by the General Post Office. For almost the next 100 years the building was the central post office for Norwich. The Crown emblem was considered eminently suitable, and the words 'POST OFFICE' can still be seen where they were added underneath it. At the turn of the 20th century the post office expanded the building to the south, copying elements of the original design and dramatically changing the streetscape by cutting off Crown Road and demolishing a number of earlier buildings. By 1969 however the post office had

once again outgrown the site, and no further expansion was possible. The central post office moved into Bank Plain in 1970, and later into The Mall Norwich.

Hardwick House stood empty again for a period but was then refurbished, and heavily altered inside, to create a base for Anglia TV. This involved joining it to the Agricultural Hall with the glass extension you see today. In 2003 Hardwick House was sold again and converted into a mixture of residential apartments and office accommodation.

Hardy Road

See *Railway Cottages*.

Harford Bridges

The first bridge recorded on the Norwich to Ipswich Road is credited to the de Hereford family in the reign of King John. This was swept away by flood water and rebuilt in 1697 but history repeated itself in 1767. In 1832, a pair of brick bridges were built to carry the main Ipswich/ Norwich Road over the two sections of the river but these were demolished for a single, new, wider bridge in 1965. Just south of the road crossing, the six arched Harford Rail Viaduct was

constructed in 1848/9 to carry the newly developed Norwich to London railway line and it still fulfils that function.

Harmers

Lost clothing company. Formed in 1825 by Messrs Harmer and Rivett the company began as an importer of Manchester and Bradford Piece Goods (cotton textiles) from the north of England. This cloth was then sold on to tailors to make up into clothing – there were no ready made, 'off the peg' suits at the time. Frederick William Harmer discovered a French tailor who had developed a machine which could stitch two cloths together making 20 stitches in a minute – he claimed that this was the first sewing machine, although Elias Howe had secured the first American patent for a sewing machine in 1846 and Isaac Singer improved on this subsequently. Interestingly an Englishman, John Fisher, had produced a functioning machine in 1844 but the loss of his patent papers undermined his claim to be first. These points aside, Harmer bought two of the French machines and went into the production of made

Left: Harmers interior, early C20th.
Above: Early C20th view of Harmers in St Andrew's.

up suits. Adding other mechanisation he adopted steam power and became one of the first clothing companies to do so. The Steam Clothing Factory in Bethel Street was so successful that by 1887 it had outgrown its premises and a major new site was developed in St Andrews Street with a further innovation of electric lighting. By the turn of the century, the company had grown to such stature that Thomas Harmer became the first Chairman of the Wholesale Clothing Manufacturers association (Great Britain). During the First World War, Harmers produced uniforms for the military including over 1 million khaki garments. The company grew between the Wars and again responded to demand for service uniforms in 1939 but on May 1st 1942 the St Andrew's factory was obliterated by a devastating air raid. The company persisted however and developed a new, state of the art factory at Havers Road, creating significant employment for the Mile Cross area. Eventually an inability to compete with the production costs in developing countries led to the company closing in December 1989. The site remained vacant for some time and was eventually redeveloped for housing.

Harvey Family

Influential merchants. The Harveys made their fortune from the wool trade and, in return, provided eight mayors and seven sheriffs to the City. Thomas and Robert had substantial Georgian town houses on Colegate, which survive today as offices, and one is said to incorporate the recycled doorway to the now lost Duke of Norfolk's palace in St Andrews. A snapshot of this astonishing dynasty is captured in a 'portrait' by Joseph Clover in 1820, entitled 'The Harvey Family of Norwich.' It includes portraits of 26 different members of the family from four generations. An impressive collection of Harvey family memorials survive in St Clement, Colegate.

Haymarket

Historic space. Originally the term Haymarket applied to the large space to the south of St Peter Mancroft and this is where hay was sold. In the early C19th the Hay Market moved to the Castle Ditches so for a time the original site was called the Old Hay Market. In its hey day the space was surrounded by pubs including the White Horse, where the hangman resided, the White Hart, where prize fighters performed, and the George and Dragon (now McDonald's) which hosted a range of unusual acts including a 'female Samson'. Up until the end of the C19th, there were ancient buildings within the space including the appropriately named Barley Mow Inn but these were swept away in 1905 to provide a statue of Sir Thomas Browne by Henry Pegram. Haymarket is now applied to the street which runs up the east side of the former market space as far as Gentleman's Walk. With the Walk this provides an interesting microcosm of Norwich architectural history. The modernist Primark store (formerly Littlewoods and briefly M&S) is on the site of the C16th Star, one of the City's oldest coaching inns, and previously the medieval synagogue. Slightly further north, on the east side, the smart Georgian façade hides the Elizabethan mansion of John Curat, Sheriff in 1529, and a much earlier undercroft, possibly dating back to the time of the synagogue.

Haymarket Picture House

See *Picture House*.

Haymarket Synagogue

Lost Synagogue. The exact location of this building is unknown but excavations in 1962, prior to the building of the Primark store (formerly Littlewoods), yielded evidence to suggest that a synagogue once stood nearby. In particular, a large stone column was recovered and this is believed to have come from a synagogue. Also, at some point before 1696 a C13th bronze bowl was discovered close by. This, the Bodleian Bowl, is now in the Ashmolean Museum, Oxford and is decorated with a Hebrew inscription. It was likely used by the rabbi to wash his hands during services and it is thought that this bowl came from the site beneath the current Primark store.

The Haymarket Synagogue was built in about 1154 but may have only been in use for about 130 years. It is possible that the synagogue burnt down in 1286 or perhaps it was demolished in 1290 when Edward I expelled Jews from England. All Jews were ordered to quit the realm on pain of death by the 1st November 1290 and the land owned by Norwich's Jew was seized by the King.

Hearne, Richard

Children's entertainer.
Popular children's TV
personality of the 1950s Mr
Pastry was born, in 1908,
Richard Hearne at 21 Lady
Lane, formerly located on
the site of The Forum and
demolished to build the then
new central library in 1962.
His family had a theatrical
background with his father
being an acrobat and his
mother a serious actress.
At the age of just six weeks,
Richard made his first stage
appearance, in his mother's
arms, in a play at the
Theatre Royal Norwich. He
developed his TV show, as a
bumbling, walrus
moustached, bowler hated
old duffer, from a 1936
stage act with Fred Emney
and went on to be an
entertainment phenomenon
of the era to the extent that
he was invited onto the Ed
Sullivan Show in 1954 and
several times subsequently.
During these appearances
he is estimated to have had
audiences in excess of 120
million and commanded
enormous fees for the
period – as much as £125
per minute. It is said that he
was the first artist to be
known as a "television star"
and also the first to have his
own regular programme. In
1958 Hearne did a pilot TV
show with the legendary
Buster Keaton but Keaton
fell ill and returned to the
States before the pilot could
be developed. He was
offered the staring role in
Doctor Who but fell out with
the director about how the
Doctor should be played
and didn't take up the offer.
The move to the big screen
wasn't a success and by the
mid 1960s he had been
eclipsed by other rising
stars. He was awarded an
OBE for his charity work and
died in 1979 in Kent.

Heartsease

**Out of centre Council
estate.** The name
'Heartsease' derives from
the common name for the
viola tricolor, a flowering
plant of the genus viola. The
estate is located to the north
east of Norwich City Centre,
north of the Outer Ring
Road, and was built partly
on the former Mousehold
aerodrome and partly on
formerly undeveloped land
between 1954 and 1957 by
City Architect L.G. Hannaford
after the 1950 Norwich
Extension Act which
extended the City boundary.
The parish church is St
Francis', was built in 1956 in
part with money from War
Reparations grants,
distributed after the
destruction of six Medieval
churches within Norwich by
bombing during World War
II. Further residential
development followed in the
1960s including the City's
first tower blocks.

Heigham

Hamlet. Located on the
upper Wensum just west of
the early emerging borough
the hamlet derives its name
from the Old English
meaning homestead at a
'grate to catch fish at a
weir'. During this formative
period and at this point on
the river, the Wensum was
braided and provided the
later location for a number of
water mills. The medieval
parish church of St
Bartholomew, built in 1254,
was the original focus of the
community but was
destroyed in 1942 during
the Baedeker Raids,
although the tower still
stands today. The other
significant surviving historic
building is the remains of the
Dolphin, also known as
Bishop Hall's Palace, badly
bombed during the War and
restored subsequently. St
Phillip's church was built
sometime around 1872 but
was demolished in 1975
after three years of disuse.
As the City expanded in the
Victorian period, the term
'Heigham' was applied to a
much wider area of terraced
housing reaching south
towards the old Norfolk &
Norwich Hospital site.

Heigham Gate

Lost City Gate. Also known
as the Hell Gate, this
connected the hamlet of
Heigham to the City. The
Gate is recorded as having
existed in 1221 and was
rebuilt in the early C14th.
Blyth states that the gate
fell down in the mid C18th.

The Heartsease estate, home of the City's first tower blocks.

The Heigham or Hell Gate.

Heigham Park

Public park. Heigham Park was the first of the new, post WWI City Parks and was opened in 1924 to serve the large area of Victorian/Edwardian terrace housing to the west of the Walled City and to provide employment during the Depression. A key feature of the park is the Sunflower Gates, originally forming part of the Chapelfield Pagoda, designed and built by Thomas Jekyll and built by Barnard, Bishop and Barnards. The park contains the Royal National Rose Society's trial gardens, a bowling green and pavilion, lawn tennis courts, pergola, and a children's play area. It is located on the Avenues to the west of the City Centre in what is now referred to as the Golden Triangle.

Heins, John Theodore.

Portrait painter. Born in 1697 in Germany, Heins moved to Norwich at the age of 23 and settled to become a prolific portrait painter of the local aristocracy and merchant class. His subjects included

no less than 12 Mayors, the architect Matthew Brettingham, Nelson's mother, Thomas Gainsborough, George Frederick Handel and Sir Robert Walpole. A large number of Heins' portraits reside in the Civic Portrait Collection.

Hellesdon

Suburban parish. Located remotely to the north west of the early borough, close to the Brancaster Roman road, on the upper reaches of the Wensum and meaning Haegel's Hill from the Old English, Hellesdon now has 11,177 inhabitants. Historically the settlement straddled the City boundary with most of the early development on the City side and all of the modern development in what is now Broadland. There are signs of early settlement here going back as far as 4,000 years indicated by the discovery of flint instruments, and later bronze axe heads. A skeleton dating from 600 AD was discovered next to Hellesdon Lodge on Low Road. Buildings of historic

interest in Hellesdon Conservation Area include the C19th Hellesdon Lodge, featuring patterned brick chimneys probably originating from the demolished Costessey Hall. The site of Hellesdon Mill, which dates from 1851, and includes a sluice bridge and mill cottages is also of interest although the mill itself is now lost. There were two mills in Hellesdon in the Saxon period, but only one existed by the mid C16th. In 1683 the mill was rebuilt and then renovated in 1719. Fire had destroyed this structure by 1805, when it was rebuilt and was almost as large a structure as Costessey Mill. However, by 1864 the mill had fallen into disuse, but was bought by the Norwich Corporation in 1920 when it was gradually dismantled for timber to be used in the construction of the Angel Estate. A small section at the eastern end of the building remains, and a mill stone can still be seen today protruding from mud in the mill pond. The remains of the structure and its buildings, including the granary and malthouse, were developed as residential property in the early part of this century.

St Mary's church has its origins as far back as 1040 with the walls of the chancel and nave of the present day church dating from around that time. It has been argued that the earlier church may mark the place where King Edmund was intered in 869 after his martyrdom by the Danes, and before the relocation of the body to Bury St Edmunds in 880. However, it is now generally thought that this battle took place at Hoxne in Suffolk rather than Hellesdon. Present day St Mary's saw some alterations in the late C14th and was renovated in the mid 1800s.

In 1880 the Norwich Pauper Lunatic Asylum was established on the Drayton Road and became Hellesdon Hospital. The Royal Norwich Golf Club was founded in 1893 just north of the City boundary and straddling the Drayton Road. The majority of modern Hellesdon developed in the C20th well to the northeast of the original village, principally for relatively low density private housing although Mann

Egerton developed an engineering plant on the Cromer Road and built aircraft in WWI – this is now a series of car showrooms. The Boundary Park Stadium brought greyhound racing to the parish in 1932 and, with a short break for the War, this continued until 1962 when the site was used as a depot and eventually redeveloped as a major DIY superstore. The City's first hypermarket (a food and durable retail store with at least 60,000 sq ft of net selling space) appeared in the early 1980s north of Boundary Road and beside the 'Norwich Sport Village' – swimming pool and indoor sports courts. The latter has been extended recently to provide an ice rink.

Hellesdon Old Hall

Lost Hall. Neither within the parish of Hellesdon nor within the original hamlet, the Old Hall was located just north of the hamlet of Heigham to the west of what is the modern Mile Cross Road roughly on or close to the site of the former Council depot. It is probable that the Hall was demolished when the railway line was built.

Henderson, James Frederick

First Socialist councillor. Born in Norwich in 1867 and educated in Norwich and Manchester, Henderson's early career was as a journalist and poet. In 1885 he was sentenced to four months imprisonment at Norwich Castle following food riots and was one of the last people in England to be forced to work on a treadmill. He was elected to the Board of Guardians in 1890 and in 1902 became Norwich's first socialist councillor. His wife later joined him on the Council to become the first husband and wife to be elected as local councillors. He became Lord Mayor in 1939 and authored a number of influential books including 'The Case for Socialism' (1911), 'The Economic Consequences of Power Production' (1931) and 'Capitalism and the Consumer' (1935). The author Sir Henry Rider Haggard described Henderson's writing as "some of the most brilliant and yet most sound journalistic work of the period". He died in 1956 and was remembered by a school being named after him.

Henry I

King. In 1122 Henry I spent a week in Norwich over Christmas at the recently completed Royal Castle and reputedly granted the City a charter with the same franchises as the City of London.

Henry III

King. In 1256 Henry III came to Norwich and while there he granted a charter of Liberties to the port of Yarmouth, granted a Charter

The sluice at Hellesdon Mill.

Left: B24 Liberator of the type serving with the USAAF at Hethel. Below: Memorial in Hethel Churchyard to the USAAF 389th Bombardment Group.

to Norwich and spent £18 on candles for devotion in local churches. He returned in 1272, in one of the last acts before his death, to preside over a 13 day trial of the citizens responsible for 'the Riot'

Henry IV

King. In 1406 Henry IV visited the City following his grant of a new Charter in 1404 granting it the right to elect a mayor, sheriffs and aldermen.

Henry V

King. In 1415, Henry V pawned a gold coronet – containing 56 rubies, 40 sapphires, eight diamonds and seven pearls – with the City Corporation for 1,000 marks to fund his expedition to France which included the successful Agincourt campaign. Since prominent Norwich resident Sir Thomas Erpingham captained Henry's Archers at Agincourt, it is possible that the King may have visited Sir Thomas during his time in Norwich.

Henry VI

King. In 1448 the king paid a royal visit to Norwich and,

in celebration, the king's arms were displayed on six of the City Gates. In the following year he returned staying with the Earl of Suffolk at Costessey and then with Bishop Walter Lyhart for a week at his Palace.

Henry VII

King. In 1485 Henry VII was in Norwich for Christmas and 'was very honourably entertained by the corporation' before going on a pilgrimage to Walsingham. 14 years later he returned, with the queen, Elizabeth of York, and her mother for a further visit to the City.

Hethel

Suburban village. Hethel is a village of 445 people located 16km (10 miles) south west of Norwich. Its name comes from the Old English and means 'hill overgrown with heather'. The Saxon origin church of All Saints has a strange collection of styles ranging from the square Saxon tower, with later additions, to the C14th/C15th body of the church then the rather incongruous brick mausoleum dating from

1730, to the Branthwaite family. The churchyard also has the distinction of supporting the oldest living hawthorn tree in East Anglia and probably in the UK at 700 years old. The village also includes three attractive C17th farms and some early barns. RAF Hethel was developed here in 1941 and was occupied by the USAAF 389th Bomb Group from June 1943 until May 1945 when it reverted to the RAF who decommissioned it in 1947. Surviving structures include the Watch Office, three T2 type hangers and the HQ site complete with operations block and a restored gymnasium/chapel now housing a museum. In 1964 Colin Chapman set up Lotus cars here and the company continues today. In 2006 Norfolk County Council supported by the Regional Development Agency EEDA set up the Hethel Engineering Centre to support the growth and success of high performance engineering and manufacturing companies.

Hethersett

Suburban parish. Located 8km (5 miles) south of Norwich and deriving its name from the Old English meaning 'stag deer fold', Hethersett is a major dormitory village for Norwich with a population of 5441. Although the vast majority of the village is made up of largely unremarkable, post War residential development, Hethersett is relatively rich in historic buildings. The connection between the City and the parish is a long standing one with no fewer than 12 mayors holding land and properties in the parish throughout its history. There has been a church in the village since before the Conquest and the dedication to the C5th Bishop of Rheims, who converted the French king Clovis to Christianity, suggests an early connection with this saint. A dedication to Remigius is quite rare with only six such dedications in England (four of these in Norfolk). The present church is essentially C14th with C15th additions and a major refurbishment in 1874. There are a number of significant, surviving historic houses around the core of the village including the

C16th Manor House at Cann's Lane, the C16th Priory (Norwich Road) which was remodelled and added to in 1607/8, Wood Hall (Norwich Road), which is C17th around an earlier core, Hethersett Old Hall (now a school) built in 1774 and the C18th Whitegates with later additions by the County Architect in 1976 for the Norfolk Fire Service. Cantley House has a C16th wing and a C17th main structure and is the only remnant of the lost Cantley village. The other major historic structure is Thickthorn Hall which commemorates the lost hamlet of Thickthorn and medieval manor, now lost, on the site of the estate. The present house was built in 1812 for William Clarke of Ketteringham but he had to forfeit the property to Norwich banker Richard Hanbury Gurney when he failed to pay off the loan which had financed construction. It passed from the Gurneys to the Colmans in 1930 who added an Adam chimney piece in the drawing room and a Gibbons chimney piece and matching doors in the master bedroom, recycled from nine Nash properties demolished in London to

accommodate the Savoy Hotel. The 'salvage' came mainly from the house of Sir James Barrie, creator of Peter Pan. There is a range of other interesting structures in the village including the C17th Queen's Head pub and the C18th King's Head pub, the Smithy probably dating from 1700, the C16th Beech Cottage, the C16th Myrtle Cottage, the early C17th Cedar grange, a number of barns and four milestones from the 1767 Norwich Turnpike.

Hildebrond's Hospital

Lost caring institution. Founded in c.1200 by Hildebrond le Mercer and his wife (Maud) in King Street, to the south east of St Etheldreda's church yard, on land purchased by Roger de Dunewiz. The founder also built, for use of the brethren, a chapel adjoining the west end of St Edward's church (dedicated to Edward the Confessor). The hospital was a facility where poor people could find lodging, warmth and food and would, in return, pray for the quick passage of their benefactors' souls through Purgatory. It consisted of a hall with a large chamber above, with

From left: Hethersett King's Head Public House, Hethersett County Fire Service headquarters.

several small rooms for lodgings. This was dedicated to St Mary. After the parishes of St Edward and St Julian were united in 1269, the church became dedicated entirely to the hospital. It was intended for poor travellers and pilgrims who were given a fire, lodging, and provisions for a certain period. In 1547 the hospital was dissolved, and granted to the City. The church was demolished but the hospital continued under the name Ivy Hall or St Edward's hospital. Nothing now remains of the site.

Hills & Underwood

Lost vinegar works.
Established in 1792, the Norwich Vinegar Works and Gin Distillery went on to be the largest plant of its kind in East Anglia. Started by Francis Gosling, the enterprise was taken over by Squire & Hills in 1817 and ultimately became Hills & Underwood. A new factory was built in 1865 between Prince of Wales Road and St Faiths Lane including offices, fermenting rooms,, vat stores, gin stills, spirit stores, boilers and warehouses. The site incorporated an ancient stone bridge which had formed part of the dissolved Greyfriars Friary. The company was incorporated with Sir Robert Burnett & Co in 1911 and subsequently closed and entirely redeveloped.

Hindes

Now lost silk manufacturer.
Ephraim Hinde founded a silk manufacturing company in 1810 in St Marys and it went on to became one of the largest and certainly longest sustained in the City. St Mary's Silk Mills was a the core of a multi site

empire and, despite devastation by WWII bombing in 1942, it prevailed to be the last surviving remnant of what had been a key Norwich industry when it finally closed in 1965. The site is now largely developed for sheltered housing although its name, Silkfields, commemorates it rich past.

Hippodrome

Former theatre and cinema.
Built as the Grand Opera House in 1903, on the site of the Norfolk Hotel, and renamed the Hippodrome in 1904, the venue specialised in variety acts but was showing films in the Hippodrome Bioscope before the first 'proper cinemas' came onto the scene.

Between both world wars, some of the greatest names in entertainment, such as Charlie Chaplin, Marie Lloyd, and Gracie Fields, performed on the Hippodrome stage. The Hippodrome became a permanent cinema in 1930 but reverted to variety in 1937. During the Baedeker Blitz in 1942, the building suffered a direct hit when the manager, his wife and the trainer of a group of sea lions were killed. The Hippodrome re-opened after the war and in the early 1950s it was again a popular venue for variety acts including Laurel and Hardy, Max Miller, Morecambe and Wise and the Goons. There was also an annual Christmas Pantomime.

The last variety show was performed there in 1958 and for the next two years, the Hippodrome became the home of The Norfolk Playhouse Repertory Company. The old building

gradually fell into disrepair and finally it stood empty and vandalised until, in 1964, it was demolished to be replaced in 1966 by the St Giles Multi-storey Car Park and St Giles House offices for the Council.

HMSO

Former major employer.
In the late 1960s a major Government initiative to move civil service jobs out from London to 'the provinces' saw Her Majesty's Stationery Office transferred to Norwich. This triggered the redevelopment of a large area of the northern City Centre and the construction of Sovereign House by Alan Cooke associates, to accommodate the move, as the cornerstone of the much unloved Anglia Square development.

Hobart House

Post-Medieval mansion.
A third significant house, after the Palaces of the Dukes of Norfolk and the Earl of Surrey, in post medieval Norwich, was that of Sir John Hobart which had 50 hearths. This consisted of reused and reconstructed elements of the surviving buildings of the College of St Mary in the Fields (currently parts of the Assembly House). These were first acquired by the last Dean, Miles Spencer, and then the Cornwallis family after his death. The Hobarts of Blickling bought the property in 1609 and developed a two winged town house around the monastic cloister, probably joined to the original Great Hall of the College which had survived the Reformation demolition which had removed the collegiate church.

Hodgson, David

Local artist. Hodgson's father was a founder member of the Norwich Society of Artists and Hodgson himself became one of its most active and articulate members. Making his living as a drawing master, he specialised in architectural subjects and his paintings, along with those of Ninham, provide some of the most detailed and evocative records of life on the streets of central Norwich in the mid C19th. The best examples include Norwich Fishmarket 1849, St James Norwich 1826, Norwich Market and Norwich Castle (1834 and 1844).

Holkham House

Georgian town house. Located on the west side of Cow Hill, Holkham House was built, probably by Matthew Brettingham, architect of Holkham Hall in North Norfolk, in the same materials and in a similar but scaled down style.

Holmstrete

See *Bishopgate*.

Holmes

See *Edwards & Holmes*.

Holy Cross Church, Stoke Holy Cross

Medieval parish church. This is principally a C13th structure with C14th alterations and a porch of 1501. There was a major restoration in 1879. Leaning against the tower outside is a C15th font. Inside there is a monument from 1719 to Thomas Havers and quite a lot of Victorian stained glass by Kings, Ward & Hughes.

Holy Trinity, Saxon Burgh

See *Christchurch*.

Holy Cross Church, Stoke Holy Cross.

Holy Trinity, Trinity Street

Victorian, suburban parish church. Built in 1859-61 by William Smith in response to the development of large areas of terraced housing just outside the western City Walls, the successful design was selected from 60 contenders. Although the tower was originally intended to be developed later, pressure from the local media resulted in the development taking place as a single piece. With a capacity of 1200 seated, this represents one of the larger parish churches in the City and remains an active Anglican venue.

Holy Trinity Church, Trinity Street.

Hooker, Sir William

Botanist. Born in Norwich in 1785, William Jackson Hooker was one of the most eminent botanists of his age. He went on to be Regis Professor of Botany at Glasgow University and the first Director of the Royal Botanic Gardens at Kew. He was made a Knight of Hanover in 1836. His son Joseph Dawson Hooker was an equally eminent botanist and succeeded him to the directorship of Kew.

Hopkins, Matthew

Witchfinder. In 1645, Witchfinder General Matthew Hopkins visited the City and singled out 40 unfortunate

Local publication of Witchfinder General, Matthew Hopkins.

From left: Horsford Hall and Horsford Mill.

women to be tried as witches at the Norwich Assize Court. He produced a book, first published in Norwich, cataloguing his activities in Norfolk.

Horsford

Suburban Parish. Horsford is located approximately six miles north-northwest of Norwich City Centre on the Holt Road and has a population of around 4,000 people, which has grown from only 750 in 1945. There are various ideas as to the derivation of the name, but 'Horsford' may refer to the River Hor, (also known as the River Beck), or to 'Horse Ford', although Horsa is also the word for a Saxon chief. There are a number of sites of historical interest located in Horsford. Horsford Castle, located off Church Street, is an C11th motte and bailey castle that was built for Walter de Cadomo but abandoned after 1431. Unfortunately the bailey was ploughed in the 1980s but a management agreement now ensures that it is a well maintained earthwork. All Saints church has the year 1703 inscribed in red tiles on the side of the thatched chancel, which

possibly corresponds to the year of a great storm. There is a Norman font, as well as a collection of C15th glass in the north aisle window, and allegedly the region's finest example of a C19th stained glass window by the Royal Bavarian Institute for Stained Glass. The late C18th Horsford Hall stands opposite the church and was built for the Day family. Horsford smockmill was built in 1819 on Mill Lane at St Helena, but was demolished between 1860 and 1865 to make way for Horsford towermill, also known as St Helens mill, which was derelict by 1922. However, the mill still exists today in the grounds of a residential property and is being renovated. In terms of flora and fauna, the nearby Horsford Woods have been made a County Wildlife Site and are the home to a colony of rare Silver-Studded Blue butterflies.

Horsham and Newton St Faiths

Suburban parish. Located around four miles north of Norwich City Centre, north of Norwich International Airport off the A140 are the villages of Horsham and Newton St

Faiths. Newton lies one mile north of Horsham. The name 'Horsham' derives from the River Hor which runs through the village. A Benedictine priory was founded here in 1105 in the name of St Faith and after the dissolution of the monasteries around 1536 was granted to Richard Southwell along with Horsham Manor. Southwell had the majority of the buildings and the priory church demolished, but converted the refectory into a residential property which still stands in the village today. A C13th painting portraying the founding of the priory, and incorporating apparently the earliest depiction of a wheelbarrow in England, was recently discovered in the house behind Tudor panelling. The painting is of exceptional quality and of national importance. Local folklore has it that here is an underground tunnel which connects the motte and bailey castle at Horsford to the priory of St Faith. There are records of Horsham dating back to the Saxon period and in 1186 William Malet was the Lord of the Manor, when the settlement is recorded in the Domesday Book as having two watermills and a population of 200. Interestingly, Catherine Howard spent her childhood with the Dowager Duchess of Norfolk in Horsham St Faith. Horsham St Faiths was the site of one of the largest cattle fairs in the country held annually on the 17th of October between the time of the founding of the Priory and 1872. It is said that, in its later years, over 20,000 beasts passed through the St Faiths Cattle fair within a three week period. St Mary and St Andrew's church is a grade I listed property dating from the C13th. The West Tower dates from 1290, although the church was restored in 1873 after a donation from the Twinings family, to which the windows are dedicated. Located opposite the church is the C18th Waytes House and the Church Sunday School and Mission Room dating from 1880

which features a Norman doorway taken from the St Faiths Priory. Horsham St Faiths has historically been the site of three mills, sadly none of which exist today. The water mill was recorded as early as 1325 but had ceased operation before World War II and was demolished. Horsham St Faiths postmill existed by 1794, but had ceased working by 1849. The smockmill was located on a hill above the old Norwich Road on land now owned by St Faiths crematorium and was recorded in 1849, although by 1891 it had fallen into disuse.

Horsham St Faith's Aerodrome

Former RAF base now Norwich International Airport. Started in 1939 as part of the hurried air defence programme for Britain, and opened in June 1940, the formerly empty site north of Norwich began

P47 Thunderbolt as flown from Horsham St Faiths.

life with grass runways, five 'type C' hangers and an art deco style 'Villa' type watch office, both of which still survive. While Blenheims, operating out of RAF Watton, were dispersed there during construction, to avoid damage during enemy raids, the first operational aircraft were Spitfires from 19 and 66 Squadrons. Boulton Paul Defiants of 264 Squadron were also early residents. The aerodrome's first bombers, for which it was originally intended, were Bristol Blenheim IVs of 114

Clockwise from top left: Horsham St Faiths – historic cottages, Priory mural, Priory mural (wheelbarrow), Priory.

and 139 Squadrons. In 1941 the Mosquitos of 105 Squadron replaced the Blenheims and they operated until September 1942 when the airfield was handed over to the US Army Air Force and B26 Maurauders from the 319th Bomb Group arrived. After a short stay, these were replaced by P47 Thunderbolts of the 56th Fighter Group led by the inspirational Col Hubert Zemke. In 1943 the site closed for the construction of three concrete runways designed to receive the B24 Liberators of the 458th Bomb Group in 1944 and they maintained occupation until the site passed back to the RAF in June 1945. RAF Fighter command continued to operate the site with a mix of Mosquitos, Hornets, Meteors and Hunters until the site became Norwich Airport, operated jointly by the City and County Councils from 1965.

Horsefair/ Horsemarket

Lost market. This is a small triangle of space in St Faiths Lane which was used for horse fairs annually on the Thursday before Good Friday, Whit Sunday and Trinity Fairs. The fairs were prevalent in the reigns of Edward I and II (1272-1327) but later moved to the Castle Ditches. The more frequent horse market however, was located in Rampant Horse Street outside the C13th Rampling Horse Inn (Debenhams) but this also moved to a site closer to the castle and remained at Bell Avenue well into the C20th.

Hospital

See *Norfolk & Norwich Hospital and Norfolk & Norwich University Hospital.*

Hotels

Visitor accommodation current and past. The City has had examples of the hospitality industry from the earliest times. The Maids Head claims to be one of the oldest continuously running hotels in England and, although recorded as an inn in 1287, there is evidence that it was accommodating guests to the Benedictine Priory before that. Although hostelries appeared all over the historic City, the bulk were concentrated around the Market with icons such as the Angel and the King's Head on the east side. In the Victorian and Edwardian period, 'grande dames' such as the Royal came and eventually went. Today, little remains of the great hospitality legacy apart from the historic Maids Head. Most are long gone although some, such as the Bell, have survived in other guises. Current offerings, from top end to budget, including some recently deployed 'high end' B&Bs are as follows:

Hotels

- **Sprowston Manor** – Marriott, 4 star, 3 miles N of centre
- **De Vere Dunston Hall** – 4 star, 4 miles S of centre
- **St Giles House** – boutique, in centre
- **Holiday Inn Norwich North** – 2.7 miles N of centre
- **Holiday Inn Express Sport Village** – 3 miles N of centre
- **Ramada** – 3 miles N of centre
- **Holiday Inn South** – 2.4 miles S of centre
- **Maids Head** – beside Cathedral
- **Old Rectory** – 2 miles E of Centre
- **Best Western Annesley** – 1 mile S of centre
- **Georgian House** – just outside City Walls
- **Best Western George** – 1.5 miles S of centre
- **Beeches** – beside the Catholic Cathedral
- **Holiday Inn Norwich City** – just outside City Walls beside football club
- **Premier Travel Inn Nelson** – opposite Railway Station
- **Premier Inn Duke Street** – City Centre
- **Travelodge** – beside bus station.

B&Bs

- **Catton Old Hall** – 2 miles N of centre
- **No 17** – in Colegate, City Centre
- **The Grove**, Bracondale – south edge of centre.

Howard, Henry Earl of Surrey

Poet and soldier. Born the son of Thomas Howard, 3rd Duke of Norfolk, Henry courted controversy for most of his short life. He was first cousin to Anne Boleyn and accompanied her and Henry VIII to the court of the King of France in 1532, where he stayed for a time. Later he served Henry VIII as a soldier in putting down rebellions at home and securing territory overseas. When Anne Boleyn was executed and the Seymores came to prominence, fortunes changed for the Howards and Henry oscillated in and out of favour but was eventually tried for treason and executed. A talented poet, he is thought to have been the first English writer to use blank verse. Along with Thomas Wyatt, he introduced sonnet form to England. Together, the couple are known as the 'Fathers of the English Sonnet.' His father had Surrey Palace built for Henry in Surrey Street and he also occupied Mount Surrey, a 'sumptuous' house on St Leonards Hill during his visits to the City. Holbein painted him in 1542 just five years before his death.

Howard House

Howard House, the Garden House of the Dukes of Norfolk is located on the southern junction of King Street with Mountergate and was built by Henry Howard in 1660. It is possible that the building incorporated remnants of the gatehouse of the medieval Austin Friary which had occupied the site prior to the Reformation. Howard House contains one of the most elaborate Jacobean stair cases in England. The adjoining 'fair garden' as Thomas Baskerville called it in 1681 had 'a good bowling green and many fine walks'. Following the departure of the Dukes of Norfolk from the City, the site became My Lord's garden – one of the principal pleasure gardens in the City. Ultimately it was taken over by Morgans King Street Brewery and then by Watney Mann before they closed down brewing in the City in the 1980s. It has remained vacant ever since and is currently (2011) a building at risk.

Howlet & White's

See *Norvic*.

Hungate Medieval Art

Museum of church art. After centuries of use as a church, St Peter Hungate had become delapidated by 1931 and was threatened with demolition. Norfolk Archaeological Trust stepped in to refurbish the building and St Peter's became the first church in the country to be used as a museum and indeed the first church museum. In 1995, however, budget cuts forced the museum to close and the contents were removed to other county museums. The building remained empty until 2009 when a new charitable organisation opened it as Hungate Medieval Art – a centre to promote and showcase the art of the medieval churches of Norfolk. The building is open to the public on Thursdays, Fridays and Saturdays with group visits possible at other times.

Hunt, John

Ornithologist. Now virtually unknown, Hunt's three volume work, British Ornithology, published between 1815 and 1822, is one of the earliest and most

Howard House from King Street.

ambitious works seeking to catalogue and describe the wild bird species of Britain. Born, probably in St Clement's parish in 1777, the son of a weaver, Hunt had worked his way up to be a stationer and bookseller by 1801 and had married well. It is probable that his wife, the daughter of wealthy merchant and twice mayor Sir John Harrison Yallow, brought resources to the family coffers that enabled Hunt to indulge his passion for ornithology. His first volume of British Ornithology was published in 1815. He had engraved all of the plates himself and hand coloured a proportion of them – his son had coloured the rest. The second volume followed subsequently and the third was printed in 1822. In all he had described 220 species supported by 180 hand coloured plates. He worked not with live specimens (in an age before cameras and effective field glasses) but relied rather upon dead specimens being brought to him by local sportsmen and wildfowlers. A large proportion of these were subsequently stuffed and sold from his shop in St Stephens. British Ornithology was a scientific milestone but not a commercial success which is probably why less than a dozen complete copies survive today.

St Peter Hungate medieval Art Centre.

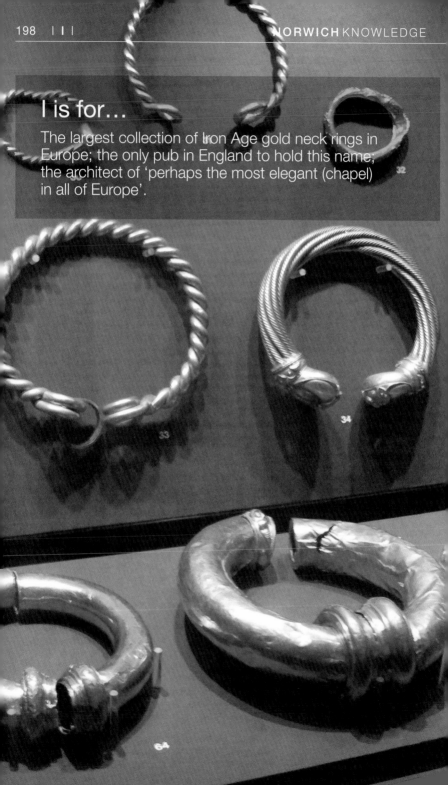

I is for...

The largest collection of Iron Age gold neck rings in Europe; the only pub in England to hold this name; the architect of 'perhaps the most elegant (chapel) in all of Europe'.

Ice House Lane

Surviving ice house. Years before the refrigerator, Colmans constructed an ice house in the garden of No. 7 Carrow Hill. Ice was taken from the frozen river and stored in a brick lined subterranean pit to provide ice in the summer months. As well as using it for commercial purposes, Colmans made it available for more philanthropic purposes.

Ignatius, Father

Born Joseph Leycester Lyne in 1837, Father Ignatius was a colourful character. From an early age his religious fervour dominated his life, owing it is said to an intense fear of hell and damnation. Despite styling himself 'Father Ignatius', Lyne was never ordained as a priest but his passion and skill as a preacher meant that the congregations of churches at which he assisted often increased dramatically. Over the years he gained an interesting reputation. He was reputed to have performed several miracles, including the resurrection of two people and a horse. Equally he was accused of cursing those with whom he argued, and who subsequently were said to have fallen down dead. Father Ignatius came to Norwich in 1861 during his quest to re-establish monasticism in the Anglican Church. He had already tried to establish a monastery elsewhere but its failure brought him to Norwich. Initially he was welcomed by the local clergy and in 1864 a lady admirer put up the money for Father Ignatius to build a monastery on Elm Hill. The Monastery survives as a red brick building to the right of the car park

entrance. It was later used as a factory and is now part of University College of the Arts.

The monastery began to flourish but soon the outspoken zeal of Father Ignatius bred enemies amongst Norwich citizens. Mobs of angry people and police are said to have surrounded the monastery and even Father Ignatius' monks began to turn against him. They were aggrieved by his strict rules and the fact that he did not practise what he preached. Each of these problems he overcame but when Father Ignatius discovered that a dance had been held on formerly consecrated ground, he severely chastised his congregation and those who had attended the dance he debased and cruelly humiliated in front of the others. This was the final straw and support for the community began to wane. It is said that his monks were half starved and in need of fuel for their fires and his own health had begun to deteriorate. To try to relieve his condition, Father Ignatius travelled to Rome. On his return in 1866

he discovered that his monastery was all but empty and up for sale. The Archbishop of Canterbury advised him to take legal action but despite spending his entire inheritance fighting the closure, the twelve year legal struggle ended in failure. Father Ignatius had long since fled to Llanthony, South East Wales where he tried to rebuild his life and to establish another monastery.

Inner Ring Road

Orbital road. The brain child of City Engineer Horace Rowley, the Inner Ring Road first appeared as a concept in the 1945 City of Norwich Plan but as an addendum which criticised the proposals within the Plan. While the 1945 Plan proposed a Ring Road around the edge of the City Walls and used Rosary Road with a new viaduct crossing the river at Carrow in the east, Rowley suggested an alternative which cut through the medieval City in the north, effectively following the present route, and in the south he proposed a link from Brazen Gate to Riverside in the form of a 'cut and cover' tunnel.

Opposite: Iron Age torques, Castle Museum.
Below: Inner Ring Road under construction, 1970s.

Houses on Ipswich Rd.

He also favoured a route which created a dual carriageway all the way along the River on the east side. Not a great deal happened until the 1960s when Colin Buchanan published his seminal work Traffic in Towns and used Norwich as a case study, recommending a 'Ring and Loop' solution to its traffic problems. The newly established City Planning Department under Alfie Wood subsequently produced the Draft Urban Plan which put forward a solution remarkably close to Buchanan's and using Rowley's 'Ring', with some minor tweeking in the south. The fundamental difference between the two was that while Rowley's scheme also created dual carriageway 'boulevards' through the historic centre, the Ring and Loop/Draft Urban Plan (DUP) closed the centre to through traffic.

Implementation of the scheme progressed in the late 1960s with the construction of the western (Barn Road/Grapes Hill) section, necessitating the demolition of Victorian terraces along the City Wall, but also and most outrageously, the demolition of the Wall itself along Grapes Hill. The northern section (St Crispins) was developed at the same time as Anglia Square and the Queens Road/Chapelfield section came in the 1970s. Work did not progress on the east and south however, and with the County Council taking over responsibility for highway matters in 1974, there was a polarisation of views between the two Councils about how things should progress. This came to a head in the 1990s when the County Council proposed the construction of the southern section of the road including the 'cut and cover' tunnel beneath Ber Street. The proposals were opposed strongly by the City Council, who ironically engaged technical support from Malcolm Buchanan (Colin's son) and received enthusiastic support from environmental campaigners and the Norwich Society. The Inner Ring Road completion went to a major public inquiry and eventually the Conservative Secretaries of State for both Transport and the Environment threw out the scheme, upholding the City Council's case that it would be too damaging. At around the same time, the emerging Riverside development allowed the Ring Road to be taken away from the old Riverside and realigned behind the redevelopment scheme, along the new Koblenz Way. The Inner Ring therefore remains a partially complete road with the most congested section being the part from Carrow bridge west to Bracondale where the Inner and Outer Rings share the same road space. The situation was alleviated to a degree in the 1990s by the construction of the Southern Bypass.

Intwood

Suburban village. Located 4.8km (3 miles) south west of Norwich, the tiny village of Intwood has its origins in Saxon times. This is reflected in Intwood's oldest building, the church of All Saints, which has a round Saxon tower and a Norman origin nave. There was a major restoration in 1590 and a further Victorian restoration in 1852. Sir Thomas Gresham built a six bay, hall at Intwood in 1560 and this was occupied by Sir Henry Hobart in 1590. While the surviving walled garden and garden buildings, including a gazebo, date from this period, the original house is gone, replaced by the present Hall, by Arthur Browne in 1807, in the Tudor style. The thatched lodge dates from 1844.

Ipswich Road

Radial Road. With Newmarket Road, this has been the historic, principal entry to the City from the south and from London. The 1838 Ordnance Survey reveals that the road is virtually undeveloped apart from some lime kilns north of Marston Lane, two nurseries, the Prussia Gardens, an out of City pleasure garden, and probably only two major residential properties – Harford Hill House, half way down on the east side, and an un-named house close to the junction with Newmarket Road, which is probably the early C18 villa destined to eventually become Town

Close School. By the 1898 Ordnance Survey, there is much more intensive development in the 'Townclose triangle' with a number of Victorian villas appearing as well as the Grove on the opposite side of Ipswich Road, forming part of the Trafford Estate. Chris Barringer singles out No. 13, built in 1887, as perhaps the best example of Queen Anne Revival in Norwich. Harford Hill House had been developed to become Harford Hall but apart from this, development remained sparse. Between the Wars and then following the Second World War, more infill development occurred at the 'City end' of the road but the substantial additions were the City College scheme which opened in 1953, the Eaton Rise Estate of mainly private

bungalows, west of the road, and the Tuckswood Council Estate which was developed on the former Harford Estate and incorporated Harford Hall as the residence of the Clerk of the Markets until it was demolished in the 1950s. The Post House Hotel, designed by John Sansom, was developed on allotments in 1972.

Iron Age
See below.

Ironmongers Arms

Historic pub. A house has occupied this site since at least 1303 and the present structure dates from the early C17th. For a long period it acted as a baker's shop, this building has served as licensed premises since 1869. Until 2003 it

Iron Age

Activity between 800 BC and 43 AD. Despite spectacular finds in Norfolk, such as the Snettisham Treasure, evidence of Iron Age activity within the Norwich area remains sparse. Significant rescue archaeology along the line of the Southern Bypass in 1990 revealed at least six

square ditch enclosures at Harford Farm which could date from the Iron Age. Other finds include a late Iron Age field system at Eaton in 1971 and five silver Iceni coins at Weston Road before 1940. It is possible that an Iron Age settlement pre dated the Roman town of Venta Icenorum at Caister and current (2010) archaeological investigations

Iron Age torques, Castle Museum.

should cast more light on the early history of the site. However, within Norwich, the Castle Museum does hold the largest collection of Iron Age gold neck rings in Europe, coming from the discovery at Snettisham.

Italian ice cream vendor, Ber Street.

The Italian community was further swelled by post First World War immigration and by prisoners of war from the Second World War who made their homes in the City once the conflict had concluded. One significant expatriot was Moray Smith (his surname was adopted from his Costessey born wife), an Italian gypsy artist, whose work included the monumental pub murals at the Coachmakers in St Stephens, the Berstrete Gates and the Prince of Denmark. Arguably his best work is a set of six bas-relief plaques in the Woolpack (Golden Ball Street) depicting the wool trade.

Ives Family

Mayors and Sheriffs. This influential mercantile dynasty of the C18th is confusing because four of the prominent members were all called Jeremiah. The first significant Ives (Jeremiah I) came from Bourne in Lincolnshire and was born in 1692. He had established himself to such a degree in Norwich by the early C18th however, that he had become Sheriff by 1726 and Mayor by 1733. His memorial in St Clement tells us "for three years(he) endured the torture of the stone with invincible fortitude of mind" until he finally succumbed in 1741. Jeremiah I's nephew, also Jeremiah (known as the Elder of St Saviours), was Sheriff in 1748 and Mayor in 1756. The next Jeremiah Ives (the Younger of St Clements) was cousin to 'the Elder of St Saviours' and son of 'Jeremiah I'. 'The 'Younger' was born in 1729 and died in 1805. He was Sheriff in 1763 and Mayor in 1769 and 1795. Originally he lived opposite St

was called the Ironmongers' Arms – believed to have been the only pub so-named in England. After a brief spell as 'Bolts' then 'Mikes' it was thoroughly refurbished and opened in 2011 as a restaurant/deli called The Ironhouse.

Italians

Italian Immigrants. During the early C19th a significant Italian community, seeking a new life, settled in the City. Some early arrivals had included Italian goldsmith, George Rossi, who had fought with Marshall Soult, Napoleon's Chief of Staff at Waterloo, before making a career move to Norwich and establishing a business in Guildhall Hill which survived for four generations. Italian sculptor Pellegrino Mazzotti, from Lucca, also established a studio adjoining Strangers Hall in 1819. Towards the end of the C19th there was a more significant influx of Italians who arrived by boat

at Great Yarmouth – some thinking that they were landing in New York – and others, such as Elizabeth Marcantonio, who made the three month trek from Italy to Calais on foot then reached Norwich via London. They brought with them a range of trades and skills including leather working but most notably the introduction of ice cream making to the City. A 'Little Italy' blossomed around Ber Street where there were at least six ice cream kitchens, including that of 'Big Peter' Chiesa, the City's first ice cream man. The Italians ran pubs, including the Fox and Hounds in Ber St (Mr Banalari), the cheapest café in the City apparently (Mr Parrivanni), restaurants (Marcantonios), fishmongers and demolition businesses (Valori). Others included specialist Italian craftsmen who contributed to the detailing of St Peter Mancroft, the Royal Arcade and the Marble Hall.

Clements in Colegate but then moved to Town Close House 'His unbounded, though undivulged benevolence and his exclusive charities were the more convincing proofs of an humane disposition and Christian philanthropy.' He is also buried in St Clements. His sister Lydia married Thomas Harvey, Mayor in 1748. Lydia and Thomas had a son called Jeremiah Ives Harvey who became Mayor in 1783 and is also buried in St Clements. The next Jeremiah (of St Georges Tombland and Catton) was sheriff in 1782 and mayor in 1786 and 1801. His sister Ann also married a Harvey – Robert Harvey, Mayor in 1787. Jeremiah moved from his house in Tombland and took over the Catton estate in 1788 commissioning Humphry Repton to lay out Catton Park. He died in 1820 and is buried in

St Margarets at Old Catton. To confuse matters further three Jeremiah Ives' as well as Jeremiah Ives Harvey were all alive at the same time.

Ivory, Thomas

Pre-eminent Georgian Architect in Norwich. Born in 1709 and starting his working life as a builder and joiner, Ivory became carpenter at the Great Hospital in 1851 although this role was much more significant than the title suggests, being more an estate manager and architect. His success is reflected in the stature of the house that he designed for himself adjacent to the Hospital (St Helen's House) which, even for the time, was grand both outside and in. In 1751 he built what was later to become known as the Tabernacle (demolished in 1953) in Bishopgate and this was followed by the commission for the Octagon

in 1754, described by John Wesley subsequently as 'perhaps the most elegant one in all Europe'. In the same year he got to work on the transformation of the former College of St Mary in the Fields into the Assembly House, with the interior work taken on by Sir James Burroughs, Master of Gonville and Caius College, Cambridge. The new Theatre Royal followed this, based on Drury Lane in London. His final, and terminal, commission was the remodelling of Blickling Hall, where a large piece of timber fell on his leg during construction and resulted in his eventual death in 1779 – his son finished the work. Other buildings produced by Ivory include Ivory House in 1771 (which became the Militia Barracks in 1860 and subsequently the Artillery Barracks) and St Catherine's House in All Saints Green and 25-35 Surrey Street.

Ivory House Bishopgate, and interiors.

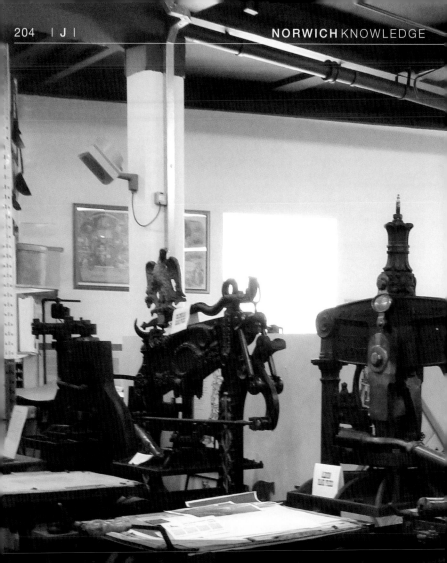

J is for...

The earliest domestic dwelling in Norwich and one
of the earliest in England; first provincial, in-patient
children's hospital in the country; wealthiest,
provincial, medieval Jewish community; earliest
recorded private herb garden in England; City's first
female MP and one of the first woman MPs in the
UK; author of the first surviving book by a woman
in the English language.

Entrance to James Stuart Gardens.

The Jacquard loom.

James Stuart Court and Gardens

Designed by Edward Boardman & Son in 1914 these Dutch gabled, alms house style cottages were built in memory of Privy Councillor James Stuart, husband of Laura Colman and paid for by the Colman family. Stuart had been an enthusiastic campaigner for improving the housing conditions of the poor and elderly. The gardens on the opposite side of Recorder Road were a gift from Laura Stuart to the City of Norwich and were opened in 1922.

Jacquard club

Former music venue. Located on the east side of Magdalen Street in a surviving C17th jettied house, the Jacquard was established by local impresario Albert Cooper as a folk, jazz and blues club in the 1960s. It supported all kinds of alternative performers until the early 1990s. The club took its name from the Jacquard loom.

Jacquard loom

Weaving innovation. This was a mechanised loom invented in 1801 by Joseph Marie Jacquard and was the first machine to use punch cards to control the operational sequence. As such it was a crude ancestor of the computer. Jacquard looms were imported into Norwich in the early C19th and were employed in the production of high quality Norwich shawls. The firm Willett & Nephew was the first to use them. An original Jacquard loom survives in the Bridewell Museum.

Jarrold

Major local company. Jarrold started life in Woodbridge, Suffolk, as a drapers and grocers in 1770. By 1823 it had moved to the south side of London Street – to sell books and stationery – into what had traditionally been the printing and bookselling quarter of the City. Printing joined the book selling operation at Jarrold in 1830. In 1840, the company moved to the present site on London Street, between Exchange Street and Little London Street. Coincidentally, the

Below: Jarrold advertising from 1860.
Opposite: John Jarrold Printing Museum.

site had previously been occupied by one of the City's leading booksellers, William Oliver, who had set up there in 1662 and his descendants had maintained his business on the site until the mid C18th. Jarrold expanded both its business and range and by 1903 had commissioned the iconic Norwich Architect George Skipper to build them a new department store. The store was extended further in 1964 when Jarrold bought and redeveloped T.D. Barry's Corn Exchange. In 2004, the surviving medieval building on the corner of Little London Street was sensitively incorporated into the store. In parallel with the company's retail expansion it developed its printing and publishing role. In 1860, a new printing works was developed in London Street. It took over the St James' Yarn Mill in Whitefriars in 1898 and after a succession of uses it ultimately became the headquarters of the Jarrold printing and publishing empire. The operation expanded during the C20th and was credited with a number of printing firsts including Black Beauty and Winnie the Pooh. The company was also at the cutting edge of printing and publishing innovation, installing the latest equipment from around the world. It prospered until, in the new millennium, it was unable to compete with the production costs of overseas printing, and the works closed in 2006. The John Jarrold Print Museum survives on the site as a record of the company's 200 years in printing.

The contraction then closure of the print works heralded a further diversification in the company's role as it moved more assertively into property. Building upon its earlier refurbishment and letting of parts of St James' Mill, the company developed former warehousing in Cowgate for new offices for Mills & Reeve (LSI Architects) and then began an ambitious redevelopment of the old print works site for offices and residential uses. The first new offices, by Aukett Fitzroy Robinson, were built to a BREAM excellent standard and occupied by DEFRA, the Broads Authority and the Environment Agency in 2008. The second phase development, at St James Court, was completed in early 2011 and is one of the most sustainable office buildings in the region.

Jarrold has supported a range of cultural and social activity within the City, including sponsoring the new stand at Norwich City Football Club.

Jenny Lind Hospital for Sick Children

Children's hospital.
Jenny Lind, the Swedish Nightingale, was one of the most famous and popular singers in mid C19th Europe. She performed in Norwich in 1847 and again in 1849 when she gave two concerts in St Andrew's Hall and raised £1,253 for the poor of the City. The citizens deliberated for some years about how best to employ her donation and eventually, in 1853, they agreed to establish an infirmary for sick children. This was to be the first inpatient facility outside London for the care of sick children. A property was secured in Pottergate and it opened in April 1854, delayed slightly by concerns from some quarters about admitting children with infectious diseases. In its first full year of operation it treated 51 inpatients and 275 outpatients. The inpatient function continued on the Pottergate site until 1898 and outpatients were admitted until 1929. In 1897 funding was obtained from the Queen Victoria Diamond Jubilee Fund and Jeremiah James Colman donated a site for a new hospital on the Unthank Road. Edward Boardman produced the design and it was opened in 1900 by the Prince and Princess of Wales. Jenny Lind's son and daughter were also in attendance. During the interim period a building in Tombland was used as a temporary measure. In 1905 the new hospital treated 334 inpatients. The facility expanded over successive years and in 1929 an outpatients department was completed and opened by Princess Mary, and Jenny Lind's daughter was again a guest. In 1948 it was taken over by the National Health Service and given the financial stability which it had previously lacked. Economies of scale forced the eventual closure of the Unthank Road site in 1975 and children's services moved to the old Norfolk & Norwich Hospital. In 1982, following the conversion of old wards, the new Jenny Lind Children's Department became operational in the N&N. In 2001 the new Norfolk & Norwich University Hospital opened at Colney and children's services were transferred there.

Jesuit Chapel
See *Willow Lane Chapel*.

C13th cartoon of the Norwich Jews – possibly the first documented English caricature.

Jewish Burial Ground plaque.

Jews

Hebrew community in Norwich. A Jewry was established between the Castle and the French Borough for Jewish immigrants from northern France and the Rhineland, shortly after the Conquest. There is documentary evidence for a synagogue within the Jewry (on the site of what was Littlewoods and is now, in 2011, Primark), a 'Jews' School' and 'Abraham's Hall' just beyond. However, the name Isaac appears in the Domesday Book in a list of Frenchmen living in the new French Borough and the most wealthy Norwich Jews, the Jurnets, lived in what is now Wensum Lodge in King Street, indicating that Jewish occupation was not exclusively within the Jewry. The Jewish community in Norwich formed one of the most important and financially powerful in England, evidenced by the fact that in 1159 their 'taxable capacity' was second only to London. By this time they constituted about 7 per cent of the City's total population. They certainly provided financial support for major projects and it is possible that this included the cathedral.

As well as financiers, there is documentary evidence of wine merchants, cheesemongers, fishmongers, butchers and at least three Jewish physicians including Isaac who lived in Saddlegate, the modern White Lion Street, his son Solomon and Benjamin, son of Deulecresse. There is additionally documentary reference to the herbarium (herb garden) of Solomon which is thought to be the earliest reference to a private herb garden in England. Artistic vestiges of the community include the Bodleian Bowl, found in 1696, and now kept in the Ashmolean Museum in Oxford. This bronze vessel is inscribed with a legend which suggests that it was donated by Yehiel, the son of the famous Rabbi Yehiel of Paris. It was made in France then taken to Acre, in the Holy Land, where it was possibly used as a collecting bowl by the Jewish community. It then passed into the hands of the Norwich Hebrew community. A further art treasure, and outstanding literary survival, is a set of poems by Meir, son of Rabbi Elijah of Norwich, preserved in a manuscript in the Vatican Library. They include a long, 108 line poem dealing with the Bible from the creation to the Exodus and 16 short poems written for a friend. Scholarship within the Hebrew community is also evidenced by the fact that four members of the Jurnet family are given, in Hebrew sources, the title HaNadid (the Generous) denoting a patron of learning – a title only accorded to ten English medieval Jews.

In 1144 the body of a young apprentice was discovered at Mousehold and some factions accused the Jews of William's ritual murder. This 'blood libel' was the first of its kind and remains unproven. The Sheriff at the time declared that the Jews were under the King's protection and prevented the Bishop from instigating a trial. A minor 'St William' pilgrimage cult emerged but found little support.

The Jews were expelled from England in 1290 by Edward I although it is likely that some converted to Christianity, under duress, and remained in the City.

While there is no firm evidence to support this proposition here, there is a record of three Norwich women who did convert and moved to the House of Converts in London.

There had been a slow trickle of Jewish returners to the City following Cromwell's lifting of the ban in 1656, but the first concrete documentary evidence is of David Moses who had been resident in Norwich for 34 years in 1798. The earliest place of worship, for the returning community, was a room in a house in Gowing's Court (St Stephens Street) but a new synagogue was established, subsequently, in 1828 in Tombland. By the mid C19th, the community had been expanded by immigrants from Russia and Poland – fleeing from persecution and pogroms – and they built a new synagogue off Mountergate in Synagogue Street – the only street to bear that name in England.

Jewish Burial Grounds

Jewish burial sites. The original Jewish burial ground was located adjacent to the synagogue, just east of Gentleman's Walk. This ceased to be used after the expulsion of 1290. After Cromwell lifted the ban in 1656, the Corporation granted a site in Mariners Lane to be used as a burial ground. A letter to the Jewish Chronicle from a Mr Levy in 1842 talks of the Mariners Lane site (now lost) being granted by the Corporation 'about a century and a half ago to Mr Solomon Levy and his heir, upon payment of ten shillings per annum,' suggesting that the site

John Jarrold Print Museum

Printing museum. Founded in 1982 the John Jarrold Print Museum, located close to St James' Mill in Whitefriars, aims to preserve the historic printing equipment associated with the Jarrold printing and publishing company and to pass on the traditional techniques of printing. Open Wednesday mornings or by special arrangement, the Museum is staffed by volunteers who demonstrate the equipment and former printing techniques.

Interior views of the John Jarrold Printing Museum, Whitefriars.

was established in the late 1600s. A second site (still surviving) was established near Talbot Square (just north of the current St Crispin's Road) by the Jewish Community in 1813 and this continued in used until 1854. Once a new City Cemetery had opened off Earlham Road, it made provision for a Jewish section.

Jewson, Dorothy

First female MP. Elected to Parliament in 1923, Dorothy Jewson became the City's first female MP and one of the very first in the whole country. She also sat as a City Councillor between 1929 and 1936.

Jex, Frederick

Educational reformer. Born in 1886 and brought up in Cowgate, Fred Jex began his working career as a turnshoe maker and became a full time official with the National Union of Boot and Shoe Operatives. He was elected Labour councillor and ultimately became Council Leader. He was Lord Mayor in 1933. Fred's passion was educational improvement and when he stepped down, after 44 years on the Council, it was said that 83 per cent of children then in school were in premises either built or radically improved during Fred's term of office.

John Jarrold Print Museum

See opposite.

Jubilee Terrace

Early extra mural housing. Some of the earliest housing to be developed beyond the City Walls, in the early C19th, survives at Jubilee Terrace to the east of City Road.

Julian of Norwich statue at Norwich Cathedral.

Julian of Norwich

Author of the first surviving book by a woman in the English language. One of England's most celebrated mystics, Julian had a series of 16 religious visions in May 1373 as she emerged from a serious illness for which she had been given the last rites. This experience prompted her to become an anchoress in St Julian's Church in King Street and to lead a devout life. She had further visions in 1393 and wrote them down in Revelations of Divine Love in the same year. This is thought to be the first surviving publication by a woman in the English language.

Jurnet

Hebrew leader and financier. Born in 1130 and died in 1197, Jurnet was a key financier for the English crown and a nadiv (patron of learning) in the local Hebrew community. There is speculation that he financed or part financed the building of the Cathedral and it is of note that the same mason's marks appear there as can be seen on the surviving stone house developed by Jurnet in King Street (Music House/Wensum Lodge), possibly adapting and extending an earlier structure. Jurnet is commemorated by Jurnet's club which occupies the vaulted undercroft of Jurnet's House. Jurnet's son, Isaac, is thought to have been the wealthiest Jew in medieval England and is the subject of what is claimed to be the first caricature in England.

K is for...

The oldest and longest street in Norwich; record holder for the highest number of appearances for Norwich City Football Club; Shakespearian clown and instigator of the 'Nine Daies Wonder'; birth place and home of the shortest reigning English queen, Lady Jane Grey; the man who had championed 'the common people of England to escape from a servile life into the freedom of just conditions'.

Kabell, Henry

The first Australian immigrant. In 1783, Henry Kabell or Cabell, his father and another accomplice were convicted of burgling a widow's house and sentenced to hang. The sentence was carried out at Norwich on two of the felons but Kabell the younger had his sentence commuted to 14 years transportation. He was then held in Norwich prison until transportation could be arranged. During his time there he fathered a baby with Susannah Holmes, another convicted felon, and by 1786 the Government were ready to transport the prisoners – a three year delay having resulted from the loss of the American colonies and therefore the former location for transported convicts. Things started badly for the transported couple however, as first Susannah and the baby were sent for transportation from Plymouth, leaving Kabell at Norwich, then the prison ship's captain refused to accept the baby. In an uncharacteristic gesture of humanity for the time, the turnkey John Simpson, who had been charged with Susannah's delivery, went personally to plead the case of the convicts to the Home Secretary, Lord Sydney. Remarkably, Sydney not only heard Simpson's pleas but agreed that Kabell and Susannah could be married and that the three could travel into transportation together.

When the first convict fleet arrived at the New South Wales colony in 1787, Kabell waded ashore with the colony's first Governor on his back, making Kabell the first white colonist to set foot in New South Wales. Kabell's first continued in spectacular fashion from then on. He took part in the first marriage service in the new colony, later went on to become chief constable, opened a hotel and ran the first stage coach service in Australia.

Keelan, Kevin

Norwich City goalkeeper. Born in Calcutta, Kevin Keelan joined Norwich City in 1963 and in 17 years notched up the highest number of club appearances, at 673, of any NCFC player. After leaving Norwich he went on to play and coach for the Tampa Bay Rowdies in Florida.

Kemp, Will

William Kemp was a famous Elizabethan comic actor and contemporary of William Shakespeare. In 1599 after arguments with Shakespeare and in an attempt to upstage him, Kemp wagered that he would Morris dance from London to Norwich in nine days. He did this, starting on 11th February 1600, and, on reaching Norwich, jumped the wall of St John Maddermarket. A plaque now commemorates the site and Kemp wrote a book about his journey, 'A Nine Daies Wonder'. Kemp is also commemorated in Will Kemp Way which runs to the rear of The Forum.

Opposite: Reconstruction of medieval King Street.
Below: Will Kemp commemorated on a new street name to the rear of The Forum.

WILL KEMP WAY

1599, the Elizabethan actor Will Kem
a contemporary of Shakespeare,
s danced' from London to Norwich i

plaque commemorates this feat and cele
long history of the performing arts in No

Kempe, Margery

Mystic and pilgrim. Born in Kings Lynn in 1373, Margery Kempe's apparently conventional life took a turn for the unusual when, following a bout of mental illness, she had a vision of Christ. In time she decided to pursue a life of chastity and embarked on a range of pilgrimages to Jerusalem, Rome, Santiago de Compostela, Norway and parts of the Holy Roman Empire. During her travels she met and spoke with Julian of Norwich as well as a range of international influential religious figures. Her thoughts and adventures were written down by two scribes in the 1430s and survive as the 'Boke of Margery Kempe'. This is thought to be the first autobiography in the English language.

Kennon, Sandy

Professional footballer. Born in South Africa, Neil Sandlands Kennon made 213 appearance for Norwich City between 1958 and 1965. He was part of the famous 1959 Cup Run squad and played a key role in the club's promotion to the Second Division the following season. He went on to play for Colchester and then became a bookmaker, as well as having his own band, Sandy Kennon and the Blazers. He also played cricket and made three appearances in the Minor Counties Championship.

Keswick

Suburban parish. Situated approximately 4.8km (3 miles) south-west of Norwich's City Centre, Keswick had a population of only 431 in the 2001 Census. There are a number

From left: Keswick (New) Hall, Keswick Old Hall.

of buildings of historical interest in the village including Keswick Old Hall, which dates from 1600 with C18th additions and sits within an attractive walled garden. The 1817 Keswick Hall, to the south, by William Wilkins, was owned by the Gurney family during the Regency period, and between 1948 and 1984 acted as a college of education. The hall is currently used for residential purposes. Keswick All Saints is a round-towered church. A previous church existed on this site until it was demolished in 1598, and a new church was constructed at Intwood instead using materials from the demolished church when the parishes of Keswick and Intwood were consolidated. It was the Gurneys who restored All Saints in the 1890s. The original east wall of the chancel still remains to the east of the current church structure and part of the tower may be of Saxon origin although it was heavily restored in 1893. There has been a watermill on the current site in Keswick since the C13th, although the current building dates from 1760, and is now a listed

building. The western end of the mill was demolished and then rebuilt in the C19th and is now used for residential purposes; the dovecote also remains. A second watermill of Anglo-Saxon origin was known to have stood in Keswick at Harford Bridge, although this seems to have disappeared in the C14th. Keswick Postmill, which stood to the east of the watermill, existed here from at least 1762 and worked together with the watermill, but was demolished in 1847. Along Low Road, Low Farmhouse dates from the C16th with a C14th barn and Honeysuckle cottage is also of C16th origin.

Ketteringham Hall.

Ketteringham

Suburban parish. Situated 10km (6.2 miles) south of Norwich, Ketteringham is a tiny parish with a population of 169. The name derives from the Old English meaning 'homestead of the Cytringas'. This is a pre C7th name (the people of Cytringa) and also appears in Saxon records of 956. The Church of St Peter has a C11th core but with significant restoration in the C18th and again in 1837. There are interesting monuments inside and some medieval glass. Ketteringham Hall, next door, is C16th rebuild of an earlier house and is thought to be the birth place and early home of the short reigned queen Lady Jane Gray. Passing from the Grays to the Heveninghams – Sir William sat in judgement on Charles I – and then to the Atkyns – Charlotte Atkyns apparently attempted to rescue Marie Antoinette and the Dauphin – eventually ending up with the Boileau family. It was Sir John Boileau who employed architect Thomas Allason to remodel the hall in a Gothic style then Thomas Jeckyll did further work on it in 1852.

Kett's Rebellion

Popular insurrection.
Following the Dissolution of the monasteries, the gentry had bought up former monastic estates and this had led to the enclosure of vast areas of common land which constrained the ability of the poorer classes to compete in arable production. This underscored a much wider and growing gulf between the rural and urban poor, who were becoming poorer, and the gentry who were profiting from these changes. The response to the enclosure issue had increasingly been direct action and, in July 1549, a large crowd which had gathered for a fair in Wymondham decided to pull down the enclosures of a local land owner called Flowerdew. His response was to bribe the protesters to demolish fences belonging to his land owning rival Robert Kett. Instead of reacting against this, Kett supported the demolitions and offered to lead the protestors. A growing band marched on Norwich, demolishing fences on the way, and established a camp on Mousehold where they set out their demands. While relating to the enclosure issue, the demands were more focussed on social justice but consistently confirmed the loyalty of the protesters to the Crown. On 21st July, Kett was offered a pardon by a Royal Herald but he refused and the City locked its gates against him. The rebels then stormed the City and captured various key figures including the Mayor.

From top: Landsknechts, of the kind deployed against Kett's citizen army.
Mural depicting incident between Kett's staff and the Royal Herald.

Protector Somerset, acting on behalf of the Crown and the Privy Council, sent the Earl of Northampton with a force of 1500 troops to put down the rebellion but they were no match for Kett's citizen army of about 30,000 and were soundly beaten in Palace Plain, with Lord Sheffield being killed in the melee. The rebels occupied the City and the Castle, taking more hostages. Somerset then sent a second force, under the Earl of Warwick, but this time the force was 14,000 strong and included Landsknechts (professional mercenaries) from Switzerland, Germany and Italy. A further pardon was offered and rejected. Warwick stormed the City and three days of intensive fighting ensued after which the rebels withdrew to Mousehold. Misreading an ancient prophecy as an omen of good fortune, the rebels relinquished their topographical advantage at Mousehold to engage the Warwick army at Dussindale

where they were no match for professional troops in a set piece engagement and they were slaughtered. The leaders were summarily executed and Robert Kett and his brother were tried in London for treason. Both were found guilty and Robert Kett was returned to Norwich to be hanged at the Castle on 7th December – his body was left to rot on the gibbet as a symbol to others. Kett's brother was hanged at Wymondham. Commentators on the rebellion either paint Kett as a brutish traitor or a champion of the common people. At the 500th anniversary of the Rebellion, the citizens of Norwich erected a memorial at the Castle in honour to the memory of a man who had championed 'the common people of England to escape from a servile life into the freedom of just conditions.' Apart from this memorial, Kett is now commemorated in many road and public building names locally.

The Boileaus stayed until 1943 when it became headquarters for the 2nd Air Division of the USAAF with James Stewart as its commander. After the War it became a school, then a college, then the head quarters for Colin Chapman's Lotus Group and it is now used for offices. Close by, Church cottage is an early C16th timber framed hall house and Hall Farmhouse is also C16th. Some distance away in the High Street there is a range of C16th and C17th houses.

Kett, Robert –
See *Kett's Rebellion*, page 213.

Kett's Heights
Viewpoint and public open space. Located half way up Kett's Hill, on the south side, Kett's Heights provides spectacular views over the City and an attractive and secluded oasis for wildlife. Originally the site of St Leonards Priory and St Michael's Chapel and later, Mount Surrey, the 'sumptuous' residence of the Earl of Surrey, the site was occupied by Robert Kett's citizen army during the 1549 Rebellion. After some neglect, the manager of the Victorian Gas Works created some paths and ornamental gardens in the area but these were first turned over to allotments then abandoned. In 1986 the Norfolk Wildlife Group regenerated the site and in 1988 a beacon was erected to celebrate the Spanish Armada's defeat.

Kett's Rebellion
See page 213.

King of Hearts
Historic arts venue. Beginning life as a merchants house in the

From top: King of Hearts stairwell, King of Hearts upper room.

Tudor period, the building was subsequently divided into shops and residential tenements and by the late C20th, its original provenance had been all but forgotten. When the Norwich Preservation Trust in collaboration with the City Council set about restoring what were thought to be fairly unremarkable shops for a 'Living Over the Shop' scheme, they were amazed to discover remarkable surviving remnants of the original merchant house including ceilings, a huge bricked up window, a stair well and door cases. The restoration transformed the building to its original glory and local philanthropist

Aude Gotto took over the lease of the unit for the King of Heart's arts trust. She subsequently bought the next door property to provide a cafe and meeting rooms. The King of Heart's trust ran the property for over 20 years before deciding to pass it on to another arts organisation in 2010.

King Street
Ancient thoroughfare. Probably the oldest and longest thoroughfare in Norwich, King Street is thought to form part of a Roman route connecting Pye Strete, and the regional cantonal capital Venta Icenorum (Caister), to Roman settlements in the

north of the County. It was originally Conesford, a name deriving from Old Danish and Old English and meaning King's Ford – although where the ford was and indeed which king this refers to, has never been clarified. The name Conesford was in use from the earliest times until the mid C18th and 'King Street' is only in common use after the late C18th. Like the street itself, settlement was also early with the pre Conquest defended borough reaching as far south as modern Mountergate and Stepping Lane but other early development extending further south of the borough including a significant number of probable pre Conquest churches, such as St Julian, St Clement, St Edmund, St Etheldreda, St Michael and St Olave, indicating extensive early, extra mural activity. After the Conquest, more church development continued as did the establishment of significant secular buildings such as Junets/Isaacs House (the Music House). Larger ecclesiastical sites developed including the Carrow Nunnery at the south end of the Street, the Austin Friars in the middle and the Greyfriars at the north end. By the medieval period, the great families of England had colonised the street. Some surviving examples included Sir John Heydon's House (Raven Yard), Recorder of the City in 1431, Sir John Paston's House in 1488 and later the house of Lord Chief Justice Coke (Music House), Sir William Boleyn's House, grandfather of Anne Boleyn (next to Dragon Hall) and the garden house of Henry Howard, 6th Duke of

Aerial view of King Street in the 1920s, depicting its very industrialised nature.

Norfolk. When the gentry fled the increasingly crowded Walled City, their splendid mansions were subdivided into squalid tenements and their gardens were either developed for more substandard housing or for industry. By the C19th, King Street was one of the most densely occupied parts of the historic City with slum families living cheek by jowl with breweries, malthouses, iron works and mills. After the War, brutal redevelopment swept away much of the historic character of the street, particularly around the Morgan's Brewery, but sensitive regeneration by the City Council, Norwich Preservation Trust, Norfolk & Norwich Heritage Trust and thoughtful developers/architects (e.g. Andi Gibbs Netherconnesford) are helping to restore both character and vitality to the street.

Kirby Bedon

Suburban hamlet. With a population of only 186, Kirby Bedon is located approximately 5.6km (3.5 miles) south east of Norwich City Centre on the road to

Bramerton. There was originally a hall here built around 1604. However, Kirby Bedon was reputedly haunted and after 1836 was sold to H. J. Stracey of Rackheath Hall who consequently demolished most of the building in 1841. Only the lower part of the construction remained and was occupied by labourers, before demolition was fully completed at the turn of the century. Two churches have served the village: the round-towered St Mary's probably survived the Reformation but then fell into disuse by 1700, and located opposite is St Andrew's, the present structure is likely to be Norman in origin although there was a major rebuild in 1876.

Kirkpatrick, John

Noted historian. Born in 1682 Kirkpatrick went on to be one of the most eminent historians in the City's history. His most noted work was the Streets and Lanes of the City of Norwich. He married Mayor John Harveys daughter, Ann, and was a sufficiently prominent figure to have his portrait painted by Theodore Heins.

L is for...

The UK's first pedestrianised shopping street; the first municipally owned library and also the first city to adopt the 1850 Public Libraries Act; builder of the Anglican Cathedral's fan vaulted roof.

*Night and day views of
Lady Julian Bridge.*

*Opposite: London Street,
looking towards the Cathedral.*

Lads Club
See page 264.

Lady Julian Bridge
Iconic pedestrian bridge.
Opened in 2009 to connect
historic King Street to the
new Riverside Quarter, the
bridge, with its elder sister,
the Novi Sad Friendship
Bridge, provides an
interesting architectural
punctuation on the river.
It was designed by architect
Gary Young and received
substantial funding from the
East of England
Development Agency. The
name was the result of a
public voting competition
and commemorates Julian
of Norwich, author of the
first surviving book by a
woman in the English
language.

Lakenham Cricket Ground
Home of County cricket.
Lakenham Cricket Ground
was laid out for the Norfolk
Cricket Cub in 1827. south
of the Walled City in the
New Lakenham suburb off
City Road. After just one
season the club failed and
matches moved to Dereham
or Swaffham. Attempts were
made in 1862 and 1876 to
reconstitute the Club but
little activity took place at
Lakenham until 1879. Early
visitors were the Australian
Aborigines Touring Team in
1868 who played against
Carrow and beat them by
an innings and 52 runs.
W.G.Grace played at
Lakenham in 1903 and
1904 for London County
against Norfolk while the
young Jack Hobbs also
played in 1904, for
Cambridgeshire, scoring 92
runs. The ground saw
Norfolk playing at its peak in
the early part of the C20th
when the team won the
Minor Counties Championship
in 1905, 1910 and 1913.
The ground closed in 2000
and has been unused since.

Lakenham, New
Early suburb. New
Lakenham developed to the
south west of the Walled
City, and north of the historic
hamlet of Old Lakenham,
in the early C19th. Small
worker's terrace housing,
of the type still surviving in
Jubilee terrace, extended
rapidly over the area and in
1844 St Mark's was built to
serve the growing
community. The Cricket
Ground had been laid out in
1827 and other facilities
arrived subsequently
including the Girls School
and Hospital (1863),
Lakenham Reservoir, and
the Boys School.
Employment was provided
by a number of small
enterprises, at least two
mills and the expanding
Colman's Carrow Works
to the east, which also
provided new worker's
housing in the area in the
late C19th. After the First
World War, the Aldous family
established the Lakenham
Creamery there, which
produced ice cream, while
the Council developed local
authority flats on a large
scale. Following the Second
World War there was a
significant amount of

New Lakenham Girls School.

From left: Commemorative plaque for The Lamb, and The Lamb in the 1930s.

demolition of the earlier terrace housing which was replaced by Council flats. One of the largest post War developments was the Hewitt School (1956) by City Architect David Percival, and the Lakenham Secondary Modern which were ultimately unified to provide the biggest secondary school in the City catering for over 1100 pupils.

Lakenham, Old

Urban hamlet. Located on the Yare at the likely crossing point of the north/south Roman road just north of the Tas and to the south of the City Centre, Old Lakenham was designated a conservation area in 1980. It takes its name from a settlement near a body of water. Lakenham was held by Stigand prior to the Conquest and was mentioned in the Domesday Book. The oldest surviving building in the village is C13th St John and All Saints church, which has a C15th tower. The church attracted grave robbers during the C18th. Old Lakenham Hall, once the headquarters of the Norfolk

Scouts, was demolished in 1971 and the C17th house Villa Gardens on Martineau Lane was also demolished in the 1950s after sustaining damage during World War II. The open air swimming pool was opened in 1908, with the river water passing through the pool, although this closed in 1992 and is now part of a campsite. Surviving points of historical interest include the Old Post Office on Mansfield Lane which dates from the C17th, 'The Lodge' on Sandy Lane which was built in the C18th, the watermill and The Cock public house. The mill is first mentioned around 1830 as a yarn mill, although due to the decline in the wool industry, by 1892 the mill was being used for crushing grain. In 1908 a great fire destroyed both the mill and the Cock Inn. Both buildings were subsequently rebuilt. After ceasing production, the mill buildings continued to be used for other purposes such as a toy workshop until 1937, and for pumping water into Lakenham baths until 1942. The mill today is used as residential property.

Lamb Inn

Ancient inn. Located just off the Haymarket and just south of the Jewry, which was evacuated following the expulsion of the Jews in 1290, the site is thought to have associations with the Mass of Jesus and was originally known as 'The Holy Lamb' for that reason. Some sources refer to the building being so named because it incorporated fabric of an early church but there is no documentary or archaeological evidence for a church in this location, only the Jewish Synagogue. It is first referred to as an Inn in 1574 but the licensee records begin in 1761. The building has an unfortunate history. The landlord between 1783 and 1797, John Aggas, had discovered his brother in law and a band of drunken friends helping themselves to the beer in his cellar and when he challenged them, the brother in law stabbed him to death – he was hanged at Norwich Castle. The ghost of Aggas is said to inhabit the premises. The second misfortune was flooding. During the severe thunder and hail storm in August 1843 flood water rose well up the wall of the main bar and used to be commemorated by a brass plate just under the mantlepiece. Fire ravaged the building in 1939 resulting in the removal of part of the top floor. A further death was associated with the Inn in 1972 when a Yarmouth 'Wall of Death' rider was found dead in Lamb Yard in the middle of the night. Despite this the Lamb seems to have prospered over many centuries. It had a brief name change to the Rat and Parrot in 1996 then became Henry's Bar at the Lamb in 2002.

Lanfranc, Bishop

See *Guader, Emma de.*

Larkman

Out of centre Council estate. The name 'Larkman' comes from an Anglo-Saxon surname, possibly originating in Norfolk. Larkman is located to the west of Norwich, and the estate's demographic can be characterised as largely white working-class and the area constitutes one third of the NELM (North Earlham, Larkman and Marlpit) New Deal for Communities area, which is one of the most economically deprived areas in the UK. The Larkman estate was constructed between 1936 and 1939 to house ex-slum dwellers from the City Centre. The area was the subject of the first area-wide traffic calming scheme in the UK in the late 1980s which saw a significant reduction in road traffic casualties.

Lawrence Scott in the 1950s.

Lawrence, Scott & Electromotors

Principal manufacturers. The company is one of the longest established manufacturers of electrical equipment and was born when in 1884 E.A.Paris, then working for the Hammond Electrical Company, persuaded J.J.Colman that William Harding Scott could provide the necessary plant to deliver electric light at his Carrow plant. Colman agreed to pay for all the business start up costs and Paris and Scott quit Hammonds to set up their new business in modest premises in King Street. R. Lawrence provided an injection of finance into the new company in 1887. As well as electrical equipment, they developed a generating station in Stamp Office Yard, off St Andrews, in 1888 and sold power to the Corporation to light the Library and St Andrews Hall and to businesses. The King Street site continued to prosper with orders from as far afield as Russia and South Africa and success was so great that they moved to a new site at Hardy Road where the workforce expanded to over 500 by the outbreak of WW1. The War brought significant work for the armed forces and after the War demand increased necessitating further site expansion and the development of a new foundry just off Thorpe Road. The marine business grew and in 1924 the company supplied a major installation for the Canadian Pacific 'Empress of Britain'. The company struggled during the Depression and this was exacerbated by the suspension of work on the Queen Mary. This was eventually resolved and with diversification into areas such as the manufacture of traffic lights and equipment of diesel electric locomotives, the company was employing 3,000 people on three sites by the outbreak of WW2. The War provided further opportunities and the company made everything from controllers for tank landing craft to switchgear for submarines. This success continued after the War with LSE products being used in a wide

Exterior views of the Norman Lazar House or Leper Hospital.

selection of defence and marine applications ranging from Royal Navy submarines to the off shore oil and gas industry. One of the company's electric motors even drove the tunneling machine which dug the UK side of the Channel Tunnel. Although rationalisations over the last two decades have reduced the scale of operation in Norwich the company remains one of the world's premier producers of electric motors.

Lazar House

Leper Hospital. There were a number of Leper Houses located beyond the Walled City and founded mainly between the 12th and 14th centuries. They were located to the north and west of the City but not to the south, because of topographical reasons (river valley) nor to the east because it was thought that the prevailing east wind might blow contagion into the City. They included St Giles (1343), just beyond St Giles Gate, St Benedicts, just outside St Benedicts Gate, St Mary and St Clement, beyond St Augustines Gate and on the modern Waterloo Road and St Leonard's on Magdalen Road. All of these have now disappeared. There was a further example just outside St Stephen's Gate which

may survive partly in the fabric of the Trowel and Hammer pub. The most notable example is the St Mary Magdalen Leper Hospital, from which Magdalen Street takes its name. Now known as the Lazar House, and located at the southern end of modern Sprowston Road, it was founded before 1119 by Bishop Herbert de Losinga. The Norman range, with two impressive Norman doorways survives. It was supported partly by rents from nearby agricultural land and partly from funds received from the annual Magdalen Fair held for three days on and either side of the feast day of St Mary Magdalen. This occurred on a site at the top of modern Sprowston Road close to the Mousehold Lane junction – it was discontinued in 1826. The hospital was suppressed in 1547 and passed into agricultural use before being used as cottages. Sir Eustace Gurney saved it from demolition in 1902 and it was restored by J. Owen Bond. It was presented to the City and became the first Norwich branch library. This use ceased relatively recently and it is now used by the Assist Trust which helps people with learning difficulties.

Le Genereux Ensign

Unique, historic flag.
'Le Genereux' was a French, Téméraire class, ship of the line and one of only four French ships to escape capture or destruction at the Battle of the Nile (1 Aug 1798). Their escape was led by Admiral Villeneuve, who was on 'Le Guillaume Tell'. The Battle of the Nile was one of Nelson's most significant victories, assuring Britain regained power over the Mediterranean after over a year of Napoleonic dominance. Nelson's flagship at the Battle of the Nile was the Vanguard, captained by Edward Berry. Shortly after, a British 4th rate ship, the Leander, was attacked by Le Genereux and, after a ferocious battle, was captured. Berry, a passenger on the Leander, was captured but exchanged subsequently. Berry and the Leander's captain were knighted for their bravery. Two years later 'Le Genereux' and 'Le Guillaume Tell' were engaged off Malta by a squadron including Nelson's flagship HMS Foudroyant, then captained by Berry. After a short engagement, Berry's ship captured Le Genereux. The Norfolk Chronicle of January 18 1871, recording the death of Christopher Bunting of

Alexandra Road Norwich, reported that Bunting had witnessed the capture of the French ship 'Le Genereux', saw the flag arrive on 'Foudroyant', and watched it being parcelled up by Berry and addressed to Robert Harvey, then Mayor of Norwich, as a trophy for the City much as Nelson had sent the sword of the defeated admiral at the battle of Cape St Vincent some years before. The ensign was displayed at St Andrew's Hall in the C19th, although it isn't clear for how long. It was also part of the early displays at the Castle Museum from 1894, where it was draped under the balcony. The ensign is currently in store at Gressenhall. It is a simple French tricolor, measures 15x8m, made of woven wool but is in a poor state of conservation. Estimates of the cost of conserving it to enable it to be displayed range from £70,000-340,000 depending on the extent of the work required. It is a unique, surviving artifact from the Napoleonic period.

Letter Boxes
See *Post Boxes*.

Libraries
Historic and contemporary library provision. Over the centuries, the City has been in the forefront of library development. The Benedictine Priory Library, founded by Herbert de Losinga, had 2,000 books by 1386 and the other priories boasted significant volumes between them. In May 1608, Norwich was the first city to establish a municipally owned library, in a house adjoining St Andrew's Hall. In 1784 a subscription library (the Public Library) was established followed by the Norfolk & Norwich Literary Institution in 1822 and the two libraries had a combined stock of 60,000 volumes. There were also libraries for the working class including one in a factory in St Augustines and others at the Mechanics Institute and the Atheneum. Norwich was also the first city to adopt the 1850 Public Libraries Act and in March 1857 the Norwich Free Library was opened in St Andrews. The Norwich Central Library was one of the most modern in the country when it opened in the early 1960s and its replacement, the Norfolk and Norwich Millennium Library was the most modern library in the UK when it opened in 2001. Today the libraries available in the area include:

- **2nd Air Division Memorial Library** at The Forum – 5,000 American books and 25 US periodicals
- **Costume and Textile Study** Centre at Colman House, King Street – one of the largest specialist costume/fashion book collections in the UK
- **John Innes Centre** at Norwich Research Park – some of the largest collections on genetics in the world
- **Norfolk & Norwich Children's Library** at The Forum
- **Norfolk & Norwich Millennium Library** at The Forum – the busiest public library in the country
- **Norfolk Heritage Library** at The Forum
- **Norwich Cathedral Library** at the Cathedral Hostry – principally ecclesiastical and historical volumes
- **Sainsbury Institute for the Study of Japanese Art and Culture Library** in the Cathedral Close – one of the largest Japanese libraries in the UK
- **UEA Library** on campus – volumes targeted to the University's courses.

Lind, Jenny
See *Jenny Lind Hospital for Sick Children*.

Anglican Cathedral Library.

Lion Wood.

London Street before (top and bottom left) and after (above right) pedestrianisation.

Lion Wood

Public woodland. Lion Wood is a 9.2 ha local nature reserve and contains many large mature trees, especially sycamore and oak. The canopy also includes other species (chestnut, beech, hornbeam and birch) and has a varied age structure. The shrub layer contains holly and elder and in one area cherry laurel. The ground flora is not diverse but includes localised bluebells. Jays and green woodpeckers and bats are likely to be seen. Parts of Lion Wood are ancient woodland forming a small element which originally covered a huge area from the margins of the old City almost out to the coast.

Little Plumstead

See *Great and Little Plumstead.*

Lollards Pit

Place of medieval execution. Located in a hollow on the hillside adjacent to Riverside Road and on the site of the modern Bridge House pub and the adjacent DIY store, Lollards Pit was used predominantly in the C15th and C16th to dispatch Lollards particularly but also others who offended the established order. Lollards were those who were regarded by the then religious and political establishment as heretics and were brought here to be burned alive after a short incarceration in the Guildhall. One of the first victims was

priest William White in 1428 although the most notable victim was Thomas Bilney, said to be the' first Protestant martyr'. Most burnings took place during the five year reign of Queen Mary when nearly 50 people were put to the torch. The 'other offenders' referred to on the commemorative plaque on the site included women accused of witchcraft who suffered the same fate.

London Street

First pedestrianised street. Historically, a pleasant but unremarkable early shopping street linking the Cathedral and the commercial heart of the City, London Street sprang to fame in the mid 1960s when a burst water main necessitated its closure to traffic. During that period, the traders noticed an increase in takings and the newly appointed City Planning Officer, Alfie Wood, was astute enough to grasp that there might be a connection. He developed an experimental scheme which then evolved into a permanent close. This was the first conventional shopping street to be 'pedestrianised' in the UK and one of the first in the whole of Europe. It proved to be a remarkable success and remains one of the most attractive shopping streets in the City. Its pleasant, traffic free environment is augmented by a range of attractive buildings including the former London and Provincial Bank (now GAP) by George Skipper (1907), opposite, an attractive jewellers dating from 1830 beside a C17th range, then attractive C18th buildings and what appears to be a Wren church but is actually the National Westminster Bank of 1924 by Palmer & Holden. Further up is an elaborate Boardman building built as the offices for the Eastern Daily Press in 1900. The street also contains one of the only surviving shoe making firms in the City, Bowhill & Elliott, which maintains an industry that once employed 15,000 people.

Lord Mayor

See *Mayors*.

Losinga, Herbert de

Cathedral Founder and Diplomat 1045 – 1119.
There is a possibility that Herbert was born at Hoxne in Suffolk but he was educated at the Benedictine abbey of Fecamp in Normandy where he rose to

Lotus Formula 1 racing car.

become prior. William Rufus made him abbot of Ramsey in 1087 then Bishop of Thetford in 1091 and around the same time the king appointed Herbert's father Abbot of Winchester. This gave rise to accusations of simony or bribery since he had given £1,900 to the king after the appointments and this was reflected in a poem of the time:

Both Bishop and Abbot are made,
By the terrible power of gold.

However, it was customary for persons receiving high office to reciprocate with gifts to the king so the bribery accusation is unlikely to have had any foundation. Herbert moved the see to Norwich in 1094 and began construction of the Cathedral in 1096. Henry I appointed Herbert Clerk to the Closet of Queen Matilda and this helped to develop his relationship with the Court. In 1107 the King sent Herbert on a mission to Rome to resolve with Pope Paschal a long running dispute between the Pope and Archbishop Anselm, which he did successfully. En route, however, he was imprisoned by Count Guido in Lyons and had to forfeit all of the money he was carrying for his freedom and that of his retainers.

As well as the cathedral, Herbert constructed a sturdy stone keep to function as the Bishop's Palace and beyond this, his holdings were significant. They included mills, Thorpe Wood with 1200 pigs, salt pans at Gaywood, a deer park at Homersfield and an eel marsh at Hilgay. Herbert's other foundations included hospitals, including the Lazar House in Norwich and a house for the aged at Kings Lynn, and the churches of St Nicholas in Great Yarmouth and St Margaret in Lynn also. He was a scholarly man, interested in studying the Latin poets such as Ovid, as well as the scriptures, he was a benefactor, an astute politician but first and foremost he was the power behind the establishment of one of western Europe's truly great Norman cathedrals.

Lotus

Iconic car manufacturer.
Established by Colin Chapman in Hornsey in 1952, the company moved subsequently to the old Hethel WWII airfield in Norfolk and developed both production cars and Formula 1 racing cars. The former produced a range of iconic sports cars including the famous Lotus Elan. The F1 side of the company won a total of 79 Grand Prix during its long association and boasted the likes of Jim Clark, Graham Hill, Jochen Rindt, Emerson Fittipaldi and Mario Andretti as its championship winning drivers. Chapman died in 1982 and the company was taken over by General Motors in 1986 and subsequently by the company that owned Bugatti. The Malaysian

Lamberts C19th tea merchants in Lower Goat Lane.

company Proton bought a controlling share in 1996. Lotus continues to manufacture production cars and announced five new models at the 2010 Paris Motor Show. Lotus returned to Formula 1 in 2010 when the Malaysia Lotus Racing Team was granted a license to use the name. In Dec 2010 Proton announced the creation of Lotus renault GP which would also compete in the 2011 Formula 1 series.

Lower Goat Lane

Ancient lane. Originally called Stonegate Magna from at least the C13th there is speculation about the origin of the name. A street in York with the same name is interpreted as 'stone paved street' but commentators have dismissed this on the basis that orders for paving Norwich streets didn't appear until the C15th. However, this neglects the strong probability that the current Lower Goat Lane formed part of a Roman Road which ran from Berstrete to Oak Street. If this was the case, that road would have been paved and such a paved road would

have justified the exceptional name of 'stone paved street' distinguishing it from the majority of other streets. From 1781, the New Goat Inn appeared in Upper Goat Lane and probably gave its name to both streets. A Golden Goat is listed in 1820, which may have been the same pub, but by 1822 there was a Goat as well as an Old Goat. By 1830, there was an Old Goat and a Young Goat. The Old Goat's licensees are listed until 1861 and similarly the New Goat survives until the same year. By the time of the

1884 Ordnance Survey, both Goats had gone.

Lyhart, Bishop Walter

Diplomat and Cathedral Builder 1446 – 1472.
Lyhart was the son of a Norwich family and after a distinguished career at Oxford, rising to become Provost of Oriel College, he was consecrated Bishop of Norwich at Lambeth Palace 1446 due principally to the Duke of Suffolk's direct intervention with the Pope. When Henry VI visited in 1449 he stayed with Walter for a week. The King sent him on a mission to persuade Pope Felix V to resign in favour of the rival Pope Nicholas V and the mission was successful.

His legacy to the City was the works instigated by him at the Cathedral. His first act was to pave the floor which had previously remained as beaten earth but his greatest act was the replacement of the fire damaged wooden nave roof with the remarkable stone fan-vaulted roof which survives today – possibly the finest example of its kind in the country.

The porch of Bishop Lyhart's house in the Cathedral Close.

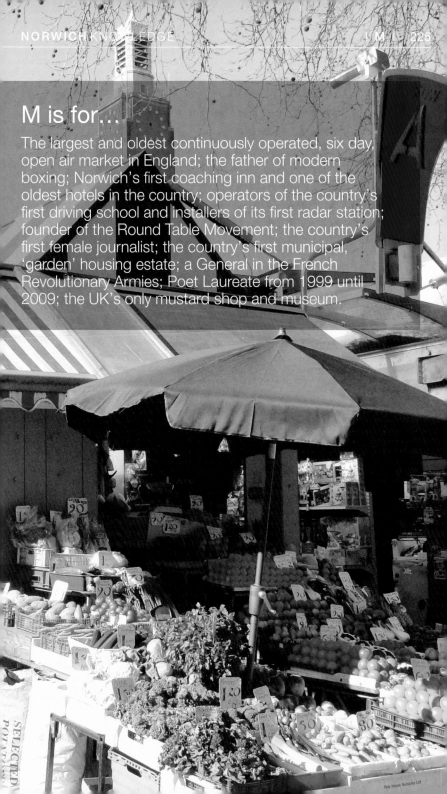

M is for...

The largest and oldest continuously operated, six day, open air market in England; the father of modern boxing; Norwich's first coaching inn and one of the oldest hotels in the country; operators of the country's first driving school and installers of its first radar station; founder of the Round Table Movement; the country's first female journalist; the country's first municipal, 'garden' housing estate; a General in the French Revolutionary Armies; Poet Laureate from 1999 until 2009; the UK's only mustard shop and museum.

From left: The Maddermarket Theatre, and view of St John's Alley at night.

Mace, Jem

English boxing champion. Regarded as the 'father of modern boxing', Jem Mace (1831-1910) was born at Beeston and for some years was the landlord of the Swan in Swan Lane. He won the World Championship in 1862 after defeating the then champion, King, in a 43 round bout. Although losing the return bout, Mace claimed the title when King retired and went on to successfully defend it in the United States.

Mackintosh

Former major employer. Mackintosh's took over the innovative Norwich chocolate manufacturing firm of Caley in 1932. It merged with the York based Rowntrees in 1969 and prospered until being taken over by Nestle and closed down in 1995.

Maddermarket

Former ancient market. The Maddermarket is referred to in records from as far back as the early C13th. This was the place where red vegetable dye made from the root of the Madder plant was sold to textile manufacturers. Much of the Madder was grown locally in the parishes of St Peter Mancroft, St Margaret and St Olave. Apart from St John's church and the Maddermarket Theatre, other significant features in the street include the surviving parish pump.

Maddermarket Theatre

Place of worship, now a theatre. In 1794 Father Beaumont moved his congregation from three small rooms in a building on Willow Lane to their newly built, licensed chapel in the Maddermarket. This move signified a time of open and free worship for the Catholics of Norwich as Catholics had been forbidden to worship publicly until 1778 and to have public places of worship until 1791. The Maddermarket chapel was the first Roman Catholic chapel to be built in Norwich and was in use until 1880. The building and Strangers Hall, where the priest lived, were sold in 1896 and in 1921 the chapel was converted into what has become the world famous Maddermarket Theatre. This was the first to be recreated as an Elizabethan theatre and was opened by Walter Nugent Monck, founder of the amateur dramatic society, the Norwich Players. In 1940 George Bernard Shaw wrote to Monck: "There is nothing in British theatrical history more extraordinary than your creation of the Maddermarket Theatre..." Monck's creation was the first theatre in the world to Stage all of Shakespeare's plays as they were originally intended.

Reconstruction of the Magdalen Gate.

From left: The Maid's Head in the Coaching Age and the Maid's Head after a dramatic mock Tudor transformation in 1903.

Magdalen Gate

Lost City Gate. This was the gate in the City Wall at Magdalen Street and, taking its name from the Magdalen (Leper) Hospital further to the north, it was one of the three principal gates in the City Walls. It was built as part of the last phase of the City Walls in the mid C14th and was demolished in 1808. Despite the fact that the Gate has been gone for 200 years, until very recently buses would be said to stop at 'Magdalen Gates' and the term is still in common usage with local people.

Magdalen Street
See *Fybriggate*.

Magpie Road

Orbital route. This is an historic, extra mural, orbital route running between St Augustines and Magdalen Gates. It was undeveloped until the C19th when a line of terrace houses were built on the filled ditch of the City Wall. The Magpie pub, from which the street takes its name, was first recorded as being licensed in 1806. Later, in the 1840s, it was known as The Weighing Machine due to the

construction of a public weighbridge in front of the pub where wagons where weighed before being allowed entry into the City.

Maiden Troop

Civil war cavalry. In 1643, the 'maidens' of Norwich provided subscriptions for a troop of horses to fight in Cromwell's army and it therefore took on the title of the Norwich Maiden Troop.

Maid's Head

Ancient hotel. The Bishop of the East Anglia's see had a house on the site of the current Maid's Head prior to

Cromwell's Maiden Troop.

the Conquest and it is probable that Norman bishops lived here until the new Bishop's palace was built north of the Cathedral. Following the relocation of the Bishop, the site was used to entertain guests of the Cathedral priory and then became a general hostelry. Records as early as 1287 refer to an inn on the site supporting the claim that this is the longest continuously used hotel site in the country. In 1350 it entertained the Black Prince at a cost to the citizens of £34 7s 6d. It was originally known as the Molde Fish but by the time that Sir John Paston was referring to it in 1472 it was 'the Mayd's Hedde'. One explanation of this curious name change is that the Norfolk colloquialism for the skate was 'the old maid' and that the Molde Fish may thus have become the Old Maid then Maid's Head. In the reign of Henry VIII, both Cardinal Wolsey and Queen Catherine of Aragon stayed there while in 1549, the Marquis of Northampton breakfasted there before being soundly thrashed by Robert Kett's rebel army. This didn't deter the Earl of Warwick who also partook of the breakfast then thrashed Kett. Despite ambitious claims, Queen Elizabeth I didn't stay here during her visit of 1587 but rather stayed with the Bishop just across the road. In the C18th, this became Norwich's first coaching inn and in 1762 a coach called the Norwich Machine left here on Mon, Wed and Fri at 11.30am arriving in London that evening – four passengers inside paid 25 shillings each and outside costs 12s 6d. Additional to coaching, the Maids Head of that period offered a range of dining and musical delights but also the much celebrated presentations of Dr Graham who lectured on the 'Propagation of the Joys of the Marriage Bed' using the future Lady Hamilton as his semi naked demonstration model. Walter Rye, local historian, bought the site in 1889 and undertook various renovations and extensions. In October 1933, J.B. Priestley stayed at the hotel while on the last leg of his 'English Journey' and described the place as a 'fantastically rambling but comfortable old place'. During the remainder of C20th, famous guests included Morecambe and Wise, David Niven, Reg Varney and Derek Guyler of 'On the Buses' fame, Sir Harry Secombe, Wilfred Hyde White, Cilla Black and Torville and Dean. The hotel also features in The Norwich Victims – a detective story by Francis Beeding (aka John Leslie Palmer) and in P.D. James' Devices and Desires where one of the suspects attends a stag party at the hotel. The hotel is probably best known for its links with L.P. Hartley's The Go-Between (1953) and Joseph Losey actually used the

Norwich Mail Coach.

hotel as the location for the lunch scene in his film.

Mail Coaches

Early public transport.
Although other periodic and scheduled coaches had run previously, the first Mail Coach (stage coach which also carried the Royal Mail) did not run between Norwich and London until 1785. By 1802 there were two Mail Coaches daily running to London from the King's Head on the Market Place, one via Ipswich to the Swan with Two Necks and the other via Newmarket to the Golden Cross in Charing Cross. The journey time was in the region of 13 hours when not delayed by weather, mechanical failures or highwaymen. Other Mail Coaches made runs to a variety of destinations locally and regionally. The London Mail ran continuously until1846 when it made its final run on 6th January following the opening of the Norwich to London railway line in 1845.

Mancroft

Historic Ward. Named after the 'Magna Crofta' or great field, upon which the post Conquest Norman borough was constructed, Mancroft was one of the early wards of the City and originally included just the parishes of

St Stephen, St Giles and St Peter Mancroft. As the City expanded, Mancroft Ward encompassed the whole of the Walled City but revisions to the boundaries in the recent past have resulted in the historic ward losing half of its territory to Thorpe Hamlet and gaining parts of West Pottergate.

Mangreen

Rural hamlet. Part of the parish of Swardeston, Mangreen, meaning 'commonly owned grassy place' represents a tiny cluster of properties between Swardeston and the Ipswich Road. The only significant structure is Mangreen Hall which was built on the site of a moated, medieval manor for Henry Davy in 1700. It contains elaborate interiors and a fireplace with Dutch tiles. More recently, proposals have emerged as part of the Norwich Growth Point designation, to locate a new town of 4,000 houses at Mangreen.

Mann Egerton

Local automotive and aeronautical pioneers.
In 1899 Gerard Noel Cornwallis Mann bought an electrical contracting business from Laurence, Scott & Co and expanded into the still surviving, imposing site on the corner of Queen Street and Bank Plain. In 1900 he took a partner, Hubert Wingfield Egerton, and Mann Egerton was born. They began in the early car trade in Prince of Wales Road, manufacturing bodies as well as selling new and used cars and by 1909 they were manufacturing bodies for Rolls Royce. At the outbreak of WWI they were asked by the Admiralty to build aircraft and this they did at Cromer Road where

they constructed an impressive, 200 ft long bow string roofed hanger. Their repertoire was extensive including Short Bombers, Sopwiths, Spad Scouts, De Haviland Bombers and Short Seaplanes. With the end of the War, production ceased as soon as it started and the company had to diversify its plant and workforce into alternative products – to begin with, custom made furniture. In 1919 their automotive theme expanded as they opened the first driving school in the country. A major fire at Alysham Road caused a production hiccup in 1934 but the company recovered and the Second World War brought a further increase in production as they switched from car bodies to troop carriers and ambulances. The first radar station in England was installed by Mann Egerton and they supplied over half a million pieces of office furniture for the Government. After the War both the car division and the furniture division prospered and the company also moved into commercial vehicles. In 1964 the electrical division was sold to Westinghouse and in 1973 Inchcape bought the

motor division but continued to use the former name in car dealerships. The old flagship site at Prince of Wales Road was developed for offices and flats while the Cromer Road site was redeveloped as a car retail park, with the loss of the aircraft hanger.

Manne, Katherine

Medieval anchoress. In the early C16th, the Dominican friary at St Andrews housed an anchoress, a deeply religious woman who chose to live a solitary life in confined quarters, whose life was dedicated entirely to prayer, mediation and spiritual counselling. Katherine Manne took over from former anchoress Katherine Foster in 1530, and seems to have been very popular and widely known. Indeed, Mann survived the Reformation and was given a pension, provided that she 'minded her own business'. Katherine was also involved in the death of Norwich's first Protestant martyr, Thomas Bilney. Thomas presented Katherine with a copy of Tyndale's English translation of the New Testament, and was arrested. As a relapsed heretic, he was burnt at the

stake in 1531, but defended her from any charges of heresy. It was then illegal to read the Bible in English.

Marchesi, Louis

Founder of the Round Table Movement. Emilio William Louis Marchesi, the son of Irish and Swiss parents, was required to deliver his maiden speech at the Norwich Rotary Club at the Suckling House (Cinema City) in 1927. During his talk he introduced the idea of a club for young business and professional men. The idea had been prompted by a speech in which the Prince of Wales, at the Birmingham Trades and Industries Fair, had talked about the need for young business and professional men to get around the table, 'adopt methods that have proved so sound in the past, adapt them to the changing needs of the time, and wherever possible, improve them.' Marchesi held an inaugural meeting at Suckling House the same year and the world wide Round Table Movement was born, under the motto 'adopt, adapt and improve'. The Round Table Movement now flourishes in every continent in the world with over 44,000 members in over 70 countries.

Mann Egerton pioneering the first UK driving school.

Louis Marchesi, founder of the Round Table Movement.

Louis Marchesi
1898 - 1968
Founder of the Round Table Movement
and owner of Langfords Restaurant
which stood on this site, where
Table No 1 meetings
took place.

Norwich Market

Main market

The Great Market was established in the new French Borough by Earl of Norfolk & Suffolk Ralph de Guader between 1071 and 1075, following the Norman Conquest, and has survived there ever since to be the largest six day market in the UK. The Market originally stretched from the Tollhouse, later the Guildhall in the north to the southern frontage of the Haymarket in the south and from St Peter's street to Le Nethere Rowe (Gentleman's Walk) although later, parts of the site were built upon. The centrally located Murage Loft, where tolls were paid, sat in the middle although the building is now thought to be lost. The original market was an amalgam of many specialist, smaller markets although most have now been superceded by modern shops. These included the Apothecary Market, forming part of the Meatmarket; Barleymarket huddled around the Guildhall initially then relocated west

of Mancroft; Cheesemarket southeast of St Peter's churchyard at least until 1390 when it was referred to as the old cheese market, suggesting a new one was somewhere else; Cloutmarket selling cloth, north of Mancroft; Cobblers' Row, denoting shoe repairers, along the east of St Peter's churchyard in Weavers Lane; Cordwainers' Row denoting shoe makers, along the modern Walk, north of White Lion Street; Drapery being the principal cloth market located north of St Peter Mancroft; Fishmarket, originally running north/south and parallel to St Peter's Street, this became a permanent set of buildings before being demolished and rebuilt grandly in the mid C19th. It is probably the only distinct sector of the old market to survive and now sits on the east of the site roughly opposite the Arcade; Girdlers' Stall were the girdlemakers and were located with the needlers; Glovers' Stalls sold gloves

and were at the south end of Needlers' Row; Hatters' Row was north of the Guildhall; Ironmongers' Row was north of the Murage Loft and south of the Guildhall; the Leekmarket was where herbs were sold and was located in the west of the Meat (Butchers') Market which was between the Fishmongers' Row and Ironmongers; Linen Drapery was in St Peter's Street; Maltmarket, selling malted barley for brewing beer, was at the south east corner of St Peter's church; Meatmarket or Butchers' Row ran parallel to and east of the Fishmarket; Needlers' Row provided a critically important product in a City where textiles were the principal industry and it was located north of the linen drapers and south of the woolsellers; Oatmarket's location is unknown but it is reasonable to assume that it was close to the Barleymarket; Omanseterow sold cloth made on a one man loom and was located west of Mancroft; Parmenter

From left: the Market in the C19th, and the Market refurbishment under way in the early C21st.

Deighton's prospect of the Market in 1799.

Row sold skins and furs and was north of Mancroft; Poultrymarket was south of St Peter's churchyard; Puddingmarket, where sausages and haggis-like concoctions were sold, was in the surviving Pudding Lane, north of the churchyard; Ropery was east of the butchers; Scudders' Row was where the dressers of white leather traded and this is peculiar to Norwich; Sheepmarket was in the Haymarket before being moved to the Castle Ditches; Skeppers Row where the basket (skep) makers traded east of the Murage Loft; Soapers' Lane, adjacent to the needlers and glovers; Sourbreadmarket, selling leavened bread, was between St Peter's Street and the Parmenters; Souter Row was an early name for shoemakers and was in the same place as the Cordwainers; Spicers' row was north of the drapers and south of the Breadmakers; Tallowmarket sold fat for candles but the location is unknown; Tanners' Market was east of the needlers; Wastelmarket sold white bread and was between St Peter's Street and the Parmenters although, at the same time (C14th) the white bread sellers were also recorded in Westlegate or Wastelgate; Wheatmarket was south of the churchyard in the Haymarket; Woodmarket was beside the sheepmarket in the Haymarket; Woolmarket was beneath the Murage Loft and Worsted Row was between St Peter's Street and the Linendrapers, north of Mancroft.

The physical form of the Market has changed quite radically over its 900 year life. By the late medieval period, permanent buildings (e.g. Fishmarket, Murage Loft) had been developed on the site. Redevelopments in the C19th transformed things further with a new fish market. The remainder of the site was, however, a large open space where temporary stalls were located but where they could be cleared from to create a gathering space. When Gladstone came to the City, for instance, 40,000 people reputedly gathered in the Market Place. At the time when City Hall was developed, a major clearance took place of permanent buildings which had occupied the Market space, notably a terrace running south from the Guildhall, roughly on the site of the current Memorial Gardens. There were also buildings within the Haymarket and on the east side of St Peter's churchyard at Weavers Lane, which were also cleared in the C20th. Another major renovation of the Market took place in the late 1960s when the stalls became more permanent. Most recently in the early

C21st, the Council examined how the Market could be refurbished to meet the needs of the new Millennium. A number of radical schemes were put forwards, including proposals to create more routes and spaces through the site. Vocal opposition to anything too radical resulted in the Council essentially sticking with the existing layout and replacing the old, wood and canvas topped stalls with permanent metal alternatives. Although more functional than their predecessors and welcomed by many users and traders, the new look stalls have attracted some criticism for the uniform and institutional visual impression they now create. The Market itself however, remains successful and a vibrant core to the historic centre with an interesting and varied range of fresh and speciality foodstalls ranging from award winning sausages to Asian, Middle Eastern and Eastern European foods, and an eclectic choice of other goods from alternative clothing through Reggae goods to somewhere that you can buy every vacuum cleaner spare part that ever existed!

From left: Reconstruction of the historic Market Cross, and the foundations of the original Market Cross revealed during the Market refurbishment.

Market Cross

Lost feature. The first Market Cross was built in 1411 but there is no detailed record of what it was like. This was replaced between 1501 and 1503 at the expense of Mayor John Rightwise. It was 70 feet tall and sat on an octagonal plinth that was 30 feet across. The whole structure was ornately decorated and contained a central chapel, occupied by an officiating priest but at the Reformation the chapel was converted to a grain store. In the C17th it became the 'Market House' where official City measures for grain and other materials were kept. The feature continued to decline and the citizens objected to being taxed for the upkeep of something which they regarded as having very little value. Consequently it was demolished in 1732 and the stone was sold for £125. It is likely that the foundations of the Cross were damaged during the remodelling of the Market in the 1930s and in 2005, when the Market was again being renovated, the foundations were uncovered briefly as part of the archaeological excavations. The surviving structure was recorded and the outline of the octagonal base is now preserved in the repaving beneath the new Market stalls.

Markshall

Lost Village. Located north of Caistor St Edmund, Markshall had become deserted by the late medieval period and its church had fallen into dereliction. A rectangular, roofless ruin was described in 1737 and the surviving remnants were demolished to make way for the Norwich to London Railway line in 1847, when construction unearthed a stone coffin and skeletons. The only surviving building in the parish is Markshall Farm which dates from 1730 and was built for a member of the Pettus family.

Marriotts Way

Long distance foot and cycle path. This is a 24 mile long foot and cycle path running from the site of the former City Station, at the junction of Barn Road and St Crispins Road, to Aylsham, along the former Midland and Great Northern Railway line. The Norwich section is entirely off road and the remainder is predominantly also off road with a few exceptions, like Drayton and Taverham where you have to cross radial roads or estate roads. This is part of the Sustrans National Cycle Route No.1 which runs from Harwich to Hull. Marriotts Way links to the Weavers Way at Aylsham (another former railway line) and this runs to North Walsham from whence it is possible to get a train back to Norwich.

Marston Marshes

Public open space. This 26 ha. local nature reserve comprising floodplain grazing marsh on the northern side of the River Yare. There are numerous dykes throughout the site, which are managed on a rotational basis. The grass is managed through summer grazing by cattle and mowing. Also included in the site are some small areas of damp woodland. Willows on site are managed through pollarding. There are five wildlife ponds. Species of interest include water voles, otters and orchids, as well as general good marsh flora and dragonflies. Geese use site in winter and a snipe was also recorded recently. Access is possible from Marston Lane.

Martineau, Harriett
Women's rights campaigner and author.

Harriet Martineau, was born into a Norwich Unitarian family and lived for much of her youth at 24 Magdalen Street, at the later named 'Martineau House'. Her parents held progressive views on the education of their daughters, but expected them to stay at home. Harriet thought this was very unfair and in 1823 the Unitarian journal, Monthly Repository, published her anonymous article, On Female Education. Instead of choosing marriage, Harriet continued writing articles for the Monthly Repository. In 1829, Harriet moved to London where the journal paid her a regular wage. Martineau's career as an author began with religious books such as Devotional Exercises for the Use of Young Persons (1826) and Addresses for the Use of Families (1826). She then turned to the ambitious project of writing books on politics and economics for the ordinary reader, which revealed her passion for social reform. Illustrations of Political Economy (1832) was a great success and brought her financial independence. This was followed by another bestseller, Poor Laws and Paupers Illustrated (1834).

After two years travelling in North America, she published Society in America (1837), a critique of America's failure to live up to its democratic principles and the treatment of women who she claimed were treated like slaves. Martineau argued for an improvement in women's education, so that "marriage need not be their only object in life." In 1839 Martineau had her first novel, Deerbrook, published and others followed. In 1851 her book Letters on the Laws of Man's Nature and Development created a sensation as it was a complete rejection of religious belief. In 1852 Martineau joined the staff of the Daily News. Over the next sixteen years she wrote over 1600 articles for the newspaper, including articles on the employment of women and state education for girls. In 1866 she presented a petition asking Parliament to grant women the vote. She also wrote articles in favour of women being allowed to enter the medical profession. In 1869 Martineau began writing articles attacking the Contagious Diseases Acts, which had been introduced in the 1860s in an attempt to reduce venereal disease in the armed forces. Martineau objected in principal to laws that only applied to women. She subsequently formed the National Association for the Repeal of the Contagious Diseases Act and continued to write articles about women's rights, until her death in 1876.

Martineau, James
Philosopher and author.

James Martineau was born into a Norwich Unitarian family and lived for much of his youth at 24 Magdalen Street in Norwich, at the later named 'Martineau House'. After being educated at the local grammar school and in Bristol under Dr Lant Carpenter, Martineau was ordained in the Unitarian Ministry and in 1828 and served as a Minister in both Dublin and Liverpool. In 1841, Martineau was appointed professor of moral philosophy at Manchester New College. While at Manchester he developed a reputation as a leading religious philosopher after the publication of Endeavours After the Christian Life (1843). In 1869 he became Principal of the college and wrote several books on religion and philosophy including A Study of Spinoza (1882), Types of Ethical Theory (1885), A Study of Religion (1888) and the Seat of Authority in Religion (1890). In his books Martineau was a strong critic of materialism and was one of the first philosophers to recognise the importance of Darwin's theory of evolution.

Site of the lost village of Markshall.

*Interior views of the
Masonic Hall, St Giles.*

Masonic Hall

**Surviving masonic
buildings.** The Masons were
one of the first associations
to establish a Provincial
Grand Lodge in the UK
(after Cheshire and
Cornwall). In 1759, Edward
Bacon of Earlham was
appointed the first Provincial
Grand Master for Norwich,
Norfolk and Beccles. The
Lodge first met in the Three
Tuns in London Lane but by
the early C20th they were
sufficiently successful to be
able to commission a newly
built Hall. The Masonic Hall
in St Giles was designed by
Albert Havers in 1907 and
the Temple and Banqueting
Hall were added by
S.J.Wearing in 1927. The
building is available for
public hire.

Mazzotti, Pelligrino

Italian sculptor. A sculptor
from Lucca, Italy, Pellegrino
Mazzotti established a
studio in Charing Cross,
adjoining Strangers Hall, in
1819. In the years 1821-29
he exhibited with the
Norwich Society of Artists.
Subjects for his work
included Shakespeare,
Norwich School painter
John Crome, Lord Nelson
and founder of the
Methodist Church John
Wesley.

Mayor

**Historic head of the
Corporation.** Henry IV's
Charter of January 1404
gave the City the right to
elect a Mayor and two
Sheriffs, effectively making
the City an independent, self
governing entity. The Mayor
was given the right to have a
sword carried erect before
him in the presence of all
lords and magnates, except
kings. The first Mayor was
William Appleyard and

Mayors were elected
annually until 1909 when the
position was elevated to
Lord Mayor by Edward VII.
All of the Mayors were men.
The 100th Lord Mayor
(Evelyn Collishaw), elected in
2009, was a woman and the
first female Lord Mayor
(Ethel Colman) was elected
in 1923. The post today is
essentially ceremonial and
apolitical.

Meadows, Bernard

Sculptor. Bernard Meadows,
educated at the City of
Norwich School and
Norwich School of Art, was
sculptor Henry Moore's first
assistant and long time
friend. He was professor of
sculpture at London's Royal
College of Art from 1960 to
1980. A plaque
commemorating him and
funded by the Henry Moore
Foundation is located on
Prospect House.

From left: Mayor Making 2011, the Mayor's Sword and Mace Bearers in the C19th.

Medieval and Merchant Houses

There are about 200 surviving houses from the period 1450-1680 within the Walls, most of them dating from after the Great Fires of 1507 when 718 houses were lost – probably more than a third of all the houses in the City at the time. While virtually all of the non domestic surviving buildings are still with us because they were in the hands of the church or the state (in the form of national or local government), many of the houses survive principally because most of them, after being held by great property owning families or individuals, passed into the stewardship of breweries. This third property holding institution managed to preserve these great houses well into the last century so it is unsurprising that the majority of the surviving medieval houses will have been pubs for substantial proportions of their histories. Some of the most notable examples include Wensum Lodge (formerly a brewery), Suckling House in St Andrews, the Briton's Arms, and other properties, in Elm Hill, the former Hampshire Hog in Hampshire Hog Yard

off St Benedicts and the former Barking Dicky in Westlegate. Survivors which weren't under the wing of breweries include Bacon's House in Colegate, Augustine Stewart's House in Tombland, Strangers Hall and the Bridewell.

Mereholt

Lost wood. Referred to as early as the pre Conquest period this was a great wood which was located to the north of the current St Augustines area. It seems to have disappeared by the 1500s with the last mention of it being in a record of 1506.

Midland and Great Northern Railway

Former railway company. Established in 1893, the Midland and Great Northern Railway was a joint railway company created by a merger of the Midland Railway and the Great Northern Railway. At a time when the majority of railways ran south to north, the M&GN capitalised on the links between the industrial Midlands and the East Coast seaside resorts and ports. At the time of its creation it was easily the longest joint railway system

in the UK, exceeding 180 miles (295km). In Norwich its base was City Station and the principal route ran west from there, via Melton Constable (the Crewe of North Norfolk), to the Midlands. The railway was incorporated into the LNER in 1936 and being immersed into British Railways in 1948 it finally closed in 1959. The line west from City Station became a highly popular pedestrian and cycle route in the 1980s despite proposals in the Norwich Area Transportation Strategy to make it into a major radial road.

Mile Cross

C20th estate. Mile Cross is essentially the area of housing west of the Aylsham Road and it takes its name from the boundary marker (the St Faiths Cross or Le Whytecrosse) which denoted the City boundary and was located a mile from St Augustines Gate.

The Mile Cross Estate was begun between 1918 and 1920 and represented the first example of a municipal garden housing estate in the country. The initial 200 houses between Drayton Road and Aylsham Road

Mile Cross – the first Municipal Garden Housing Estate to be developed in the UK.
Aerial view of Mile Cross Gardens and early council houses.

were developed in the 'English cottage tradition' and were supplemented by shops, pubs, six schools, parks and other facilities. As well as a traditional style and layout, designers sought to enshrine a local distinctiveness in the estate by naming streets after notable characters from the City's history such as Herbert de Losinga, Richard Spynk, Luke Hansard and Margaret Paston. The estate grew eventually to several thousand units with more high rise development taking place south of Boundary Road in the 1960s. In the more recent past the Norman Centre has been developed to offer a wide range of community, educational and recreational facilities at affordable prices while the Phoenix Children's Project runs a number of projects including a youth club, an after school club and the Duke of Edinburgh Award. For some years the area has been characterised by poverty and deprivation. In 2003 it was the 6th most deprived ward in the East of England Region and in 2007 it remained as one of the 10 per cent most deprived wards in England.

Mile Cross Marsh

Public open space.
Mile Cross Marsh and Sycamore Crescent Wood Mile Cross Marsh is adjacent to Sweet Briar marsh, which is a SSSI. The marsh consists of an area of fen and an area of damp grassland. A number of years ago a local resident dug a pond and this is used in spring by breeding frogs. There are a number of dykes dissecting the site, one of which is a storm drain which often contains foul water. Species of interest include toads and water voles and orchids. Access is possible from Marriotts Way long distance footpath.

Mills, Sir John

Actor. Oscar winner and star of over 100 feature films Sir John Mills went to school at the surviving building at 94, Upper St Giles when it was the Norwich High School for Boys. Apparently he hated it and claimed, as one of his achievements, that he broke the school bully's nose.

Mischief Tavern

Former merchant house.
Located just north of Fye Bridge and originally built as the City house for Alexander Thurleston, Mayor in 1600 and Burgess to Parliament in 1601 (buried next door in St Clement's), the house is predominantly C16th with major C19th alterations. Thurston's merchant mark adorns the surviving fireplace of 1599. Its use as the Mischief Tavern dates only from 1960 when it was a Bullard's house and took on the name from the original Mischief located in St Paul's Back Street, which closed in 1915. Prior to that the Fye Bridge house had been called the Fyebridge Tavern from 1915 and prior to that, the Ribs of Beef since 1760 – a title taken on subsequently from the pub facing it across the river from 1985.

Monastery

Former chapel. Located to the north of Elm Hill and built in 1864 in a Gothic revival style for an order founded by Father Ignatius, it survived as a chapel for barely two years then became a factory. It is now used by the Norwich University College of the Arts and was recently converted, by Hudson Architects, to provide a state of the art technology studio.

Monck, Nugent

Theatrical innovator. Born in Shropshire and trained in Liverpool, he was influenced by William Poel who was a devotee of producing Shakespeare plays in the 'pure' form which the Bard had originally intended. Monck came to Norwich in 1911 to produce a pageant and stayed. He developed an empathy with other enthusiasts and they started to put on plays, first in the Music House, which held just 97 people. After WWI Monck set up a home for his productions in a former Roman Catholic Chapel, which was to become the Maddermarket. He built a Globe-style interior and raised money from supporters to create his vision of pure Shakespeare. He managed to set a record by producing all of Shakespeare's plays in the form that they were originally intended. A Mrs Pym let him live in the stunning medieval Ninhams Court for six shillings a week and he stayed there for 40 years until his death in 1958. His remarkable contribution is reflected in the fact that the Maddermarket legacy continues successfully 50 years after his death.

Money, Colonel John

Soldier of fortune. Regarded locally as something of a 'character', Col. Money was a professional soldier and a veteran of the American War of Independence. He had named his Crown Point Estate at Trowse after a battle in that war. He was a prime mover in Norwich society and gave an annual ball to which the leading citizens were invited. In 1789 he undertook one of the first hot air balloon flights

Demolition of the Morgans King Street Brewery in the 1990s.

from the City to raise money for the Norfolk & Norwich Hospital. The balloon took off from Quantrell's Gardens in the presence of 1,000 spectators and, having 'ascended higher than any of the former balloons' it took off towards the coast, passed over Lowestoft and finally came down in the sea off the coast of Southwold. The colonel remained in the sea until 11.30 at night when he was picked up by the Argus revenue cutter of Harwich commanded by Capt Haggis.

In 1792 the French National Assembly passed a decree allowing four foreign generals to raise legions to fight with the French Army and they invited Money to be one of these generals. He reached Paris in July of that year and was commissioned Marechal des Camps et Armees. He witnessed first hand the 'Reign of Terror', including the storming of the Tuilleries and saw the Paris mob carrying the heads of the Swiss Guard on pikes and bayonets. Despite his distaste with the new Republican Government he continued in their service, fighting the Austrians in Belgium, until the end of the

year when he resigned his commission, feeling that war between Britain and France was imminent – 'When I engaged to serve these people they had a King and Constitution; now they have neither.'

Monuments

See *Sculpture.*

Morgans

Lost Brewer. In 1845, John Brandram Morgan and Walter Morgan took over the Conesford Brewery from the Thompson family which in turn had taken on an enterprise started by John Barnard in 1563. Things didn't start well since Walter Morgan was found `drowned in a Gyle Vat' in March of the same year, presumably overcome by alcohol fumes. By 1887 it was a registered company trading as 'The Old King Street Brewery Established 1720' and was controlling 188 pubs. The 1 Ha (2.4 acre) site, on both sides of King Street, between Stepping Lane and Thorn Lane expanded further into the C20th as Morgans absorbed breweries in Chatteris, Grimston, Wymondham, Kings Lynn and Letheringsett, and increased production. By 1904 they owned or leased 600 pubs. Expansion continued with further takeovers but in June 1942 the Luftwaffe obliterated the Old King Street Brewery. A new brewery was swiftly constructed after the War on the King Street sites and production resumed in 1950 but the days of independent breweries were numbered and in 1961 Morgans fell victim to a joint take over by Bullard's and Steward & Pattesons, who in turn were absorbed by the Watney empire and closed down just a few years later. Although Watneys initially centred their Norwich production on the King Street Brewery site, they, in turn, closed it and the site remained derelict for many years. Eventually the western half was redeveloped by regional developer Hopkins Homes for houses and flats while the eastern half, now cleared awaits a secure future after a number of false starts.

Moray-Smith, John

Mural sculptor. It is easier to say what Moray-Smith did than who he was since he was something of an enigma – even his real name is unknown. What is known is that he moved to Norwich shortly after WWI, married a woman from Costessey and adopted her name. He is famous because in the 1930s he worked for local brewers Morgans to produce some of the first art installations for 'theme pubs' in the UK. His most prominent work is the massive relief on the exterior of the Coachmakers Arms, produced in 1937 and depicting St Stephen's Gate. He produced another 'Gate' mural for the Berstrete Gates. Equally impressive was the enormous 1939 representation of the Prince of Denmark (consort of Queen Anne) on Sprowston Road. In 1938 he was commissioned to produce six plaster reliefs depicting the medieval wool trade for Morgans new pub the Woolpack in Golden Ball Street (five survive in the pub and an internet record suggests that the 6th was sold at auction in 2001). Other, now lost, works include a coach and horses in the former Coach and Horses, Red Lion Street, and a prospect of Norwich from St James' Hill, in the Cock, King Street. Recent research by the Norwich Society has indicated that he also produced a Viking for the Viking in Sprowston as well as works beyond Norwich in Carbrook, Stalham, Cromer and March. Intriguingly there is a bronze plaque attributed to Moray-Smith and dated 1957, located at the Burrell Museum in Thetford.

Morse, George

Brewer and politician. A major figure in the brewing company of Steward, Patteson, Morse, Finch & Co, Morse was Mayor in 1898 and Lord Mayor in 1922, making him the first person to hold both posts. He was on the Council for nearly 35 years and was rewarded for his civic works by a knighthood. He was an accomplished mountaineer and President of the Alpine Club from 1926 to 1929.

Morton Peto, Sir Samuel

Railway innovator. Samuel Morton Peto was a hugely successful railway contractor in the mid C19th working not only in the UK but also in Canada, Algeria and Russia. He built the first railway line from Yarmouth to Norwich in 1844 and between 1847 and 1854 he was Liberal MP for the City, living during this time in Bracondale. He is commemorated by a bust in Norwich Station.

Mosley, Sir Oswald

Leader of the British Fascist Movement. In 1935 Sir Oswald Mosley addressed a 'lively' crowd of

---

From left: St Stephen's Gate by Moray-Smith, on the wall of the Coachmakers. The Prince of Denmark, on the wall of the pub of the same name.

10,000 in the Market Place but due to the City's long history of radicalism and socialism, he was not well received and had to be protected by the constabulary.

Motion, Andrew

Poet Laureate. Poet Laureate from 1999 until 2009, Motion was Professor of Creative Writing at the University of East Anglia from 1989.

Mottram, Ralph Hale

Writer. Born the son of Gurney's chief clerk at their bank in Bank Plain, Mottram worked at the bank during his youth but began writing in his spare time and received encouragement from the likes of John Galsworthy. His experiences in the First World War formed the basis for his first and most famous book The Spanish Farm which secured him the Hawthornden Prize in 1924. He followed this with Sixty Four, Ninety Four in 1925 and The Crime at Vanderlynden's in the same year and a biography of John Galsworthy. He left the bank in 1927 to devote more time to writing and broadcasting. Mottram became Lord Mayor in 1953 and had long associations with the Libraries Committee, the Norfolk and Norwich Subscription Library and the Norfolk and Norwich Archaeological Society. He was also elected President of the General Assembly of Unitarian and Free Churches. In 1966 he received an honorary degree of Doctor of Letters at the UEA. He died in 1971, is buried at the Rosary Cemetery and there is a memorial to him on St James's Hill.

St Faith's House Mountergate.

Mountergate

Ancient thoroughfare. A corruption of Parmentergate or 'street of the leather workers', the present form of the name has only been in use since the 1890s. Prior to that it was known as Inferior Conesford or various versions of St Faith's Lane. The latter is unsurprising since, during the pre Conquest period, the southern, intra mural route running from King Street, followed a line in an arc along the alignment of the present Mountergate (or more accurately just south of it) and the north/south section of St Faith's Lane, cutting across the later Cathedral Precinct to join up with the north/south section of modern Bishopgate.

One of the surviving Mousehold Aerodrome bow string roofed hangers.

Today the street is something of a wasteland, devastated horribly by the 1942 Blitz and clueless post War redevelopment, the street contains only one building of distinction (the Georgian St Faith's House and the adjacent Weavers House) and some partial remnants of Bolton & Paul, later the Co-op Shoe Factory, and the Fishmarket.

Mount Pleasant

Historic suburban street. Mount Pleasant was, historically, an area at the heart of the Golden Triangle but today it survives as one street running between Unthank and Newmarket Roads. It contains 11 grade II listed structures, predominantly mid C19th, yellow brick houses sitting in attractive gardens.

Mount Surrey

Lost mansion. Following the Dissolution, the King granted the site of St Leonard's priory to Thomas Howard, Duke of Norfolk. Howard's son, Henry Howard, Earl of Surrey, built a fine mansion there called Mount Surrey. Following the Howard's fall from favour and the execution of Henry for treason, the house reverted to the Crown and while Elizabeth restored it to the Howards, and indeed visited while in Norwich in 1578, the family let it fall into ruin. Some remnants of the original structure may survive in the current buildings on the site.

Mousehold Aerodrome

Former aerodrome now redeveloped. Formerly used as a training ground for the locally billeted cavalry regiments from the Nelson Barracks, the site was taken

*Above and right:
Mousehold Heath today.*

*Below and right: The original
extent of Mousehold Heath,
reaching to Mousehold
House, Great and Little
Plumstead and Mousehold
Farm, Woodbastwick.*

over by the Royal Flying Corps (RFC) in 1914 and redesignated Mousehold Heath Aerodrome. It was initially used as a training depot until 1916 then it became a Wing HQ and was ultimately used by Number 3 Aircraft Acceptance Park whose job it was to commission aircraft into the RFC made by local companies such as Boulton and Paul. After the 1st World War, Boulton and Paul took the site over for aircraft assembly and flight testing and it remained in their use until the 1930s. The Norfolk & Norwich Aero Club was formed in 1927 and also used the site. After Boulton & Paul's departure the site became Norwich Airport, and during the Second World War was laid out as a decoy airfield to tempt enemy bombers away from Horsham St Faiths but ultimately fell into disuse when the former Horsham

St Faiths aerodrome became the new Norwich airport. The site was subsequently developed for housing, industry and a school. Two bow string roofed hangers survive from the original aerodrome on Salhouse Road and have been adapted for industrial use.

Mousehold Heath

Major urban green space.
Mousehold Heath is an area of heath and semi natural, broad leaved woodland covering nearly 200 acres (81 ha) just to the north east of the Walled City. In 1880 it passed from the Dean and Chapter to the care of Norwich Corporation who, in 1884, established the Mousehold Heath Conservators to oversee its care and protection. The Mousehold Heath Defenders, formed in 1972, act as an unofficial 'public conscience' to protect the Heath and have supported

popular protests to resist threats to the integrity or character of the space. These threats have been significant over the years including unsuccessful proposals by the war Office in 1947 to take over 150 acres as a military training ground and the Norwich Area Transportation Strategy in the 1970s to drive a major radial road broadly along the line of Gurney Road.

Originally the Heath stretched far out into the adjacent countryside to South Walsham and Faden's Map of 1779 shows it reaching to Salhouse Broad. The original extent is hinted at by surviving remnants, such as Mousehold House in the parish of Great and Little Plumstead, now nearly three miles away from the edge of the current Heath, and Mousehold Heath Farm in the parish of Woodbastwick, five miles from the Heath.

Enclosure in 1801 reduced much of the outer areas but the 'City' Heath survived principally because its poor quality made it unsuitable for productive agriculture then the Corporation's takeover protected it. It was peppered with a rash of brick and lime kilns but these have, over time, been restored back to a natural state. Even the Vinegar Pond (then the only standing water on the Heath), apparently created by Bren Carriers compacting the earth in World War II training exercises, now looks like a natural feature.

Historically the Heath is famous or infamous for a number of events. The St William 'Blood Libel' incident began here in 1144 when the body of an apprentice boy was discovered apparently the victim of ritual murder. St William's Chapel was then erected (or possibly rededicated from the existing chapel of St Catherine) and served as a pilgrimage site until its demolition at the Reformation. Vague remnants of earthworks remain. Robert Kett's Rebellion made its camp on Mousehold Heath although

this was more likely to have been in the Gas Hill/Kett's Hill area. George Borrow wrote about gypsies camped upon the heath and Norwich artists made the Heath the subject of their paintings. There were previously three mills on the Heath but all have now gone, including, most recently, Sprowston Mill, an impressive post mill built in 1780 but which burned down in 1934 just as it was about to be protected formally. There were also two farms close to the present boundary and one, Hill Farm, survives.

Today the Heath provides a wildlife oasis with semi rural walks, spectacular views out over the City and more formal attractions like sports pitches, pitch and putt, a bandstand and a restaurant.

Mousehold House

Merchant House. Built in 1760, and enlarged in 1821 by William Mear as a substantial mansion for Major General Sir Robert John Harvey, Mousehold House is located off modern Pilling Park Road. Harvey had been an enormously distinguished soldier in the Peninsular War, and

innovator in guerrilla warfare. He was honoured by the King of Portugal and the Prince Regent. Wellington supported his promotion after distinguished service at Salamanca and Victoria. The house looks like a plantation owner's mansion from the southern United States and survived into the 1960s, when it was threatened by demolition. Fortunately, it was conserved by the Council and converted to six flats by City Architect David Percival and survives today, surrounded by Council flats from the 1960s.

Mousehold Waterworks

See *Waterworks*.

Mulbarton

Suburban parish. Located 9.6km (6 miles) south of Norwich, Mulbarton is spread out around a huge, triangular common. The church of St Mary Magdalen dates predominantly from the C14th, with a tower of 1393, but the church was substantially restored in 1875. South of the church is the early C17th Old Hall, formerly the manor of the Rich Family. A C17th barn, now converted to other

Views of Mousehold House.

Clockwise from top: Mulbarton Old Hall, Mulbarton (New) Hall, Barn associated with Old Hall.

uses, is located close by. Mulbarton Hall, on the south east corner of the Common, is early C18th in origin and one of its first occupants was wealthy Norwich textile merchant Philip Stannard. The Malt House, on the Norwich Road side of the Common, is a C17th timber framed house refaced in brick. The World's End pub also dates from the C17th with C18th additions.

Munnings, Alfred

Artist. Internationally famous for his equestrian subjects, Munnings came to Norwich, from Mendham in Suffolk, at the age of 14 as a poster designer and spent his evenings honing his talent at the School of Art. His success as a painter is reflected in his having had 289 pictures exhibited at the Royal Academy from 1898 and his eventual election as Academy President in 1944, when he was also knighted. Over 30 of his works are held by the Castle Museum.

Murderers/ Gardeners Arms

See *Timberhill*.

Museums

Origin and provision. The eminent botanist James Edward Smith suggested the establishment of a Norwich Museum to supplement the book collection of the Norfolk & Norwich Literary Institution in the 1820s. The Institution was housed in the Haymarket and in 1825, the first Norwich Museum opened there. These premises were very modest and in 1833 the first purpose built museum, by John Brown, was provided in Exchange Street and survives as part of Jarrold stationers. Initially it was open to the public but then restricted to members of the Institution only. The Institution had been using the 1764 Duke of Norfolk's Catholic Chapel in St Andrews as a subscription library, but when this moved to new premises in 1838, the institution converted the

Sir Alfred Munnings.

Mulbarton Common looking south.

Chapel to a new Museum. Exhibits were principally natural history collections with elements of ethnography and archaeology. To begin with this was also for Institution members only but in 1840, on Queen Victoria's wedding day, it was opened to the public at large and 5,000 people visited. Subsequently the public were regularly allowed in free. In 1883 the Corporation acquired the Castle, following the relocation of the prison, and, with a donation of £5,000 from John Gurney, Edward Boardman was commissioned to convert the surviving structure to a new museum and gallery. The museum collections from St Andrews were transferred there and as were collections from the East Anglian Art Society. The new facility was opened by the Duke and Duchess of York on 23rd October 1894.

The Castle Museum remains the principal museum and art gallery in the East of England. Other museums include the Royal Norfolk Regimental Museum (adjacent to the Castle), the Bridewell (currently being regenerated and due to reopen in 2012), Strangers Hall, the John Jarrold Printing Museum and the City of Norwich Aviation Museum. The St Peter Hungate Church Museum (the first of its kind in the country) closed in the 1990s but has reopened recently as a centre for medieval art. The Norfolk & Norwich Pathological Museum can be visited by appointment at the new University Hospital. The Telephone Museum, formerly in the remnant of Francis Rugge's mansion in St Andrews, closed in the 1990s.

Music

Current Music scene.

Norwich boasts an extensive, diverse and innovative contemporary music offer. Major venues such as the UEA Lower Common Room (LCR) and the Waterfront host regular concerts ranging from cutting edge contemporary, festival favourites and charting bands to legends such as Motorhead and Dr John. Smaller venues such as the Playhouse and Norwich Arts Centre augment the larger sites offering performances from touring bands, up and coming performers, folk singers and individual artists. Local talent performs in a wide spectrum of venues with pubs playing a key part. The Brickmakers won the 'Best Live Music Pub of the Year 2011' award in the national Best British Pub Awards. Norwich also hosts the UK's only dedicated music video festival, annually in September. Jazz is also well represented in the City with the three day, annual Jazz Party in May attracting international stars. Classical music has a huge following and attracts performers of global stature. The Theatre Royal has a long record of internationally reknown performers in orchestral music, opera and ballet. The Britten Sinfonia has a residency in the City, along with Cambridge and Brighton, and performs here regularly. The Norwich Philharmonic has been performing since 1841 and puts on a regular programme of concerts while Chamber Orchestra Anglia celebrated its 10th birthday in 2011/12 with a programme of concerts in Norwich 12, the City's most iconic heritage buildings.

The first purpose built Norwich Museum.

Music House

Ancient house. Thought to be the oldest surviving house in Norwich, the first element of the building, consisting of a two storey structure at right angles to King Street, was started in the early C12th. This building sat on a five bay vaulted undercroft which survives as Jurnet's Club. In 1175, the building was extended south, along the King Street frontage, in the form of a three bay single aisled hall open to the roof timbers. A surviving pier base which formed part of the aisle is identical to those in the Cathedral Infirmary. Identical masons marks on both sites lend credence to the proposition that both buildings were not only constructed by the same people but that Jurnet, the Jewish financier for whom the Music House was probably built, may have also provided funding for the Cathedral. The Norwich Jews were associated with the building until 1267 when the property passed to Thomas de Weseham, a minor Crown official who sold it on to Alan de Freston,

Archdeacon of Norfolk. He extended the site and built a chapel in the house. The next major changes to the house came in 1480 when a brick undercroft was constructed in the former aisled hall and the surviving scissor braced roof was added. This heralded a takeover of the site by the Paston family who held it from 1488 until Sir Edward Coke bought it in 1612 for £850. Although one writer claims that Sir Walter Raleigh was a guest there, that seems unlikely since Coke, as Lord Chief Justice tried him and had him executed in 1618. The Cokes stayed on there for the next century. The House was taken over by Edward Hunton in 1723 and this started the Music House's association with brewing (Hunton was a brewer) which was to be formalised by the takeover by John Youngs in 1812 – this was ultimately to become Youngs, Crawshay and Youngs and was to maintain its occupation until the company disappeared in 1958 when Bullard's and S&P jointly took it over. In parallel with being part of a larger brewery site, part of the building was pressed into use as a pub (The Music House) and this continued until 1933 when the license renewal was refused because 'its defects are beyond question'. In 1964 the site was taken over by the Norfolk Education Authority as a teachers' centre. Today the site remains in educational use as an adult education centre.

The term Music House emerged in the Elizabethan period when the City's official band of Musicians, the Norwich Waits,

The Music House.

practiced there. The Waits had a national reputation, performing at court and were taken by Sir Francis Drake on a voyage to Lisbon in 1589. The Waits used the site until they were disbanded in 1790. Other cultural occupation included the use of part of the site by Nugent Monck and the Norwich Players from 1913 until 1921 when the Maddermarket opened. In 1933 the Music House Singers and Players (later the Music House Guild) were based there and this continued into the 1950s. Today the undercroft functions as a bar/club and folk club.

Muspole

Former watercourse.
The relatively minor Muspole rose at the north end of Muspole Street and, flowing along the present Water Lane, entered the Wensum at St Georges.

Mustard Shop and Museum

Industrial heritage institution. The Colman's Mustard Shop opened in Bridewell Alley in 1973, to commemorate the 150th anniversary of the founding of Colmans in 1823, and moved to its present location in the Royal Arcade in 1999. It was threatened by closure in 2008, when the then owners Unilever decided that a Mustard Shop no longer fitted with their corporate business. The Heritage Economic and Regeneration Trust (HEART) negotiated a takeover with Unilever and became the new owners in 2009. It provides a shop selling predominantly mustard related products and small, free museum illustrating the story of the Colman company both as an important component in the area's industrial heritage and as a pioneer in Victorian social philanthropy.

Reconstruction of My Lord's Garden in King Street.

My Lord's Garden

Earliest City Pleasure Garden. Developed on the site of the Austin Friars in King Street, on what was later to become the Norwich Brewery distribution depot and, latterly, a housing redevelopment site (St Anne's Wharf), the gardens were laid out by Henry Howard (brother of Thomas, Duke of Norfolk) in 1663. In the following year, journal writer Edward Browne noted the provision of recreational walks and proposals for a bowling green, 'wilderness' and flower garden. The bowling green in particular became a popular local amenity late into the C18th. In 1770 the site was put up for sale but its continuing appeal was reflected in the fact that it was acquired by William Curtiss, who not only introduced public breakfasts but also fireworks including line rockets running 'from the Top of the Summer House to the Top of the Booth'. Spurred on by early success, Curtiss diversified into 'topographic views and curios' including St James Park, the Duomo of Florence, Ranelagh Gardens and the Quirinal in Rome. In 1772 he imported workmen from London's Vauxhall Gardens who produced an artificial cascade with watermill. After a flirtation with extravagant pyrotechnics, Curtiss decided to concentrate on 'museum curiosities' and sold on to Mr Graves who introduced a series of set piece tableaux including a 'sea fight' with five ships, the storming of a castle and Versuvius. 1775 saw the ultimate competition between the four principal pleasure gardens and the return of the firework experience par excellence. Graves' imported the Italian Giuseppe Gatti to create a firework spectacular including 'Gobo la Luna' and 'Peca Curiosa Che va Arestal'. Competition from the two principal venues, the New Spring Gardens (later Vauxhall) and Quantrell's (Later Ranelagh), was intense and as they went on to do even more spectacular events, My Lord's Garden faded into just a pleasant garden until, ultimately, being taken over and developed by Morgan's Brewery.

Mustard Shop & Museum.

N is for...

The largest life insurance provider in the UK; England's greatest naval hero; England's first provincial newspaper; one of the most modern archive centres in Europe; the oldest city based music festival in the UK; the largest Victorian shoe factory in England; the UK's finest provincial collection of individually outstanding urban heritage buildings spanning the last millennium; one of Europe's largest single-site concentrations of research in Health, Food and Environmental Sciences; the only regional school of painting in England.

Nedeham Gate

See *St Stephen's Gate*.

Needham

Historic quarter. Previously thought to be a pre Conquest, small, proto-urban settlement in the vicinity of the site of the later Castle Fee, the current view is that Needham, probably meaning 'poor meadow' or 'cattle meadow,' was located on the west side of the Great Cockey, somewhere around the northern end of modern St Stephens. It would be logical for a large grazing area to be outside but close to the Anglo-Scandinavian settlement, on primary routes from the rural hinterland (the later Ipswich/Newmarket Roads and the probable Roman Berstrete) and to be near to water. The later, alternative naming of St Stephen's Gate as the Needham Gate also lends credence to this proposition.

Nelson, Admiral Lord

England's Greatest sailor. Born in 1758 at Burnham Thorpe in North Norfolk, Nelson was the son of the local rector, Edmund Nelson, and Catherine Nelson whose father came from the influential Suckling family and whose mother was grand niece of Sir Robert Walpole, England's first prime minister. On Boxing Day 1767, Nelson's mother died and his grandmother died within the space of 11 days, removing two of the most influential people in his life. He was despatched to board at the King Edward VI Grammar School in Norwich, with his brother William, where he remained briefly until transferring to Paston School at North Walsham. In 1780 Nelson read that the Royal Navy was preparing for war and asked his elder brother if he would ask their father to write to Maurice Suckling, already a serving officer in the Navy, 'and tell him I should like to go to sea with my uncle Maurice.' Nelson joined HMS Raisonnable on 24 April 1771 but shortly transferred to a merchant ship captained by one of Suckling's former colleagues for his first voyage, to the West Indies. This modest beginning saw Nelson go on to develop a meteoric and illustrious career in the Navy with one of the milestones being the orchestration of the English victory at the Battle of Cape St Vincent in 1797 by the unprecedented action of capturing two Spanish ships. He commemorated the action by sending the sword of the Spanish fleet commander, Rear Admiral Don Xavier Francisco Winthuysen, to the Mayor of Norwich. The sword is now displayed with the Civic Regalia in the Castle. Nelson made periodic visits to the City during his returns to England. With Admiral Lord Duncan he dined with Mayor

Opposite: The home of the largest life insurance provider in the UK, Norwich Union, now Aviva. Below (clockwise from bottom left): Burnham Thorpe, the first pub to take Nelson's name, Nelson's bust in the Castle Museum, Nelson's statue in Bridgetown Barbados, The Nelson Museum on Nevis, where he married his first wife, and Nelson's flagship at Portsmouth.

Nelson Barracks enlisted men's quarters before their demolition in the early 1960s.

Nelson Street Methodist Chapel, now the City Church.

Alderman Herring, in his home in St Faith's House, in the same year as his Cape St Vincent victory, shortly after Admiral Duncan's victory over the Dutch, for instance. Although Nelson's illustrious career was prematurely cut short by his death at the successful conclusion of the battle of Trafalgar, he remains the most successful English naval figure and one of the country's most popular historic icons – he came 9th in the BBC's poll of the 100 greatest Britons undertaken in 2002.

The 'local hero' is remembered by a marble statue, now in the Upper Cathedral Close, which was sculpted by Thomas Milnes and originally erected in the Market Place in 1854, at a cost of 700 guineas (raised by public subscription) before being moved to its present position in 1936. There is also a substantial portrait by Sir William Beechey, painted in 1801 and now hanging in Blackfriars Hall. Other Norwich recollections of the great man include some mementos in the Castle Museum, the extra mural Nelson Street, which includes the Nelson pub, named after him, just off Dereham Road and the former Nelson Hotel, now a restaurant associated with

the Premier Travel Inn. There is an extensive Nelson Museum at Great Yarmouth and the hero is remembered further afield with the most substantial memorials being the famous column in Trafalgar Square and his flagship at Portsmouth. More remotely though, he is remembered by a statue in the centre of Bridgetown, Barbados, and a Nelson Museum in Nevis, where he met and married his first wife.

Nelson Barracks

Lost cavalry barracks.
Started in 1792 and completed within two years the barracks were built on the ten acre site occupied formerly by Blennerhasset House (latterly Hasset's Hall). This was a substantial Elizabethan mansion, sketched by John Ninham just before its demolition in 1791 and subsequently reproduced by his son Henry. Intriguingly, there is a reference to a Hasset's Hall pub in 1836 which could suggest a surviving remnant being reused. The barracks were designed by architect James Johnson to a U-shaped plan, located north of modern Barrack Street, to accommodate 500 troopers and support staff and 340 horses. They were among the first batch of purpose built barracks in the country,

instigated by Colonel Oliver De Lancey, deputy adjutant-general at the Horse Guards, as a device to separate troops from a possibly seditious population in the wake of the French Revolution. In 1815, the Cavalry Barracks was home to the Duchy of Brunswick's Hussars of the 'Black Legion', so called because of their all black uniforms. They performed with distinction at Waterloo in that year and were called upon to exercise control over civic disorders in the City. Another notable regiment at Waterloo was the Royal North British Dragoons, or Scots Greys, who were also stationed at Nelson Barracks along with a host of other cavalry and artillery regiments including the King's Royal Irish Hussars, the 16th (Queen's) Lancers and the 8th Kings Royal Hussars. In 1905 a model barrack design was approved by the War Office and was to be piloted in Norwich. The Secretary of State for War laid the foundation stone for new Cavalry Barracks on the site of the later Mousehold Aerodrome, which had, for some time, been used as the cavalry's training ground. The stone was taken up and the barracks were never built. The Nelson Barracks site continued in use until 1965 when it was redeveloped for housing by the City Council and no elements of the original complex remain.

Nelson Street Methodist Chapel, Heigham

Converted, Victorian Methodist chapel in Heigham. Built in 1878 to serve the growing artisan's suburb of Heigham, the chapel remained with the Methodists until 1956 when it served as a relatively short term replacement for the congregation of St Bartholomew, Heigham, which had been bombed in 1942. In 1975 it became the Mount Zion Pentecostal Church and then the 'City Church'.

Nest

Former football ground. Established in 1908, the Nest was the second home of Norwich City after the club moved from Newmarket Road. The name derived from the obvious association with the Canaries. The ground was built into a former chalk pit on Rosary Road and the site was stabilised by a number of concrete walls. Some presented hazards not only to the spectators but also

the players, notably Jimmy Stokes who broke his leg by running into the wall. The facility was upgraded in 1910 with additional terracing and improved drainage. The terraces, however, remained perilously close to the pitch and in 1922, against Northampton, the fencing gave way on top of one of the concrete walls and over 50 spectators fell onto the pitch, fortunately without any serious injuries. The ground's record attendance was for an FA Cup tie against Sheffield Wednesday in 1935 when 25,037 people were crammed into the ground. Perhaps this kind of overcrowding and the need for the Club to respond to its 2nd Division status provoked the closure of the Nest and a move to Carrow Road in the following season. The site was eventually redeveloped for industry and was the home of Bertram Books before their recent move to Thorpe Business Park.

Nest Public House

Football Ground Pub. The Nest was the first example in the UK of a pub attached to a football ground. Taking its name

from the club's former football ground and located in the River End Stand (now Norwich and Peterborough) it changed its name to 'Strikers' then 'Scores'. It is now an American style restaurant called 'Yellows' and forming part of Delia Smith's food offerings at the ground.

New Common Staithe

Lost quay. Located off King Street, roughly opposite to the lost St Edward's church, the Quay is first referred to as Calves Staithe in 1397. The term New Common Staithe was still in use in 1830 but had disappeared by the time of the 1884 Ordnance Survey along with its namesake Newcom Lane.

Newmarket Road

Radial Road. This is the main Norwich to London road and is the location of some of the most 'high end' housing in the City. It is characterised by substantial trees, a spacious and wide aspect and a very significant level of planting provided by the large gardens of the predominantly detached villa-style houses. Moving outwards from the Ipswich Road junction, the two pairs of Georgian, 1830 Town Houses on the left (nos. 12-14 and 16-18) are fine examples of some of the first houses for the upper middle classes to be developed beyond the City Walls. Opposite is a terrace of more modest, but still relatively early, Georgian cottages. Next to these, the Eagle pub was also built in 1830 and has maintained its license since then. No. 45 is a substantial villa from 1830 and the very imposing, Albert Terrace next door,

Newmarket Road – the early C19th Albert Terrace.

From left: The very rare machinery surviving in New Mills, exterior view of New Mills.

fronted by an attractive mini wood, is also of that date. The remainder of the buildings in the road are predominantly late Victorian or Edwardian with a smattering of more modern additions. The key elements of note are two major school complexes – the Norwich High School for Girls and the Town Close Preparatory School – and the first home of Norwich City Football Club, the large green space to the south of the Road just beyond the Outer Ring Road. The Club occupied this site from 1902 until 1908 when it moved to the Nest on Rosary Road.

New Mills

Watermills. The 'New Mills' were preceded by a series of earlier mills dating from before the Norman Conquest. Early mills included Appleyard's Mill, Bumpstede's Mill and the Caulke Mills. The first record of a piped water supply for Norwich was achieved by the establishment of a pumping plant close to the New Mills site, on the Wensum between Westwick Street and Oak Street, in about 1401. In 1430 the Mayor and wealthy citizens funded the development of a corn mill referred to as the 'New Mills'. By 1584 two 'citizens and plumbers of

London' had contracted with the Corporation 'to build and set up a mill at or near the New Mill to drive water through certain pipes of lead… to the Market Cross.' In 1710 New Mills were rebuild with 60 per cent of their capacity used for grinding corn and the remainder for pumping water. By 1780 wood milling was being undertaken as well. In 1794 the Corporation made a new agreement for two Norwich citizens to pump water from New Mills to a new reservoir in Chapelfield. In 1850 the new Heigham Waterworks replaced all of this and in 1868 a new pumping station at new Mills was constructed to pump sewage to Trowse. It was rebuilt again in 1897 and the machinery inside is one of only two examples surviving in the UK, the other being in the Houses of Parliament. New Mills was decommissioned in 1972 and despite attempts to turn it into a visitor attraction in the 1990s, it remains empty.

Newspapers

Popular publishing innovation. The first provincial newspaper in England was published by Francis Burgess in September 1701, in Redwell Street. The

Norwich Post was a weekly publication and its early success provoked imitation so that by 1706 Norwich had more newspaper titles than any other English provincial city. In that year, the two leader titles were born – the Gazette and the Post Man. The former became the Norfolk Chronicle and the latter the Weekly Mercury then the Norwich Mercury which claims the record as the longest continuously printed local newspaper. The City's newspaper provenance continues to the present day with Archant, producers of the Eastern Daily Press and Eastern Evening News, claiming to be the largest provincial newspaper and magazine publishing company in the UK.

Norwich Post – the first provincial newspaper.

New Spring Gardens

Lost Pleasure Gardens.
Exploiting the success of My Lord's Garden, slightly to the west, gardener John Moore launched his competition in 1739 by laying out a garden with walks and bowers on St Faith's Lane (Mountergate), where genteel folk could 'regale themselves at the choicest fayre while indulging in garden related diversions and even a trip on the river'. Taking its inspiration from London's New Spring Gardens, the site was essentially rural to begin with but as the competition developed (the Wilderness at Butter Hills) Moore felt the need to provide more structured entertainment such as concerts, fire works and illuminations. Moore's gardens prospered under the stewardship of his widow during the mid C18th and managed to hold its own against the opposition. In 1776, theatre set designer and engraver James Bunn took over the New Spring Gardens and introduced an innovation – a rotunda named the Pantheon enabling him to entertain 1,000 people in covered accommodation and to extend his entertainments beyond the spring and summer months. Performances varied radically from the works of great composers through militia bands to local variety turns. In the late 1700s Bunn continued to diversify, adding exhibitions of paintings and transparencies to his repertoire and extending his outdoor offers by purchasing the artificial waterfall and landscape from the Wilderness. Fireworks, however, remained a public favorite

and in 1780, Bunn invited Quantrell's former firework engineer to produce a spectacle to outshine his rival. While the upside was continued public support, this strategy also had downsides. In 1782 Bunn's engineer had a mishap while preparing a demonstration and the ensuing explosion killed one man. This blunted Bunn's pyrotechnic enthusiasm but soon he was back with another innovation. After the first manned balloon flight in Paris on 1st December 1783, Bunn had an unmanned balloon over the Pantheon in January 1784 but was soon eclipsed again by Quantrell who managed three manned flights. After a brief session of equestrian circus acts, Bunn finally sold the site to John Keymer of the Dove Tavern in 1789. The new owner employed a relative, Matthew Keymer, to re-arrange the lamps in the garden and to produce new transparencies and he undertook a general refurbishment of the site. In Assize week he enacted a Royal Progress to St Pauls using model figures that attracted so many spectators that it had to be repeated. After a retaliatory strike by Quantrell depicting the Storming of the Bastille with real actors, Keymer produced his own Bastille spectacular, a Bastille based pantomime. This major showdown finished Quantrell and with a few years both he and his son were working for Keymer and his gardens had been sold to a Mr Coe.

Keymer renamed the New Spring Gardens the Vauxhall Pleasure Gardens and set off with a new programme of pantomimes supported by former owner James Bunn who took on the role of

scenery provision. These new initiatives were augmented by more fireworks and circuses but just when it seemed that Keymer had eradicated the opposition, he retired to a local inn.

The site seems to have ticked over as just a pleasant garden for some time but, well after the demise of all of the competing, large scale pleasure gardens, there is then reference to 'The Old Spring Gardens' opening a Pavilion in 1910 which was a large green canvas structure with a stage built by Boulton and Paul. The Pavilion staged a wide range of shows and attracted stars of the time such as Stanley Holloway and even Ronald Coleman. In 1930 the canvas Pavilion was replaced by a permanent structure which could accommodate 500 people. In the same year, the Lord Mayor opened a new indoor bowls facility at the Gardens. Within a short time though the Gardens had disappeared beneath timberyards and industrial development to re-emerge in the 1980s as a sculpture garden, developed by local entrepreneur Paul King and associated with the Hotel Nelson (now the Nelson Premier Inn).

Newport

Historic quarter. Probably meaning 'new town', the name applies to the French Borough built by the Normans after the Conquest on the area to the west of the Great Cockey, approximately between modern St Giles and Theatre Street. The point is reinforced by the naming of the two principal streets, later Bethel Street and St Giles, as Over or Superior Newport and Nether or Inferior Newport respectively. It is also suggested that 'port' could mean 'town with market rights' and this again resonates with the newly founded Norman Great Market.

Ninham Family

Local artists. Originally the de Ninhams, the family were Huguenot refugees and, like many others, made their home in Norwich after fleeing Catholic persecution. Although both significant Ninhams were artistic professionals in their own right, their value to the City's heritage is that they were recorders of, now lost, architectural history. John Ninham (1754-1817) was a painter of heraldic arms for coaches as well as an engraver and copper plate printer. His most remarkable work is the Views of the Gates of Norwich, produced in 1792/3 but not published until 1861. The etchings illustrate the inside and outside view of 11 of the 12 Gates since Heigham had been demolished before Ninham made his drawings. 'Old' Ninham also produced map etchings including a plan of Norwich in 1802 and a plan of the Battle of the Nile in 1789. One of his strangest commissions however, was to produce a pasteboard replica of the Bastille for John Keymer's New Spring Gardens.

'Young' Ninham (1793-1874) continued his father's skills of etching, printing and lithography but also developed as an accomplished, if relatively unsung, painter of architectural subjects. Probably his best known picture is a view of the Cathedral from across Whitefriars Bridge at Cowgate although other examples of

Ninhams Court between Bethel Street and Chapelfield North.

his subjects include several views of the Wensum, Elm Hill, Mancroft, St Martins and Strangers Hall as well as many architectural details in churches, the Cathedral and the Castle.

The Ninham family became famous in the Victorian era as a producer of baking powder and cake mixes with Henry Christian Ninham heading the operation from a factory in Ber Street. The business was absorbed by a national brand, in the 1960s, which subsequently failed. However, the name and recipes were bought by a member of staff and the brand now exists as a Norfolk based cake mix company.

Ninham's Court

Medieval gem. Located between Chapelfield North and Bethel Street and named after artist Henry Ninham, whose house stands at the Chapelfield end, this tiny alley contains a remarkable gem from the medieval period. The complex sits on a well preserved C15th undercroft and the core of the development is C16th with C17th additions. Apart from its architectural quality, the site is notable as the home of Nugent Monck, founder of the Maddermarket Theatre. He lived there from 1918 until his death in 1958. The successor tenant maintained much of Monck's original possessions at the house.

No. 26 Bus to Hellesdon

The disappearing bus. On 3rd March 1988 the No. 26 double decker bus to Hellesdon was travelling west along the Earlham Road when it disappeared, partially. Former chalk workings below the road had collapsed and the bus disappeared into a 30 foot deep hole. Miraculously none of the crew or passengers were injured.

The No. 26 bus to Hellesdon disappears into Earlham Road.

The incident made international news and appeared as far afield as TV news reel programmes in the United States. The 'bus in a hole' photograph remains an iconic image of the period. Shortly following the incident Cadbury used the photograph with the caption 'Nothing fills a hole like a Double Decker' to market their Double Decker chocolate bar.

Nonconformists

Dissenting church members. 'Nonconformist' describes churchmen who didn't conform with Matthew Parker's Elizabethan Statement. Significant nonconformists associated with Norwich included 'Separatist' Robert Browne, William Bridge, John Collins, Thomas Grantham, Robert Govett and prominent Baptists Joseph Kinghorn and Mark Wilks. A history of Nonconformity in Norwich was published by Ted Doe in 2009.

Norfolk Archive Centre

Innovative archive facility. Historically the City's records and archives were administered by the Norwich Public Library and when this moved to the new Norwich Central Library in 1962, a new Norfolk & Norwich Record Office was included. Following the devastating Library fire of 1994, the records and archives which survived were without a home and temporary arrangements were put in place pending the development of a replacement facility. A bid to the Heritage Lottery Fund in 1997 for a site at the UEA failed but a subsequent proposal the following year was

successful and a new Archive Centre opened adjacent to County Hall in 2003. The centre holds in the region of 7,000 archival collections in state of the art facilities. There is also a sound archive. This is thought to be one of the most up to date archive centres in Europe.

Norfolk & Norwich Archaeological Society

Local archaeological society. Founded in 1846, the society is one of the oldest of its kind in the country.

Norfolk & Norwich Asian Society

Local Asian society. Formed with the intention of promoting Asian culture, racial goodwill and harmony and relieving poverty and sickness, this is a membership organisation.

Norfolk & Norwich Benevolent Medical Society

Oldest benevolent medical society in the UK. Founded in 1786 this subscription based society was intended to assist those in the medical professions in times of need and having been established in the same year as the first society of this kind (Essex & Hertfordshire, which was dissolved in 1951) the N&NBMS claims to be the oldest surviving society of its kind in the UK.

Norfolk & Norwich Festival

Long running cultural festival. Established in 1772 as a device to raise funds for the construction of the Norfolk and Norwich Hospital, this is now the oldest city based music festival in the country. Over its long history it has attracted performers ranging from Elgar, Spohr, Bliss and Vaughan

Norfolk & Norwich Festival (clockwise): The modern Festival attracting acts from across the globe, Greening the Wensum – one of the 2011 Festival events, and a festival installation outside The Forum in 2010.

Clockwise from top: The now demolished Norfolk & Norwich Hospital 'blocks', the 'old' Norfolk & Norwich Hospital, now restored and converted, and the Norfolk & Norwich University Hospital.

Williams to Philip Glass, Ute Lemper and Laurie Anderson. Since the arrival of director Jonathan Holloway in 2004, the Festival moved into the top league making it the 4th most successful city arts festival in the UK in 2010, attracting nearly 300,000 visits. In 2011, former director of the Cork Festival, William Galinsky, took over the artistic directorship.

Norfolk & Norwich Horticultural Society

Local horticultural society.
Founded in 1829 by Thomas Starling Norgate, the N&NHS claims to be the oldest regional society of its kind in the UK.

Norfolk & Norwich Hospital

Pioneering hospital.
Founded by William Fellowes, with early funding coming from the proceeds of the Norfolk & Norwich Festival, the new hospital was built by William Ivory between 1770 and 1775 to an H shaped plan, just outside St Stephen's Gate on an empty site. Soane made revisions in 1788 and Edward Boardman, supported by T.H.Wyatt, added a chapel and substantially rebuilt Ivory's blocks in 1879-84 leaving only a small element of the original structure on the east of the site. The hospital was the first general hospital of a modern type in Norfolk and one of the most forward

looking in the country. Its surgeons were some of the first to use anaesthetics and antiseptic techniques and they were leaders in the treatment of bladder stones – the largest collection of bladder stone specimens in the world survives in the hospital's museum collection. Pressure on the historic buildings resulted in the acquisition of Crooks Place at the rear of the site and the development of first the ten storey Maternity Block in 1966-8 by Guy Aldis, followed by the 12 storey Main Block next to it in 1971-4 by Feilden and Mawson. Increasing pressure continued to make operation on the constrained site difficult and in the 1990s the decision was made to replace the old hospital with the Norfolk & Norwich University Hospital at Colney. The old site was redeveloped for a major housing scheme called Fellowe's Plain, which incorporated parts of the old buildings and named the new streets and courts after characters associated with the former hospital.

Norfolk & Norwich Museum
See *Museums.*

Norfolk & Norwich Naturalists Society

Local Naturalists' society.
Formed in 1869 the society claims to be the oldest in the country. Its aims include to research and improve knowledge of the county's flora and fauna, to protect endangered species by recording changes in the presence of species and to educate all in aspects of the natural sciences through field meetings and lectures.

Norfolk & Norwich Operatic Society

Local operatic society.
This is an amateur musical theatre company founded in 1925 which has put on annual productions since its founding year.
www.nnos.co.uk

Norfolk & Norwich Pathological Museum

Early medical museum.
Founded in 1843 by surgeon William Dalrymple, this was the first provincial, non-university pathological hospital to be founded in the country. Additional to the largest collection of bladder stones in the world, it holds interesting collections of medical equipment and portraits of eminent doctors. It can be visited at the Norfolk & Norwich University Hospital by appointment.

Norfolk & Norwich Philatelic Society

Local stamp society.
Founded in 1911, the Society runs an active programme of lectures relating to stamps and postal history. It meets at the Princes Street United Reform Church and runs a successful Stamp and Post Card Fair every August.
www.norphil.co.uk

Norfolk & Norwich Subscription Library

Former innovative library.
Known first as the Norwich Public Library, the Subscription Library was established in August 1784, initially in a room in St Andrew's Hall, and was the first of its kind in Norfolk and one of the first in the country. In 1794, the need for expansion moved it to the former Catholic Chapel of the Duke of Norfolk in St Andrew's Street. The Library was run on a subscription basis with members paying an annual fee but by 1821 there was severe dissent about the paucity of new books and the following year, a faction broke away to establish the Norfolk & Norwich Literary Institution in the Haymarket. In 1825 the Norwich Public Library received a boost in the form of the permanent loan of 2,000 books from the old City Library, which had been established in 1608, and ten years later it acquired the lease of the old City Gaol on Guildhall Hill. John Thomas Patience was awarded the contract to design a new library and through a combination of reusing parts of the Gaol structure and new build, the first purpose built Subscription Library emerged by 1838. Within ten years the Library contained 14,000 volumes and by 1880 this had risen to 50,000. In 1886 the Norwich Public Library and Norfolk & Norwich Literary Institution merged to form the Norfolk & Norwich Public Subscription Library. Despite a severe fire in 1898, which necessitated an internal rebuild, the Library survived until 1976 when it closed with the books passing to the Norwich School. In 1986 the main building and east wing were converted to an innovative Advice Arcade by the City Council but this in turn closed in 2002 and the premises were eventually converted into a restaurant where local artists exhibit.

Norfolk & Norwich University Hospital

Principal hospital. The Norfolk and Norwich University Hospital is a modern teaching hospital designed by Anshen and Allen and opened in 2001 (formally opened by the Queen in 2004) on a substantial, formerly undeveloped site at Colney, across the Yare Valley from the University of East Anglia and adjacent to the Norwich Research Park. It was the first large, Private Finance Initiative hospital in the NHS and the first new NHS teaching hospital to be built in England for 30 years and provided just under 1,000 acute beds.

Norfolk & Norwich World Family

A unique international community. Uniting the 53 places across the world called either Norfolk or Norwich into a connected community has been the 20 year vision of Derek Bickford-Smith. Through visits and lectures, radio interviews, press articles, internet activity and a series of 'family gatherings', Derek and other enthusiasts have sought to bring together the diverse communities across the world that share the Norfolk or Norwich names. The Norwichs include 18 in the US located in Connecticut, North Dakota, Iowa, Kansas, Massachusetts, Michigan (2), New York (4), Ohio (3), Pennsylvania (2) and Vermont (2), two in Canada, and two in Jamaica.

Norfolk Broads

See *Broads*.

Norfolk County Council

County Local Government administration. Norfolk County Council is the local government body responsible for administering a range of services across the whole county of Norfolk and this includes service provision for the City of Norwich and the surrounding parishes.
In the last financial year, the County Council spent a total budget of £559.9m on a range of services including Adult Social Services, Children's Services, Planning and Transportation, Environment and Waste Management, Fire and Rescue, Cultural Services and Trading Standards. The County Council also spent a further £423.2m on schools. The County Council is an elected body made up of 84 Members each representing a seat covering up to 10,000 people. At the 2009 election the councilors representing the following political parties were returned: Conservative 60, Liberal Democrat 13, Green 7, Labour 3, UKIP 1. The County Council is based principally in County Hall at Martineau Lane Norwich.
www.norfolk.gov.uk

Norfolk House

1950s office building. Built on the site of the former Trevor Page furniture shop, which was destroyed by bombing in 1942, Norfolk House is one of the very few post War, 'Festival of Britain' designs to survive in the City. It was inspired by a visit made by local property developer Raymond King and his wife to southern Sweden in 1938 when they discovered Halmstad Town Hall (Radhuset), built in a clean, modern, Swedish style. Norfolk House replicates the Radhuset very closely, even down to reproducing the ship, crest and clock at the top of the building but in Norwich, the architect (Alec Wright) has used a Norfolk Wherry and the arms of East Anglia. Built in 1951, the design takes its cue from the 1945 Plan which proposed widening Exchange Street and is therefore stepped back from the historic street line. Preparatory works for the development revealed Saxon wells and the probable crypt of the C13th church of St Crowche, which had ceased to be used by 1551. The building continues in use as offices.

Norman's Hospital

Lost caring institution. The Hospital, also known as the Hospital of St Paul, and the adjacent church were founded after the Conquest and completed in the first half of the C12th on a site roughly on the line of St Crispins Road, west of Whitefriars. The title refers not to the Normans but to the first master who was called Norman. In 1429 the institution was restricted solely to the care of poor sisters. At the Reformation, no more masters were appointed but the Hospital survived for a short time further and in 1571 passed to the control of the Corporation and became a bridewell and house of correction for 'lazy and idle beggars'. Nothing survives from the original site.

Norman House

Surviving remnant of a Norman House. Located beneath the City's Magistrates Courts and discovered during the pre development excavation, this represents the substantial remains of a C12th town house, often referred to as a 'stone house', and is contemporary with the Music House in King Street. The remains are a Scheduled Ancient Monument. Visits are possible by prior arrangement with the Magistrates Court.

Norman Norwich

See opposite.

Norman School

Early educational foundation. Founded in Cowgate in 1723 by Alderman Norman the Norman School was intended to be a charitable educational institution, but one which would benefit the sons of himself and his first wife and their descendents. It survived into the 1930s when it was absorbed into the newly founded Mile Cross School which took its name in 1935. Ultimately replaced by newer and larger schools, the Norman School became the Norman Centre, a venue for community activities and events on the Mile Cross Estate.

North Park/ South Park

Out of centre Council estate. North and South Park Avenues are located around Eaton Park close to the UEA and west of Norwich City Centre. Eaton Park was built in 1928 as part of the unemployment relief scheme and opened by the Prince of Wales. The plans for the park were created by the Parks Superintendent Captain Sandys-Winsch, who

Norman Norwich

Post Conquest borough

The Normans' radical transformation of the City's townscape after 1066 set the pattern for the Norwich we still see today. Four significant elements changed the look and functionality of the place from the pre Conquest Anglo-Scandinavian borough. In order of magnitude, the greatest impact was made by the development of the cathedral Precinct over an area of 18 Ha (44 acres). Not only did this involve a huge constructional enterprise being imposed upon the City but, more significantly, it represented carving a large part out of the civic, commercial and spiritual heart of the pre Conquest borough. Most significantly, the Normans demolished the most important church (St Michael Tombland) and the second most important church (Christchurch) as well as clearing a large area of urban development. They probably encroached onto the principal market place and flattened the Earl's Palace. They even diverted the principal highway network around the Precinct and finally they effectively removed this part of the borough from the inhabitants by placing a wall around it. The second and almost equally large impact was the development of the Castle and its defensive enclosures. Although this only covered half of the area taken by the Cathedral (9.3 Ha./23 acres) it involved the demolition of at least 98 houses and two churches and the eradication of another section of highway network. The third element was the French Borough and although larger in extent than the Cathedral precinct, this did not represent such a dramatic development physically because it was outside the pre Conquest Anglo-Scandinavian Borough and therefore required minimal demolition. Functionally though the impact was dramatic, as it moved the centre of commerce and administration across the City to a new location and it established new churches, including St Peter Mancroft, second only to the Cathedral at the time. The fourth element was less about the development of distinctive quarters and more about the nature of urban development. Prior to the Conquest, all secular buildings were almost certainly made of timber – a possible exception may have been the Earl's Palace but this is only speculation. After the Conquest the power and wealth of the new elite was reflected in a new urban element – the stone house. There is evidence that at least 18 of these structures were developed after the Conquest but it is highly probable that others existed. The only relatively complete, standing example is the Music House (Wensum Lodge) in King Street, home to one of the wealthiest Jews in England. The substantial remains of another stone house also survive beneath the Magistrates Courts. Evidence for other stone house locations include sites around the Norman Market, including The Forum site, sites in King Street, sites around Tombland (evidence in the Maids Head and documentary evidence outside the Ethelbert Gate) and locations north of the Cathedral.

Additional to these four initial interventions, the Norman Invasion ultimately brought a second wave of change in the form of monastic complexes – five major ones in addition to the Cathedral priory, hospitals (the Great Hospital and Norman's being the largest), leper houses and a major ecclesiastical college (St Mary in the Fields).

The changes wrought by the Normans were so extreme that it is very difficult to unpick what Norwich would have been like before they arrived. The section on the Anglo-Scandinavian Borough, although informed by excavation and documentary sources represents 'educated guesswork'.

From left: Remains of Norman House preserved beneath the Courts, and an extensive archaeological dig reveals remains of Norman House.

incorporated into the design water features and the use of concrete for pavilions, much of which can still be seen today following a recent major renovation funded by the Heritage lottery Fund.

Northwic

See opposite.

Norvic

Lost shoe manufacturer.
In the second quarter of the C19th, Robert Tillyard started a leather currying (the transformation of tanned hides into shoe upper leather) business in Elm Hill and moved to Princes Street, following a substantial financial investment by James Warnes Howlett in 1846. By 1856 the business had established itself as Tillyard & Howlett, Shoe Manufacturers, on the site of the later Norvic factory, opposite St George's Colegate. A new warehouse and factory were designed by Robert Kitton and the former survives behind later buildings. Howlett's son, John Godfrey Howlett, joined the business a year later and, as well as working in the factory, he 'went out on the road' drumming up business for the company. At about the same time, George White joined the business as a junior clerk. He was the son of Thomas White, a valued customer of Tillyard & Howlett, based in Bourne, Lincolnshire. Within 20 years, George White had made a major impression on the development of the shoe manufacturing side of the business, leaving Howlett to drive the leather currying, and the Company became Howlett & White. At this time the new partnership acquired a range of

properties on Colegate and commissioned local architect Edward Boardman to build a new factory. This was extended and elaborated with a central tower in 1894, making it the largest shoe factory in England at the time. The huge premises enabled the company to transform the shoe production process from one which was largely home based ('outdoor work') to a modern factory production process. White's success in business was reflected in his growing role within the City. He became a councillor in 1876, then an alderman, chairman of the Education Committee and Sheriff. He then became MP for North West Norfolk in 1900 and was knighted in 1907. With White's growing interest in civic affairs and Howlett's failing health, the sons of the founders joined the business in the 1880s and took an increasing role in its development. By the First World War, the company had become highly proficient at making and exporting women's satin and brocade dress shoes. The War changed things in respect of the product and the workforce. H&W were soon awarded a major contract for army boots for the French Army. This was followed by a contract for brogues for Highland Regiments and for British Army Boots. The success of these contracts led to others for Russian ankle boots and Cossack Cavalry Boots, Italian Alpine Boots and remarkable sheepskin, thigh length boots for the Royal Flying Corps. Over the Wartime period, H&W made over half a million boots of various sorts. The other significant change was that women

Northwic

Danish, pre Conquest settlement

Evidence suggests that the principal settlement emerged on the north bank of the Wensum running along the accessible river margins and being contained by a defensive D shaped mound and ditch (see reconstruction image opposite). The settlement was known as Northwic and eventually gave its name to the whole borough.

The main north-south thoroughfare of the borough would have been Fybriggate (now Fye Bridge Street/ Magdalen Street), taking its name from the first wooden causeway crossing of the river. Excavations for a drainage trench in April 1896 revealed piles driven into the river bed, suggesting a support structure for a causeway and earlier building works 'for foundations at Messrs Geldart's in Wensum St' revealed a roadway paved with round cobble stones sloping down towards the river and likely to have been the approach to the causeway. In 1999 archaeological excavations produced a further pile with bark but it was not possible to date it. The suggested early date of the crossing is perhaps supported by the discovery of C10th Thetford type ware close to the site in 1974.

Just north of the crossing, the church of St Clement, the patron saint of sailors and a popular Scandinavian dedication (examples in Arhus, Schleswig and Trondheim), is a likely Danish foundation. The original church, being pivotal to this part of the borough, may well have been built of flint although the current church is of a later date. In London there is a St Clement Danes and in other cities this church dedication will often be where a street crosses a river.

To the east, and running parallel to the river, Fishergate – the street of the fishermen – suggests an obvious riverside activity confirmed by the discovery of C11th fish hooks and net weights during recent excavations. Other finds including a Viking age linen 'smoother' made of glass – a sort of primitive iron used for flattening yarns and textiles. These would have been used in cloth making or the laundry process to smooth garments, particularly seams. This find provides evidence of glass making and probably flax growing and linen production. Fishergate runs down to the church of the martyr king St Edmund who, despite being killed by the Danes, was venerated by them 25 years after his death when he was honoured as a saint and celebrated by the Danish rulers issuing special St Edmund Memorial coinage. Again, therefore, this church is likely to have been a Danish foundation. The present building is of a later date.

Running north from the church Tolthorp Lane (modern Blackfriars Street) takes its name from torp meaning small or secondary settlement and Toki, a Danish personal name. Turkil or Thorkell the Tall was a renowned Viking warrior who had fought with Ethelred in 1012 but then changed sides to fight with Cnut who gave him command of Norfolk and Suffolk in 1017 – it is plausible that Toki and Turkil may have been the same person. Tolthorp Lane follows the eastern boundary of a D shaped defensive ring mound and ditch which bounded this northern part of the borough from about 900. This section would have probably taken advantage of the defensive benefits of Dalymond watercourse which flowed into the Wensum at this point from north of the borough.

Continuing north, the route crosses Cowgate – street of the cows or more probably a street leading to a cow pasture beyond the defences. Turning west along Cowgate, to the north of its junction with Fybriggate just inside the gate of the defences, or

even part of the gate structure, the church of All Saints (demolished in 1550) would have been located. Crossing Fybiggate and continuing west, St Botolph's church (demolished in 1548) would have, again, been located just inside the defences on Botolph Street, before it becomes modern St Augustines. The defences then turn south along Gildengate (modern St Georges Street) and are paralleled on the inside by Snaylgate (modern Calvert Street). It is possible that the Muspole watercourse which flowed into the Wensum at this point, also supplemented the western defences. Eventually Snaylgate joins Colegate which rejoins Fybriggate. It is probable that Northwic was 'the borough' that was 'completely ravaged and burned' by Sweyn Forkbear in 1004 (as opposed to the whole of the urban area). This event signalled a major topographical shift with former Northwic ceasing to be the epicentre of the borough and the centre of administration moving just south of the river to Tombland.

Reconstruction of pre Conquest Northwic.

largely filled the roles previously dominated by men and this continued after the War. Post War production returned to high quality women's fashions. A squeeze on potential export markets then required the company to diversify into walking shoes, sports shoes and children's shoes (the Kiltie Division). In the 1930s the company became Norvic. Again the firm's principals became prominent in local affairs with Arthur Howlett becoming a City Councillor, alderman and Sheriff while Ernest White became Lord Mayor in 1932 and was knighted in the same year. The War again brought a switch to Service related production and after the War the company went through a relatively successful expansion phase before falling victim to the malaise of the industry in general – a failure to compete with cheaper foreign competition. The company finally succumbed in 1981 and the historic factory was converted to offices and a wine bar, appropriately called 'The Last'.

Norwich 12
Unique family of heritage assets. This is the UK's finest collection of individually outstanding urban heritage buildings spanning the Norman, medieval, Georgian, Victorian and modern eras. The overall aim is to develop the 12 iconic buildings into an integrated family of heritage attractions which will act as an internationally important showcase of English urban and cultural development over the last 1,000 years. Norwich 12 is a pioneering heritage initiative developed by the Heritage Economic and Regeneration Trust (HEART), initially with funding from HM Treasury. The buildings include Norwich Cathedral (begun 1096), Norwich Castle (1100), the Great Hospital (1249), St Andrew's/ Blackfriars Halls (1271), the Guildhall (1408), Dragon Hall (1427), the Assembly House (1754), St James' Mill (1836), St John's Cathedral (1884), Surrey House (1900), City Hall (1938) and The Forum (1999).
www.norwich12.co.uk

Norwich 800
Celebration of self government. Norwich 800 was a year long celebration running from May 1994 to commemorate the charter of self government granted to the City by Richard I in 1294. The event consisted of a year of community celebration and exhibitions and a year long display of the City's history in a shop unit in Castle Mall.

Norwich Alabasters
In the mid C15th, a remarkable altar piece of gilded and painted Derbyshire Alabaster was commissioned probably for the Cathedral from Nottingham craftsmen. Following the Reformation it was probably broken up and dispersed. In 1892, Norfolk Archaeology reviewed four fragments which, in all probability, represented components of the original piece. They included the nine orders of angels which resided in the Bishop's Palace; nine female saints from St Peter Mancroft (pictured); nine male prophets from St Stephens and a group of male apostles or saints from a private collection.

Norwich Buddhist Centre
Buddhist Centre. Norwich Buddhist Centre has been established in Norwich for some years and is part of the Friends of the Western Buddhist Order. The Centre has recently moved from All Saints Green to No. 14 Bank Street.

From left: A surviving historic sign from the pre Norvic days of Howlett & White, the surviving Norvic factory, now converted to offices.

Norwich Alabasters.

No. 14's mock Tudor façade hides a Grade II listed building built in the C16th. The first floor of the building is timber-framed and is jettied outwards. The building still retains some C16th features such as a timber batten ceiling. The centre provides a quiet relaxed space for meditation and meetings, and organises Buddhist retreats, training courses in meditation, yoga classes and other events. The Centre also has a small shop selling Buddhist literature, videos, CDs and DVDs.

Norwich Central Library
See *Central Library*.

Norwich Citadel
See *Salvation Army Citadel*.

Norwich City College
See *City College*.

Norwich City Council
Local Government administration.
Norwich City Council is the successor of the old Norwich Corporation which ran Norwich for most of its history. The Council was responsible for providing all local government services until 1974 when Local Government Reorganisation in England and Wales created a two tier system which allocated strategic services to County Councils while leaving more local services with District Councils. Currently Norwich City Council is responsible for local services within the administrative area of the City of Norwich. In the last financial year the City Council spent £145m on Housing Services, Central and Corporate Services, Environmental Services, Cultural Services, Planning and Highways, Roads and Transport. The Council is overseen by 39 elected councilors representing 13 wards. After the local elections in 2011 the political balance was Labour 18, Greens 15, Liberal Democrats 4, Conservatives 2.

Norwich City Football Club
See overleaf.

Norwich Corporation
See *Norwich City Council*.

Norwich, Edward of (2nd Duke of York)
Statesman and soldier.
Born in 1373 in Norwich, Edward went on to be a key figure at, his cousin, Richard II's court and in the late C14th became Constable of England. He features prominently in Shakespeare's Richard II (as Duke of Aumerle) and during the reign of Henry V he participated in the French Wars. He was also a writer having translated the French hunting treatise the "Livre de Chasse" by Gaston Phoebus, Count de Foix, adding five chapters of his own. His version was called 'Master of the Game' and, as the first book in English on hunting, is considered the most important source on its medieval practice. A scholarly edition, with a 1909 foreward by Theodore Roosevelt, is still in print. His principal claim to fame is that he was commander of Henry V's right flank at Agincourt where he suggested using pointed stakes hammered into the earth (Cheveux des fris) to protect the English archers but he was also the most high ranking English casualty of the battle.

Norwich Electric Theatre
Former cinema now redeveloped. Designed in 1912 by Francis Burdett Ward as an ornate picture theatre at 102 Prince of Wales Road, the Electric hosted variety acts as well as films and had its own resident orchestra. It prospered in its early life and was refurbished and reopened as the Norvic in 1949. It closed in 1961 and was demolished for an office development.

Norwich Fringe Festival
Alternative cultural festival. This is a 16 day festival of art exhibitions, music, performance, film, animation, workshops and experimental happenings. It runs 'as an independent intelligent entity under and around and outside the Norfolk and Norwich Festival'. 'The concept for the Fringe is to redefine the cultural landscape of Norwich over sixteen days of events designed to inform and entertain in equal measure by a loosely knit cabal of leading local arts practitioners, promoters and genuine, home-grown, grass-roots talent.' It runs in May in parallel with the Norfolk & Norwich Festival.

Norwich City Football Club

Principal football club

Norwich City Football Club was formed on 17th June 1902 at the Criterion Café in White Lion Street. It was initially an amateur team in the Norfolk & Suffolk League and played their first competitive game against Harwich & Parkeston in September on their first site, Newmarket Road. In 1905 they were elected to the Southern League as a professional club and moved to their new ground at the Nest on Rosary Road in 1908. The club went into voluntary liquidation at the end of 1917 and were reformed in February 1919. City were founder members of Football League Division Three in 1920 and the following season became founder members of Division Three South. Their first League fixture was against Plymouth on 28th August 1920. After an unremarkable first ten year league history, they improved in the next decade beating Coventry 10-2 and getting promoted to the Second Division in the 1933-4 season. Increasing

Above: Norwich celebrates promotion in 2011.

popularity and larger crowds led to them quitting The Nest for a move to the purpose built Carrow Road where they played their first game on 31st August 1935, against West Ham. Sadly, the club slumped back into the Third Division at the end of the decade.

After the War things didn't improve with the Club having to apply for re-election to the League and finishing bottom of the entire League in 1956-7. In 1959 they rallied, getting to the semi final of the FA Cup and beating Spurs and Manchester United in the

process. The following season they returned to the Second Division and the season after they won the League Cup. In 1971-72, under Ron Saunders they reached the First Division for the first time in their history and lost 1-0 to Spurs in the League Cup Final in 1973. They were relegated in 1974 but bounced back the following season under John Bond and reached the League Cup Final but lost again to Aston Villa.

In the early 1980s they were down then back up again and this time they won the League (Milk) Cup against

From left: League Cup celebrations at City Hall, and Norwich lift the League Cup at Wembley.

*From left: Promotion celebrations in 2004,
Promotion celebrations in 2010.*

Sunderland but were relegated once more. They won the Second Division Championship in 1985-6 and returned to the top flight for their most successful and sustained presence there.

The inauguration of the Premiership in 1992 saw Norwich as one of the founder members, beating Arsenal away on the first day of the season and leading the League for most of the season before finally finishing 3rd. In the next season they performed in the UEFA Cup for the first time beating Bayern Munich in the Olympic Stadium but ultimately going down to Inter Milan. A season later and the club slumped back into the former Second Division, then the First Division. Martin O'Neil was brought in to reinvigorate the squad but left after only six months when Chairman Robert Chase seemed determine to sell all of the best players. Chase stepped down after major supporter protests and Delia Smith ultimately took over the majority share holding with her husband.

The arrival of Nigel Worthington as new manager in 2000 saw City first reach the play offs in 2002-3 then get promoted in as outright champions the following season. Despite beating the likes of Manchester United and Newcastle, City struggled and went straight back down at the end of their first season back in the Premiership. Mediocre performances not only saw Norwich fail to 'bounce back' but resulted in them plummeting into League 1, the old Third Division where they hadn't been since the 1960s. After a 7-1 drubbing by Colchester on the first day of the 2009-10 season the popular, former goalkeeper and then manager Bryan Gunn was sacked and replaced by the former Colchester manager Paul Lambert, who delivered a remarkable run of successful results and the highest goal tally in the Division by Christmas. By the end of his first season with the club, Norwich had been projected from near bottom to divisional champions.

The following season Norwich sought to become one of the few clubs to achieve automatic promotion in concurrent seasons and succeeded, by finishing 2nd to QPR.

At time of publication they sit in the top half of the Premier League.

*Norwich City manager Paul Lambert (left in picture)
celebrates promotion in 2011.*

Norwich Fringe Project

Green space enhancement initiative. Founded in 1990, the Norwich Fringe project has the aim of enhancing and managing the countryside around Norwich and its surrounding urban fringe for conservation, bio-diversity and recreational value. The project represents a collaboration between local authorities and the Broads Authority and has worked with a range of community and disability groups to generate a range of enhancement schemes which have received awards from bodies such as the CPRE. The NFP is supported financially by a partnership of local authorities in the area.

Norwich High School for Girls

Principal independent girls' school. Founded in 1875 on an extensive site on Newmarket Road around a Regency villa, this independent, fee paying school now provides for girls between three and 18 years old. Facilities include playing fields, tennis courts, a 25m indoor heated swimming pool, a gym, a sports hall, a state-of-the-art performing arts studio and a variety of learning tools including Language Labs, five Computing Suites and several Science Laboratories. Alumni include Edith Cavell, the local nurse martyred by the Germans during the First World War, and Dorothy Jewson, the City's first female MP.

Norwich International Airport

Principal regional airport. Established in 1963, when the former Horsham St Faiths RAF fighter station

Norwich International Airport.

was decommissioned, the facility was originally administered jointly by the City and County Councils who developed a new terminal building in 1988. The airport has maintained scheduled flights to Amsterdam, from its establishment and more recently has extended its route network with the arrival of Flybe. It has also become a successful charter airport with a growing number of flights to summer holiday resorts and winter ski destinations. Its other role since its establishment has been as a service base for the off shore oil and gas industry, for helicopters. In 2004 the local authorities sold 80.1 per cent of the airport to a private company Omniport who have improved the facilities with the aid of a passenger levy for each traveller.

Norwich Lads Club

Youth institution. The Norwich Lads Club, founded in 1918 by the then Chief Constable John Henry Dain, was the first club of its kind anywhere in the World. It was aimed to get poor boys off the streets and give them an interest in sporting activities. Starting off in St Georges Street, it moved to the former Boulton & Paul

Norwich Lads Club before closure and conversion to the Kings Centre.

Smith's Shop and Foundry in King Street in 1925 before purpose built premises were provided in 1936 in a mock Tudor building by Buckingham & Berry which was extended to the south by the same architect in 1950 (later redeveloped for the King's Centre by Andi Gibbs). Boxing was a principal activity of the Lads Club and it became a training ground for some of the region's top fighters, including middleweight Ginger Sadd, welterweight Jack Forster, heavyweight world champion Herbie Hide and British lightweight title-holder Jon Thaxton. The Club moved from King Street in the 1990s to Whiffler Road, then to Lakenham and finally to the Hewitt School.

Norwich Lanes

Distinctive shopping area. When shops first started to appear in Norwich, in the late C16th/early C17th they congregated around the area north of the Market in the block bounded by London Street, St Andrews, St John Maddermarket and Guildhall Hill. One of the earliest, original, C16th shop fronts in the country survives at 15 Bedford Street in the epicentre of this area. As the retail centre of the City

A flavour of the Norwich Lanes.

developed, smaller, independent shops spread west into Dove Street and Lower Goat Lane and north to St Benedicts. By 2005 much of the centre was occupied by national or international chain stores and, with the impending arrival of a new batch of 'High Street' multiples at the Chapelfield Shopping Centre, there was concern that the remaining, small scale independents, who still inhabited the birthplace of Norwich shops, might struggle to survive. Consequently, the Heritage Economic and Regeneration Trust worked with local traders and the City Council

to create a unique and compelling destination, able to compete in a modern retail environment. The Norwich Lanes was born from about 300 small retailers and other businesses trading largely from historic premises. The initiative created a brand and web site and reinforced this with a wide range of physical reference points in the local environment including paving, street art, signage and way marking, blue plaques and historic interpretive signs. A study funded by EEDA, the regional development agency, and undertaken by the New Economics

Foundation concluded that an investment of £500,000 in the Lanes would have created an economic benefit of £17m for the local economy in terms of additional spend, new business start ups and additional jobs.

Today the Lanes provide an eclectic mix of individual fashion and jewellery retailing, music shops, gift and collectables stores as well as cafes, bars and restaurants. The traders augment the regular offer with special events including street fairs and Christmas festivities. www.norwichlanes.co.uk

Norwich Machine

Stagecoach. The first regular coach service between Norwich and London was provided by the Norwich Machine in 1762 although there is evidence that periodic coach runs occurred as early as the mid C17th. The Machine left the Maid's Head at 11.30am on Mondays, Wednesdays and Fridays, and went to the Green Dragon in Bishopsgate Street, arriving on Tuesdays, Thursdays and Saturdays. One and a half days was considered to be 'good time' for completing the 111 mile journey. Inside passengers paid 25 shillings each (£1.25) and outside 12 shillings and 6 pence (62.5p).

Norwich Mercury

See *Newspapers*.

Norwich Philharmonic Society

Local musical society. Founded by Frank Noverre in 1839, initially with the intention of enabling musicians to practise together, the Society developed into an organisation to promote choral and orchestral music. The Society now organises four or five concerts annually covering a broad and diverse repertoire. www.norwichphil.org.uk

Norwich Playing Field and Open Space Society

Voluntary amenity body. The Society was formed in the early C20th to access funds and work with the Corporation to develop public open spaces.

Norwich Post

See *Newspapers*.

Norwich Pride

Lesbian, Gay, Bisexual and Trans celebration. The annual Norwich Pride event, taking place in 2011 on 30th July, brings thousands of people onto the streets for a day long celebration. This year (2011) the parade was augmented an arts trail and exhibitions, by a Pride Show and by speeches from invited guests such as Peter Tatchell. Beyond the annual event, the Gay scene is thriving. The Castle is one of the principal gay pubs and the Loft has been the gay club of choice for some time. Future Radio provides a regular spot on events for the gay community.

Norwich Prison

Principal prison for Norfolk & Suffolk. Norwich Prison is a category B/C prison, located at Knox Road, just north east of the Walled City, and was opened in 1887 replacing the prison at Norwich Castle and the Norwich Gaol on Earlham Road. In 2004 the Prison became the only one in England and Wales to have a unit exclusively for elderly prisoners, mainly serving life sentences. As a result Norwich has hosted a number of high profile criminals including:

Ronald (Ronnie) Biggs, one of a gang who stole £2.6m from a mail train in 1963 and went down in history as the most famous of the 'Great Train Robbers'. He was convicted and jailed but escaped from Wandsworth Prison in 1965. After changing his identity he moved to Australia and eventually to Brazil in 1970 where he lived openly for three decades due to a lack of any extradition procedures between the UK and Brazil. In 2001 he

John Innes Centre at the Norwich Research Park.

returned voluntarily to the UK following an exclusive publishing deal with the Sun. He was imprisoned and in 2007 was moved to Norwich Prison on compassionate health grounds. Appeals for his release on health grounds resulted in him being finally released in August 2009.

Anthony Sawoniuk, the only Nazi war criminal to be convicted after a full trial in a British court was imprisoned in 1999 in Norwich prison where he died of natural causes in 2005.

Donald Neilson, the so called 'Black Panther' is a multiple murderer and armed robber convicted in 1976 and now serving out his life sentence in Norwich.

Reggie Kray, one of the infamous Kray Twins, was moved to the healthcare wing at Norwich in 2000. He was later diagnosed with bladder cancer and released on compassionate grounds before dying in the Townhouse Hotel.

Norwich Research Park

Hub of Research and Development activity. Located to the south west of the City, across the Yare Valley from the University of East Anglia and adjacent to the Norfolk & Norwich

University Hospital, the Norwich Research Park is a collaboration between UEA, the Norfolk and Norwich University Hospital, and four independent research centres; the John Innes Centre, the Institute of Food Research, the Sainsbury Laboratory and from July 2009 The Genome Analysis Centre. With over 9,000 employees, the Norwich Research Park has one of Europe's largest single-site concentrations of research in Health, Food and Environmental Sciences. The site is recognised as a centre of excellence for research in the fields of plant and microbial sciences, food, health, environmental sciences, computer and information systems and chemistry. An analysis of the most highly cited scientists in the UK over the past 20 years reveals that Norwich is ranked 4th after London, Cambridge and Oxford (New Scientist, 1 July 2006/ Thomson ISI). The six partner institutions work together in integrated, multidisciplinary teams to address the challenges of the 21st Century. They include the Earth and Life Systems Alliance, the Norwich Centre for Preventive Medicine and multi disciplinary teams working on Plant and Microbial Natural Products.

Norwich School
Long established school. One of the oldest established schools in the world, the Norwich School has its roots in the Episcopal Grammar School founded by Bishop Herbert de Losinga in 1096. Vincent of Scarning appears as Master of the Episcopal School in documents dating from 1240. From 1285 there are

documentary references to the Almonry School, associated with the Cathedral Almonry. In 1516 the two schools were merged and after the Reformation the school was refounded as the King Edward VI Grammar School under the control of the Mayor and Corporation. Today it is an independent, co-educational, fee paying school with a very good academic record. The school site includes the former Bishop's Palace, probably just predating the Cathedral itself and the early C14th Carnary College. Alumni include Lord Nelson, Lord Chief Justice Coke, Elizabethan novelist Robert Greene, George Borrow, a number of members of the Norwich School of Painters and Humphrey Repton.

Norwich School of Art and Design
See Norwich University College of the Arts.

Norwich School of Monumental Masons
Local monumental masons school. For about 200 years, from the Elizabethan period, there was an explosion of monument development in Norwich churches and an indication

that this work was orchestrated by the City's first School of monumental masons operating between 1570 and 1630. The legacy is the largest collection of church monuments of any city in the UK and some individually unique examples.

Norwich School of Painters
Unique collective of artists. Started by John Crome and Robert Ladbrooke in 1803 as the Norwich Society of Artists, this became the only regional school of painting in England. The aim of the organisation was to establish 'An Enquiry into the Rise, Progress and present state of Painting, Architecture and Sculpture, with a view to point out the Best Methods of study to attain the Greater Perfection in these Arts.' Eventually 30 local artists were to participate in the 'School' with the most famous, aside from the founders, being John Sell Cotman, George Vincent and Joseph Stannard. The largest collection of their works is held at Norwich Castle.

Norwich Shawl
Fashion icon. Norwich had been a textile production centre of European stature from the C12th. In 1714 it was referred to as 'the chief seat of the chief manufacture in the realm.' The Industrial Revolution, however put Norwich at a competitive disadvantaged compared with the emerging textile towns of the North of England and by 1780 it was beginning to lose the battle. At the same time, quantities of high quality shawls began to arrive from Asia and some Norwich manufacturers saw an opportunity to replicate

A Norwich Shawl.

these and develop a specialised niche textile market to redress the general decline. Entrepreneur John Harvey produced a shawl made of finely spun Worsted weft and silk warp in 1788 which won a Royal Society Commendation. Harvey was subsequently joined by P.J.Knight, who produced a 3.6M (12 ft) square Royal Counterpane for George III and Queen Charlotte – this earned him the appointment of 'Shawlmaker to Her Majesty.' In the early C19th, Norwich weavers developed the Norfolk Pine design, later to be referred to as Paisley. Another early innovation at this time was developed by Michael Stark, (father of the painter) who perfected a technique to exactly match dyed silk and worsted to produce 'Norwich Red'. By the 1840s there were 26 shawl makers working in the City and taking advantage of the Jacquard loom. Designs seemed to pre-empt the later Art Nouveau style and became extremely popular with companies such as E&F Hinde recording 39,000 shawls being made in 1849 alone. Thomas Claburn was one of the leading manufacturers and produced a shawl for the Danish Pricess Alexandra when she married future Edward VII as well as one for Queen Victoria. Claburn, Son & Crisp won a first Class award at the Paris Exposition of 1855 while other Norwich manufacturers performed well at the Exposition of 1862. Claburns though are thought to be the producers of the quintessential Norwich Shawl in terms of their luxury and size. Fashions changed however, and the shawl passed from favour as quickly as it arrived – by the 1870s the Norwich Shawl had had its day. Today examples survive in the collections of the Norfolk Museums Service and can be viewed at the Costume and textile Study Centre at Carrow House. Examples are also in private collections and are periodically exhibited by the Costume and Textile Association. www.ctacostume.org.uk

Norwich Society

Civic Amenity Society. The Norwich Society is a local membership organisation affiliated originally to the now disbanded Civic Trust. Its aims are to encourage high standards of architecture and town planning in Norwich, to stimulate public interest in and care for the beauty, history and character of the City and its surroundings and to encourage the preservation, development and improvement of features of general public amenity or historic interest. The Society was formed in 1923 in response to proposals to demolish the medieval Bishop Bridge and they were successful in getting it listed. The Society has a string of other successes including leading the campaign to prevent the demolition of Elm Hill in the 1930s. More recently, the Society has worked with the Heritage Economic and Regeneration Trust (HEART) to regenerate the Wensum in the City Centre.

Norwich Society of Artists

See *Norwich School of Painters*.

Norwich Spiritualist Church

Modern church. In 1919 a small group of Norwich citizens who were practising Spiritualists decided to advertise locally for others with a similar interest. The Christian Spiritualist Church was formed and for many years held services in hired halls. In 1936 a plot of land on the north side of Chapelfield that was owned by a naval club was bought but the construction of the church was not without its troubles. Only three weeks after the land was acquired, the naval club asked to buy it back. Needless to say the church declined the offer. Moreover, during the construction of the church the builder demanded extra money and one of the founders had to remortgage their home. The red brick building was completed and its plain design reflects the architecture of the time. James Duffield, a former key member of the church, designed the stained glass windows which display the emblems of all of the major religions of the world and George Anderson, one of Norwich's prominent architects of the 1950s and member of the church, designed collapsible healing cubicles for the lower hall.

During the Second World War good use was made of the church and early on, the lower hall was offered to the Jewish community as a temporary synagogue after their building on Synagogue Street was destroyed by bombing. The Jewish congregation did not wish to enter the building by the front door as it had a cross above it so a side door was added for their access. Later the hall was also employed as a canteen for

*From left: Norwich Union archive material,
Norwich Union's Board Room, Surrey House.*

US servicemen and the church was also damaged when a bomb landed in Chapelfield. After the war the Christian Spiritualist Church resumed its normal activities and in 1948 became affiliated to the Spiritualist National Union, changing its name to Norwich Spiritualist Church in 1975. In 2005 the church celebrated sixty years of worship on the site.

Norwich Union

International insurance giant. Recently rebranded 'Aviva' and now the largest life insurance provider in the UK, the company started life in 1797 when banker and wine merchant Thomas Bignold formed the 'Norwich Union Society for the Insurance of Houses, Stock and Merchandise from Fire'. The fire insurance society had its own fire brigade which survived until 1929.

In 1808, Bignold formed the 'Norwich Union Life Insurance Society' and as the company expanded it began to open offices overseas – Ireland in 1816, 1824 Portugal and eventually the company had agencies across Europe, the Middle and Far East, Australasia and North and South America. In 1866 Norwich Union acquired the Amicable Society, established in 1706 and the world's oldest mutual life

office. In 1877 the company adopted Norwich Cathedral as its trade mark. In 1900 the company was sufficiently robust to commission a lavish new head office, Surrey House, on the site of the Earl of Surrey's palace, by local architect George Skipper. Norwich Union grew steadily but saw its greatest period of expansion, locally, between the 1960s and 80s. The eight storey Surrey Street building, dwarfing Skipper's masterpiece, was developed by T.P. Bennett in 1960, the two reflective glass towers appeared in St Stephens in the early 1970s, the All Saints Wing was developed in 1974 and the Sentinel House block in Surrey Street emerged in the late 1980s. By the turn of the Millennium, Norwich Union was the biggest employer in Norwich, providing nearly 10,000 jobs on over 20 sites, with most being located on their Surrey Street 'Island Site'. At its bicentenary the company floated on the Stock Exchange and in 2000 Norwich Union merged with Commercial Union to form CGNU. It renamed itself Aviva in almost all of its worldwide incarnations but retained the Norwich Union name here. In 2006, the company entered into a sale and leaseback arrangement for its local property portfolio

with Land Securities/Trillium which saw a £192m refurbishment of its core site, including the development of a new atrium, by LSI Architects, and the restoration of the Marble Hall as the company's 'foyer and reception'. In 2009 the company rebranded the whole operation as Aviva and the Norwich Union name disappeared, although the symbolic cathedral spire remained as part of the company logo.

Norwich University College of the Arts (NUCA)

Arts university. In 1845 the Norwich School of Design was established as one of the earliest of its kind in the country by followers of the Norwich School of Painters, to provide high quality designers for local industries. In 1899 Douglas W. Wiles, the Assistant City Engineer, designed the Norwich Technical Institute in St Georges Street, which continues to house a large element of the University College. Degree level status arrived in 1965 when the School of Art was able to award Diplomas in Art and Design validated by the National Council for Diplomas in Art and Design. In 1975 the School offered its first BA Hons Degree courses validated by the

From left: Norwich University College of the Arts – Duke St Building, Degree Show time in St Georges, and Norwich Technical Institute.

Council for National Academic Awards. In 1989 the School merged with the Great Yarmouth College of Art and Design and the Norfolk Institute of Art and Design and two years later it became affiliated to the Anglia Polytechnic. The first MA course in Fine Art commenced in 1993 and a year later it was incorporated as a higher education institution. In November 2007 it was granted the power to award degrees and renamed Norwich University College of the Arts. As well as being based in the old Technical Institute, NUCA occupies elements of the former cloister of the Blackfriars, the Monastery behind Elm Hill and the old Gunton & Havers factory building in St Georges as well as the old Duke Street Board School (1888) and the former Eastern Counties Newspapers offices in Redwell Street, dating from 1958, by Yates, Cook & Darbyshire. NUCA, now, is host to almost 1,500 students, studying a wide range of arts, design and media disciplines at Undergraduate, Postgraduate

and Doctoral level and in 2011 inaugurated an architecture course. Alumni include Alfred Munnings, Bernard Meadows, Neil Innes, Colin Self and Tim Stoner, winner of Beck's Futures Prize.

Norwich Waits

Elizabethan musicians. Founded in 1408 and surviving until the end of the C18th, this was a band of nationally renowned, Norwich based musicians who, legend has it, were given their instruments by Queen Elizabeth the first on her visit to the City in 1578. They were so well regarded that Sir Francis Drake asked the Mayor if he could take them on a voyage to Spain and Portugal in 1589. Although originally based in Blue Boar Lane (now Bank St) they later moved to

Norwich Work cushion.

Jurnet's House (now Wensum Lodge) in King St and renamed it the Music House.

Norwich Work

Distinctive local fabric. Norwich Work, also known as Turkey Work or Setwork, was a knotted pile fabric with a linen or hemp warp introduced by immigrant weavers from the Low Countries to Norwich in the late C16th. Usually floral designs similar to the embroidery designs of the period were used. The fabric was employed for cushions for buffit stools, window seats and for early upholstery when it was usually trimmed with braid. Rare examples of the work survive in the Costume and Textile collection in the form of cushions made as a set for Aldermen in Blackfriars Hall in the C16th.

Notre Dame Convent School

Catholic school. Opened in 1864, the school was established by the Sisters of Notre Dame and extended five years later to accommodate 70 female students. Extended further in 1926 to take the capacity up to 238 the school continued to develop and, in 1979, ownership of the school was transferred from the Sisters of Notre Dame to the Catholic Diocese of East Anglia, and the school's status changed from girls' direct grant grammar school to a voluntary aided mixed comprehensive school. The school is now a specialist Language College, a Science College, Training School and a Sixth Form College, teaching 1400 11-18 year olds, 400 of whom are in the sixth form.

Nourriche, Guillaume de

European Master Mason 1280-1340. Guillaume (William) was a Norwich stone mason and possibly a graduate of the Norwich School of Stone Carving which, during this period, would have produced pieces such as the remarkable Prior's Door in the Cathedral dating from 1310 and the ornate roof bosses. While other members of the School worked on St Paul's Cathedral in London, St Stephen's Chapel Westminster, the Octagon Chapel at Ely and King's College Cambridge, Guillaume's skills took him to work in Paris between 1297 and 1330 and a life sized apostle produced by him is currently in the Musée de Cluny.

Noverre Cinema

Former cinema. The Noverre was developed in 1950 to create a 272 seater cinema out of what had been the former Noverre ballroom at the Assembly House. It was always regarded as the 'up market' end of the genre and tended

Novi Sad Friendship Bridge.

to specialise in films not generally available on commercial circuits – a sort of Cinema City ahead of its time. It closed a 1992 following a period of declining ticket sales.

Noverre Family

Cultural innovators. Augustin Noverre was Swiss and brother to the noted Chevalier Jean Georges Noverre who had been a member of the Imperial Academy of Dance in Paris at the time of Marie Antoinette. The Noverre brothers were invited to England by actor John Garrick in 1755 but, following a minor, anti French riot in London, Augustin fled to Norwich where he remained with French Huguenots until the issue had been resolved. He went back to London to pursue his interests as a dance master and on the stage. In 1797 he came back to Norwich to live at the Chantry and when he died in 1805 he was buried in St Stephen's church. He was referred to as 'the most finished, elegant and most gentlemanly minuet dancer that ever appeared.' Augustin's son Francis continued the family tradition of teaching dance at the

Assembly House but was also active in the City's commercial life, being a founder of the Norwich Union Fire Insurance Society and also an original director of the Norwich Union Life Insurance Society. He died in 1840 and was also buried in St Stephen's. Frank Noverre, the son of Francis, was also a director of the Norwich Union Life Insurance Society but threw his principal energies into cultural activity. He was founder of the Norwich Philharmonic Society in 1841. Later, he bought the west wing of the Assembly House and an adjacent site to construct a 'ball and concert room'. It became the base for the Philharmonic Society and for Frank's dancing academy as well as the location for a regular series of concerts. Frank died in 1878 and, like his father and grandfather, was also buried at St Stephen's. Frank's 'room' remained popular for dances and concerts until 1901 when his son sold it to the Girls High School. It became a cinema in 1950 and following the post fire restoration of 1996 it became a hall for conferences and concerts.

Novi Sad Friendship Bridge

Iconic footbridge. Opened in 2001 by the Yugoslav ambassador to connect the recently developed Riverside scheme to the historic King Street Area, and funded by EEDA and Norwich City Council, the bridge's name sought to commemorate the close links between Norwich and its twin city Novi Sad, particularly during the break up of the former Yugoslavia when Novi Sad had suffered under the Milosevic regime.

O is for...

'Perhaps the most elegant (chapel) in the whole of Europe'; one of England's most iconic C14th artists; the largest and most fully equipped organ works in the country; the oldest non conformist meeting house in the City and one of the oldest in the country.

Oak Street

Ancient thoroughfare.
Originally part of the Roman route running from Venta Icenorum to Roman settlements in North Norfolk, and crossing the site of the later City, the street was formerly called Coslany Street and St Martin at Oak Street. Today, Oak Street runs from the western end of Colegate to the site of the former St Martin's Gate in the City Wall. Until relatively recently, the street would have appeared as a narrow thoroughfare, full of ancient buildings but a combination of Wartime bombing and slum clearance have despatched much of its character. The jewel of the street remains St Michael at Coslany, also known as St Miles and formerly a science discovery centre but now vacant. Opposite the church on the west side of Oak Street, and now occupied by recent town houses by Hopkins Homes, is the former site of two storey Tudor cottages, bombed during the War and, to their rear, former Dial Yard, the site of the mansion of Gregory Clerk, sheriff in 1497 and mayor in 1505 and 1514. Panelling with his merchant mark was recorded in 1886 but stripped out and sold to J.J. Colman then Dr Nelson of Liverpool. The mansion fell victim to slum clearance in the 1930s. Opposite to this site, on the east side of the street, was Greenland Fishery Yard named after the unusually titled Greenland Fishery pub which operated there from 1760 until the First World War. Further up on the east side, the shoe factory of Sexton Son & Everard replaced another oddly named ancient pub, the Bess o' Bedlam. North of this, St

Opposite and above: Interior of the Octagon Chapel, Colegate.

Martin at Oak was damaged by wartime bombing and rebuilt by J.P. Chaplin in 1953 then converted to a night shelter in 1978 by Anthony Faulkner & Partners before becoming an artists' studio. North of the church, and on St Martin's Lane, was a house with its origins in 1300 which survived until 1981 when its state of repair apparently resulted in its demolition. Across the 1960s aberration of the Inner Ring Road, a tiny vestage of the street's original character can be glimpsed in Nos. 98-108 which were preserved by the Norwich Amenities Preservation Society although numbers 114-110 were destroyed by Wartime bombing. On the west side, the C15th Great Hall was destined for clearance as the 'worst slum in Norwich' but fortunately survived. Finally, the northward extension of Oak Street, now St Martins Road, was the location of the remarkable mansion of Henry Fuller, mayor in the reign of Henry VIII. Like many other great houses, this fell victim to 1930s slum clearance.

Octagon Chapel

Unitarian Chapel.
The Octagon Chapel, designed by Thomas Ivory, was built between 1753 and 1756 to replace an earlier meeting house that had become unsafe. The previous meeting house is said to have been built of brick and timber and when demolished some of these materials are thought to have been salvaged for the new building. The funds for the new building, £5174.15s.8d, were raised solely by the congregation. Like the nearby Old Meeting House, the Octagon displays the prior wealth of Norwich which was once England's second city.

John Wesley, visiting in 1757, described the chapel in his journal to be 'perhaps the most elegant one in all Europe.' It has also been described as 'one of the most spacious, noble, and elegant buildings of its kind in the new kingdom' and has a splendid interior. The chapel's domed ceiling hides an arched roof, which is supported by eight fluted Corinthian columns featuring impressive wood carving.

Cosseyware detail in Old Bank of England Court.

Also worthy of note are the gilded sword and mace rests as the chapel is said to be the first Nonconformist church to have them.

There has been little alteration to the chapel's interior over the years. However, between 1877 and 1899 the original 'wine-glass' pulpit was replaced by a large rostrum, which incorporated the front and stairs of the original. The most significant alteration or addition is the splendid organ, which dominates the chapel. Originally minister Dr John Taylor had allowed no musical instrument other than the human voice. The organ was first played in 1802 by Norwich Cathedral's organist Mr Beckwith and air was blown into the pipes of the organ by 'pumping boys' at the bellows. The organ is said to feature a number of pipes that were removed from the cathedral's own organ. Also of interest is a comprehensive display of past ministers, local dignitaries and past pictures of the chapel in the vestry.

Odeon

Former and current cinemas. The original Odeon was built in Botolph Street in 1938 and was a classic example of 1930s Art Deco cinemas, designed by Basil Herring, a well regarded cinema architect of the time. It boasted a colossal capacity of 2054 seats and was hailed as the biggest cinema north of London. The cinema prospered until the 1960s when it fell victim to the Anglia Square redevelopment. It was replaced in 1971, just to the east and south of its original site, by the new, modernist Odeon, by Alan Cooke & Partners, with a vast auditorium and a capacity of 1016 seats. Eventually subdivided into three smaller cinemas then abandoned by the Odeon Group this cinema became the Hollywood and is now (2011) operated as an independent cinema. The third Odeon is now what was originally developed as the 14 screen UCI multiplex on the Riverside site by Higgs Young Architects in 1999.

Okell, Thomas de

Artist and artisan. Okell was entered into the freedom of the City in the craft of painter in 1387 and it is probable that he was responsible for painting the Despenser Reredos in St Luke's Chapel of the Cathedral, evidenced by the presence of oak leaves in the background of the Resurrection scene – a possible rebus of his name. He is also credited with the Wilton Diptych, now in the National Gallery.

In a time when the formal profession of architect was undertaken by a combination of masons and painters, de Okell was given responsibility for managing the construction of the Guildhall in 1411 and he became Sheriff in 1415.

Were it not for the eradication of the majority of the City's art history by the Reformation and the Civil War, it is likely that de Okell and his contemporaries would now be regarded with the same distinction as the Italian Masters of the time.

Old Bank of England Court

Historic courtyard. Following a national banking crisis in 1825, the Government decided in 1826 to establish branches of the Bank of England in key centres to avert future runs on the Pound. The branch opened in 1828 on the north side of what was to be renamed Old Bank of England Court, in Queen Street. The Bank closed in 1852. It is said that the modestly proportioned courtyard of Georgian and C17th buildings, with later additions, was the subject of an interesting wager. In 1810, Sir Lambert Blackwall

Old Cattle Market looking towards Farmers Avenue, in the C19th.

bet that he could drive a coach and four into the court, turn it round and drive it out again without scraping the walls – he did, with two inches to spare. The Norwich Art Circle were also established here in 1885 and local Architect Edward Boardman had his office here in the east wing, which he remodelled with the extensive use of terracotta tiles.

Old Cattlemarket
Lost cattle market.
As the Castle lost its original role and the surrounding Castle Fee fell victim to encroachment by development, it was decided, in 1617, that 'The Cattell market shall be kept in the castell dykes and not elsewhere.'
This developed into a huge institution within the City spreading beyond the trading of just cattle, to include distinct markets for horses, pigs, sheep and other creatures and, by the C19th, sale rooms off Timberhill, an Agricultural Hall and dozens of pubs around the whole site. By WWII the site was handling 200,000 cattle, sheep and pigs a year in addition to poultry, rabbits and other livestock. As early as 1938 the principle of relocating

the Market was floated but it took until 1960 for a new Market to be constructed at Harford. After this, the former market became a surface car park and coach park until being absorbed into the Castle Mall Shopping Centre development in 1988 and re-establishing something of its original form by becoming a rooftop park.

Old Common Staithe
Landing quay. First referred to in 1378, the Old Common Staithe was where 'aliens' bringing cargoes to the City were to land them and 'not elsewhere'. It was in the parish of St Clement in Conesford and, later renamed the Town Staithe, it remained the principal place for loading and unloading ships up until the C18th.

Old Meeting House
City's oldest purpose-built Nonconformist meeting house. The congregation which formed the Old Meeting House was founded by William Bridge. Bridge (previously rector of St Peter Hungate and curate of St George Tombland) fled to Holland in 1638 as a result of Bishop Wren's enforcement of Roman Catholic principles. He was

amongst approximately 500 dissenters who left for the Netherlands and America. Bridge returned after two years with other exiles and in 1644 the church was formed. The Old Meeting House was built in 1693; its construction was permitted after the 1689 Act of Toleration permitted freedom of worship to Nonconformists. Prior to the act, Nonconformist groups were not permitted to own land or buildings and their members were persecuted. The congregation of the Old Meeting House was previously forced to meet in private houses, a small nearby brewery and in part of Blackfriars' Hall. The building is Norwich's oldest purpose built Nonconformist meeting house and can seat 700.

Until the middle of the C19th, Nonconformist churches tended to keep a relatively modest outward appearance and the Old Meeting House is a good example. Its exterior is more like a high-class town house than a church. The building is tucked down an alleyway out of view from the street. An alleyway such as this could easily be blocked and is said to have been used in order to defend the church

The Old Meeting House – exterior and interior.

from rioters if necessary. The front of the building is dominated by four large Corinthian capitals above brick pilasters. The link to the Netherlands is plain to see, with the yard paved in Dutch brick and a large stone vault (located below the sundial) that records the burial of a congregational member from Rotterdam. The interior of the building features an original pulpit and clock. On the north wall close to the pulpit is a memorial tablet to William Bridge. The church features a pulpit chair belonging to John Cromwell, minister in 1645, and cousin to Oliver Cromwell. Also of interest are an ancient crucifix window, discovered during redecoration work in 1993 and the Deacon's vestry which contains a display of photos and drawings of historical interest.

Old Skating Rink

Former skating rink.
Opened in September 1876, the Norwich Skating Rink operated just north of Bethel Street but survived for only just over three years as the activity failed to attract sufficient support as a leisure activity. It closed and

was acquired by the Salvation Army in 1882 who converted it for services. This use only survived for ten years when the Salvation Army moved to its new Citadel in St Giles. After a time it became a builders merchant's depot and warehouse which it remained for many years before being reused for a showroom by Country and Eastern for the sale of exotic oriental antique furniture. The building also contains the South Asia Decorative Arts & Crafts Collection. A remarkable timber framed roof remains an imposing attraction of the building.

Open

Multi purpose youth venue.
Located in what was formerly the largest banking hall in England, on Bank Plain, Open is a £12m venue built especially for 12-25 year olds who live in Norwich and Norfolk. The venue includes a café, live music venue, nightclub, dance studio, recording studio, media laboratory, climbing wall, information and guidance. Opening in 2009 the venue was converted by Hudson Architects.

Opening Hours

Most shops open from 9am until 5.30pm from Monday to Saturday with a few staying open until 6pm. Thursday night is late shopping night when some City Centre shops will stay open until 8pm. On Sundays most 'high street' shops and a number of independents open between 11am and 4pm – some of the shops in the enclosed shopping malls open earlier for 'viewing'. Food shops tend to have longer opening hours, including M&S and Tesco in the centre, while some major food supermarkets operate 24 hours a day, apart from Sunday nights when they close late afternoon until the following Monday morning. Bank opening hours in the centre are generally 9am-5pm. Pubs, as a general rule, open 11am-11pm Sunday to Thursday, extending to midnight Friday and Saturday, with pubs in the 'evening economy' area (Prince of Wales Road/ Riverside) not closing until the early hours. Restaurants will normally open from 11am but some will take last orders at 2pm and not serve dinner until 6.30pm. Last dinner orders are usually 10pm.

The Old Skating Rink, Bethel Street.

Opie, Amelia

Romantic author. Daughter of noted local physician James Alderson and wife of portrait painter John Opie, Amelia was a prolific author and poet. She wrote 'Dangers of Coquetry' when she was just 18 and there followed one of her most noted novels 'Father and Daughter' (1801) of which Sir Walter Scott commented that he had cried over it more than he had ever cried over such things. Subsequent publications included a volume of verse (1802), Adeline Mowbray (1804), Simple Tales (1806), Temper (1812), Tales of Real Life (1813), Valentine's Eve (1816), Tales of the Heart (1818), and Madeline (1822). She associated with leading radicals of the time and was a friend of writers Sir Walter Scott, Richard Brinsley Sheridan and Madame de Stael. She later joined the Quakers and devoted herself to charitable works. In her early years she lived in Colegate and when she returned to retire in Norwich she lived at the junction of Castle Meadow and Opie Street. She died aged 84 and is buried at the Gildencroft.

Orford Arms and Cellar

Former Pub and Rock Music Venue. The Orford Arms was a product of George Skipper's remodeling of the medieval Red Lion Street in 1899-1901 to make way for the trams. Skipper's elaborate Art Nouveau and Flemish revival frontages included the Orford which took its name from the Earl of Orford who had paid for the reworking of the adjacent public space at the bottom of Timberhill. By 1925, the pub and associated hotel was the only venue in the City offering a 'Silver Grill' on Saturday nights and this regularly attracted over 200 diners paying half a crown each. The venue was popular during the War but by the 1960s, the cellar located beneath the Orford Arms had developed cult status. On October 12th 1966 Cream, one of the great rock bands of all time, featuring Eric Clapton, Ginger Baker and Jack Bruce, appeared at the Orford and Ginger Baker was apparently a relatively regular act, attracted by the lure of local fishing opportunities! The legendary Jimi Hendrix played there on 25th January 1967 and other pop and rock music icons including David Bowie and Rod Stewart also played at the venue as did other popular performers of the time including Geno Washington. Local impresario Howard Platt was responsible for attracting all the acts to the venue, which was often regarded as the place to try out a new line-up before touring. The Orford also featured long lived and popular local acts including Lucas and The Emperors and The Continentals. It closed in the 1970s and is currently a tanning studio with a Portuguese chain chicken restaurant on the ground floor.

Orford Hill

Historic space. Originally known as Swynemarket, when the market for pigs was moved here from All Saints Green in the late

Bust of Amelia Opie.

Organs, Church and other

Musical instruments. With such a large number of ecclesiastical institutions it is unsurprising that Norwich also has a significant heritage in organs reaching back at least to a documentary reference in the C14th, particularly church and chapel organs with over 50 examples surviving within the City boundary. Additionally, at the turn of the century, the local firm of Norman & Beard operated an organ works which Ralph Bootman describes as 'the largest and most fully equipped in the country' from the still surviving premises at St Stephen's Gate. Although they ceased trading in 1998, many of their creations survive today as do many other remarkable organs. Some of the most interesting can be seen in the following locations:

Clockwise from top: The surviving building which accommodated Norman & Beard's organ works in St Stephen's Square, organ in the Old Meeting House, and organ in St Helen's church.

- **Anglican Cathedral** – largest in the City and second largest cathedral organ in the country, designed by Hill, Norman & Beard and completed in 1942. The case was designed by Stephen Dykes Bower and added in 1950. The first documentary reference to an organ in the Cathedral is 1381 but a succession of others were all superseded. A further small organ resides in the Lady Chapel, by Snetzler, dates from 1754 and had a number of homes before being gifted to the Cathedral after the War.

- **Carnary College** – originally built in 1879 by Rayson of Ipswich, for St Peter Parmentergate, it was rebuilt by Bishop's of Ipswich and relocated to the Norwich School's Chapel in the College, within the solo case of the former Norman & Beard Cathedral organ

- **Old Meeting House** – built in 1660, this is the oldest surviving organ in the City and may have come from the Cathedral

- **St Elizabeth, Earlham** – the smallest pipe organ in the City, by W & A Boggis of Diss

- **St George, Colegate** – built in 1802 by George Pike England on the gallery,

the organ was moved to the north side of the chancel in 1880 by E.W. Norman but returned to its original position, where it remains, by Boggis in 1949

- **St Helen, Bishopgate** – built in 1855 by Norwich organ builder Mark Noble Snr

- **St John's Catholic Cathedral** – originally built in 1876 for the Maddermarket when it was a Catholic Chapel and subsequently moved to St John's

- **St Peter Mancroft** – one of the largest and most modern organs in the City, this was built by Peter Collins of Redbourn in 1984.

C13th, the space retained this name association (Hogge Market, Hoghill) until it was changed to commemorate George Walpole, the 3rd Earl of Orford and grandson of England's first prime minister Robert Walpole. George was said to have given generously to public subscriptions for planning improvements. This public largess was however rather out of character since his principal preoccupation was to squander the family fortune on gaming and sporting while the family estate at Houghton fell into decay. The space was originally enclosed on the north side before the trams broke through to Castle Meadow in 1900. Notable buildings include the Bell Hotel and, opposite, the former Darlow's gunsmiths dating from 1890 with an impressive stag on top. No. 7 is a C17th building sitting on a C15th vaulted undercroft.

Orford Hill Baptist Chapel

Little is known about this chapel except that it was converted from a warehouse in 1833 at a cost of £1,150. It could seat 550 people but this high figure was not reflected in the return made in the 1851 Census of places of worship. Morning and evening services were held in the chapel and there was an additional service in the afternoons which was attended by servants, invalids and those who couldn't attend at any other time on a Sunday. When the chapel was examined for a survey in 1989, major renovations were underway and all that remained of the original

interior features were some pillars and a stair-rail. It is in use currently as a bar and restaurant.

Orford Place

Changing topography.
Like Orford Hill, Orford Place takes its name from the Earl of Orford but where and what it is has changed significantly over two centuries. The name appears on an inscribed stone plaque in Orford Street and dated 1809, while a century later it was applied to the whole area occupied by the tram terminus developed around 1901. Today it is the small alley connecting Brigg Street to Red Lion Street.

Organs, Church and other

See opposite.

Over the Water

Historic Ward. This historic City ward encompassed all of the area north of the Wensum and south of the City Wall and included the parishes of St Michael at Coslany, St Mary at Coslany, St Martin at Oak, St George Colegate, St Augustine, St Clement, St Edmund, St Saviour, St Paul and St James, and the dissolved parishes of St John, St Olave, St Margaret Newbridge. Over the Water ceased to be a ward when Mancroft became the single ward for the Walled City. The term was coined in the 1970s when the area became the focus for historic building regenerations as part of the European Architectural Heritage Year initiative. The previously common name for the area had been Ultra Aquam.

Prince Philip reviews work undertaken as part of European Architectural Heritage Year 'Over the Water'.

P is for...

'Nosey' Parker, chaplain to Elizabeth I; a unique collection of 1930s parks; the Paston Letters; the only order of Pied Friars in England; unique, Dutch inspired public spaces; the first UK use of the postcode system; one of only two English puppet theatres.

Panks

Local engineers. Abraham Pank moved from Bawburgh to Norwich in 1842 to set up business in Pottergate as a brass worker, gas fitter and bell hanger. 16 years later his business had grown to such a degree that it necessitated a move to Bedford Street where he expanded into adjoining properties soon after. Sons subsequently took over the company and by 1879 the Norwich Postal Directory was referring to it as 'PANK & SON: Gas engineers and fitters, bell hangers and metal workers, lamp, beer-engine, bath and hot water apparatus manufacturers, ventilating and sanitary engineers.' By 1896 they had extended their repertoire to include electric lighting, drain testing, plumbing, telephones, oil engines and being contractors to H.M. Office of Works. Five years later they'd taken over the old established company of Holmes who had made their name particularly in the field of engineering and steam engines and Panks occupied Holmes' Prospect Place Works on Cattlemarket Street. Following the First World War they purchased the goodwill of engineers Riches & Watts and in 1926 they started an auto electrical department, purchasing electrical engineers C.E. Gates three years later. By 1933 they were advertising themselves as 'agricultural, electrical, wireless, mechanical, heating

Opposite: St Andrew's Plain, one of the unique collection of Norwich Plains.

engineers and contractors, mill furnishers and church furnishers, providing electric lighting for country houses, and official repairers of C.A. V. batteries, and district agents for Crossley's gas and oil engines'. In 1944 they sold the Bedford Street site for a very large sum and subsequently split the business into Engineering, Electrical and Radio subsidiaries. The electrical arm installed a Luminous Indicator Call System at the Norfolk & Norwich Hospital and a similar system at City College as well as installing flood-lighting at the Boundary Park Greyhound Stadium. The engineering arm provided boilers for Norwich Union and for a range of local industries. The radio business expanded and was boosted enormously by the arrival of TV. By 1967 Panks Radio had retail outlets in Orford Place, Davey Place and Prince of Wales Road. In 1982 the engineering company took over an old tannery in Heigham Street, moving out of Cattlemarket Street, taking with them the ornate cast iron lettering from the old Holmes site. The company is still prospering in Heigham Street and now specialises in pumps for dirty water, bore hole drilling, water treatment, site installations, food processing, irrigation and water features.

Parker, Bishop Matthew

Former Archbishop of Canterbury. Born in the parish of St Saviour in 1504, Parker came to the attention of Henry VIII while at Corpus Christi Cambridge and was appointed as Anne Boleyn's chaplain. Immediately before her execution she placed

Matthew Parker commemorated on a London Street sign.

her three year old daughter in his charge and she became Elizabeth I. A year after ascending to the throne she made Parker Archbishop of Canterbury – the only Norwich born cleric to reach that position. It is said that he was a remarkably inquisitive man which earned him to label of 'Nosey Parker', a titled now in common usage. His principal achievements included a new translation of the Bible – the Bishop's Bible – and the Thirty Nine Articles of religious settlement which sought to chart a balanced way between extreme Puritanism and Catholicism. This balanced approach to life was also illustrated in his early years when, in 1549, he tried to intercede with Kett's rebels but without success.

Parks and Open Spaces

Outdoor recreation opportunities. There are 23 parks, 95 open spaces and 59 natural areas in Norwich, within the control of the City Council plus a number of other open spaces managed by private institutions, independent organisations or trusts

Above: Early volume from the Cathedral Library containing the Paston Letters.
Right: Painting from Norwich Castle depicting the treasures of the Paston family.

(e.g. Plantation Garden, UEA Broad). Beyond the City boundary there are further parks and open spaces in the adjacent parishes. The significant parks and spaces are covered under specific, individual entries e.g. Mousehold Heath.

Park and Ride
See *car parking*.

Paston Family
Influential family. The Pastons were significant in the affairs of Norfolk and Norwich from the C14th for 300 years. They emerged from relative poverty and obscurity but took advantage of circumstance after the Black death to amass a significant land holding and fortune. A local saying states 'There was never a Paston poor, a Heydon a coward or a Cornwallis a fool'. They are know most famously for the Paston Letters which represent a unique surviving record of social life in the C15th. Margaret Paston owned a substantial house in Elm Hill which was severely damaged by the fire of 1507 and rebuilt by Augustine Steward (now the Strangers' Club). She and John Paston were

benefactors to St Peter Hungate and paid for the rebuilding of the nave and transepts in 1460. The family also gifted the roof-beams for Blackfriars and the hammer-beams in St Andrews Hall roof together with the superb C15th doors which bear their arms. Sir John Paston bought the Music House in King Street and remodelled it in 1488. John Paston was lawyer and confident to Sir John Fastolff and when he died the Pastons inherited his substantial land holdings

The surviving tower of Peafield Mill in New Lakenham.

and fortune. Following John's death, his sons (John the Elder and John the Younger) had to defend the lands inherited from Fastolff both legally and through force of arms. Much of the detail is captured in letters between the sons and their mother Margaret. The family continued to prosper but during the Civil War, Robert backed the wrong side and had his fortune confiscated. With the Restoration, Robert was back in favour but not sufficiently to get his wealth back from Charles II. He was, however, made Earl of Yarmouth as a consolation. Robert's son William died without a male heir and the title became extinct and the family's fortunes similarly declined.

Pastry, Mr
See *Hearne, Richard*.

Peafield
See *Lakenham, New*.

Peafield Mill
Converted historic flour mill. Located in Eleanor Road and built by Henry Lock in 1824 as a flour mill, it closed in the 1960s and was converted to housing in 1973 by the City Council.

Peters, Martin

Norwich City footballer.
Legend of the English World Cup victory in 1966, Peters joined Norwich in 1975 and for a five year period put in 232 appearances for the club. He scored 50 times and provided inspiration in notable victories against the likes of Arsenal, Chelsea, Liverpool and Manchester United.

Peter the Wild Boy

Ferrel child. Peter the Wild Boy (c.1713-1785) was a feral child found near Hamelin in the forests of Hanover in about 1725, who was brought back to England by King George I, and kept as a curiosity by Caroline, Princess of Wales. Initially he was regarded as a celebrity and writers such as Jonathan Swift and Defoe wrote about him. Eventually he lost his curiosity value when he failed to respond to his tutors and was 'retired' to a farm at Northchurch. However, he was in the habit of escaping and in 1751 he remarkably turned up in Norwich and was briefly imprisoned in the Bridewell as a supposed Spanish spy because he couldn't communicate. Once this misunderstanding was cleared up he was fitted with a leather collar bearing the message 'Peter, the Wild Man of Hanover. Whoever will bring him to Mr Fenn at Berkhampsted, Hertfordshire, shall be paid for their trouble.' He was returned to his guardians in Berkhampsted in Hertfordshire and died there in 1785 at the remarkable age of 72, considering his hardships. His presence in Norwich is commemorated in the name of the Wild Man pub in Bedford Street and a HEART blue plaque on the same building.

1966 World Cup hero and former Norwich City player Martin Peters.

Pettus Family

See overleaf.

Picture House

Former cinema. Claiming to be the City's premier cinema, the Picture House, or Haymarket Picture House as it became known, started life in 1911 as a modest conversion of the former London and Provincial Bank designed by the interestingly named Norwich architects Stoddart, Pine-Coffin and Imrie to provide a 372 seater auditorium. After the First World War it was almost completely rebuilt, reopening in 1921 to provide a new 1687 seat cinema with its own resident orchestra and the building was blessed by the Canon of St Peter Mancroft. In 1929 the Picture House was refurbished and became only the sixth cinema in England to be converted for the 'talkies' – the first showing was, perhaps predictably, Al Jolson's 'Singing Fool'. The Picture House was also the first City venue to install a cinema organ and this arrived in

1931. In 1955, a change in ownership changed the Haymarket's name to the Gaumont but this incarnation was short lived and it closed in 1959. The site was redeveloped to provide a Peter Robinson clothing store which subsequently became Top Shop.

Pierce, Stephen Rowland

Architect. Noted architect and town planner, and professional partner of Charles Holloway James, Pierce's greatest achievement was Norwich City Hall, won in open competition in 1932 and completed in 1938. He also designed Slough Town Hall (1936) and Hertfordshire's County Hall (1940). He was co-author of the City of Norwich Plan in 1945 and also provided town planning advice to Leamington Spa, Southampton and Malta.

Pierrepoint, Albert

Public Hangman. In 1951, Albert Pierrepoint, the longest serving public executioner in the 20th century, presided over the execution of Dennis Moore and Alfred Reynolds at Norwich Prison on 19th July. This was to be the last execution in Norfolk.

Pied Friars

Unique Order. The Friars de Pica or Pied Friars (so called because of their black and white habits) settled in King St at the north east corner of St Peter Parmentergate churchyard – it was their only order in Britain. Their stay was brief when, in 1307, the Council of Lyons required the order to join one of the four greater orders.

Pettus Family

The Pettus family were associated with Norwich as far back as the mid C16th, when wealthy mercer John Pettus moved from London. His son Thomas Pettus rose to prominence in the local community becoming Sherriff in 1566 and Mayor in 1590.

The family's City House was at Pettus House between 1550 and 1683, originally a substantial mansion in Elm Hill, extending from the surviving remnant at 41-43 Elm Hill as far as St Simon and St Jude's church. Monuments to Thomas Pettus and his family and to Sir John Pettus survive in this church while subsequent family memorials were placed in the now redundant All Saints at Rackheath Magna close to the country seat at Rackheath Hall.

The family line ceased in England with the death of Sir Horatio Pettus who died in 1772 but migration to the American colonies in the C17th ensured the continuation of the line there.

Colonel Thomas Pettus went to Virginia in 1638 with a military detachment to assist the Jamestown colonists in combatting the Powhatan natives. He built a substantial house close to Jamestown and became a Governors Council in the mid C17th.

Above: Sir John Pettus, former Mayor.

Clockwise from left:
Pettus tombs in the church of St Simon & St Jude, Elm Hill, Sir Thomas Pettus, and reconstruction of the Pettus House in Elm Hill.

Places of Worship

Religious institutions.
Norwich has a wide variety of places of worship meeting the needs of all denominations. Key sites, mainly located in or close to the City Centre, include:

- **Anglican** – Anglican Cathedral; St Andrew in St Andrew's Street; St George at Colegate and Tombland; St Giles; St Helen Bishopgate; St John Timberhill; St Julian; St Peter Mancroft and St Stephen
- **Baptist** – Norwich Central Baptist Chapel, St Mary's Plain
- **Buddhist** – Buddhist Centre, Bank Street
- **Christadelphian** – Cow Hill
- **Christian Fellowship** – New Hope Christian Centre, Martineau Lane
- **Christian Science** – Recorder Road
- **Community Church** – King's Centre, King Street
- **Congregationalist** – Old Meeting House, Colegate
- **Evangelical** – Surrey Chapel, Botolph Street
- **Jehovahs Witness** – Kingdom Hall, off St Crispin's Road
- **Judaism** – Norwich Synagogue, Earlham Road; East Anglian Progressive Jewish Congregation, Octagon Chapel; Adat Yeshua Messianic Synagogue Thorpe St Andrew Village Hall, Yarmouth Road
- **Methodist** – Chapelfield Road
- **Mormon** – Church of Jesus Christ of the Latter Day Saints, Greenways, Eaton
- **Muslim** – Ihsan Mosque, Chapelfield East; UEA Masjid, UEA Campus; East Anglian Bangladeshi Islamic Centre, Rose Lane
- **Pentecostal** – Elim Pentecostal Church, Trory Street
- **Orthodox** – St John the Theologian, Ber Street
- **Quaker** – Meeting House, Upper Goat Lane
- **Roman Catholic** – Cathedral of St John the Baptist
- **Salvation Army** – Citadel, St Giles Street
- **Seventh Day Adventist** – Dereham Road
- **Spiritualist** – Norwich Spiritualist Church, Chapelfield North
- **Strict Baptist** – Zoar Strict Baptist (Reformed), St Mary's Plain
- **Unitarian** – Octagon Chapel, Colegate
- **United Reform Church** – Princes Street; Trinity, Unthank Road.

Plagues

Historic pestilence.
The worst visitation of disease upon Norwich was the Black Death which arrived in 1349 and came again in 1362 and 1369. This series of plagues probably claimed a third of the population and resulted in some parishes disappearing entirely. Margaret Paston, in the famous Paston Letters talks about epidemics in Norwich in 1465, 1471 and 1479 as 'the most universal death that I ever knew in England.' A further outbreak of plague followed Elizabeth I's visit of 1578 and, although the local folklore claims that her entourage brought it with them, this is unproven. 4193 people died of the plague in that year and further outbreaks followed in 1603, when 3,000 people were taken, and in 1625 and 1665. After the last incidence of the plague in 1666, which took nearly 2500 people, smallpox became the most feared disease. In 1669/70 Sir Thomas Browne wrote that more than 300 families had succumbed in less than a fortnight and it returned in 1681/2. Smallpox continued into the C18th and C19th as a significant threat until vaccination became prevalent. In 1819 530 people died of the disease. Typhus also briefly had an impact and was probably the cause of an unusually high death rate in 1710. Cholera replaced smallpox in 1832, when 128 people died and outbreaks continued to the end of the C19th. Typhoid was also a significant epidemic disease with nearly 100 deaths from it in 1898.

Plains

Distinctive public spaces.
Inspired by immigrations from the Low Countries, and particularly the large scale influx in the mid C16th, 'Plains' take their name from the Dutch term 'Plein'. The Norwich Plains are public open spaces unique in this part of Eastern England and have been a distinctive part of the local topography since at least the mid C16th. Writing of Kett's Rebellion of 1549, Nicholas Sotherton describes the battle 'in the playne before the Pallace gate of the Bishop'. While only five formally named Plains appear on street plans now (Agricultural Hall Plain, Bank Street, St Catherine's Plain, St Martin at Palace Plain and St Mary's Plain), many have been referred to on earlier maps and some remain in informal local

The Plantation Garden, Earlham Road.

usage. Examples include Maddermarket Plain, Redwell, St Andrew's Plain, St Benedict's Plain, St George's Plain (Colegate), St Gile's Plain, St Margaret's Plain, St Paul's Plain, St Stephen's Plain and Theatre Plain. Continuing the tradition, newer Plains have included University Plain, Millennium Plain and Chapelfield Plain.

Plantation Garden

Hidden urban garden. Nestling out of public gaze behind the Catholic Cathedral, just off Earlham Road, the Plantation Garden began life as a chalk quarry. Cabinet maker Henry Trevor saw the potential of the site in 1856 and spent the next 40 years creating a spectacular hidden gem until his death in 1897. By 1883 he had succeeded to such a degree that White's Directory stated 'The Plantation, situated in a deep dell, the site of ancient and extensive chalk-pits, is a gem of landscape gardening, and its tropical and sub-tropical collections are in high repute.' The Garden is open to the public daily and it is cared for by the Plantation Garden Preservation Trust, formed in 1980. Its patron is Sir Roy Strong.

Playhouse Theatre

Theatre. The Playhouse, located in St George's Street in the heart of the City's creative quarter, opened in 1995 as a 300 seat venue providing a wide range of entertainment from plays through music to stand up. The design work was undertaken by Lambert, Scott & Innes with Henry Burke, the founder, being the driving force for the project. 80 per cent of the £2.5m development cost was raised from donations by individuals and companies. The site started life as a maltings in the 1840s and subsequently was used as the Crown Public House, the head office of the Norwich Mercury Newspaper, the depot for Ruymps builders' merchants, the warehouse of a motor-cycle dealer and a Greek restaurant. In 2003 it came under the wing of the Theatre Royal in a merged management agreement. The venue also operates a very popular public bar.

Pleasure Gardens

Now lost, private C18th/19th outdoor leisure venues. Pleasure Gardens were privately managed venues for outdoor public entertainment, including eating and drinking, theatre, exhibitions, circuses, fireworks and even hot air balloon spectaculars, and they flourished mainly in the C18th and C19th. Norwich apparently had the largest number of such establishments of any provincial English city. Over the period of their popularity they divided between large scale enterprises on the London model and smaller attachments to pubs providing not much more than food, drink and modest entertainment like bowls. The former included My Lord's Garden (the earliest) in King Street, Cater's Garden in St Faith's Lane (Mountergate), later to be renamed New Spring Gardens then Vauxhall Gardens following the fashion to name places after their London originals, Ranelagh Gardens on Queens Road, the Wilderness, just south of the Walled City and the Prussia Gardens on the Ipswich Road. Major gardens related to pubs included the Angel Gardens on Angel Road, Gibraltar Gardens at Heigham, Greenhills Gardens near St Augustines Gate, gardens at Trowse White Horse, at Pockthorpe, at Thorpe and in Julian

Place off Chapelfield Road by the Vauxhall Gardens pub. Somewhere between the two extremes, Pages Greyhound Gardens in Ber Street was targeted at a more working class audience.

Plumsteads

See *Great and Little Plumstead*.

Plunkett, George

Documenter of local change. George Plunkett had a rare passion for photography and Norwich. Over a period of 75 years, George accumulated a unique record of change to the fabric of Norwich. He began his photographic mission with a box camera at the age of 18 but for his 19th birthday acquired an Ensign Carbine No. 7 folding camera which cost the equivalent of a month's wages. George's photographic record was remarkable for three reasons. Firstly, he began taking pictures at a time when the Council were pursuing a slum clearance programme with a vehemence which saw dozens of medieval gems disappearing. Closely behind this, the War saw the Baedeker Blitz removing further elements of the City's heritage and thirdly, in the late 1950s and 60s, the appalling institutional vandalism of post War redevelopment, erased other historic gems. Over a long and distinguished crusade to capture and document these important changes, George took over 8,500 photographs and published two books. In 2000, his collection was made accessible to a much wider audience on the internet and organised by his son Jonathan it can now

be viewed at www.the-plunketts.freeserve.co.uk

Pockthorpe

Urban hamlet. Located on the Wensum, just north east of the Anglo Scandinavian D shaped, defended enclosure of Northwic, the name means Poka's village, from the old Norse. St James Pockthorpe is probably C12th in origin but saw C19th restorations and has an octagonal tower dating from 1743. The church now houses Norwich Puppet Theatre, founded in 1978. Pockthorpe smockmill was built in 1769 but demolished around 1813, to be replaced by Pockthorpe towermill. It was located somewhere between Magdalen Road and Silver Road, most likely around St Olaves Road. By 1882, the mill had lost its sails and was steam-driven. However, the mill was demolished around 1896. Steward and Patterson's brewery was begun by John Patterson in 1793. It was positioned close to the River Wensum so that the brewery could transport beer along the river to Yarmouth and have coal brought back by boat. By 1895 Steward & Patterson

Bethel Street Police Station.

controlled 489 pubs in total. In the C20th, the brewery joined with Bullard's, but was then taken over by Watneys in 1963. Brewing eventually ceased in 1970 although a remnant of the brewery survives on the eastern junction of Barrack Street and Silver Road.

Pockthorpe Gate

See *Barre Gate*.

Police, Norwich City

Local constabulary. England had been slow to embrace the idea of a professional law enforcement and crime prevention body. Continental Europe had introduced measures well before the British Isles (the word 'police' is of French derivation) and even the Scots and Irish had adopted police forces before London led the way for England in 1829. It took until January 1836, following the adoption of the Municipal Reform Act the year before, for Norwich to establish then recruit a Norwich City Police Force. To begin with the Force numbered 18 supplemented by 32 night watchmen and the Police Station was in the eastern end of the Guildhall. Numbers rose to 24 by 1839. They wore blue uniforms and leather top hats and were equipped with truncheons and handcuffs. The first statistics, produced in 1838, showed that the police dealt with 69 felonies, 56 assaults, 113 disorderly persons and five cases of uttering false coins. By 1853 the size of the Force had risen to 61 constables and 12 officers and more locations were secured across the City Centre to serve as police stations. In 1871, the helmet replaced

The Port of Norwich in the 1970s.

the top hat. The police ultimately moved to the new police station following the completion of City Hall and Norwich retained its own police force until Local Government Reorganisation in 1974 when the force was absorbed into the Norfolk Constabulary, then based at County Hall. The Norfolk force is now head quartered at Wymondham.

Population

Local population. The administrative area of the City of Norwich contains 132,200 residents (2007 mid year estimate) while the Greater Norwich Area supports 223,200 people and the Travel to Work Area, 376,500. Within the City 15.6 per cent are 15 years old or under (18.9 per cent in England) and 19.2 per cent are over 60 (21.7 per cent in England).

Port of Norwich

Historic harbour. The early topography of east Norfolk, with a wide estuary stretching from Caister on Sea to Gorleston, facilitated access to the City by sea going ships from the earliest period. It is clear that European trade flourished with the Port of Norwich from the pre Conquest period well into late medieval times. Initially focussed around Fishergate and Bychel (St Martins), port activity eventually took root along much of the Wensum within the City Walls. Photographs taken as late as the Victorian period show intense wherry-based activity around the Quayside area with larger ships occupying the wharves from Foundry Bridge southwards. Even up to the 1970s sea going ships were bringing cargoes to Reads (grain),

Kings (scrap), Colmans (raw materials) and to the timberyards along the river. It was only when the riverside industries disappeared that the industrial nature of the Port ceased giving way to exclusively leisure use, based around the Yacht Station.

Post Boxes

Convenient and historic posting locations. Up until the mid C19th letters were taken to receiving houses but in 1856, the first post box appeared in Norwich. These early boxes were green and the first red boxes appeared in 1874 and a few of the Victorian boxes still survive. Today the principal locations for posting letters in the City Centre are at the Railway Station (inside), Prince of Wales Rd (at St Faith's Lane), Castle Mall Main Post Office, Castle Meadow (near Arcade St), All Saints Green (John Lewis), Queens Rd (bus station), Orford Hill, Lower Close, Bank Plain, Gentleman's Walk (London St junction), Haymarket, Theatre St (Assembly House) and Maddermarket/St Andrews. The significant surviving historic post boxes include: Queen Victoria – Haymarket; Bell Hotel; Prince of Wales – St Faith's Lane; Carrow Hill; Upper St Giles; King Street; Edward VII – St Georges; St John Maddermarket; St Giles; George V – Theatre St (double).

Postcode

Pilot postcode use. Norwich was the first city in Britain to pioneer the use of the postcode system, in the 1960s, and the successful piloting of this system resulted in it being applied subsequently across the UK.

From left: Victorian wall mounted post box in Upper St Giles, and a Victorian replica post box, St Peter's Street – the original was demolished by a truck on the Walk.

Post Offices

Post office history and locations. References to the 'Post' go back in Norwich to the 1500s when the Mayor and Duke of Norfolk made pronouncements on the use of post horses. Postmasters were appointed in the City from the mid C17th and a range of locations served as the Head Post Office. The first recorded site was at the King's Head on the Market Place (site of current Davey Place). From 1766 it moved to Hungate Street (now Princes Street), then to Jack of Newbury Yard off Pottergate in 1783, then Old Post Office Yard off Bedford Street in 1789, then Upper St Andrews in 1792 and a year later, Old Post Office Court, off the Market Place and forming part of the Half Moon pub. The Head Post Office moved to Museum Street (now Exchange Street) in 1836 and the street changed its name to

Post Office Street from 1842. In 1875 the Head Post Office moved to Hardwick House in Agricultural Hall Plain where it remained for nearly 100 years before moving to Bank Plain. That Office in turn was closed as part of a series of rationalisations in the new Millennium when the post office in Castle Mall became, and remains, the new main office.

Postwick

Suburban parish. Located around 7km (4.5 miles) east of the centre of Norwich, Postwick with Witton parish has a population of 323 and was recorded in the Domesday Book as 'Possuic'. The probable meaning is the farm belonging to Poss. Postwick's All Saints church is a medieval flint and stone construction which was restored in 1866. St Margaret's church at Witton

has a square C15th tower and a C17th octagonal second stage. It was partially rebuilt in 1857. A ferry previously ran between Postwick and Surlingham on the River Yare, although this service ceased after a collision in 1939. Postwick is the location of one of Norwich's Park and Ride sites at the junction of the A47 and the A1042.

Pottergate
Ancient thoroughfare.
Originally the name given to Lobster Lane and Bedford Street in the Pre Conquest, Anglo-Scandinavian period and meaning 'street of the potters'. A number of early kilns have been found here. The name migrated west following Post Conquest urban development reaching beyond the Walls where it became West Pottergate, which is interesting since there was no Gate in the City wall at this point. Starting from the extreme eastern end, the Edinburgh Arms sat on the south side from 1586 although its cellars were much earlier and occupied at one time by the City's first printer, Anthony de Solempne, from Brabant in the Netherlands. In August 1898 a fire devastated the area around the Edinburgh but the pub itself miraculously survived – weakened though, it collapsed four days later. Opposite the site of the lost pub is the medieval church of St John Maddermarket, now run as a 'show church' by the Churches Conservation Trust. Next door, No. 7 retains two C17th brick doorways but was substantially restored in a Gothic Revival style by George Skipper in 1916. The intervening buildings are C17th/18th but further

From left: Colman House, Pottergate, and the view west along Pottergate.

along, on the north side, Nos. 17-19 are C16th with a renovated C18th facade while Nos. 19-21, with a carriageway arch, are of a similar date. Finally, completeing this otherwise entirely listed run of frontages, is the 1930s, Art Deco Pottergate Tavern (now the Birdcage) referred to by the authors of 1945 City Plan as 'incongruous in design and out of place'. This is indeed a remarkable judgement from the people who were responsible for the demolition of a whole ancient street block of Norwich and its replacement by the City's largest Art Deco building – City Hall. Opposite to this is the very clearly incongruous and out of place Seld House, by City Architect David Percival, which replaced more ancient and attractive buildings in 1964. Eastwards, Bagleys Court demonstrates how C18th buildings can be brought back into beneficial use. Moving west, and on the north side of the street, the gigantic Kiln House (1978 by Piper Black) is followed by Nos. 61-3, C17th with a C18th top storey and in a courtyard, behind these, is the early C17th Colman House. This fine building was the City's Eye Infirmary from 1854 until 1913, then it became a shoe factory and was converted into flats in 1984. Also in front of Colman House, No. 65 is C17th with an extensive C15th undercroft reaching beneath the pavement. Next, Nos. 69-71 are a C16th house with a C19th top floor followed by a group of C17/18th houses. Opposite these the Jenny Lind Children's Hospital was established but subsequently relocated. At the end of Pottergate, a stunning collection of Tudor and Georgian houses were destroyed either by slum clearance or the Wartime bombing campaign. Nos. 100-104 survived, the latter being the striking C17th house later occupied by Joseph Kinghorn, baptist minister and scholar. Beyond the Inner Ring Road the West Pottergate Council housing development of the late 1960s swept away streets of Victorian terraces and a row of Georgian alms houses dating from 1827.

Premier League

Top football league.
Norwich City's first appearance in the newly inaugurated Premier League (formerly League Division 1) was on 15th August 1992 when they beat Arsenal 4-2 away at Highbury after coming from 0-2 down. Mark Robbins came on as sub and turned the game by taking the record as the first scorer for Norwich in the Premiership and then scoring the fourth goal. During that season, Norwich secured 39 points from their first 18 games and led the table by eight points just before Christmas, eventually finishing 3rd at the end of the season. Norwich were relegated in the 1994-5 season returning briefly in 2004-5 to be relegated again at the end of that season. After plummeting to the bottom of the old 3rd Division (League 1) in 2009 they were reinvigorated by new manager Paul Lambert and achieved promotion back to the Premiership in 2011 – a remarkable feat of moving through two divisions in just two seasons.

Prince of Wales Cinema

Former cinema. This 900 seat conversion of the New Assembly Rooms opened in June 1912 but survived only ten years and then became the Grosvenor Rooms dance hall. It survived until the 1960s and apart from being a very popular dance venue from the War until its closure, it had the distinction of hosting the only performance of the Beatles in Norwich, in 1963. It was redeveloped for the Grosvenor House office block by British Rail.

Prince of Wales Road

New street. Built on the former orchards and hopfields of the Austin friars,

Prince of Wales Road was one of the very few new streets to be added to the predominantly medieval street pattern. Begun in 1860 by the Norwich New Street Company to produce a new 'grand approach' from the railway station, work had to be taken over by the Corporation five years later. The grand vision only developed as far as a terrace of grey brick villas on the north side. While Agricultural Hall Plain did deliver some more distinguished buildings at the top of the road, the remainder of the development consisted of unremarkable Victorian/Edwardian edifices and

awful modernist accretions from the 1960s. The street now serves as a 'key element of the 'evening economy' with a high concentration of pubs, bars and clubs.

Princes Street

Ancient thoroughfare. Connecting Tombland to St Andrew's Plain, this street was originally part of the Holmestrete-Westwick Roman Road and was called Hundegate for most of its history apparently reflecting the probability that the Bishop's hounds were kept there. In 1830 the name changed to Princes Street, after the Princes Inn, dating from 1391, whose carved lintel was relocated from here and now survives at 168 King Street. In a 'tit for tat' gesture, No. 24 incorporates a carved lintel taken from the surviving Fye Bridge Street City house of Edmund Wood, Sheriff in 1536 and Mayor in 1548. The northern run of frontages, referred to by Pevsner as 'one of the best street sequences in Norwich', includes C17th and C18th buildings and No. 20 which has a C15th vaulted undercroft and a C16th barrel vaulted cellar. The 'book ends' are provided by St Peter Hungate, now a medieval art centre, and St George Tombland, still in use as a church. On the opposite side of the road, similar delightful ancient houses, including the timber framed Sussex House dating from 1500, survived until Bally & Haldestein's shoe factory was built on the south side in 1939. It in turn was redeveloped in 1974 for the St Michael at Plea housing and office development.

From top: A rare moment of joy for Norwich in the 2004/5 Premiership season – a sound home victory over Manchester United. Return to the Premiership celebrations in May 2011.

Princes Street Congregational Church.

Princes Street Congregational Church

Non Conformist church.
Princes Street Congregational Church, now Princes Street United Reform Church, was founded opposite St Peter Hungate in 1819 by the Rev. John Alexander. Alexander was a key figure in Norwich life and counted Norwich's Gurney family, Elizabeth Fry and writer Amelia Opie amongst his social circle. Under his inspiring and active ministration, worship at Princes Street flourished. Alexander's good work was continued by George Barrett, an equally dynamic minister, who took over in 1866. Membership was such that in 1869 Barrett commissioned Norwich architect, Edward Boardman, to design an extension to the church and ten years later additional space that was used as a the lecture hall and Sunday school. Boardman's buildings still stand today and remain much as they were designed. The exterior of the buildings and the church interior have changed little over the years but modern glass doors were added to the front of the church to reflect the church's conviction that there should be no barrier between the Church and the outside world.

As well as Alexander and Barrett, Princes Street church has had several other members with an interesting personal history. Ethel Mary Colman was the second daughter of Jeremiah Colman, founder of the world-famous mustard company. Miss Coleman was active in both Princes Street church and in Norwich's social and political circles. She became the first female deacon of Princes Street, possibly the first in the country, and continued this trend in 1923 by becoming the first female Lord Mayor of Norwich and in England. Oliver Tomkins, another interesting member, pursued his calling much further afield. He joined the church in 1890 at the age of seventeen and had a very strong religious conviction. By the summer of 1895 he was certain that he wanted to join the London Missionary Society and in December 1899 George Barrett ordained Tomkins at Princes Street church. There was a great celebratory atmosphere to the farewell proceedings as jokes were made about the perils of venturing into cannibal country. Tomkins was to join the celebrated missionary, James Chalmers, in New Guinea. Chalmers had cheated death on many occasions and was seen by the Congregational Church as a hero. It was felt that Tomkins would be in safe hands. Tomkins found his missionary life quite challenging but fulfilling and was determined to bring Christ to the 'heathen'. In April 1901 Chalmers, Tomkins and twelve students travelled to a place called Dopima on the Island of Goaribari in New Guinea. A tribal dispute was underway on shore and Chalmers decided to try to mediate. Against Chalmers' wishes Tomkins insisted on following him ashore. Trouble escalated and both men, plus the students in their care, were clubbed to death and eaten by the natives.

Prior's Hall

House of the Prior then Dean. Initially the Prior would have lived with the other monks in the common dormitory but separate lodgings developed by the C12th and by 1284 the Prior's Hall existed in Norwich Cathedral's Benedictine friary east of the cloister. By 1330 a separate Priors Chapel (now lost) had been developed adjacent to the cloister. In the early C16th a major development took place which inserted a new floor into the Hall, added a new residential wing to the north and created a gallery access to the chapel. It is possible that this work was completed to accommodate Catherine of

Aragon and Cardinal Wolsey on their visit in 1520. While subsequent adaptations changed the look of the Prior's Hall/Deanery to something more like a substantial Victorian house, much of the early architecture is still visible externally and internally. Very early features including painted ceiling beams still survive.

Prospect House

Modernist newspaper headquarters. Designed by Yates, Cook & Derbyshire and opened in 1970 as the new corporate headquarters for Eastern Counties Newspapers (now Archant), relocated to the redeveloped Cattlemarket Street, this modernist concrete slab incorporates a sculpture of lacquered bronze balls by Bernard Meadows.

Public Art

Art outside. While the bulk of outdoor public art in Norwich tends to be in the form of sculpture there are a few examples of graphic art of various sorts. The most impressive is perhaps Norwich Images at Wensum Lodge, produced in 1985 by the acclaimed international muralist Walter Kershaw. An example of temporary mural art on a building destined for demolition is Thomas More's Utopia, inscribed on the walls of the old Eastern Electricity Board Meter Testing Building off Westwick Street.

Left to right, from top: Temporary public art on the Walk, poster art in Castle Meadow, Walter Kershaw's impressive mural at Wensum Lodge, Art on Bicycles in Upper St Giles, and Thomas Moore's Utopia on the old Duke St EEB site.

Public Houses and Bars

Profusion of pubs. Norwich has a reputation for having a church for every week of the year and a pub for every day although the latter, historically at least, represented a serious under reflection of the situation in reality. During the latter half of the C19th, the City boasted something approaching two pubs for every day of the year and this was for a geographical area reaching only just beyond the Walled City. The Market Place alone, for instance, boasted 49 pubs while the 'King Street Run' offered a similar number. While many of the physical buildings still survive, few have remained in pub use and it would now be fair to say, in the City Centre at least, that Norwich has a pub for every week of the year. The following attempts a rough categorisation, picking out those pubs and bars in the Norwich area most worthy of a visit from a range of perspectives.

Good Beer Pubs

Pubs with exceptional ranges of draught and/or bottled beers.

- **Fat Cat** – 49, West End Street. Best beer pub in Norwich with astonishing choice (25 draughts alone), excellent staff, nice 'local' atmosphere, small outside seating area and pleasant Victorian building with lots of pub memorabilia. 20 min walk from the City Centre along Dereham Rd.

Top: The Ribs of Beef in Wensum St.
Right: Recently refurbished and historic Plough in St Benedicts St.
Opposite (from left): the Mischief in Fye Bridge Street, and the out of centre but very popular Unthank Arms.

- **Coach and Horses** – 82 Thorpe Rd. Rare micro brewery in Norwich with good range of Chalk Hill beers, pleasant food, outside seating area and nice early C19th building. Ten mins walk from the City Centre along Thorpe Rd.
- **Plough** – St Benedicts. Combines a very rare historic rear wing with a showcase for local beer.
- **Cidershed** – 98, Lawson Rd. A mecca for cider drinkers, run by the proprietor of the Fat Cat and lauded by the Guardian, this venue offers a unique drinking hole for beer and cider drinkers. Ten mins north of the Walled City.
- **Belgian Monk** – 7 Pottergate. Very impressive selection of Belgian regional draughts

and bottles, good Belgian food, pleasant historic building with Belgian memorabilia all located in the epicenter of the City.

- **Kings Head** – 42 Magdalen St. Good range of cask and bottled beers. Winner of local CAMRA branch Pub of the Year twice.
- **Ribs of Beef** – 24 Wensum St. Good range of draught real ales, good food, friendly staff located in a building which contains vestiges of an early structure and gained a new license in 1985. On the river and close to tourist sites.
- **Duke of Wellington** – 93, Waterloo Rd. 20 cask beers available, folk nights and a WWII air raid shelter! Just north of City Centre.
- **White Lion** – 73 Oak Street. Rare outpost of the

Cambridge based Milton Brewery but also featuring a range of guests. Food recently introduced and located within a building dating back from 1558. North western City Centre.

- **Playhouse** – 42 St Georges St. Although the bar of a small theatre, this is regarded as one of the coolest bars in the City. Innovative beer choice, nice staff, pleasant atmosphere, outside seating area and very central location.

- **Murderers/Gardeners Arms** – 2-4 Timberhill. Named by Lonely Planet as one of the best pubs in the world in 2009 it sells a range of cask beers and food in a partly reproduction historic atmosphere.

- **Trafford Arms** – Trafford Rd. Award winning real ale pub with extensive range and occasional beer festivals.

- **Cottage** – 9, Silver Rd. Rare outpost for the Mauldons Brewery offering ten draughts including guests. Snack food. Located ten mins north of City Centre.

- **Coachmakers Arms** – St Stephen's Gate. Former C17th coaching inn selling wide range of real ales just outside Walled City.

- **Bell** – 5, Orford Hill. Wetherspoons House so the usual package of beer and food, tends to be rammed with 'the evening economy crowd' in the evenings but is in an interesting and very well interpreted historic building and does sell interesting beer at reasonable prices. Next to the Castle.

- **Glass House** – Wensum Street. Another Wetherspoons House with a very similar description to the Bell except the building is less interesting and the location is slightly less central.

Historic Pubs
Pubs in significantly historic premises.

- **Adam and Eve** – 17 Bishopgate: claims to be the oldest pub in Norwich, located just north of the Cathedral.

- **Bedfords** – Bedford St/ Old Post Office Court: a bar set in one of the oldest medieval vaulted cellars in Norwich.

- **Coach and Horses** – 51 Bethel Street: C16th inn with C17th additions, characterful interior.

- **Maid's Head** – Tombland: parts of the building date from at least the C15th and possibly earlier, tap bar is quaint.

- **Mischief** – Fye Bridge St: outstanding former C16th merchant house with interesting internal details.

- **Take 5** – 17 Tombland: dating from 1480, with a C15th undercroft and C16th rear wing, formerly called the Louis Marchesi after the founder of the Round Table Movement.

- **Wig and Pen**, 6, St Martin at Palace Plain: C17th building formerly the house of the Broomfield family.

Bars
Bars favoured by the clubbing set.

- **Rocco's** (Prince of Wales) – Bar and restaurant, at night local dj's perform. Cocktails and champagne.

- **Rehab** (Prince of Wales) – Playing music from the 70s all the way through to the newest dance tracks.

- **Shoosh** (Prince of Wales) – A boutique bar offering a wide selection of cocktails which can be enjoyed on the two exclusive beds. Music ranges from RnB to club to reggae.

(continued over the page)

(bars continued)

- **Bar X** (Prince of Wales) – Music ranges from club anthems, Rnb and garage. Karaoke every Tuesday.

- **Vodka Revolution** (Queen street) – Open seven days a week with food available. Also serving cocktails, pitchers and wine. Music is a cool eclectic party.

- **Havanas** (London Street) – Late night bar open till 4am every night. A laid back vibe. Live dj's every weekend, music ranges from hip hop, dub step, jazz and electro, suiting everyone.

- **The Dog House** (St Georges Street) – Reopened November 2010 after refurbishment. Urban chic playing music throughout the night. Karaoke every Thursday. The kennel bar is available for hire (up to 150 people) which can include a buffet.

- **The Playhouse** (St Georges Street) – Converted from a 160 year old maltings. Alongside the 300 seat theatre there is a family friendly bar where you can relax with a coffee or juice or enjoy a range of ales from many brewers in East Anglia. Patio seating by the Wensum River.

- **The Mustard Lounge** (All Saints Green) – Underground alternative music spread on two floors. There is a large cocktail bar and a fully equipped dj booth. Free entry every Thursday until 3am.

- **Karma Kafe** (Bedford Street) – An eclectic mix music spread out on three floors.

- **Chain bars** including All Bar One (Tombland), Beluga (Queen St), The Glasshouse Wetherspoon (Wensum St).

Pulls Ferry

See *Cathedral Close*.

Puppet Theatre

Unique theatre. Founded in 1979 as a conversion of the medieval church of St James in Barrack Street, this is one of only two puppet theatres in England. It houses a 185 seat raked auditorium, 50 seat Octagon Studio, workshops, an exhibition gallery, shop and licensed bar. It is the only theatre in the East of England with a year-round programme of family-centred entertainment. As well as hosting a variety of touring puppetry companies from Britain and overseas, and featuring the best of British and international theatre of animation for all ages, the theatre presents an ongoing programme of craft based workshops for children, with special sessions for adults. www.puppettheatre.co.uk

Pykerell's House

Medieval Merchant House. Pykerell's house was built in the late C15th and was the home of a textile merchant who died in 1545. Pykerell was an important Norwich citizen who became sheriff in 1513 and then Mayor in 1525, 1533 and 1538. The building has had a turbulent history and was originally much larger: All that remains now is the former pantry and buttery plus the main hall or living area. The Zoar Chapel now stands where the kitchens probably were and another wing, containing the private rooms of the Pykerell family, would probably have stood at the other end of the hall. In 1860 the building was used as an inn, later called the Rosemary Tavern and was nearly demolished in the 1930s as part of the slum clearance scheme but saved by the Norfolk Archaeological Trust. The house was bombed on August 2nd 1942 and lay vacant and almost derelict for six years until it was restored to become one of Norwich's oldest inhabited houses and one of only five surviving thatched buildings within the City Walls.

Pykerell's House in St Mary's.

Q is for…

Award-winning 'green' building; one of England's principal Quaker foundations; one of the principal examples of pleasure gardens outside London.

Above: The Quaker Meeting House in Upper Goat Lane.
Previous page: The Queen's Building at the University of East Anglia.

Quakers

Religious Society. The Religious Society of Friends has its origins in the mid C17th, during the Commonwealth period, when dissenting groups, seeking simpler alternatives to priests and establishment church ceremonials, were united by Charles Fox. They were nicknamed Quakers because they were said to quake in the presence of God and the title has remained with them since. In 1654 Thomas Symonds instigated the first Norwich meeting of the Society and by 1670 they had acquired a site in the Gildencroft for a burial ground, which survives today. This was followed shortly after, in 1676, by the purchase of a site in Upper Goat Lane for a Meeting House, which opened in 1679. A second Meeting House opened at the Gildencroft 20 years later. By the end of the C17th Norwich had become one of the principal centres for the Society in England and the organisation had over 500 members. Although the Friends

endured significant individual and institutional persecution during their early years of their Norwich existence they had become an acceptable part of the local establishment by the C18th, endowing alms houses and a school and supporting poor members of their community. Respectability was underpinned by support from powerful and influential sectors of society and individuals such as the Gurney family (founders of the banking empire that was to become Barclays) their daughter Elizabeth Fry who was well connected to powerful reformers nationally like Wilberforce and Thomas Fowell Buxton, and by the authoress Amelia Opie. John Gurney was responsible for commissioning the new Meeting House in Upper Goat Lane by Patience in 1826 in an attempt to bring new impetus to the movement when it was flagging in the early C19th. Later in the C19th grocer John Eddington arrived in the City and as well as becoming the Society's biographer he set about

improvements to the Upper Goat Lane site. The Gildencroft however, suffered from falling attendances and was let to the Baptists in the 1880s. It was destroyed during a bombing raid in April 1942 and although rebuilt, reusing salvaged elements, in a replica style in 1958 it never returned to a Quaker use and today supports a private nursery. Today the Quaker community remains active in the City with regular meetings at the Upper Goat Lane Meeting House.

Quantrell's (or Ranelagh) Pleasure Gardens

Lost Pleasure Gardens. These gardens first appeared at the top of St Stephen's (currently the Sainsbury's/Marsh sites on Queens Road) in 1763 as nurseries but by 1766 'Smith's Rural Gardens' began to turn them more into an entertainment venue and a year later, fireworks had become a feature. By 1768 widow Smith had taken on William Quantrell, something of a pyrotechnic master, and he created for her the largest piece of firework display ever seen in Norwich, in 1771. The next year, Quantrell took over the gardens. In 1775 Quantrell engaged enthusiastically in the contest between the four Norwich principal pleasure gardens and introduced Baptista Pedralio, a star of Marylebone extravaganzas, to orchestrate a 'large globe 21 feet in circumference which will turn around its axis and fall into four parts and will discover Vulcan on the inside who will be attended by his Cyclops.' This established Quantrell as the 'industry standard' in the City and the following year he delivered 'the taking of Bunker Hill with fire ships' and 'Hercules delivering Thetis from out of the infernal Regions' the year after. Concerts and musical performances provided a more staple diet for the regular clientele, including appearances by famous London performers of the day, but competition with the other pleasure gardens, and Bunn's in particular, spurred Quantrell on to innovate further. In 1780, responding to Bunn's poaching of his former firework engineer, Quantrell engaged a new Italian engineer to create 'a capital Firework call'd Harlequin from the Globe, With a Dance of Furies, and Sig. Antonio Batalus will Fly across the Garden with Fire from different Parts of his Body.' Further innovations followed and shortly after the first manned balloon flight in 1783, from Paris, Quantrell produced a number of small, unmanned balloon ascent the following year and the year after he announced the first manned flight by James Decker and

his 13 year old companion, Miss Weller. Despite problems of rips in the silk fabric and bad weather the balloon eventually rose 'in the most beautiful manner, with considerable rapidity' (but without Miss Weller unfortunately) and eventually came down near Loddon. When Decker returned to the City the same evening he was mobbed by an excited crowd. Subsequently, Major Money rose from Quantrell's in the British Balloon but after an impressive ascent he had problems with the release valve and floated out to sea, being rescued by a cutter after five hours adrift. Balloons then lost their novelty and Quantrell moved on to slack wire shows.

With Bunn's Gardens passing to new and more innovative hands, Quantrell had to raise his game and in 1790 commissioned painter John Ninham to produce a pasteboard replica of the Bastille and on Guild Day 1790, following a concert

and fireworks, Quantrell's Bastille was stormed by real actors who beheaded the governor and released the prisoners. Competition reached new peaks and almost closed Quantrell as his costs escalated. Although he built a new amphitheatre in 1792, he gave up in 1794 to become his chief rival's chief engineer. Quantrell's Gardens were sold to a man called Coe who failed to make a success of them and sold on to Samuel Neech two years later. Neech rechristened them Ranelagh Gardens. With the unexpected demise of Keymer's Vauxhall Gardens in 1800, Neech was left as effectively the 'only show in town' and erected a rotunda capable of holding 2,000 people which he named the Pantheon. During this period there was a return to the more standard diet of concerts and performances but these were, nevertheless, regarded as

Site of Quantrell's Gardens in 1946 after development for Victoria Station but retaining the pleasure gardens buildings.

the 'golden years' of the gardens, particularly in terms of patronage. In 1805 R.M. Harper took over from Neech and business began to decline. In a last bid to turn things around, Harper invited the eminent balloonist Windham Sadler to make a flight from Ranelagh in 1815 but, although hugely popular, this did little to avert the decline and by 1817 Harper had given up. W. Finch took up the challenge and as a man 'of very creative imagination' he created a Chinese saloon and installed Mrs Jones from London's Vauxhall to run his firework displays. 9,000 people attended Ranelagh during Assize Week in 1819 and this prompted Finch to redecorate the Saloon with extensive murals, employ one of the popular Pandean bands and introduce Fantoccini puppetry. He prospered for some years but finally left in 1827. It ticked over for some years and after a takeover and rebrand as the Royal Victoria Gardens in 1842 it finally gave up the ghost in 1849 to be redeveloped as Victoria Station but with much of the Pleasure Garden's buildings recycled to provide facilties for the station. The Saloon became waiting rooms and the Amphitheatre a ticket office and luggage rooms.

Quarries

See *Underground Norwich*.

Quayside

Historic wharf. This wharf connects the ancient Fye Bridge with Whitefriars Bridge on the south side of the Wensum. It was the focus of port related activity for much of the City's history and paintings from as recently as the C19th show the quay heavily congested with wherry traffic. At the western end, remnants of C17th and C18th houses survive and have recently been sensitively restored and incorporated into a new housing scheme by Hopkins Homes which effectively reinstates the ancient wharf frontage. Sadly, next door and on the corner of Pigg Lane, the New Star Inn suffered a different fate. Thought to be Tudor in origin the building had been neglected and was allowed to be demolished in 1963. During this process it was discovered that the Inn was part of a Hanseatic Warehouse of much earlier date and one of the few examples of its kind surviving anywhere in England. The street's cobbles were also taken up at the same time. The other interesting survivor is the School, built in the early C19th and inspired by Joseph Lancaster 60 years before the 1870 Education Act introduced a national education system and Board Schools. This school survived only until 1927 when it lapsed into warehouse use for many years. By the end of the C20th the street was looking rather desperate but a combination of public realm (reinstating some of the cobbles) and street art improvements promoted by the City Council and funded by the EU, combined with imaginative conversion of the Quayside Board School and sensitive new housing at Beckwith's Court have transformed the street wholly into a reasonable reflection of its former picturesque glory.

Queen's Building, University of East Anglia

Used by the School of Occupational Therapy and Physiotherapy, the building was designed by John Miller

Quayside wall sign, and Quayside looking east.

The Queen's Building at the University of East Anglia.

& Partners and built in 1993. It is a 'green building' and received an RIBA award in 1994. It was opened formally by the Queen in May of that year.

Queens Road

Orbital road. Once an extra mural track running around the south western perimeter of the City Walls, Queens Road had become heavily urbanised by the late Victorian period, first with the arrival of the Ranelagh Gardens succeeded by Victoria Station, then various chapels and terrace housing, on the north side backing onto the City Wall. By the 1960s the scene was about to change dramatically. The canyonesque gash of the Inner Ring Road tore a huge swath through the area leaving nothing but devastation on the north side except for a tiny, beleaguered tower and small stretch of wall, with very early gun loops, hinting at the City Wall which had once been here. On the south side the stark edifice

of Bland Payne, now insurance brokers Marsh, and the Sainsbury supermarket replaced the former station. Further down the Road the stately former Co-op Bakery survives as an office conversion as do the former 1872 Primitive Methodist Chapel, by Edward Boardman, and its neighbour. Further east a terrace of mid C19th houses also survives.

Queen Street

Ancient thoroughfare. Probably pre Conquest in origin, linking the Anglo Scandinavian market place of Tombland to the site of the Plea Court at St Michael Motstowe (now St Michael

at Plea), the street still retains many historic vestiges. Aside from St Michael and the virtually hidden, C13th St Mary the Less, No. 1 is a late C17th jettied building with a vaulted undercroft and although originally a pub, was for many years a notable local eating establishment called Gundrey Whites. The next door building was originally a C15th house occupied at one stage by Robert Ferrier, mayor in 1526 and 1536. In 1922 a wooden spandrel dating from 1475 and an extensive ceiling of probably C15th date were discovered there. The building later became the premises of the famous Norwich furnishers and upholsterers Robertson & Colmans. Unfortunately the building collapsed in the 1980s and although redevelopment – for the Bank of Scotland – by Lambert Scott & Innes in 1988 created a strikingly modern replacement, the site retains a C15th brick undercroft. Next door, No. 5 also retains an undercroft. Opposite Old Bank of England Court retains some interesting buildings while most of the other buildings in the street are of local interest historically.

Queen Street.

R is for...

The first non denominational cemetery in the UK; a notable riot leading to the City being the only one to be excommunicated by the Pope; the first evidence of Romani DNA in the UK; the most expensive hat maker in the world.

Rackheath

Suburban parish. Located approximately 4km (2.5 miles) north east of Norwich on the A1151, Rackheath is a large village with a population of around 1500. Rackheath appears in the Domesday Book as 'Racheitha' meaning a 'landing place on a water-course' and by the C14th Rackheath had been divided into Rackheath Magna to the north west and Rackheath Parva to the south east. Rackheath Parva was predominantly heathland until the C19th, and extended over to Mousehold. The C14th All Saints Church stands in what was Rackheath Magna and contains monuments to the Pettus family, although the church was declared redundant in 1971. Holy Trinity stood in Rackheath Parva in the area around Round Hills but this had been demolished as early as the mid C15th. The new Holy Trinity church in New Rackheath was built on the Salhouse Road in 1959 and

memorial gates and a plaque commemorating the 467th Bombardment Group were added in 2008.

Rackheath was historically closely associated with two local families, the Straceys and the Pettus. The families' coats of arms can be seen on the village sign today, and memorials to both families exist in All Saints Church. Mayor of Norwich Sir John Pettus lived at Rackheath Hall and he was succeeded by Thomas and Sir Horatio before the estate was purchased by the Stracey family in 1773 who had the Hall rebuilt in 1852-4.

The secret underground army, the British Resistance Organisation, or Auxiliers, which were established to create guerrilla chaos in the event of a German invasion in 1940, had one of their main Control and Communications Centres secreted in Rackheath Park. The USAAF 467th Bombardment Group occupied the park and hall during World War II but the

BRO's base was so well hidden that the Americans were blissfully unaware of it. The Hall went on to be an antiques showroom and warehouse for the next 30 years. It was then vacant for the subsequent 20 years and was the victim of vandalism and neglect before finally being sold in 1988 and converted into residential flats. The airfield at Rackheath was the home to the USAAF 467th Bombardment Group, known as the Rackheath Aggies, who carried out a total of 212 missions between April 10th 1944 and April 25th 1945 losing only 29 aircraft in combat. Disaster was only narrowly averted on October 4th 1944 when a V2 rocket strike missed the Rackheath Bomb Dump by only a quarter of a mile. A memorial plaque to the 467th Bomb Group and the base can be found on the Rackheath Industrial Estate while also on the eastern extremity of the estate, the original airfield control tower

Opposite: The Rosary Cemetery – the first of its kind in the country.
Clockwise from left: Old airfield control tower Rackheath,
Rackheath memorial to the 467th Bomb Group, and Rackheath Woods.

Clockwise from top: Rackheath Hall stained glass, Rackheath Hall, Rackheath Park and Rackheath Hall interior.

was restored in 2007 for use as offices. Rackheath saw substantial development post-World War II, with the development of almost exclusively bungalows in what is now known as New Rackheath. Additionally, Rackheath is set to expand further with the potential development of the proposed Eco-Community scheme.

Radical Club

Workers club. Located in Cowgate, the club was an association of working people who wished to discuss and debate radical politics of the time. All that now remains is a reused, stone plaque on the wall of No. 55.

Radio Norfolk

Local BBC radio station. Launched in September 1980 at Norfolk Tower, Radio Norfolk has become one of the BBC's most successful and popular regional networks providing a combination of news, sport, local features and music. The move to the new Forum building in 2002, in association with the BBC East television production facility, served to raise its profile and consolidate its presence in the City.

Raes, Maurice

War hero. Commemorated in the name of a new housing development (Maurice Raes Close) between Sprowston Road and Denmark Road, Sergeant Maurice Raes was a 'free' Belgian pilot flying with Royal Air Force 350 (Belgian) Squadron out of RAF Debden in Essex. On 13th June 1942 his Spitfire crashed just off Sprowston Road as he was returning from convoy patrol.

Railway Cottages

Railway workers housing. These unusual single storey cottages with dormers were developed in Cozens Road and Hardy Road in 1847 for railway workers at the new Norwich Station, built three years earlier. Designed and built by Grisell and Peto this early development outside the City Walls also included a grander, detached manager's house at No. 10 Hardy Road. Shortly after, the construction of Victoria Station in 1849 also generated some rather grander railway workers housing in Victoria Street on the western side of the City Centre.

Railway Mission

Place of worship. The Railway Mission is situated on Prince of Wales Road close to Thorpe railway station. The Mission building, with its Art Nouveau exterior, is striking, and stretches back to Rose Lane. Inside, the space has recently been renovated and partitioned to provide modern facilities. Even so a coal cellar (now converted into a kitchen), and many original features including wooden flooring and a pulpit remain. The pulpit is towards the back of the building and is set with brass memorials to the chapel's organists.

When built in 1901, two 'lanterns' or glass atriums set within the roof were proposed by architects and numerous beautifully-detailed ink and water-colour plans of the lanterns still exist in the Norfolk Record Office. The lanterns survived air-raids during the Second World War but finally succumbed to damage and water leaks in 2005. They were removed

and the spaces left in the roof were boarded over. The Railway Mission was used as a place of worship by workers, and their families, employed on the Great Eastern Railway (GER) from 1884 onwards. The building could accommodate up to 400 people and was run by evangelical Christians with the aim of providing a space for temperance and religious meetings. Eventually, it was hoped, 'a reading-room and coffee palace' would be added to provide an alternative venue to public houses and other perceived sources of potential vice.

A newspaper article of 15th April 1885 reported on the opening of the Mission the previous day. The GER chairman added his support to the venture, observing that 'anything which tended towards making the men... temperate and sober would naturally have the heartiest co-operation of the directors'. The venue proved popular and four years later the Mission was overcrowded with up to 500 people attending the Sunday evening service. At this time, the annual running costs were around £100 which included payments for training the choir and band.

In their 1891 report, the Railway Mission committee noted that the low ceilings and high number of participants caused ventilation problems. They considered raising the roof but in the same year the accounts show that payment was made for adding 'skylights' so they presumably chose a cheaper option and postponed making major changes. The 1901 plans suggest the problem was not resolved and eventually had to be tackled by more substantial building modifications. The building underwent minor renovations in 2004 and repainting showed that the window frames were made of excellent quality oak which had survived years of neglect with minimal damage.

Railway Station

Main railway station. The first railway station was opened in May 1844 to accommodate the recently developed Eastern Counties Railway from Great Yarmouth. It was a low building with an Italianate bell tower and while most of the station was subsequently demolished, a small element survives on the south side of the station forecourt. A spectacularly larger station was developed in 1886, in the French Renaissance Chateau style by W.N. Ashbee, the architect for the Great Eastern Railway. It was named Norwich Thorpe to distinguish it from the other two Norwich stations. Following closure of Victoria Station to passenger services in 1916 and City Station in 1959, Norwich Thorpe became the only Norwich station. It was

From left: Railway cottages in Victoria Street, and railway cottages at the Clarence Harbour.

From left: Thorpe Station in the C19th, and Norwich Station (formerly Thorpe Station) today.

the subject of a £5m refurbishment in the 1990s which restored the forecourt and re-established the symmetry of the main building which had been damaged during the war. Today National Express operate half hourly services to London and hourly services to Cambridge. East Midlands Trains operate services to the Midlands and the West including Nottingham, Liverpool and Birmingham. The station includes all of the usual terminus facilities including a recent, maltings inspired, car park by LSI Architects.

Rampant Horse Street

Historic Walled City street. Named after the C13th Rampling Horse inn which in turn took its name from the Horse Market in the same location, the street has been a centre for commerce since its development shortly after the Norman Conquest. The Rampling Horse became the Rampant Horse and was popular for over 100 years as a venue for travelling shows. In 1784 Dr Katterfelto amazed audiences with his

performances of 'perpetual motion and occult secrets' including raising his daughter to the ceiling using a huge, hidden magnet. In the following year, famous local diarist Parson Woodforde noted that he had been entertained by 'the sagacity of a learned pigg', a black boar with a magic collar that could spell and add up figures. The Rampant Horse was also a popular haunt for the medical fraternity and in 1823 suspicion was aroused by the passage of several large trunks – when one was opened by the authorities it was found to contain a fresh corpse from the Lakenham

The only remaining vestige of the historic Rampant Horse Inn.

churchyard on its way to the dissecting room of one of the London Medical Schools.

During the coaching age the street became a terminus for His Majesty's Mail and the Royal Mail Coach but with the change of retailing styles in the Victorian period it was eventually redeveloped for large shops. Although the Baedeker Raids of 1942 destroyed one side of the street entirely and gutted the Buntings store on the other, the sites were redeveloped for Woolworths, Marks & Spencer and Curls (now Debenhams) in the 1950s.

Ramsey, William

Master Mason. William Ramsey III was the most prominent of a long line of masons from the Ramsey family. Thought to be the 'father of Perpendicular architecture' and Edward III's leading mason, Ramsey probably hailed from Norwich and his early work included the rebuild of Norwich Cathedral cloister in the 1320s and the chapel in St Ethelbert's Gate after the Norwich Riot. He worked on St Stephen's Chapel Westminster and the Chapter House at Old

Master Mason William Ramsey was responsible for rebuilding the Cathedral cloisters.

St Paul's where the Perpendicular style of architecture is thought to have emerged first. Ramsey continued to work in Norwich as well as Ely but his national stature saw him working in London and he was one of the Commission reporting on the fabric of the Tower. He is also thought to have worked in Paris. Ramsey was employed on other Norfolk churches including the rebuilding of St Margaret at Cley. He died of the plague in 1349.

Ranelagh Pleasure Gardens

See *Quantrell's (Ranelagh) Pleasure Gardens*.

Reads

See *Albion Mills*.

Rede, Sir Peter

Adventurer. Peter Rede, or Reade, was a successful mercer and wealthy merchant although his early life was as a soldier and mercenary. Sir Peter's memorial by the high altar in St Peter Mancroft shows him in full armour and tells us that not only had he worthily served 'hys Prynce' (intriguing since for the last 17 years of his life both Mary and Elizabeth were on the throne so presumably this refers to Edward VI or Henry VIII) but also the Holy Roman Emperor Charles V at the Conquest of the Barbaria and at the Seige of Tunis in 1535 for which he was awarded the Order of Barbaria. He registered his status in the local community with a bequest to 'the Mayor, Shreves, Cittizens in remembrance of my good will £20 wch they shall put in som peace of plate beying eyther a salte or a boll with a cover, and my arms to be set upon the same to remayne and serve the mayor and successors for ever'. The Corporation acquired the Reade Salt with the bequest and this is now the 'jewel in the crown' of the Civic Regalia and one of the finest examples of its kind in the country. His house was formerly in Old Post Office Court. His portrait forms part of the Civic Portrait Collection. His wife, Anne Reade, is buried in St Margaret's Church and records indicate that 'This ancient family dwelt in the black flint house opposite to the north side of the churchyard, in which many of their arms remained lately.' Peter Rede died on 29th Dec 1568.

Red Lion Street

Edwardian landmark. With probably pre Conquest origins and maintaining a confined and ancient character up until the end of the C19th, Red Lion Street, taking its name from an Elizabethan Inn, was devastated by the coming of the trams in 1899 and all the historic buildings, apart from the tiny remnant on the corner of Orford Hill, were swept away. The rebuild on the east side however is an imposing and attractive mixture of Dutch and Flemish revival and Baroque styles. George Skipper's Norfolk & Norwich Savings Bank (now Barclays) and originally intended for Stump Cross is perhaps the most exuberant of the new buildings. Boardman's Dutch inspired Veterinary Surgery for J. Pollock, with a very unusual two storey Livery Stable at the rear is nicely detailed and reflects the City's long standing Low Countries connections. Similarly the plainer, former Orford Arms and Anchor Buildings continue the Dutch theme. The Blitz intervened on the opposite side of the road, flattening the whole area, and the current Debenhams building was produced in a rather bland, faux Georgian style by A.F. Scott & Sons in 1954.

Regal Cinema

Former cinema. Designed by J. Owen Bond, the 914 seater Regal opened just outside the former St Benedict's Gate in April 1938. It was badly damaged in the April 1942 Baedeker

Restaurants

Past and current eateries

Although the City has an impressive range of eateries, it has struggled to quite meet the top flight since the demise of the 1 Michelin Star Adlards some years ago. However, Adlards chef, Roger Hickman, is now back, occupying the old Adlards unit in Upper St Giles, and has recently (June 2011) been awarded the accolade of the Good Food Guide's Best Restaurant in the East of England. Creative fine dining combined with relaxed but attentive service and the use of local ingredients make this the restaurant of choice in the area.

Beyond the City, Norfolk boasts two Michelin starred establishments, both on the coast. Galton Blackiston's Morston Hall has become something of a gastronomic institution over the last decade while the relatively new kid on the block, The Neptune at Old Hunstanton is growing in reputation.

Back in the Norwich area, Richard Hughes has established a strong fine dining/local ingredients reputation at the Lavender House in Brundall over many years and has recently taken up residency at the Assembly House with Iain Wilson from Byfords in Holt, in Ivory's. And no review would be complete without reference to the UK's best selling TV cook, Delia Smith, whose restaurant is a popular venue at Carrow Road, home of Norwich City Football Club.

From top: Restaurants The Last Wine Bar and Roger Hickman.

Dining within the old City tends to be clustered in areas including:

Norwich Lanes – Ironhouse, Lobster Lane (new Modern British in totally refurbished old pub); Bedfords, Bedford St (dining in an historic location); Belgian Monk, Pottergate (Belgian); The Vine, Dove St (Thai in Norwich's smallest pub), The Library, Guildhall Hill (wood-fired grilled food in a former library); The Waffle House, St Giles (a long established institution);

St Giles House, St Giles Street (Modern British); Italia Nostra, St Giles (Italian); St John's (Modern British); The Wine Cellar, off Guildhall Hill (subterranean Modern British); Captain America's, Exchange St (very long established American); Bar Tapas, Exchange St (Tapas with a South American twist); Thai Lanna, Bridewell Alley (Thai); Sweet Chilli, St Gregorys (Thai); Lam Thai, Upper St Giles (Thai), Pulse, Labour in Vain Yard off Guildhall Hill (Vegetarian,

From top: Restaurant By Appointment and Tombland restaurant concentration.

respectable chains including Café Uno, La Tasca, Zizzi's, Ha Ha's and All Bar One.

Chapelfield Plain – Mackintosh's Canteen (Bistro) supplemented by higher end chains such as Carluccio's, Wagamama's, Giraffe, ASK, Yo Sushi.

St Benedicts – St Benedicts Restaurant (Modern British); Pinocchio's (Italian); Umberto's (Italian); Don Pepe (Spanish); Bengal Spice (Indian); supplemented by Pizza Express.

Magdalen Street – Brummells (seafood); Torero (authentic Tapas); Ali Tandoori (Indian); Passage to India (Indian).

Beyond the 'clusters' a few distinctive 'singletons' are worthy of a look, including Three Ways, Brigg Street (Lebanese), Pedro's, Chapelfield Gardens (Mexican), Zaks, off Barrack Street and at Mousehold (American Diner), Sakura Yakiniku, White Lion St (Japanese), Sugar Hut, Opie Street (Thai), Figaro's, All Saints (Italian), Baby Buddha, Ber St (Cantonese), Krasades Tavern, Prince of Wales Rd (Greek), Thai on the River, opposite the Station (a floating Thai restaurant), Yellows, Carrow Rd (American) and, although a chain, Pizza Express at The Forum offers some of the best dining views in the City. Finally, Jamie Oliver is destined to open one of his restaurants in the centre later in the year.

located in the stables of the Old Fire Station), Paulo's, St Giles (Italian) supplemented by chains like Café Rouge and Loch Fyne.

St Andrew's/St Georges – The Dining Rooms at Cinema City, St Andrews (Modern British); Bishops, St Andrew's Hill (Modern British), Elm Hill Brasserie (Modern French); Last Wine Bar, St Georges (long established, Modern British); By Appointment, St Georges (eclectic Fine Dining).

Tombland – Tatlers (long standing institution, relaxed Modern British); Farmer Browns (recent Modern British addition), Shiki (top of the range Japanese); Spice Lounge (higher end Indian); the Wine Press @ Wensum is the newly formatted British with a modern twist at the Maids Head Hotel; Reads, also Modern British, was a private club and retains a club-like feel; the independents are supplemented by a café cum pub (Take 5) and

Blitz but opened again after the War. Its moment of glory was screening Bill Haley's 'Rock Around the Clock' in 1957 when exuberant fans caused a near riot and had to be dispersed by the police. The innovation of a panoramic screen wasn't enough to halt its decline and in 1958 it closed. It stood vacant for a period and after a brief reincarnation as a bingo club it was converted sensitively by the J. D. Wetherspoon chain into a theme pub but retaining much of the character of the building.

Regent Theatre

Former cinema. The last of the Prince of Wales Road cinemas, the Regent was originally called the 'Alexandra Picture House and Theatre Company' and taking its name from the buildings it replaced, this 1800 seat venue appeared in 1923 and was destined to become the City's longest surviving cinema. Originally it included a stage for variety acts and also incorporated elaborate internal décor including a goldfish pool in the foyer. It was taken over by the ABC chain in 1961 and enjoyed its moment of glory a decade later when

Regent Theatre, Prince of Wales Road (1934).

the Queen Mother attended the Royal Premiere of Joseph Losey's The Go-Between, a film made entirely in Norwich and Norfolk and staring Julie Christie, Michael Redgrave and Alan Bates. The cinema changed its name to ABC becoming a three screen 'multiplex' in 1973. Eventually it became the Canon with four screens before closing, ultimately, and being transformed into the Mercy nightclub.

Regimental Museum

See *Museums and Collections*.

Restaurants

See pages 308-309.

Richard I's 1194 Charter

First real instrument of self government. Prior to 1194, Norwich 'belonged' to the King. The King's Bailiff collected rents, tolls and taxes and effectively controlled the commerce of the City. In 1194 the Charter of Richard I provided a landmark in the City's status. For an annual payment of 200 marks (£108) to the King it freed the City and its citizens from all rents tolls and taxes previously paid and allowed Norwich to elect its own Reeve and be self governing, effectively giving Norwich the same rights and privileges as London.

Richard II

King. Richard II and his queen Anne of Bohemia, sister of 'Good King Wenceslas' and daughter of Holy Roman Emperor Charles IV, visited the Great Hospital where the Eagle Roof was said to have been painted in honour of her visit. The queen amazed the

local population by riding side saddle through the streets.

Riches & Watts

Engineers. The earliest references to the origins of the company are in the 1830s when Thomas Watts had a foundry in the King Street area and James Watts was referred to at the same location, as a manufacturer of steam engines while Henry Smith Riches was identified as a brazier and tin plate worker, also in King Street. By 1854 the former company was Watts Brothers and just five years later, a catalogue appeared for Howard, Riches & Watts describing them as 'Engineers, Millwrights, Iron and Brass Founders, General Machinists and manufacturers of improved high and low pressure expansive - condensing steam engines, non-condensing engines, corn mills, draining mills, water wheels etc' and trading from the Duke's Palace Iron Works. They prospered up until the end of the century with offices in London and a prolific output of products but particularly steam engines. One engine produced for Youngs, Crawshay & Youngs' King Street Brewery was installed in 1879 and survived until 1960. Another brewery engine powered Steward & Patteson's at Pockthorpe but was also scrapped in the 1960s. An earlier model, dating from 1872, which powered the Bishop Bridge Gas Works, has survived at the Gressenhall Museum of Rural Life and a small steam water pump from the company survives in the Bridewell collection. In 1900 the company was taken over by the Norwich Electricity Company. During its relatively short history it built probably more than 500 engines, many powering the great industries of Norwich and Norfolk but others travelling as far afield as New Zealand.

Rigby, Dr Edward

Multi-talented doctor.
Edward Rigby came from Lancashire but by the age of 24 he was established in Norwich and became involved in the founding of the Norfolk & Norwich Hospital. He was a brilliant surgeon and excelled particularly in the field of 'the stone'. He was responsible for the introduction of vaccination into the City, he ran a smallpox hospital and he held a licence to hold '12 lunatics' in a house at Lakenham to enable him to study mental disorders. He was made a freeman of the City in recognition of his services in reorganising the processes of catering in workhouses. In 1789 Rigby was in Paris at the time of the Revolution and heard speeches from its leaders and saw the crowd which had stormed the Bastille.

In Norwich he practiced in St Giles, where he also had an apothecary's shop, and he lived at Framingham Earl where he cultivated medicinal plants including opium poppies. He also persuaded the Council to embark upon an ambitious tree planting programme within the City. He died in 1822 aged 74 and is buried at Framingham Earl.

Riot of 1272

Major civic/religious dispute. Ever since the Normans arrived in Norwich, shortly after the Conquest, and levelled a substantial part of the civic heartland of the former Anglo Scandinavian Borough to build a precinct for the Cathedral and Benedictine Priory, there had been animosity between the citizens and the Priory establishment. In the summer of 1272, this boiled over into a full blown riot after priory servants killed a citizen then retreated into the sanctuary of the Cathedral precinct. They then re-emerged to rampage through neighbouring properties, plundering and wrecking houses and taverns. The citizens responded by storming the Priory, burning down the gates, bakehouse, stables and St Ethelbert's Church. Although the belfry, dormitory, refectory, infirmary and part of the cloister were also engulfed in the fire, the citizens claimed that the Priory servants had been responsible for this by allowing a watch fire to burn out of control. The Prior fled from the riot returning shortly with barge loads of mercenaries from Yarmouth who retaliated by 'wounding, killing and destroying many houses'. The King, Henry III, arrived in person to restore order and to preside over a 13 day trial as one of the last acts of his reign. The judgements were relatively even handed. The Prior was imprisoned and his lands were confiscated. 29 rioters were executed, some were hung, drawn and quartered and others were 'dragged to death' behind horses while the woman alleged to have set fire to the Priory gates suffered the Anglo Saxon penalty for arson – death by burning. Royal officials took charge of both the Priory and the City which had its rights and privileges suspended. The Pope excommunicated some of the citizens and placed the City under interdict which had the effect of denying the citizens all religious rights including marriages and funerals. Special pleading by a delegation to Rome eventually resolved the situation. The citizens had to pay a 3,000 mark fine and agree to rebuild the Ethelbert Gate, with a chapel dedicated to St Ethelbert in lieu of the destroyed church, before the City's rights were restored three years later.

Riverside

Mixed use development.
For most of the City's history, the water meadows to the east of the Wensum, opposite King Street, remained undeveloped. With the coming of the railway and C20th industrialisation, these areas were drained and occupied first by the marshalling yards of Thorpe Station then, south of these, by the extensive premises of Boulton & Paul.

By the 1980s Boulton & Paul had been taken over and the site closed, and British Rail were considering rationalisation of their operations. Norwich had a 17 Ha (42 acre) site in the heart of the City and took a proactive view of city centre regeneration when the authorised Government view at the time was that developers should be allowed, if they wished, to develop outside town centres on green field sites. Initial proposals for regeneration, brokered by the Council in the late 1980s, combined with a market down-turn, stalled

Riverside entertainment quarter.

redevelopment but a new impetus in the mid 1990s augmented by Single Regeneration Budget funding impelled the scheme forward. The resultant scheme delivered by a partnership of the local authority, Gazeleys and Railtrack, using Higgs Young Architects, supported locally by LSI Architects on scheme elements, delivered:

- 224 residential units, including 15 per cent affordable
- Leisure facilities including a 14 screen UCI multiplex cinema (now Odeon), a bowling alley (Hollywood Bowl), nightclubs (Square, Brannigans, and Time)
- Restaurants (Frankie and Benny's, Nandos, Pizza Hut, Old Orleans), bars (Wetherspoons, Norwegian Blue), and a health club (Fitness Exchange)
- Format retailing functions including a Morrisons food superstore and an associated shopping centre containing Boots the Chemist, JD Sports, Argos; Mamas and Papas, JJB Sports, and Going Places Travel)
- A new major section of public, landscaped Riverside Walk
- A new and re-orientated

portion of Norwich's inner ring road, and associated internal service roads
- 1800 car parking spaces, including a new build six storey car park (730 spaces) serving rail and leisure development users
- A £5m restoration and improvement of the existing Norwich Railway Station, a Grade II listed building
- Redesign and landscaping of the Railway Station's forecourt to integrate it into the adjoining development
- A major swimming and recreation centre
- Two new pedestrian and cycle swing bridges which link Riverside with the historic King Street area, another major regeneration project on the opposite side of the River Wensum
- A bioremediation process that involved large scale, on-site blending and volatilisation of hydrocarbons which saved about £0.5m compared to off-site disposal while heavy metals were hauled off-site by rail, eliminating the need for more than 4500 lorry journeys, and minimising the need to import clean material.

Although criticised for not delivering a fine enough grain of townscape, the scheme has achieved regeneration, jobs and local facilities. The leisure component underpins an evening economy which attracts 30,000 young people to the City on a Friday or Saturday night while the swimming, leisure and cinema facilities have been a definite benefit for families. The retail facilities have helped to support one of the top ten most successful retail economies in the UK rather than undermining it by allowing the haemorrhage of out-of-town development.

Riverside Walk

Linear leisure resource.
The Riverside Walk, or more properly the Wensum Riverside Walk, was a concept launched by the City Council in the 1970s and is now substantially complete. Starting from the Railway station it is possible to follow the Walk northwards, hugging the Wensum, as far as Hellesdon – a distance of about four miles. There is currently only one break in this link, between St George's Bridge and Duke Street bridge although the Heritage Economic and Regeneration Trust (HEART) and the Norwich Society are collaborating currently to complete this link. The route takes in a wide range of heritage and natural sites and connects to the Marriotts Way long distance footpath and cycle way. An illustrated guide was produced for the section within the City Walls, by HEART in 2009. From the station south it is possible to walk as far as the football ground but longer term

ambitions to link up to the Whitlingham Country Park and thus to the Wherryman's way long distance footpath and cycle way require the development of new bridges across the Wensum and Yare. This developing project is part of a major lottery funded initiative called Connect 2.

Ritz Cinema

Former cinema. Opening in the same year as the Regal and designed to the same pattern, the Ritz appeared at the other end of Dereham Road and provided a 638 seat venue for the expanding local authority housing estates in the Larkman area. It survived until 1960 and immediately became a tyre depot until being redeveloped for a new housing scheme in 2008.

Robinson, John

Free Church pioneer. John Robinson was pastor for the Pilgrim Fathers, the first English colonists in America. He honed his Free Church philosophy when he was curate of St Andrew's, from 1603, but after suspension by the Bishop and further sanctions he moved to establish a Free Church in Leiden, from whence he became pastor to the Pilgrim Fathers.

Romani presence

Evidence of early Romani occupation. A skeleton discovered during excavations of an C11th churchyard close to Timberhill has been found to have a mitochondrial DNA marker unique to the Romani people. This is the earliest evidence for a person of Romani descent in the British Isles, and is 400 years earlier than historical records previously

identified their first presence in these islands. The other major local connection is through the works of author George Borrow, notably Romany Rye, who engaged with local gypsy families and reflected their lifestyles and culture in his writings.

Romans

Possible Roman occupation. Contrary to the view held by early historians, that the Castle was built by a British King Gurguntus and strengthened by Julius Caesar, the modern consensus is that there was no significant Roman occupation on the site of the later Norwich. Although 1500 years of continuous development and up to 900 years of relatively undisturbed occupation on some sites have prevented a thorough archaeological testing of this view, there are strong pointers to this proposition being accurate.

Firstly, the cantonal capital of Venta Icenorum (Caistor), 5km (3m) to the south of the site of later Norwich, was an important settlement covering a fortified area of 15 Ha (35 acre) with external features including an amphitheatre. It is extremely unlikely that the Romans would have constructed another major settlement so close to the capital.

Secondly, an ancient rhyme tells us: 'Caistor was a city when Norwich was none, Norwich was built with Caistor's stone.'

This relates to the third piece of evidence, or rather lack of it. There have been no Roman period building discoveries during archaeological excavations in Norwich apart from the inclusion of reused Roman bricks in later buildings (e.g.

the Cathedral). Looking at the parallel experience in similar historic cities with Roman origins (e.g. York) it is difficult to see how evidence of significant occupation could have remained undiscovered, if it existed. Finally, while there is documentary evidence of Caistor and other local Roman foundations, there is no Roman, or indeed any early, documentary reference to Norwich, or anything that might be construed as early Norwich. It can therefore be reasonably concluded that no settlement of any stature existed here in the Roman period.

While there is no evidence of a Roman City of Norwich, there is evidence that the Romans left some traces on the site of the later City. The most significant legacy was a basic road infrastructure which helped to shape the later borough. There is a reasonable case to support the proposition that roads picked up the alignment of the Roman Pye Strete (roughly the modern A140), running north from Colchester to Venta Icenorum, and continuing north, via the site of later Norwich, to the Roman camp at West Runton – and north west to the coast and the Roman fort of Brancaster via the Roman road running virtually due north from Sculthorpe.

The Caistor-Brancaster road passed through the site of Norwich probably crossing the Yare near the current Lakenham Bridge and rising along Long John Hill to the Ber Strete ridge. The historians Kirkpatrick and Hudson note the use of the Latin 'strete' to describe this route from the earliest documentary sources, denoting its probable

Roman origin. Berstrete continued as far as the site of the present Bell Hotel. The road then probably cut diagonally across the site of the later Market, descending to the Wensum valley via Goat Lane (known subsequently as Stonegate) and, via an island in the previously wider river somewhere between the modern Duke Street Bridge and St Miles Bridge, joining Oak Street on a straight alignment (modern Oak street kinks to the west at its southern end). The road would then have connected to the modern Drayton Rd to Fakenham, via the Roman settlement of Billingford – and a crossroads with an east/west Roman road – and thus to Brancaster.

The second possible, but unconfirmed, north/south road across later Norwich connected to another important Roman centre. Located at a river crossing and cross roads, Brampton was a large producer of pottery, with over 140 known kilns, exporting its products as far afield as Scotland. The Caistor-Brampton road is likely to have started in the same entry point to the later City but then branched off along modern King Street and Magdalen Street with a river crossing at Fyebridge. Commercial development in 1961 identified a possible Roman wharf 30m (100ft) below the confluence of the Wensum and Yare and it is possible that Roman King Street may have originally connected to this, forming a south east arching spur. After leaving the later Magdalen Gates the route would have passed through Catton and Spixworth and thus to Brampton. It is probable that the route then went north to the Roman camp at West Runton.

Additionally a further probable Roman road, also with the Latin suffix 'strete', was Holmestrete or the Holmestrete Way. This ran from the possible Roman port at Brundall in the east to the settlement of Ashill (south east of Swaffham) forming a junction with the north-south Roman Peddars Way in the west. It entered the City at modern Pilling Park and crossed the river at the site of Bishop Bridge. A causeway along Bishopgate lifted the road above the level of the marsh and the road then passed through the site of the later Cathedral, along the alignment of the nave, to emerge in Tombland. It passed through the site of the later St Georges church to Princes Street and via St Andrews Street, where it crossed the Great Cockey and the Berstrete route, to exit the City via St Benedicts and Dereham Road.

In summary then, it is likely that the site supported at least two and possibly three Roman roads, and two or possibly three river crossings and crossroads. In other situations these would have resulted in some, but not necessarily significant, development. In Norwich, there is evidence of some development close to the main routes. Near the Holmestrete/Westwick road a Roman burial site, with a body in a lead coffin and another skeleton close by, were discovered in 1861 at Woodlands Park. At the other end of the same road, two first century cremation burials were discovered at Stanley Avenue in 1950. Along the probable north-south roads, Roman pottery finds were made adjacent to Magdalen Street in 1974 and 1987, indicating a possible farmstead on the site of modern Anglia Square. Additionally, coins of Aurelian, Claudius II and Diocletian were found at the Dove Street junction with the Market Place and a further Vespasian coin, in St Peter Mancroft churchyard. Add to this the evidence of reused Roman bricks in the fabric of the cathedral – at the junction of two probable Roman roads – and in the hearth of a sunken floored Saxon house near King St, Roman rotary querns reused in 8th century houses at Barn Rd (on the Holme Strete Way) and pottery finds throughout the centre, this provides at least a possibility of some Roman occupation during this period.

Rosary Cemetery

Oldest non denominational cemetery in the UK. This is a 5.25 Ha (13 acre) site on the north of Rosary Road/Thorpe Road established by Thomas Drummond on a former market garden and opened in 1821 as the first ever non denominational cemetery in the UK. It is estimated that, since 1821, 18,500 people have been buried there and it still takes burials today. 'Residents' include members of the great families who shaped the local economy and therefore the City we see today. They include the Colmans, Gurneys, Jarrolds, Harmers and shoe barons Henry Holmes and George White. Others include artists Ladbrooke, Sillett, Stark and Thirtle, architect Edward Boardman and writer R.H. Mottram. Architecturally the site contains a range of striking and evocative monuments as well as over 130 species of flowering

Views of the Rosary Cemetery.

plants, 40 species of birds and 20 species of butterflies. The site received the accolade of Grade II* Listed status from English Heritage in 2010.

Rose Lane

Historic thoroughfare. A pre Conquest route which originally supported the early churches of St Vedast (St Vaast and St Armand), at its eastern end, and St John the Evangelist, at the west end. Today though virtually nothing remains of the ancient street apart from the tiny C16th shop on the south side and the former Tudor Hall, which dates only from 1899 but incorporates salvaged timbers and an arch dated 1596, recycled from ancient buildings in King Street. The remainder of the street has been disfigured by a petrol filling station and a range of bland 1960s offices.

Rossi family

Italian emigres. Italian goldsmith, George Rossi, who had fought with Marshall Soult, Napoleon's Chief of Staff at Waterloo, before making a career move to Norwich, established a goldsmith's business in Guildhall Hill, right on the doorstep of the Goldsmiths' Guild. The business survived for four generations until Theodore Rossi, who had been associated with the business for 54 years, retired in 1936.

Rowley, Horace

City Engineer. Horace Rowley was the City Engineer from 1944 until 1966 and as such also undertook the role of Planning Officer. A charitable view would be that he was a very efficient highway engineer aiming to shape the City to accommodate future traffic demand and also make a competent contribution to the engineering aspects of civic projects like the St Augustines Baths and the Livestock Market. A less charitable view would be that, like many other 'old school' highway engineers, he focused on the car to the exclusion of everything else. His worst legacies were the

Views of the Royal Arcade.

dreadfully destructive Inner Ring Road, cutting a swath through the northern section of the historic centre, and the appalling intrusion that is modern St Stephens. Fortunately some of his more extreme proposals didn't see the light of day. These included moving the Provision Market because it was in the way of a proposal for a dual carriageway along the Walk and down Exchange Street, creating a major north/south through route; widening Magdalen Street on the west side; creating a gyratory around the Royal Hotel; completion of the Inner Ring to the south on a direct line from the All Saints Green junction to Abbey Lane in King Street; a new link road continuing Cleveland Road through to Pottergate then on a widened alignment to Exchange Street; a gyratory around Debenhams and finally the dualling of St Augustines. He noted that

his ideas involved 'the destruction of rather more property of interest' than those contained within the 1945 Plan, although that was destructive enough. He felt though that this 'limited sacrifice of property must be made' in the interests of efficiency. Although the Council did make some dreadful decisions in the two decades following the War, to their credit, they did not take on board the entirety of Horace Rowley's vision. It is also an interesting postscript that a number of the steel reinforced concrete buildings that appeared in the City during Rowley's currency, had to be demolished in the new Millennium due to 'concrete cancer'.

Royal Arcade

Art Nouveau masterpiece. Built in 1899 to a design by George Skipper on the coaching yard of the old Royal Hotel the 'Arcade' was a rather clever piece of

recycling rather than an entire new build. It retained Joseph Stannard's original facade of the Royal and utilised the stables and loose boxes of the hotel, in some cases refaced with a single skin of brick and tile. It is referred to by Nikolaus Pevsner as having a 'perfectly innocent front' but 'is very naughty once its back is turned'. The original scheme included 24 bow fronted shops, the Arcade Stores pub and the Conservative Club. The real jewel, however, is the Arts and Crafts style decoration of tiles and stained glass peacocks, trees, flowers and women designed by W.J. Neatby, who also produced the tiles in Harrod's food hall. Doulton manufactured the tiles and Italian craftsmen executed the work. During its life the Arcade suffered a degree of vandalism, first by the mutilation of the Arcade Stores after the closure of the pub then by the installation of electric strip lighting. Fortunately, architects Ley Colbeck undertook a sensitive regeneration from 1986 to 1991, which replaced the floor, added new lamps and generally restored the original striking quality of the building. Today it is the home of a range of speciality shops including the unique Colman's Mustard Shop and Museum.

Royal Hotel
Former iconic hotel.
Designed by Edward Boardman and built in 1897 in an exuberant Flemish style, with 'Cosseyware' detailing, this was the focal point at the conclusion of the recently built Prince of Wales Road. The new Royal replaced Joseph Stannard's old Royal Hotel in the Market Place. The new Royal's site, on the northern side of Agricultural Hall Plain, originally supported a range of buildings, including the Georgian offices of Messrs Foster and Burroughs, but all were cleared away for the new hotel.

However, an impressive Georgian plaster ceiling was salvaged and reused in the Royal's Drawing Room. Other hotel facilities included a winter garden lounge, with palms, a billiard room with tables by Burroughs and Watts, a stylish smoking room and a grand entrance hall with marble and stained glass. Local firms made contributions to the building including Youngs as main contractor, stained glass by J & J King, ironwork by Barnes & Pye, lifts by Laurence Scott and furniture by Trevor Page. As well as the hotel, the new development included a major restaurant with Japanese decoration.

In 1899 the Royal Hotel's specially produced guide reveals that private suites cost 15/- (75p) but that a servant's bedroom could be had for 2/6d (12.5p). The hotel continued to operate for many years but in 1973 the owners sought approval to demolish it and replace it with 'a strong modern building which makes its own music'. The Council resisted and in 1977 it was converted to offices for Anglia TV. The site was subsequently refurbished in 1989 with the brickwork being cleaned and the interior being converted to serviced offices and a night club on the ground floor which has passed through a number of incarnations, including Chicago and Po Na Na's and is currently (2011) Lola Lo.

Drawing Room of the Royal Hotel from the promotional booklet produced in 1899.

Royal Norfolk Show
County agricultural show.
'The Show' started life in 1847 as a showpiece for the local agricultural industry and attained its 'Royal' prefix in 1908 from Edward VII. It remained itinerant until 1954, first alternating between Norwich and Swaffham then moving between the east and west, then north and south of the county, before finally settling at its current location at the Costessey Showground. In its first year at its permanent home it attracted nearly 66,000 visitors but the popularity of the occasion was such that by 2006 it attracted record attendances of over 106,000 visits over two days. As well as a showcase for agriculture both in terms of equipment and prize breeds, it has

Images from the 2011 Royal Norfolk Show.

expanded to become the largest two day agricultural show in the country with a wide range of public events including equestrian displays, human cannon ball spectaculars and motor cycle display teams.

Royal Observer Corps, Chartwell Road

Cold War feature. The Royal Observer Corps 6 Group Headquarters was located at Chartwell Road, just south of the northern section of the Outer Ring Road. It consisted of a three level, semi sunken bunker, built in 1961 to a standard pattern, and intended for use as an operations room in the event of nuclear attack. Decommissioned in the 1990s it was sold at auction in 1997 to a developer who sought planning approval for a variety of uses including petrol filling station and 'drive thru' restaurant – all were refused although a residential scheme was recommended for approval in 2006. Although there was some local support for developing the site as a visitor attraction, the owner demolished the surviving ROC structures in 2008.

Rumsey Wells, Herbert

Remarkable hat maker. S & G Wells was established in Cockey Lane (London Street) in 1815 as a company of 'Club, School and Regimental Outfitters'. By 1879 the company was manufacturing hats from three storey premises in St Andrew's Hill. Thomas Wells won many prizes for his hats and was the first maker of sporting caps for hunting, racing, bicycling, boating, riding, smoking, shooting, and travelling. He made Forage caps for the services and noted that the hussars stationed in Norwich were 'highly satisfied with the articles supplied to them.' Herbert, the son of Thomas, joined the business just as it moved to St Andrew's Street. Herbert Rumsey Wells designed the 'Doggie' cap in a number of local variants named after Norfolk localities. The first included the Blofield and Brancaster while the Westwick and Conesford followed after the First World War. He claimed that he was the most expensive cap maker in the world and that his products were bought by people from all over the globe. Herbert died in 1937 but the business continued to trade until 1974 when the shop became the St Andrew's Tavern. Herbert is remembered by the pub which has changed its name in 2009 to the Rumsey Wells, a newly completed apartment development on the site next door – Rumsey Wells Place– and by a HEART blue plaque.

Rush, James Blomefield

Infamous murderer. In 1848, James Blomefield Rush, shot the Recorder of Norwich, Isaac Jermy, along with his son at Jermy's Stanfield Hall home near Wymondham. The murder was the result of Rush's attempt to evade repayment of a mortgage and attracted national media attention. Rush defended himself at the six day trial and claimed his innocence on the basis that the real perpetrators were a branch of the Jermy family who had been swindled out of the Stanfield Hall inheritance by Isaac Jermy (actually Isaac Preston). This assertion Rush substantiated by the presence of notes at the murder scene stating 'There are seven of us out here… and we have come to take possession of the Stanfield Hall property. Signed – Thomas Jermy, the Owner'. Rush's case fell apart when Thomas Jermy was called to the stand and admitted that he couldn't write. It took the jury ten minutes to find Rush guilty and he was hanged at Norwich Castle on 21st April 1849 when a very large crowd gathered to witness the event and special trains were laid on. His death mask is maintained in the Castle Dungeons on public display and his body was buried within the Castle precincts.

The execution of James Blomefield Rush, from the local newspaper of the time.

NORWICH CASTLE.

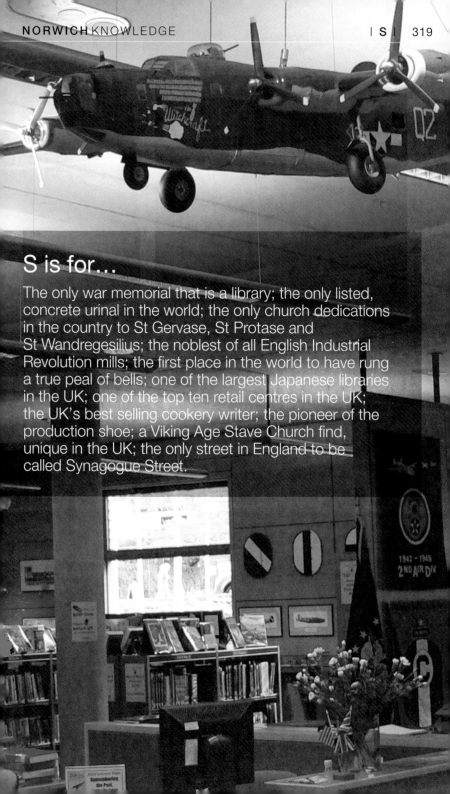

S is for...

The only war memorial that is a library; the only listed, concrete urinal in the world; the only church dedications in the country to St Gervase, St Protase and St Wandregesilius; the noblest of all English Industrial Revolution mills; the first place in the world to have rung a true peal of bells; one of the largest Japanese libraries in the UK; one of the top ten retail centres in the UK; the UK's best selling cookery writer; the pioneer of the production shoe; a Viking Age Stave Church find, unique in the UK; the only street in England to be called Synagogue Street.

From left: St Andrew's Plain – the eastern end of St Andrew's Street,
Sir Thomas Rugge's House, St Andrew's Street.
Previous page: Second Air Division Memorial Library.

Sack Friars
See *Friars de Sacco.*

Saddlegate
See *White Lion Street.*

Sainsbury Centre for the Visual Arts
See opposite.

Sainsbury Institute for the Study of Japanese Art and Culture (SISJAC)
Japanese art research centre. The Sainsbury Institute was founded in 1999 through the generosity of Sir Robert and Lady Sainsbury to promote knowledge and understanding of Japanese arts and cultures. The Institute is an active source of and conduit for innovative research: positioning, revealing and interpreting the arts and cultures of the Japanese archipelago from the present to the past in regional, European and global contexts. It holds one of the largest Japanese libraries in the UK and has affiliations with the University of East Anglia (UEA), the School of Oriental and African Studies (SOAS), University of London, and the British Museum. It is located within the Cathedral Close. www.sainsbury-institute.org

St Andrew's Plain
Historic space. Compared to the chaotic, hotch potch that is St Andrew's Street, St Andrew's Plain is a delight in architectural, aesthetic and functional terms. Originally Elm Hill continued directly into the junctions of Holmestrete/ Westwick Way and St Georges but the King's approval for the Dominicans to stop up the street and build their Hall changed all that. As a result we now have the only intact friary to survive the Reformation on the north side, facing the attractive early C16 Suckling House, recently the subject of an award winning conversion to Cinema City. To the east is the surviving element of the C16th Garsett House. Opposite, an attractive range including a C17th extension to the C19th Festival House, frames the space. Perhaps most significantly though, the recent, attractive paving scheme helps to emphasise the unity of the space, encouraging continuous and occasional activity such as outdoor cafes, the annual Ice Sculpture Trail or just sitting and watching the world go by.

St Andrew's Street
Ancient thoroughfare. Originally part of the Roman Homestrete/Westwick Way, the Street has been named variously after the church, founded in the pre Conquest period but rebuilt between 1477 and 1518, and the medieval leet of Wymer. Confusingly therefore we have Wimer's or St Andrew's Street in 1746, Wymer Street in 1789 and St Andrew's Broad-street in 1819. Running from St Andrew's Plain to Charing

Sainsbury Centre for Visual Arts

Major art centre

The Sainsbury Centre is one of around 100 university museums in the UK which are regularly open to the public. Sir Robert (1906-2000) and Lady Lisa Sainsbury (1912-) donated their collection of world art to the University of East Anglia in 1973 and the Sainsbury Centre first opened its doors to visitors in 1978. It was the Sainsbury's hope that students, academic staff and the general public would grow to appreciate the works on display in much the same way as the Sainsbury's themselves had done, by being able to look frequently and closely at them without the distraction of too much museum-style text and labelling. When the Collection was offered to the University in 1973 it numbered around 300 works but by the time the Centre opened five years later in Norman Foster's building, 300 had become 600.

Now, the Robert and Lisa Sainsbury Collection contains more that 1700 objects. By the late 1980s the Collection and the staff had outgrown the original building and the Crescent Wing was added, with new office, exhibition and technical spaces.

In 2002, to mark his mother's 90th birthday, Lord David Sainsbury gave her – and thus the University – the promise of a new gallery linking the two parts of the Centre, together with new education and studio spaces. These opened to the public in May 2006, making the Collections even more accessible. The Centre is located at the western extremity of the UEA campus. www.scva.org.uk

Sainsbury Centre for Visual Arts – exterior and interior views.

Reconstruction of St Augustines Gate.

Cross the Street has, on the north side, the C19th Festival House, sitting on a C15th undercroft; next to the late C18th No. 37 and next to this, the vaguely 'Festival of Britain' St Andrew's House, designed in 1954 by Ernest Buckingham and now occupied by City College's National Skills Academy for Financial Services. Next door is the very attractive, three gabled range of C17th buildings where the historian John Kirkpatrick once lived and next to these, the slightly Japanese-esque new Telephone Exchange dates from 1981 by the Property Services Agency on the site of the old Free Library, built in 1857 and demolished in 1964. On the south side, the C19th buildings cornering St John Maddermarket were previously the Shrub House pub, from 1842, and Rumsey Wells 'the most expensive cap maker in the world'. Further along the

vaguely faux Georgian, old Telephone Exchange, which opened in 1942, towers over the tiny remnant of the C15th mansion of MP and Mayor Sir Thomas Rugge. The heavily trafficked street is now a rather discordant mixture of brave architectural survivors and randomly distributed large scale, interventions including, most dramatically, the recently contrived St Andrew's Car Park, although to be fair, this is a vast improvement on its hideous concrete predecessor.

St Augustines Gate

Lost City Gate. This was the point at which St Augustines Street left the Walled City. There is a record that the Gate was rebuilt in 1343 but probably existed before that time and it survived until 1794 when it was demolished.

St Augustines Swimming Baths

Demolished swimming pool. Built on the site of the bombed St Augustine's School, the baths were designed by City Architect David Percival and built between 1959 and 61. The style was typical of other modernist Norwich buildings of the time including the use of flint panels. The baths were closed in the 1990s following the discovery of 'concrete cancer' and they were demolished in 1998. They have been replaced by a mixed use development of flats and shops.

St Augustines Street

Ancient route. Although taking its name from the possible Pre Conquest church of St Augustine, the street does not use that name until the C18th. It is one of the main routes into the City from the north and runs from the site of the now demolished St Augustines

Gate to the junction of Pitt Street and Botolph Street. Although the street has seen better days it still acts as the 'high street' for the rather independent parish of St Augustine and contains a wealth of historic and interesting features. From the south end of the east side No. 5 was the Rose Tavern, with a pub on this site stretching back to the C14th and surviving until the 1970s. The remaining building is substantially C17th with an C18th façade. The pub gives its name to the next door Yard which claims to be the largest yard in Norwich. On its south side, jettied extensions originally forming part of the pub still survive while on the north side were the premises of De Carle's Drug Stores, who produced their own bottled fruit drinks and cough linctus. Rose Yard, in its time, had supported a number of residential tenements, a boot and shoe factory and even a Primitive Methodist Chapel. Next to the former Rose on the main street are the C18th and early C19th Nos. 7-11, then Nos. 13-15

St Augustines Street.

contain a late C16th range back from, but parallel to, the street frontage forming the back range of an original courtyard house. No. 21 is C18th but has the remains of a two storey, C17th house embedded within it while Nos. 23-25 are a five gabled C17th house. The remaining frontages on the east are principally C19th with the occasional, earlier punctuation, but of particular note is the very attractive, flint faced C16th range No. 57. Further up and on the corner of Catherine Wheel Opening, the Catherine

Wheel pub was recorded as operating in 1742. Originally thatched, it was partly rebuilt in the 1800s but retains elements of the earlier structure. On the west side, the buildings at the south end exhibit evidence of early development. Nos. 22-24 are externally of C18th appearance but incorporate a C16th house with remains of a queen post roof. Similarly Nos. 26-30 appear C19th but contain a C16th timber framed building. On the corner with Sussex Street the two storey (south side) then three storey (north side) buildings represent some of the earliest surviving C19th development in the City. The Street is targeted by the Council for improvement and regeneration so over the next few years, its fortunes should improve. www.staugustinesnorwich. org.uk

St Benedict's Gate

Lost City Gate.
St Benedict's Gate or the Porta de Westwyk, was recorded as early as 1118. It guarded the principal west entry to the City and was

Reconstruction of St Benedict's gate.

From left: St Benedicts Street looking east, interior of a C16th building off Queen of Hungary Yard, and St Benedicts Street summer festival.

rebuilt in the early C14th. The gate was unique among the 11 around the City Walls in that it had a square crenellated stair turret built against the west side that rose above the gate itself to provide access to the roof. The gate was demolished in 1793 though the south side of the gateway, incorporated into the side of a house built against the gate in the C18th, survived until the 1940s when it was severely damaged by bombing in this area.

St Benedicts Street

Ancient street. Part of the Roman Holmestrete/ Westwick Way this is the principal entry into the City from the west. Over its length from the demolished St Benedict's Gate to Charing Cross, it probably has the densest clutch of medieval churches of any street in the City including the surviving St Benedict's tower, St Swithin, St Margaret de Westwick, St Lawrence and St Gregory. The street was important in the medieval period and a hive of activity as a local shopping centre, with its own mini department stores, up until the 1960s. It struggled for about a decade and managed to

avoid some ill considered ideas for regeneration including a ten storey office block straddling the west end and a Tesco superstore between St Lawrence and St Margaret. Instead it saw small scale restoration and residential rehabilitation. Beyond its impressive churches, the other buildings aren't quite so imposing being mainly a mixture of C19th and earlier shops and pubs with a few generally sympathetic modern additions. Highlights include the surviving C17th remains of the Cardinal's Cap pub at No. 86, named originally, apparently after visits by Cardinal Wolsey and surviving as a pub until 1963. Further up, Nos. 45-49 are of C16th origin and the later incorporates a crown post roof. This was the former Queen of Hungary pub with licence records running from 1760. The Plough further up on the south side is C17th with an attractive C19th pub front and C16th elements at the rear. In Plough Yard to the rear are the surviving C19th St Swithin's Alms Houses. Further east, Nos. 26-28 are C18th and Nos. 18-20 also incorporate C18th elements, with the remains of a C16th

house at the rear. No. 14 has a C19th front but a timber framed C17th rear and sits on a C16th vaulted undercroft. No. 4 is an attractive C18th shop with carriageway arch and was the Alexandra pub until 1933. It sits on a C15th brick undercroft. The street today contains a lively and eclectic mix of very individual, speciality shops as well as pubs, restaurants and the Norwich Arts Centre in the converted St Swithin's church. The other redundant churches are also used for a range of occasional or semi permanent cultural uses. The street forms a key element of the Norwich Lanes.

Unique, listed concrete urinal on St Crispin's road.

St Crispin's Road Urinal

Listed concrete urinal.
This ten sided public urinal is made of patterned concrete and dates from 1919 when it stood opposite to the entrance of the then City Station (now closed and demolished). It is the only listed concrete public urinal in the world and the earliest of its kind in England.

St Ethelbert's Gate

Medieval Cathedral Precinct gate. Dating from 1316-20 the gate replaced its late C11th predecessor, and the nearby Anglo-Saxon church of St Ethelbert, both destroyed during the Riot of 1272, although the current gate incorporates surviving elements of the earlier example. Architecturally, the Ethelbert Gate is of great importance. All four of its sides are decorated in flush-work, which is a decorative technique developed in Norfolk. The technique uses hard to come by freestone, such as limestone, to edge panels of the more readily available knapped flint. The decorative panels are in a geometric design and the work on this gate probably represents the earliest

known example of this technique. It is also one of only nine gatehouses with flushwork on them. The chamber above the gateway was used as St Ethelbert's Chapel and built most probably by master mason William de Ramsey. William Wilkins undertook major restoration in 1815 revising the original pattern of windows at the upper level. The carvings were replaced by Sir Bernard Fielden in 1965 (sculptor Frank Beverley). The Gate is a Scheduled Ancient Monument.

St Faith's Aerodrome

See *Horsham St Faith's Aerodrome*.

St Faith's Lane

'Moveable street'. Today, St Faith's Lane is the back street running along the south side of the Cathedral Close Precinct Wall from the Ethelbert Gate to Prince of Wales Road. It has very little of any consequence on it apart from the backs of some very attractive buildings in The Close, the Precinct Wall and the James Stuart Gardens. Originally though St Faith's Lane was

the present Rose Lane. In 1549 it is recorded as Seynt Vayst Lane after the pre Conquest church of St Vaast and St Armand, on the north side of St Faith's (Rose) Lane. The original church/ street name was shortened to St Vaast then corrupted to Vayst, Fastes (1567), Fasse (1609) and eventually Faith's (1613). To confuse matters further, the church name itself became corrupted to St Vedast. After the church was demolished in 1541 the street name migrated curiously to the present Mountergate where it remained until 1889 when it became restricted to its present location.

St George's Bridge

Historic bridge. The original bridge was known as New Bridge suggesting that it may have been the last of the medieval bridges in the City. Also known as Blackfriar's Bridge, the current structure was designed in 1784 by Sir John Soane, architect of the Bank of England and designer of the dining room interiors of 10 and 11 Downing Street. The bridge was closed to traffic in 2008 and renovated.

St Ethelbert's Gate viewed from outside the Cathedral Close.

St George's Bridge, designed by Sir John Soane.

St George's Street

Historic thoroughfare.
St George's Street existed before the Conquest and was an extra mural route around the Anglo Scandinavian defenses of Northwic, known as Gildengate, suggesting a route to the Gildencroft to the north. Later dissection by the more important Colegate, as well as the dramatic truncation caused by the Inner Ring Road in 1974, have destroyed the north/south integrity of the street. There are a few vestiges of how this ancient street might once have appeared. From the north, all is lost north of the Ring Road but just south, a tiny C17 house survives on the east side and more substantial C17th houses further down on the west. More houses of a similar date survive south of the Colegate junction while, south of the River, the Dog House (previously the Red Lion) has a C17th frame and Delaney's (former Festival House) hides a C15th undercroft and the remnant of a small C17th, timber framed building.

St George's Street looking south.

St Giles Gate

Lost City Gate. St Giles Gate is first recorded in 1288 and was of relatively modest proportions compared with the two adjacent examples. It was rebuilt in the first half of the C14th and demolished in 1792.

St Giles Hospital

See *Great Hospital*.

St Giles House

Former telephone exchange. Designed by George Skipper in 1906 in an exuberant Baroque style, this was Telephone House until the exchange moved to St Andrews. It is, in some respects, Surrey House in miniature although the marble interior is by no means as opulent.
It functions now as a restaurant and boutique hotel.

St Giles Street

Historic thoroughfare.
Originating from the development of the Norman New Town (Neuport), the street was known originally as Nether or Inferior Newport refecting its relative distance from the centre of Norman urban development around and to the south/east of Bethel Street (Superior Newport). In consequence, the street was lightly developed until the C15/16th when substantial town houses began to appear and the street's name begins to change to St Giles Street, after the church. There was

Reconstruction of St Giles Gate.

George Skipper's exuberant Telephone Exchange, now a hotel, St Giles Street.

St Gregory's Alley looking south.

a significant building boom in the Georgian period when either new houses with large gardens were constructed or older houses were refronted in the 'modern style'. Later some imposing Victorian and Edwardian additions supplemented the street's architecture. The high quality of the street is reflected in the fact that virtually all of the buildings are listed, apart from the gap left by the stately Hippodrome, demolished in the 1960s. Starting from the east end and the north side, on the corner of Upper Goat Lane, is the striking, terracotta office designed for the Norfolk Daily Standard by George Skipper in 1899. Between this and the site of the former Hippodrome is an attractive range of C17th/C18th gabled buildings sitting on C15th and C16th undercrofts. Obliquely opposite is Gladstone House, the late C18th home of John Harvey, Mayor in 1792. Back on the north side, a pleasant Georgian terrace leads to a striking pair of 1740

Georgian town houses with a C16th timber framed, flint rear section and an extensive C15th undercroft. More well mannered Georgian houses lead to George Skipper's exuberant, Baroque Telephone Exchange of 1906, and now a hotel and restaurant. Next door is another stately Georgian house and next to this, Albert Havers' Masonic Hall of 1907, added to by S.J. Wearing in 1927. Next to this, more Georgian buildings take the street down to St Giles church. Returning to the south side, more restrained Georgian development leads to the Salvation Army Citadel and then the early C18th former Conservative Club. No. 38 next door is also early C18th with C19th alterations while Nos. 42-44 date from 1680. The former YMCA, further down the street, dates from the late 1700s although sits on C15th undercrofts. The range next door date from 1727. The street today is extremely attractive and is home to a range of eating establishments, galleries and small shops.

St Gregory's Alley

Ancient thoroughfare.
Taking its name from the adjacent church, there is a strong possibility that the alley existed before the Conquest. It contains an interesting range of buildings with the early C17th No. 5 and 6 and No. 4, which dates from 1830, being listed. No. 7 sits on a medieval undercroft. Half way down the Keir Hardie Hall is, unsurprisingly, home to the Norwich Working Men's Club but also a dizzying array of dance and music events as well as other groups – such as the anarchists. A beleaguered K6 listed phone box sits at the bottom.

St James' Mill

'The noblest of all English Industrial Revolution Mills'.
Norwich had been the principal English textile producing city for most of the medieval period and a cloth producing/exporting city of international significance. With the coming of the Industrial

St James' Mill, south elevation, and St James' Mill at night.

St Miles Bridge.

Revolution, the textile towns of the north of England began to assert a new prominence and Norwich responded by developing its own mills. Although it had ceased to be the 'second city' by the 1780s. Three mills were built north of the Wensum in the 1830s and the largest, St James's Mill of 1839, by either John Brown or Richard Parkinson, survives. The lack of coal for steam power and fast flowing water finally saw the death knell of the once supreme Norwich textile industry. Jarrold printing company eventually took over the premises. The site

of the Mill was originally occupied by the Carmelite friars between 1256 and the dissolution and remnants of an impressive, two-cloistered friary complex were unearthed during recent excavations. The building survives today as a range of sensitively converted offices suites.

St Lawrence's Well
See *Gybson's Well.*

St Martin at Palace Plain

Ancient space. In the pre Conquest period, this was an important urban space located at a crossing point

between a now lost north/south route from the probable river crossing (now Whitefriars Bridge), through the later Cathedral and south to Mountergate and an east/west route running from Elm Hill to the now lost Worlds End Lane. 'Palace' refers to the Bishop's Palace, located the other side of the Precinct Wall but accessed via the Alnwick Gate located in the Plain. 'St Martin' commemorates the church which was an early foundation and includes pre Conquest 'long and short work'. The church contains a substantial monument to late Elizabeth

Reconstruction of St Martin's Gate.

Calthorpe who lived in a mansion previously occupied by Sir Thomas Erpingham, just north east of the church. While the house was demolished, subsequently, a two storey bay window probably dating from the very early C15th was saved, however, and relocated onto the gable end of No. 10, a late C18th town house. Next door another modest Georgian townhouse with carriageway arch butts up to the very imposing Cotman House, built by Samuel Pye on the site of the old White Swan around 1767 and possibly designed by Robert Brettingham, brother of the nationally famous Matthew. Next to that is the C17th former White Lion, now the Wig and Pen while just to the west, on the corner of what used to be Busseys garage, are some attractive, C17th gabled buildings. The attractive, listed buildings, with the precinct Wall frame a very pleasant and tranquil space, enhanced by the Council in the 1990s by a landscaping scheme.

St Martin's Gate

Lost City Gate. This was the point in the City Walls where Oak Street left the City. The Gate was first mentioned in 1275 as the Porte de Coslayn, reflecting its proximity to the Coslany area of the northern City Centre, and was rebuilt in 1340. It was demolished in 1808 but the side wall survived for some time as part of an adjacent cottage.

St Miles Bridge

Very early iron bridge. The site of one of the very earliest river crossings in the City. The current bridge, by James Frost, dates from 1804 and is the earliest iron bridge in the City.

St Stephen's Gate

Lost City Gate. The principal entrance to the City and the most elaborate of the 12 City Gates, the St Stephen's or Needham Gate was built by 1285. During Kett's Rebellion the Earl of Warwick broke into the City through the Gate with a Master gunner demolishing the portcullis. The gate was demolished in 1793.

St Stephen's Street in the 1950s.

St Stephen's Street

Ancient thoroughfare. The principal entry to the Walled City from London, this street was typical of many stately, historic streets within the City until the War and post War redevelopment intervened. The first blow came to the street in 1793 when the great Gate was demolished. The remainder of the street survived remarkably intact however until the War. Widening the street was first floated in 1915 but the Council struggled with which side should be sacrificed. The east side included the

Reconstruction of St Stephen's Gate.

Boar's Head, dating from 1456, and the Crown and Angel dating from between 1434 and 1492 and built by the Clere family. On the same side of the street, and opposite the Boars Head there was a splendid four storey, late C17th building with weavers' windows, the incased remnants of medieval alms houses at the top of the street and also an attractive run of at least a dozen buildings described in the 1945 Plan as being 'of minor interest but good design'. On the west side of the street, the presence of two major department stores had inhibited widening but there were also buildings of historical worth. Barwell's wine merchants at No. 12 contained a magnificent, moulded, C17th plaster ceiling while the building itself probably had its origins in the mid to late C15th and incorporated extensive undercrofts. The maze of yards running back from the Street were also a cornucopia of fine medieval and Georgian buildings. It is fair to say that the Baedeker Blitz of April 1942 inflicted severe damage on the Street. It is interesting though that at the most severely damaged end (St Stephen's Plain) it was possible to salvage the structure of the former Buntings Store (now M&S) and rebuild it while down the remainder of the street, medieval gems were demolished, whether or not they were restorable. The key was partly the 1945 Plan's desire to create a dual carriageway through the street and partly a post War civic pride obsession to shake off the chaotic, muddled past and look 'modern'. 'Modern' in the context of St Stephens

Salvation Army.

started in the 1950s as faux Georgian at the northern end, east side and by the 1960s was degenerating into some bland, modernist reproduction of post War Coventry at the top end, culminating in the starkly hideous multi storey car park, to be crowned eventually by two monstrous glass towers. The west side degenerated into a sort of 'dog's dinner' mélange running from the awfully bland Co-op building through a couple of C19th/early C20th survivors to the Saxone's building of the 1950s. It is certainly, architecturally the most awful street in Norwich and no surprise that the Commission for Architecture and the Built Environment (CABE) gave it the accolade of the 'Ugliest Street in the East of England' recently.

Functionally it remains an important shopping street and still a gateway. To their credit, the Councils (Norwich and Norfolk) recently sought to ameliorate the 'horror' by improving the pedestrian environment and removing the ridiculous miles of guard rail. The addition of a new entrance to the Chapelfield

shopping centre also helped. Even more recently the City Council commissioned a master plan to transform the street into 'A High Street for the 21st Century'. Let's hope it isn't too long before that vision starts to become a reality.

Salhouse Road

Radial road. This is a radial road running north east roughly from Mousehold Heath to the village of Salhouse. It runs through what used to be the Heath before it was radically reduced in size although some remnants of Thorpe Wood survive along the way. From the south end, Mousehold Aerodrome used to straddle the Road but now this has been redeveloped as Heartsease School to the south and a retail park and industry to the north. Some hangars survive within the industrial area. Further along the route, the Heartsease Council estate occupies the area predominantly to the south while post War private housing and industry occupy the area to the north. Tom Smiths, who were inventors of the Christmas cracker, previously had a factory north of Salhouse Road but this has now closed.

Salvation Army Citadel

Salvation Army HQ. Following the founding of the Salvation Army by William Booth in 1865, the Norwich branch was established in the, still surviving, Old Skating Rink in Bethel Street in 1882 and launched by William Booth himself. A more permanent base was established in 1892 when the purpose built Norwich Citadel was opened in a complex on

From left: Courtyard of the Samson and Hercules with the two statues, prior to the space being enclosed, and Samson and Hercules in the 1930s.

St Giles Street on the site of a former cycle repair yard. Subsequently the former Mortimer Hotel (1858), next door, was bought to provide a day centre for the elderly and administrative facilties. The acquisition of the former Conservative Club further along St Giles provided opportunities for additional facilities in the 1990s.

Samson and Hercules

Historic merchant house. Samson and Hercules House stands on the site of a significantly older building, erected in the C15th. This early mansion was built by the important military captain, Sir John Fastolf (1380-1459) who fought in the campaigns of Henry V in France. After Fastolf's death, Samson and Hercules House was occupied by the Duchess of Suffolk, who often resided there with her family, and later by the Countess of Lincoln. John Pye, a Norwich cordwainer lived here in 1539. Popular folklore has it that the Samson and Hercules House is haunted by victims of the great plague in 1578.

Up to around 5,000 bodies were buried beneath the site.

The present structure is attributed to Christopher Jay to mark the year of his mayoralty, 1656-7. However, it is probable that the building incorporated much of the earlier house rather than being started as an entirely new building – indeed, the undercroft and other C15th walls formed part of Jay's house. The building also contained ornate mantelpieces, paneled walls and a heavily framed oak doorway.

After the death of Christopher Jay, Samson and Hercules House was sub-divided so that it housed several residences. The building was occupied by numerous people during the 17th, 18th and 19th centuries; a wool combing business, the local excise offices, and a surgeons practice, are just a few examples of the diverse use this building had. Some structural changes were made to the building while it was in the hands of Thomas Hancock, the City treasurer. He also ran a grocer's business from there.

Hancock covered in the courtyard and removed a smaller building attached on the west side. Not long after, the house was acquired by George Cubitt (who also owned Augustine Steward's House next door), a valuer and collector of antiques and art. Cubitt did much to restore the building, including returning the two figures that support the entrance portico.

It is from these two figures that the house takes its name. They represent Samson ('the sturdy'), who is carrying a lamb and gripping the jawbone of an ass, and Hercules ('the heavy'), who wears a lion skin and is holding a club. The originals were carved from wood, painted and enamelled. They were placed outside the building in 1656-7 and removed to an inner court in August 1789. 100 years later Cubitt restored them. By the C20th only the original Samson remained and Hercules had been replaced by a C19th copy. In the late 1990s, after Samson lost an arm, the statues were removed. Replica statues were

Sir Arthur Samuel.

installed in 1999, made out of more durable material. The original wooden ones were removed to the Museums Service for restoration.

After fears that it was going to be used for commercial purposes, Samson and Hercules house was bought by the Norfolk and Norwich Archaeological Trust and the YWCA jointly. The YWCA was opened by the Duchess of York (later the Queen Mother) in 1924. During the 1930s the building served as a social centre, a dance hall (frequently used by Allied troops), and a ballroom. There was also an underground swimming pool (100 ft by 35 ft) that was opened in 1935.

There was a major fire in the building in 1944 which resulted in the loss of the upper floors of half the building as well as the roof. It was reconstructed in 1952-55 by J. P. Chaplin, who restored the interior and exterior to its pre-fire appearance. The 'Samson' was a popular local dance venue for most of the mid to late C20th. During the 1990s it was the home of Ikon nightclub, which closed in 2004. The building was converted and redeveloped as apartments in 2008.

Samuel, Sir Arthur

First Jewish Lord Mayor.
Arthur Michael Samuel was born in 1872 in Timberhill into part of the Haldestein shoe making family that went on to become Ballys. He became the 4th Lord Mayor and first Jewish Lord Mayor of Norwich in 1912 and when elected he said "I am the first Jew who has ever been Mayor of the City and I thank you not only in my own name, but, in the name of the local community of British-born Jews for this honour." He was a passionate advocate for Norwich and his activities ranged from supporting victims of the 1912 Floods to making donations to the civic office and being an active president of the Norfolk & Norwich Archaeological Society. He left the City to become MP for Farnham, Secretary for Overseas Trade (1924–1927) and Financial Secretary to the Treasury (1927–1929). He was created a Baronet in 1932 and became first Baron Mancroft, choosing the name in recognition of his strong links to the City. When he died in 1942 he left donations in his will to the Norfolk & Norwich Hospital, the 'Magistrates Poor Box' in the Police Court at the Guildhall, the Jewish Synagogue, the Norwich School, the Cathedral and All Hallows Mission.

Scrope, Thomas

Remarkable hermit.
Thomas Scrope was the possible illegitimate grandson of Baron Scrope of Bolton. He entered the Carmelite friary as a normal friar but left wearing a hair shirt and sack to preach the gospel in the streets. His extreme behaviour brought

From top:
Sculpture in the garden of the Assembly House.
Sir Thomas Browne, by Anne and Patrick Poirier, Hay Hill.
Sea Form, by Barbara Hepworth (and Ice Copy), St George's Green.

Sculpture
Public art locations

The City has a relatively wide range of public sculpture ranging from conventional statuary to more contemporary installations. The Norwich Society and the Norfolk Contemporary Art Society are currently (2009/10) promoting a campaign to achieve more public sculpture.

Major installations that can be viewed relatively easily include:

Installation	Location	Date made	Date installed	Artist
Abstract Sculpture	Earlham House Centre	1961	1961	Matthew Frere-Smith
Angel of Light	Chapelfield Gardens	1999	1999	Kevin Lee
Armed Science	Norwich Cemetery	1878	1878	John Bell
Bird Flight	N & N University Hospital	2004	2005	Ros Newman
Boulton & Paul	Riverside/Novi Sad Bridge	2003	2004	Andi Gibbs
Dragonfly	Earlham Millennium Green	2000	2000	Jamie Sargeant
Draped Reclining Woman	Sainsbury Centre	1957	1980	Henry Moore
Edith Cavell	Tombland	1918	1918	Henry Pegram
Extrapolation	UEA (moved1994)	1982	1982	Liliane Lijn
Gaea	Sentinel House	1990	1990	Colin Miller
Gildencroft entrance	Gildencroft, Pitt Street	2006	2006	Garry Breeze
Girder Structure	St Crispins Roundabout	1973	1978 moved 2004	Peter Hide
Helios	N & N University Hospital	2001	2002	Keith McCarter
Heraldic Lions	City Hall	1936	1938	Alfred Hardiman
Homage to Sir Thomas Browne	Hay Hill	2005	2007	Anne & Patrick Poirier
Lady Julian and St Benedict	Anglican Cathedral	1996–2000	2000	David Holgate
Low Ebb	Wendene, Bowthorpe	1991	1991	Neville Ward
Monument to Daedalus	Castle Green	1993	1998	Jonathan Clarke
Mother and Child	Old Nflk & Nrwch Hospital (moved 1965)	1874	1876	Sir Joseph Boehm
Mother and Child	Upper Close	1978	1978	George Fullard
Mother and Child	Upper Close	1984	1984	Naomi Blake
Nelson	Upper Close	1847	1854 moved 1936	Thomas Milne
One For Bristol	UEA, Suffolk Rd	1968	1996	John Hoskin
Parrot Head	Castle Green	1993	1994	Bernard Reynolds
Pencils	Premier Inn Gdn (Nelson)	1996	1996	Peter Logan
Reclining Figure	Sainsbury Centre	1956	1985	Henry Moore
Sea Form	St Georges Green	1964	1968 moved 2008	Barbara Hepworth
Sir Samuel Bignold	Surrey House	1904	1904	Leon-J Chavaliaud
Sir Thomas Browne	Hay Hill	1905	1905	Henry Pegram
Symbol of Norwich	Top London Street	1974	1974	Tadeusz Zielinski
The Guardian	Parmentergate Court	1991	1991	Beatrice Hoffman
The Wader	Hotel Nelson	1986	1986	Colin Miller
Two Piece Reclining Figure	Sainsbury Centre	1961	1979	Henry Moore
Untitled	Prospect House	1969	1969	Bernard Meadows
Variations on a Square	UEA, Suffolk Rd	1964	1964	Henry H Clyne
'Victory' Boer War Memorial	Agricultural Hall Plain	1903	1904	George Wade
Wellington	Upper Close	1854	1854 moved 1936	George Adams
Will Kemp	Chapelfield Gardens	2000	2000	Mark Goldsworthy

disapproval from the prior provincial of the English Carmelites so he returned to the friary as an anchorite where he remained for about twenty years writing a number of books. He then went to Rhodes as legate to Pope Eugenius IV and was subsequently consecrated as bishop of Dromore in Ireland. He then held the post of suffragan bishop in the Norwich diocese for twenty eight years before a partial reversion to his old habits when he walked the City streets preaching barefoot every Friday. He died in 1492 aged almost 100 – a remarkable age for the period.

Sculpture
See page 333.

Seago, Edward
Landscape painter.
A nationally regarded landscape painter, Seago was born the son of a Norwich coal merchant. He was a favourite of the Royal family and accompanied Prince Philip on a visit to Antarctica in 1956.

Second Air Division
US 2nd World War Air Force presence. The 2nd Air Division of the US 8th Army Air Force was responsible for 20 US operated air force bases focussed around Norwich but reaching down to north Suffolk between 1942 and 1945. These included 13 bomber stations, six fighter stations and one operating both. Divisional headquarters was at Ketteringham Hall just south of the City and, for a time at least, the famous Hollywood actor James Stewart was Divisional Commander. During this period the 8th Air Force dispatched 3,000

aircraft on daily operations involving more than 20,000 personnel.

Second Air Division Memorial Library
Memorial to WWII US aircrew. At the end of WWII, senior officers of the 2nd Air Division conceived the notion of a library to act as a living memorial to those Americans 'who, flying from bases in these parts, gave their lives defending freedom.' Almost 7,000 Americans lost their lives while serving with the 2nd Air Division. The Memorial was also regarded as an educational and friendship bridge between the two nations. An appeal was launched at the end of the War and funds were placed in the care of the 2nd Air division Memorial Trust. It was not until 1963 that the first Memorial Library opened as part of Norwich Central Library, designed by City Architect David Percival, along with a commemorative water feature with stones from each of the 50 States. In the devastating fire of 1994, the entire library, including the Memorial, was destroyed. A new Memorial Library rose from the ashes as part of the Norfolk & Norwich Millennium Library in The Forum, designed by Sir

Michael Hopkins, completed in 2001 and opened formally by the Queen. The library now contains 5,000 American non fiction and fiction titles and 25 periodicals as well as a vast amount of record material, including films, prints and CDs, concerning the history of the 2nd Air Division.

Sedan Chair
Mode of transport. In the C19th a Sedan Chair hire point was located at the junction of what is now Opie Street and London Street. A plaque commemorates the site and a surviving Sedan Chair is held within the collections of the Norwich Museums.

Sewell, Anna
Author. Born in Great Yarmouth, Anna spent most of her life in Dalston, Stoke Newington and Brighton but when she was given only 18 months to live in 1871 she moved to a house in Catton where she was tended by her mother. Anna wrote the novel Black Beauty, from her sick bed, over the next five years, drawing from her experiences locally. It was eventually published by Jarrold and became an international success although Anna died too soon to see it and, as her mother had sold the

From left: B17 of the USAAF Second Air Division, Second Air Division Memorial Library located in The Forum.

From left: Sewell Park, the Whalebone pub in the Sewell area, and the Sewell Barn Theatre. Inset: an illustration from Black Beauty by Anna Sewell.

copyright for £20, the family did not benefit. Anna Sewell is commemorated in the City by Sewell Road and Sewell Park.

Sexton, Sons & Everard

Former major shoe manufacturer. In 1886 Henry Sexton worked for Howlett & White in Colegate and when his request for a pay increase met with a rebuff, he left and established his own company. Employing 30 staff in a business in St Edmund's Mills the company enjoyed early success but a disastrous fire in 1913 resulted in both a relocation, to the Upper Market, and the involvement of A.A. Everard in the company to create the new firm of Sexton, Sons & Everard. The company grew rapidly and after an initial move to Oak Street, they built the new St Mary's Works in St Mary's Plain in the 1920s where they employed over 500 people. The company focussed on the 'high end' of the market, seeking to rival the designers of Paris and Vienna and when the First World War effectively halted the import of shoes from Mainland Europe, S,S&E were there to fill the breach. During the 1920s and 30s the company modernised and expanded to become one of the largest producers in the City. The company's principal, Harry Sexton, felt that he should give something back to the City which had helped him to make his fortune so he regenerated the Assembly House as a public resource and gave it to the City. Following the Second World War, the company continued to prosper and, among other products, produced Joyce shoes from America under license. Like most other Norwich shoe companies, S,S&E were feeling the pinch from overseas competition by the late 1960s and in 1972 they called in the receivers, making 750 people redundant. Since closure, the factory has contained a range of small businesses as well as a gym and snooker cub. There are plans to develop it for homes, offices and a hotel but the recession has stalled progress.

Images of shoe production at Sexton, Sons & Everard in the early and mid C20th.

Sheffield, Lord

Victim of Kett's Rebellion.
Sheffield was second in
command of the Royal Army
under the captaincy of the
Earl of Northampton sent to
put down Kett's Rebellion in
1549. On 1st August the
Royal Army engaged the
rebels in Palace Plain and in
the heat of the fighting, Lord
Sheffield fell from his horse.
He removed his helmet and
indicated to the rebels that he
was a noble and therefore a
valuable hostage. A butcher
called Fulke was clearly
unimpressed and crushed
his skull with a club. Sheffield
and 86 others were buried
at St Martin at Palace. A
stone plaque in the flint wall
on the south of the Plain
commemorates his death.
The plaque was originally
located at the corner of the
Cupid and Bow pub which
stood on the opposite side
of the road facing the
church but was demolished
in 1968. It is said that Lord
Sheffield's ghost haunts the
Adam and Eve pub.

Sheriffs of Norwich

Civic official. Deriving from
the Anglo Saxon term Shire
Reeve the post was
essentially a keeper of the
peace within a municipality.
The City was granted the
right to elect its own two
Reeves by the Charter of
Richard I in 1194. Henry IV's
Charter of 1404 allowed the

City to elect two Sheriffs
to administer the separate
'City & County of Norwich'.
The Municipal Reform Act
of 1835 restricted the
Council's ability to elect
Sheriffs, to just one post.
Norwich is now one of only
15 towns or councils with a
Sheriff – an entirely ceremonial
post, elected annually. The
post holder is apolitical and
invariably someone who has
served the community with
distinction.

Shirehalls

**Seats of county
administration and law.**
The Shirehouse or Shirehall
was the centre for the
County of Norfolk's
administration and law
within Norwich. From the
time of the City's charters of
self government, which
made Norwich an
independent County in its
own right, the City was
administered separately,
principally from the Guildhall.
The first Shirehouse is
mention in 1219 but a new
Shirehouse is recorded as
being constructed on a
raised rampart in 1270
south of the Castle, within
the Bailey. Despite extensive
excavations prior to the
development of Castle Mall,
no remains were discovered.
In 1326, this Shirehouse
was reconstructed and while
there is no information about
what form this took, a

reference in 1466 talks
about it being thatched. In
1345 the Charter of Edward
III gave the Castle Fee, with
the exception of the Castle
Keep itself and the Shirehall,
to the citizens of Norwich. In
1578 a new Shirehouse was
built on the top of the Castle
Mound adjacent to and
north of the keep. The only
evidence that remains of this
structure are a modest
representation on
Kirkpatrick's North East
Prospect of the City of
Norwich (1723) and an
illustration on Corbridge's
plan (1729). It appears as a
two storey timber framed,
brick built structure, with
pitched roof and Flemished
gabled eastern end. The
interior included a Grand
Jury Chamber. On 13th
September, 1746, at 1pm,
the Shirehouse burned
down. In 1748 architect
Matthew Brettingham
constructed a new
Shirehouse, north of the
keep. This was an elegant,
two storey stone faced
structure with a low pitched,
slate roof and castellations.
It appeared not unlike a
meeting house. In 1784 a
single storey vestibule was
added on the west side and
in 1792 William Wilkins
senior renovated
Brettingham's building.
In 1789, eminent architect
Sir John Soane was
commissioned to build a

Matthew Brettingham's original plans and elevation for the Shirehouse.

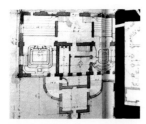

new Prison and Shirehall east of the keep. The structure was built in a style which replicated the keep including castellations. The building was labeled a 'monstrosity' by William Wilkins senior and, ironically, in 1822 William Wilkins junior was selected from 30 applications to build a new Shirehall at the base and east of the Castle Mound. Soane's building was demolished in 1824 to make way for a new prison. Wilkin's new Shirehall was refaced in 1846 by Joseph Stannard who also had to solve the problem of the building 'sinking'. Architect John Brown added two new wings. In 1907 the County Council required further administrative space and architect Edwin French was successful in winning the commission for an extension in the French Renaissance style, faced with Bath stone. In 1988 the County Courts moved to the new Courts complex in St Martins and four years later, part of the Shirehall was converted into the Royal Norfolk Regimental Museum. Following a major Heritage Lottery Fund award for the regeneration of the Castle in the 1990s the majority of the Museum and Archaeology Service administration moved into the Shirehall and it also became a study centre.

Shoe Industry

Former principal employer. Although the textile industry dominated the Norwich economy for hundreds of years until its eventual demise in the late C18th/early C19th, shoe making had always been important and this stature made it well placed to take over the leading mantle when textiles finally faded.

Pub sign commemorates the one time chief employer in the City.

In 1569 cordwainers (shoemakers) were the 4th largest occupation in the City and by the C17th they were 3rd out of 200 trades. Before the mid C19th, shoemakers were small scale, craft operations, often working out of their homes and making bespoke shoes to order. The first significant change to this came when James Smith started to make readymade shoes in 1792 from his premises on the site of the current City Hall – possibly the first example of production, pre-sized shoes. This developed in the latter half of the C19th to entrepreneurs like Tillyard and Howlett setting up shoe factories which sourced large proportions of the production process to 'out door workers' under a system run by 'garret masters'. Although by the end of the century, the process was getting more mechanised and more of the process was being undertaken within factories, it was noted by C.B. Hawkins in 'Norwich: A Social Study' in 1910 that 'boot manufacture is still in a transition stage in Norwich, up to 12 years ago production being mostly in the hands of small employers.' He noted that a dozen firms undertook the

'team system' of shoe production (all production in house with division of labour into specific processes) and a further 20 had a more or less complete set of machinery (so almost reaching the team system) but 40 garret masters survived indicating that there was still significant outsourcing. Between the Wars, the industry flourished as the biggest employer in the City led by the likes of Howlett & White (later Norvic), Haldestein (later Bally), Sexton & Everards, Edwards & Holmes, Shingler & Thetford and James Southall (later Startrite). With over 10,000 employees, 26 firms and six million pairs of shoes produced in 1935, the industry specialised in high quality women's shoes for the national and international market. The War had a dramatic impact with many of the factories falling victim to the bombing campaign but after the War the industry rallied and flourished again in the 1950s. Foreign competition and particularly cheaper overseas labour had a dramatic impact on the industry in the 1970s as the number of employees halved and, one by one, the great shoe making names closed – Sextons in 1976, Norvic in 1981, the Co-op in 1987 and W.H. Clarke (K Shoes), Edwards & Holmes and Bally in the 1990s. Shoe making, once employing 20,000 people directly and in connected trades, is now nearly extinct in the City. The only bright note perhaps is that the company which was started by James Smith then became Southall's and Startrite, retains a presence in Norwich for design and administration. Also, Van Dal

From left: One of the UK's largest provincial Marks & Spencer, small scale independents in the Lanes, major antiques venue at the centre of many antique shops around Magdalen Street.

still manufacture in the City and are one of the few shoe factories left in England.

Shopping

Past and current retail role. The shopping role of Norwich has always been key to its function and development, from its extensive medieval street markets to its innovation in speciality shopping and department stores. From its position 20 years ago as 49th in Experian's league of the top 1100 retail centres, Norwich now sits within the top ten and rose to 5th in 2006. In the same year, the centre was voted in a Goldfish Credit Card shopping satisfaction survey as the best centre in the UK. The quality of the centre flows partly from a very high proportion of independent speciality retailers (Norwich Lanes, Timberhill, Elm Hill) but also a very large number of department/variety stores (House of Fraser, JLP, Jarrold, M&S) and extremely good representation by the multiples, primarily within the two shopping centres (Chapelfield and The Mall). The ancient market still represents a key component of the retail offer while niche sectors such as antiques (Magdalen St and Old Skating Rink) and food/beverage (Lanes and Market) are growing in strength. The main line retail offer is augmented by a strong representation in the restaurant/café sector again providing a good mix of higher end chains (Carluccio's, Jamie Oliver) with quality independent offers.

Sir Garnet Wolseley

Iconic pub. The distinguished soldier who led the unsuccessful relief force for General Gordon at Khartoum in 1882, and in 1895 reorganised the British Army, becoming its Commander in Chief, gave his name to the impressive pub in the centre of the Market Place. The pub, formerly the Baron of Beef, is the sole surviving hostelry of the 44 inns and taverns which once served the Market Place. Prior to being a pub it was a butcher's shop and also the birthplace of the eminent botanist Sir James Edward Smith in 1759. After the Guildhall and St Peter Mancroft, this is probably the oldest building on the Market Place, with a C15th timber framed core, the predominant façade facing the Walk dating from 1626 and C18th additions.

Skipper, George

See page 340.

Sloughbottom Park

Public park. Sloughbottom is located west of Drayton Road and was developed in the 1920s to serve the Mile Cross Estate. It contains a range of conventional sports pitches and, since 2005, a BMX track. The site is located adjacent to the Marriotts Way long distance foot and cycle path and there is a linking footpath cycle route running from Marriotts Way, through the Park to Mile Cross. The name derives from a notation on early maps indicating 'The Slough' which referred to a dip around the Drayton Road at this point which had a tendency to be swampy or boggy.

Sir Garnet Wolseley pub, sole survivor of 44 pubs originally ranged around the Market.

Smith, Delia

The TV Cook and Football Club Funder. TV cook and the UK's best selling cookery writer Delia Smith, became a majority share holder in Norwich City Football Club, with her husband Michael Wynn-Jones, in 1996. She set about reorganising the catering, which she had described as the worst in Britain, and commissioned Bruce Oldfield to design the team kit. She has remained passionate about and supportive of the Club during their difficulties in 2001, their triumph of promotion to the Premiership, their immediate fall from grace and their inexorable plummet to League 1, despite interest from other funders to step into the majority shareholder role. In 2010, as the Club walked a tightrope between remarkable success on the field and financial challenges off, Delia was there for the 'long game' seeing them move back eventually to the top rank of English football and financial stability. In 2011 she announced that she was stepping down from the catering operation but remained committed to the Club as a majority shareholder.

Smith, James

Shoemaking innovator. James Smith, previously a travelling leather seller, opened a shop in the Upper Market (broadly St Peter's Street) in 1792 and began to sell ready made shoes for ladies as opposed to bespoke shoes to order. It has been argued that this was the first example of stock shoe production in the country, and the business prospered, eventually becoming the Startrite company.

Smith, Sir James Edward

Founder of the Linnaean Society. Born in 1759 at the Sir Garnet Wolseley pub, James Edward Smith went on to become one of the country's most eminent scientists, being a member of the academies of Stockholm, Upsala, Turin, Lisbon, Philadelphia and New York and a Member of the Royal Academy of Sciences in Paris. He had developed an enthusiasm for botany at an early age but at that time the subject could only be studied as part of a medical degree. He therefore studied medicine at Edinburgh and went on to secure a degree at Leyden, in the Netherlands. A close friend of Sir Joseph Banks,

One of the surviving original snap dragons, in the Castle.

Captain Cook's botanist, Smith developed a deep interest in the work of the eminent Swedish scientist Carl Linnaeus. When Linnaeus died in 1778, his wife offered his library and research papers for sale and Smith bought them, despite efforts by the Swedish King to prevent the purchase. He formed the Linnaean Society in 1788 and brought the collection back to Norwich where he established a Surrey Street study and lecture facility in a house designed by Thomas Ivory which still survives. He was knighted for his contributions to science.

Snap

Ceremonial beast. Snap is technically a hobby horse and formed a key part of

From left: An understated garden tribute to the Norwich City icon Delia Smith, and Delia celebrates Norwich's return to the Premiership with a chorus of 'Come on, lets be avin you'.

George Skipper

Norwich's Gaudi

Dereham born and educated at the Norwich School of Art, Skipper began his architectural career articled to London architect John Lee in Bedford Row in 1873. He returned to Dereham in 1876 to work for his father, a building contractor, then set up his own practice there three years later. Winning a competition in Shepton Mallet in that year gave him early access to more work in Somerset, some of which still survives, but by this time he was also winning commissions in the East of England. By 1889 he had been elected a fellow of the Royal Institute of British Architects, nominated by notable local members of the profession including the eminent local architect Edward Boardman. His early local work focussed on the coast and included town halls at Cromer and Hunstanton and a profusion of hotels at Gorleston, Lowestoft and Sheringham and most notably the French Chateau style Grand, Metropole and Hotel de Paris at Cromer. In 1896 he built his new offices at 7 London Street with striking terracotta panels which advertised his art to the passing public. His first big commission in Norwich followed shortly with the Art Nouveau Royal Arcade which allowed him to demonstrate his flair and imagination. This work involved a collaboration with Neatby (also responsible for the decoration of the Blackpool Ballroom and Harrods Food Hall) who was

From top: Royal Arcade, former Daily Standard offices in St Giles. Inset: George Skipper's office, London Street.

to work with Skipper subsequently. Close on the heels of the Arcade came the Daily Standard offices in St Giles (still surviving at the junction of St Giles and Upper Goat Lane) with thematic reliefs of Caxton and Defoe, the Haymarket Chambers (inspired by the C16th Pallazzo Pietro Massimi in Rome) and the remodelled Jarrold department store. These were followed by the offices

for the Norwich & London Assurance Company in St Giles (later to be Telephone House then the St Giles House Hotel), the remodelling of Red Lion Street as part of the introduction of the trams and the London & Provincial Bank at 30 London Street. Skipper's 'tour de force' is however the design of Surrey House as the new headquarters for Norwich Union. Skipper's work here,

From top: Boardroom of Norwich Union's Surrey House, Skipper's 'tour de force' the former London & Provincial Bank in London St, and Haymarket Chambers.

regarded by Pevsner as one of the most assured Edwardian office buildings in the country', was supported again by Neatby as well as George Murray (paintings) and the Minns Family (woodwork). Overlapping with Surrey House, Skipper was commissioned by the grandson of travel agent Thomas Cook, to extend and develop Sennowe Park at Guist.

civic ceremonial processions up until the early part of the C20th. It has its origins in the Guild of St George and played a key role in Guild Day festivities for over 400 years. The earliest reference to the Dragon appears in the minutes of the Guild assembly for 1408. The Guild Days involved the inauguration of the new Mayor and when the Guild was eventually disbanded, the Mayor making procession continued to include the Dragon. Eventually the use of the Dragon died out and preserved examples survive in the Castle Museum. More recently, a replica dragon has formed part of the Lord Mayor's procession in July although this is some time after the formal Mayor making in May.

At the end of the C18th mock guilds were established in Pockthorpe and elsewhere and on Guild Day, a mock mayor was elected to process through the area led by their own snapdragon. This developed into a fund raising initiative whereby the dragon would snatch people's hats and return them for a small forfeit. The practice died out by the early C20th.

Soane, Sir John

Prominent architect. Considered to be one of the most inventive European architects of his time, some of Soane's most notable achievements included becoming architect for the Bank of England and designer of the dining rooms at 10 and 11 Downing Street and the Dulwich College Picture Gallery in London. During his earlier career, Soane designed Blackfriars Bridge in St Georges Street in 1783,

Sir John Soane's Blackfriar's – or St George's – Bridge.

and a new gaol at the Castle in 1789. He undertook alterations to the Norfolk & Norwich hospital, and also to 9 Surrey Street for John Patteson who had accompanied him on his Italian study tour in 1777.

Solempne, Anthony de

City's first printer. The first printer in Norwich, Anthony de Solempne was a refugee from Brabant in the Southern Netherlands. He arrived in 1567 and established his business at the sign of the White Dove, later the Edinburgh Arms, Dove Street. Although his productions were mostly in Dutch, Solempne also printed in English and French. He also traded in wine and is thought to have been one of the wealthiest members of the Stranger community in Norwich.

SOS Bus

Evening economy support facility. The SOS bus is a specially fitted out Optare, single decker bus providing medical and social support facilities to people in the evening economy. The unit is staffed by a clinician from the East of England Ambulance Service, a St John Ambulance member and other support staff.

Sir Arthur South.

Interior of Southall's shoe factory in the early C20th.

Members of the team are trained in drug and alcohol intervention and clients are able to be signposted to other agencies who can help them. The bus and other support vehicles are located on Prince of Wales Road from 9pm, overnight. The project was started ten years ago as a six month pilot with support from the local press, Norfolk Police, YMCA Norfolk, Norwich City Council, Norwich nightclubs, LVA, local businesses, public donations and local churches – including free donation of the bus from the Proclaimers Church. Staff were seconded from a broad range of organisations. Grants followed subsequently from the Government and the range of public, private and third sector sponsors has expanded significantly. The project has been a huge success locally and has attracted praise from a wide range of bodies and individuals including the former Home Secretary.

The SOS Bus.

South, Arthur

Local politician. Arthur South was the youngest councillor in Britain when he was elected to the City Council in 1935 at the age of 21. By 1956 he had become the youngest Lord Mayor in Norwich history at the age of 42. At this time he championed a successful appeal to save Norwich City Football Club from financial ruin and in 1973 he became club chairman. South championed a range of social causes as a councillor, from public health issues to the founding of the University of East Anglia, and eventually went on to become Council Leader, a position he held for 18 years. He was knighted in 1974 for his services to the local community.

Southall, James

Pioneer shoemaker. James Southall and Company was started by James Smith, on the site of the present City Hall, in 1792. Innovative in that it made pre made shoes in different sizes rather than tailored shoes to order, the company was taken over by the founder's grandson, Charles Winter in 1816 and he mechanised the business by the introduction of American machines for sewing uppers and subsequently stitching soles. Winter's success in the business community was reflected in him becoming Sheriff in 1846 and Mayor in 1851. The company was taken over by John Willis and James Southall who developed the export trade to the colonies. When Willis died, Southall continued to drive it forward and ultimately passed it over to his sons. Mechanisation and expansion continued and, in 1907, the company moved to a new factory on Crome Road just north of the Pockthorpe Brewery. In the Norwich tradition of high quality shoe making, the company received a host of accolades including the

Southern Bypass.

Diploma of Honour at the Franco-British exhibition of 1908, the Diploma of Honour at Brussels in 1910 and the Grand Prix at Turin in 1911. In the 1920s the company developed a children's shoe range but with a radically different shape to adult shoes and they purchased the Startrite brand. The company grew and by 1936 was employing nearly 1,000 people and producing 600,000 pairs of shoes a year and in the same year the famous Startrite Twins advertising image was introduced. In 1943 the company undertook a major national survey of children's feet which provided the basis for further improvements to their children's ranges. By 1952 Southalls had developed such an expertise in children's shoes that they decided to abandon adult shoes and concentrate solely on children under the Startrite brand. In 1955 they secured a Royal warrant to supply shoes to the Royal children and in 1989 they received a second, from the Price of Wales. In the new Millennium Startrite closed its Crome Road factory, which has been redeveloped for housing,

and moved to Broadland Business Park. Although there is no longer any production in Norwich, the company remains headquartered here and still operates successfully in the children's shoe business servicing over 400 retail outlets and trading over the internet.

Southern Bypass

Radial Road. The Southern Bypass began construction in 1990 and was a device to take through traffic away from the City. It was the first high capacity, dual carriageway road in Norwich with grade separation at key junctions. 25km in length and with eight junctions, it runs between Easton and Postwick. In practice, it functioned more as a distributor, moving traffic around the City and avoiding bottle necks rather than essentially acting as a bypass. This experience has generated a strong pressure from local Councils to now deliver a Northern Distributor Road, mirroring the bypass in the south.

Spirit of Coltishall

War memorial. This is a memorial to the service personnel at the former RAF Coltishall airfield, which closed in 2006 (previously located to the north of Norwich), who gave their lives in times of war and peace. The memorial is located adjacent to the Norfolk Archive Centre at County Hall and is a 6.5m tall structure incorporating the airframe (engines and all functioning equipment removed) of the second pre production Anglo French SEPECAT Jaguar strike aircraft which was 'retired' in 1977 and was previously located, as a memorial, outside the airfield.

Spitaldyke

Lost water course.
Rising east of Norman's Hospital, (roughly on the site of modern St Crispin's Road, west of Whitefriars) from which it takes its name, it flowed south then west into the Dalymond Dyke.

Spixworth

Suburban village.
Approximately five miles north of Norwich's historic centre, Spixworth was recorded in the Domesday Book. The origin of 'Spix' is either a personal name, Spic, or derives from the Old English for bacon while 'worth' comes from the Anglo-Saxon for a 'small settlement' or enclosure. At this time there was a mill in the village, although this is no longer present, and it is recorded that along with the mill there were only ten men and thirteen sheep present. There has been a church on the current site on Buxton Road for more than 900 hundred years. St Peter's was remodelled between the C13th and C14th, although the font is Norman. Very little of Spixworth Hall survives today. The hall was acquired by the Southwells in the late C15th, but by 1600 it was owned by the Peck family. Remodelling was in the Jacobean style, although there were further modifications made in 1693 after the sale to Francis Longe. The Longes did not then leave Spixworth Hall until 1912. During World War II the Hall was used as a furniture depository, but was finally demolished in the 1950s. The dovecote and stable do however remain today, and were converted into holiday accommodation in 1997.

Spong Man.

Pavilion at Sprowston Recreation Ground.

Spong Man

Ancient human representation. Spong Man is a pottery lid of a cremation urn in the shape of a seated figure. It was excavated in 1979, at Spong Hill Anglo-Saxon cemetery site located at North Elmham and is unique in Early Saxon archaeology, being the earliest Anglo-Saxon three-dimensional human figure that has ever been found. It is displayed in the Anglo Saxon and Viking Gallery at the Castle Museum.

Sport, Participatory

Participatory sporting opportunities. Norwich offers a broad range of opportunities to participate in sports. Separate entries cover the main areas but the range includes American Football, archery, athletics (including a number of running clubs), badminton, basketball, bowls (over a dozen clubs and pay to play opportunities), boxing, canoeing, capoeira, climbing, cricket, croquet, cycling (including cycle speedway), dance, fencing, football (over two dozen clubs), golf, gymnastics, hockey, horse riding, ice skating, korfball, lacrosse, martial arts, motorcycle racing, netball, petanque, roller hockey, rugby, scuba diving, short mat bowls, skiing, snowboarding, squash, swimming (six clubs), synchronised swimming, table tennis, tennis, trampolining, triathlon, ultimate Frisbee, walking and water polo.

Sport, Spectator

Opportunities to watch sport. A range of spectator sports are available in the area with the largest, in crowd terms, being Association Football represented professionally by Norwich City, who regularly attract home game crowds of around 25,000, and a vast array of amateurs performing on local parks, recreation grounds and village greens. Other opportunities include:

- **Athletic meetings** – UEA Sportspark
- **Bowls** – various parks and the N&N Indoor Bowling Club, Unthank Road
- **Cricket** – various parks and village greens
- **Rugby** – Norwich Rugby Club, North Walsham Road
- **Swimming** – UEA Sportspark
- **Tennis** – parks, Norfolk Tennis and Squash Centre Lime Tree Road, and the UEA Sportspark
- **Water sports** – Whitlingham Country Park.

Sprowston

Suburban parish. Located to the north east of Norwich City Centre, Sprowston is the largest parish in Norfolk and the most populous in Broadland District, with a population of 14,027. Sprowston is enclosed by Heartsease to the east, Mousehold Heath and New Sprowston to the south, Old Catton to the west and Beeston St Andrew to the north. Sprowston is recorded in the Domesday Book as 'Sprowestuna' meaning 'settlement belonging to Sprow'. St Mary and Margaret's church on Church Lane dates from the C14th although its brick tower is early C18th and there is substantial C19th remodelling by Boardman. St Cuthbert's on Wroxham Road is much later having been built in 1886 by Fleming. The original Sprowston Hall was built in 1560 by the Corbets, but John Gurney bought it in 1869 and rebuilt it as

Sprowston Manor in 1875. It is now one of the two 5 star hotels in the area and the grounds provide a golf course. Sprowston Tower Mill was demolished circa 1860, but Sprowston Post Mill which features on the village sign, survived a good deal longer, although sadly it no longer exists today. Built in 1780, and also known as Mousehold Mill, the mill was destroyed by fire in March 1933 just before it was due to be handed over to the Norfolk Archaeological Society.

Sprowston Road

Radial Road. This is a radial road leaving the Walled City from the former Magdalen gates and heading north east to the suburb of Sprowston. Its most significant historic feature is the C12th Lazar House (or leper house) on the east side at the extreme southern end. Other features of note include St George's Church just north of the Lazar House, designed by A.J. Chaplin in 1962.

Spynke, Richard

See *City Gates and Walls*.

Stannard, Joseph

Artist. Stannard was predominantly a landscape and marine painter but also produced portraits. He developed early, exhibiting at the age of 14 and by 22 his work was on show at the British Institution in London. He was hampered by ill health which contributed to his early demise at the age of just 33 from tuberculosis. During his short career he travelled little, apart from visits to Holland, where Dutch painters of marine subjects had a marked influence on his style and where he exhibited in Amsterdam in 1822.

He focussed principally on local river and coastal subjects with pictures such as 'Water Frolic at Thorpe' (Norwich Castle), which was produced under the patronage of prosperous merchant John Harvey. Other pictures included 'The River at Thorpe', an interesting painting of nine local Norwich characters standing outside a pub and a profusion of seascapes and pictures of Yarmouth beach. He is buried in St John Maddermarket where there is a memorial. Beechey painted a portrait of him.

Stark, James

Artist. Stark was a prolific landscape painter, born in Norwich in 1794 and he was a pupil of Crome and in 1812 he became a member of the Norwich Society of Artists before leaving to study at the Royal Academy Schools in 1817. Returning to Norwich he continued to paint local landscape subjects until 1830 when he moved permanently to London, after a short intervening spell at Windsor. In 1834 he produced a book called 'Scenery of the Rivers of Norfolk' which included

Stave Church in Aarhus, Denmark, identical to the type excavated on the Anglia TV site.

his own work and that of other artists. A large number of his works are held at the Castle Museum while others are in the care of institutions as far afield as the Huntingdon Library in California and the Art Gallery of New South Wales while the Fitzwilliam, Ashmolean, Tate and Courtauld Institute also have examples.

Startrite

See *Southall, James*.

Stave Church

Lost pre Conquest church. In 1979 excavations on the site of Anglia TV's car park revealed the remains of an Anglo Scandinavian church and associated graveyard. This church was previously unknown as there is no documentary evidence for it or its dedication. The building began as a simple square structure but in time developed into a slightly more substantial rectangular building. It measured 10m (33ft) by 5m (16ft) and had a nave and a chancel. The walls of the church were constructed by setting timber posts into a bedding trench and a large posthole at the centre of the nave is thought to have supported a belfry. This central posthole is a unique find in Britain but parallels can be found in the central-mast stave-type churches of Norway and Denmark.

To the northern and eastern sides of the church archaeologists uncovered part of the graveyard which contained some 130 individuals and analysis of the skeletons revealed some interesting data. The adult males seem to have had a physically demanding life and most of the group appear to have been malnourished. Indeed,

Clockwise from above: Steward & Patteson's Brewery in 1975, just prior to demolition, the Pockthorpe Brewery in the early C20th, and the surviving remnant of the lost brewery on a former Steward & Patteson pub in Wensum Street.

many of the child burials suffered from rickets and they represent the earliest undoubted cases of rickets in Britain.

The church was probably only in use for about 75 years and was destroyed when the north-east bailey of the castle was built after the Norman Conquest. Such destruction was not unheard of in Norfolk or nationally. Castle Rising castle near King's Lynn replaced parts of an earlier settlement, as did Eaton Socon in Bedfordshire.

In addition to this unnamed church and graveyard, the 1979 excavations revealed more burials in the north-eastern part of the site, at the northern end of Crown Road. These burials could be part of the other graveyard discovered on the site but this would make that graveyard massive. It is more probable, therefore, that these individuals were buried in another graveyard associated with another previously unknown church.

Stephen

King. In 1140 King Stephen arrived to take control of the Castle from Hugh Bigod and to pass it to his third son William de Blois.

Steward & Patteson

Brewing dynasty. The Pockthorpe Brewery was established north of Barrack Street in the mid C18th and in 1793 John Patteson bought it from previous owner Charles Greeves. Two years later he acquired the breweries of James Beevor on Magdalen Street and Jehosophat Postle in Cowgate and developed the Pockthorpe site. Patteson was already an established figure within the Norwich power structure having been Mayor in 1788. In 1797, he entertained Prince William Frederick at the brewery for lunch which he ate within a newly manufactured vat. In 1800 the North Quay Brewery at Yarmouth was added to the portfolio and the company continued to expand, now producing 20,000 barrels a year. Patteson served the City as

MP from 1806-12. In 1820 he retired from the company, while remaining active in the Norwich Union Life Society, and the business was taken over by John Staniforth Patteson, William Steward and his brothers, Ambrose and both Timothy the elder and younger. The company became Steward, Patteson & Stewards. Pockthorpe was by now a state-of-the-art facility with horse mill and steam engine adjacent to the three storey fermentation block. George Morse's brewery was absorbed in 1831 and the company became Steward, Patteson & Co. Six years later, Peter Finch's brewery, one of the longest established in the City, amalgamated creating Steward, Patteson, Finch & Co. By the mid C19th the company had set its ambitions beyond the local market and was 'exporting' as far afield as Newcastle while their move into Porter brewing put them in direct competition with the big London brewers. Between then and the turn of the century, the company absorbed breweries in Great Yarmouth, Gorleston, Reepham, Swaffham, Weybourne, Eye, Dereham, Kings Lynn and Spalding. In 1908, brewery architect W.A. Trollope developed a pneumatic maltings plant which was the largest of its kind in the country. In the early years of the C20th S&P expanded to be the biggest and most successful brewery in the City. After WWII the number of breweries diminished and S&P collaborated with Bullard's to eradicate the local opposition, in 1962, by gobbling up Morgans, the only other surviving Norwich brewery. It was said that the two Norwich giants decided on how they would divide Morgans pubs by cutting a pack of cards. After Watney Mann had taken over Bullard's they acquired S&P and closed it in 1968. While they produced an S&P Bitter as a gesture to the heritage of the company, this was a Watney beer under another name. The brewery at Pockthorpe closed in 1970 and the chimney was demolished in 1974 with the fermentation block following shortly after. The site was developed for housing and all that remains today is the administration block fronting Barrack Street probably also designed by brewery architect W.A. Trollope and built in 1928.

Steward, Augustine

Influential City Leader. Born in 1491, son of twice Mayor John Steward, Augustine, or Austine as he was more commonly known, went on to be three times Mayor and a burgess to Parliament. Steward was active in the City's affairs both in terms of its political management and the protection and

development of its physical fabric. An early achievement involved him directing the rebuilding of the Guildhall in 1534 after its partial collapse. In 1540 he negotiated the purchase of the Dominican Friary (St Andrew's and Blackfriars Halls) from Henry VIII for the remarkable sum of £81 although the King did come back with a demand for an additional £152 for the lead on the roof. Not only did this astute deal provide the City with a hall for assemblies, a school, a reserve granary, a civic chapel and many other things over the ensuing centuries, but it ensured the survival of the only intact medieval friary complex in the UK.

During Kett's Rebellion, Steward deputised for Mayor Thomas Codd while he was being detained by the rebels and, having offered his house in Tombland as headquarters for the Earl of Northampton's army, saw it pillaged when the Earl was defeated. Steward sought to maintain some sort of order during the rebel occupation and when the second Royal army arrived, under the Earl of Warwick, Steward opened St Benedicts Gate to let them in. Steward had

houses in Tombland and Elm Hill, both of which survive today.

Stewart, James

Actor. In 1943, Hollywood icon James Stewart, was stationed with the USAAF at Tibenham, Old Buckenham and, as Divisional Commander of the 2nd Air Division of the 8th Air Force, at Ketteringham Hall and he visited the City in his leisure time, during this period. He returned in 1975 to tour his old wartime haunts and to visit the 2nd Air Division Memorial Library in the then Norwich Central Library.

Stoke Holy Cross

Suburban parish. Located 8km (5 miles) from the centre of Norwich, Stoke's greatest local claim to fame is that it was the birthplace of the Colman empire before it moved to Carrow. The legacy to the Colmans survives here as the 1776 Stoke Mill, extended by Colmans in 1814 and converted to a restaurant in 1962. The village has possible Roman origins and by the time of the Conquest had already established its 'Holy Cross' title. The present Holy Cross church was begun in the C13th and developed subsequently.

Augustine Steward.

James 'Jimmy' Stewart.

Clockwise from above: Stoke Mill, Stoke Hall Lodge, Stoke Mill Cottage.

Of a contemporary date is Blackford Hall Chapel which formed part of the moated, but now lost, early mansion and was converted to a house in the C16th with some remodelling in 1703. The present Blackford Hall is a relatively ordinary, C18th house. Stoke Holy Cross Hall was commissioned by Henry Birkbeck in 1852 from one of England's great architects Anthony Salvin at a cost of £8,300 (£500,000 at modern prices) but it was completed without electricity or hot water plumbing. The Tudor revival style, Flemish gabled mansion met the needs of the Birkbecks until just after WWI when it was sold. It struggled to find a new use and was demolished in 1938. Salvin's Lodge survived however and was restored as a private house in 2007. Salvin also built Abbot's Farmhouse for Birkbeck in 1860. Other significant structures include Gostleyns, on Shotesham Road, which dates from the mid C16th with C17th additions, the C18th, timber framed Old House on the Norwich Road, the former Stoke Rummer pub dating from 1700, and Dairy Farmhouse dating from 1760.

Strangers

See *Dutch and Flemish*.

Strangers Club

Historic club. Founded in 1927 by six local men the club was intended to be a device to welcome people that moved into the local community – 'strangers'. Club membership reflects this aim by requiring 51 per cent incomers and 49 per cent local people. It is located in Elm Hill in a house built by former Mayor Augustine Steward after the fire of 1507. The club has entertained many 'notable persons' including Queen Mary, Princess Alexandra, the Lord Mayor of London, Ambassadors from the Netherlands, Belgium and Mexico, Lord Birkenhead, Lord Baden-Powell, Sir Henry Wood and Sir Alfred Munnings.

The Strangers Club, Elm Hill.

*Clockwise from above:
Strangers Hall – main hall,
undercroft, kitchen, and the
view from the garden.*

Strangers Hall

Medieval Merchant Hall.
Probably the most complete
surviving example in
Norwich of a Great House
developed substantially over
the two centuries from 1450
is Strangers Hall. Although
the early undercroft dates
from about 1320, William
Barley rebuilt the Great Hall
in 1450 and Thomas
Sotherton added the King
Post roof, the stunning oriel
window and further
elements in the 1530s.
Francis Cock added the Hall
staircase and the window
that lights it in 1627.

Street Names

Name derivations. Of the
just under 2,000 roads,
street, lanes, yards, alleys
and courts currently or
originally in, or immediately
adjacent to, the old Walled
City, the vast majority take
their names from people

who either lived there or had
businesses there, such as
textile manufacturer John
Wright from Wrights Court
or the Earl of Surrey in
Surrey Street. Next in line
come pubs and with nearly
two pubs for each day of
the year by the late C19th, a
tendency for pubs to
change their names and a
propensity for relatively
frequent pub closures and
openings, it is perhaps
unsurprising that a third of
the thoroughfares have pub
name origins – everything
from A for Adam and Eve
Yard (3 of them originally) to
Y for York Alley. Next most
numerous are thoroughfares
inspired principally by
churches, surviving or lost,
but also by other
ecclesiastical institutions,
some long gone (Greyfriars
Road). The penultimate
largest group commemorate
landmarks – Castle Street,

Exchange Street, Theatre
Street etc. While finally,
about a dozen very old
streets are Scandinavian in
origin, indicated by the suffix
'gate' and are inspired by
the use of the street (potters,
fishermen, white bread
makers, parmenters, saddle
makers), by topography
(Hollowed Out Lane, Sandy
Lane) or, like the first
category, by the people that
lived there (Cole).

As the City developed
beyond the Walls, adding
thousands of new streets
and roads, the Council was
called upon to be ever more
inventive in its naming. The
network of radial roads was
pre existing and, sensibly,
related to where the road
was destined either locally –
Drayton Road, Sprowston
Road – or ultimately –
Newmarket Road, Ipswich
Road. The first significant
'spillage' beyond the Walls

Dave Stringer.

was for large tracts of Victorian terrace housing to the west and north. Here the fashion, predominantly, was to adopt the names of other cities or counties – Newmarket Street, Gloucester Street, Cambridge Street, Cardiff, Swansea, Northumberland etc. Subsequent developments celebrated the famous families and individuals of the City – Bignold, Hansard, Suckling, Appleyard, Elizabeth Fry and George Borrow. After the War, estates began to be named to specific themes, some more than a little bizarre. With no other connection than the name Tuck's Wood Farm on the 1834 Ordnance Survey, the Council decided to transplant the Robin Hood Legend to Lakenham and named the streets of characters from the folk tale. Elsewhere, later Council estates such as the Heartsease, returned to local celebrities such as Munnings, Rider Haggard and Paine. Developments around the Airport commemorated flyers or aircraft and the Council co-ordinated development

at Bowthorpe made a virtue of applying Norfolk dialect terms such as Bishy Barnebee, Pishmire and Dodderman. Finally, the relatively new suburb of Dussindale, within Broadland District, has curiously adopted a street naming system themed around the English Civil War. This is odd because the overall estate name Dussindale, relates to Ketts Rebellion which took place over 100 years before the Civil War, an event in which Norwich played very little part. With Norwich planned to grow by 30,000 homes over the next 20 or so years it will be interesting to see how the names of new housing areas reflect any elements of local distinctiveness and place.

Stringer, David

Norwich City footballer. Local boy (born in Great Yarmouth) Dave Stringer holds the 3rd place appearance record for the club with 499 appearances between 1965 and 76. After finishing his playing career with Cambridge United, he returned to Norwich, first as Youth Team coach then Reserve Team manager until

Barclays in Stump Cross prior to its demolition for Anglia Square.

taking over as club manager in 1987. During his tenure he managed to take Norwich into the top four in the old First Division in 1989 and achieved two FA Cup semi final appearances. Resigning in 1992 he returned again to be Assistant Director of Norwich City's Academy and finally retired in 2001.

Stump Cross

Lost feature. The name is associated with an area of the City, now lost, but formally opposite St Saviour's church, at the junction of Magdalen Street and Botolph Street (destroyed by Anglia Square in 1970). The site was originally the location of a stone cross, known in Henry VII's time as the Guylding Cross. In 1673, £20 was given to the parish to rebuild it. Just over 50 years later however, Kirkpatrick noted 'There is a piece of the lower part of the shaft of a stone cross now lying upon the top of St Saviour's churchyard wall next the lane leading to Rotten Row (Peacock Street) which is about a yard long and I suppose part of the old Stump Cross.' It can be assumed that the name derives from the fact that only a stump of the Cross remained. Today nothing survives of the Cross but the name is still in use.

Subterranean Norwich

See *Underground Norwich*.

Suckling House

Medieval merchant house. Suckling House is mainly a C15th merchants' building, which was once owned by John Cambridge who was both Sheriff and Mayor of Norwich. During the C16th the building was owned by the notable Suckling family who worshipped at St Andrew's church. Part of the property was eventually turned into the City Arms Pub that was partly demolished along with more of the Suckling home to make way for a tramway. The remaining building fell into disrepair but was saved in the early C20th by the Norfolk News Company and members of the Colman family. In the 1920s the Colman's built Stuart Hall, designed by the son of famous local architect Edward Boardman, on wasteland next to Suckling House and the buildings were used for a range of community purposes until Cinema City was opened in 1978. Following a major refurbishment, the new Cinema City, now run by the Picturehouse Group, opened in 2008, using Suckling House as the café bar and restaurant.

Suckling, Robert

Eminent citizen. Robert Suckling, born in 1520, was the eldest son of Richard Suckling, a baker and Alderman. Robert too became an Alderman, and was admitted to the Freedom of the City as a mercer. At various times he held the positions of Sheriff (1564), Mayor (1572 and 1582) and a Burgess in Parliament (1571 and 1586). The Suckling family's crest had been a buck or a stag and in 1578 Robert Suckling was granted the privilege to add a piece of honeysuckle to the crest. The Suckling Crest survives in the glass in the oriel window in the Great Hall of Suckling House. Robert's son Edmund became Dean of Norwich in 1614 – he was buried in Norwich Cathedral in 1628.

Interestingly, one of Robert's daughters, Mary, married John Hassall of St Peter's, Cornhill in London. She became the mother of John Hassall (junior) who succeeded Edmund Suckling as Dean of Norwich in 1628. Robert died in November 1589 and was buried in St Andrew's Church, where there is a monument commemorating him. In his will he left his messuage in the parish of St Andrew's (i.e. Suckling House), with all the adjoining lands and tenements, to his youngest son, John.

Suffield, Walter de

Philanthropist Bishop. Born in Norfolk, de Suffield was educated in Paris and consecrated Bishop of Norwich, at Carrow Priory in 1245. He was a generous man and used his consecration to appeal for funds to restore St Paul's. He was well regarded in the Royal Court and when, in 1247, Henry III carried the Holy Blood in a crystal vase from St Paul's to Westminster Abbey, Walter preached the sermon. His greatest legacy to the City was the Great Hospital, or hospital of St Giles, founded in 1249 for the care of 'poor and decrepit chaplains'. The institution was co-founded by William of Dunwich who provided the site.

In 1253 and 1254 Walter's status within the church is reflected in the fact that the Pope appointed him to complete a valuation of all property held by the clergy in England – the so called 'Norwich Taxation'. When he died, his will included extensive donations to the poor and needy and to hospital institutions.

Surrey Chapel

Lost chapel. The chapel was founded in 1854 by Robert Govett. In 1841 he was appointed curate of St Stephen's church, Norwich, but in 1845 he suffered a crisis of faith over baptism of infants. After witnessing baptism by immersion, he felt he could no longer baptise infants, resigned as curate and withdrew from the Church of England. A number of sympathisers followed him and he held services in Victoria Hall on St Andrews Street. The number of the congregation expanded so rapidly under his care that a new building became necessary. A large grey brick and split flint chapel called the Ebenezer Chapel (later known as the Surrey Chapel) was constructed between Ber Street and Surrey Road. It seated 1500 and was one of the largest chapels in Norwich. Govett paid for most of the cost of construction himself. The Ebenezer Chapel was non-denominational and offered extreme simplicity of worship, having no music, though there was a choir. The chapel was without a pastor from 1951 until 1963 and suffered a decline, but the congregation increased again after a new pastor was appointed in 1963. In the 1980s, the Victorian chapel was in need of repair and was eventually demolished to accommodate the expansion of the Bonds department store and car park so the congregation decided to relocate to Pitt Street. The new chapel has retained the name of the Surrey Chapel.

Top and bottom left: views of the Marble Hall, Surrey House.
Top right: Surrey House clock from the Great Exhibition. Bottom right: stained glass.

Surrey House

'Perhaps one of the finest, most beautiful non-ecclesiastical buildings in Britain'. Norwich Union

- One of the most elaborate marble interiors in the UK

- An Edwardian air conditioning system unique in its period

- Remarkable interior design elements including an Adam fire place, and a skeleton chiming clock made for the Great Exhibition in 1851.

Built on the site of the Earl of Surrey's medieval city house, and incorporating some recycled details from it, the Marble Hall was built between 1900 and 1904 as the new corporate headquarters of Norwich Union by local architect Edward Skipper. Although the exterior is a striking representation of the Palladian style, it is the interior, which portrays the English Renaissance at its most sumptuous. £6,000 worth of marble – a king's ransom at the time – was redirected from Westminster Cathedral for the project. The Main Hall provides not only the most striking architectural expression of the interior spaces but exhibits the greatest diversity of marble including columns of Cipollino and Verde Antico and wall panels of Skyros Rosso, Carrara and Rosso Antico capped with alabaster arches and entablature. The staircase has steps of Piastraccia marble, the handrails of Pavanazzo, other details of Breccian marble and wall insets of Istrian marble. Belgian Blue and Siennese marble, now worked out, decorate other parts of the Hall.

Swardeston

Rural Parish. Swardeston is a village located 6.4km (four miles) to the south of Norwich. It had a population of 540 in the 2001 Census compared to 378 (1901) and 277 (1801). It was mentioned in the Domesday when it had 34 households as well as a church (probably the surviving St Mary's) and a chapel. St Mary's is the village's oldest surviving building dating largely from a C14th rebuild but with a Norman nave and some earlier windows. The other key building in the village, or more accurately, in the manor of Gowthorpe is the listed Grade II* Gowthorpe Manor built as a timber framed house, by the Styward Family, around 1520. It was enclosed in brick and extended in 1574 and an east range was added in about 1630. At about the same time, a gazebo and barn were developed in the grounds. Further additions were made to the house in

1908. Over the years, the manor had been owned by the Boleyns, Augustine Steward and his son – referred to at the time as the Stywards – and Sir Thomas Berney. The manor was sold to the Steward family in the early C19th. The other manor of the parish is Mangreen where a hall dating from 1700 survives with a south wing developed in the C19th. Back in the village proper, the Croft at High Common (there are extensive High and Low Commons) is a C16th timber framed cottage, the Garden House is C17th while the Dog PH dates from 1700. The Old Rectory is C16th with C19th additions and includes a stair light with glazing bars incorporating panes of

C16th Norwich School glass depicting Kings of England from William I to Henry VII. The Old Cavell Vicarage, remembering the childhood house of Edith Cavell, dates from 1865.

Sweetbriar Marshes

Important open space.
This is a substantial 9.53 Ha (23.55 acre) Site of Special Scientific Interest (SSSI) located east of Sweetbriar Road and represents the best remaining example of a type of wetland habitat which at one time was more widely occurring in the river valleys of east Norfolk but which has been lost or progressively altered in post war years due to drainage and agricultural improvements.

Clockwise from top left: Swardeston – Garden House on the Common, Gowthorpe Manor, The Dog Public House and Cavell House.

Sweetbriar Road

West section of the Outer Ring Road. Sweetbriar Road was part of the Norwich Town Planning Scheme of 1925, approved in 1930, and formed a component of the 1930s public works schemes implemented by the Council to relieve unemployment. It was an element in the development of an Outer Ring Road for the City and in its early life, didn't have much in the way of development associated with it, essentially being constructed through what had been agricultural land or marsh. The adjacent areas, however, had signs of ancient occupation and an archaeological survey to the east of Sweet Briar road in 1982 provided evidence of Bronze Age Barrow and various associated finds including pottery and a Romano-British brooch. The road now links Farrow Road to Boundary Road and its key sites include the Sweetbriar Marsh open space, the extensive Bayer Crop Science site and the Sweetbriar Road industrial estate.

Sweyn Forkbeard

Danish King. Sweyn Forkbeard, King of Denmark, son of Harald Bluetooth and father of Canute the Great, came with a great fleet in 1004 and 'completely ravaged and burned the borough' (Anglo Saxon Chronicle)

Synagogue Street

Lost Street. Synagogue Street was the only street of that name in England – named after the synagogue that stood there from 1848. Joel Fox who was president of the Jewish congregation in Norwich and later became the first Jewish member of

Norwich City Council, laid the foundation stone. The building was designed by an architect called Bunn and was built by Gage and Underwood at a cost of £1,600. It was designed in an elegant classical style with a large pedimented and pillared entrance. Inside, the building was planned in a traditional way with an upper gallery for the women, with men seated separately around the walls on the ground floor. In September 1849 the synagogue was consecrated and nine years later a house and vestry was added for the Rabbi. When the census of places of worship was administered two years after the Synagogue's consecration, the return showed that twenty-four people attended on the day in question. The signatories of the return were Simon Caro and Myers Levine whose occupations appear in the City records as a linguist and silversmith.

The Jewish community in Norwich flourished during the late C19th and C20th despite the inevitable disruption caused by the First World War. The Second World War also had an impact upon the community. In 1942 the Norwich Synagogue was destroyed by enemy action. The

Jewish community of Norwich was dispossessed but did not lack offers of help. The congregation of the Octagon Chapel offered the use of their building, rooms were found in Redwell Street and members of the Christian Spiritualist Church in Chapelfield also offered their hall. After the war, in 1948, the current site on Earlham Road was found and rented from the Norwich Corporation. Restrictions on building and limited finances meant that initially only a prefabricated building was erected. Even so, several pillars from the Synagogue Street building had been salvaged and were incorporated in the new development as gateposts. These pillars can still be seen today at the entrance and exit of the Norwich Synagogue. In 1951 the community built a communal hall with a small flat above for the Rabbi. It was not until the 1960s that action was taken to replace the prefabricated synagogue building and in 1968 the current buildings were erected. The Norwich Hebrew Congregation now worships at this synagogue and follows a traditional orthodox Judaism with services in Hebrew.

From left: Plaque commemorating the lost street, Synagogue Street, prior to destruction during WWII.

Saints – the churches

This entry combines, in a unified section, all of the ecclesiastical institutions commemorating a saint thus providing a handy source and cross reference for virtually all of the churches and excluding only those without a specific 'saint' dedication (eg All Saints, Christchurch, Holy Trinity).

St Alban's Church, Grove Road.

St Andrew's, Colney.

St Andrew's, Eaton.

St Alban, New Lakenham

1930s church in Grove Walk. Designed by Cecil Upcher and built on Grove Road between 1932 and 1938 the church contains a font relocated from Knettishall in Suffolk, a bell founded in 1828 and relocated from Fulmodestone, a glazed nativity screen by Robert Hendra and an altar painting by Jeffrey Camp. Upcher also designed the vicarage to the east.

St Andrew, Colney

Suburban, Medieval parish church. Probably a pre Conquest foundation with a round tower and some potentially early work at the west end of the nave. The surviving building is predominantly C14th. Inside the attractive font is C15th and there is some rather odd glass dating from 1870 by Harry Wooldridge. There

is a C16th tomb chest to John Tomson in the sanctuary and a memorial to Richard Browne (d. 1674).

St Andrew, Eaton

Suburban, Medieval parish church. St Andrew's church, just off Church Lane, dates from the C13th with a C15th tower, and is the only thatched church within the City boundary. Its most notable features are a

St Andrew's, Kirby Bedon.

set of C14th wall paintings discovered during restorations in 1860 by Thomas Jekyll. The church also has an unusual extension on the south side built in 1993-3.

St Andrew, Kirby Bedon

Medieval parish church. Although a Norman foundation with C14th/C15th additions and retaining a few vestiges of its original structure, St Andrew's underwent a major reconstruction in 1876 at the hands of R.M. Phipson. Inside there is a C15th octagonal font, a C18th pulpit, an attractive wall monument of 1600 to Robert Sheppard, a tomb slab to Diocesan Architect Richard Phipson, who had been responsible for restoring nearly 100 East Anglian churches, and some stained glass including fragments of medieval glass.

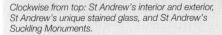

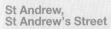

Clockwise from top: St Andrew's interior and exterior, St Andrew's unique stained glass, and St Andrew's Suckling Monuments.

St Andrew, St Andrew's Street

Medieval, Walled City church. The church of St Andrew, located on part of a former Roman road, St Andrew's Street, was a possible, pre Conquest foundation at a time when dedications to St Andrew were popular. The area around the church has yielded fragments of Anglo-Saxon pottery but the current church is much later in date. The 29m high (96 ft) tower was completed in 1477 and the nave, chancel and porches between 1499 and 1518. During the C15th

many of Norwich's churches were 'modernised' but St Andrew's was completely rebuilt. It was the last of the City churches to be 'updated' and John Antell, the mason, took his inspiration from St Peter Mancroft and built the second largest parish church in Norwich. There are some similarities between St Andrew and the rebuild of Mancroft notably the nave and chancel under one great roof; the large Perpendicular aisle windows, the two sets of 11 clerestory windows and the east window. Five panels of

C15th glass also appear in the east aisle windows.

Evidence of an earlier church at the site has survived. Documents dated 1386 and 1467 detail money given by parishioners to re-lead the roof of the church and to build a new porch. The eastern wall of the current church, facing onto St Andrew's Hill, also has a stone frieze from the earlier building reset into it. The frieze shows several shields including those of Bishop Henry Despenser (1370-1406), William Appleyard, first mayor of

Norwich in 1403 and the earliest known depiction of the coat of arms of Norwich.

The interior of St Andrew's was greatly restored in 1867 and the font, reredos (wall decoration behind the altar) and most of the furniture was installed during this restoration. The ornate sedilia (stone seat for the priests) set into the south wall of the chancel is C15th as is the screen to the tower. On the southern side of the chancel is a set of misericords. These chairs with folding seats have a built in 'pity shelf' on which clerics could lean during long services. These misericords are thought to have originated in Blackfriars, the Dominican Friary over the road and notably one of the seats has a carving of a monkey portrayed as a doctor. The same monkey doctor is also portrayed in the beautifully illuminated fourteenth-century East Anglian manuscript, the Macclesfield Psalter, which is in the Fitzwilliam Museum in Cambridge. Also of interest is the medieval stained glass panel in the south west window of the south aisle. This is one of possibly seven original panels and it shows a skeleton and a bishop dancing on an empty chessboard: the game is over and death has come to claim him.

St Andrew's church has the largest and finest collection of memorials of any of the City churches. Brasses next to the altar show Robert Gardiner and his wife. Gardiner was mayor of Norwich three times in the late C15th. The Suckling chapel at the east end of the north aisle contains a number of impressive monuments. A monument to Sir Robert Suckling, mayor of Norwich in 1572 and 1582 can be seen on the east wall and his daughter-in-law and son, Sir John, are commemorated in an elaborate marble tomb on the north wall. This rather macabre appearance, with its carved skulls and carving of a shrouded corpse, was fashionable at the time. Sir John held positions in the court of James I and Charles I, while John's son, also called John, was a famous poet and is depicted on the tomb at the head of his father and mother. The Sucklings were the ancestors of Horatio Nelson but are not the only members of the former congregation of St Andrews to have famous descendants. The ancestors of Abraham Lincoln are also said to have worshipped at St Andrew's and there is a monument to a man of that name. Three times mayor and burgess to Parliament Francis Rugge also has an elaborate memorial in the church. A remnant of his house survives in St Andrew's Street. Another local resident, whose house survives just across the street from the church, was Robert Garsett, who also has a more modest memorial in the church.

Several of St Andrew's former clergy led distinguished lives too, in particular Jacob Mountain and John Robinson. Mountain left England for Canada and in 1793 became the first bishop of Quebec. Nearly two centuries earlier Robinson had become the pastor of a group of Nonconformists who left England for the Netherlands in search of a place to practise their religious views without persecution. Encouraged by Robinson, many of this group were later to sail to the Americas on the Mayflower, becoming the celebrated Pilgrim Fathers.

St Andrew's Hall

The only intact English friars' church. In about 1250 the Friars de Sacco (Brethren of the Sac), or Friars Penitential, came to Norwich and William de Gissing gifted them a house opposite the church of St Peter Hungate. Subsequently the friars were given further land and in 1271 they were granted permission to build and worship on the site. Little evidence remains of the Friary now but it would have been located where Blackfriars' Hall now stands. Nevertheless, excavations in 1958 proved that the foundations of Beckett's Chapel, directly north of the Hall and east of The Crypt, are in fact the remains of a structure built by the friars. It would have been a simple single storey building with six small windows along its sides and a large east window with tall statue niches to either side. The southern wall also had a simple arched piscina (a stone basin used to pour away the water used during mass). The site was given to the Dominican Friars, or Black Friars, who had outgrown their site on Colegate, north of the River Wensum, provided that they took care of the former prior, William de Hoo, who was blind and too old to leave.

From top (left to right): The nave of the church of the Blackfriars (St Andrew's Hall) as it appeared in the C19th.
St Andrew's in Thorpe St Andrew – ruin of an earlier church and St Andrew's today, and St Andrew's in Trowse.

The Dominican friars flourished on the site and in 1310 built a priory for 60 friars and a church dedicated to St John the Baptist. The church was probably constructed around the earlier chapel of the Friars de Sacco and the 1958 excavations showed that the Dominicans added a rib vaulted ceiling, external buttresses, larger windows and an upper storey to the older chapel. Despite the addition, this new church was soon superseded and the lower floor became a chapel dedicated to St Thomas Becket while the upper floor became a library. The grand new church was built between 1325 and 1345 but stood for less than 70 years since in May 1413 the church and friary were devastated by fire. Ironically the library and Becket's Chapel survived the conflagration.

Plans were soon made to rebuild the Dominican Friary and the halls and buildings that we see today are the remains of that work. The C15th masons began by building a magnificent church, St Andrew's Hall was its nave and Blackfriars Hall its choir. Six windows from the earlier church survived the 1413 fire and five were incorporated in the new nave while one large window was set at the east end of the choir. Sir Thomas Erpingham, captain of the English archers at Agincourt, donated large amounts of money to the rebuilding. Erpingham's coat of arms can be seen between the clerestory windows of St Andrew's Hall. The Paston family, famous through the survival of many of their letters and papers, also gave generously, paying for the roofs of the halls and the C15th doors which bear their coat of arms. The tower was hexagonal and built over the chancel arch but unfortunately collapsed in 1712. The Friary cloisters were built to the north of the church and the cloister walks originally had an upper storey. The dormitory stood on the eastern side of the cloisters and the refectory, or dining hall, took up the western side.

When Henry VIII dissolved the monasteries in the 1530s a majority of the religious complexes in the country passed into secular hands and as a result the buildings have not survived. The Corporation, however, asked Henry if they could buy the Dominican friary buildings for £81 and by pledging to use the halls for the good of its citizens, for fairs and for feasting, most of the Dominican friary has survived intact. The nave of the church, St Andrew's Hall, became a banqueting hall and the choir, Blackfriars Hall, was later used for worship by Norwich's large Dutch community who had settled in the City to rejuvenate Norwich's textile industry. A memorial to the Dutch pastor, Joannis Elison, can still be seen on the wall of the hall. The King reflected on the deal and demanded a further £152 for the lead on the roof.

After the Dissolution of the Monasteries in the 1530s, the cloister buildings became granaries and storerooms and during the C17th the refectory was used for worship by Presbyterian, Baptist and Roman Catholic congregations. Between 1696 and 1698 the Norwich mint was established in the corner of the cloisters and minted £259,371 worth of silver coins. In the early C18th the former cloister buildings were employed as a workhouse; in the C19th they were used as a school that later became the City of Norwich School and at the beginning of the C20th they became the Norwich Middle Class School. Only the south, east and west ranges of the cloister buildings survive. The northern portion is taken up by a late C19th building designed by Norwich architect George Skipper as Norwich Municipal Technical Institute. This school later became Norwich City College and the building now houses the University College of the Arts.

During the Victoria period, the Halls were much restored but while much of the work did ensure the longer term survival of the complex, 'restoration' included serious acts of civic vandalism such as the demolition of the vaulted roof of Becket's Chapel, in 1876, and its infilling to the top of the walls. It remained 'hidden' until 1972 when it was excavated and in 1983 was covered by a polycarbonate roof.

Between them the Halls also hold a major part of the country's largest collection of civic portraits, totalling 127 late C16th to C19th paintings. The two-storey porch on the south side of St Andrew's Hall, heavily restored and rebuilt in the C19th, even became the home to a public lending library set up in 1716 and is said to be the first in the country. Despite all of these changes and probably because of the diverse civic uses to which the buildings were put, the Dominican friary complex survives as the best preserved in England.

St Andrew, Thorpe St Andrew

Suburban, parish church. Sitting close to the Yarmouth Road, the redundant C15th tower survives from the original medieval church, with ruinated remnants of the medieval structure, which probably date from the post Conquest period. A new church, just to the north, was designed by Thomas Jekyll in 1866 with the tower, by J.B. Pearce, following in 1882. An impressive set of eight bells was commissioned from the highly regarded bell founders Holmes, Moore and McKenzie but although hung in 1883, their first use was delayed until 1886, due to concerns about the ability of the tower to sustain the vibration from a full peal. Concern persisted after the first full peal and, in consequence, the last complete ring of eight in full circles was in 1886. A WWII air raid destroyed the substantial Victorian spire of the tower which was replaced by a pyramid in 1944. The 'new church' incorporates the original, C13th font and some memorials including one from 1810 to Elizabeth Meadows Martineau.

St Andrew, Trowse

Suburban, parish church. St Andrew's church was founded around 1281 by William de Kirkby and the most significant feature surviving from that period is the east window, made by Cathedral Master Mason Nicholas before 1288.

The chancel dates from the same period with the tower dating from the C14th and the nave from the C15th. The church was restored in the late Victorian period after a period of dereliction. Inside there is a C15th font, a monumental brass to Elizabeth Dalyson (1585) and a painting by Heins.

St Andrew, Whitlingham

Suburban, parish church. Ruinous remains of medieval parish church on a promontory at the extreme east end of Whitlingham Lane just before the Southern Bypass. The church became abandoned some time after the Reformation and there is speculation that Victorian tracery was the result of creating a picturesque ruin. Although there was a bequest for an octagonal belfry in 1620, surviving photographs show that this was never added, suggesting abandonment after this date. The Norman round tower with Norman arch and twin tower openings, collapsed in 1940 and all that survives now is the south wall of the chancel, with two windows, and the south wall of the nave.

St Anne's Chapel

Lost Walled City chapel. Standing close to St Anne's Staithe at St Ann Lane (curiously different spelling) on King Street, this early foundation survived until 1370 when it was demolished and the parish united with St Julians.

St Anne, Earlham

Suburban, parish church. Built on Colman Road to serve the new Council housing estate of West Earlham in 1927, the church was burnt out by wartime bombing in April 1942 and rebuilt as a simple red brick structure by C.H. Dann in 1951. It has a bell relocated from St Edmund in Fishergate.

St Augustine

Redundant, medieval, Walled City church. St Augustine's church mostly dates to the C14th/15th but is thought to be located on the site of a much earlier church as the proportions of the nave are similar to that of an Anglo-Saxon church. However, the most striking feature of the church is its much later distinctive C17th red brick tower – the only one of its kind in Norwich. So famous is the tower, that the parishioners of St Augustine's were formerly known as 'Red-Steeplers'. The tower was rebuilt in brick in the 1687 after the original tower's collapse ten years earlier. The original medieval sound holes were retained and incorporated in the new tower. A five bell frame was also installed inside the tower, although no more than three bells were ever hung. The church became redundant in 1998 and in the same year the three church bells were removed from the tower and taken to the village of Carleton Rode, Norfolk. Nevertheless, St Augustine's still has a congregation, which meets in the hall behind the church.

Inside, St Augustine's still retains some early features. A painted panel hanging at the church's west end is all that remains of the medieval Rood screen. The figure on this panel represents St Apollonia who is depicted holding a tooth in a pair of pincers. It was commonplace in medieval times to summon her aid in cases of toothache as St Apollonia suffered the torment of having her teeth forcibly extracted during her martyrdom. The church also contains two quite plain but significant monuments: one to Matthew Brettingham, the C18th architect of Holkham Hall, the other to Thomas Clabburn, a master weaver who died in 1858.

St Barbara's Chapel

Lost Guildhall chapel. The Guildhall was built in 1407 to accommodate the civic needs of the City, the law courts and the prison. Situated in the upper storey of the south eastern corner (near the current taxi rank), St Barbara's chapel was small, not big enough for the full needs of the council but adequate for prayer, private services and for the use of the prisoners. During the C16th and early C17th the chapel was neglected and religious imagery was smashed from the windows and replaced with plain green glass. Eventually St Barbara's was demolished in 1625 and, ironically, all that remains are fragments of C15th glass from its windows, now incorporated with later glass in windows of the Guildhall Council Chamber.

St Barnabas

Edwardian church in Heigham. Built in Russell Street in 1903-6 and designed by A.J. Lacey, the church is in the Mechanical Perpendicular style and includes attractive stained glass war memorial window.

St Bartholomew

Lost, Walled City church.
The church was probably a post Conquest foundation, being located outside the pre Conquest Anglo Scandinavian borough, on the east side of Ber Street. It was secularised after the Reformation but survived, miraculously, into the C20th. Architect Claude Messent sketched a plan of its surviving fabric in 1931 and George Plunkett photographed its interior. At that time the surviving nave and chancel were encased in other buildings including a factory, a slaughterhouse and some houses. It was bombed during the War and now only a stump of the tower survives.

St Bartholomew, Heigham

Ruined medieval church in Heigham. The church was the parish church for the hamlet of Heigham, located on Waterworks Road, and the substantive style of the building, which survived until the 2nd World War, is described as plain Perpendicular although it is likely that the original building was earlier, possibly pre Conquest. Nearby resident Bishop Hall was buried beneath the chancel and was commemorated by a monument. The church was gutted by the late April 1942 Baedeker Raids and all of the remains, apart from the 44 foot tall tower, were demolished in 1953.The remains are a Scheduled Ancient Monument.

St Bartholomew, Heigham

(New church) – See *Nelson Street Methodist Church.*

From top (left to right): St Andrew's, Whitlingham – complete ruin 2011 and ruined tower 1935, St Augustine's, St Augustines Street, the ruin of St Bartholomew Ber Street, St Barnabus, Heigham, and the ruined tower of St Bartholomew, Heigham.

From top (left to right): St Benedict's tower – only surviving remnant of the bombed church, St Benedict's font, before the War, St Benedict's as it appeared in 1935, St Catherine's, Mile Cross, St Clement, Colegate.

St Benedict

Medieval, Walled City church remnant. St Benedict's church tower stands alone in Wellington Green at the extreme western end of St Benedicts Street. The rest of the church was pulled down after sustaining severe bomb damage in April 1942. The south wall and roof collapsed, so the north aisle, nave and chancel were pulled down to leave only the tower. Thirty years later a thorough archaeological investigation determined the complete story of St Benedict's church. The late Alan Carter and his Norwich Survey team discovered four phases of development. The earliest building, dating to the C11th, was a simple rectangular nave with an apsidal eastern chancel. Religious activity on the site appears to predate this building, however, as three earlier burials were discovered. By the late C12th or early C13th the apsidal chancel had been replaced with a larger rectangular one and a western round tower had been added. The nave was later enlarged, engulfing the chancel, and a northern porch was added. This was probably completed by the beginning of the C14th. Later still, a five bay northern aisle was added to the nave, with a porch at its western end and a chapel at its eastern end. A southern porch was also built but no archaeological evidence was discovered to indicate a date for any of these later alterations. Nevertheless, photographic evidence of St Benedict's show that the church was built in the C15th Perpendicular style and medieval documentary evidence supports this date

The Victorian era prompted an aggressive restoration programme after the parishioners became increasingly concerned about St Benedict's state of repair. The church floor was replaced, as was the lead and tile roof. Sadly the exterior walls, except the tower and south porch, were resurfaced with mortar and some of the aisle pillars were replaced with iron posts. St Benedict's probably suffered one of the less sympathetic church restorations in Victorian Norwich.

St Botolph

Lost Walled City church. The dedication of St Botolph's suggests that the church was probably founded prior to the Norman Conquest. St Botolph was a popular Scandinavian dedication at this time and has strong East Anglian associations. He founded the monastery of Ikanhoe in the C7th and this is said to have been at Iken in Suffolk.

St Botolph is regarded as the patron saint and protector of wayfaring men, and churches dedicated to St Botolph were often built close to gates in City defences so that travellers setting out on a journey could stop at the church to pray for guidance and assistance for a safe trip. Likewise, they could offer their thanks upon a safe return. St Botolph's in Norwich was located on the street (now Botolph Street) that passed right through the original Anglo-Scandinavian defences of the town. The burh ditch, as these defences are known, is thought to date to the C10th, suggesting that St Botolph's was founded after this date.

St Botolph's was demolished and the parish amalgamated with St Saviour's in 1548. As a result of this, little is known about the building, but human bones were discovered at the site during building work in the 1960s. In the 1970s the rest of the site was destroyed without record to make way for the

Anglia Square development, making it impossible to discover more about the church's history although remnants of the church could still survive below ground.

St Catherine, Mile Cross

Suburban, parish church. Located on Aylsham Road, this substantial brick church was funded entirely from a gift by Violet Wills. The church was designed by architect Alban Caroe and the Queen laid the foundation stone in February 1935 with the church being consecrated subsequently in 1936. The bells were 'recycled' from the ancient church of St Mary at Coslany in the Walled City.

St Catherine

Lost Walled City church. This was dedicated to St Winewaloi or Winewaloy, also known as Winall. It was rededicated to St Catherine at Domesday. The church was given to the nuns at the Carrow Priory by King Stephen. The whole parish was almost depopulated by the Black Death in the middle of the C14th and the church became a subsidiary chapel of Carrow Priory. Stone remnants in the wall of Notre Dame School are likely to have been recycled from the remains of the church.

St Christopher

Lost Walled City church. This dedication is very rare with only nine pre Reformation examples existing in England. St Christopher's church was built by 1190 but little is known about the building because it burnt down before 1286. The former site of the church lay almost

directly in front of St Andrew's Plain, where a triangle of buildings now stands between Princes Street, St Andrew's Street and Redwell Street. The church was never rebuilt and the parish was divided up. Most of the land went to the church of St Andrew but a small portion went to St Michael-at-Plea. One of the C18th houses on the site of the church was used as the Rectory of St Michael-at-Plea. Some of the land was also taken up by the C16th Garsett House. The house is also called Armada House because it is claimed that its timbers come from an Armada ship wreck and it has a plaque bearing that name decorated with a ship on its southern chimney stack.

St Clement, Colegate

Redundant, medieval, Walled City church. It is probable that the church of St Clement was founded by Danish settlers as early as 900. Clement was a popular saint in Scandinavia. He was the patron saint of sailors and in many instances, as here, town churches dedicated to St Clement were sited near to a river at its main crossing point. Evidence suggests that the centre of C10th Danish activity in Norwich is likely to have been north of the Wensum in this area.

The parish of St Clement's was once vast and took in areas both inside and outside the C13th/14th City walls. It is evident that this church once held extensive influence. A number of other medieval parishes north of the Wensum (such as St George Colegate) appear to have been carved out of the original large parish of St Clement's. Not only did St Clement's claim tithe payments (one tenth of annual incomes paid to the church) from its own parish, but at one stage also claimed two thirds of tithes from land in these other parishes.

The church is built from flint with stone dressings, predominantly in the Perpendicular style of the late C14th early C15th. It also features a good example of 'Decorated' tracery in the eastern windows. This tracery is a Victorian replacement of original C14th stonework that had been damaged or eroded.

There are several important memorials in St Clement Colegate. Of particular interest is a monument in memory of John Harvey, a prominent manufacturer who was at various times elected sheriff, alderman and mayor. This tribute can be found close to the south door. Opposite, another memorial records Jeremiah Ives who was Mayor of Norwich in 1733. These families intermarried and lived at Numbers 3, 18 and 20 Colegate. There is also a memorial to the wife of Edmund Wood, mayor of Norwich during the C16th. Wood built the house now called the King of Hearts near Fye Bridge. His son was knighted by Elizabeth I and greeted her when she visited Norwich in 1578.

The churchyard contains a tomb to the parents of Matthew Parker who was the first Elizabethan archbishop of Canterbury. During Kett's famous rebellion in 1549, Parker is said to have preached in St Clement's churchyard against the uprising. Another tomb known as 'The Leper's Tomb' can also be found in the churchyard. Legend has it that a leper was buried here after being turned away by several other parishes while searching for a burial site when alive. Because of his acceptance at St Clement's he gave a number of parish houses to the rector, the income from which was to be used for the repair of the church forever. However, this tale remains uncorroborated.

St Clement, Conesford

Lost pre Conquest, walled City church. This pre Conquest foundation church was located half way along King Street on the east side, south of Abbey Lane. Also known as St Clement the Martyr or St Clement at the Well (from a nearby public well) it survived until 1472 when the parish was joined with St Julian. In 1550 Leonard Southerton and John Rede bought it and put it to secular use then sold it on to Thomas Keteringham nine years later. It had survived in 'private use' by the time the General History of Norfolk appeared in 1829 but was demolished subsequently. Archaeological investigations on the site revealed the bones of seventeen children and twenty-four adults and an indication of both high child mortality and poor physical health in the medieval population.

St Crowche

Lost Walled City church. Very little is known about St Crowche's church. The church was also known as St Cross as it was dedicated to the Holy Cross and the name Crowche is a corruption of the Latin word for cross – Crux. The church was built at some point before 1272 and had gone out of use by 1551. Several sources suggest that the building was demolished at this time but other dates for its demise include 1744 and 1838. Even the exact location of the building is uncertain. Possible sites include west of the junction of Exchange Street with St Andrew's Street; east of the junction or even straddling the end of Exchange Street. Human bones have been found to the east and during the C20th, a C13th font was dug up from the site, then the garden of St Andrew's Parsonage. The font was given to St Luke's church, New Catton, but when this church was rebuilt in the 1990s the font was dismissed as too ancient for the new church so was given away. Its new owners are a mystery. Other remains thought to originate from St Crowche's church lie on the north side of St Andrew's Street. Built into a flint and brick wall that makes up the western side of an office almost opposite the telephone exchange there is a medieval stone corbel. The corbel is carved in the form of a head and can be seen just behind the metal gates leading into a private car park. During the redevelopment of the site to the west of Exchange Street for Rumsey Wells Court, some wall and arch remnants were revealed at the rear of the site and an old crypt, possibly belonging to the church of St Crowche, was also disclosed, perhaps for the first time since the C16th.

St Cuthbert

Lost Walled City church.
Cuthbert was a monk who became abbot and later Bishop of Lindisfarne, Northumberland during the C7th. After his death on 20th March 687, Cuthbert was made a saint and was a very popular dedication in the Saxon and earlier medieval period, particularly in the northern parts of England. It is unusual, therefore, to find a church dedicated to St Cuthbert as far south as Norwich. This dedication does suggest, though, that St Cuthbert's church was probably founded prior to the Norman Conquest. Very little is known about the church as it appears to have gone out of use by 1492 when the parish was added to that of St Mary the Less. St Cuthbert's was demolished between 1530 and 1535 and the churchyard was leased to Thomas Godslave who built a house on the land.

The majority of information available about St Cuthbert's church has been gathered through archaeological excavation. Work on the eastern side of Upper King Street in 1939, 1952 and again in 1999 appears to have confirmed the site of the church. In 1939 a substantial flint rubble wall, almost 3m in height (9 ft), was discovered and probably represented part of the south wall of the church. The 1952 and 1999 investigations both uncovered human burials in the area suggesting the location of St Cuthbert's graveyard. Three excavations in the 1970s, however, failed to find any more evidence of the church

From top (left to right): Stonework remnants of the lost church of St Crowche in adjacent buildings, St Edmund's, Caistor St Edmund.

itself and it is likely that later activity on the site had destroyed most of the remains of the building. The site now has a number of typically Georgian buildings on it, which are used as estate agents and solicitor's offices.

St Cuthbert, Sprowston

Suburban Victorian chapel.
Built on Wroxham Road in 1886 by A.R.G. Fenning, this was intended originally as an overspill for the medieval Sprowston parish church of St Mary and St Margaret. It soon developed its own community and this has been sustained with a major refurbishment in 1990-2. Internal features of note include a reredos, dating from that refurbishment, painted by

local people and a medieval font, relocated from the redundant parish church in Kempstone, now a roofless ruin.

St Edmund, Caistor

Medieval parish church.
The church is located in the south east corner of the Roman Town and has stood in this location at least since the time of Edward the Confessor. Its rather unusual rendered exterior adorns a largely early C14th construction with the nave as probably the oldest part of the building and there have been several alterations to the church over the centuries, including the addition of red tiles taken from the walls of the Roman town. Inside there is a faint, large wall painting of St Christopher and a small

From top (left to right): Rarely seen south prospect of St Edmund's, Fishergate, St Edmund's, Old Costessey, St Edmund's, Taverham, St Etheldreda's, King St, looking west and St Etheldreda's interior.

one of St John. There is also an early C15th octagonal font.

St Edmund, Fishergate

Redundant, medieval, Walled City church.

Probably a pre-Conquest foundation, St Edmund's is the only church in Norwich dedicated to this East Anglian saint, who was martyred by the Danes shortly after their arrival in Norfolk in the late C9th. King Edmund of East Anglia tried to repel the attacks of the Danish raiders. He was captured in 870, and beaten before being tied to a tree and whipped while he continually called upon Jesus. The Danes fired many arrows into his body 'until he bristled with them like a hedgehog or thistle' at which point he was decapitated. His show of religious faith throughout this ordeal ensured his martyrdom and numerous miracles were attributed to him after his death. One of many locations put forward for the murder of King Edmund is Hellesdon to the north west of Norwich.

St Edmund's church was reputed to possess a number of relics of St Edmund including a piece of his shirt that was kept in a box of crystal. The church therefore became a popular pilgrimage place during the medieval period.

The church is in the ornate Perpendicular style of the late C14th but is simple in layout. It has a chancel, nave with south aisle and a rectangular tower that originally housed only one bell. It does, however, feature an impressive central wooden boss on its fine butt-purlin roof. Famous

Norwich architect Edward Boardman, who designed many of the City's Nonconformist churches during the C19th, replaced the earlier furnishings of St Edmund's with Victorian Gothic examples. These furnishings disappeared when the church went out of use. It eventually became a warehouse for a factory that had been bombed and was forced to move from its premises. The building fell into a bad state of repair and became redundant but was restored in 1992, when it was converted back into a church. The interior of the building has recently been modernised and is now used as a pregnancy advice centre.

St Edmund, Markshall

Lost, medieval church. Abandoned when the village of Markshall became deserted, ruinous by 1737 and eventually demolished for the railway in 1847, nothing now remains of this medieval parish church.

St Edmund, Old Costessey

Suburban, medieval parish church. The majority of the church is C14th in origin but with considerable Victorian renovation including the nave windows, which are replacements. The square tower has a C14th base and a conical topped stair turret on its south side. The top of the tower collapsed in 1768 and, principally through funding by Sir William Jerningham (of Costessey Park), it was rebuilt in 1800 in brick with a lead covered spire. The position of the tower, at the north west corner of the nave, is a result of the church being widened in the C14th. Four

of the towers five bells date from the mid C17th while the fifth dates from the 1520s. The porch is C15th with attractive flushwork. Inside there is a C14th font and Jacobean pulpit, recycled from Booton. The original rood beam survives and beneath, a C15th screen. There are several memorials to the Jerninghams including one in marble by Thomas Rawlins to Mary Jerningham (d. 1733).

St Edmund, Taverham

Medieval parish church. St Edmund's is a probable pre-Norman foundation, with a round tower. The church is recorded as having stood in Taverham in 1086, and this is supported by the survival of a Norman north doorway, although the chancel and south aisle would have been added in the late C13th/early C14th. Lightning struck the church tower in 1459 and the church would have sustained some substantial damage, as at this time the roof was constructed of thatch and wood. Considerable repairs and renovation are recorded throughout the C17th/18th. Inside there some stained glass dating from 1450, a medieval timber screen, medieval choir stalls and a late medieval communion rail.

St Edward

Lost, Walled City church. Located to the west side of King street between St Peter Southgate and St Etheldreda this church was probably pre-Conquest. It contained a cell for a female recluse on the north side, the remains of which were still visible at the start

of the C19th. By 1305 St Edward's had been joined with St Julian's church and was used as the chapel for Hildebrond's hospital until 1540 when it was desecrated. The church was demolished in 1547, though some ruins remained until 1738.There are no obvious remnants surviving.

St Elizabeth, Earlham

Suburban parish church. Built originally in 1938, on Cadge Road, for the expanding local authority housing population, the church was replaced by a new building in the 1990s. The church contains two stained glass windows by Lillian Shaw and a dramatic winged sculpture, by Rebecca Kemp, 'recycled' from the former wrought iron gates.

St Ethelbert

Lost Walled City church. Originally a pre Conquest foundation and located on Almary Green just inside the present Cathedral Close, the church survived the building of the Cathedral (unlike other earlier churches in or close to the precinct) but succumbed to the 1272 Riot, when it was burnt down. The parish was united with St Mary in the Marsh and when St Ethelbert's Gate was rebuilt, a chapel dedicated to Ethelbert was included above the gate.

St Etheldreda

Redundant, medieval, Walled City church. The surviving church is Norman. The church was rebuilt in 1305, and the chancel was repaired in 1376. Little of the Norman church remains, but it can be detected in the typically Norman aisleless nave, the zig-zag Norman string course in the north and south walls and in the rounded Norman archway inside the porch. The lower part of the tower is Norman with a Perpendicular top added in the late Middle Ages. The octagonal belfry dates from 1723. The porch is C15th Perpendicular and, just above the doorway, the coats of arms of donors to the church still advertise their piety and family connections. There is also a niche which was probably intended to hold a statue of St Etheldreda, Abbess of Ely. The location of the original sanctuary is indicated to the right of the doorway where the string course drops to a lower level. The original sanctuary which was probably apsidal was replaced by a rectangular church.

A hermit who offered advice on matters both religious and secular lived in the churchyard throughout the medieval period. Also in the churchyard, as recorded by Francis Blomefield, were the ruins of an almshouse which had been founded in 1611 for five poor widows.

At the Reformation in the mid-sixteenth century, St Etheldreda was granted to the mayor and citizens of the Norwich for a term of 500 years at an annual rent of four pence. It declined thereafter and by 1597 it was described as 'greatly ruinous'. It remained dilapidated until an energetic vicar in the 1880s took on the restoration of the church in the idealised medieval style. In 1884 the Norwich architect, Edward Boardman, carried out extensive restoration which included

replacing the thatch with tiles and in the process uncovered a long-forgotten rood-stair. Much of what is seen today dates from this period of restoration. The church was declared redundant in 1975 and has now been converted into artists' studios, and an upper floor, roof light, toilets and a kitchen have been installed.

St Francis, Heartease

Suburban parish church. Built on Rider Haggard Road in 1956 by J.P. Chaplin this low brick structure was designed to serve the expanding Heartease Estate. The bell, dating from 1636, comes from the Walled City church of St Benedict, gutted in April 1942 air raids.

St George, Colegate

Medieval Walled City church. It has been said that St George Colegate is perhaps 'the greatest example of medieval parish church architecture in Norfolk and one of England's best'. The church was probably established in the mid to late C11th or early C12th. The parish of St George appears to have been carved out of the earlier, larger parish of the nearby church of St Clement. The dedication to St George was popular after the first crusade of 1096, during which Richard I is said to have had a vision of St George who assured him of victory over the Saracens. Carvings in the spandrels (the roughly triangular space between an arch and the rectangular framework surrounding it) of the south doorway show St George being dressed in his armour by angels.

The church was mostly rebuilt between 1458 to 1513. Work began with the tower and nave, then a south porch was added giving access to the tower's upper stage and finally the chancel was rebuilt. John Antell, a mason of some renown has been recognised as responsible for the nave interior and he also completed work at the nearby churches of St Martin-at-Oak and St Michael Coslany. The expense of the work carried out at St George Colegate during this time reflects the wealth of the church's parishioners. The textile trade had brought wealth to Norwich and many of the City's merchants lived in St George's parish.

Inside the church are a number of points of interest. Featured in a south aisle window is a C15th roundel depicting a man sheltering from the rain. This scene was popular for medieval windows but they are usually found in people's homes rather than in a church. St George's also contains the C16th terracotta tomb of wealthy merchant Robert Jannys, twice mayor of Norwich. The tomb features the same moulding as was used in the famous Bedingfeld tombs at Oxborough and may well have been made by the same craftsman. A memorial tablet to John Crome, who founded the Norwich School of Painters, lies in the south aisle chapel. Crome lived in the parish and frequently brought his pupils to worship at the church. Additionally, there are monuments to John Herring (Mayor of Norwich in 1799) and the Calvert family, after whom nearby Calvert St is named.

St George, Tombland

Medieval Walled City church. St George Tombland is situated opposite the Erpingham Gateway, one of the main entrances into the cathedral precinct and as a result was often known as St George-at-the-Monastery-gate. It was also built across Hungate, a road possibly of Roman origins that formerly ran along the line of Princes Street and Tombland Alley. The church was probably one of the later churches to be founded within the medieval City because dedications to St George did not become popular until about 1095 when the first Crusade was undertaken. St George Tombland could have been built in the late C11th or early C12th but may have been built as late as the C13th when the first references are made to it in medieval documents.

Unlike most of Norwich's medieval churches, St George Tombland was not completely rebuilt in the C15th. The church retains its C13th nave and chancel but did not escape some redevelopment and enlargement. Between 1430 and 1450 the tower was replaced and in 1445 the north porch was added. Shortly after this, the north aisle was built and at the end of the C15th the south aisle and porch were added. The nave retains its C13th hexagonal Purbeck marble font and the central window of the north aisle is in the Decorated style of the late C13/14th. It is likely that this window was once part of the earlier church but was moved to the north aisle when it was built. The columns of the north arcade

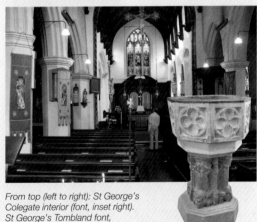

From top (left to right): St George's Colegate interior (font, inset right). St George's Tombland font, stained glass and interior.

are not positioned opposite those in the south arcade which is unusual but probably reflects the piecemeal redevelopment of the building and that the

north and south aisles were added at different times.

St George's church has been restored several times over the years and the interior furnishings reflect

From top (left to right): St Giles interior and north side, St Gervase and St Protase, Little Plumstead. St Gregory's – interior, now an arts centre, in 1825 with spire still intact, St Gregory's south side, and the outstanding medieval mural.

this. In the north aisle is a Flemish or North German painted panel showing St George and the Dragon, which dates from the mid C16th. The cover to the font is C17th in date, as is the ivory inlaid oak pulpit. The wooden chancel reredos, the screen behind the altar, dates to about 1730 and is one of only three similar examples remaining in Norwich. More often the modest Georgian screens were replaced by more ornate Victorian ones and the survival of this one owes much to Ewan Christian who restored the building in 1883. A small amount of medieval stained glass is also preserved in the middle window of the south aisle. A roundel depicting 'Spring' from a series called the Labours of the Months lies below another roundel containing fragments of medieval glass.

Most noteworthy is the collection of monuments within St George Tombland. The earliest monument, dated 1609, can be found by the font and commemorates John and Olive Symonds. The Symonds left money so that bread could be doled out to the poor of the parish every week. Beneath their monument is a 'dole table' or 'bread table' from which the bread was handed out. The practice continued until 1890. In the chancel is a monument to Mary Gardiner who died in 1748. The monument is by the Flemish sculptor, Peter Scheemakers, who is probably best known for his sculpture of Shakespeare in Westminster Abbey. Next to the organ in the former Lady Chapel of the north aisle is the Anguish monument created by the renowned sculptor Nicholas Stone. It commemorates Thomas Anguish who died in 1617 and who lived in a house on the site of the Maid's Head Hotel in Tombland. Anguish was mayor of Norwich in 1611 but it is for founding a children's Hospital to care for and educate the poor children of the City that he is most celebrated. The resulting boy's and girl's hospitals closed in 1941 Anguish's legacy continues to this day with the work of the Anguish Education Foundation.

St George, Sprowston Road

Modern, suburban Catholic church. The only Roman Catholic place of worship in Norwich apart from the Catholic Cathedral, St George was built in 1962 and designed by A.J. Chaplin.

St Gervase and St Protase, Little Plumstead

Medieval parish church. Little Plumstead's church St Gervase and St Protase is the parish's oldest building, and interestingly the only church in the country to be dedicated to these saints. The church has a Norman round-tower dating from 1150 and a nave from 1120. Although Victorianised in 1851 the building retains much of its original character. Inside there is a C17th font, stained glass by Robert Allen from 1834 and monuments to Sir Edward Warner (1565) and Thomas Penrice (1816).

St Giles

Medieval Walled City church. St Giles boasts the tallest tower in Norwich at 120 feet, completed, with the rest of the reconstruction, a little earlier than the other rebuilds, by about 1430. It does not share the open nature of the former examples since it lost its chancel in the C16th and it was not replaced until the Victorian period. Additionally, the clerestory windows are widely spaced. Most noteworthy features are the striking nave hammer beam roof, supported by large winged angels on the hammers, and the elaborate fan vaulted roof in the porch – a unique feature in Norwich.

St Gregory

Redundant, Medieval Walled City church. One of the earliest pre Conquest foundations in the City, St Gregory's preceded the other churches along St Benedicts but is first recorded in 1210. The chancel dates from 1394 and the church experienced a massive program of rebuilding in the Perpendicular style in the C15th. During the first half of the C15th the chancel, nave and aisles were all altered and, unusually, porches were added to the north and south sides of the tower. The tower also dates from the C15th and carried a spire until 1840. Known for providing sanctuary, St Gregory's retains its wonderful C14th sanctuary ring or door knocker, now on the vestry door. Its design shows a wolf holding the head of a man with a forked beard. This is probably St Edmund, the C9th King of East Anglia, who is often depicted with a forked beard and is the patron saint of wolves, kings, plague sufferers and torture victims. St Gregory's also contains a nicely decorated C15th font; a brass eagle lectern dated 1493 and four striking misericordes. Of particular note, however, are its C15th wall paintings. On the entire west wall of the north aisle is a depiction of St George and the dragon, and recently, paintings of the Annunciation, St Ambrose, St Augustine, St Gregory and St Jerome have been discovered. These paintings are remarkable and some of the best C15th paintings in the country. The church is now used as an arts centre and is in the stewardship of the Norwich Historic Churches Trust.

St Helen

Medieval Walled City church. The church of St Helen and the Great Hospital were established in 1249 when Bishop Walter Suffield decided to found a hospital for the sick and poor clergy of Norwich. In doing so, Suffield demolished the original parish church of St Helen that stood within the cathedral precinct on the south side of Bishopgate and constructed his hospital beyond the cathedral precinct on the north side of Bishopgate. A substantial flint wall of the pre Conquest church survives in the north wall of No. 44 The Close. Only a small portion of Suffield's original building, the simple southern porch to the church, survives. The remaining parts of the church and hospital date to a redevelopment during the late C14th/early C15th.

From top (left to right): St Helen's – south side, interior detail, pew end detail of St Margaret of Antioch, the patron saint of women in childbirth – a curious choice for an elderly people's caring institution, and ceiling bosses.
Wall remnants of the lost church of St Helen, Bishopgate.

The hospital buildings and layout resemble those of a monastery or priory and are set around a small cloister. On the south side of the cloister is St Helen's church with a nave plus three-bay north and south aisles; a south porch, south transept; and an unusually large chancel. On the opposite end of the nave to the chancel is an equally large aisled infirmary hall and on its south west corner, a tower. The tower was built in 1375 after a bequest by John Derlington who was the Master of the hospital from 1372 to 1375 and the chancel was built in the 1380s by Bishop Despenser. It was completed by 1385 in time for the visit of King Richard II and his queen, Anne of Bohemia. The 252 panels of the roof are decorated with eagles and these are said to be Anne's emblem. In 2003 roof timbers from the nave and south aisle were dated through tree ring dating techniques (dendrochronology) to between 1378 and 1403. Previously the nave was thought to have been built along with the south transept by Bishop Goldwell in about 1480. The nave contains fine furnishings including a C17th table, a mace rest and an interesting collection of both bench and box pews. Some of the bench pews are C16th with poppy head carvings to their ends and one has a carving of St Margaret emerging from the dragon. The south transept contains a box pew of the Ivory family that is inscribed with the date '1780' and the name 'William Ivory'. William Ivory was the son of the famous architect who designed St Helen's House within the grounds of the Great Hospital, the Tabernacle, the Octagon and the Assembly House. The transept also boasts a spectacular stone vaulted roof with a central boss of the Virgin Mary surrounded by bosses of the Nativity, Annunciation, Ascension and the Resurrection. In turn these bosses are surrounded by St Catherine, St Edward, St Edmund, St Margaret and each of the twelve apostles.

During the 1530s Dissolution of the Monasteries, the hospital of St Giles and the church of St Helen were taken from the cathedral priory by Henry VIII but returned eventually to local control. When the hospital was re-founded the medieval buildings were modified. The church was reduced in size by separating off the chancel with a wall and turning it into a dormitory for the female patients. Access from the church into the Infirmary Hall was also blocked and the infirmary was turned into lodgings for the male patients. To increase capacity, both the chancel and infirmary were divided into two floors and a fireplace was inserted at either end. By 1839 both floors of these halls had been divided into individual cubicles with a small living room next to the fires. By the late twentieth century the ground floor of the chancel was named the Pump Ward and the first floor the Eagle Ward, the ground floor of the infirmary was called Parker Ward, and the first floor Fawcett Ward. In the 1970s the residents were re-housed in modern flats nearby but most were sad to leave their comfortable little bed-sits

From top (left to right): St James Cowgate, interior in the 1930s, C14th font, and in its new guise as the Puppet Theatre.

in the medieval hospital. The core of the building remained as the parish church and the church for the residents of the Hospital.

St Helen

Lost medieval church.
Located on the south side of Bishopgate, west of the current St Helen's, the church was a probable pre Conquest foundation. It was absorbed into the Cathedral precinct, along with St Mary in the Marsh and St Ethelbert, but eventually demolished in 1270. Substantial sections of flint wall, probably forming part of St Helen's, survive to the rear of 60a/61 The Close and form part of the north wall of 44.

St James, Carrow

Lost medieval church.
Located near the junction of King Street and Bracondale, this was a fishermen's church but disappeared centuries ago and nothing remains of it today.

St James, Cowgate

Redundant, medieval, Walled City church.
St James is correctly known as SS James as it is dedicated to two apostles: St James the Great (also patron saint of Spain) and St James the Less (first bishop of Jerusalem.) The church is of Norman origin but the earliest documented reference to this parish dates to 1180.

During the C14th a porch was added to the church, although this is not in use today. It was built slightly to the east of the current porch entrance. Also in the C15th, a rood-stair turret was built into the north wall of the nave and the present tower to the west of the church was added. In 1743, the distinctive upper octagonal part of the tower was built on a flint square and the original south wall of the nave was knocked down to accommodate the south aisle.

During the medieval period two local guilds used the church and through their generosity the church became relatively wealthy. However, from the C17th onwards the affluence of the Pockthorpe area, in which the church stands, began to decline. It became poorer still from the C18/C19th and Pockthorpe became a recognised slum. During this period policemen reputedly would not dare to patrol the area alone.

SS James was converted into a puppet theatre during 1979-80. It is one of only two puppet theatres in England and has, by their own assertion, 'the best facilities of any puppet theatre in the UK'. Work done during the conversion of the building showed that the church originally consisted of an aisle-less nave with a long narrow chancel made of roughly knapped flint.

St John the Baptist, Colegate

Lost Walled City church. The church of St John the Baptist probably originally occupied the site just to the west of the Octagon

From top (left to right): St John and All Saints, Old Lakenham, south side and north side. St John Maddermarket – tower west side, interior, and monument.

chapel. The Dominicans, or Black Friars, arrived in the area in 1226 and acquired the northern side of Black Boys Street in the parishes of St George and St Clement. They took over St John the Baptist church and founded a Priory. Through gifts from various wealthy citizens of Norwich the Friars eventually owned land that ran from the river at the south to the church at the north. This land was enclosed by a large wall in 1281 but the popularity of the Dominicans meant that they continued to receive substantial gifts of land. In 1308 they moved to the site that is now St Andrew's and Blackfriars' Halls. The church was then used as a chapel and was looked after and lived in by a hermit. When Henry VIII dissolved the monasteries in the 1540s St John's was granted to the City but was demolished in 1540.

St John (Catholic) Cathedral
See Cathedral of St John the Baptist.

St John the Baptist and All Saints, Old Lakenham
Suburban, medieval parish church. The oldest parts of the church date from the C13th, however the unbuttressed tower dates from the C15th and bears a remarkable similarity to the towers at Trowse and Arminghall which all stood on estates belonging to the Cathedral Priory and, in all likelihood, were the work of Cathedral masons. The north porch dates from 1824, the south aisle was rebuilt in 1825 and the chancel was constructed in 1864 by John Brown. The

bulk of the church is constructed of flint but the chancel is of brick construction and rendered with a hard cement. The church contains a C14th font and an imposing monument to William Crowe dated 1778.

St John the Evangelist
Lost Walled City church. This church was situated at the corner of Rose Lane and King Street. It was bought by the Greyfriars and demolished in around 1300. The hermit who dwelt in the churchyard was allowed to remain in the anchorage and was permitted to use the churchyard as his garden.

St John Maddermarket
Redundant, medieval Walled City church. St John's was possibly founded in the Anglo-Scandinavian period, although there is no firm evidence to support this. The beautiful east window, dated to around 1340-1350, now contains Victorian stained glass but is the finest and most complete example of a C14th Decorated style window surviving in a Norwich church today. Nevertheless, the window is not in its original place and was possibly put there during Elizabethan alterations. The majority of the present building belongs to a major redevelopment campaign of the late C15th from which period some glass survives in the north aisle windows. Of particular note is the unusual design of the north porch, which makes it look octagonal in shape, and the lack of a chancel. The chancel is thought to have

been demolished, along with the original churchyard walls around 1578 when St John's Street was widened in preparation for Elizabeth I's visit to Norwich.

St John's contains a particularly impressive collection of monuments and possibly the finest collection of brasses in Norwich. Nicholas Sotherton, mayor of Norwich in 1539 and owner of Stranger's Hall, is one of several mayors commemorated. A plaque to Lady Margaret, the second wife of the fourth Duke of Norfolk was only erected in 1791 by her ancestors. Until then, Lady Margaret's death in 1563, aged just twenty three while visiting Norwich, had been overlooked for more than 200 years. There is also a plaque to Walter Nugent Monck, founder of the Norwich Players and the Maddermarket Theatre, who died in 1958.

St John Maddermarket is managed by the Churches Conservation Trust and is no longer used for worship. It remains consecrated but is now used as a display church. For a time prior to this the church was used for worship by the Greek Orthodox community of Norwich.

St John de Sepulchre
Medieval Walled City church. The original church was probably a pre Conquest foundation and is mentioned in Domesday (1086). The church was probably founded during the reign of Edward the Confessor (1042-1066) by Bishop William of Thetford. Bishop Eborard bought the advowson (the right to

nominate the priest and receive an annual income from the church tithes) and gave it to the Cathedral Priory for maintenance of the infirmary. The church we see today was built in 1472 and was restored in 1866.

The tall tower is C15th and built in three steps or stages. The flushwork parapet and corner pinnacles date from 1901. In 1492 the church fabric was enriched by Robert Cok who bequeathed lead for the roof. The groined porch is C15th with a parvise, its flintwork is knapped and squared. There are two friezes of shields over the doorway of the porch. The nave windows are in the C15th Perpendicular style and provide a striking contrast to the flatter arches in the later chancel windows. The corner of the chancel has been cut back to allow heavy market day traffic to pass by.

The church is entered through the porch and the carved medieval inner door. The narrow recess to the south of the tower arch was used for storing staves on which processional banners were carried through the street. The font is in the East Anglian style and decorated with lions. The chancel is hidden by a curtain and contains several wall monuments and a medieval consecration cross on its south wall. The church also contains a palimpsest brass of the arms of George II.

St John de Sepulchre underwent extensive reconstruction from the mid C15th. Largely paid for by parishioners, the new nave was complete by 1475 and building work started almost immediately on the chancel.

By 1492, when a bequest was received for leading the roof, work began on two transept chapels, the southern one being described as 'new' at the turn of the century. Work on the north chapel commenced in 1536, just before the Dissolution irrevocably altered the form and function of the parish church.

Additional alteration took place during the high church Oxford Movement in the C19th. Pews, a painted rood screen, choir stalls, a new organ, an elaborate reredos and a stained glass window over the altar were all added in the C19th. When a window dedicated to the memory of the Reverend Samuel Stone was erected by church members in 1914, it was hoped that the sight would provide "an opportunity of cultivating taste in a poor parish".

The church was declared redundant in the 1980s but underwent extensive repairs to the fabric of the building to reduce further deterioration. It was leased to the Russian Orthodox Church and had been rededicated to St John the Theologian. It is now vacant.

St John, Timberhill

Medieval Walled City church. Once known as St John at the Castle Gates, the church was the burial place for prisoners from the gaol. The church was probably founded in the C11th by the priest Wodowin who gave it to the Norwich Benedictine Priory. The church possibly dates from around 1070; certainly the north-east corner of the chancel dates after 1066 as

it uses Caen stone which was introduced to Norwich by the Normans. Archaeological investigations in 1989 found a bell founding pit and fragments of bell moulds in the graveyard to the north of the church. The Timberhill area of Norwich, in addition to hosting the timber market, housed a number of bell founders in the C15th who also made goods from copper alloy. In the cell to the north of the tower dwelt an anchorite.

The church is made of flint with stone and brick dressings and on the corners of the east wall of the chancel C11th long and short work survives. The present church dates from 1420 and is in the early-fifteenth-century Transitional style between the Decorated and the Perpendicular, though the east window is in the earlier Decorated style. In 1794 the tower collapsed. All of the windows were restored in the C19th. The concave part of the south side of the churchyard wall is where there was a well or pump.

By the C19th the church was in disrepair. However, when Father Ram arrived in 1871 he undertook to restore the church and recreate a medieval interior; he is said to have carved one panel of the pulpit himself. Inside the church is a plain Norman font with a modern font cover. The brass chandelier, which dates from c1500, is German or Flemish and depicts the Virgin and Child amid the branches of the 'mystical vine' at its centre. The life size statue of the Virgin by the south chancel pier was by a local Norwich artist, Martin Travers. The Stations of the Cross and the Oberammergau rood were restored and repainted by artists in the congregation.

Of the memorials in the church, the north-east corner of the sanctuary contains a memorial to Robert Page, the gifted Norwich sculptor who carved the wall tablet himself. His work is to be found in many Norfolk churches and in this example, his death in 1778 is mourned by a putto. One of the best wall tablets in Norwich is also found in St John the Baptist. In the north wall of the nave is an inscription to the Elizabethan benefactor John Forster, whose donations to the church continue to aid repairs.

St Julian

Medieval Walled City church. Today's church has been substantially rebuilt after the original was bombed during the Second World War. Reconstruction included rebuilding the cell and shrine to Mother Julian of Norwich who lived at the church for four decades. Mother Julian wrote 'Revelations of Divine Love' in 1396, the first book written in English by a woman. The church doesn't take its name from Mother Julian, rather she adopted the name of the church when she began her life there as an anchoress. It is probable that the church is dedicated to St Julian the Hospitaller, the patron saint of ferrymen; though some assert it is dedicated to the Norman bishop Julian of Le Mans.

The church was a pre-Conquest foundation,

From top (left to right): St John de Sepulchre interior when used as an Orthodox church, St John Timberhill interior, and St Julian's in 1933 prior to wartime bombing and reconstruction.

probably one of the oldest churches in Norwich. Its round tower remains though it is now half its original height. St Julian's was neglected and fell into disrepair until, in 1845, the east end of the chancel collapsed. The church was repaired during the C19th by the Oxford Movement.

During reconstruction of the church in 1953, two early, circular windows were revealed in the north wall. The cell and shrine have been rebuilt close to the site of the original cell which was destroyed during the Reformation. The window

between the cell and the chancel is in its original location although there would not have been a connecting doorway. The doorway entry to the cell is Norman and was taken from St Michael at Thorn which was destroyed in the same air raid that destroyed St Julian's.

The C15th font was relocated from All Saints. The high altar reredos dates from the 1930s and is from Oberammergau, a town in the south of Germany long famous for its exquisite woodcarving and religious pageant.

From top (left to right): St Laurence – rare view of west tower elevation, interior, vaulted ceiling of north porch, detail of martyrdom of St Edmund on west door. St Margaret's Drayton.

continuous hammer beam roof sitting above a great space lit by 11 clerestory windows, large aisle windows and a great east window are typical of the period. Also, fragments of surviving medieval glass have been brought together in one of the east windows. The 112 foot high tower is also typical of the Perpendicular Norwich type (with the exception of the unusual Victorian spirelet feature over the stair turret). The chancel is distinguished from the rest of the building by the more elaborate design of its arches and by a rood screen and rood loft. The chancel steps were added by the Victorians, as was the impressive eastern window dated 1894.

There are several interesting monuments in the church, including Geoffrey Langley, Prior of Horsham St Faith's who died in 1436 and a 'skeleton brass' of Thomas Childes, a priest, dated 1452. A more recent memorial is a brass in the eastern end of the northern aisle. It commemorates Sarah Anne Glover who developed a method for teaching music (the Norwich Sol-Fa). She died in 1867 but has been little recognised for her achievements.

Of particular interest on the outside of the building is the decoration above the western doorway of the tower. The spandrels in either side of the arch depict St Edmund (on the right) and St Laurence (on the left). Laurence was cooked to death on a gridiron in 258 and it is said that his mummified head is kept amongst the collections of the Vatican.

St Laurence

Redundant medieval church in the Walled City.
On the former site of an ancient fishing quay, the church of St Laurence was built between 1038, when the site is described as land in Bishop Aelfric's will, and 1086, where the church is mentioned in the Domesday Book. Nevertheless, the present church bears little resemblance to this early structure, owing most of its Perpendicular style and design to a piecemeal rebuilding in the late C15th. Almost equal in size to St Andrew, St Laurence, rebuilt by 1472, resembles it in many ways. Again the

St Leonard's Priory

Thorpe Hamlet. Dedicated to St Leonard (a French noble), the priory was founded by Herbert de Losinga, before he built the Cathedral. It was a 'cell' of, and dependent on, the Cathedral Monastery, and was inhabited by associated Benedictine monks (a Prior, with several monks) who maintained the Priory through the receipt of donations. It is thought that such gifts and bequests were almost entirely responsible for the Priory's survival. The friars of St Leonard's Priory used the adjacent chapel of St Michael on the Mount to perform their daily ceremonies. Despite its following and success, the Priory was closed at the Reformation and the site was passed to the Crown. In 1538 it was granted to Thomas, Duke of Norfolk. The Duke's son, Henry Howard, Earl of Surrey, built Surrey House on this site soon after this. However, after Henry was beheaded in 1547 for 'treasonous activities', the site again came into the hands of the Crown.

In 1562, Queen Elizabeth I granted St Leonard's Priory and the site surrounding it to the Duke of Norfolk (the son of Henry Howard) and his heirs. Despite this, the family largely abandoned the area, and the once grand Surrey House was left derelict. Other houses were periodically built on the site, perhaps incorporating parts of the Earl's original residence.

Of the old priory, only a few fragments of wall remain today, on private land but these are preserved as a

Scheduled Ancient Monument. There is also a very early, 160 feet deep well, south-west of the site.

St Luke, New Catton

Suburban, parish church. Originally built in 1913 by C.J. & A.C. Blomefield, St Lukes was demolished and rebuilt in 1991.

St Margaret in Combusto

Lost Walled City church. St Margaret's was an early foundation at the northern end of Magdalen Street and was the most northerly church in the medieval Walled City. 'In Combusto' translates as 'in the burnt area', possibly a reference to the Viking raid of King Sweyn of Denmark in 1004, during which he comprehensively burned large parts of Norwich or alternatively the name relates to damage resulting from one of several fires recorded to have damaged the City during the medieval period.

The church has also been identified by a further suffix: 'ubi sepliunteur suspensi', which translates as 'where those who have been hanged are buried'. Evidence from excavations of St Margaret's graveyard in 1973 and 1987, when 436 undisturbed bodies and the remains of 4-600 others were excavated, supports this proposition. Bodies were found buried face down with their hands behind their backs, implying that they had been tied as a criminal might. In addition, the church stood just 100m inside the City's defensive walls and near to Magdalen Gate, outside which the common gallows were

located. Evidence was also uncovered that a significant number of local residents are likely to have died from plague or an epidemic.

St Margaret's ceased to be used for worship by the end of the C15th. The parish was added to that of All Saints Fyebriggate (c 1468) and the church is likely to have been demolished by the C16th. Little of the building was recorded during the excavations in the late C20th as it had been destroyed during the construction of the Norwich Blind Institute cellars in the C19th. The only possible traces of the church were some flimsy flint footings and some C14th painted window glass

St Margaret, Drayton

Medieval parish church. St Margaret's dates from the C13th, although the tower collapsed in 1850 resulting in extensive restoration with the tower being rebuilt in 1852 followed by the nave and aisles in 1860 and the chancel in 1866. A stone entrance to an old stairway, which had existed prior to the restoration, was rescued after the addition of an aisle and the moving of the chancel and this entranceway now stands alone in the north arcade. Inside there is some medieval and C17th glass.

St Margaret, Newbridge

Lost Medieval, Walled City church. St Margaret Newbridge is known to have stood off St Georges Street, near to the river, by the year 1157. In 1349 the plague arrived in Norwich and depopulated the parish, after which the parish church was converted in to a hermitage chapel. The hermit in residence took charge of the bridge on St Georges Street. The building was demolished some time in the mid to late C14th and by the mid C19th the site was occupied by Weston's brewery. The site is now occupied by the Playhouse Theatre.

St Margaret, Old Catton

Medieval, suburban parish church. Although the parish is mentioned in the Domesday Book, there is no reference to a church. It is probable that the surviving round tower, and indeed the original church, date from the late C11th and Victorian records refer to apparent C11th Caen stone remnant mouldings which had been reused in a nearby barn. The present nave was built in 1350 with the clerestory added in the C15th although most of the church was restored or rebuilt by Robert Kitton in 1850-2. Slightly later, the unusual North Transept was added, extending the seating capacity but orientating half of the congregation southwards, out of view with the altar. The linenfold pulpit, dated 1537, was relocated from St Georges Colegate. There is an impressive selection of monuments, including the Greene family (1745) and Mayor Jeremiah Ives (1820). There is also a good range of Victorian glass (much of it from the King studio in Norwich), including a commemorative window to the Bignold family.

St Margaret de Westwick

Redundant, Medieval Walled City church. St Margaret's church is first recorded in 1254 and is often mentioned with its neighbour St Swithin's. It has had a turbulent history and, as with most of Norwich's other churches, was extensively redeveloped in the C15th. During the Second World War both the tower and the main body of the church were damaged during bombing raids but the tower's ornamental tracery survived. The tower was repaired in 1948 and the remainder of the church was restored by 1951. Since then it has had all of its bells removed, four being sent to St Andrew's church in Holt and the rest going to Morley St Botolph. St Margaret's was even used as a gym in the 1980s but is now used as an art gallery periodically.

Excluding the tracery on the tower, St Margaret's C15th structure bears few particularly remarkable features, possibly due to the twentieth century restoration. Points of interest, however, are the C15th decorated door and a medieval stone cross set into the north wall of the modern vestry. This cross likely originates from the churchyard.

More impressive is the collection of furnishings that St Margaret's held prior to it falling redundant in the 1970s. The C14th octagonal font had a beautifully carved bowl with shield decoration inside quatrefoils and further quatrefoils were carved on its deep base. There was also an intricately carved

C15th wooden chest very similar to one at Licham church. An C18th reredos showing the Ten Commandments flanked by Moses and Aaron hung above the south doorway and parts of a C17th communion rail were incorporated in the tower screen and gallery.

St Mark, Lakenham

Suburban, Victorian parish church. Built by John Brown on City Road in 1843-4 in the Perpendicular revival style, to serve the expanding extra mural suburb of New Lakenham, it was extended by the same architect 20 years later with the provision of an apse and vestry. Inside there is a striking art nouveau Bignold Rood Screen.

St Martin in the Bailey

Lost Walled City church. This church was also known as St Martin in Baliva, St Martin at the Bale, St Martin at Ber Street, and St Martin at Timber Hill. It was situated close to the site of the former Golden Ball public house. Of ancient foundation, it was, according to Francis Blomefield, "given by the Conqueror to that Ralf Fitzwalter who is mentioned in Domesday". The church held the right to bury everyone who died in the castle, plus all executed criminals. After the church was demolished in 1562 (the bells and lead reaching the princely sum of £76) its burial rights passed to St Michael's at Thorn and St John Timberhill.

St Martin at Oak

Redundant, medieval, Walled City church. St Martin at Oak was probably founded in around 1100 and by the mid C14th had gained the name 'at oak'. 'At Oak' was coined from an oak tree growing in the churchyard that had a branch that was said to have grown in the shape of an effigy of the Virgin Mary. Pilgrims flocked to the site and the oak became a good source of revenue for the church. Subsequent oak trees were planted to replace the original tree in 1656 and 1830.

Like virtually all the churches in this area, St Martin's was bombed during the blitz of 1942. As a result the belfry was destroyed, large holes were burnt in the roof and all the windows were blown out. The church lay derelict until 1953. At the end of this period, the War Damage Commission agreed to its restoration as a church hall and it was divided into its current layout. The nave was made into a congregational hall, the aisle divided off into separate classrooms and a kitchen, and by building a wall across the chancel arch, a separate chapel was created to accommodate thirty to forty people. The tower was also lowered to the level of the nave roof and some of the stringcourse of carved stonework from the church's battlemented top was re-used lower down. A year later, during alterations to the holy water stoup in the south porch, two late C14th Nottingham alabaster tablets depicting the resurrection and the beheading of St John were found.

From top (left to right): St Margaret's Old Catton, St Margaret de Westwick interior, St Mark's New Lakenham.
St Martin at Oak – east elevation 1825, and west elevation 1938 prior to wartime bomb damage.

The church originally contained an early C18th wall tablet to Jeremiah Revans, rector of East Tuddenham featuring an almost life-size kneeling figures of Revans and his wife. It has since been removed to a 'museum' but it is unclear which one. On his death in 1727, Revans reportedly left a sum of money to assist in the education of six poor girls of St Martin's parish. There are several other memorial

From top (left to right): St Martin at Palace Plain, note Saxon long and short work on end of chancel, St Mary's Arminghall, St Mary & All Saints Little Melton, St Mary & St Andrew Horsham St Faith, St Mary & St Margaret Sprowston.

partitioned into work areas and the post-1953 chapel is used as an office.

St Martin at Palace

Redundant, medieval, Walled City church. The church of St Martin at Palace is so called as it lies opposite the gate into the medieval Palace of the Bishops of Norwich. Despite this medieval link, the church is noted in the Domesday Book of 1086 and is likely have been founded before the Norman Conquest. Certainly, in 1987 and 1988 archaeological excavations of the nave and part of the chancel provided evidence to suggest such early origins and there is pre Conquest style 'long and short work' at the east end. The excavations within St Martin's revealed at least three phases in the development of the site prior to a stone church being built. The earliest evidence discovered was not structural but was a burial. This burial was radio carbon dated to the eighth century and provides strong evidence to suggest a church on or near the site at that time. A C10th/11th post-trench that originally contained wooden posts to make up the wall of a building was also discovered and to the north of this there was an C11th building. This later building was constructed using postholes and seven of these were found set out in an L-shape making up the south west corner of the building. Furthermore, one of these postholes contained a fragment of a C10th/11th limestone grave cover with a knotwork design on it. Stonework with carvings like

tablets remaining in St Martin's. The grandest commemorates a brewer named Thomas Newton and his wife Rebecca. Newton was a sheriff and Alderman of Norwich, who later became mayor in 1722.

After a period of use as a night-shelter for the City's homeless, the church was occupied by the internationally renowned 'On-Oak' artists' studios and exhibition space. What was once the nave is now this are rare finds in Norfolk and again this grave cover firmly suggests a church nearby. The burial and grave cover both point to the probability that the timber buildings were early churches.

Above the two timber buildings, foundations for a more substantial post-Conquest building were established. The building was constructed of flint with chalk and gravel foundations. It had a nave and small chancel and these provided the structural basis for the current church. The original stone building is defined inside the current St Martins by the east wall of the tower, the nave and chancel arcades and the east wall of the chancel

The tower, south porch and the north and south aisles of the nave and chancel are all C14/15th. At this time most Norwich churches were being enlarged or modernised in the latest Perpendicular styles of architecture. St Martin's was clearly not exempt from such alterations and it did not escape the usual program of restoration during the Georgian and Victorian periods either. In 1783 the tower collapsed and was rebuilt, albeit a storey shorter. In 1854 St Martins underwent a major restoration and in 1874 the tower was again restored but this time the upper storey was replaced. Unfortunately, St Martin's also fell foul of the spate of church closures during the 1970s. In 1973 worship came to an end on the site and the Norwich Historic Churches Trust took over its care. By the late 1980s the church was converted into a Probation Centre and is still used for this purpose today.

St Mary, Arminghall
Suburban, medieval, parish church. The body of the church is C13th with an early C14th tower. Inside, the Herne family are well represented by memorials including an elaborate wall monument to John Hurne (1661) and incised coats of arms in the Sanctuary.

St Mary and All Saints, Little Melton
Medieval, parish church. The core of the church dates from about 1300 although there was major restoration of the roof and other parts of the structure in 1896. Inside there is a C15th painted chancel screen, C14th wall paintings, a C13th Purbeck marble font and a mural monument, of 1656, to Richard and Bridgett Scottowe.

St Mary and St Andrew, Horsham St Faith
Suburban, medieval, parish church. Principally Perpendicular but with earlier west tower and east end chancel wall exhibiting very interesting chequerboard work. There was a major restoration in 1874 when the roof was replaced. Inside there are 12 impressive screen paintings dating from 1528 and also pulpit paintings dating predominantly from 1480. The octagonal font is C15 and the font cover is a fine Jacobean example. There is a brass of Geoffrey Langeley dated 1437 (and moved from St Laurence, in the City Centre) and stained glass by King, 1855.

St Mary and St Margaret, Sprowston
Suburban, medieval, parish church. Although principally C14th, the tower was added in the C18th and the nave clerestory was remodeled in 1725 while significant Victorian Gothic revival was imposed by Edward Boardman in 1890, including re-roofing. Interesting glass includes work by Heaton, Butler and Bayne in 1867, Jones and Willis in 1907 and King & Son in 1961. There is a profusion of monuments inside. The Corbet family – John, 1559, Thomas, 1617 and father of one of the Parliamentarians responsible for dispatching Charles I, 2 Miles Corbets from 1607 and 1662. Also and bizarrely there is a monument to Sir Thomas Adams, Lord Mayor of London and intimate friend of Charles II, who bought the Sprowston Estate from the Parliamentarian Corbets in 1645. Others include Christopher Knolles (1610), a fine brown and white marble memorial to Nathaniel Micklethwaite (1757) by Robert Page and one in white marble to Lady Micklethwaite (1805) by John Bacon Jnr.

St Mary and St Walstan, Bawburgh
Suburban, medieval, parish church. The foundation is pre Conquest reflected in the dedication to St Walston who was apparently buried there by the Bishop in 1016. The round tower is early and the chancel was rebuilt in 1309 when a shrine chapel was also added. The Reformation, however, resulted in the destruction of the Walstan relics and the shrine chapel as well as significant neglect of the

church. In 1633 repairs were made and parts of the restored structure date from this period. Inside there is a fragmentary survival of a wall painting near the door, on the west wall. There is some surviving medieval stained glass including C15th angels and a figure of St Barbara. The pulpit came from the Cathedral in 1892. A further interesting artifact is a medieval, lathe turned 'poor box', probably intended for pilgrims to make donations for the parish poor.

St Mary Combuste
See *St Mary Unbrent*.

St Mary, Coslany

Redundant, medieval, Walled City church. St Mary Coslany is one of only three surviving round towered churches in Norwich; the others being St Julian's and St Etheldra's (and the tower of St Benedict). St Mary's dates from the pre Conquest period as evidenced by the round tower and pointed Saxon style heads of the bell openings.

Although it has been argued that Caen stone shafts in the openings suggest a post Conquest date, these could have been later modifications to a pre Conquest tower. Much of St Mary's was rebuilt in its current form by 1477. The church has two porches, of which the northerly contains two rows of wooden pegs. These pegs are often mistaken as having been for poor children to hang their coats on when arriving for lessons with the parson. However, it is more likely that they were used to hang the parish fire buckets. In 1570 it was ordered that

each parish should provide a certain number of pegs according to the parish's size and need. St Mary's required eighteen and there are several references to these in the church warden's accounts.

Fire, however, was not the enemy that St Mary's faced in the seventeenth and eighteenth centuries. The church is situated in a low-lying area and was prone to flooding. The floodwater of 1762 reached a depth of about one metre (3 ft) and destroyed numerous valuable books and manuscripts. The church registers were under water for three days. This was not the first or last time that flooding caused a problem. The church warden's accounts note in 1615 that payment was made for 'putting stooles into their places that were removed by the flood' and in 1647 flooding caused subsidence in the floor. In 1794 water again overflowed the courtyard, but was kept at bay 'by building the south door up'.

Towards the end of the C19th, St Mary's fell into disrepair. In 1898 the Norfolk and Norwich Archaeological Society visited the church, stating in their annual report that it was 'sad to see the state of ruin into which this fine building [had] been allowed to fall'. By 1904 a sizable section of the tower had collapsed, and in 1905 the church was described by one newspaper correspondent to have been left to the mercy of 'stone throwing street urchins'. The building was rebuilt in 1908 but lasted only thirty-two more years before it was hit by firebombs in August

1942. The roof caught fire but the church survived largely intact, and was repaired and re-opened in 1950. Sadly it was rarely used and was declared redundant in 1974.

The church contains what is reportedly the oldest mural tablet in the City. This can be found on the interior of the nave's west wall, to the north of the tower arch. In Norman French it records that Thomas de Lingcole (a tanner and bailiff of the City who died in 1298) made gifts of a wax taper and a lamp to the altar of the Holy Trinity. The arch braced roof is also worthy of note, particularly where it meets the transept crossing. Here it has a centre boss showing the church's patron saint, Mary, surrounded by rays of light. The stained glass windows in both the north and south transepts also feature impressive coats of arms. Those in the northern transept represent Thomas Osborn Springfield (Mayor in 1829 and 1836) and Osborn Springfield (Mayor 1863). The six bells that previously resided in the tower were all cast in Norwich. Due to their uncommonly small size they were said in their day to have a 'toy' peal. They are now housed in St Catherine's Church, Mile Cross.

Luke Hansard was born on 5th of July 1752 in St Mary's parish and was baptised at the church. Hansard was the printer of the House of Commons Journal from 1774 onwards and much later, in 1943, his name was leant to the official reports of the proceedings of Parliament, the Hansard Reports.

St Mary, Earlham

Suburban, medieval parish church. The round tower and core of the nave are probably Norman although the presence of some long and short work could suggest a pre Conquest date. A bequest in 1524 suggests a degree of rebuilding then and the hammerbeam roof is slightly earlier. Inside there is a C15th screen and a C14th traceried font. The stained glass is relatively recent by King & Son (1956). There is a C17th alabaster monument to the Petty children, moved from the demolished London church of St Giles in the Fields in 1731, to be near the graves of their parents.

St Mary, East Carleton

Medieval, Parish church. A pre Conquest dedication with a reference in Domesday, but the present structure was originally C13th with most of the evidence of this in the chancel and north aisle. The rather heavy Victorian restoration dates from 1881 while the tower was rebuilt in 1895 and the porch in 1918. Inside there is little trace of the original structure or ornaments apart from a memorial slab of 1676 and a tiny fragment of medieval glass.

St Mary, Great Melton

Medieval, Parish church. Only the dilapidated tower, dating from 1440, survives in the churchyard of All Saints. Both churches operated until after 1728 when the parishes were consolidated. At first St Mary's was used as the principal church but it

From top (left to right): St Mary & St Walstan, Bawburgh – exterior and interior, St Mary's Coslany, St Mary's Earlham, St Mary's East Carleton, and the surviving tower of St Mary's Great Melton.

became too small for parish needs and All Saints was restored and took over. St Mary's then became dilapidated and fell into ruins leaving only the tower standing.

St Mary, Great Plumstead

Medieval parish church. The parish church St Mary the Virgin dates originally from the C13th. The tower was rebuilt in 1711, and the church itself underwent a major redevelopment in 1875 after a fire destroyed the majority of the building. There are two medieval brasses in the nave.

St Mary, Hellesdon

Suburban, medieval parish church. A small, towerless church and a pre Conquest foundation, with the walls of the nave and chancel probably dating from that period. There is a vaulted C14th porch and the north aisle is also C14th as are the doors. There was a substantial renovation in 1869 and the chancel roof was restored again in 1954. Inside there are C14th brasses, a C14th font and glass by King & Sons dating from 1942.

St Mary in the Marsh

Lost, Walled City Church. As stated in Norwich cathedral's records, the church of St Mary in the Marsh was founded before the Norman Conquest. Two wills that date to about the C10/11th mention the church, proving that it was in existence by this time. St Mary's name, 'in the Marsh', refers to a time when the land around the church was still marshy. The church was located to the south of the

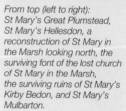

From top (left to right): St Mary's Great Plumstead, St Mary's Hellesdon, a reconstruction of St Mary in the Marsh looking north, the surviving font of the lost church of St Mary in the Marsh, the surviving ruins of St Mary's Kirby Bedon, and St Mary's Mulbarton.

current Lower Close, on the corner of a probable pre Conquest west/east route running from Tombland to the river and a north/south route running from St Martins, through the later Cathedral to Mountergate. Cathedral records say that it was not initially taken into the cathedral precinct but that it had been incorporated by the mid C13th.

Few details are known about the church building as worship at St Mary's stopped in the mid C16th, the last rector, John Toller, being appointed in 1559. By 1564 the dean of the cathedral is said to have sold the lead from the church roof and the chancellor of the diocese is thought to have removed the interior furnishings, fittings and stonework. The bells were also sold and records show that by 1564 St Mary's had been turned into two houses. Even so, most of the church must have remained intact. A map of the site, drawn as late as 1761-1775, shows the land of Ann and Rachel Brigham lying directly north and south of what is clearly a church with a round tower, nave, porch, south transept and a chancel. In 1775, however, the site was developed into a terrace of elegant Georgian houses known as St Mary's Chant (Nos. 10-12 The Close). What had survived of St Mary's was either destroyed or incorporated in the terrace. The spine wall of Nos. 10-12 is clearly medieval in date and represents the north wall of St Mary's church while No. 12 has two C16th windows preserved within it.

Once St Mary's church was made redundant, the congregation did not disperse. The congregation was given use of St John the Baptist chapel, in the south aisle of the cathedral, for their services and the cloister garth (the green or courtyard at the centre of the cloister) for burying their dead. Later the congregation was given use of St Luke's chapel and this was furnished with St Mary's former font. The font remains there to this day and is one of thirty-eight fonts of a similar design that are found only in Norfolk and Suffolk (there are only two elsewhere in the country). St Mary's former font is octagonal with ornately carved faces depicting scenes of the Baptism, Confirmation, Ordination, Holy Communion, Marriage, Death, the Crucifixion and Penance. Unfortunately the carved figures on the font were all defaced, reputedly during the English Civil War of 1642-1651. The congregation of St Mary in the Marsh still worships at the cathedral and is possibly the only parish and congregation to survive the destruction of its church.

St Mary, Kirby Bedon

Lost medieval parish church. Probably originating in the C12th, the church survived the Reformation but was abandoned in the late C17th. It is located just 50 m from Kirby Bedon's other church and all that now remains is a C13th round tower with C14th belfry, and some masonry remnants.

St Mary Magdalen Leper Hospital, Sprowston

See *Lazar House*.

St Mary Magdalen, Mulbarton

Medieval parish church. Principally dating frim the C14th with a tower of 1393, the church was substantially restored in 1875 by Phipson. Inside there is some C15th stained glass and two large monumental tablets to Sir Edwin Rich (1675) and his son of the same name (1651).

St Mary Magdalen, Silver Road

Extra mural Edwardian church. Although only built in 1903, by diocesan architect A.J. Lacey, this church contains a remarkable screen relocated from St James in Barrack Street in 1946. Dating from 1505, the screen represents St Barbara, St Sitha, St Agnes, St William of Norwich, St Joan de Valois, St Martin, St Blaise, St Walstan, St Helen and St Nicholas. The medieval font also originated from St James.

St Mary, Baptist Chapel

Post War Baptist Chapel. Originally erected in 1714, at the junction of St Mary's Plain and Duke Street, the chapel was under the stewardship of Joseph Kinghorn, until his death in 1791. It was rebuilt in 1811 and enlarged in 1838. It was badly damaged by fire in 1939 and restored shortly after but after being hit twice by enemy bombing raids in 1942 it was gutted. A service was held in the ruins to celebrate VE Day in

1945 and the present building is the result of a rebuild undertaken in 1951-2 by Stanley Wearing.

St Mary, Swainsthorpe

Lost, medieval parish church. Formerly contemporary with the surviving St Peter's, St Mary's was dissolved at the Reformation and demolished with the building material being recycled. No trace remains of the building or churchyard.

St Mary, Swardeston

Medieval parish church. Although the foundation was probably pre Conquest, the core of the building is Norman with C14/C15th additions and a tower dating from 1470. Inside there is an early C15th screen, a plain octagonal font with an elaborate C17th cover, C15th bench ends and some nice stained glass including C14th fragments and a 1917 commemorative window by Ernest Heasman to the vicar's daughter Edith Cavell.

St Mary's Swardeston.

St Mary the Less

Redundant, medieval, Walled City church. Absorbed on three of its four sides by modern shops, restaurants and estate agents, St Mary the Less is rather hard to find. Only the square tower, roof and the face of the south porch can be seen through a small gap in the buildings on Queen Street. St Mary's may have been founded prior to the Norman Conquest but there is little evidence relating to its foundation or the early history of the church. Much of the current building dates to the C13th, as the architectural style of the tower and parts of the aisle-less nave attest. The chancel contains windows of C14/15th date proving that the building did not entirely escape the remodelling that most Norwich churches seem to have experienced in that period.

At the Dissolution of the Monasteries in the 1530s St Mary the Less was made redundant and the building was handed over to the Dean and Chapter of Norwich cathedral. In June 1544 the dean decided to rent out the building so, at a cost of £43, it was converted into a Drapers' Hall. The Dutch and Walloon weavers of Norwich sold their cloth from the Hall until 1623, at which point and for a further eight years it was used for the sale of worsted yarns. Commercial use of the building saved the redundant St Mary's from demolition but unfortunately it did not help preserve its internal fittings. Most of the fittings were sold in 1544 and ten years later the roof lead was stripped off to be sold and the roof was covered in cheaper tiles.

St Mary the Less did eventually revert to its original religious purpose. After the cloth trade moved to St Andrew's Hall, the church was leased for worship to the French Huguenot and Walloon populations of Norwich. Carved into one of the doors of St Mary's is the date '1637' which records the date on which worship resumed there. The French ancestry of the congregation is confirmed by a late C18th memorial to Paul Colombine, the son of a French refugee. The French and Walloon congregation continued to worship at St Mary's until 1832 but by then so many of their number had joined other religious communities in the City that they had to give up the church. In 1862 it was leased to a religious organisation called the Swedeborgians and seven years later to the Catholic Apostolic Church who worshipped on the site until 1953. St Mary's was then used as a furniture store and became the only privately owned church in Norwich. Its owner's ambition since his purchase over 20 years ago, has been to develop the church as a study centre for the Dutch and Walloon heritage of the City.

St Mary Unbrent

Lost Walled City church.
St Mary's probably dated to the pre-Conquest period and stood at the corner of Magdalen Street and Golden Dog Lane in the heart of the early C10th defended D shaped enclosure. In later documentation, the area around Magdalen Street is referred to as 'in combusto', in the burnt area. It is possible that this, like the church's alternative title 'St Mary's Combuste', refers to King Sweyn of Denmark's attack of 1004 in which he sailed up the Wensum 'with his fleet and completely burned and ravaged the borough' (the Anglo-Saxon Chronicle). Alternatively, the burnt reference may be to damage sustained by the area during one of several fires that swept the City during the medieval period. St Mary's was amalgamated with St Saviour's church in the early C16th, but went out of use around 1540. It was demolished before 1558 and as a result little is known about the building.

St Mathew

Lost Walled City church.
The church of St Mathew is also known as St Mathew the Apostle and St Mathew at Palace. The latter name refers to its former location opposite St Martin at Palace, on Palace Plain and next to the gate leading into the Palace of the Bishops of Norwich. Many of St

From top (left to right): a very rare view of St Mary the Less south side before being encased in development, Mary the Less interior in the 1930s and Priest's Door on the north side, and probable reuse of materials from the lost church of St Mary Unbrent, formerly in Golden Dog Lane.

Mathew's parishioners succumbed to the Black Death in 1349 and the congregation became so small that it joined the congregation of St Martin's over the road. This move became permanent after 1377 when St Mathew's last Rector died by which time the building was already becoming a ruin. The date of the church's final destruction is unknown and, as with many Norwich churches that disappeared during the medieval period, little is known about the building itself.

St Matthew, Thorpe Hamlet

Converted, former Victorian church. Built in 1851 by John Brown in the Romanesque Revival style, the church was restored in 1951 but had become redundant by the 1970s. Narrowly escaping demolition, it was converted to offices in 1983 by the Peter Codling Partnership.

St Matthew, Thorpe Hamlet

Modern, suburban parish church. Built in 1982 in Telegraph Lane to replace the Victorian church of the same name, on Rosary Road, and St Leonard's Chapel of Ease on Ketts Hill, built in 1907 and demolished in 1981, the new St Matthews was designed by Peter Codling and furnished with artefacts from its predecessors. These include the altar and rood figures, pipe organ and war memorial from the old St Matthews and the pulpit from St Leonards.

From top (left to right): St Michael at Plea – south side, and interior, prior to the recent conversion.
St Michael at Thorn in 1938 prior to wartime bombing, interior 1938, and the site today with surviving thorn trees.

St Michael at Plea

Redundant, medieval, Walled City church.

St Michael Wymer and St Michael de Motestowe are both alternative names that have been used for St Michael at Plea. St Michael Wymer simply refers to the location of the church: it stands in an area once called Westwyk, which was renamed Wymer in the C13th. St Michael de Motestowe is a much earlier name and originates from the Anglo-Saxon period when St Michael's was probably founded. 'Motestowe' means 'meeting place' so the church may have been the focal point for the 'folkmoot', the means of local government at that time. Alternatively, St Michael at Plea may have inherited the name 'Motestowe' from St Michael Tombland when it was destroyed to make way for the cathedral precinct in the early C12th. This would make sense as Tombland was the market place and centre of pre-Conquest Norwich.

Nothing survives from the earlier building of St Michael at Plea. The chancel is the earliest part of the building and dates from the C13th. It retains a single 'Y' tracery window characteristic of architecture at that time. Other than the chancel, work in the nave in 2004 uncovered a small portion of a wall from an earlier nave. No other evidence of the earlier church has been found, probably because during the late C14th/early C15th the majority of the churches within Norwich were updated with the latest Perpendicular style of architecture. St Michael at Plea is no exception and it

was given a new nave, transepts, south chancel chapel and south porch. The large windows of the nave are typical of the Perpendicular style of that time, as is the base of the nave, transepts and chapel. This base is decorated in flushwork, a decorative technique developed in Norfolk that uses scarce freestone, such as limestone, to edge panels of the more readily available knapped flint. Flushwork is often designed in the form of window tracery or, as is the case at St Michael's, in the form of shields, quatrefoils and rosettes. The two-storey porch of St Michael's is also highly decorated and unusually the front face is completely faced in stone which would have been expensive. A carving of St Michael and the dragon can be found above the arched doorway and a frieze of crowned M's which represent Mary rather than St Michael. Above this frieze two rectangular windows light the first floor room or parvise that would have been used by the clergy.

St Michaels became redundant in the 1970s and since then has been used as an exhibition centre, antiques shop and antiquarian book dealers. Currently the church is in the care of the Norwich Historic Churches Trust and is being used as a Christian bookshop and a café. As a result of these various uses and of a Victorian restoration, few of St Michael's internal fittings remain. The nave has an impressive arch-braced roof decorated with winged angels that were repainted during the 1887 restoration. The C15th octagonal font was also retained along with

its remarkable C17th cover with a carved dove near its top. Unfortunately however an important collection of medieval panel paintings can no longer be found in the church. The paintings date between 1389 and 1445 but during the 1887 restoration several of them were made into an altarpiece. This was later bought by the Norfolk Regiment and can be seen in the Regimental Chapel of St Saviour in Norwich cathedral.

St Michael at Thorn

Lost Walled City church.

Located on the north corner of Ber Street and Thorn Lane, the church was probably a Norman foundation just outside the pre Conquest Borough. Its only feature surviving from that period was the Norman doorway, which was re-erected within St Julians after the War. The slender west tower was built in 1436 but collapsed in November 1886 and was re-erected in the following year in the same style. It had a nave, north aisle, south porch and chancel originally rebuilt in 1430 but virtually rebuilt in a C15th style in 1887. Internally there was an attractive Victorian roof and screen but the only ancient features were a C15th font and lectern. The church also contained a chapel dedicated to St Martin in commemoration of St Martin in Balliva which was demolished in 1562 when its parish was united with St Michael's. On 27th June 1942 the church was completely gutted following a fire bomb raid and only the tower and walls survived. While other bombed churches were restored, St Michael's was entirely flattened in 1952 leaving no trace at all on the site. This may have been because the church was regarded as a Victorian reconstruction rather than a medieval church so the best bits were salvaged (e.g. the Norman doorway) and reused but the remainder wasn't regarded as worthy of restoration. The name of the church and the Lane where it once stood derive from the presence of Thorn trees in the church yard and some still survive.

St Michael, Bowthorpe

Redundant, medieval parish church. The original church is now a ruin. The remnants of the nave suggest that it was essentially C15th as was the chancel although there is excavated evidence of a round tower. By 1602 the church was used as a barn and despite renovation in 1636, the roof collapsed in 1792 and the structure became derelict. Standing beside it is a modern church built in 1975.

St Michael, Conesford

Lost Walled City church. Demolished to make way for the expanding Austin Friary between 1360 and 1368, no obvious signs of the church remain.

St Michael, Coslany

Redundant Walled City church. St Michael Coslany stands on the site of an earlier church known to have been in existence by 1254. The current building is the greatest of a key group of City churches rebuilt by master mason John Antell in the late C15th and early C16th. It has been described as 'the finest late Gothic achievement in any

of the churches of Norwich'. The tower still contains eight bells, second only to the thirteen bells of St Peter Mancroft. St Michael's is sometimes known locally by the abbreviation 'St Miles' to distinguish it from other churches dedicated to St Michael within Norwich.

St Michael's church is most well known for its Thorp Chapel. In the late medieval period it was the fashion for rich parishioners to pay for masses to be sung for the redemption of their souls. This resulted in the foundation of chantry chapels. At the start of the C16th, Alderman Robert Thorp paid for the construction of a chantry chapel at the east end of the south aisle. The walls of the aisle, the chancel and the chapel were decorated in flushwork, a decorative technique developed in Norfolk. The technique uses scarce freestone such as limestone to edge panels of the more readily available knapped flint. The decorative panels are often designed in the form of window tracery and such decoration can be seen at St Michael's: it is said to be the finest example of this technique in England. Despite the great promise of the remodelling work supervised by Thorp, it was never completed. You can still see parts of the earlier church at the west end of the south aisle wall where a mid C14th window and door remain. The north aisle has a chantry chapel dedicated to St John the Baptist. Both the aisle and the chapel were paid for by William Ramsey (Mayor of Norwich in 1502 and 1508) whose altar tomb can be found inside the church.

The churchyard of St Michael's suggests that the parish was ravaged by the Black Death. The high level of the ground around the church in relation to the floor level inside suggests serious overcrowding in the churchyard and thus a high level of mortality in the parish. Before 1910, the ground almost reached to the top of the churchyard wall so work was undertaken to lower the level of the surface by several feet.

St Michael's also has the misfortune of being the lowest lying church in Norwich and the land on which it stands was originally marshland. The church suffered significantly in 1912, when Norwich experienced the worst floods in the City's history. Over one metre of flood water rose in the church's chancel, ruining the organ bellows, and blocks of pews on wooden platforms reportedly floated about the church 'like huge rafts'. Early church registers held in the vestry safe were also badly damaged, some irretrievably. The overall repair costs came to some £600. The church was converted to a sports centre in the 1970s and then a science discovery centre but at the time of publication, was vacant.

St Michael, Chapel, Ketts Hill

Lost chapel. Built by Bishop Herbert in 1101 outside the precinct of St Leonard's priory and just north of it, the chapel was intended to replace the demolished church of St Michael at Tombland. It measured 5.5 M (18 ft) by 12.8 M (42 ft) and stood roughly where Ketts Heights now is. It was

abandoned at the Reformation and damaged during Kett's Rebellion although a substantial proportion survived for some time being celebrated in paintings and lithographs as Kett's Castle. Only a remnant survives today as a section of garden wall.

St Michael, Tombland

Lost Walled City church.
St Michael's is recorded in the Domesday Book of 1086 as the richest of Norwich's churches and may even have been one of the first churches to be built in Norwich, although its foundation date is uncertain. St Michael's was probably the most important church in Norwich prior to the building of the cathedral and this importance is reflected in its prominent location in Tombland, the open space used for the Anglo-Scandinavian market.

The church was demolished, before 1119, by Bishop Herbert de Losinga to make way for the building of the cathedral precinct but also, probably, to make a point about the new dominance of the Norman Bishopric. As a result nothing is known about the building itself and the site of St Michael's can only be inferred from finds discovered when the Tombland public lavatories were installed below ground in the 1870s. Most significant of the finds was a pectoral cross made of walrus ivory that would have been worn on the chest of a cleric. The cross is a very fine example of pre Conquest artwork and was exhibited in the Victoria and Albert Museum but is now on loan to the Castle Museum's Anglo Saxon and Viking Gallery.

From top (left to right): Ruined remains of St Michael's Bowthorpe, St Michael at Coslany interior when used as a science centre, and showing elaborate flushwork on the east end of the chancel. Reconstruction of the pre Conquest church of St Michael at Tombland.

From top (left to right): The lost church of St Paul – south side in 1825, interior in 1938, and prior to wartime bombing in 1938, and St Peter's Cringleford.

with an elaborate entrance arch, at 45 deg to an aisled nave measuring about 8.2m (27ft) by 7m (23ft) with a flat wooden ceiling set about 4.7m (15 ft 6 in) above floor level. Today, the altar sanctuary survives in the south east corner.

St Nicholas, Bracondale

Lost chapel. This was a chapel located somewhere in Bracondale but virtually nothing is known about its history.

St Olave, King Street

Lost pre Conquest, Walled City church. Located just inside the Conesford Gate on the east side of King Street and in the area later to be developed for Read's Mills this was a pre Conquest foundation reflecting the City's early Danish connections.

St Olave, Pitt Street

Lost Walled City church. St Olave's church was probably one of the earliest churches to be founded in this area. St Olave (Olaf) was King of Norway and he had tried to forcibly convert his country to Christianity. During this struggle he was banished and in 1030 was killed when trying to regain his throne. He was popular with Scandinavian settlers in England and it is likely that the church was founded by such settlers in Norwich. By the C14th the church was all but redundant but was not demolished until 1546 when the parish was amalgamated with that of St George Colegate. St Olave's was in time corrupted to 'Tooleys' and, as in Southwark, the adjacent street became Tooley Street, next to Cherry Lane. During the C18th

St Miles

See *St Michael Coslany.*

St Niclolas Chapel, Norwich Castle

Chapel remnant. This was the chapel for the Castle and the garrison, developed at the same time as the keep in about 1100. It is located on the balcony level of the keep in the south east corner. It consisted of an apsidal, vaulted altar space,

Cherry Lane also lent its name to the churchyard which became known as the Cherry Ground. Prior to this, during the C17th, a large pit at the west end of the graveyard had given its name to Pitt Street.

St Paul

Lost Walled City church. St Paul's was dedicated jointly to St Paul the Apostle and St Paul the first Christian hermit. The church was gutted on 27th June 1942 by Second World War incendiary bombs, yet stood for a further ten years with no roof before its demolition. The church originally had a round tower, Norman in origin, and possessed an octagonal belfry until 1819 when this was removed and replaced with a shallow coping of white brick and stone. The remainder of the building was largely of late C15th and consisted of a nave without clerestory, a north aisle and a rib-vaulted south porch with a chamber above. A small semi-circular chancel was added in 1870. Most of the interior was modern having been renovated in 1921 and again in 1933 although a remarkable survival was a C15th screen. When the church was finally demolished, there were pleas from local people that the impressive round tower should remain but to no avail, probably because the church ruins sat on the line of Horace Rowley's proposed northern Inner Ring Road alignment. Consequently, part of the site was absorbed as part of the St Crispin's Road scheme and a children's play area now occupies the remainder.

St Paul, Hellesdon

Modern, suburban parish church. A rather unusual church, dedicated in 1950 and having a corrugated iron Nissen hut for a nave. Architects Wright and Mason added a brick chancel and west front subsequently.

St Paul, Magdalen Road

Modern, suburban parish church. Designed by J.P. Chaplin and built in 1958, St Paul the Hermit was intended to replace the bombed and subsequently demolished St Paul just off Cowgate and now incorporates the bell from the old St Paul.

St Paul, Tuckswood

Modern, suburban parish church. Designed by Peter Codling and opened in 1969 it replaced the 'old' St Paul which survives next door and had been built to serve the Tuckswood Council Estate in 1951.

St Paul's Hospital or Norman's Spital

Lost medieval hospital. St Paul's Hospital or Norman's Spital (Norman, a monk from the Cathedral Priory, being the first Master and spital being a corruption of hospital) would have stood south of St Paul's, now lost, church and south of today's Inner Ring Road close to modern Whitefriars Street, but nothing remains now. The hospital was founded by the Cathedral's first prior, Ingalf, during the lifetime of Bishop Herbert de Losinga but was completed by the second Bishop, Eborard de Montgomery. It was consecrated by Archbishop Theobold of Canterbury. Eborard also founded a small community around the church and hospital. The hospital was granted several gifts of land and its benefactors included the King and four bishops. Eborard had given the incentive of granting forty days' pardon to any benefactors and this prompted numerous gifts and bequests. The hospital catered for 14 poor men and women who were helpless due to chronic sickness although by 1429 it was reserved for women only. It was the only institution in the City that catered for pregnant women and nursing mothers. It was closed in 1565 and leased to the City for use as a hospital. Five years later, the lease was revoked so that a new lease could be issued, which allowed the buildings to be used for any purpose. The City then turned it into a bridewell or prison for 'the correction of idle and lazy beggars'. The building gradually disappeared but in 1934 it was noted that remnants of the walls and reused materials were identifiable in later buildings. All were swept away for the inner Ring Road in the late 1960s.

St Peter, Cringleford

Suburban, medieval parish church. Probably a pre Conquest foundation with a suggestion that original fabric might survive in the nave and chancel walls. There are also small traces of Norman work. The north and south aisles were demolished in the C15th and the church was substantially restored in 1898. Inside there is a C14th font and a C17th painting of the Virgin.

St Peter, Crostwick

Medieval parish church.
St Peter's is principally C15th with an early C16th porch and C17th roof but there was a major Victorian restoration. Inside there is a fragment of a C15th wall painting of St Christopher, some attractive glass by William Wailes of 1853, an attractive font and some pleasant memorials.

St Peter, East Carleton

Medieval parish church.
Mentioned in the Domesday Book this was a medieval contemporary with its very near neighbour, St Mary, but by 1441 its parish had been united with St Mary's and although bequests had apparently been made for a new tower in 1503, the site was abandoned and ruinous by 1550. Today all that remains is an 8m stretch of wall within the graveyard.

St Peter, Easton

Medieval parish church.
A possible pre Conquest foundation, evidenced by long and short work to the south west corner of the nave. There are interesting Norman survivals including the south doorway. Much of the structure dates from the C13th with the clerestory, raised in the mid C15th followed shortly by the roof. The tower collapsed in 1778 and in 1883 Richard Phipson undertook an exterior restoration. Inside there is a C13th, octagonal Purbeck marble font and a C16th pulpit. There is also a surviving roundel of medieval glass in the east window.

St Peter Hungate

Redundant, medieval, Walled City church. St Peter Hungate was named after Houndes Gate the street on which it stood and so named because the bishop kept his kennels nearby and now called Princes Street. St Peter's was in existence by the C13th since John Bonde was buried there in 1248 and bequeathed money to the church and its clergy. Records show that in 1285 cloth merchant Nicholas de Copesty escaped imprisonment in Norwich Castle and claimed sanctuary in St Peter Hungate. He eventually gave himself up, was tried and was acquitted. The location of St Peter Hungate on the corner of two streets is thought to be a key characteristic of Norwich's pre Conquest churches so its foundation may be of that period. There is little other firm evidence to support this theory and not much is known about the church up until the C15th. At this time St Peter's became yet another of the City churches to undergo major refurbishment and rebuilding.

St Peter's was redeveloped in quite a simple and understated way in comparison to the new designs of other C15th Norwich churches. The earliest part of the church is the tower which was built at the expense of Mayor Thomas Ingham in 1431. By the early C17th, the tower was too unsafe to ring the bells but it was not until 1906 that the upper portion of the tower was removed and a pyramidal cap added in its place. The chancel that

Ingham built in 1431 had fallen down and was rebuilt in 1604. The former windows from the chancel were reused and the east one now holds all that remains of the C15th stained glass. The glass includes beautiful depictions of the Archangel Gabriel and the Apostles. Besides the tower and chancel, Ingham built the two-storey south porch by 1497 and was later buried in it.

Between 1458 and 1460, John and Margaret Paston paid for the nave and transepts of St Peter Hungate to be rebuilt. This rebuilding is commemorated by an interesting inscription on one of the buttresses by the north door of the church. The inscription says 1460 and shows an old tree trunk without any branches except for one new shoot. The tree trunk is said to represent the old church and the shoot, its renewal. The Paston family's famous letters refer to St Peter's on numerous occasions and the head stops on the window of the south transept are thought to depict John and Margaret. The beautiful part-gilded hammerbeam roofs with carvings of angels and a central boss of Christ's Judgement are also a notable feature.

Despite the great rebuilding of St Peter's in the C15th, the parish was small and the church income was meagre. This often meant that Rectors did not stay for long and were neglectful of their duties. Records of building work reflect periods when less committed Rectors were in charge and the building was in need of major refurbishments or modernisation in the early C16th, the early C17th, the late C19th, and the early C20th. By 1931 the building was so dilapidated that it was under threat of demolition. Norfolk Archaeological Trust stepped in to refurbish the building and St Peter's became the first church in the country to be used as a museum. The museum housed church art and ecclesiastical artefacts but was closed in 1995 and the contents moved to the Castle Museum. Even so, a few of the artefacts may have been left behind: a rather plain font bowl and the remains of another can be found outside, to the left of the south porch. One of the fonts may be St Peter's original font as the current one dates to the early C15th. The church has recently become a museum of medieval church art.

St Peter, Ketteringham

Medieval parish church. The core of the building is Norman with evidence of it in the nave. The chancel is early C15th and the tower was rebuilt in 1609. There was major restoration in the C18th and again in 1837. The interior is particularly impressive and includes a C15th octagonal font, a C16th Flemish reredos, C15th stained glass in the east window, a C15th door and a large range of memorials from 1470 to 1869 commemorating the Heveningham, Gray, Atkyns and Boileau families of the next door Hall. There is a Boileau mausoleum in the churchyard.

From top (left to right): St Peter's Crostwick, St Peter's Easton – late Norman doorway and view of the south side. Examples of medieval stained glass in St Peter Hungate, and St Peter's Ketteringham.

From top: St Peter Mancroft – south side, and outstanding medieval stained glass. Opposite (top): St Peter Mancroft east end and roof.

St Peter Mancroft

Medieval, Walled City church. St Peter Mancroft was founded between 1071 and 1075 by Ralph de Guader, Earl of Norfolk. The earlier structure is thought to have included a central tower, transepts and a lady chapel. The total rebuilding of the immediate post conquest church from 1430 to 1455 represents one of the most complete and striking examples of the Perpendicular style in the country. Mancroft's most notable features include the dramatically imposing tower, quite unlike any other in the City, the huge, single span hammer beam roof – with it's hammer beams concealed under fan-like groining; the large, unbroken expanse of the interior with no structural division between the nave and chancel; the 'wall of light' effect generated by the two sets of 17 clerestory windows, the large aisle windows and the magnificent east window with its stunning medieval glass. In May 1648 the Royalists in Norwich revolted exploding a gunpowder store near to the church. The incident killed 40 people and blew most of the glass from Mancroft's windows. The glass was collected up, restored in the eastern window and is now seen as an internationally important collection of work from the Norwich School of Glass Painters.

Mancroft also claims to have been the first place in the world to have rung a true peal of bells. Recorded on 2nd May 1715, the Norwich scholars rang Mancroft's 13 bells, changing their order over 5,000 times without repetition. A plaque commemorating the feat can be found in the church.

The Theatre Royal, just over the road, also has a curious friendship with St Peter Mancroft, which is often referred to as 'the actor's church'. The churchyard contains the tomb of Sophia Ann Goddard, an actress at the Theatre and "the darling of Drury Lane", who died in 1801 aged just twenty five. The church has continued this association with the Theatre for over 250 years, still ministering its acting community.

Sir Thomas Browne (1605-1682) is buried at St Peter's too. Known as a writer, physician, botanist, antiquarian and philosopher, Browne is reputed to have invented the words 'electricity', 'hallucination' and 'antediluvian'. As a famous character of Norwich he is also commemorated with a statue in the Haymarket. The interior of the church boasts a number of treasures including a C11th linen chest, a C15th font with cover, a C16th Flemish tapestry and a small museum containing historical and religious artefacts from Roman coins and stained glass to a collection of plate and early paintings.

Above: St Peter Parmentergate, rare view of north side during redevelopment of adjacent site.

St Peter Parmentergate

Redundant, medieval Walled City church.
The church was probably built in the C13th. The advowson originally belonged to Roger Bigod, Earl of Norfolk, who died in 1221 and he left it to the cathedral-priory. However, the church was completely rebuilt in 1486 and paid for by bequests. The stalls in the church were used by the Pied Friars whose friary was adjacent to the church. The tower has a double crenellated parapet and richly moulded openings. The porch is also C15th and has two storeys, the upper storey is called a parvise and was used by the clergy. The windows are in the C15th Perpendicular style. There are shields over the west door commemorating the families who paid for the rebuilding of the church. The doorway also contains Victorian spandrels showing St Peter and a woman holding a rosary. The turret houses the stairs to the former rood loft and blocks off part of the window, suggesting it was a later addition.

The interior is plain with an elegant chancel arch. Parts of the medieval screen exist on the north side; the southern section is a reproduction. The stairs to the rood loft survive. Some painted consecration crosses have been uncovered. These are circles enclosing geometric crosses and would have been anointed with oil when the church was consecrated. Each church had twelve consecration crosses around the interior walls. The nave roof is one of only two in the City employing tie beams. The old roof was sold in 1497 for £1 3s 4d, by which time rebuilding had been underway for thirteen years. In common with other churches in the City, St Peter Parmentergate was completely rebuilt in the late C15th, and in 1512 the vestry was still described as 'new'.

The tomb in the chancel is dated 1623. It has an elaborate Jacobean canopy and the recumbent figures of Robert Berney and his wife. The font is C15th and decorated with wild men and women and lions. Thomas Codd, Mayor of Norwich who failed to repress the 'rebellyous' crowds encamped at Eaton Wood during Kett's Rebellion in 1549, is buried in the church. A certificate of church goods dated 1548 indicates how the previously colourful church changed in the Reformation. Everything in the church was sold except the font and the northern portion of the rood screen dado. The proceeds of the sale were used to pay for the painting and erection of boards showing the Ten Commandments and for installing clear glass in the windows. The remainder helped to pay for paving of the highways and to poor relief. In the C19th the church fabric and fittings including a new roof, choir stalls, panelling, screen dado, a reredos and stained glass were restored and replaced in the popular 'medieval style'.

In 1981 the church was declared redundant and the nave pews, pulpit and organ were removed. Since then it has undergone extensive repairs. In 2004 the church was awarded a grant to install toilets, heating and lighting and to decorate the nave. It is used now as a martial arts centre.

St Peter Southgate

Lost Walled City church.
The church was founded before 1217 and was known as St Peter de Bither. It was used by fishermen as their guild headquarters. The church was rebuilt in the C15th Perpendicular style. All that remains is a fragment of flint rubble from the west tower and a brick Tudor arch. The church's wall monuments, bells and registers were removed to St Etheldreda's.

St Peter, Spixworth

Medieval parish church.
A Norman foundation, begun in 1160 by the Bardolfe family, the church originally had a round tower but this collapsed in 1804 and the rather odd, spindly tower seen today is a part reconstruction around the surviving elements. The majority of the surviving fabric is C14/15th. Inside there is a Norman font, an impressive alabaster monument to William & Alice Peck (1635) by Edward Marshall and a large amount of attractive, Victorian stained glass.

St Peter, Swainsthorpe

Medieval parish church.
Probably a pre Conquest foundation but the surviving building has a C12th round tower with the remainder dating from the C14th and the south windows being added following a bequest in 1443. There was major restoration in 1885 when the south porch was rebuilt. Inside there is a recut C13th Purbeck font, four C15th stalls and a memorial to Gilbert Havers from 1628 who was a captain of infantry for Elizabeth I.

St Peter's Wesleyan Methodist Chapel

Lost, Walled City, Methodist Chapel. In 1751 James Wheatley came to Norwich and from Castle Hill or Tombland, he preached Methodism. He faced fierce opposition and despite John Wesley, leader of the Methodist movement, preaching here only three years later it took a little while for Methodism to take hold in Norwich. By 1824, when St Peter's Wesleyan Methodist chapel opened, there were over 2,000 Methodists in Norwich but fierce opposition to Methodism remained. Indeed, until 1845 St Peter's chapel paid a constable to stand guard outside the chapel during Sunday services in case of disruptions. St Peter's was built on the site of an old theatre where early Methodist preachers once gave sermons. It stood on Lady's Lane, between the Swan Inn and a private house and was named after St Peter Mancroft, the parish in which it lay. The building was designed by architect, John Thomas Patience and was built in light-coloured brick. It looked much as an ordinary town house of the period with two impressive, classically styled, columned porches and sash windows. Inside it had a brick floor, two aisles of slim pillars, wooden galleries on all four sides and straight backed pews. St Peter's held 866 worshippers but both the congregation and the building had a turbulent history.

By 1850 serious infighting amongst the different factions of Methodism saw numbers drop. St Peter's only managed to attract a congregation of about 300 people, only a third of its total capacity, and as a result suffered financial difficulties. By 1868 matters had improved and the chapel was able to buy the Swan Inn's old stable block and some alterations were made to the chapel. In 1879, however, the congregation suffered a tragedy when two of its young members were drowned as a wherry smashed into their rowing boat while they were on a Sunday school outing to Whitlingham Broad. Ten years later the building was in need of major refurbishment so the organ was repaired, the heating renewed and the walls were repainted. The pews and sash windows were replaced and a bow fronted rostrum was added to the furnishings. Despite modernising the building the congregation again began to dwindle. People were beginning to move out of the inner city and industry was taking their place. In 1937 the City Council compulsory purchased the Sunday school buildings from the chapel and it was agreed that the congregation should merge with that of Park Lane chapel. On the 3rd September 1939, the day on which the Second World War broke out, St Peter's Wesleyan Methodist chapel held its last service. After the war the chapel was demolished to make way for Bethel Street car park and later, the Library. Nowadays the site of the chapel lies beneath The Forum building.

From top (left to right): Ruinous remains of St Peter Southgate, and as it appeared in 1825. St Peter's Spixworth, St Peter's Swainsthorpe, and the lost St Peter's Wesleyan Methodist Chapel.

From top (left to right):
The lost St Philip's Heigham,
St Remigius Dunston,
St Remigius Hethersett,
St Saviour's interior view after
conversion. St Simon & St
Jude – interior view in the
1930s, detail of arch spandrel,
and the Pettus monument.

St Philip, Heigham

Lost, Victorian, suburban, parish church. Built on Heigham Road in 1871 by Edward Power, the church struggled for some years to complete its tower, which took until 1879, but the intended spire never materialised. Redundant after the War, the church was finally demolished in 1975. All that now remains is the original dedication stone set in a garden wall of one of the new houses on the site.

St Remigius, Dunston

Medieval, parish church. St Remigius is dedicated to the C5th Bishop of Rheims who converted the French king Clovis to Christianity. A dedication to Remigius is quite rare with only six such dedications in England (four of these in Norfolk). The present church is C13th in origin with C15th alterations and a major Victorian refurbishment in 1898. The inside is more spectacular than the exterior with a remarkable C15th rood screen, some lovely medieval glass, a C15th font and a brass from 1647.

St Remigius, Hethersett

Medieval, parish church. There has been a church in the village since before the Conquest and the dedication to the C5th Bishop of Rheims who converted the French king Clovis to Christianity, suggests an early connection with this saint. A dedication to Remigius is quite rare with only six such dedications in England (four of these in Norfolk). The present church is essentially C14th with C15th additions and a major refurbishment in 1874.

Inside there is a C14th, octagonal font, a C14th monument to the Berney family, a 1704 memorial to Isaac Motham by William Swanton and, unusually a marble ledger slab from 1816 to 'John Luke Iselin Esq' a native of the City of Bazil in Switzerland. Eminent Merchant and Manufacturer in Norwich". There is some stained glass in the Arts and Crafts style produced by R. Anning Bell in 1913.

St Saviour

Redundant, medieval, Walled City church.
St Saviour's church is built in the Perpendicular style of the late C14th and is dedicated to the 'Transfiguration of Our Saviour'. It was restored in 1852 and a year later the tower was 'cropped' losing its top storey. The south porch was rebuilt in 1728 and the chancel was restored in 1923. An attractive scissor brace roof survives. There are several monuments surviving, including Edward Nutting (Sheriff 1602) and John Greene Baseley (Mayor 1791), but the font was moved to St George Tombland. The church was taken over by the King's Church in the 1990s, who renovated the building and now use it as a youth centre.

St Saviour's Hospital (St Saviour in Coslany)

Lost medieval hospital.
Founded early in the reign of Edward I (1272-1307) by Richard de Brekles (Breccles), chaplain but abandoned by 1306. Little is known about where the hospital was sited, but probably either in the parish of St Michael Coslany or St Saviours.

St Simon and St Jude

Redundant, medieval, Walled City church. The church of St Simon and St Jude was founded prior to the Norman Conquest an is thought to have begun as a small chapel within the house of the Bishop of Elmham. Bishops Æthelmær, Herfast and William are known to have lived in the house on the site and they would have needed a place to worship within the City prior to Bishop Herbert de Losinga building the cathedral in 1096. The church of St Simon and St Jude is certainly in existence by 1086 as it is mentioned in the Domesday Book.

The current church was built in the C14/15th and replaced the earlier building. The tower was begun in 1446 and much of the nave is in the late C14/15th Perpendicular style of architecture. The chancel is built in the C14th Decorated style and the vestry doorway is of particular note. The doorway has a carving of St Simon on one side and three fishes, which are thought to represent the Trinity on the other. The chancel is also the last resting place for two soldiers who were killed by Kett's rebels during the uprising of 1549. Little remains of the furnishings within the church. The C15th octagonal font with a foliage carved bowl has been removed and the organ was sold in 1920. The C16th stained glass was relocated before the Second World War and was set in a window of the ambulatory at Norwich cathedral. The glass includes the Coats of Arms of Sir Nicholas Bacon, Lord Treasurer to Elizabeth I, and William Cecil, Lord

Burleigh. Despite the removal of these treasures, the Pettus monuments have been preserved within the church and are the most notable feature of St Simon and St Jude's.

The Pettus family lived on nearby Elm Hill from 1550 to 1683. They were prominent Norwich cloth merchants and Thomas Pettus became sheriff in 1556 and Mayor in 1590. He died in 1597 and a monument to Thomas and his wife, Christian, can be found on the south side of the chancel of St Simon and St Jude. Thomas and Christian are depicted kneeling at a prayer desk and their four sons and four daughters are carved to either side. One of Thomas' sons, Sir John Pettus, was mayor in 1608 and on the east wall of the nave is a monument to him, his son Sir Augustine Pettus and his daughter-in-law Abigail. Sir John is depicted reclining in full armour but propped up on one elbow. Above is a carving of Sir John's two sons and four daughters and above again is a depiction of Sir Augustine and Abigail. The Pettus family's link with the church also extend as far as the United States of America. In 1638 Sir John Pettus' nephew, Colonel Thomas Pettus, was asked to travel to Jamestown, the first permanent English colony in the United States of America, to help the townspeople with their struggle against the Powhaton Indians. Colonel Pettus liked the area so much that he settled there, beginning a strong bond between Norwich and Jamestown that survives to this day. Several members of the American Pettus family have given money to help preserve the church and in the 1960s James T. Pettus brought his children from the United States to be christened in the church.

The churchyard of St Simon and St Jude's is noticeably small but would have been just as heavily used during medieval times as any other parish burial ground. In 1988 a small excavation in the car park of the Maid's Head Hotel discovered six burials. Documentary research revealed that they were probably part of an overspill burial ground owned by the church of St Simon and St Jude. It is thought that the church had acquired the site by 1316 and continued to use it for burial until 1400.

As is often the case, the church of St Simon and St Jude was not well maintained over the years and in 1892 the number of services diminished. In 1911 the top portion of the tower collapsed and after a small programme of restoration, the Rev. W F Crewe used the church as a Sunday school. After Crewe died the church became redundant again and by 1934 was condemned to be demolished. The church was given a reprieve and the Norwich Amenities Preservation Society raised enough money to begin restoration. A plaque detailing their work and dated 1939 can be seen in the nave. World War Two prevented further refurbishment but in 1950 the Norwich Society oversaw further work and in 1953 the building was officially reopened as the headquarters of the local Scouts Association. Over the years, the Scouts used

the church as a store, outdoor centre and shop, but by 1973 the building proved too small for their purpose and was hard to heat. Permission was given to insert a concrete floor and to partition off the chancel and other areas into separate rooms. All of the work is removable and was undertaken without affecting the fabric of the building. Although unattractive, the extra floor offers the chance of a closer view of the roof and upper parts of the building. The church is maintained by the Norwich Historic Churches Trust and now accommodates a dance school.

St Stephen

Medieval, Walled City church. One of the three churches to be developed in the post Conquest Norman borough, St Stephen's church was the last of all Norwich's churches to undergo the great redevelopment which began in the C15th. The redesigning of St Stephen's was underway during the Dissolution.

The chancel reflects this as there is no rood loft, thus keeping in line with the strict reforms introduced in the 1540s. The chancel dates to the 1520s or 1530s while the nave is as late as the 1540s or 1550s. The tower is said to be the prettiest in Norwich and was heavily restored in 1610. It contains much of the earlier structure as its lowest level dating from the late C14th. None of the church survives from its founding date at the end of the C11th. Inside, St Stephen's is a fine church seating up to 900 people. As with several other Norwich churches it has an

impressive hammerbeam roof and a large number of memorials and brasses. There are three commemorations to the Brownson family and a brass dated 1546 to Eile Buttry, Prioress of Campsey Abbey. At the eastern end of the church is a large and attractive window containing a fine array of C15th to C17th glass, including some work from England and Germany. Of particular note, however, is the screen or reredos behind the altar. A beautiful piece of work, it was given to the church as a gift from Miss Lucy Bignold in 1894. Miss Bignold was granddaughter of Thomas Bignold, founder of Norwich Union.

The recent Chapelfield development has transformed the formerly dingy churchyard, opening it and the church to greater public access and adding some interesting public art reflecting the history of church.

St Stephen's Leper Hospital
See *Trowel and Hammer*.

St Swithin

Redundant, medieval Walled City church. Almost next door to St Margaret's and with an even more turbulent history is the church of St Swithin, C9th patron saint of drought relief. Due to its dedication, the church likely has a late ninth or early tenth century foundation date and was first referred to in records of 1200. A good proportion of the current architecture dates from the C14th. Decorated style so St Swithin's appears to have escaped the massive rebuilding trend of the C15th. Even so, the church has undergone several restoration projects beginning with the western tower, condemned as unsafe in 1881. The tower was demolished but by 1883 the rest of the church had gone out of use. At the turn of the C20th St Swithin's came under the control of Rev. John Sawbridge who decided to refurbish the building and add a church hall. This was helped by a mysterious anonymous patron, whose donation allowed the project to be completed by 1910. At some point the beautiful font was also restored and its design shows the Trinity along with the three crowns of East Anglia. The only other detail of note is a monument commemorating the death, in 1767, of Catherine Suckling mother to Lord Nelson. After the Second World War St Swithin's again became redundant as a result of dwindling membership but the building was reborn as the Norwich Arts Centre and Café Bar.

St Thomas à Beckett Chapel
See *St Andrew's Hall*.

St Thomas, Heigham
Victorian, suburban, parish church. Built in 1888 on Earlham Road by Ewan Christian, the church was bombed badly, destroying the roof and central bell turret, during the infamous Baedeker Raids of April 1942. A.J. Chaplin restored the surviving shell after the War.

From top (left to right): St Stephen's west end and south side, St Swithin's south side, and the base of a pre Conquest cross shaft from the church of St Vedast.

St Vedast
Lost Walled City church. Also known as St Faith's, this church was founded in the pre-Conquest period. Documentary evidence from the C13th shows the church was dedicated to the Flemish saints St Vaast and St Armand, Vedast being a corruption of these and Faith being a sequential corruption of Vaast. The lane which took the church's name changed as follows – Vayst (1549), Fastes (1567), Fasse (1609) and eventually Faith's (1613). The advowson was in six parts: one part held by the cathedral-priory, the others in private hands. It is assumed that this church is the one mentioned in Domesday as having been 1/6 owned by Edstan. The church was demolished in 1540-41 and the parish was added to St Peter Parmentergate around

From top (left to right):
Ruined church of St
Wandregesilius, Bixley –
tower and south side.
Image of 'St' William of
Norwich commissioned in
the C15th for St John
Maddermarket church.

1562. However, the churchyard remained in use until at least 1744. A Mammen style stone, thought to have formed part of the churchyard cross shaft, was recovered from the fabric of a demolished house on the site in 1896 and is now displayed in the Castle Museum.

St Wandregesilius, Bixley

Derelict, medieval, parish church. The church of St Wandregesilius dates back to 1272 and is the only church dedicated to the C7th Frankish abbot St Wandregisel or Wandrille, the patron saint of weavers. Although the church was refurbished in 1868, the structure was severely damaged during an arson attack in 2004 and now stands derelict, in isolation from any other buildings.

St William of Norwich

Norwich's saint. William was a twelve year old apprentice tanner who disappeared in March 1144.

His mutilated body was discovered in Thorpe Wood (present day Mousehold). The body was initially buried where it was discovered but shortly after the grave was reopened and the body was identified by William's uncle, a priest called Godwin Stuart. Stuart accused the Jewish community of Norwich of abducting William to re-enact the Crucifixion and gain blood for their Passover feast. Bishop Eborard and the diocesan synod met to hear the accusations from Stuart who offered to prove his accusation by ordeal. This was the first recorded 'blood libel' (accusation of ritual murder) against the Jews. However, the Sheriff pointed out that the Bishop had no jurisdiction in the matter and that the Jews were effectively 'the property' of the King and under the Sheriff's protection. The case was, consequently, left unresolved. William's body was removed to the Cathedral and few a small miracles were attributed to

him but the cult did not gain in popularity until some years after his death when Thomas of Monmouth wrote about St William in The Life and Miracles of St William of Norwich and along with the prior and bishop encouraged the cult. The cult was disapproved of by the Pope because of its anti-semitic origins and eventually the cult lost popularity. More recently a chapel of the Holy Innocents has been established in the cathedral to pray for those who have suffered at the hands of others and for the reconciliation of the different faiths.

St William's Chapel

Lost chapel. Following the alleged martyrdom of William of Norwich, a chapel was consecrated to him on the spot of his death, by Bishop Turbe in 1168. It was demolished at the Reformation and virtually nothing apart from some earthworks remains today but the site is a Scheduled Ancient Monument.

St Winevalcy/ St Winwaloy

See *St Catherine.*

T is for...

The UK's largest teapot collection; England's leading advocate of C19th German literature; the first long distance, commercial telephone call in the country; the 'chief seat of the chief manufacture in the realm' from the medieval period until the C18th; the first purpose built provincial theatre.

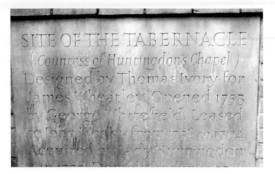

Plaque commemorating the lost Tabernacle.
Previous page: The largest teapot collection in the UK.

Tabernacle

Lost chapel. In 1751 one of John Wesley's preachers brought Methodism to Norwich. At the time this preacher, James Wheatley, had been disowned by John Wesley as he had been accused of and had admitted indecency with several of the young female members of the Bristol organisation. Nevertheless, Wheatley began his Norwich career preaching at a temporary tabernacle on Timberhill. His sermons were unpopular in Norwich and he was often attacked when preaching. Even so, in January 1753 a license was granted for a meeting house on Bishopgate and this meeting house, the Tabernacle, was built near to the Adam and Eve pub.

Funds for the Norwich Tabernacle were raised from at least forty four members of the organisation. The land and building cost £1,760 and the Tabernacle was designed by famous architect, Thomas Ivory, who later designed the Octagon and the Assembly House. The design was typically Georgian and austere with round headed sash windows and a double

entrance. Inside, the building was also rather plain and had a large upper gallery, high pulpit and straight-backed mahogany pews. Wheatley continued preaching at the new Tabernacle but unfortunately fell into his old ways. Almost as soon as it was opened, Wheatley was again accused of adultery and indecency with members of the congregation. Wheatley was expelled from the Methodist organisation in 1754, the same year that Charles Wesley promised Norwich a new larger place of worship which was to be at a former foundry on Timberhill but both buildings continued in use simultaneously for some time.

In 1775 Selina Hastings, Lady Huntingdon, bought the Tabernacle. She was one of England's most prominent Methodist leaders and had founded numerous Methodist chapels across the country. The Tabernacle became known as 'Lady Huntingdon's Connection Chapel' but by the 1930s was no longer in use. The Eastern Gas Board bought the former chapel and it was demolished by 1953.

Tas, River

Minor river. With tributaries emerging at Hempnall and Carleton Fen and joining at Tasburgh, the river flows for 20 miles north and joins the River Yare south of Norwich at Trowse. Originally the river would have provided a significant transport link for the inhabitants of the Roman town Venta Icenorum, now though it is a picturesque, modest river offering reasonable fishing and pleasant walks as part of the Tas Valley Way. The river has inspired poetry from Edwin Brock and Anthony Thwaite.

Taverham

Suburban parish. Located north of the River Wensum some 9.6km (6 miles) to the north west of Norwich City Centre and to the west of Drayton, Taverham has a population of 10,233 people. Taverham also incorporates the Thorpe Marriott housing development which has been constructed within the last twenty years to accommodate a major proportion of Norwich area growth. Taverham was recorded in the Domesday Book as 'Taursham'. The patron saint of Taverham is Saint Walston, as seen on the village sign where he is pictured with a scythe. St Walston is the patron saint of farms and farmers, and interestingly he died while scything a hay crop after allegedly experiencing a vision from an angel in 1016. Taverham's parish church is St Edmund's, a grade I listed, round towered structure, with a probable pre-Norman foundation. The church is recorded as having stood in Taverham in 1086, although the chancel and south aisle would have been added in the late

The former Norwich Institute for the Blind being demolished.

A very early taxi rank at the Haymarket.

C13th/early C14th. Lightning struck the church tower in 1459 and the church would have sustained some substantial damage, as at this time the roof was constructed of thatch and wood. Considerable repairs and renovation are recorded throughout the C17th/18th. Taverham Mill was recorded in the Domesday Book and began as a corn mill, although was better known as a paper mill after 1701. The mill was attacked during the Swing Riots in 1830, and eventually closed in 1899. Today only the wheelrace and marks from the waterwheels remain. Taverham Hall was built in 1858 in the neo-Jacobean style and now functions as a private school. A V-2 rocket exploded in woods near the Hall in October 1944.

Tawell, Thomas

Philanthropist. Born the son of a Wymondham draper, Tawell was brought up by a guardian from the age of ten after his father died, leaving his estate to his son. He was visually impaired and was moved to use his position of relative privilege to help blind people who, he felt, society was largely

ignoring, relegating them to a life in asylums or on the street as beggars. In 1804 he wrote to the Norfolk Chronicle expressing his desire to establish an institution that would care for the elderly blind and provide a school for blind children. A year later, a public meeting chaired by Mayor James Marsh launched the initiative and Tawell went on to buy a substantial house on the west side of Magdalen Street for the proposed institution to which 250 people had subscribed by the end of the year. It catered for blind people over the age of 65 who had not been in a workhouse or a 'beggar or wandering minstrel' and had a complete 'suit of apparel'. Children had to be 12 or over. Tawell continued to support the institution until his death in 1820. The institution itself has survived its founder and continues to prosper today as a major facility to support visually impaired people.

Taxis

Hailable public transport. Horse drawn carriages which could be hailed in the street operated in London

from the early C17th with the first stand being on the Strand. Legislation appeared in the mid C17th to allow the licensing of Hackney Carriages in London and environs and the trend soon spread to other cities. In the C19th, Norwich had a major horse drawn cab rank at the Haymarket and with the coming of the motor car in the C20th, motorised ranks followed. Norwich now has 217 'black cabs' and over 300 private hire vehicles. Principal taxi ranks within the City include the main rank east of the Guildhall and north of the Market, Norwich Station, Tombland, Norwich Airport, Castle Meadow and St Stephens. Taxis can be hailed on-street and conform to a standard, black format while private hire vehicles, coming in all shapes and sizes, have to be booked.

Taylor, William

Radical writer. Taylor was the son of a wealthy Norwich merchant involved in European trade but although the young man was schooled in Latin, French and Dutch, as a precursor to him taking over the family business, he found that this preparation

A wide selection of tea and coffee venues, including the 'smallest in the world'.

stimulated him into a life in politics and literature. He was a vocal supporter of the French Revolution and a proponent for universal suffrage. Although a nonconformist, his outspokenness and excessive drinking didn't endear him to the mainstream of nonconformists in the City. In parallel to his politically radical activity he was England's leading advocate for German literature. He visited Detmold, Göttingen, and Weimar in 1781-2 and in 1790 made his name with a translation of Bürger's narrative poem Lenore. He had met Goethe in 1782

and 1793 and produced a translation of Goethe's 'Iphigenia in Tauris'. Between 1793 and 1799 he wrote 200 reviews introducing the principle of philosophical criticism and in 1799 he toured Germany, France and Italy. His magnum opus was a three volume work called 'Historic Survey of German Poetry' and published in 1830. His writings were influential with poets such as Coleridge and Wordsworth. Taylor died in 1836 aged 71 and is buried in the Octagon graveyard.

Teapots

See *collections*.

Tea and Coffee Shops

Historic and Current Provision. The first coffee house opened in London in 1652 and Norwich followed with its first establishment recorded in 1680, although the first formal property record is of a coffee house in St Andrew's Hall in 1700. A William Browne, however, was running a 'Coffee Roome' well before this date and by the early C18th, the selling of tea and coffee by Norwich grocers was commonplace. By the mid 1700s there was a cluster of these establishments in the Market Place as well as other locations and they provided venues for political discussion. Today the usual chains abound, but notable independent tea and coffee shops include:

- **Assembly House**, Theatre Street – Regency Assembly House setting for elegant tea rooms
- **The Britons Arms**, Elm Hill – traditional English tea room in England's only medieval beguinage
- **Caley's**, The Guildhall – Chocolate themed café in England's most elaborate guildhall
- **Expresso**, St Georges St – popular café close to historic attractions
- **Harley's**, Yarmouth Rd, Thorpe River Green – attractive, riverside 'diner' style café
- **Hostry** – Anglican Cathedral's café set in stunning, modern building
- **Jarrold Dept Store** – top floor corner restaurant offers good views and elegant setting
- **King of Hearts**, Fye Bridge street – stunning medieval setting for traditional tea room
- **Morello**, Orford Yard – pleasant café in a former livery stable yard

- **No. 33**, Exchange St – popular café in central location
- **Olives**, Elm Hill – contemporary tea/coffee house in former medieval merchant house.

Telegraph Lane
Telegraph

Innovative communication medium. Developed in the late C18th as a means of high speed communication during the Napoleonic Wars, and therefore as an early warning device of possible invasion, the Shutter telegraph was a device using six large shutters in two vertical columns which could be arranged in different combinations to represent letters of the alphabet. Shutter stations were placed on high points 12 miles apart and the Norwich station was on the site of the present water tower at Telegraph Lane. It passed messages on from Strumpshaw and to Wreningham. A message could be flashed from the Admiralty in London via Norwich to Great Yarmouth along the 19 station chain in just 17 minutes. It operated at its peak from 1808 to 1814 and fell into disuse after peace with France.

Telephone Exchange
History of telephone development. In 1878, on 1st November, the first commercial long distance telephone call in the UK was made between Colmans Carrow Works and Cannon Street in London. The first Norwich exchange opened in 1883 at 12 Exchange Street but was superseded in 1891 by the 2nd exchange above the Great Eastern Railways Parcels Office in the Haymarket (currently Top Shop). In 1904 the exchange had moved to a 3rd site between Exchange Street and Dove Street, accessed off the Market Place. The 4th Exchange was set up in George Skipper's Baroque building in St Giles, built in 1906 for Norwich Union and occupied subsequently by the City Council. Increasing demand resulted in a new exchange being built in St Andrew's and although this started in 1938, the War delayed its opening until 1942. A dramatic proposal emerged in 1973 for a five storey building with a tall 'stack' beside it on the north side of St Andrew's but bridging across to the earlier exchange on the south side.

From left: Original switchboard from the old Norwich Telephone Exchange, a proposal to redevelop the Telephone Exchange which was never realised.

Early C20th textile factory, and a pattern book of C18th textile manufacturer.

This scheme did not progress and instead the current building, designed in 1981, was developed.

Telephone Kiosks, traditional

Phone boxes first appeared in the UK in 1884 but by 1912, when the Post Office took over responsibility for them, there were three favoured designs – the Norwich, the Birmingham and the Wilson. Following a national competition, Sir George Gilbert Scott's K2 was established as the favoured design and variants of this have appeared subsequently as the familiar red phone box. Due to the advent of mobile phones and the now limited use of pay phones as well as the substitution of the traditional design by hideous advert phone boxes, few of the original designs now survive.

Surviving traditional phone boxes, to the original or variant Gilbert Scott designs can be seen within the City Centre at St Andrews Street/Hill (two boxes), St Gregorys Alley, St Saviours, Tombland (two boxes) and Weavers Lane.

Terrace Houses
See opposite.

Textile Industry

Lost staple industry. Early cloth production in Norwich was centred around the production of heavy woollen products. The first mention of lighter Worsted cloth appears in 1315 when an alnager was appointed to regulate Worsted measurements made in 'NORTHWYC'. The Worsted industry flourished during the reign of Edward III when the King invited Flemings to help to develop the industry.

Edward III and his queen, the Flemish Philippa of Hainault visited the City on numerous occasions, presumably to monitor progress and for Philippa to engage with her countrymen. This proposition is endorsed by the large numbers of aliens recorded in the traditional textile districts of St Giles and St Andrews during this period. In the C15th the woollen and Worsted industries flourished and the manufacture of Dornix – fine linen thread combined with short woollen fibres – also developed. By the early C16th, Norwich was specialising in superior worsted fabrics and by the mid C16th Worsted Russells had been developed by the influx of Flemish and Walloon weavers whose numbers were initially only 30 families but within a few years they represented over a third of the City's population. The key here was that these immigrants would introduce 'New Draperies' not then being produced in Norwich, to reinvigorate the flagging textile industry. Production of Norwich Stuffs continued into the next century and developed on a massive scale to such an extent that wool had to be sourced from Lincolnshire and Liecestershire. Despite war and plagues, the industry continued to grow particularly in the last three decades of the century. A key element at this time was a use of silk as a subsidiary fabric which gave a major boost to the Norwich products. Additionally, Norwich Crape was introduced – a cloth made with a twisted weave to create a crimpled effect – and it is thought that

Terrace Housing

Volume working class housing. Although terraces first appeared in London, for the more affluent classes, in the late C17th, and similar terraces were developed in Norwich, the term is more commonly associated with cheap, volume housing for the working classes. This is reflected in the 1875 Artisans' Dwelling Act. Cole's plan of Norwich from 1807 shows large underdeveloped areas between the principal streets (Ber Street/King Street, Oak Street/St Augustines) and no residential development beyond the City Walls. Just 23 years later, Millard and Manning were still showing sparse development in the centre but significant, extra mural, terrace development at Crooks Place/Union Place (behind the N&N Hospital), further north between Dereham Road and Heigham Street and to the south, north of City Road. By the 1873 Morant Map, infilling was under way in the centre and Crooks Place and Heigham had expanded significantly. Between 1875 and 1919, 15,000 terrace houses were developed in a huge arc predominantly around the west and north of the City, with a smaller proportion in Thorpe Hamlet. In the 1950s/60s there was a drive to clear much of the older terrace housing but from the 1970s, improvement was the priority. The City retains one of the highest levels of terrace housing in the UK.

From top: general view of terrace housing, early terrace housing in Sussex Street, very early surviving terrace housing off King Street, early terrace housing development in the south of the City Centre.

Huguenot immigrants helped to refine this product. In 1714 Norwich was referred to as 'the chief seat of the chief manufacture in the realm'. Wars disrupted the export trade and recessions threatened the domestic industry but manufacturers rode out the storms to make the period 1743 -1763 the Golden Age of Norwich Textiles. In 1751 for instance, one of the Worsted Damask manufacturers recorded visitors from Cadiz, Venice, Leipzig, Weimar, Zurich, Frankfurt, Cologne, Bremen, Lubeck, Copenhagen, Oslo and Stockholm – all coming to order his products. Other manufacturers reported orders from as far afield as Oporto, Leghorn and St Petersburg. Access to the Russian market created demand in Siberia and there were even reports of large quantities of Norwich manufactures being re-exported from Spanish ports to Central and South America, while the East India Company was taking Norwich products to China. As the industry approached the end of the C18th two impulses contrived to undermine then destroy it. First the American War of Independence impacted badly upon export markets while the growing textile industry in the West Riding, able to exploit close supplies of coal and adopt higher levels of mechanisation, began to out compete the Norwich products. An output of £1.2m a year in the 1760s had dropped to £800,000 by 1798. The decline had set in and was irreversible. The Norwich Shawl helped to cushion the decline for a time, until it in turn fell out of fashion, while brave attempts to deploy

The Hermitage, one of six thatched buildings surviving in the centre.

new, mechanised factories at Whitefriars and in King Street failed before they started. Vestiges, however, hung on for a long time and the last textile factory, Courtaulds in St Mary's, didn't close until the 1970s. www.norwichtextiles.org.uk

Thatched Buildings

The use of thatch was outlawed following the fires of 1507 and although this order was repealed in 1532, later laws again sought to limit the spread of fires by requiring the use of other materials. It is therefore unsurprising that, of the surviving houses from this period, the thatched examples within the City Walls number six only. Apart from the Britons Arms, the others include Pykerell's House, in St Mary's Plain, which is a late C15th survivor and the only thatched house north of the river. This small but fine merchant house retains a queen post roof in its thatched hall at right angles to the street range and derives its name from Thomas Pykerell, three

times mayor of Norwich in the early C16th. This house later became the Rosemary Tavern. Another thatched survivor is a late C15th house in Hampshire Hog Yard – taking its name from the house when it later became a pub. The building's former occupants included Mayor Sir Peter Seaman who bequeathed the property to provide an annual income to train apprentices. The other three thatched survivors are the C15th Hermitage on the south side of Bishopgate, the C16th Barking Dicky (a local corruption of the sign of the Light Horseman pub formerly occupying the building) in Westlegate – the old Pastry Market – and the tiny cottage in Lion and Castle Yard. Beyond the Walls another remarkable survivor is the thatched church of St Andrew at Eaton.

Thatched Theatre

Former cinema. Located next to the fashionable Bonds department store and owned by the same family, the Thatched started life as a restaurant and ballroom. The latter was converted to a cinema in 1915 and quickly became the 'quality venue' for local audiences, augmented by a quality string orchestra and a tea room. It also had the additional novel feature of a sliding roof which was opened in pleasant weather, although how this worked with the cinema black out isn't clear. It was never equipped for 'talkies' and struggled on until 1930 when it reverted to its former ballroom use before being absorbed into Bond's store, then succumbing to enemy bombs in 1942.

Theatres

History and provision. Theatres have a long tradition in Norwich, beginning with players companies in inns along the Walk and in venues such as the White Swan in St Peter's Street. They developed into more formal venues such as the Theatre Royal – only the second purpose built theatre in England – as well as other venues such as the Hippodrome. Today there is an extensive range of theatre offers including:

- **Theatre Royal**, Theatre St – recently completely refurbished offering 1,300 seats and top West End entertainment
- **Norwich Young People's Theatre**, Hewitt School – focusing on productions by 5-25 year olds
- **Norwich Playhouse**, St Georges St – 300 seats, broad range of theatre, music and performance
- **Norwich Arts Centre**, St Benedicts St – variety of music and performance
- **Norwich Puppet Theatre**, Whitefriars – 185 seat auditorium presenting a range of puppet productions

- **Maddermarket Theatre**, St John's Alley – reproduction Shakespearian theatre, amateur productions
- **King of Hearts**, Fye Bridge St – small venue specialising in music, recitals etc
- **Sewell Barn**, Constitution Hill – amateur productions
- **UEA Studio**, University – theatre and other performance.

Theatre de Luxe

Former cinema. Norwich's first 'proper' cinema, the Theatre de Luxe (pronounced locally as 'theatre de lue') was converted from an early C19th building, including the former 1831 Technical Institute, and was opened by Electric Theatres 1908 Ltd, who operated a chain in London and the south. Initially, the cinema's capacity was 560 seats but it proved to be so popular that its capacity was almost doubled in 1920 by a major reconstruction which provided 1,000 seats. It was the last cinema in Norwich to convert to 'talkies' but the first to become equipped for 3D, in 1953. It closed in 1957 and after years of neglect, was eventually demolished and the site is now an access yard for the adjacent telephone exchange.

Theatre Royal

Principal theatre. Thomas Ivory built the first Theatre Royal, 'The New Theatre in Chapelfield', in 1758. It was the second purpose built theatre in England and in 1759 it was renamed 'The Grand Concert Hall'. In 1826, changing tastes provoked William Wilkins to redevelop the site. At £6,000, the new theatre cost ten times what Ivory's had cost to build. A new manager, Fred Morgan, improved the fortunes of the business and stayed from 1855 for nearly 50 years when he left to work on the Grand Opera House (Hippodrome) in St Giles. Morgan returned in 1904 to the renamed Theatre Royal. The institution continued successfully until 1934 when a catastrophic fire destroyed it. The ruin was quickly replaced by what was a standard Art Deco design for Odeon cinemas at the time and it reopened in 1935. Despite some close shaves during the War the Theatre Royal was very

From left: The recently refurbished Theatre Royal, and Theatre Royal after the 1930s fire.

successful but by 1956 it had been taken over by a cinema chain who used it for pantos at Christmas and occasional concerts as well. The Theatre Royal operated as a cinema from 1956 and was the first in the City to introduce stereophonic sound but as audiences diminished it was used as a bingo hall before eventually being bought by the Council in 1970. City Architect David Percival's refurbishment scheme served it well in its new incarnation and the inspirational manager Dick Condon turned around its performance to make it the only financially successful provincial theatre in the country. A further refurbishment in 1991 maintained audience figures and Condon's successor, Peter Wilson continued the success, masterminding a £10m refurbishment in 2010.

Thorns

Historic ironmonger. Thorns was founded in 1835 in the newly developed Exchange Street by a wealthy London merchant called Robert Elliott Thorns just following the completion of the first Corn Exchange. Thorns owned a run of property in the street, including nos. 16-22, and could,

potentially, have been one of the developers of the new street. Thorns went into partnership with Charles Fisher Ishbill and Robert Paston, whose descendents are still partners in the company. In the late C19th the company also occupied the Old Iron House, which survives further north in Exchange Street. Despite the virtual eradication of the independent DIY sector by 'big sheds' and globalised trading formats over the last 30 years, Thorns has survived as a remarkable monument to personal service and speciality retailing. Today, 20 expert staff from seven different departments will be happy to sell you all manner of obscure ironmongery items or to get it for you if they don't have it in stock. The labyrinthine premises are also a delight to explore, stretching between Exchange Street and Dove Street, and even under ground – long may they prosper.

Thorpe End

Suburban 'garden village'. Thorpe End village, located to the west of the Plumsteads, was founded by Percy and Leonard Howes in the 1930s following Ebenezer

Howard's garden village model, with properties being built on individually owned plots in rural styles. The north end of the village was further expanded throughout the 1970s and 1980s. The church of St David's was built in 1992.

Thorpe Hamlet

Hamlet beyond City Walls. Located just to the east of the City Centre on the wooded escarpment, Thorpe Hamlet derives its name from the middle English 'thorp' meaning a hamlet or small village. According to archaeological evidence, the Pilgrim's Way, an old Roman track passed through this area. The manor of Thorpe was granted to Bishop de Losinga by Henry I in 1101 and he then went on to establish St Leonard's Priory and St Michael's chapel. Subsequently, the Duke of Norfolk acquired the site of the Priory at the Dissolution and in 1544, his son Henry Howard, the Earl of Surrey, built a house known as Mount Surrey, although shortly after, in 1547, the Earl was executed for treason. The house, as well as the remains of the priory and St Michael's church, were used by Kett in the 1549 rebellion as the headquarters of the 'King's Great Camp'. Mount Surrey fell into disrepair subsequently and two farmhouses occupied the site from the C18th and one was used for the headquarters of the Royal Flying Corps during the First World War, although the last house was demolished in the 1970s. Very little of St Michael's chapel remains today. Lollard's Pit was a chalk pit which had been dug into the hills opposite Bishop's Bridge and was

Views of Thorpe End Garden Village.

Clockwise from top: Thorpe Hamlet – Taylor Green housing, St Michael's Terrace and the lost St Leonard's Church. Inset: historic detail.

used for the execution of witches and heretics.

Parish status was granted to Thorpe Hamlet in 1852, when it was known as the parish of St Matthew's, and considerable growth was seen throughout the C19th. The Norwich School painter John Berney Ladbroke had his house Kett's Castle Villa built on St Leonard's Road, notable for its gardens which incorporated some medieval arches, possibly taken from St Michael's. The gas works had been established in 1830 on St Leonard's Hill, now Gas Hill, and the gas manager developed terraced houses built of old kiln lining bricks and laid out terraced gardens in the late C19th, which are now known as Kett's Heights, and were previously known as Jubilee Gardens. North of the St Michael's chapel site are the remains of orchards, stables and a drinking trough dating from the time when the land was used for allotments in the early C20th. The parish church of St Matthew had been built on Rosary Road by John Brown in 1851 with a capacity of 600 and

served the local population for 130 years when a new St Matthew's was built on Telegraph Lane West in 1981 to a design by Peter Codling Associates. After being declared redundant, the original 1851 church was converted into offices by the same architects. Thorpe Hamlet Towermill, or Gallant's Mill, was built in 1834 to the back of the gas works. The mill house still remains today. Between 1881 and 1911 most of the escarpment overlooking the City and beyond was developed for terraced housing. The surviving Jubilee pub was built to commemorate Victoria's Golden Jubilee in 1887. In 1908, Norwich City Football Club moved to its second home at 'The Nest' on Rosary Road. After the First World War, housing spread eastwards and water tower of Mousehold Reservoirs, located off Quebec Road and Telegraph Lane, was constructed between 1932-33. New Council housing was developed in the late 1960s/early 1970s and incorporated, in the north of the area, the Taylor & Green model of housing

development, innovative for its time. The area was designated a conservation area in 1991.

Thorpe Road

Radial Road. This is the principal east bound radial running from the City Centre to the village of Thorpe St Andrew, and thus to Great Yarmouth. The City end of the road, from the Rosary Road junction, didn't exist prior to the development of the first Foundry Bridge in 1810. One of the first buildings on the new section of Thorpe Road was the attractively balconied 'Yarmouth Coach' pub which still survives as the Coach and Horses pub and Chalk Hill Brewery. Moving eastwards from the City end, one of the oldest and indeed most impressive buildings is the 1886 Thorpe Station, in the French Chateau style. On the opposite side of Thorpe Road, a pleasant, late C19th terrace leads to No. 22, a Flemish revival villa by A.F. Scott, dating from 1894 and employing Cosseyware decoration. Opposite again, Nos. 7-9 are attractive, late

From left: Elevated view of Thorpe St Andrew, and the Buck PH, Thorpe St Andrew.

C19th villas, recently converted to flats. Next to these is the Post Office Sorting Office, designed by T.F. Winterburn for the Ministry of Works in 1956 and represents one of the few good 1950s buildings in the City. Further eastwards on the south side the Jonathan Scott Memorial Chapel commemorates the Reverend Scott who ministered to the parish of Thorpe Hamlet for 44 years. The building was designed by one of Reverend Scott's sons, A.F. Scott and opened in 1902. This is thought to be the best of Scott's many Gothic revival churches in Norwich and one of the finest Methodist chapels in England. By the 1980s it had been vacant for some time and was converted to offices in 1986. Further east a range of late Victorian villas and terraces typify the character of the road, interspersed with later development. The former Redan pub (1873), named after a defensive work in the Crimean War, is a good example of a suburban Victorian pub but it went out of use in 1986 and is now a Chinese restaurant. Thorpe Road then becomes Yarmouth Road and continues eastwards.

Thorpe St Andrew

Suburban parish. Located two miles to the east of the historic City Centre, Thorpe St Andrew is a large civil parish with a population of 13,762, whose history dates back to Roman times as evidenced by the discovery of Roman archaeological findings in the area, such as a 32 inch sword inlaid in gold. Thorpe is recorded in the Domesday Book as 'Torp', originating from the Scandinavian word for 'village', although 'Thorp' is also a Viking word for 'daughter settlement'. Up until 1536, Thorpe St Andrew was known as Thorpe Episcopi (Bishop's Thorpe), when it became Thorpe-next-Norwich until taking its current name in 1954. The original village centred around Yarmouth Road with the river to the south, and included the Thorpe Narrows, a narrow street whose building frontages came right up to

Thorpe Old Hall before and after restoration.

Views of Timberhill.

the carriageway, which was demolished in the 1950s. The parish originally incorporated Thorpe Hamlet, and also incorporated parts of Mousehold Heath; Plumstead Road East for example, was a track running through the heath and woodland in former centuries. The area has a wealth of historic buildings, and accordingly parts of Thorpe St Andrew have been designated a conservation area by Broadland council. Thorpe Old Hall, located off of Thorpe Hall Close, probably dates from the C14th when, as a courtyard house, it was in the possession of the Bishops of Norwich, although the surviving part is only a small portion of the larger house remodelled in the C16th by Edward Paston. Other buildings of note include: The Rushcutters pub (formerly known as The Tuns in the C19th), which was built circa 1600; the school on Old School Lane, built 1841; the Manor House (12 Yarmouth Road) dating from the mid C17th and the

addition to this at 16 Yarmouth Road from the C18th, which includes a gazebo overlooking the river; and St Andrews Hospital, originally the County Asylum, dating from 1814 but closed in 1998 before being developed into residential properties. Thorpe Lodge on the Yarmouth Road was built by John Harvey in 1792; interesting features of the Lodge which remain today are the gazebo (1a Yarmouth Road) which originally housed a camera obscura, and Harvey's so-called 'crinkle crankle' boundary wall, which ran through the grounds of the Lodge and marked the City boundary. The parish church of St Andrew was built between 1866 and 1882 to replace the former C13th church, although a church has been on this site since at least 1086. The C13th font remains, as does a sundial dating from 1694. The spire was damaged in an air raid in the WWII and was replaced by a pyramidal roof in 1944. Thorpe St Andrew

has seen considerable growth throughout the C20th, and has expanded beyond the historic heart of the village around Yarmouth Road towards the east to incorporate the late C20th housing estate at Dussindale and Broadland Business Park.

Thorpe Station
See *Railway Station*.

Timberhill
Ancient route. Probably originally part of a Roman route running from Ber Street to Oak Street, the street was originally called Durnedale (secret or hidden valley) but takes its present name from the Timbermarket that used to be at the Ber Street end from the time of Edward III. Before the Second World War, the Street had many ancient and interesting buildings but the April 1942 Baedeker Raids demolished most of the east side, including the knapped flint faced Star and Crown – a medieval gem, and left an unsightly gap in the west

frontage. Starting from the southern end, the pre Conquest origin St John's church survives and opposite there is a run of attractive buildings including 43-41 dating from 1707, then an imaginative, contemporary infill building next to the attractive C17th No. 35. The C17th No. 33 was formerly the Red House pub from 1830 until 1894 when it became the Museum Café. Next to this the attractive, jettied No. 31 is C16th in origin. Through the gap to the north, in Lion and Castle Yard, are a pair of C17th Weavers cottages sporting one of only six thatched roofs in the City Centre. No. 25 is late C17th with C19th shops at Nos. 23 and 21, then No. 19 is C18th as is No. 17 with a jettied first floor. The Orford Hill Baptist Chapel dates from 1833 and is now in restaurant use. C19th link northwards to the C17th Nos. 1-3 which sit on a C15th brick undercroft. On the opposite, east side, the C17th Murderers/ Gardeners pub takes its 'popular' name from a murder there in 1895 and its extension occupies a C19th shop. The remainder of the east side is a reconstruction of the bombed façade by Lambert, Scott and Innes in a pleasant, vernacular reinterpretation of the historic form. Today the street provides an attractive combination of independent speciality shops and eating/drinking outlets.

Tinkler, Capt Robert

Bounty loyalist. In 1789, Robert Tinkler was part of Captain Bligh's crew on the Bounty in the South Seas of the Pacific. When the crew engaged in the famous mutiny, Tinkler and his brother-in-law were amongst the 19 who remained loyal to Captain Bligh and were set adrift in a 23 foot boat by the mutineers. Bligh and his companions endured a voyage of 41 days, during which the only sustenance was one ounce of bread and a quarter of a pint of water each day, and eventually arrived at the Dutch settlement of Cupan in the island of Timor although they had landed at other islands (uninhabited or hostile) en route. The mutineers had allowed 28 gallons of water, 150 lbs of ships biscuits, 20 lb of pork, five gallons of rum, three bottles of wine, some coconuts and bread fruit, no guns but four cutlasses in the boat. After they reached Timor, six more men died of disease, because of their weakened state.

The only mention of Tinkler in Bligh's log of this journey was on Timor on 7th July 1789. 'Robert Tinkler and the Master, his brother-in-law, having behaved Saucy and Impertinent to the Boatswain, received some little chastisement for it, upon which it appears the Master interfered and ordered him to stick his knife into the Boatswain. As soon as I became acquainted with this matter, I publicly reprimanded the Master, making him responsible and equally Criminal with Tinkler in case any such violence is committed.'

Tinkler was not called as a witness in the mutineers' trial, probably due to his absence from England at the time. He was promoted Lieutenant on the 'Isis', on which ship he fought at the Battle of Copenhagen in 1801 with Lord Nelson's squadron, which attacked the Danish line. The 'Isis' was heavily engaged for four and a half hours with two of the enemy's ships at close quarters. 27 members of the crew were killed and 84 wounded. Tinkler later rose to the rank of Post-Captain and Commander. In 1820 he died, aged just 46, he was buried in St Margaret's churchyard in St Benedict's. "He signalised himself by his intrepid bravery in several engagements, in which he received 21 wounds".

Tombland
See page 422.

Tombland Fair

Lost Fair. The Tombland Fair was an annual fair held around Christmas time with its origins in the C12th and possibly earlier. In 1818 it was moved to the site of the Old Cattle Market, previously known as the Castle Ditches, where it remained for over a century and a half. In the C19th and first half of the C20th it was characterised by fairground rides and the kind of freak shows that had previously appeared in inns around Gentlemans Walk. With the development of the Castle Mall shopping centre in the early 1990s the fair was variously relocated to the Livestock Market at Harford, streets around the centre, including Castle Meadow, and Chapelfield Gardens.

Tombland Synagogue

Lost synagogue. In 1818, Barnet Crawcour, a dentist and leader of the Jewish community in Norwich, began raising funds to build or rent a synagogue in Norwich. The room in a house on Gowing's Court off St Stephen's Street that was being used for services was no longer suitable but it

Houses in the Town Close Estate.

took ten years to find a better space. In July 1828 a small synagogue measuring only 5.8 x 4.3m (19 x 14 ft) was opened in Tombland Alley, on the corner of St George's churchyard and next to Augustine Steward's House. The synagogue was a simple room and had a small cupboard or Ark set into one of the walls used to store the synagogue's scrolls. When the Jewish community moved to Tombland, it was still small, just twenty-nine members, but within twenty years a new synagogue was needed to accommodate the growing congregation. In 1848 construction of a new synagogue was begun on St Faith's Lane off King Street and the synagogue in Tombland was vacated. It is uncertain what the building was then used for but by 1961 it was the coke store for the Samson and Hercules club. The location of the Tombland Synagogue is uncertain but the early C19th three-storey building, now Tombland Jewellers and Silversmiths, may have housed it.

Toppes, Robert

Medieval entrepreneur. Toppes was a significant figure in C15th Norwich but his principal reason for being remembered is that he was probably responsible for the construction of Dragon Hall to provide a huge display facility for his goods. Essentially he was a merchant trading cloth and other goods principally to the Low Countries and importing a wide range of goods from the Continent. His stature is reflected in the remarkable achievement of becoming Mayor in 1435, 1440, 1452 and 1458 as well as being a Burgess to Parliament. He donated a stained glass window to St Peter Mancroft where he is buried. The window includes an inset depicting Toppes and his family.

TIC (Tourist Information Centre)

The tourist information centre is located in The Forum and is open six days a week. It provides a wide range of information on local attractions, facilities and events and is able to help out with accommodation.

Town Close

Historic District. The Domesday Book refers to 80 acres between Lakenham, Eaton and Harford and south of Needham (St Stephens Gate) over which the townsfolk had grazing rights. For the next 450 years, disputes continued between the Prior and the City as to who controlled 'The Town Close' but the Reformation finally settled it confirming the rights of the City Burgesses over the area. From the C19th control was exercised by the Freemen and the area began to be developed to meet the residential needs of the more affluent classes seeking to avoid the congestion and insanitary conditions of the Walled City. Income from this development was managed by the Freemen, going into a fund operated for charitable benefit of local people and organisations. Town Close is now, broadly, the area bounded by Newmarket Road, Ipswich Road and the Outer Ring Road. It has been developed substantially for large villa

Tombland

Ancient market space

Deriving its name from the Anglo Scandinavian term meaning empty space, the area was the principal, pre Conquest market place and the epicentre of the Anglo Scandinavian Borough, supporting the principal church of the period and the Earl's Palace. Even after the Conquest and the development of the Priory Precinct on the east side, Tombland continued to be an important space for civic events, including the Tombland Fair, and a fashionable place to live with nine Mayors having residences there. Moving clockwise from the junction with Queen Street, No. 3/3a is a substantial C18 house as is No. 4 but the latter sits on a C15th undercroft. No. 5 is also C18th with an impressive Georgian staircase inside while No. 6 although predominantly C18th, connects to 19 Princes Street which sports an exposed C16th timber ceiling with dragon beam. On the opposite corner of Tombland and Princes Street, the corner pub was

built in 1870 and originally the Army and Navy Stores before being renamed the Edith Cavell in 1981, then Coles, then Edith Cavell again in 2008. Next door the applied timber framing hides a C15th house with C18th additions while next to that is a C17th house. Nos. 10 and 11 used to be an impressive Georgian house which collapsed and was replaced by a replica in the 1970s. Next again, No. 12 is of C17th origin while on the corner of Tombland Alley an early C19th house (possibly the site of the Tombland Synagogue). On the opposite corner is the remarkable C16th Augustine Steward House and next to that the surviving remnant of the Samson and Hercules, dating originally from 1657, and on the site of a mansion owned by Sir John Fastolf. The one time Waggon and Horses pub, now Take 5, again has applied revival timber framing hiding a building with its origins in 1480 standing on a C15th undercroft. Opposite, the Maids Head is of even earlier origins despite its Tudor revival façade,

although the recently restored east range in Palace Street gives a feeling of where the building comes from. Crossing to the east side of Tombland, the imposing Erpingham Gate, built between 1416 and 1425, still retains an effigy of its builder, 'stout Sir Thomas', in a niche above its arch. Just south of the gate is a bust commemorating the Norfolk heroine Edith Cavell. The first building of the eastern range is a mid C18th house, now a restaurant and next to it is the C19th Erpingham House as is No. 23. Next south is the very elaborate No. 24 designed in 1888 by E.P. Wilkins next to No. 25 which has an C18th northern portion with the remainder being early C19th. Completing the range is the St Ethelbert Gate which is predominantly a 1320 rebuild of the earlier gate destroyed in the 1272 Riot. The southern range is a very attractive run of Georgian town houses but predictably perhaps, they are not all they seem – No. 26 sits on a C15th brick undercroft. This was

allegedly the site of the Saxon Earl's Palace and in the early C16th Sir William Denny developed the site for a building called 'Stonehall', parts of which were incorporated into the Georgian redevelopment. Next door, No. 27 had a very grand doorway up until the 1930s when it was relocated to West Bradenham Hall and the opening was replaced by a sash window. The buildings therefore represent an impressive ensemble which is degraded severely by the awful space which they sit around, disfigured by a hideous, concrete, underground toilet, pock-marked with at least two dozen sorts of randomly scattered street furniture, fragmented by probably a dozen different surface materials and dislocated by heavy, fast moving traffic. It could be one of the most delightful urban squares in England, a fitting entry to the Cathedral Close, but instead it's an appallingly wasted opportunity.

Below, from opposite left: Tombland on a map of 1530, Undercroft beneath 26 Tombland, and Tombland Fair after its move to the Old Cattle Market, 1950s. Above: Tombland at night.

type houses in substantial grounds, and a large private school (Town Close). The income from the estate is today managed by the Town Close Charity which continues to dispenses grants to a wide range of educational and charitable causes.

Town Crier
See *Bellman*.

Trafford Estate
Housing development outside the City Walls. The Trafford housing estate was developed between New Lakenham and Town Close on the 'Trafford Estate at Lakenham' in the ownership of the Trafford Family of Wroxham Hall, from the 1890s. Prior to this the area had been occupied largely by allotments and nurseries and a pub, the Nursery Tavern, is recorded just off Southwell Road/Grove Road from 1865. With the impending development of terraced housing, the Nursery transferred its licence to the new Trafford Arms on Trafford Road in 1885. The first phase of terraced housing development was concentrated between 1890 and the early C20th and after a lull around the First World War there was a second phase of building in the 1930s when St Alban's church was also developed. The roads took their names largely from the Trafford Family and, additional to Trafford Road itself, include Cecil Road, Eleanor Road, Lady Betty Road, Lady Mary Road and Sigismund Road. The pub and a few houses were destroyed in the 1942 Baedeker Raids and rebuilt after the War. The Council also acquired the City College site from the Trafford estate in the late 1930s and

Trafford Estate.

developed the College after the War. Much of the site had been occupied principally by the Grove, a substantial residential property whose tenents had included the Gurneys and the Chamberlains. Now all that survives is a lodge to the original house. Further new housing followed with the redevelopment of Grove Road and Grove Walk in the 1960s. One curiosity of the area is the Ring also known as the Sheep Pen. This is a railinged and grassed enclosure on Trafford Road. Its original purpose is unclear and although a Norfolk Chronicle Report of 1739 talks about a mass grave on the site with an association to a coin of 1664 it is more likely that the Ring is merely an early example of a landscape feature.

Trams

Lost urban transport system. The tram network was developed under the impetus of Town Clerk George Butler Kennett and the supervision of architect George Skipper. It was installed from 1899 and represented the most dramatic impact on the City's streetscape since its development just after the Norman Conquest. It was the first street tramway in the Eastern Counties to be powered by electricity. Over 17 miles of tracks were laid originally and a terminus was constructed at Orford Place with a depot at Silver Road. One rather unusual addition was an electric light railway extension across Mousehold to transport materials to aircraft factories at the Mousehold Aerodrome. Aside from half a dozen electrical conductors on buildings in the City Centre, the Silver Road Depot is the only surviving physical manifestation of the network which opened on 30th July 1900 and closed 35 years later, with the last tram running on 10th December 1935. Ultimately, the trams were seen as inflexible and anachronistic as the advent of new motorbuses offered greater flexibility, range and comfort.

Trinity Presbyterian Church

Lost Victorian church. Opened in 1867 opposite the Theatre Royal, this imposing building with bell tower and rose window, had a capacity of 550. It was destroyed during the air raids of 1942.

Trinity United Reform Church

Post War Presbyterian Church. The construction of Trinity Presbyterian Church was begun, on the eastern end of Unthank Road in October 1954 on the site of a former Baptist chapel designed by the firm of architects Edward

From left: Surviving former Tram Depot, Silver Road, and a Norwich Tram.

Boardman and Son in the 1870s. The current church cottage and hall were part of this complex. The chapel had gone out of use in 1941 and was being used as a store by Caley Mackintosh, the famous Norwich chocolate company. The Presbyterian Church bought the site after its Trinity Church, Theatre Street, had been bombed during the Second World War and it was the first war damaged church to be rebuilt in Norwich, albeit on a new site. The 250 seat church thrived on the site despite being in the shadow of the mighty Church of St John the Baptist and in the early 1970s Trinity became part of the United Reformed Church.

The unusual design of Trinity was the inspiration of Sir Bernard Feilden, then a young designer working for Boardman and son. The design has a very modern look from the outside, with a detached tower or 'Campanile': the only example in Norwich. Inside the building you climb the stairs to reach the airy main church, leaving the ground floor to more practical uses. Feilden's design for Trinity has caused much debate and people wonder about his source of inspiration. He dismissed notions of it being Scandinavian in style or inspired by churches in Norwich, saying that his inspiration came from a very early church near Ravenna, Italy. He also made a careful study of Presbyterian beliefs to help inform his work and he even designed all of the church furniture. Trinity was Feilden's first church and was recently listed but he went on to design several buildings in and around Norwich and to become

Former Leper Hospital, now the Trowel and Hammer public house.

Norwich Cathedral architect. He is now celebrated nationally and internationally for his contribution to architecture throughout England.

Trowel and Hammer

Pub, formerly a medieval Leper House. There is a strong probability that the medieval St Stephen's Leper Hospital, which is recorded in 1315, survives in the fabric of the current public house. The 'Lazar House' survived the Reformation as a hospital and by 1700 a tavern on the site was known as the 'Spittle House' – a corruption of hospital. The proposition is further confirmed by the fact that the tavern was called the Lazar House by 1755. It wasn't until 1824 that it became the Trowel and Hammer. The back bar had previously been used as stables and in the early C19th had accommodated the horses of a cavalry troop brought in to quell agricultural riots. The pub also has connections with the famous artist Sir Alfred Munnings who was given a bay mare by the landlord as the subject of his first large scale horse painting, The Suffolk Marshes. The pub

was also the lodgings for painter William Martin before he became locally famous. After a brief spell as Finnegans Wake in the 1990s it got its proper name back in 2002.

Trowse

Suburban parish. Located around 2.4km (1.5 miles) to the south east of the City Centre on the River Yare, the parish of Trowse with Newton can be divided into a number of distinct parts: Trowse Common, or the main village; Crown Point, or Upper Trowse, where Newton was originally located; Trowse Magna, a gated development at Whitlingham Hall; New Newton, an extension to the original village around Newton Close built in 1968; and Nether Trowse, located at the far end of Whitlingham Lane, and originally part of the hamlet of Whitlingham prior to the dereliction of St Andrew's church. The name 'Trowse' is thought to derive from the Old English or Scottish word 'trouse' meaning a wood or iron grate which controlled the flow of water into a mill race. Trowse is recorded during the Saxon period when it was owned by the Bishop Stigand, although

Clockwise from top left: Trowse village centre, Trowse Pumping Station, the ruins of Trowse Newton Hall, and Colman's workers' cottages in Trowse.

the land was acquired in 1205 by the Cathedral Priory of Norwich. St Andrew's church was founded around 1281 by William de Kirkby, although the tower is C15th. The church was restored in the late Victorian period after a period of dereliction. Many church records were lost during the 1912 flood when the water level rose to 3 feet deep in the nave. Crown Point Hall, formerly Whitlingham Hall, was built in 1784, and then rebuilt by the Colman family in 1865. Trowse was developed as a model village in the C19th, to house workers at the nearby Colman's factory. The development pre dated the more famous model communities developed by the Cadburys or Rowntrees and as well as terraced houses for the workers and semi detached houses for management levels, the Colmans built a chapel and a school. Crown Point Hall was sold off in 1955 and was used for some time as a hospital, although it is currently being used as residential property. Norwich Ski Club's dry ski slope was founded in 1972 and is based in Trowse. The completion of the Trowse Bypass in the 1990s had a beneficial traffic impact on the village.

Trowse Millgate

Suburban hamlet. Situated around one mile to the south east of the City Centre north of the river Yare and forming part of the City of Norwich separate from the parish of Trowse, Trowse Millgate centres on the mill itself, which was first mentioned in the Domesday Book. In the C18th, a later mill was a target for grain riots and then in 1792 a fire destroyed the mill, although it was rebuilt subsequently and was one of the largest mills in Norfolk with two waterwheels. In 1967 the mill was completely demolished, and it was only in 2001 that the mill was rebuilt to a design which reflected the original mill building, for a residential development. The bridge was also a significant feature of Trowse Millgate first being recorded in 1430, although the present structure dates from only 1863. The railway line was constructed in 1845 and trains stopped at Trowse station, which dates from 1854 and was used principally for transporting cattle destined for the Old Cattle Market adjacent to the Castle. A tram line extended down to the station from the turn of the C20th, although this had closed by 1934 and the station ultimately closed in 1939. A sewerage plant consisting of a pumping station and six artisans cottages was constructed in the area between 1866 and 1867 and extended in 1909. Post-World War II saw a period of industrial decline which left many of the area's buildings derelict and in disrepair. Bracondale Millgate has, however, seen a renaissance in more recent times with the restoration of some of its historic buildings. Buildings of historical interest include the Pineapple Public House, dating from the mid to late C19th and destined to be developed as part of a new fire station; Mill House, dating from the C17th; Trowse House, dating from 1703; and the Trowse House Cottages, built in 1884.

Tudor Hall

Industrial remnant. Tudor Hall, located on Rose Lane, is a Tudor revival, Arts and Crafts Movement building designed in 1899 by Boulton & Paul's architect, Thomas Plaford. This building formed the 'front door' headquarters office for the company's substantial factory site which occupied a majority of the street block between Rose Lane and Mountergate and King Street and St John's Street. The company had acquired premises in King Street, two years earlier, to develop a new Smiths and Fencing Shop but when they started to demolish what they thought were 'dilapidated cottages' they uncovered a substantial medieval Hall House (like Strangers Hall). Since it was beyond restoration, they salvaged substantial roof timbers which were reused in the new building as well as a major medieval moulded ceiling which they reinstated in Dawson Paul's office (Governing Director) within the new headquarters. During the demolition work, a very well preserved C14th crypt was also uncovered, in 'splendid condition' and local historian Walter Rye prevailed upon the company to retain it although it was lost subsequently when the Boulton & Paul site was redeveloped. They also relocated a door frame dated 1586 and a nine light window from the same period, from a house on the junction of William Street and St John's Street, into the east façade of the Tudor Hall. After Boulton & Paul vacated the building it was used for a range of uses but most recently a series of night clubs including Tudor Hall, Henrys and Peppermint Park. After a long period of vacancy it was recently converted to ten flats.

Tunnels

Subterranean passages. Norwich tunnels fall into two basic categories, legendary and actual – either still existing or lost but with verifiable evidence that they did exist. The former category are part of local folklore and while they may have existed, there is no evidence to that effect and they do not exist now. Principally quoted examples of the folklore type include a tunnel between the Castle and the Guildhall and one between St Andrew's Hall and the Cathedral. This issue is explored in more depth in the *Underground Norwich* entry.

Tussaud, Madame

Wax museum innovator. Born Marie Grosholz, Marie learned her skill in wax moulding from a Swiss Dr. Curtius and when he died she inherited his entire waxwork collection and toured it around Europe. In 1819 she exhibited at the Angel on the Walk and returned in July 1825 for a more impressive and extensive exhibition at the Assembly House.

U is for...

The largest number of architectural awards for a campus university in the UK; the UK's largest collection of medieval undercrofts; the country's largest university sports centre; Sir John Mills' school; a bid for the first UNESCO City of Literature in England.

UEA – the University of East Anglia

Principal university.

The University of East Anglia (UEA) is situated on a 270 acre campus in the western suburbs of Norwich. UEA comprises 19 schools of study. Alongside the traditional humanities, sciences and social sciences, there are many vocationally orientated courses.

UEA enjoys an excellent academic reputation, attracting students from all over the world, contributing to a cosmopolitan atmosphere. The University gained its Royal Charter in 1961 and took its first students in 1963.

- The University has a student population of over 13,000, of whom more than 2,000 are from over 100 countries outside the United Kingdom.

- The University employs over 2,100 members of staff, of which over 700 are academic and research staff.

- The University is ranked eighth best for science amongst United Kingdom universities.

- The University has well over 3,000 student rooms on campus so all international undergraduate students are guaranteed accommodation for the duration of their studies, and all new international postgraduates are guaranteed accommodation for their first year.

- Out of over 150 degree award institutions in the country, UEA is consistently ranked in the top 20 for most academic subjects, in the top ten for some and ranked top in the country in several subjects.

- UEA has the largest sports complex of any UK university and is rated in the top ten UK universities for music, entertainment and social events.

UEA is divided into Schools of Studies covering a wide range of subjects: Biological Sciences, Chemical Sciences, Computing Sciences, Development Studies, Economic and Social Studies, Education, English and American Studies, Environmental Sciences, Health, History, Language Linguistics and Translation, Law, Management, Mathematics, Music, and World Art Studies and Museology. UEA has been graded "excellent" for the quality of its teaching by the HEFCE in ten subjects: American Studies, Film Studies, Development Studies, Law, Social Work, Communication and Media Studies, History of Art, Mathematics, Statistics and Operational Research, Molecular Biosciences and subjects allied to medicine.

Undergraduate Degrees follow a modular system and continuous assessment means students avoid the panic of 'final examinations at the end of their course'.

Opposite: The University of East Anglia (UEA). Clockwise from left: UEA from the Sainsbury Centre for Visual Arts, Thomas Paine Centre UEA, and UEA Panorama.

Underground Norwich

Subterranean attractions

Beyond the obvious and generally very visible heritage attractions of the City, there is a wealth of hidden heritage which is cloaked from public view and goes largely unnoticed. This is the City's underground heritage which falls broadly into undercrofts, other structures, former 'workings' and folklore. The undercrofts are medieval, vaulted cellars, constructed originally as masonry-built, fire-proof basements to store valued goods. Since they were built so well, many have survived intact beneath much later buildings. Norwich is distinguished in having the largest collection of medieval undercrofts of any City in the UK. There are two basic types – barrel vaulted and ribbed and the footprint sizes vary from 10 sq m to almost 100 sq m. Of the 69 known and surviving sites (there is documentary evidence of a further 33 which have been demolished and a strong suspicion that others are waiting to be rediscovered) the best examples are:

- **Bedfords**, 21 Bedford Street – late C14th date and fine example. Open to the public as part of a bar

- **Blackfriars Crypt** – imposing C13th structure. Previously used as a café but now closed. Accessible by request to staff

- **Bridewell** – the largest undercroft in Norwich dating from the C14th. Closed for renovation until at least 2012

- **Dragon Hall** – C14th/C15th undercroft and vaulting. Open regularly as part of Dragon Hall

- **The Guildhall** – one of the very earliest brick vaulted undercrofts in the UK and predating the Guildhall itself by at least 100 years. Visits by arrangement

- **Strangers Hall** – dating from 1320. Open as part of the Museum

- **Take 5** Tombland – impressive undercroft. Occasional access from bar/pub above when used for exhibitions

- **Wensum Lodge/Music House** – undercroft of the C12th house of one of the wealthiest Jews in early medieval England, with mason's marks common to those in the Cathedral. Now used as Jurnet's Bar and can be visited in the evenings or by appointment.

A unique feature of some of the Norwich undercrofts is side and end chambers which basically allow an increase in the floor area without an increase in the height and span of the principal vault. These chambers have given rise to local folklore tales of tunnels that connected all of the undercrofts along particular streets and allowed merchants to conduct their business without suffering the inconvenience of inclement weather. It is also contended that one tunnel functioned as a subterranean waterway connecting the undercrofts with the river although why the undercrofts were not flooded was not explained. More often, it is claimed, the tunnels gave access to the Castle, Cathedral or Blackfriars and one legend talks about a tunnel link between the Cathedral and Ludham. A more colourful legend reports a tunnel extending from the Cathedral to the Blackfriars Church and allowing the monks access to ladies in an undercroft strategically positioned between the two institutions. Two monks and their lady friends were discovered in flagrante delicto and consequently killed for partaking of their pleasures and their bodies were entombed in the blocked-off tunnel. Needless to say all the tunnels, if they ever existed, are now blocked and in reality the supposed blocked tunnel was, in all probability, simply the rear wall of the side chamber.

Romantic as the notion of tunnels might be it does not stand up to reasoning, primarily because if one building was broken into the other buildings connected by the tunnel would have been easily accessed by the felon. In no cases is there evidence for a door to block off the entrance to the 'tunnel'. While the legends are compelling and are often reinforced by modern day commentators who recount

discoveries made by their ancestors, there is little or no hard evidence of any surviving tunnel network – shame.

Additional to the undercrofts there are various other interesting, below ground assets. The so called Castle dungeons are one example, which are actually the vaulted basements of the lost drum towers at the top of the Castle Bridge, and are now deployed to give a feel of what the historic prison would have been like. Similarly, the Guildhall retains below ground cells dating from the original construction date of the building (1407-12). One actual tunnel leads from the Castle, down through the Mound to the Regimental Museum. Another fascinating underground feature is an excavated Norman 'stone house' surviving to about two metres in height and preserved beneath the courts

in St Martins. It can be visited by prior arrangement with the court authorities.

Finally, the underground geology of Norwich has given rise to other interventions in the form of flint or chalk workings. Ever since the No. 26 bus to Hellesdon disappeared into a hole in Earlham Road in 1988 and created international news, the workings have formed part of the Norwich underground legends. Principally located under Earlham Road, the Thorpe Ridge east of the Wensum (Ketts Hill to Rosary Road) and around Marston Lane, these workings have now been largely sealed and closed off.

There is then much myth and legend associated with underground Norwich but still a good deal of interesting surviving heritage infrastructure to go and see.

Opposite: Bedford's undercroft, Bedford St. This page, top left: Bridewell undercroft. Top right: Assembly House undercroft. Right: Norman House beneath the courts.

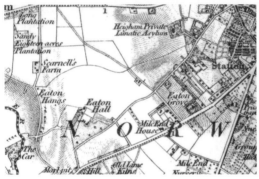

Clockwise from top: Georgian terrace on Unthank Road, The Elms, former alms houses of the Mackintosh Company, and The Unthank Estate as it appeared in 1838.

Postgraduate Masters courses also include continuous assessment. With regard to research, UEA has top rated departments in: Environmental Science, Scandinavian Studies, Biological Sciences, Education, History, Social Work, Pure Mathematics and Communications and Media Studies. Several well regarded research centres and links to the Norwich Research Park (NRP) make the UEA an important national and international centre for research in a number of subject areas.

The campus is reckoned to have the largest number of award winning buildings of any campus university in the UK with architects including Norman Foster, Sir Bernard Feilden, Denys Lasden and Rick Mather.

Ultra Aquam
See *Over the Water*.

Undercrofts
See *Underground Norwich*.

Underground Norwich
See page 430.

UNESCO City of Literature
International accolade.
Over the last few years, the Writers Centre Norwich has been co-ordinating a bid to UNESCO for the coveted accolade of UNESCO City of Literature. Melbourne, Iowa City, Edinburgh, Dublin and Reykjavik already have this status but there is, currently, no English representative.

With a pedigree that includes luminaries ranging from the first English Hebrew poet and the first woman to write a book in English, running through Britain's first provincial newspaper and the first public libraries in the country to the establishment of the UK's first creative writing course, the City has a strong pedigree. The outcome will be known in Spring next year and if successful this will enable the creation of an International Centre for Writing in the City: a physical space and a platform from which to build the City's literary profile, focus attention of the built and natural heritage, market the City, attract tourists and engage residents of City and county alike.

University College of the Arts

See *Norwich University College of the Arts*.

Unthank Road

Arterial road. Named because it was originally the drive across Colonel Unthank's parkland estate, Unthank Road was developed in the C19th as one of the early urban extensions from the Walled City. The new City Gaol by Philip Barnes of 1827 was one of the first new buildings on the road. Attractive C19th buildings line the northern end including a fine Georgian terrace. Also, north of the junction with Park Lane is a set of interesting alms houses, provided by the Mackintosh chocolate company for their retired employees. The bulk of the remaining buildings of note are early C20th villas. Today the street provides the service centre for the Golden Triangle.

Upper St Giles

Historic street. Once part of the entry from the west into the Norman new town (Newport) Upper St Giles (previous just the west end of St Giles) was transformed into a slightly dislocated stump first by the construction of the Inner Ring Road in the late 1960s, which created a cul de sac, and secondly by the construction of Cleveland Road in the 1970s. This unfortunate dislocation aside, the street still provides a delightful range of speciality shops, galleries and eateries as well as some fine historic architecture. Starting from the medieval splendour of St Giles church, with the tallest tower of the set in Norwich, and moving west, No. 75 has a mock Tudor façade which hides a C18th shop with an attractive C19th shop front. Next door Nos. 77-79 are late C17th/early C18th with C19th refacing and the latter was, for some time, the location for the City's only Michelin starred restaurant, Adlards. A run of pleasant Victorian shops, including No. 89 which dates from 1887, continue until No. 91, which is dated 1738, No. 95 which is C17th with C19th additions and No. 97, a pleasant C18th house. There are several examples of nice mosaic tiling and shop fronts. Opposite, No. 94 is a substantial C18th house by local architect Thomas Rawlins, later converted to a school, where Sir John Mills studied, and now flats. Next door, No. 90 is a quaint C17th building, which had been the Queen's Head between 1763 and 1982. Nos. 84-88 are C18th with a C17th rear block while the gabled No. 82 is also C17th in origin. The gabled No. 76 further east sports an attractive C19th chemist shop front (the chemist was once a local institution but is now sadly gone) and next is a substantial C16th mansion with interesting C17th internal panelling and stairs. Until the War, a substantial Tudor mansion had existed at No. 72 while No. 70 was probably of C16th origin with a Georgian façade – both were destroyed by bombing.

Upper St Giles.

V is for...

Roman cantonal capital and one of only three undisturbed Roman sites in Britain; Norwich City's holder of the highest average goals per game record; one of the very last surviving shoe production plants in England.

Above: Panorama of Venta Icenorum.
Opposite: Ramparts of the Roman Cantonal Capital for Venta Icenorum.

V1 and V2 Strikes

WWII ballistic missile attacks. Being relatively close to the launch sites for Hitler's 'vengeance' weapons, Norwich was a potential target during the latter part of the War. Fortunately although there were numerous over flights by V1s, none fell within the City boundary. V2 interventions were more dramatic since more of them fell in the area, their payload was significantly larger and there was absolutely no defence. In the last few months of the War around 1,000 missiles were fired at London and Norwich alone. The assaults on the Norwich area came from Battery 444 deployed principally in Rijsterbos, in the Netherlands, from 19th September 1944 to 21st October 1944. The most violent incident was on October 3rd 1944 when a V2 broke up over Mile Cross and the war head impacted at the Royal Norwich Golf Club, damaging 400 houses and killing one person. Other V2 strikes during this period included Botany Bay Farm, Horsford, the City Sewage Works (2 minor injuries), Coltishall (missing the airfield but causing two minor injuries), a sugar beet field at Thorpe St Andrew, causing damage to 27 houses, near a school at Rockland St.

Mary, at Crostwick, very close to the US air base at Rackheath, at Spixworth (this rocket fell apart before impact scattering parts over a large area and the largely intact components were sent to the Royal Aircraft Establishment at Farnborough for analysis), in a forest near Taverham, at Surlingham (10 injured and 36 houses damaged) and at Bramerton Woods End,

Van Dal shoes

Shoe makers. Van Dal, who this year (2011) celebrate 75 years in the City, is the last of the large scale shoe manufacturers in Norwich. Specialising in women's fashion shoes the company sells thousands of pairs of shoes a year and still makes shoes here in Norwich at its Dibden Road factory. The company has been based in Norwich since 1936 when the founder Adelman Goodman bought the Florida shoe factory on Salhouse Road. Originally a refugee from Russia, Goodman had owned a shoe factory in London before deciding that Norwich offered better opportunities. The Salhouse Road factory was destroyed by bombing in 1942, forcing Goodmans to share the Northumberland Street premises of W.H.H. Clarke

until their own factory could be rebuilt after the war.

The Van Dal brand was launched in 1946 and proved to be extremely successful over the next few decades – by 1990 the three hundred strong company workforce was making 600,000 pairs of shoes a year in Norwich. Today, only about 15 per cent of Van Dal shoes are made in Norwich with the remainder being made abroad, largely in India.

Varco, Percy

NCFC Striker. Holder of the record for the highest goal average per appearance, Varco arrived at Norwich via Aston Villa and QPR in 1927 and, before leaving two years later to play for Exeter then Brighton, had managed to net 47 goals in just 65 appearances for Norwich, coining in the process the chant from Nest fans 'give it to Varco'.

Vauxhall Gardens

See *New Spring Gardens*.

Venta Icenorum (Caistor St Edmund)

Roman cantonal capital. This was the location of the major Roman period settlement in the area. If, as evidence suggests, there was no significant Roman occupation on the later Norwich site and bearing in mind that Norwich's site attributes led to the founding of a substantial later settlement, it is reasonable to ask why the Romans chose not to build at Norwich in the first place, rather than at Venta Icenorum. There are three propositions for Caistor being developed as the cantonal capital. First, that it was a new settlement located for topographical reasons. This seems unlikely since the locational characteristics of Norwich were more beneficial, relatively, even 2,000 years ago so if there were no other determining factors then it is unlikely that Caistor would have been the first choice. The second proposition is that Caistor was developed on a former British site. While it is reasonable to assume that the Romans may have prudently 'recycled' an earlier site – as did subsequent settlers on the early site of Norwich – there is no archaeological evidence to this effect and the distinctive pattern of Roman town planning would

not have sat comfortably with a relatively cruder British settlement form. The third, and most likely, proposition is that the Romans built their settlement close to an existing British one. This could have either been to 'stamp their authority' on a subjugated British tribe – as the Normans later did to the Saxons in Norwich – or it could have been a gesture of symbolic and tangible support for a client British tribe, who had supported the Romans militarily and were established close by. Recent speculation suggests the former, that after the Revolt led by Boudicca, the Romans constructed Venta Icenorum as a clear gesture to emphasise their subjugation of the defeated tribe.

Venta Icenorum was the largest Roman settlement in northern East Anglia. Founded around 60 AD in the Tas Vally, its name means 'market place of the Iceni'. It is one of only three Romano British towns to have escaped destruction by layers of subsequent urban development.

Set on a predictable grid iron pattern, excavations in the 1930s have revealed the Forum and two other groups of buildings while inter war investigations revealed the basilica and two temples. A substantial flint wall, rising to 7m in height, surrounded the core of the settlement and this represents the most visible surviving element. Beyond the Walls substantial suburban development has been identified including an amphitheatre to the south of the walled site and a major temple complex to the north east. Following the Roman evacuation of England in the 5th century, there is evidence of subsequent Saxon occupation from artefact finds on the site and the presence of burial grounds nearby. The site is now owned and managed by the Norfolk Archaeological Trust and public access is permitted.

Victoria station

Lost station. Following just four years after the opening of Norwich's first station at Thorpe, Victoria Station, located just outside the

The lost Victoria Station.

From top: City skyline from City Hall, and winter evening skyline from Mousehold.

Walled City at the top of St Stephens, opened in 1849 on the site of what had been the Ranelagh Pleasure Gardens, to serve the Great Eastern Railway. Some of the former Ranelagh buildings were pressed into service for the new station including the Saloon which became waiting rooms and the Amphitheatre became a ticket office and luggage rooms. Amalgamation of railway companies obviated the need for a separate station at Victoria but it hung on as a passenger terminal until 1914. The site continued as a freight depot well into the 1980s focussing particularly on

coal. When it closed finally, the station and goods shed were developed for offices by the insurance group Bland Payne, now part of the international group Marsh. The old coal yard was later developed by Sainsbury's for a superstore and car park.

Viewpoints

Best panoramic views. Contrary to Noel Coward's pithy observation ('flat, Norfolk') Norwich is one of the hilliest cities in the country and consequently provides opportunities for some impressive panoramic views. Some of the best are as follows:

- **St James Hill Mousehold** – the classic viewpoint just north east of the Walled City providing expansive, sweeping views to the west and south. Vehicle access from Britannia Road – park outside Britannia Barracks and walk across the heath.

- **Kett's Heights** – a similar orientation to St James Hill but providing slightly better views of the historic City than the Mousehold alternative with less detritus in the foreground. Best sunset view. Pedestrian access from a footpath half way up Ketts Hill on the right.

- **St John's Catholic Cathedral Tower** – spectacular views of the Walled City from the west as well as the western suburbs and on a very clear day, even the coast. Best position for sunrise although you'd be unlikely to get access at that time unless you'd negotiated special arrangements. The Cathedral does have regular tower tours but the ascent is not for the faint hearted – once on top its fine though.

- **Grapes Hill Pedestrian Bridge** – a sort of 'poor relation' to the Catholic Cathedral Tower alternative with not a lot to see of historic value but quite a good sweep of the northern suburbs. Walk from Upper St Giles.

- **Castle Battlements** – probably the most popular viewpoint venue and good for being at the epicentre of the City looking out although, from the 'warts and all' perspective it gives you particularly horrible views of the St Stephens area, probably the most unattractive part of the City after Anglia Square. Tours available on a daily basis but involving the ascent of a large number of tiny Norman steps.

- **City Hall Clock Tower** – a dramatic alternative to the Castle being equally tricky to ascend then rather small and compact once you get there – avoid

periods like 11 or 12 O'clock when the loudest clock bell in the East of England can be a trifle terrifying. Occasional access only, usually during Heritage Open Days (first full weekend in September) or by special arrangement.

- **Forum 'Bridge'** – views from the first floor (restaurant area) of The Forum looking east provide a spectacular (and free) perspective of the eastern City Centre and views out to the countryside to the south. Pedestrian access by stairs or lift.

Other options exist, such as the Anglican Cathedral spire, but these are very rarely publicly available if at all.

For an alternative, Norwich International Airport offers helicopter flights which provide really spectacular views around the edge of the City and obliquely across the Walled City although they are not allowed to overfly the centre. A variety of hot air balloon flights are also available, over flying the City.

VMS

Variable Message Signing.
This is a system of electronic signs, on the approach roads to the City and the Inner Ring Road, alerting drivers as to real time availability of spaces in car parks.

Votiers

Local coach company.
Leonard Votier was born in the parish of St Clement Without in 1902, the son of a publican. After a brief spell in the boot and shoe industry, Leonard became a driver with a number of employers and ultimately with Mr Eddie Bush who made charabancs. Leonard persuaded the owner to let him build a charabanc for an undisclosed customer and this turned out to be Leonard himself. He began running bus trips and using the vehicle for haulage at other times. He christened the new company Mascot Comfort Coaches and was soon expanding his fleet. By the outbreak of the Second World War, Mascot had half a dozen vehicles – the Votier Family also established a concert party which entertained local servicemen. After the War, business boomed and a row of excursion coaches at Bell Avenue were a regular local site. The coaches were also pressed into service for a range of special purposes including Norwich City away matches. By the 1960s, Mascot was offering a range of coach services providing up to 1500 seats. The company finally disappeared as an independent entity in the 1970s when it merged with Eastern Counties.

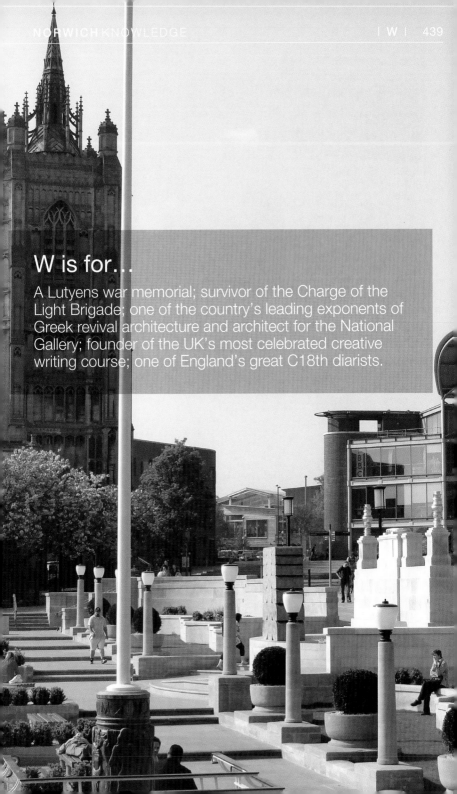

W is for...

A Lutyens war memorial; survivor of the Charge of the Light Brigade; one of the country's leading exponents of Greek revival architecture and architect for the National Gallery; founder of the UK's most celebrated creative writing course; one of England's great C18th diarists.

From left: The opening of the war memorial in 1927, and the opening of the refurbished War Memorial and Memorial Gardens in 2011 by Council Leader Steve Morphew, and Terry Fuller, CEO of the Homes & Communities Agency. Previous page: The refurbished Lutyens War Memorial and Memorial Gardens.

Walloons
See *Dutch, Flemish and Walloons*.

Walpole, George
See *Orford Hill*.

Warminger, Alfred
Local entrepreneur. Alfred Warminger began to make his mark on City life at the relatively early age of 13. He opened a childrens' cinema at the rear of his father's pub, the Globe at South Heigham, in February 1934. This proved very successful and was granted a licence by local magistrates. Just seven months later, young Alfred opened the Enterprise, in Northumberland Street. This fully fledged, if rather modestly scaled, picture house was the only one in the country to be equipped with 16mm sound apparatus. This was just a hint of Alfred's potential who went on to be not only Norwich's waste paper baron but something of an icon in the gliding world and City Sheriff in 1960/1.

War Memorial
Memorial to C20th wars. Designed by Edwin Lutyens and originally located east of the medieval Guildhall, the War Memorial was moved to its current location in the Memorial Gardens as part of the City Hall/Market Place redevelopment scheme of the late 1930s. After deterioration in the structural concrete in the early part of the C21st, the Gardens were temporarily closed. Work started in autumn 2009 with the revamped programme completed by 2011 when the memorial was turned to face City Hall and the Gardens were refurbished and made more accessible.

Warwick, Earl of
See *Kett's Rebellion*.

Waterloo Park.

Waterloo Park
Public park. Forming part of a major programme of job creation and public works, Waterloo Park opened in 1933, east of Aylsham Road, to serve the expanding population developing at Mile Cross and other areas north of the old City. Designed by Parks Superintendent Capt. A. Sandys-Winsch this was a formal, landscaped park with a pavilion and bandstand. A recent Heritage Lottery Fund grant has enabled a major refurbishment.

The Heigham Waterworks.

Water Works
Victorian waterworks.
A new waterworks at Heigham Common was established in 1850 to replace the former provision at New Mills. The initial buildings were developed by Lynde but these were subsequently substantially replaced by much more impressive structures both at Heigham and the Lakenham reservoir, designed by architect and engineer Thomas Hawksley, something of a monument nationally in terms of waterworks construction, following his appointment in 1858. New reservoirs were also developed at Thorpe Hamlet, off Quebec Road/Telegraph Lane in the late C19th and the surviving water tower was built in 1932.

Watneys
UK brewing giant. In 1963, Watney Mann took over the two surviving independent Norwich breweries of Bullard's and Steward & Patteson, which themselves had absorbed Morgans and Youngs, Crawshay and Youngs shortly before. The historic Anchor and Pockthorpe Breweries were closed and production focussed on the former

Wensum Park.

Morgans King Street Brewery with a massive new distribution depot being developed between King Street and Mountergate. The new company branded itself as the Norwich Brewery Company but increasingly became a distribution portal for beers brewed elsewhere in the Watney Mann/Grand Metropolitan empire. In 1985 the King Street Brewery closed, ironically with a special commemoration beer called Ketts Finale, bringing to an end one of the largest brewing centres in the UK after London and Burton on Trent.

Weavers
See *Textile industry*.

Wellington's Statue
Like the Nelson statue, this bronze monument, by George Adams, was erected by public subscription in the Market Place in 1854 and was also moved to the Cathedral Close in 1936. The 2nd Duke subsequently told the sculptor that the likeness was 'the best by far that has appeared.'

Wensum Lodge
See *Music House*.

Wensum Park
Public park. Forming part of a major programme of job creation and public works, Wensum Park opened in 1925, west of Drayton Road. In the early days the park included a bathing area but today the facility offers a substantial, equipped, children's play area and riverside walks.

Watney's Brewery.

The Wensum Parkway with one of the new interpretive signs.

The River Wensum as it would have appeared as a great port in the Medieval period, and sunset over the Wensum.

Wensum Parkway

River regeneration. This is a joint project launched by the Heritage Economic and Regeneration Trust (HEART) and the Norwich Society, supported by the City Council and Greater Norwich Development Partnership, to regenerate the River Wensum within the heart of the City, making it a viable link within a chain connecting the Marriotts Way and Weaver's Way long distance foot paths and cycle ways. The initiative has delivered landscape improvements, a guided trail, interpretive and information boards, educational work and wildlife improvements.

Wensum, River

River running through Walled City. The City was founded on the Wensum (old English Wændsum meaning winding), just north of its confluence with the Yare. The Wensum rises in mid Norfolk by the village of Whissonsett and enters Norwich, from the north west. Turning east, the river flowed originally between a chain of small islands, later to be exploited as locations for mills and intermediate bridging points. Here, the Wensum is constrained to the south by a ridge running roughly along modern St Giles and sloping relatively steeply down to the river valley. To the north, the rise was more gentle towards a promontory at the end of the modern Aylsham Rd and another ridge forming the southern edge of Mousehold. As the Mousehold ridge turns south into the north-south Thorpe ridge, the Wensum valley becomes a minor canyon defined by the steep Ber Street ridge to the west and the Thorpe ridge to the east, both rising to about 40m above sea level. Although the river is of modest proportions today, at the time of the City's foundation Norwich sat at the head of a great estuary stretching from what is now Caister on Sea in the north to Gorleston in the south – Gt Yarmouth did not exist. Consequently, the flow of the tide caused the estuarine river level to fill the valley at high tide and to leave substantial marshy river margins at low tide. Substantial sections of the modern Cathedral Close and the Great Hospital Meadow were part of this marshy river margin. An impression of how the landscape would have appeared 1500 years ago can be gained by photographs of the great flood of 1912.

This point on the river was attractive for settlement because it was the first bridgeable point on the Wensum up stream from the sea and, at its narrowest points, the first bridges or causeways were developed. Upstream of the marshy areas and on the west bank of the Wensum around modern King Street, the river was narrowed by well drained gravel terraces, suitable for development.

John Wesley.

Westlegate Tower.

Wesley, John

Non conformist leader. Wesley was a frequent visitor to the City either preaching or visiting members of the non conformist community. He was associated with both the Tabernacle in Bishopgate and the Foundry on Timberhill, where he narrowly escaped injury during a fire on one visit. Visiting in 1757, he described the Octagon chapel in his journal to be 'perhaps the most elegant one in all Europe.' Two years later he observed on a visit to St Peter Mancroft 'I scarcely ever remember to have seen a more beautiful parish church.' In December 1774 Wesley gives a flavour of his attachment to the City – 'I took a solemn and affectionate leave of the society at Norwich.'

Westlegate Tower

First tower block. Designed in 1960 by Chaplin and Burgoine, this was to become the first tower block to be developed in the City, in the modernist style. The uniform glass façade is relieved by a strip of armorial crests decorating the west side. It had the dubious distinction of hosting the first McDonalds restaurant to appear in the City but after three decades of providing a home to various financial institutions it closed in the 1990s and has been derelict and decaying since – plywood panels now out number the original glass panels of the façade. The recent (2009) St Stephen's Masterplan for the area recommended its demolition. After 15 years standing empty, the site was bought by a Norwich based developer in a joint venture with Soho Developments in 2011.

West Norwich Hospital

Former General Hospital. Built as the Norwich Workhouse, on the north side of Bowthorpe Road in 1859, and the Norwich Isolation Hospital, on the south side in 1893, the site became the Woodlands Hospital in 1941 but was substantially bomb damaged in 1942. Passing to the NHS after the War it ultimately became the West Norwich Hospital with significant rebuilding in the 1940s/50s and a good deal of extension and infilling subsequently. The complex remained in use until the opening of the Norfolk and Norwich University Hospital

A local pub commemorates the Whiffler.

in 2001 when this site was largely vacated. In 2002 the north site became the Norwich Community Hospital and the south site became the Norfolk and Waveney Mental Health Partnership NHS Trust's Julian Hospital.

Westwick

Ancient district. This is an area originating before the Conquest and located in the western part of the later walled City, south of the river and focusing on Westwick Street and St Benedicts. It later became the Leet of Wymer.

Wherryman's Way

Long distance footpath. This is a recently developed 56km (35 miles) footpath running eastwards from Whitlingham, along the length of the Yare, to Great Yarmouth.

Whifflers

Processional character. Taking their name from a 'whiffle' or small flute, these characters were originally musicians but evolved into 'path beaters' for musical processions whose role was to lead the group and 'beat a path' through the crowds using a stick, which had

Whitefriars (Carmelite) Friary

Lost friary

In 1256 Philip de Cowgate (also known as Philip Arnold) settled lands in Cowgate between the Wensum and St James church, upon William de Calthorpe on condition that 'the brethren of Mount Carmel should enter and dwell there without any molestation for ever and serve God therein'. The Carmelite or White friars extended the site by the acquisition of various parcels of land and, with the aid of several generous bequests, they were able to develop a substantial friary complex.

Building of the church of the order was begun at once; however, it was not completed until c.1383. Despite the Carmelites avowed simplistic life style they clearly felt the need to compete with the friaries of the Grey and Black friars and produce an imposing edifice.

From 1322, the site of the Norwich Carmelites experienced some expansion. Further properties were added at intervals between 1332 and 1345, including additions to the church and a new cemetery. In 1359 the lane to the east of the site was enclosed. William of Worcester says that 'the cloister alongside the choir of the church is 60 paces, or 35 yards, long'. The reference to the location of this particular cloister might suggest that he was

distinguishing it from a second cloister. This proposition has been confirmed by recent archaeological excavations which have uncovered a significant principal cloister with substantial surviving buttresses footings which suggest that it was two storeys high. A second, much smaller cloister was also discovered to the east of the first. William of Worcester tells us, additionally, that the nave

Reconstruction of the Whitefriars Friary.

was 46 paces long (80 feet) and 36 wide (62 feet). He adds that 'the passage beneath the belfry between the choir gate and the door called the parclose is 23 paces' (40 feet). The church was eventually consecrated in 1382. Although more recent writers have speculated that the church was in the north western sector of the precinct, effectively north of the cloister, Kirkpatrick suggests that it was adjacent to the

river and supports this by an early documentary reference to Whitefriars bridge – 'ponta juxta Ecclesiam Fratrum Camelitarum' – the bridge beside the church of the Carmelites Brothers. The recent excavations have confirmed Kirkpatrick's position as substantial column footings and the remains of a tiled floor have been discovered adjacent to the surviving arch on the south of the site – almost certainly the south porch of

the friary church.
The order of the Carmelites was dissolved in 1543, as part of the Dissolution. After this, the site of the order changed hands many times. It was eventually divided up. Nothing remains of the original buildings of the monastery apart from the arch and an undercroft dating from the C13th and probably therefore one of the earliest monastic buildings on the site.

The former Criterion Café in White Lion Street, now a clothing shop.

superseded the whiffle. In Norwich, the Whifflers appear to date from the Tudor period and their function was to beat a path through the crowd in advance of civic processions, using a ceremonial sword. Whifflers disappeared in the 1950s but were reinstated in 1996 through a joint effort of the Norwich Society and the then Lord Mayor.

White, George

See *Norvic*.

Whitefriars (Carmelite) Friary

See page 444.

Whitefriars Bridge

Historic river crossing. Also known as St Martin's Bridge, the first bridge probably dates from before the Norman Conquest and it was certainly there by 1106. It was demolished during Kett's Rebellion by the Earl of Warwick in an attempt to keep the rebels out of the City in 1549 and rebuilt in wood shortly after. In 1591 a new single span stone bridge replaced the wooden one and iron railings were added in 1835. In 1924 A.E. Collins (City Engineer) designed a new bridge which currently occupies the site but the old bridge was dissembled stone by stone and numbered for eventual reuse. Unfortunately the stones were, apparently, later used as hard core for the construction of Alysham Road.

White Lion Street

Ancient thoroughfare. Originally known as Saddlegate (street of the saddlemakers), the street probably ran straight through to the Castle providing a direct access from the Jewry to the protection of the Royal garrison. It later became Lorimers Row (after harness makers), Bridlesmiths Row and Spurriers Row (after spur makers). By the C19th the name had changed again and the White Lion pub at No. 10 had given the street its current name before becoming the Haymarket Stores in 1914 and closing in 1974 to become a shop.

Starting at the west end/north side, the building now occupied by W.H. Smith was the former Fruiterers Arms pub which resided in a C17th building entered originally by passages from the Arcade or the Walk. The pub frontage to White Lion Street appeared only in 1896 but survived only until 1989 when the pub closed. The next door buildings are also C17th while opposite was the original entrance of the surviving C16th Curat House, now hidden behind a boarded up entry. At the other end of the street, No. 20 (Moss Bros) was the C18th Criterion Café where Norwich City Football Club was founded. The building, which contains remarkably attractive stained glass as part of an imposing shop front, originally formed part

---

From left: Substantial vaulted cellars of the ancient White Swan during demolition in the early 1960s and an historic statue mounted on the wall.

of the York Tavern or City of York which was recorded from 1760 and became the York Hotel. The run of buildings next door, although modest, are C17th in origin. The tiny building opposite is C15th in origin with attractive internal timbers but remarkably was missed by the listed building inspectors. Amongst the pleasant but unremarkable buildings on the south side is No. 13 which was the local chemist institution Claude Benton for many years.

White Swan

Lost Inn. Standing on the former section of St Peter's Street, which used to connect through to Theatre Street, the White Swan was located opposite to the west door of St Peter Mancroft. The building had been an inn since the C15th and the fabric went back further. As well as an early undercroft, the inn had a large assembly hall, with moulded plaster ceiling, used for performances and it was here that the Norwich Company of Comedians performed. The Swan became their permanent base in 1731 and prospered, with performances attracting some of the principal actors of the time, until Thomas Ivory opened the Theatre Royal in 1758 when theatrical performances declined but variety continued. Even as late as the mid C19th, concerts were still attracting patronage at the White Swan. The Inn was also a major centre for cock fighting for most of the C18th and well into the C19th and prize fighting was also a popular attraction at the inn. It ceased to be a pub in 1865 and was used for a variety of functions including as the premises of Johnson, Burton & Theobald, a wholesaler of motor cycle and radio parts. Despite its obvious antiquity, the Council, in its wisdom, demolished it in the early 1960s to provide a surface car park for the new Central Library.

Whitlingham

Suburban parish.
Whitlingham is a churchless parish 4.8km (3 miles) east of Norwich City Centre, and is positioned south of the River Yare. It is reached via Whitlingham Lane from Trowse. The area has a history of mining and flint-knapping from as far back as 4000 BC, and archaeological finds from the Palaeolithic and Neolithic eras have been unearthed in the vicinity. Chalk and lime was mined from the C18th onwards, and the chalk pits can still be seen at the lower end of Whitlingham Country Park today, although they are now in overgrown woodland. A lime kiln can also be seen off Whitlingham Lane. Whitlingham has two Broads both created by gravel extraction: the Little Broad which was created in 1990, and the Great Broad which followed in 1995. Whitlingham features some interesting historical ruins. As has been noted, the parish is currently without a church, but this was not always the case. St Andrew's church was already dilapidated by around 1630, but the round tower did not collapse until 1940. Today the ruins are overgrown, but the south wall of the chancel still stands, as well as a portion of the south wall of the nave. The ruins of Trowse Newton Hall can be seen on Whitlingham Lane. The hall was built by the Priors as a country retreat and in 1335 King Edward and Queen Philippa are said to have stayed here. However, by 1850 the hall was being used as a farmhouse and was eventually demolished by Sir Robert Harvey after falling into disrepair. Whitlingham Hall however still exists today. Originally Crown Point Hall, it was built in 1784 but was subsequently rebuilt in 1865. It belonged to the Colman family before being sold in 1955 and developed into Whitlingham Hospital. Although the hospital is now closed, the Hall is currently used as residential property.

Activity on the Broad at Whitlingham.

Wlllow Lane Chapel, and rear view of Willow Lane properties.

Wilberforce, William

Abolitionist. Wilberforce was a great friend of the Gurneys and visited them frequently at Earlham Hall. With his friend and colleague, Thomas Fowell Buxton, he spoke publicly in Norwich and campaigned against slavery. He is remembered in the name of Wilberforce Road, located just a short distance from Earlham Hall.

Wilde, George

Crimea veteran. Wilde was a plasterer, born in St Margaret's parish, when he enlisted in 13th Light Dragoons. He participated in the Crimean War and was one of 'the 600' to take part in the Charge of the Light Brigade at Balaclava in 1854 where he was wounded when his horse was shot from under him. He died in 1887 and is buried in the Rosary Cemetery. Another Norfolk veteran, Private James Olley (4th Light Dragoons) of Holt was only 16 during the charge and wrote one of the only first hand accounts of the battle.

Wilderness at Butter Hills

Lost Pleasure Garden. In 1748, Samuel Bruister joined the competition for pleasure gardens, already established by My Lord's Garden and the New Spring Garden, by planting up a wilderness on Butter Hills, south of the Walled City, and establishing wrestling bouts there. By 1768, Bruister's successor Samuel Stebbing was offering public breakfasts on the site supported by musical interludes.

Wilkins, William

Architect. William Wilkins Jnr was born in Norwich in 1778, the son of plasterer and self taught architect William Wilkins senior. His father had been responsible for Beeston Hall in Norfolk, modifications to Stanfield Hall, near Wymondham, the restoration of St Ethelbert's Gate, restoration work at Norwich Castle and the restoration of the old Shirehall, originally designed by Brettingham. Wilkins junior was educated at Gonville and Caius College, Cambridge before undertaking a three year Society of Antiquaries travelling architectural scholarship to Italy, Greece and Asia Minor. This grounding was to make him one of the leading exponents of Greek revival architecture in England during the early C18th. His major works included Downing College Cambridge (designed 1805 but built later), Theatre Royal, Bury St Edmunds (1819), University College

London (1825-32) and the Yorkshire Museum (1830). He also produced work in the Gothic style including schemes at King's, Trinity and Corpus Christi Colleges in Cambridge. His most famous work is the National Gallery, completed in 1838. More locally, he was responsible for Nelson's Monument at Gt Yarmouth and the new Shirehall in Norwich at the base of the Castle mound, ironically after his father had restored the old Shirehall.

Wilks, Rev. Mark

Radical Cleric. Born in Gibraltar into an army family in 1748, the Rev. Wilks first made his mark in Norwich as the minister in the Countess of Huntingdon's Tabernacle in 1776 where he remained until 1778. He returned in 1780 as a Calvinist Methodist. He continued to preach but in 1791 preached two eloquent discourses on the benefits of the French Revolution.

Willow Lane

Historic street. The Lane takes its name from the willows that used to grow on waste ground on the south side, according to Kirkpatrick. A cockey used to run down the Lane and from its junction with Cow Hill, down Ten Bell Lane and into the Wensum. The buildings on the south side are predominantly Regency. No. 2 is a substantial, three storey villa, Nos. 4-14 are effectively three semi detached blocks while No. 16 is another three storey villa but, curiously with a Gothic oriel window incorporated into the south elevation overlooking the church yard. Completing the run, No. 18 is C17th with C18th alterations and sports an imposing, Flemish, crow step gable. Opposite, another C17th house was the home of author George Borrow between 1816 and 1824. Next door, No. 15 is apparently Regency but this is actually a 'fashionable' façade grafted onto another C17th house. Nos. 13 (home of historian Francis Blomefield) and 11 are also C17th in origin with later additions while Willow Lane House is C18th. Next to this is the imposing former Jesuit Chapel by Patience dating from 1827 and finally, No. 1 is another Regency town house.

Willow Lane Chapel

Former Catholic Chapel. A creation of the architect John Thomas Patience, this Corinthian style chapel was built by the Jesuits in 1828 and was the first new Catholic chapel to be built in the City following the Catholic Emancipation Act of 1826. It originally had a highly decorated interior with a side altar, several statues and numerous stained glass windows. The building was later used as a Roman Catholic school and prior to its current use, as a solicitor's office, it was heavily restored.

Wilson, Angus

Writer. Angus Wilson started his career as a librarian working on the General Catalogue for the British Museum in 1937. During the War he worked at the famous code breaking centre at Bletchley Park. Following the war, he returned to the British Museum and also started writing books. His first successful novel, Hemlock and After, prompted him to resign from the Museum and write full time. His most successful book, Anglo Saxon Attitudes followed shortly. In 1970, jointly with

Malcolm Bradbury, he established the Creative Writing Course at the University of East Anglia. He was knighted in 1980 and died in 1991.

Wincarnis

Tonic wine. Wincarnis is a fortified (14 per cent) tonic wine made to a secret recipe but containing grape juice, malt extract, herbs and spices. It is very popular in some of the former British colonies. It was first made by Coleman and Co of Norwich in 1887, at their Westwick Street works, and originally called Liebig's Extract of Meat and Malt Wine. Advertisements in the late C19th refer to it as 'the finest tonic wine in the world'. The product and company were hugely successful in the early C20th and the factory expanded in Westwick Street to meet production demand. However, The Baedeker Raids devastated the site and the works had to be totally rebuilt after the War. The company was acquired by Colmans (of Mustard fame) then passed to Hedges & Butler (part of Bass) before being taken over by Ian Macleod Distillers Ltd of Broxburn in 1998. The Norwich site was redeveloped as a retail warehouse park and the product continues to be made by Broadland Wineries in Norfolk, and sold by Macleod.

Early Wincarnis advertising.

Windham, William

Government Minister. Born in London in 1750 Windham represented Norwich as Member of Parliament from 1784 until 1802. His Government posts included Chief Secretary for Ireland, Secretary at War in the Government of Pitt the Younger and Secretary of State for War and the Colonies under Grenville. He had a final 'lying in state' in the Maid's Head Hotel on 10th June 1810.

Witard, Herbert

First Labour Lord Mayor. Witard came from a poor background being brought up by his widowed mother as part of the family of 12 children. At the age of 13 he ran away to sea. Returning to Norwich he found work in the shoe industry and joined the Independent Labour Party when it was formed in 1894. In 1910 he changed careers and became manager of the Planet (later Co-operative) Insurance Society where he remained for the next 28 years until his retirement. He became a Labour Councillor in 1903 but failed twice to be elected to Parliament. In 1927 he became the City's first Labour Lord Mayor. He served for long periods as chairman of both the watch Committee and Waterworks Committee and was Labour leader. He is remembered in the name of Witard Road.

Wooded Ridge

Natural feature. The topography of Norwich is characterised by the valley of the Wensum with relatively steeply rising escarpments on either side. Historically, these have been wooded but as development has encroached over the last century, the woodland

Footpath along the western Wooded Ridge.

has receded. Today the remnants survive east of the Wensum, running from Mousehold, south to Thorpe. In the west, the surviving trees are much more sparse and, beginning at Thorn Lane, the tree line runs along the Ber Street Ridge towards the Wilderness at the junction of King Street and Bracondale. This part of the Ridge is largely accessible by a recently created footpath.

Woodforde, Parson James

Clergyman, Diarist. Although born in Somerset and educated at New College Oxford, Woodforde made his name as an often outspoken diarist while he was the incumbent clergyman at Weston Longville from 1774 until his death in 1803. His almost daily entries provide a remarkable picture of life in the later half of the C18th and cover both the daily routines of village life and Woodforde's frequent excursions to Norwich and other places with his niece and companion Nancy. The Parson had a healthy pre occupation with eating, describing many a visit to an inn or eating house in Norwich, and it is perhaps appropriate that his last diary entry states 'Dinner

today Roft Beef.' His memory is kept alive by the Parson Woodforde Society www.parsonwoodforde.org.uk/society

Woodrow Pilling Park

Public park. Located to the west of Harvey Lane, Woodrow Pilling Park was one of the 1920s/30s public works schemes promoted by the City Council to combat unemployment. Today it provides a variety of formal recreational opportunities including cricket, football, BMX and a play area.

Woolpack

Historic pubs. The name 'Woolpack' commemorates the textile trade in Norwich and specifically a bail of wool. Five pubs have celebrated the name although there are now only two trading survivors. The younger is the Woolpack in Golden Ball Street which replaced an earlier Woolpack in 1938, demolished for road widening and dating back to 1760. The present one contains a set of fine plaster reliefs by mural artist Moray Smith and was probably one of the first examples of a 'theme pub' to be developed in the UK. The St Georges Colegate Woolpack was a pub until

2008, closed briefly but reopened recently as The Woolie. In was built in the C18th and was a pub, initially called the Woolpackers, from 1760. The site was originally occupied by the town house of the Augustinian Priory of Our Lady of Walsingham, from 1298. The other three, at St Giles, Oak Street and Botolph Street, have all been demolished.

Workhouses

Former workhouses. In 1797 a survey of the poor in England reported that Norwich had two large workhouses – one a conversion of part of the former Palace of the Dukes of Norfolk, off Duke Street and the other, a monastery, the former Priory of the Blackfriars (St Andrews and Blackfriars Halls). Additionally, the former Leper House off Sprowston Road had been pressed into service as an infirmary and this was extended in 1828 and enlarged in 1838 to cope with 'pauper lunatics.' The Priory alone coped with 700 paupers and the conclusion of the survey was that conditions were not impressive. In response, a new Workhouse was erected just north of Bowthorpe Road in 1859 to a design by Medland and Maberly. It was developed in a red brick Tudor revival style and could house 885 inmates. A workhouse infirmary was added at the north-east of the original Workhouse sometime prior to 1883, and extended in 1911. A nurses home was built at the east of the Workhouse in 1903 and a new three-storey infirmary in 1939. During the Baedeker Blitz of April 1942 the original Workhouse buildings were destroyed but the nurses home and 1939 Infirmary survived. The complex later became the West Norwich Hospital.

Worlds End Lane

Lost ancient route. Originally part of the pre Conquest street grid and running east from Palace Plain, it was called Le Skolhalleyerd in the reign of Edward III and the first mention of 'World's End Lane' is on Cleer's Map of 1696. Its earlier name refers to the High School of Norwich which was located here and moved to the Carnary College after the Reformation. It is probable that the Lane takes its name from a pub formerly at No. 6, and while licence records only exist for it from 1830, it is probable that the building and use went back much further. In refusing its licence in 1906, which led to its eventual closure in 1907, the Licencing Sessions noted that 'the house was very old'. The Lane also contained Rome Hall, referred to as early as the C14th, and the C15th mansion of Sir Thomas Erpingham. Part of the Lane was demolished for the St Martin's Gas Works in 1850 and the remainder was obliterated in 1888.

Worsted Cloth

See *Textiles*.

Worsted Seld

Lost feature. The Worsted Seld was established north of the Market in 1384 as the only place that county weavers could sell their Worsted cloth. It was attached to the Common Inn, or Woolstaplers Hostel, where visiting merchants had to stay. The Seld remained there until being

The Colegate Woolpack before its recent transformation to The Woolie.

transferred to the Guildhall in 1550. It is probable that the complex of the Inn and the Seld ran from No. 1 Guildhall Hill back to Pottergate. The Seld is commemorated in the name of a set of hideous 1960s flats in Pottergate (Seld House) which, ironically, were probably developed following demolition of remnants of the original Seld.

Wrench, Sir Benjamin

Eminent physician. Sir Benjamin (1665-1747) was a physician who had qualified at Cambridge and worked at the Bethel Hospital. He was also a philanthropist and his contributions included the donation of a fire engine to the City after a particularly severe fire. He was sufficiently prominent to have his portrait painted by Theodore Heins in the year before his death. He lived at Benjamin Wrench's Court south of the current Bedford Street, in a stunning, three storied, mullioned-windowed Tudor house. The building was painted by Stannard and etched by Ninham. It later became the New Lobster Inn before being demolished for the Corn Exchange.

Wrights Court, Elm Hill, with surviving remnants of the Pettus Mansion.

Wrights Court

Surviving gem. This is one of the few examples of a surviving Norwich Court, once represented in their hundreds but now virtually extinct. The Court takes its name from John Wright who was a manufacturer of bombasin, crape, camlets and silk here in 1830 and reputedly employed 1500 hand loom weavers. The buildings are much older, dating from the rebuild of Elm Hill after the disastrous fire of 1507. They constitute the very early C16th remnant of the courtyard house of the Pettus family, along with Nos. 41-43 Elm Hill.

Wymer

Historic Ward. Wymer was one of the original City wards and stretched east/west, south of the Wensum, across the middle of the Walled City encompassing the parishes of St Peter Hungate, St George Tombland, St Simon and St Jude, St Martin at Palace, St Helen, St John Maddermarket, St Michael at Plea, St Benedict, St Swithin, St Margaret, St Laurence, St Gregory and the dissolved parishes of St Christopher, St Crowche, and St Matthew.

Y is for…

Norfolk's principal river; pioneering YMCA.

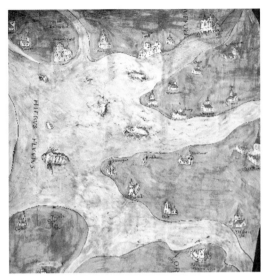

Opposite: Wherry and other boats on the River Yare.
Above: River Yare from the Southern Bypass Bridge.
Right: Very early map of the Yare Estuary (north is bottom).

Yacht Station

Berthing facility. Located at Foundry Bridge, just opposite the Railway station, the Yacht Station provides berthing facilities for hire boats and other craft within easy walking distance of the City Centre and principal facilities. Recently subject of a major refurbishment, the facility includes shower-rooms, toilets, water standpipes, washrooms and sewage pump outs.

Yards

See *Courts and Yards*.

Yare, River

Principal river skirting Norwich. The Yare rises close to the village of Shipdham, near Dereham, and flows broadly east, forming the southern boundary of Norwich, and flowing out to the sea at Great Yarmouth (mouth of the Yare). It is joined by the Wensum (which flows through the heart of Norwich) at Whitlingham and by the Chet, Bure and Waveney on its route to Yarmouth. It is tidal and navigable. Between the Postwick Bridge on the Southern Bypass at Norwich and Yarmouth, there are no other bridges although there is a ferry at Reedham.

Yare Valley Walk

Recreational walk.
The Yare Valley Walk has been developed by the Norwich Fringe Project and runs for about 12km (7.5 miles) around the southern edge of Norwich from Bowthorpe in the east to Whitlingham in the west. The rivers and railway contrive to make a continuous walk a challenge. Probably the best options are either to walk from Bowthorpe to Harford (the Yare Valley Society produced a printed guide for this section in 2000, updated in 2005) or from Trowse, via Whitlingham and over the Southern Bypass (not for the faint hearted) to Thorpe (a trail was produced by the Fringe Project in 1994 and is available online).

Yarmouth Road

Radial Road. Yarmouth Road is the principal route from Norwich to the east coast and has been since it replaced the former Roman Road running parallel and to the north of it, formerly connecting Norwich to the port of Brundall. Starting at its junction with Thorpe Road/Harvey Lane and heading east and on the north side of the Road, Thorpe Lodge (currently the offices of Broadland District Council)

The Yare Valley Walk at the University of East Anglia.

Thorpe River Green on the Yarmouth Road.

was built in the 1820s for the Harvey family and retains a pleasant crinkle crankle wall and gazebo of the same date in the grounds. Further east and opposite, Thorpe Old Hall nestles behind the trees and was the house of the famous Pastons. Built around 1600, on a site owned by the Bishops of Norwich and incorporating earlier structural elements, the house had become derelict by the C20th but was restored and converted by Anthony Rossi in 1987. East of the Hall is No. 10 dating from 1840 then the Manor House, slightly later than the Old Hall and dating from about 1650 with C18th remodelling and additions. Walpole House, at No. 16, is C17th in origin with C18th remodelling and an early C19th road frontage while there is a C18th garden house just south of the main house. Nos. 18-20 are early C19th but the Town House is mid C18th. Further east, the Kings Head pub is essentially mid C17th with licensing records indicating continuous use as a pub from 1700 to the present day although it was renamed The Riverside in 2000. Moving east and on the opposite side of the Road, Thomas

Jekyll's St Andrew's church sits beside the tower remnant of the original medieval church. Next door, the Buck pub dates from the C17th and behind it nestles the old rectory dating from the C18th. Thorpe River Green presents a pleasant interlude and here, a C17th building sits behind the later shop front extensions. The Rush Cutters restaurant, further east still on the opposite side, has a C16th core with later additions, and was originally the Three Tuns before becoming the Thorpe Gardens in 1879 and the Boat and Bottle in the 1970s. There are a few more attractive C18th houses on the north side before the Road ultimately reaches Thorpe Hospital, the former County Asylum, designed by Francis Stone in 1811-14 and added to by John Browne between 1816 and 1849. It has now been converted into flats.

Yeats, W.B.

Poet. In 1911 Poet W.B. Yeats visited his friend Nugent Monck and was put to work tying numbers onto seats in Blackfriars Hall where Monck was producing an adaptation of the Book of Job.

YMCA

Caring institution. The YMCA was founded in Norwich in 1853 by local Nonconformists to support apprentices and shop workers and improve moral and religious conditions. In 1886 48 St Giles, an impressive house dating from 1790, was bought, with the help of Jeremiah James Colman, to house the institution and two years later a gymnasium was provided. The institution supported soldiers during the First World War and in the 1920s/30s concentrated on youth work, education and physical fitness. The YMCA also provided support for the unemployed during the Recession. During WWII the YMCA again provided support including by the provision of 20 mobile tea trucks to support communities during the bombing campaign. After the War Norwich pioneered Summer Camps and developed improved sporting facilities. In 1969 Mr and Mrs Roger Chandler became the first couple to spend their honeymoon in a YMCA (in Norwich). The centre developed its work further in a range of pioneering ways under the guidance of John Drake from 1979 and 30 years later moved to brand new, purpose built premises at the bus station.

YWCA

Caring institution. The YWCA occupies an early C17th structure in Bethel Street which probably had a 3rd storey added in about 1750 and a rear extension in 1810.

Youngs

Construction business.
James Young was a bricklayer engaged principally on building bridges for the Eastern Counties Railway when he decided to set up on his own in 1851. He benefitted from the mid C19th terrace house boom and during the early 1850s built over 1,000 houses in the Heigham area. His depot, on Chapelfield Road, expanded to include a wide range of construction services. After much success in the domestic field Youngs, and his son John, took on the task of replacing the original Thorpe Station in 1884 and the Royal Arcade in 1899. The company also secured the contract for the new Royal Hotel and a major contract for Howlett & White in St Georges Plain and Caley's in Coburg Street/Chapelfield East. After the First World War they continued with a number of public projects, including a new water tower and a fire in their depot necessitated a move to City Road. After WWII they played a key role in rebuilding the bomb damaged City most notably with schemes at Mackintosh's and Bonds. In 1967 the company was incorporated within the R.G. Carter Group.

Youngs, Crawshay & Youngs
See right.

Youngs, Crawshay & Youngs

Brewing dynasty

By 1807 John Youngs was an established brewer in King Street and after several mergers and demergers, Youngs and his son merged with Charles Crawshay's St Stephens Gates Brewery in 1851 and consolidated the operation at the Crown Brewery and extending it with a new maltings in the same year. By the time of incorporation in 1897 the brewery covered three acres and included a brewhouse, millhouse, maltings, stables and offices. The brewery prospered, adding a successful wine business which kept its stock in the Music House cellars.

Following the War Bullard's took over the Crown Brewery and closed it. Unlike the other King Street brewery though, much of the Crown Brewery survived as part of the Wensum Lodge complex although part of the site was cleared for the incongruous Lincoln Ralphs Sports Hall in 1968. An interesting feature is the 1986 mural by Walter Kershaw on an east facing wall and depicting scenes from the architectural, industrial and social history of the City.

Above: Youngs, Crawshay & Youngs historic advertising, a Young's strong 'nip' and an embossed bottle, and Internal views of the old Crown Brewery, now the Wensum Lodge complex.

Fermenting Room

Gas Collecting Plant

Bottle Washing Chamber

Z is for…

One of the most energy efficient buildings in the world; home to some of the most innovative research bodies in the world.

Zeppelin Raids

WWI aerial bombardment.
During the First World War there was serious concern that, due to the proximity of Norwich to occupied Europe, the City was in severe danger of being aerially bombarded for the first time in its history. Although there were a number of 'scares', no actual bombs fell on the City itself and there were no deaths. However, as a result of warnings, the City was 'blacked out' several times to avoid detection. The most serious threat was on 1st October 1916 when four Zeppelins either overflew the City or flew close by. One passed over Magdalen Road in the early hours and another dropped its load on Easton Park then overflew the City.

ZICER Building

One of the most sustainable buildings in the world.
Home of the Zuckerman Institute for Connective Environmental Research (ZICER) the building was officially opened in 2003 by the then Secretary of State for Education and Skills, the Rt Hon Charles Clarke, MP, in the presence of special guest Dr Paul Zuckerman. ZICER is the first physical symbol of recognition commemorating Lord Solly Zuckerman, the Government's first Chief Scientific Adviser. Covering five floors, the building houses open plan office accommodation for researchers as well as a novel exhibition and seminar space on the top floor. Its core aim is to foster

Left: The award winning ZICER Building at the University of East Anglia.

C19th premises of Zipfel the watchmakers.

interdisciplinary research between the natural and social sciences. ZICER houses a number of collaborating, cutting-edge international research centres, including the Tyndall Centre for Climate Change, CSERGE and the Centre for Environmental Risk, as well as faculty, research scientists and postdoctoral researchers from right across the School. ZICER also hosts a number of bodies which are actively involved in Knowledge Transfer activities, namely CRed and Renewables East. One floor of the building houses a Virtual Reality theatre which is the centrepiece of the Social Science for the Environment, Virtual Reality and Experimental Laboratories (SSEVREL). SSEVREL also includes an

Experimental Laboratory and facilities for holding and monitoring focus group discussions. ZICER won the 'Low Energy Building of the Year' award in the Building Magazine's 2005 sustainability competition and was short listed for the Times Higher Education Supplement's 'Outstanding Contribution to Sustainable Development' award in the Higher 2006 awards.

Zipfel Family

Watch making dynasty. In a City which innovated in the field of clock making and which welcomed immigrants from across the world, the Zipfels (pronounced Ziffel) were prominent both as a successful clock making dynasty and a family from mainland Europe who, like legions of Flemings, Dutch and Huguenots before them, became part of the cosmopolitan and pluralistic population of the developing Norwich. Since the C17th there had been a quality clock making tradition in the Black Forest region of Germany but the arrival of mass production American clocks in mainland Europe provoked German clock makers in general and the Zipfels specifically to seek out new production markets in the UK. The Norwich based dynasty was founded by Charles Zipfel who arrived in Norwich at 1800 and set up business at the Lion and Castle off Timberhill. He marrried Edith Morris in 1807 and moved his business to Magdalen Street in 1811. Charles junior was apprenticed to the clock making business which was behind 113-117 Magdalen Street, later to be named Zipfels Court. The 3rd Charles Zipfel set up a jewellers and watchmakers at 167 Magdalen Street in 1855. Charles' sons and grandson ran the business until 1938 when the son of Charles' daughter (Catherine) and William Symonds took over the business and ran it until the 1970s. The shop closed in the 1980s and was eventually redeveloped for new flats which were named Zipfel House.

In parallel to this, George Zipfel also moved from Germany and married Elizabeth Butterfield in 1813. He set up business at 11 Cockey Lane (London Street) as a watch, clock and barometer maker. His son, Bernard, had established a clock and watch shop in St Gregory's church yard by 1836. A year later, a John Zipfel, from Lenzkirch, was recorded as living in Stump Cross and he

Zoar Strict Baptist Chapel.

apparently made long case clocks of excellent quality. Joseph Zipfel, also from the Black Forest, is recorded in Timberhill in 1830 and his sons continued the clock and watch making business. Finally, another German émigré, Matthew Zipfel is recorded in Ber Street in 1851.

Zoar Baptist Chapel

Victorian, Strict Baptist Chapel. Following a rift in the congregation of St Mary's Baptist Chapel in the C19th the Strict Baptists moved, first, to the Tabernacle, in Bishopgate, then constructed their own chapel, in 1886 in St Mary's Plain, on what had probably been the site of the kitchen range of Thomas Pykerell's House.

Bibliography

Anderson A.P./Storey N.R.
*Norwich – Eighty years
of the Norwich Society*
Sutton Publishing Ltd.
2004

Ash M.
*Memories of Thorpe Hamlet
Norwich* Wahnfried
Publications 2004

Atkin M.
Norwich History and Guide
Alan Sutton Publishing Ltd.
1993

Atkin M/Margeson S.
Life on a Medieval Street
Norwich Survey 1985

Avery D.
Cathedrals Wordsworth
Editions Ltd. 1995

Ayers B.
*Digging Deeper Recent
archaeology in Norwich*
Norfolk Museums Service
1987

Ayers B.
*Excavations within the
North-East Bailey of
Norwich Castle, 1979*
Norfolk Archaeological Unit
1985

Ayers B.
Norwich 'A Fine City'
Tempus Publishing Ltd.
2003

Ayers B.
*Norwich Archaeology
of a Fine City* Amberley
Publishing Plc 2009

Ayers B.
Norwich B T Batsford Ltd.
1994

Ayers B./Brown J. & Reeve J.
*Digging Ditches –
Archaeology and
Development in Norwich*
Norfolk Museums Service
1992

Banger J.
Norwich at Peace
Poppyland Publishing 2003

Banger J.
Norwich at War
Poppyland Publishing 2003

Barnes R.
*Norfolk, The Year of
Public Sculpture*
Frontier Publishing 2001

Barrett G. N.
*Norwich Silver in the
collection of Norwich Castle
Museum* Norfolk Museums
Service 1981

Bayne A.
History of Norwich
Jarrold & Sons 1869

Berwick D. A.
*Beating the Bounds in
Georgian Norwich*
Lark Press 2007

Bickford-Smith D.
*Norfolk & Norwich World
Family* The Norfolk and
Norwich World Family 2004

Bithray M.
King Street – A Guided Walk
Geo. R. Reeve Ltd. 1983

Blackwell M. & C.
*Norwich Theatre Royal –
The first 250 Years*
Connaught Books 2007

Bown J.
*Norfolk Archaeological Unit
Annual Review 1999-2000*
Norfolk Archaeological Unit
2000

Brew A.
Boulton Paul Aircraft
Tempus Publishing Ltd.
2001

Brooks J.
The Great Hospital Norwich
Norwich Colour Print 2008

Brooks P.
*Heroes, Villains & Victims
of Norwich* The Breedon
Books Publishing Company
Ltd. 2008

Brooks P.
Norfolk Miscellany The
Breedon Books Publishing
Company Ltd. 2009

Brooks P.
Norwich, Street by Street
The Breedon Books
Publishing Company Ltd.
2006

Brooks P.
Norwich, Stories of a City
Fort Publishing Ltd. 2003

Browning S.
Norwich Halsgrove 2009

Bunting J./Loveday M.
*The Heritage Trail –
The Changing Face of the
Old City of Norwich*
Norwich City Council 1987

Burgess E.
*The Men Who Have Made
Norwich* E. Burgess 1904

Cattermole P.
Church Bells of Norwich
The Golden Bell Press 2005

Childs A.
Portrait of Norwich
Halsgrove 2005

Clarke D.
*The Country Houses of
Norfolk Part One: The Major
Houses* Geo. R. Reeve Ltd.
2006

Clarke D.
*The Country House of Norfolk
Part Two: The Lost Houses*
Geo. R. Reeve Ltd. 2008

Cocke S./Hall L.
*Norwich Bridges Past &
Present* The Norwich
Society 1994

Cocke R. & S.
*Public Sculpture in Central
Norwich* Norwich Society
2007

Collins A./Nash P.
The Walls of Norwich
Jarrold & Sons Ltd. 1910

Colman M.
Norwich in Old Photographs
Alan Sutton Publishing Ltd.
1990

Cooper K.
Norwich Markets
Charles N. Veal & Company

Cotman A. M./Hawcroft F. W.
Old Norwich – A collection of Paintings, Prints and Drawings of an Ancient City
Jarrold & Sons Ltd. 1961

Davison A.
Justly Celebrated Ales
Brewery History Society 1991

Dent L/Livock J.
Wensum Lodge – The Story of a House Norfolk County Council 1990

Dorman B. E.
A Guide to Norwich
Goose & Son Ltd. 1947

Dunn I/Sutermeister H.
The Norwich Guildhall – The City of Norwich

Emmerson R.
The Norwich Regalia & Civic Plate Norfolk Museums Service 1984

Fowler E.
A Hundred Years In The Shoe Trade, 1862-1962
Jarrold & Sons Ltd. 1962

Frostick R.
The Printed Plans of Norwich, 1558-1840
Raymond Frostick 2002

Gardiner R.
The Story of Norwich Cathedral
Workshop Press 1987

Gibbs M.
English City Companion – Norwich Harrap Books Ltd. 1991

Gilchrist R.
Norwich Cathedral Close
The Boydell Press 2005

Goreham G.
Norwich Past and Present Volume One
Nostalgia Publications 1991

Green B/Young R.M.R.
Norwich the growth of a city
Norfolk Museums Service 1981

Groves N.
The Medieval Churches of the City of Norwich
HEART/East 2010

Gurney-Read J.
Trades & Industries of Norwich Gliddon Books 1988

Gurney-Read J.
Milestones to Mile Cross
The Mile Cross History Research Group 1995

Hanson-Smith C.
The Flemish Bond East Anglia & The Netherlands – Close & Ancient Neighbours
Groundnut Publishing 2004

Hartley A.
John Moray-Smith
The Norwich Society 2007

Heaton T.
Nasty Norwich
Bosworth Books 2005

Hepworth P./Ogden J.
Norwich Society 1923-1983 – Sixty Eventful Years
The Norwich Society

Hepworth P.
Norwich As It Was Hendon Publishing Co. Ltd. 1974

Hepworth P.
Norwich Central Library, Norfolk and Norwich Record Office Jarrold and Sons Ltd. 1963

Hepworth P./Alexander M.
History and Treasures – City of Norwich Libraries
Jarrold & Son Ltd. 1957

Heslop T. A.
Norwich Castle Keep – Romanesque Architecture and Social Context
The Centre of East Anglian Studies 1994

Hooper J.
The Royal Hotel
Jarrold & Sons 1899

Hudson Rev. W.
How the City of Norwich Grew into Shape

Hudson Rev. W.
The Ecclesiastical History of The Parish of St Peter Parmentergate
The King Street Research Group 2009

Ishmael G.
The Tree Trail
Norwich City Council

James C./Rowland Pierce S.
City of Norwich Plan City of Norwich Corporation 1945

James G.
Norwich on This Day – History, Facts & Figures from Every Day of the Year
Pitch Publishing 2009

Jerrold W.
Norwich And The Broads
Blackie & Son Ltd.

Jewson, Charles B.
History of The Great Hospital Norwich
Great Hospital 1980

Jones D.
Norwich Boot & Shoe Industry Norfolk CC 1986

Lane R.
The Plains of Norwich
The Larks Press 1999

Lasko P./Morgan N. J.
Medieval Art in East Anglia, 1300-1520 Jarrold & Sons Ltd. 1973

Leeds H.
Peace Souvenir – Norwich at War Jarrold & Sons Ltd.

Lely B. & P.
The City of Norwich Official Guide Jarrold Publishing 1993

Lewis C.
Norfolk in Europe Norfolk Museums Service 1980

Lindsay B.
The Jenny – A history of the Jenny Lind Hospital for Sick Children, Norwich 1854-2004
Norfolk And Norwich University Hospital 2004

Kelly S./Rutledge E./Tillyard M.
Men of property – An analysis of the Norwich enrolled deeds 1285-1311
The Centre of East Anglian Studies 1983

Kennett H.
*Elm Hill, Norwich –
The Story of its Tudor
Buildings and the People
Who Lived in Them*
Ecollectit Ltd. 2006

Kent A./Stephenson A.
Norwich Inheritance
Jarrold &Sons Ltd.

Lepper S./Rycroft I.
*Footwear Industry: Case
Study* Norfolk CC 1994

Margeson S.
The Vikings in Norfolk
Norfolk Museums Service
1997

Margeson S./Seilier F./
Rogerson A.
The Normans in Norfolk
Norfolk Museums Service
1994

McDonald D.
*A Pub Walk With a
Difference in 1883*
2000

Meers F.
A History of Norwich
Phillimore & Co Ltd. 1998

Meers F.
*Norwich – A History and
Celebration* Frith Book
Company Ltd. 2004

Messent C. J. W.
*The City Churches of
Norwich* H.W. Hunt 1932

*The Art of Faith – 3,500
Years Of Art and Belief in
Norfolk* Philip Wilson
Publishers 2010

Mitchell A.
Memories of Norwich
True North Books Ltd. 1999

Morson M.
*A Force Remembered –
The Illustrated History of the
Norwich City Police, 1836-
1967* The Breedon Books
Publishing Co Ltd. 2000

Nobbs G.
*Norwich – A City of
Centuries* Macklow
Publications 1971

Nobbs G.
*Norwich – A City of
Centuries* George Nobbs
1978

Nobbs G.
Norwich City Hall Norwich
and Norwich Arts Centre
1988

Norwich Heritage Projects
A Market For Our Times
Norwich Heritage Projects
2010

Norwich J. J./ Blythe R.
*A Country Parson – James
Woodforde's Diary, 1759-
1802* Tiger Books
International plc 1991

Osborne, M.
*20th Century Defences in
Britain – Norfolk* Concrete
Publications 2008

Palgrave-Moore P.
*Cathedral Church of St John
The Baptist, Norwich*
Errey's Printers Ltd.

Pardue B.
*Images of England –
Norwich Streets* Tempus
Publishing Ltd. 2005

Parkin D./Temple C. R.
Bygone Norwich – An A to Z
Rushmere Publishing 1990

Penfold S.
Norwich Cathedral
Jarrold Publishing 2006

Penn K.
*Norfolk Archaeological Unit
Report no. 488, Anglo-
Scandinavian Norwich: an
Archaeological Desk-Top
Survey* Norfolk
Archaeological Unit 2000

Perkins A.
Norwich Jarrold Publishing
2001

Pevsner N./Wilson B.
*Buildings of England:
Norfolk 1* Yale University
Press 1997

Pevsner N./Wilson B.
*Buildings of England:
Norfolk 2* Yale University
Press 1999

Phillips E.
*A Short History of The Great
Hospital Norwich* Jarrold
Bookprint Ltd. 1999

Platten S.
Norwich Cathedral

Plunkett J./Etheridge H.
*Plunkett's Pictures of
Norwich and Norfolk*
Grey's Publishing 2007

Plunkett G. A. F.
Disappearing Norwich
Terence Dalton Ltd. 1987

Plunkett G. A. F.
Rambles in Old Norwich
Terence Dalton Ltd. 1990

Pound J.
Tudor And Stuart Norwich
Phillimore & Co. Ltd. 1988

Priestly U.
*The Great Market – A survey
of nine hundred years of
Norwich Provision Market*
The Centre of East Anglian
Studies 1987

Priestly U./Fenner A.
*Shops and Shopkeepers in
Norwich, 1660-1730*
The Centre of East Anglian
Studies 1985

Rajnai M.
*The Norwich School of
Painters* Jarrold Colour
Publications 1985

Rawcliffe C.
*The Hospitals of Medieval
Norwich* The Centre of East
Anglian Studies 1995

Rawcliffe C./Wilson R.
Medieval Norwich
Hambledon And London
2004

Reed B.
*The Courts and Yards of
Norwich* Norwich Heritage
Projects

Roberts C. V./Frankl E.
Norwich The Pevensey Press

Rodgers M
*The River and Staithes of
Tudor Norwich* King Street
Publications 1996

Rose M./Hedgecoe J.
Stories in Stone – The
Medieval Roof Carvings of
Norwich Cathedral
Herbert Press 1997

Rowles H./Wood R.
Strangers Hall Jarrold
Publishing 1991

Rye J.
A Popular Guide to Norfolk
Place-names The Larks
Press 2000

Salt R.
Plans For a Fine City
The Victorian Society East
Anglian Group 1988

Sampson A.
Norwich Close
Portico press 1987

Sharp B.
The Story of the Norwich
Fire Marks

Sharp Rev D.
The Church of St Peter
Mancroft Norwich
Jarrold Publishing 1994

Shaw A. B.
Sir Thomas Browne of
Norwich 2005

Skipper K.
The Norfolk Companion
Jim Baldwin 1994

Smith G.
Norfolk Airfields in the
Second World War
Countryside Books 2004

Smith R.
A Norwich City Fact File –
The Canary Companion
R. J. S. Publishing 2004

Snelling S.
Images of Norwich The
Breedon Books Publishing
Co. Ltd. 1994

Solomons G.
Stories Behind the Plaques
of Norwich Capricorn Books
1981

Spencer N./Kent A.
The Old Churches of Norwich
Jarrold Publishing 1970

Spencer N./Kent A.
The Old Churches of Norwich
Jarrold Publishing 1990

Standley P./Storey S.
Norwich Then and Now –
A Third Selection John
Nickalls Publications 2003

Standley P.
Norwich Volume 1 –
A Portrait in Old
Picture Postcards
S.B. Publications 1988

Stephenson A.
A History of The Assembly
House Norwich
The Larks Press 2004

Storey N.
Britain in Old Photographs –
Around Norwich
The History Press 2009

Storey N.
A Century of Norwich –
Events, People and Places
Over the Last 100 Years
Sutton Publishing Ltd. 2000

Storey N.
Norwich – The Changing City
The Breedon Books
Publishing Co Ltd. 2002

Storey N.
A Grim Almanac of Norfolk
Sutton Publishing Ltd. 2003

Temple C. R.
Norwich – The Archive
Photographs Series
The Chalford Publishing
Company 1996

Thompson L. P.
Norwich Inns W.E. Harrison
& Sons Ltd.

Timpson J.
Norwich A Fine City Jarrold
Colour Publications 1988

Tricker R.
The Church of Saint
Laurence in The City of
Norwich 2010

Tricker R./Cook J./Young R.
All Saints Church Norwich –
A History and Guide 2004

Tyrell D.
Youngs Crawshay & Youngs
Ltd. Crown Brewery King St.
Norwich Coronation
Souvenir The Home
Publishing Co.

Walker R.
Seventy Years Young –
A history of Norwich
Lads Club, 1918-1988
Norwich Lads Club 1990

Wallace M.
Medieval People of
Norwich – Artists and
Artisans King Street
Publications 1992

Wheldon F. W.
A Norvic Century and
the Men Who Made It
Jarrold And Sons Ltd.

Williams N/Marriage J. & J.
The Rosary Cemetery,
Norwich – A Place of Decent
Interment Friends of the
Rosary 2005

Williams N.
The Norwich Blue Plaques
HEART 2010

Whittingham A.
Norwich Cathedral Bosses
and Misericords
Jarrold &Sons Ltd. 1981

Wilson J.
900 Years, Norwich
Cathedral And Diocese
Jarrold Publishing 1996

Young R.
Norwich Discovery Walks
Jarrold/Norwich Society
1983

Author Unknown:
A Guide to Norwich Castle
Museum Jarrold Publishing

The Leaf and the Tree
Boulton & Paul 1947

Norwich Floods 1912

Norwich Official Guide
City of Norwich Amenities

Old Ordnance Survey Maps
Norwich (South) 1905
Alan Godfrey Maps 2005

Old Ordnance Survey Maps
Norwich (North) 1905
Alan Godfrey Maps 2005

Norwich Past & Present
Map 1838 to present day
Cassini Publishing Ltd. 2006

Who's Who in Norwich
Pullman Press Ltd. 1961

Photo: Simon Barber (from an article on Mike in the Guardian 2007).

About the author

Michael Loveday was born in Norwich and has harboured a passion for the place from his earliest memories, including standing on the River End terraces when he was too small to see anything, being at the Central Library on the day it opened, going into Lambert's basement on the Walk to buy strange food and, as an avid and very young photographer, snapping a parked Spitfire on the site of the old Horse Market at Bell Avenue.

At school he revelled in 'local studies' visiting now long gone industries including Steward & Pattesons, Heatrae and the Co-op Shoe Factory. In the 6th Form he prepared a scheme for the pedestrianisation of the City Centre 20 years before it happened. Leaving Norwich for the West Country, he trained as

a town planner but returned eventually to work for the City Council ultimately becoming the amusingly entitled Director of Spatial Planning with European and Economic Development or DSPEED as it was acronymed – which sounded like a star ship captain, he quipped, but wasn't. During that period, the Office of the Deputy Prime Minister noted that 'the City is one of the leaders in urban renaissance in England' and, in carefully marshalling a billion pounds worth of development investment, the Planning function had been pivotal to fostering that reputation. In contrast, a former Chief Executive had referred to him as a dangerous, anarchic maverick – one of the nicest things anyone had ever said about him he reflected.

Michael has over 30 years experience in urban regeneration and in 2005 left the Council to establish the Heritage Economic & Regeneration Trust (HEART) – a unique charity which co-ordinates, regenerates and promotes heritage assets in one City – Norwich – and acts as a best practice exemplar internationally. In its brief six year history, the organisation has moved from a slightly 'maverick' one man band, to a charity employing 17 people and turning over in excess of £1.5m annually. HEART appeared last year as the first best practice case study in the Government's Vision Statement for the Historic Environment. This role has brought Michael to keynote the principal heritage conferences in Canada and in Virginia, to run workshops in Washington for the World Bank and US National Trust and to lecture to organisations as diverse as the World League of Historic Cities, the EU, the British High Commission in Canada, the Indian National Trust, ICOMOS, Euro Cities and a range of municipalities and academic institutions across the globe. He has

been Chair of the national pedestrian charity Living Streets for four years and is Executive Member of the Historic Towns Forum, a Board Member of the Centre for East Anglian Studies and a member of the Royal Society of the Arts.

Apart from 'the fine city', his passions include obscure

travel, the 'Stans' and the Caucases being recent destinations; the Canaries, a passion since his youth; photography; gastronomy, craft beer and spending time with his family – he is married and has a daughter from his first marriage and two step daughters from his second.

12 top websites

Heritage
www.heritagecity.org
www.norwich12.co.uk
www.norfolkchurches.co.uk
www.norwich-churches.org

Tourist information
www.visitnorwich.co.uk
www.visitnorfolk.co.uk

What's On
www.edp24.co.uk/events

Shopping
www.norwichlanes.co.uk
www.chapelfield.co.uk

Sport
www.canaries.co.uk

Local Council Services
(includes tourism and transport)
www.norwich.gov.uk
www.norfolk.gov.uk

Picture Credits

All pictures contained within this publication are either taken by the author or form part of his collection unless credited below:

Edward Burgess (The Men Who Have Made Norwich):
inset 10; 35; 78 top; 96 bottom; 129 bottom; 131 top left; 158; 183 top right; 185; 224; 342; 346 top right; 412 top.

George Plunkett (permission from Jonathan Plunkett):
39; 46; 47 top & bottom right; 61; 62 top left; 63; 64 bottom right; 72 bottom right; 82 top; 87 bottom; 137 top; 149 mid; 155 top right; 182; 184 bottom; 218; 331; 354; 358; 362 top right; 373 top; 377 mid right; 381 bottom; 389 top; 389 mid left; 390 mid & bottom left; 394 top & mid; 401 bottom; 402 top & mid right; 415 bottom right; 432 bottom left; 446 bottom.

HEART/ University of East Anglia, School of Computing:
20; 25; 40; 45; 53 bottom; 58 right; 59 bottom; 68 top; 84;

88-9; 101; 106 top & bottom; 116 top; 119 top right; 128; 138; 147 top right; 176 top; 188; 210; 226 bottom; 227 top right; 232 top right; 245; 322; 323 bottom; 326 bottom; 328 bottom; 329 bottom; 386 mid; 442; 445.

Jarrold & Sons: inside front cover map; 205 bottom.

Norfolk County Library/Picture Norfolk: 116 mid 2; 120 top left & right; 155 top left; 162 top; 163 top; 332; left; 409 right.

Norfolk Historic Environment Service: 213 mid; 299; 453.

Norfolk Museums Service: 81 top; 124 bottom left; 125 bottom right; 231; 284 portraits; 347; 422 bottom.

Norwich City Council: 44 top left, bottom right & left; 96 mid right; 108 bottom; 219; 227 top left; inside back cover map.

NUCA: 85, 3 down.

Additionally I would like to thank organisations that provided copies of tickets for use on the front cover.

Kindly printed in Norwich by Swallowtail Print Ltd
www.swallowtailprint.co.uk

Designed by Anne Reekie